International Law and Foreign Direct Investment

International Law and Foreign Direct Investment

Muna B. Ndulo and Abigail N. Chase

Carolina Academic Press
Durham, North Carolina

ISBN 978-1-5310-1523-7
eISBN 978-1-5310-1524-4
LCCN 2019949092

Carolina Academic Press
700 Kent Street
Durham, NC 27701
Telephone (919) 489-7486
Fax (919) 493-5668
www.caplaw.com

Printed in the United States of America

Dedicated to our parents
Temba and Julia Ndulo
and
Howard and Gisela Chase

Summary of Contents

Contents

Table of Cases

Principal cases are in bold type. Cases cited or discussed in text are in roman type.

List of Documents

Principal documents are in bold type. Documents cited or discussed in text are in roman type.

Introduction

This book is designed to provide an overview of the law of foreign investment, incorporating a thorough exposition of the legal principles that are likely to affect a commercial investment in a foreign country. It includes a discussion of the following issues: the international legal framework for foreign investments; the regulation of foreign investment; the role of foreign capital in economic development; foreign investment and the environment and human rights issues; obstacles to flow of investment to developing countries; the role of guarantees to investors and investment codes; bilateral investment treaties; nationalization and problems of compensation; the structuring of joint ventures; transfer of technology; investment insurance; project financing and infrastructure construction; international efforts against corruption in international business transactions; international commercial arbitration and other forms of dispute settlement; and the unification of trade law. The subjects have been chosen because of their common link to international law and foreign direct investment. With the worldwide acceleration in the volume of international trade and investment activity, brought about by globalization, the need for capital in developing countries, and the emergence of new forms of structuring investments and the increase in bilateral and regional investment treaties, as well as the number of disputes referred to both treaty and institutional based arbitration tribunals, international investment law has become an important area for scholars to study. This area of the law has witnessed tremendous growth and has now become one of the fastest growing areas of international law with far reaching implications for both investment receiving and investment exporting countries.

This book analyses the fundamental principles of foreign investment law and the manner in which these principles have been interpreted and applied by international courts, domestic courts, and arbitral tribunals. Relevant cases and materials are printed in the book. Most cases have been sharply edited, and we have indicated omissions through the conventional use of dots, except for omissions of citations. Generally footnotes have been omitted from judicial decisions. The materials in the book in addition to the cases, include writings by scholars who write on the field of international investment law. The book is arranged according to the following chapters: Chapter 1, Foreign Investment and International Law; Chapter 2, Attraction of Foreign Investment, Guarantees to Investors, Investment Codes and Efforts to Regulate Foreign Investments; Chapter 3, Investment Insurance, Features, Concepts; Chapter 4, The Protection of Investment Through Bilateral Treaties; Chapter 5, Nationalization, Investment Protection and Compensation; Chapter 6,

Intellectual Property Protection and Transfer of Technology to Developing Countries; Chapter 7, The Process and Value of the Unification of Commercial Law for International Trade and Investment; Chapter 8, International Commercial Arbitration and International Settlement of Investment Disputes; Chapter 9, Legal Issues in Joint Ventures; Chapter 10, Emerging Issues in Foreign Direct Investment; Chapter 11, Project Financing; Chapter 12, International Efforts Against Corruption in International Business Transactions.

Muna Ndulo

Abigail Yadav, née Chase

Acknowledgments

The genesis of this book is from a search for teaching materials for my course on international law and foreign direct investment at Cornell Law School. For a number of years, I taught the course from a set of handouts. Over the years, I saw the need to turn the materials into a book for easy access for teaching as well as a contribution to this growing area of the law. This book would not have been possible without the work of several people. We thank the students in my International Law and Foreign Investment classes at Cornell Law School for being active participants in the debates in the classes and asking questions about issues covered in the book thereby contributing to the development of materials for the book. We thank the research assistants who worked on the materials all of whom provided many hours of research and assistance in various ways to this project. These include Gabrielle Di Bernardi, Leigh Blomgren, Manasa Gummi, Patrick Meson and Dae Un Hong. We thank Megan Olivares who has provided invaluable assistance in the development and production of this book.

Muna Ndulo

Abigail Yadav, née Chase

List of Common Abbreviations

AAPL	Asian Agriculture Products Ltd
ADB	Asian Development Bank
AIA	Leahy-Smith America Invents Act (U.S.)
AIFI	All India Financial Institutions
AOC	Arabian Oil Company
AoS	Act of State Doctrine
APEC	Asia-Pacific Economic Cooperation
ASEAN	Association of Southeast Asian Nations
ATS	Alien Tort Statute (U.S.)
BEPS	Base Erosion and Profit Shifting
BIT	Bilateral Investment Treaty
BJP	Bharatiya Janata Party
BOA	Build Operate Agreement
BOT	Build Operate Transfer
BTLP	Barcelona Traction, Light and Power Company Limited
CAA	Compania De Aguas Del Aconquija S.A.
CETA	Comprehensive Economic and Trade Agreement (EU-Canada)
CGE	Compagnie Générale des Eaux
CHIPS	Clearing House Interbank Payments System
CIETAC	China International Economic and Trade Arbitration Commission
CISG	The United Nations Convention on Contracts for the International Sale of Goods
CL	Compulsory License
CLOUT	Case Law on UNCITRAL Texts
CMEA	Council for Mutual Economic Assistance
COFACE	Compagnie Française d'Assurance pour le Commerce Extérieur
CPTPP	Comprehensive and Progressive Agreement for Trans-Pacific Partnership

CSIR	The Council for Scientific and Industrial Research
DAC	Development Assistance Committee (OECD)
DCF	Discounted Cash Flow
DSB	Dispute Settlement Body of the World Trade Organization
EBRD	European Bank for Reconstruction and Development
ECGD	Export Credits Guarantee Department (U.K.)
ECT	Energy Charter Treaty
ELN	National Liberation Army (Colombia)
EU	European Union
FAA	Federal Arbitration Act
FARC	Revolutionary Armed Forces of Colombia
FCN	Friendship, Commerce and Navigation Treaties
FDI	Foreign Direct Investment
FET	Fair and Equitable Treatment
FGS	Federal Government of Somalia
FPS	Full Protection and Security
FSIA	Foreign Sovereign Immunities Act of 1976 (U.S.)
FTA	Free Trade Agreement
GATS	General Agreement on Trade in Services
GATT	General Agreement on Tariffs and Trade
GOA	Government of Argentina
GOC	Government of Chile
GOI	Government of India
GOM	Government of Maharashta
GRIP	Guaranteed Recovery of Investment Principal
ICAC	Independent Commission Against Corruption (Hong Kong)
ICC	International Chamber of Commerce
ICJ	International Court of Justice
ICSID	International Centre for Settlement of Investment Disputes
IDA	International Development Association
IEPS	Impuesto Especial Sobre Producción y Servicios
IFC	International Finance Corporation
IIA	International Investment Agreement

ILO	International Labour Organization (UN)
IMF	International Monetary Fund
IOIA	International Organizations Immunities Act (U.S.)
ISDS	Investor to State Dispute Settlement
ITT	International Technology Transfer
JASTA	Justice Against Sponsors of Terrorism Act (U.S.)
JV	Joint Venture
LCIA	London Court of International Arbitration
LDC	Least Developed Country
MERC	Maharashta Electricity Regulatory Commission
MFN	Most Favoured Nation
MIA	Maximum Insured Amount
MIGA	Multilateral Investment Guarantee Agency
MNE	Multinational Enterprise
MSEB	Maharashta State Electricity Board
NAFTA	North American Free Trade Agreement
NT	National Treatment
OECD	Organisation for Economic Co-operation and Development
OPIC	Overseas Private Investment Corporation
PCA	Permanent Court of Arbitration
PCT	Patent Cooperation Treaty
PRI	Political Risk Insurance
RCEP	Regional Comprehensive Economic Partnership
SCC	The Arbitration Institute of the Stockholm Chamber of Commerce
SCIA	Shenzhen Court of International Arbitration
SHIAC	Shanghai International Economic and Trade Arbitration Commission
SIAC	Singapore International Arbitration Centre
SOE	State-Owned Enterprise
TGS	Transportadora de Gas del Sur (Argentina)
TI	Transparency International
TPP	Trans-Pacific Partnership
TRIMS	Agreement on Trade-Related Investment Measures
TRIPS	Agreement on Trade-Related Aspects of Intellectual Property Rights

TTIP	Transatlantic Trade and Investment Partnership
UNCITRAL	United Nations Commission on International Trade Law
UNCTAD	United Nations Conference on Trade and Development
UNCTC	United Nations Centre on Transnational Corporations
UNHRC	United Nations Human Rights Council
UNGP	United Nations Guiding Principles on Business and Human Rights
USAID	United States Agency for International Development
USIDFC	United Statess International Development Finance Corporation
USMCA	United States-Mexico-Canada Agreement
VCLT	Vienna Convention on the Law of Treaties
WBI	World Bank Institute
WFOE	Wholly Foreign Owned Enterprise
WIPO	World Intellectual Property Organization
WTO	World Trade Organization

International Law and Foreign Direct Investment

Chapter 1

Foreign Investment and International Law

A. Introduction

Our book reviews the legal protections available for direct investors of tangible or intangible assets in a foreign country and the procedures that can be used to settle disputes arising with respect to those investments. It describes the relevant framework of international law and introduces the principal legal instruments dealing with foreign direct investment. A focus on the abstraction of legal norms helps to consolidate the key themes in each area discussed.

The book is divided into twelve chapters, each dealing with a practical aspect of direct investment in a foreign country. Each chapter includes a review of current case law in each area, an analysis of the relevant treaty/treaties or other relevant legal instruments, and an assessment of the related legal and political risks. Particular attention is given to the resolution of investment disputes and the enforcement of dispute settlements.

Chapters one and two provide a general introduction to international investment law, setting the background and highlighting legal norms in this area.

Chapter three explores the subject of investment insurance. Countries often create insurance schemes for investors as they invest abroad, for example the OPIC facility for U.S. companies. However, it is important to be precise on the types of risks insured, the procedures followed when nationalization or similar events occur, and the various options or remedies available in such circumstances. This chapter reviews the investment schemes available in a number of countries and also looks at the insurance provisions offered by the Multilateral Investment Guarantee Agency (MIGA), part of the World Bank Group.

Chapter four focuses on Bilateral Investment Treaties (BITs) and their development. Many capital exporting countries, the U.S., China and Germany for example, have concluded investment treaties with a range of countries, and the respective BITs provide the principal framework of investment protection for investors from these countries. This chapter explores why and how BITs developed, the legal status and function of BITs, and the typical form and structuring of BITs. BITs create special norms for investors between two countries, and a number of the key case histories in this area are reviewed and assessed. In addition, the relationship between insurers and BITs is also discussed.

Chapter five addresses the issue of nationalization, where a state expropriates or "takes over" a foreign company and/or its assets in a country, in full or in part. Questions considered include the circumstances under which a state can or does nationalize, and the constraints to such actions that may arise under international law. Attention is given to the phenomenon of indirect or "creeping" expropriation—as distinct from "direct" nationalization—whereby a state takes measures effectively forcing a company to discontinue its activities in the country. A key question arising here is the distinction (if any) between legitimate regulation by the state and actions amounting to actual expropriation. A number of key cases are reviewed, and consideration is given to the important question of compensation in the event of state expropriation, and the relevant expectations in these circumstances under international law.

Chapter six concerns the question of intellectual property protection, with a focus on the protections available under the World Trade Organization (WTO) Agreement on Trade-Related Aspects of Intellectual Property Rights (TRIPS). Consideration is also given to Intellectual Property Transfer Agreements, the issues that may arise under such contracts and the use of model contracts for this purpose. Mention is also made of the particular controversies arising in this area with respect to TRIPS and the provision of medicines for serious diseases such as TB and AIDS.

Chapter seven looks at the relationship between commercial law and international trade and investment, with a focus on the Vienna Convention on International Sales and its effect with respect to international sales contracts. Particular attention is given to the question of applicable law in the event of a dispute, and how a conflict of laws may be addressed in the context of the Sales Convention.

Chapter eight addresses the important subject of commercial arbitration and its role in the resolution of international investment disputes. It is estimated that 80%-90% of international investment disputes take the arbitration route rather than proceeding through national courts. The reasons for this are assessed, and the essential elements of the arbitration procedures applied by various national and international arbitration centers are reviewed. Particular attention is given to the International

Centre for Settlement of Investment Disputes (ICSID) treaty-based arbitral system. Finally, the role and significance of the New York Convention in the enforcement of arbitral awards is described and assessed.

Chapter nine deals with joint ventures and their particular characteristics as a vehicle for foreign direct investment. Attention is given to joint venture model agreements, how a joint venture agreement is concluded and the types of dispute resolution provisions that may be included.

Chapter ten looks at current issues in foreign investment, including the experience of direct investor initiation of dispute settlement against the state under the Energy Charter Treaty, and the European Commission's proposals for a court-based system of Investor to State Dispute Settlement (ISDS) in recent EU treaty texts (CETA, EU-Vietnam FTA, and draft TTIP). It also looks at the important area of Chinese investment in Africa, the impact of foreign direct investment on economic and social development and the relationship between investment protection and the application of regulatory measures to protect human rights, health or the environment.

Chapter eleven discusses the particular issues arising in the area of project financing, where investment is raised and secured against the proceeds of the identified project alone, rather than through general debt or equity financing. Particular attention is given to the structuring and issues arising in the implementation of Build-Operate-Transfer agreements (BOTs).

Finally, chapter twelve looks at international efforts to combat corruption and, in particular, the provisions and implications of the U.S. Foreign Corrupt Practices Act and the UN Convention on Corruption, to which the U.S. is party.

This book, and the subjects it covers, stands at the interface of international politics and international law. At the time of writing, the global political order appears to be shifting towards greater fragmentation into national and regional interests. With U.S. global leadership in relative decline, both as a cause and effect of this fragmentation, and Europe facing complex and difficult questions of regional identity and global effectiveness, the future governance and protection of foreign investment under international law is likely to be shaped by a wider range of influences than has generally been the case in the post-colonial era.

In this context, the emerging economies will play an increasingly important role in determining the international investment environment, but may also find themselves at a crossroads in terms of the direction of their own development policies and reliable application of the rule of law. The interests of state enterprises, as well as privately owned businesses, and the need for reduced exposure to commodity prices and for greater national and regional economic diversification, will be powerful factors in shaping future developments. The extent to which international law is seen as facilitating the fundamental interests of this wider group of stakeholders will do much to determine the success or otherwise of foreign direct investment law (and the investments that go with it) in the coming decades.

B. Evolution of Foreign Direct Investment Law

Before looking in detail at different aspects of current international investment law, it is useful to take a general overview of the law as it has developed in this field.

1. Historical Context

Foreign direct investment generally represents a major commitment of tangible and intangible resources by an investor of one country over an extended time period in the territory of another. Such investment may present significant risks for the investor in terms of protection of their assets in unfamiliar and/or less predictable legal jurisdictions and political contexts. In the colonial era, the question of applicable law was not an issue for investors from the colonizing power, as their jurisdiction also applied in their colonies. This situation persisted to a degree in post-colonial times, at least where the newly independent nation largely carried forward the legal system of the colonial power. However, as post-colonial nations increasingly established their own distinctive jurisdictions, firstly in Latin America and then elsewhere, the issue of reliable protection of inward investments came more to the fore. The development of international law in this area can largely be seen as a post-colonial response to this newly emerging global geopolitical reality.

2. State Responsibility and Minimum Standard of Treatment

The initial approach to protecting investors in this new context drew primarily on the doctrine of state responsibility. This doctrine is embedded in and stands as a fundamental norm in public international law. It requires states to observe a minimum standard in the treatment of foreign persons and their property, irrespective of the treatment they give to their own nationals. This means it is not sufficient for the state to follow domestic law alone, where this is below the expected minimum standard, and it is not a defense if nationals are treated in the same way as foreign persons. Thus, where a state treats an investor of another state at a level below the expected minimum standard, it is in breach of its international obligation under the doctrine of state responsibility. The country of origin of the investor then has a basis to sue the state in which the investment took place and to seek damages on behalf of the investor.

In other words, no country is obliged to admit foreign investors, and this is always a public policy choice of the country concerned. However, once an investor has been admitted, they should not be mistreated, and the country of origin may seek to intervene and afford diplomatic protection on behalf of the investor if such mistreatment occurs.

The doctrine of state responsibility is discussed in the *Barcelona Traction* case.

Barcelona Traction, Light, and Power Co., Ltd. (Belg. v. Spain), 1970 I.C.J. Rep. 3 (Feb. 5).

Case Introduction

The Barcelona Traction, Light and Power Company, Limited ("BTLP") was incorporated in Canada, where it had its head office. For the purpose of developing an electric power production system in Catalonia, Spain, it formed a number of subsidiary companies. Three of these companies were incorporated under Canadian law, and the others under Spanish law. At the outbreak of the Spanish Civil War in 1936, the subsidiaries supplied the majority of Catalonia's electricity requirements. Barcelona Traction's shares were largely held by Belgian nationals.

Barcelona Traction issued bonds, principally in sterling, and these were secured by trust deeds with the National Trust Company Limited of Toronto. In 1936, due to the Spanish Civil War, the servicing of the bonds was suspended. Several years later, payment of the interest on outstanding Spanish peseta bonds was resumed, but the Spanish government refused to allow the BTLP subsidiaries to transfer currency to service the sterling bonds and pay these bondholders the interest they were due.

In 1948, three Spanish holders of BTLP sterling bonds petitioned the Spanish courts for a declaration pronouncing BTLP bankrupt, on account of the failure to pay the interest on the bonds. The Spanish court allowed their claim, and BTLP was declared bankrupt and its assets seized. Trustees in bankruptcy were elected, and the totality of BTLP shares was subsequently sold by public auction. The purchaser was a newly formed Spanish company, Fuerzas Electricas de Cataluna, S.A. (Fecsa).

A claim was subsequently brought by Belgium in the International Court of Justice (ICJ) on behalf of Belgian nationals as shareholders in BTLP. The British, Canadian and United States governments also made representations to the Spanish government on the matter.

Principal Points of the Judgment

Edited by: E. Lauterpracht Q.C.

46. It has also been contended that the measures complained of, although taken with respect to Barcelona Traction and causing it direct damage, constituted an unlawful act vis-à-vis Belgium, because they also, though indirectly, caused damage to the Belgian shareholders in Barcelona Traction. This again is merely a different way of presenting the distinction between injury in respect of a right and injury to a simple interest. But, as the Court has indicated, evidence that damage was suffered does not *ipso facto* justify a diplomatic claim [. . .] Not a mere interest affected, but solely a right infringed involves responsibility, so that an act directed against and infringing only the company's rights does not involve responsibility towards the shareholders, even if their interests are affected. [. . .]

92. [. . .] A theory has been developed to the effect that the State of the shareholders has a right of diplomatic protection when the State whose responsibility is invoked

is the national State of the company. Whatever the validity of this theory may be, it is certainly not applicable to the present case, since Spain is not the national State of Barcelona Traction.

93. On the other hand, the Court considers that, in the field of diplomatic protection as in all other fields of international law, it is necessary that the law be applied reasonably. It has been suggested that if in a given case it is not possible to apply the general rule that the right of diplomatic protection of a company belongs to its national State, considerations of equity might call for the possibility of protection of the shareholders in question by their own national State. This hypothesis does not correspond to the circumstances of the present case.

94. In view, however, of the discretionary nature of diplomatic protection, considerations of equity cannot require more than the possibility for some protector State to intervene, whether it be the national State of the company, by virtue of the general rule mentioned above, or, in a secondary capacity, the national State of the shareholders who claim protection. In this connection, account should also be taken of the practical effects of deducing from considerations of equity any broader right of protection for the national State of the shareholders. It must first of all be observed that it would be difficult on an equitable basis to make distinctions according to any quantitative test: it would seem that the owner of 1 per cent and the owner of 90 per cent of the share-capital should have the same possibility of enjoying the benefit of diplomatic protection. The protector State may, of course, be disinclined to take up the case of the single small shareholder, but it could scarcely be denied the right to do so in the name of equitable considerations. In that field, protection by the national state of the shareholders can hardly be graduated according to the absolute or relative size of the shareholding involved. [. . .]

100. In the present case, it is clear from what has been said above that Barcelona Traction was never reduced to a position of impotence such that it could not have approached its national State, Canada, to ask for its diplomatic protection, and that, as far as appeared to the Court, there was nothing to prevent Canada from continuing to grant its diplomatic protection to Barcelona Traction if it had considered that it should do so. [. . .]

102. [. . .] Since no *jus standi* before the Court has been established, it is not for the Court in its Judgment to pronounce upon any other aspect of the case, on which it should take a decision only if the Belgian Government had a right of protection in respect of its nationals, shareholders in Barcelona Traction.

Judge Padilla Nervo opted for a separate opinion where there were certain observations which he added.

Separate Opinion of Judge Padilla Nervo

The history of the responsibility of States in respect to the treatment of foreign nationals is the history of abuses, illegal interference in the domestic jurisdiction of weaker States, unjust claims, threats and even military aggression under the flag of exercising rights of protection, and the imposing of sanctions in order to oblige a government to make the reparations demanded. Special agreements to establish arbitral tribunals were on many occasions concluded under pressure, by political, economic or military threats.

The protecting States, in many instances, are more concerned with obtaining financial settlements than with preserving principles. Against the pressure of diplomatic protection, weaker States could do no more than to preserve and defend a principle of international law, while giving way under the guise of accepting friendly settlements, either giving the compensation demanded or by establishing claims commissions which had as a point of departure the acceptance of responsibility for acts or omissions, where the government was, neither in fact nor in law, really responsible. [. . .]

The law, in all its aspects, the jurisprudence and the practice of States change, as the world and the everyday requirements of international life change, but those responsible for its progressive evolution should take care that their decisions do, in the long run, contribute to the maintenance of peace and security and to the betterment of the majority of mankind. [. . .]

[. . .] It can be said that, by the mere fact of the existence of certain rules concerning the treatment of foreigners, these have certain fundamental rights that the State of residence cannot violate without incurring international responsibility; but this is not the case of foreign shareholders as such, who may be scattered all over the world and have never been or need not be residents of the respondent State or under its jurisdiction. [. . .]

The rules of international law concerning the responsibility of the State regarding the treatment of foreigners would not make it possible to impute to a State an internationally unlawful act even in a case where the said State had only harmed an interest which was not protected by the municipal legal system of that State. [. . .]

It might be argued that in case the company is liquidated and therefore ceases legally to exist its national State loses the subject of its right and the general rule cannot be applied. In such eventuality the shareholders can undertake the defence of their interest before the courts of the State whose responsibility is invoked and exhaust the local legal remedies open to them. [. . .]

The unfavourable impact on the wealth of a nation cannot be the legal foundation of a claim when a State considers that its nationals have lost money abroad, due to an act of the territorial State which is alleged to be a breach of an international responsibility. [. . .]

3. Sources of International Investment Law

Sources of domestic law are normally clear. For example, in the United States through legislation passed by Congress. However, in the international legal field, there is no equivalent legislative organ that can fulfill the law making function. The United Nations, for example, is not a sovereign legislature and does not "make" international law. The result is that international law, whether in the international criminal, environmental or foreign direct investment fields, looks to other sources for its origins and legitimacy.

In this context, Article 38 of the statute of the International Court of Justice (ICJ) has crucial importance. The ICJ is the highest court in the world to adjudicate on international disputes. It operates on the basis that domestic law is subject to international law in those areas where relevant international law exists and can be applied. Article 38 identifies the sources of international law recognized by the Court as including conventions, treaties and customary law. Thus, where treaties governing foreign direct investment are in place, these form part of the applicable international law and may include provisions applying to corporations as well as sovereign entities.

Customary law, as listed in Article 38 of the ICJ statute, is also an important source of international law with respect to foreign investment. Indeed, it can be seen as representing a step towards codified international law in this area, in a similar manner to the evolution of contract law from the common law tradition in the UK. Customary law has particular importance in the context of foreign direct investment, as it governs the question of legal nationality of the international corporation and consequently represents the starting point for matters relating to nationalization by another state.[1]

Custom and treaties represent distinctive and different sources of international law. However, international law that starts off as treaty can end up as customary law, and the treaty may no longer be needed as it becomes a customary law rule. Customary law may then have advantages that treaty law does not have, most notably that customary law is general in application and applies to every state, whereas treaty law applies only to states that have joined the relevant convention or treaty, for example the World Trade Organization (WTO). Thus, the progressive evolution of customary norms from international treaties can generally be seen as a desirable development.

In addition to custom and treaty, general principles of law recognized by civilized nations and judicial decisions, may also be used as references in a manner familiar to the contract or tort lawyer. Together, these sources provide the applicable legal framework for direct investment by a party of one state on the territory of another.

---

1. The U.S. Supreme Court case, *The Paquete Habana*, 175 U.S. 677 (1900) (relating to the seizure of fishing vessels during an armed conflict), is of particular significance in this respect, in setting out how the court determined if customary rule is applicable law (*opinion juris*).

4. Definition of Investment

The question of what constitutes foreign direct investment is of obvious practical importance. The starting point is generally the International Monetary Fund (IMF) definition:

> Foreign investment involves the transfer of tangible or intangible assets by one country in to another, for the purpose of use in that country to generate wealth under the total or partial control of the owner of the assets.

This definition points toward four essential characteristics of investment for these purposes:

- actual investment generating wealth in the country concerned
- transfer of assets into the country concerned
- relatively difficult to withdraw the investment from the country concerned
- significant element of control retained by the owner of the assets

Investment promotion and protection and other treaties may provide different or additional definitions within the scope of the treaty, for example, to include portfolio investments or more sophisticated intellectual property protection, or to extend specified or additional rights to a particular economic sector, for example, the Energy Charter Treaty.

5. Additional Reading

The work of Sornarajah provides a valuable guide to the historical development of the law of foreign direct investment and an important reference point for current practice and potential future developments.

© M. Sornarajah, *The International Law on Foreign Investment*, 3rd edition, Cambridge University Press (2010). Published with permission of Cambridge University Press.

The sudden ending of colonialism released forces of nationalism. Once freed from the shackles of colonialism, the newly independent states agitated not only for the ending of the economic dominance of the former colonial powers within their states but also for a world order which would permit them more scope for the ordering of their own economies and access to world markets. [. . .] pressure to ensure that each newly independent state had complete control of its economy.

[. . .] multinational corporations, the principal instruments of foreign direct investment exerted power and influence akin to and sometimes exceeding those of states. As a result, they were regarded by some as posing a threat to sovereignty of states. [. . .] competition for the attraction of foreign investment has resulted. [. . .]

This interplay of various economic, political and historical factors shaped and continues to shape the development of international law on foreign investment.

If international law is generated by the eventual resolution of conflicting national interests, the international law of foreign investment provides an illustration of these processes of intense conflicts and their resolution at work. It is a field which provides for the study of international law as an interdisciplinary subject in which ideas in the sphere of economics, political science and related areas have helped to shape the arguments in the field. Yet, for all its richness, the field has seldom been looked at as a whole [....] much confusion in the international law norms which apply to foreign investment.

I. The Definition of Foreign Investment

Foreign investment involves the transfer of tangible or intangible[2] assets from one country into another for the purpose of use in that country to generate wealth under the total or partial control of the owner of the assets. [. . .] in portfolio investment, there is a divorce between management and control. [. . .] In the case of portfolio investment, it is generally accepted that the investor takes upon himself the risks involved in the making of such investments. The situation is different in the case of foreign direct investment which is entitled to protection of both the domestic law of the host state and the diplomatic protection of the home state from which it was exported. [. . .] Whereas a portfolio investor may pull out his investment readily and transfer it into other portfolio investments when he sees fit, this opportunity is not present in the case of foreign direct investment which cannot be withdrawn easily. [. . .] foreign direct investment requires the continuous presence of the foreign investor and his management staff in the host state. The protection of personnel as well as plant and other equipment is vital to the functioning of foreign investment. If such protection is not given, there will be no movement of foreign investment within the world.

[. . .] foreign investments are made largely by multinational corporations. The element of control becomes more significant as the multinational corporation will seek to implement a global strategy in making the foreign investment. Control is necessary for the implementation of the strategy. The power which multinational corporations could exert to ensure the protection of their investment is considerable [. . .] The home states of these corporations could be influenced to ensure that such claims are made meaningful and they lend their weight to the creation and maintenance of an effective system of protection of foreign investment. Such power is absent in the case of those making portfolio investments.

[. . .] The success in the area of finding common norms on a universal scale, represented in the Vienna Convention on International Sales, has been due largely to the confluence of interests of major blocs of trading nations, whereas the area of foreign direct investment is characterized more by conflict than by a confluence of interests. Foreign investment involves a more permanent relationship between the

2. Intangible assets include intellectual property rights, such as patents, copyright, know-how, etc. A transaction such as a licensing agreement will therefore fall under foreign direct investment.

foreign investor and the host state than is involved in the transitory international sales convention.[3] The physical presence of the foreign investor in the host country and the high profile of his role within the economy contribute to making the transaction more than a legal transaction of low visibility which an international sales transaction is. The foreign investment transaction has to mesh in with the local economy in which it operates. It is an active participant in the economic and, often, the political processes of the host state. [. . .] Unlike the foreign investment transaction which is centered within the territory of the host state, an international financial transaction, even with a sovereign borrower, can be located within the lender's state.[4]

Foreign investment attracts the greater attention of international law for the simple reason that it involves the movement of persons and property from one state to another and such movements have potential for conflicts between the two states. [. . .] The resulting integration of the foreign investor into the host economy makes his involvement in the internal economic and political affairs of the host state inevitable. Conflict is inherent in such situations. Whereas disputes that arise between parties to sales and financial transactions are largely settled through domestic courts, the intervention of the machinery of international law may become necessary for the settlement of disputes arising from foreign investment. Because movement of persons is involved, it is possible to link the protection of foreign investment to the already existing norms on the diplomatic protection of aliens [. . .] and of state responsibility for injuries to aliens. [. . .] The roots of the international law on foreign investment lie in the effort to extend diplomatic protection to the assets of the alien. The extension of the right was contested from the time it was attempted on the ground that it leads to unwarranted interference in the domestic affairs of the host state.

II. The History of the International Law on Foreign Investment

In the eighteenth and nineteenth centuries, investment was largely made in the context of colonial expansion. Such investment did not need protection [. . .]. In this context, the need for an international law on foreign investment was minimal. [. . .] it was the major trading companies which had first established colonial power in the states that were later integrated into the imperial system [. . .] a blend of diplomacy and force ensured that these states did not interfere with foreign investors too adversely. [. . .]

---

3. Where the exporter establishes his own distribution system through entry into a state rather than through the appointment of a local agent, he would become a foreign investor as well.

4. Deposits in foreign banks are an investment but, here again, the role of international law is limited as the deposit would be governed by local law so that if there are exchange control limitations placed by the state on its withdrawal, the remedy is seldom through international law. Here again, the risk is to be borne by the foreign depositor.

Power was the final arbiter of foreign investment disputes in this early period. The use of force to settle investment disputes outside the colonial context was a frequent occurrence.

It was in the relations between the United States, still a fledgling power, and its Latin American neighbours that the need for the development of an international law relating to foreign investment played a role during the period prior to the Second World War. [. . .] The Latin American states insisting [. . .] that provision of equal treatment to foreign investors satisfied the requirements of international law.[5] In many ways, the tussle between the United States and the Latin American states was to be replayed on a global scale in the post-colonial period. But, the law that was generated in the early period of this confrontation between the United States and the Latin American states had little to do with the taking of alien property to bring about economic reforms. It involved cases of attacks by mobs or political vendetta carried out for profit by juntas in power. The takings of foreign property that were involved in these early disputes are qualitatively different from the takings that resulted from economic reforms in later periods both in Latin America and elsewhere. The uniform application of principles to both types of interference with foreign investment is an unfortunate facet of the law which was introduced by early writers who failed to see the distinction between the two types of interference with foreign investment.

However, the Russian revolution and the spread of communism in Europe led to the taking of foreign property which was justified on the basis of economic philosophy. [. . .] Many of the claims which arose as a result of these nationalisations were eventually settled by lump-sum agreements which reflect a compromise between the two conflicting views as to the appropriateness of standards that have to be met for valid interferences with foreign property. Though important as indicating state practice, the use of lump-sum agreements did not shed any light on the resolution of the question as to the external standard that had to be satisfied for a valid interference with alien property rights.

III. The Post-Colonial Period

[. . .] The period immediately following the ending of colonialism witnessed hostility and antagonism towards foreign investment generated by nationalistic fervour. Such nationalism was itself a result of the anti-colonial movements which spread throughout the colonised parts of the world. There was also the need felt on the part of the newly independent states to recover control over vital sectors of their economies from foreign investors, largely nationals of the former colonial

5. Carlos Calvo, an Argentinian foreign minister and jurist. In his *Le Droit International* (Vol. 6, 5th edn, 1885) p.231 he had said: "Aliens who established themselves in a country are certainly entitled to the same rights of protection as nationals, but they cannot claim any greater measure of protection."

powers. The result was a wave of nationalisations of foreign property.[6] [. . .] In this period of political nationalism, there was more rhetoric generated than law. [. . .] The capital-exporting nations argued for an external international law standard protecting foreign investment, whereas the newly independent nations argued for national control over the process of foreign investment, including the ending of foreign investment by nationalisation. [. . .]

One major gain of this period was the increasing acceptance that nationalisations in pursuance of economic reform or reorganization will not be considered unlawful in international law.

The second period was a period of rationalization undertaken by the state. [. . .] This pragmatic approach was a response also to a new perception of the multinational corporation as a promoter, if development can be harnessed to the economic goals of the host state. [. . .] even small states could utilize the resources of multinational corporations to leap into economic development.[7] This explains the apparent inconsistency in the stances of developing countries which, while supporting normative changes at the global level, were busy making bilateral investment treaties and foreign investment codes providing tax and other incentives to attract foreign investment.

The modern period takes pragmatism in the area further. [. . .] the emergence of a multipolar world [. . .]. The United States and European states have themselves become host states to foreign investment. There is no single hegemonistic power which could dictate terms to others as to what the rules of the foreign investment game are.

There is a growth of multinationals centered in the traditionally capital-importing countries.[8] [. . .] The trend is reflected in the law by the existence of bilateral treaties on investment protection between developing states.[9]

In the past, the existence of oligopolies within global industries enabled multinational corporations to act together to exert leverage on host states. Now, the existence of more multinational companies to choose from, within the same industry,

6. C. Himmawan, *Foreign Investment in Indonesia* (1981) discusses the intensity of nationalistic feelings that attended the Indonesian nationalisations of Dutch interests after independence.

7. The obvious examples are provided by Singapore and Hong Kong.

8. Louis T. Wells, *Third World Multinationals: The Rise of Foreign Investment from Developing Countries* (1983).

9. See, for example, the bilateral investment treaties between Singapore-Sri Lanka and Thailand-Bangladesh. As labour gets more expensive in industrializing developing countries there will be a relocation of labour intensive industry in less sophisticated economies. This relocation is given a further impetus by the fact that products made in less sophisticated economies will still be entitled to preferential treatment under the generalised system of preferences. Hence, the movement of less sophisticated investments from Singapore and Thailand into Sri Lanka and Bangladesh. The network of treaties between such states will increase. Vietnam has treaties with Indonesia and the Philippines.

has destroyed the leverage which was previously held by multinational corporations.[10] [. . .] and with the assistance of international bodies,[11] have made it possible for an unequal balance to be redressed.

Apart from the multinational corporations, which do not have personality to shape directly the course of developments in the law, there are three principal groups that have an immediate interest in influencing the manner in which the international law on foreign investment develops. The first is the group of host states, principally the developing states which are the major recipients of foreign investments. These states seek to control foreign investment by their national legislation. Such legislation shows a clear pattern of consistency in attitudes which result either through imitation or the pursuit of common goals. [. . .] The second group consists of the home states of the multinational corporations. Quite apart from promoting rules which will enhance the protection of foreign investment, some of these states also seek to control the manner in which their corporations conduct business in international markets. [. . .] The third group consists of international organizations which have an interest in developing the law in the area. They purport to speak for the whole of the international community, but pursue the sectorial interests of the dominant interest groups within it.

C. Relationship of Domestic and International Law

Although domestic law is always applicable to a foreign investor in a country, domestic law alone may not be sufficient for the protection of an investor to the required minimum standard. For example, a U.S. corporation investing in Venezuela would be at liberty to bring a claim against the Venezuelan state in the domestic courts of Venezuela, but may consider that it will not be assured of the expected minimum standard of treatment. The corporation might consequently also consider the options for the case to be pursued in an international forum under relevant customary international and/or treaty law.

Furthermore, many countries have passed laws which are designed to attract foreign investors because of the perceived benefits in terms of investment flows, technology transfer and economic development. Such legislation typically sets out the treatment that foreign investors can expect, including the provision of incentives and procedures for resolving disputes. However, this may also raise important questions regarding the relationship between such guarantees and other domestic law or public policy decisions of the country in which the investment is made. Dispute

10. The most striking change was in the oil industry which was dominated at one stage by a few companies. Now, that dominance has dissipated and there are several smaller companies which compete effectively in the industry.

11. The United Nations Centre on Transnational Corporations, which provided assistance to developing countries on negotiation of foreign investments, the drafting of contracts and on the reform of foreign investment legislation, is the obvious example.

settlement in these circumstances may raise particular complexities, while in all cases, the question of the enforceability of a settlement, either in the country of investment or in other jurisdictions, can become a matter of considerable practical importance.

In dealing with a legal issue relating to both domestic and international law, it is crucial to clarify which parties are subject to the relevant jurisdictions. Individuals and corporations are subject to the domestic law of the country of establishment and the country of investment and have legal standing in both these jurisdictions. However, only states and international organizations are subject to and have legal standing/personality under international law.

Where an individual or corporation wishes to bring an investment case in an international forum, it consequently has two potential avenues open for consideration:

1. For the government of the country of establishment (the home state) to bring a case for violation of customary international and/or treaty law against the country in which the investment took place (the host country) in a relevant domestic or international forum, up to and including the International Court of Justice.
2. For the corporation to take the case to arbitration at the International Centre for Settlement of International Disputes (ICSID) or any other forum to which the state parties are a signatory and the corporation has given its consent (such a provision would normally be established, for example, in a Bilateral Investment Treaty, and is also available on a multilateral basis in the energy sector under the Energy Charter Treaty).

The legal and practical issues related to and arising from these two approaches are considered in more detail in the following chapters.

Chapter 2

Attraction of Foreign Investment, Guarantees to Investors, Investment Codes and Efforts to Regulate Foreign Investments

A. The Current Regulatory Framework for FDI

Foreign Direct Investment (FDI) is a powerful tool for promoting economic growth and sustainable development. For this reason, governments frequently offer incentives and guarantees to attract and strengthen the inflow of foreign investment.

Nevertheless significant risks may remain for an investor of one country making investments under the jurisdiction of another. These risks may be addressed in national law, through adherence to global and regional investment codes, and by recourse to public international law. This chapter reviews these approaches to the regulation of foreign direct investment. It also sets the scene for the development of bilateral and multilateral agreements for the promotion and protection of foreign direct investment. These agreements are considered in more detail in Chapters 4 and 10.

The legal framework for the promotion and protection of foreign direct investment continues to evolve, with international investment rulemaking taking place at the bilateral but also increasingly at the regional, interregional and multilateral levels. The policy objective is to improve market access, strengthen trade facilitation and support regional economic integration.

International codes for the promotion and protection of investment include the OECD Codes for Liberalisation of Current Invisible Operations and of Capital Movements and the OECD Declaration on International Investment and Multilateral Enterprises. Regional approaches include the North American Free Trade Agreement (NAFTA) and the APEC Non-Binding Investment Principles. These codes and agreements generally commit the signatory members to transparency of investment related legislation, not to relax domestic health, safety, and environmental regulations as an incentive to encourage foreign investment, and to minimize the use of performance requirements that distort or limit expansion of trade and investment.[12]

Since Germany and Pakistan signed the first bilateral investment treaty (BIT) in 1959, two thousand nine hundred and twelve such agreements have been put in place worldwide.[13] Thus, in less than six decades, the BIT has become the principal international legal instrument for promotion and protection of private foreign investment. While states remain the primary subjects of international law, the emergence of the BITs has created an additional level of protection for private international investors, in terms of both the standard of protection and the availability of provisions for dispute settlement.[14] There are an additional three hundred and eighty-eight treaties with investment provisions in place worldwide.[15]

Provisions for investment protection were also included in the negotiations for the Trans Pacific Partnership (TPP) and for the Transatlantic Trade and Investment Partnership (TTIP). The incoming Trump Administration withdrew the United States from the TPP negotiations in January 2017, but the remaining eleven countries reached agreement in January 2018 to conclude the Comprehensive and Progressive Agreement for Trans Pacific Partnership (CPTPP). Lack of political support

12. APEC Non-Binding Investment Principles.

13. UNCTAD: International Investment Agreements as of 28th September 2019.

14. Ibid.

15. Professor Muna Ndulo, Bilateral Investment Treaties, the Settlement of Investment Disputes, and Developing Countries in *Issues Involving Foreign Investments and International Business Transactions*, p.107.

in both the U.S. and EU member states means that progress is unlikely to be made for the foreseeable future in the TTIP transatlantic negotiations.

Meanwhile China is leading the enactment of the Regional Comprehensive Economic Partnership (RCEP) in South and East Asia, including a substantive investment chapter. This free trade agreement would be between the ten member states of the Association of Southeast Asian Nations (ASEAN) and the six states with which ASEAN has existing free trade agreements, namely Australia, China, India, Japan, South Korea and New Zealand.

There is no single global investment agreement in existence to date that covers all aspects of investment.[16] Some existing WTO agreements contain provisions relating to investment, notably the Agreement on Trade-Related Investment Measures (TRIMs) and the General Agreement on Trade in Services (GATS). TRIMs protect investment from certain types of performance requirements such as local content and trade-balancing requirements. The GATS Agreement includes provisions concerning notification, transparency, Most Favoured Nation (MFN) treatment, National Treatment, market access, subsidies, and foreign exchange restrictions on capital account and current account transactions. These rules attempt to facilitate foreign investment within the framework of reducing trade distortions.

B. Attraction of Foreign Investment

1. Investment Incentives

Governments seek to attract foreign direct investment through schemes aimed at stimulating private sector interest in identified sectors of the economy. These incentives may take the form of direct subsidies (investment grants) or corporate income tax credits (investment credit) that compensate the investors for their capital costs.

© Sherif H. Seid, *Global Regulation of Foreign Direct Investment*, pp. 34–43, Ashgate Pub Ltd; First Edition (July 1, 2002), printed with permission from Taylor & Francis Group.

As industrialisation is a priority in many countries, under the implicit assumption that it will speed up the country's economic development, incentives are regarded as a useful tool to attract the capital and technology required for that purpose. [. . .]

Appropriately designed incentives can induce the investor to undertake the investment, provided the general investment climate is conducive. However, the use of incentives can also be a loss for the host country. They undoubtedly impose both financial as well as administrative burdens on the government. They can even lead to a distortion of the country's productive structure, rendering it less efficient.

16. The European Commission is consulting stakeholders on a possible permanent multilateral investment court system (see Chapter 10).

For example, maintaining high prices for industrial products as an incentive to investment in industry may result in disincentives to agricultural production, thus reducing agricultural incomes, increasing rural-urban migration, and exacerbate problems of unemployment. Therefore, any incentive has to balance its costs against its expected benefits. [. . .]

Some studies define incentive measures narrowly and draw distinctions between factor-based incentives (that is, cash grants and tax holidays) which impact directly on the factor costs of a project, and product based incentives (e.g. tariffs and import quotas) which impact directly on returns from the sale of a project's products (Wells, 1986:58). [. . .] Since most countries wish to avoid reliance on foreign raw materials or semi-finished goods, tariff concessions on raw materials raise particularly difficult policy issues. [. . .]

Tax holidays are one of the most frequently used incentives to attract FDI. The usual form of the holiday is to allow an enterprise operating in a designated investment activity to be fully or partially exempted from income or corporate taxation for a certain period of time, with full taxation applying after the holiday period. [. . .] One way of protecting against excessive revenue loss from firms that become profitable quickly is to set a ceiling on tax benefits, that is, by restricting exempt earnings to a certain percentage of the invested capital. Another way is suspending the exemption if annual earnings exceed a certain percentage of the invested capital. [. . .]

The location decision of foreign investors is influenced by many factors, but they can be classified into two broad categories: factors other than incentives and incentives policies (Guisinger and Associates, 1985:39). The first category refers to all considerations other than government incentive policies that an investor would apply to a location decision, including all advantages of production, marketing, transportation, exchange rate and price stability, quality of public management of monetary, fiscal, and social policy, and political and social stability (Guisinger and Associates, 1985:40). The second category comprises all government incentives and disincentives that affect foreign investment, whether applied to foreign investments or to investments in general (Guisinger and Associates, 1985:40–41). These include tax holidays, customs duty exemption, various types of allowance, externalization of fund, and so on.

[. . .] the debate is whether tax incentives should be provided as instruments for inducing the flow of or attracting foreign investment (OECD, 1989; UNCTAD, 1992). [. . .] [An] argument put forward against the efficacy of tax incentives is that for many economically less developed countries the tax system is relatively unimportant, compared to other factors impeding investment. [. . .] more important obstacles are either the undeveloped state of the economy itself or a fundamental lack of natural resources, or both (Heller and Kauffman, 1963:60). [. . .] Administrative corruption, arbitrariness or ineptitude in the implementation of the tax or other laws pertaining to industrial activity are also presumed to be other factors which discourage foreign investment. Tax incentives cannot compensate for such negative factors (Heller and Kauffman, 1963:63). [. . .]

The problem of inducing business enterprises to commit their capital to overseas investment is multidimensional, complex and elusive. Incentive laws do not operate in isolation, but they function in relation to a given economic and political framework, and an existing underlying tax system. An attractive investment opportunity and an acceptable investment climate represent the optimum mix of high financial returns and low non-commercial risks. [. . .] the cost of incentives may well exceed the benefits the host country anticipate from the FDI. [. . .] if the investor's investment decision is driven largely by non-incentive related considerations, the provision of incentives may simply transfer wealth from the host country to the investor without its intended effect.

C. Guarantees to Investors

A strong investment climate is often more important than investment incentives in attracting FDI. Governments are advised to focus on clear and well-implemented policies on taxation, the protection of physical and intellectual property, and on the rule of law and clean government. In doing so, countries may create a climate that welcomes and encourages private investment.

© Sherif H. Seid, *Global Regulation of Foreign Direct Investment*, pp. 34–43, Ashgate Pub Ltd; First Edition (July 1, 2002), printed with permission from Taylor & Francis Group.

Among the most important factors an investor considers before deciding to invest in a foreign country are the host country's treatment of foreign investors and their investments, the degree of protection the host country provides to the investor and its property, and the right to repatriate earnings. [. . .]

Many countries accord foreign controlled enterprises either national treatment or "fair and equitable treatment" (OECD, 1993). National treatment requires that foreign controlled enterprises be treated by the host country no less favourably than domestic enterprises (OECD, 1976: Article II).

In many countries, including the OECD members, national treatment is accorded post entry and establishment, that is, countries may regulate discriminatorily the entry of foreign investment or the condition of establishment of foreign enterprises into their territories (OECD, 1993:14).

The principle of national treatment is aimed at eliminating discrimination vis-à-vis foreign investment, the comparison usually being between firms in the same sector (OECD, 1993:62–64).

[. . .] the principle of national treatment has no uniform application at the moment. Even though the great majority of countries apply it on already established investments, others would like to see it applied at the pre-establishment phase as well. Its current application is also qualified by numerous exceptions the selection of which is left entirely to the host country. Moreover, it is arguable whether national treatment brings its intended effect, at least in countries where the nationals themselves are subjected to a lower standard of treatment. [. . .]

Some countries accord foreign investment "fair and equitable treatment" [. . .] non-discrimination, the internal minimum standard, and the duty to protect foreign property by the host state are normally considered by classical international law as the firm ingredients of "fair and equitable treatment" (UNCTC, 1988:42).

D. Investment Codes and Efforts to Regulate Foreign Investments

1. Host States' Laws on FDI

Host countries are at liberty to take measures in national legislation to promote and protect foreign direct investment. These measures, including with respect to labor standards, may significantly affect the decision to invest in a certain country.

© Sherif H. Seid, *Global Regulation of Foreign Direct Investment*, pp. 44–45, Ashgate Pub Ltd; First Edition (July 1, 2002), printed with permission from Taylor & Francis Group.

Increasingly, the laws of host countries on FDI are taking the form of a code or a single piece of legislation that states the pertinent rules relating to FDI in the country. They specify the authority responsible for supervising investment, conditions of entry and the sectors open to FDI, the controls FDI is subjected to, remissibility of funds, performance requirements, incentives granted to investors, and the circumstances of the termination of foreign investment and other similar matters. Such codes typically apply to FDI alone, while foreign investors in other sectors must generally obey all relevant laws. The existence of a single code enables the foreign investor to acquaint itself with the laws on foreign investment of a country more easily. It is part of an attempt to communicate the certainty in the rule of law.

Example of Host Country Code:
Republic of Namibia Foreign Investment Act, 1990

PART I

Administration of Act and Principles Regarding Foreign Investment

2. Subject to the laws governing the public service, there shall be established in the Ministry of Trade and Industry a division, to be known as the Investment Centre, to assist the Minister in the administration of this Act.

3. (1) Subject to the provisions of this section and the activities of compliance with any formalities or requirements foreign prescribed by any law in relation to the relevant business nationals activity, a foreign national may invest and engage in any business activity in Namibia which any Namibian may undertake.

(2) For the purposes of any law governing the establishment and carrying on of any business activity or the taxation of the income, or any other aspect, of any business activity, a foreign national shall be in no different position than any Namibian, except as may be otherwise provided by this Act.

(3) No foreign national engaged in a business activity or intending to commence a business activity in Namibia shall be required to provide for the participation of the Government or any Namibian as shareholder or as partner in such business, or for the transfer of such business to the Government or any Namibian: Provided that it may be a condition of any licence or other authorisation to or any agreement with a foreign national for the grant of rights over natural resources that the Government shall be entitled to or may acquire an interest in any enterprise to be formed for the exploitation of such rights.

(4) The Minister may, by notice in the Gazette, specify any business or category of business which, in the Minister's opinion, is engaged primarily in the provision of services or the production of goods which can be provided or produced adequately by Namibians, and, with effect from the date of such notice, no foreign national shall, subject to the provisions of section 7(3), through the investment of foreign assets, become engaged in or be permitted to become engaged in any business so specified or falling within any category of business so specified.

(5) Any law relating to natural resources or any licence or other authorisation granted under such a law conferring rights for the exploitation of such resources, may provide for the granting or enjoyment of such rights to or by Namibians on terms more favourable than those applicable to foreign nationals. *[s.3(5) added by s.1 of Act 24 of 1993]

[. . .]

6. (1) A foreign national may apply to the Minister for a Certificate of Status Investment in respect of an investment which qualifies as an eligible investment in terms of section 5.

[. . .]

(2.) (b) the extent to which the enterprise in which the proposed investment is to be made will utilize Namibian resources, including labour and natural resources so as to contribute to the economy, by, inter alia:

(i) increasing employment opportunities in Namibia;

(ii) providing for the training of Namibians;

(iii) earning or saving foreign exchange;

(iv) generating development in the less developed areas of Namibia;

[. . .]

8. (1) Notwithstanding the provisions of any other law, the Bank of Namibia shall ensure that there is available for purchase by the holder of a Certificate, at the request of that holder, freely convertible foreign currency which the holder may use without any restriction:

[. . .]

9. (1) Notwithstanding the provisions of any other law but subject to subsections (3) and (4) of this section, the Bank of Namibia shall ensure that there is available for purchase by the holder of a Certificate, at the request of that holder, convertible foreign currency which the holder may use without any restriction:

(a) for the transfer out of Namibia of the profits of the enterprise or, where the enterprise is carried as a branch operation by a company which is a foreign national, for the payment to the head office of the company of remittances out of funds representing the branch profits, after deduction or retention in either case of any tax due;

[. . .]

11. (1) No enterprise, or part of an undertaking carried on by an enterprise, or interest in or right over any property forming part of such undertaking shall be expropriated except in accordance with the provisions of Article 16 (2) of the Namibian Constitution.

(2) Where an enterprise or any part of an undertaking carried on by an enterprise, or any interest in or right over any property forming part of such undertaking is expropriated, the Government shall pay to the holder of the Certificate just compensation for such expropriation without undue delay and in freely convertible currency.

[. . .]

(2) If the holder of the Certificate fails to carry out the obligations referred to in this section within the time or periods, if any, specified in the Certificate, the Certificate may be cancelled in accordance with the provisions of section 15.

13. (1) If a person to whom a Certificate is to be issued under section 7 so elects, the Certificate shall provide that any dispute between the holder of the Certificate and the Government in respect of:

(a) any issue relating to the amount of, or any other matter in connection with, any compensation payable in a case of an expropriation as provided in section 11;

(b) the validity or continued validity of the Certificate, shall be referred for settlement by international arbitration

(2) Where a Certificate provides for the settlement of disputes by international arbitration, arbitration shall be in accordance with the Arbitration Rules of the United Nations Commission on International Trade Law in force at the time when the Certificate was issued, unless agreement [. . .] another method of settling the dispute.

(3) [. . .] any award rendered in any such arbitration shall be final and binding on the holder of the Certificate and the Government.

[. . .]

2. The World Bank Guidelines on the Treatment of Foreign Direct Investment

The World Bank is the parent institution of the Multilateral Investment Guarantee Agency (MIGA) and the International Centre for Settlement of Investment Disputes (ICSID), which will be discussed in detail in Chapter 3 and Chapter 8 respectively.

The World Bank Guidelines on the Treatment of Foreign Direct Investment is not a treaty, and its provisions are not formally binding as international law. However, the Guidelines are widely acknowledged as "soft law" and considered "as good as binding" on states. The Guidelines provide a strong benchmark for calibrating the investment climate in a given country. For example, under MIGA, the country receiving investment is required to certify that it has a good investment climate in accordance with the World Bank Guidelines. The Guidelines may also play a role in complementing and supporting BITs and regional conventions.

Ibrahim Shihata, *The Legal Treatment of Foreign Investment: The World Bank Guidelines*, Springer Netherlands (1993).

A convention requires elaborate negotiations and must be signed and ratified before it enters into force in respect of a given country. While it is legally binding, it can only reflect the common denominator, that is what is acceptable to the potential contracting parties. Recommendations or guidelines issued by the World Bank could not have this binding effect since they would not be subject to the same process involved in the preparation of a draft convention and would not be ratified. However, they would not necessarily represent the lowest common denominator. [. . .]

[With respect to the content of the guidelines, Shihata outlines the Bank's aims:] The studies of the various multilateral instruments showed that the most vocal objection they see in this exercise is an attempt to impose on them rules which reflected what they perceived to be the interests of foreign investors and their home states: some of them probably felt that their own interests would be better served in this particular area if no hard and fast rules representing a binding law were in place. It was therefore important, in drafting the guidelines, to do so in a manner that would lessen rather than aggravate the concerns of developing countries. A sensitive approach to the position of developing countries would stress the relevance of the guidelines to the promotion of FDI in these countries [. . .]. Moreover, [the Guidelines] should be related to principles which could be demonstrated to have a strong basis in state practice, not to principles favored by a small group of countries, be they developed or developing. Yet, for the exercise to serve the purpose defined by the [Bank's] Development Committee, "so as to promote FDI", the guidelines clearly had to go beyond what was commonly reflected in state practice. The task was not simple.

Sabine Schlemmer-Schulte, The World Bank Guidelines on the Treatment of Foreign Direct Investment in *Legal Aspects of Foreign Direct Investment* edited by Daniel D. Bradlow, Alfred Escher, The Hague; Boston: Kluwer Law International (1999).[17]

The first multilateral instrument to be adopted in the 1990s was the *World Bank's Guidelines on the Treatment of Foreign Direct Investment* (*World Bank Guidelines*), issued in September 1992 by the Development Committee and the Boards of Governors of the World Bank and the International Monetary Fund (IMF). As the name suggests, the Guidelines, unlike laws and treaties, are not binding on governments but were intended to influence the formulation of new laws and treaties. [. . .]

The influence of the Guidelines may be detected in many of the multilateral instruments dealing with investment that have appeared since the adoption of the Guidelines. [. . .] regional multilateral treaties such as the 1992 North American Free Trade Agreement, the 1994 Energy Charter Treaty, and the two 1994 investment protocols to the trade agreement establishing Mercosur [South American trade bloc]. [. . .] The idea of a global investment agreement is also being discussed by WTO members.

a. The Content of the Guidelines

The Guidelines cover each of the five main areas usually dealt with in investment treaties: the scope of application (i.e. in particular the definition of foreign investment), admission, treatment, expropriation of foreign investments, and the settlement of investment disputes.[18] [. . .]

The Guidelines are formulated in a normative form or, occasionally, in the form of policy advice, depending on their substance and the degree to which they may be reconciled with general principles of contemporary international law. They aim to guide governmental behavior toward foreign investors. They do not address the conduct of foreign investors which was being discussed at the UN at the time.[19]

[. . .] they represent a general framework which complements, but does not substitute for, bilateral investment treaties, regional conventions and other instruments

17. Reproduced with the permission of Kluwer Law International from *Legal Aspects of Foreign Direct Investment* (ISBN 9789041112149), "The World Bank Guidelines on the Treatment of Foreign Direct Investment," by Sabine Schlemmer Schulte, pages 88, 91–93, © 1999.

18. For an in-depth analysis of all Guidelines along with their drafting history, see I. Shihata, *Legal Treatment of Foreign Investment—The World Bank Guidelines*, Chapters 4, 5 and 6, 61–98, 124–137 and 139–150 (1993).

19. In this respect, the Guidelines differ from the abortive attempt of a draft Code of Conduct by the UN Centre on Transnational Corporations (UNCTC) which included both rules for governmental behavior toward foreign investors and on good conduct on the part of the foreign investor. Compare also the 1976 OECD Guidelines for Multinational Enterprises which laid down standards for the activities of such enterprises.

for broader application. In a concrete case, the Guidelines would be most relevant to situations where bilateral investment treaties or other instruments do not exist or are silent on the matters provided for in the Guidelines.

Their main rationale, of course, is to promote foreign investments, so that such investments may increase in volume and spread out to as many countries as possible, and that these flows may be governed by economic considerations and not hampered by non-commercial factors. [. . .]

The absence of restrictions as to the nature of covered investments suggests that the Guidelines favor a broad interpretation of the concept so that it covers all kinds of investments.[20] In the absence of any restrictions, the Guidelines apply to indirect as well as to direct investments. This means they are applicable to any contractual and other arrangements in which funds, equipment, technology and/or service are provided, and the provider's return depends in whole or in part on the fortunes of the enterprise. [. . .] While the Guidelines may in several respects be particularly relevant to private foreign direct investment, there is no reason to exclude portfolio investment from their scope. [. . .] While the Guidelines do not address the conduct of foreign investors in their host States, they emphasize that they only apply to investments made and carried out in *good faith* and in complete compliance with local legal requirements.

World Bank Guidelines on the Treatment of Foreign Direct Investment

The Development Committee

Recognizing

that a greater flow of foreign direct investment brings substantial benefits to bear on the world economy and on the economies of developing countries in particular, in terms of improving the long term efficiency of the host country through greater competition, transfer of capital, technology and managerial skills and enhancement of market access and in terms of the expansion of international trade;

that the promotion of private foreign investment is a common purpose of the International Bank for Reconstruction and Development, the International Finance Corporation and the Multilateral Investment Guarantee Agency;

that these institutions have pursued this common objective through their operations, advisory services and research;

that at the request of the Development Committee, a working group established by the President of these institutions and consisting of their respective General Counsel has, after reviewing existing legal instruments and literature, as well as best available practice identified by these institutions, prepared a set of guidelines

20. In this respect the Guidelines are similar to most bilateral investment treaties and multilateral instruments, which either adopt broad definitions of covered investments or do not qualify them at all.

representing a desirable overall framework which embodies essential principles meant to promote foreign direct investment in the common interest of all members;

that these guidelines, which have benefitted from a process of broad consultation inside and outside these institutions, constitute a further step in the evolutionary process where several international efforts aim to establish a favorable investment environment free from non-commercial risks in all countries, and thereby foster the confidence of international investors;

and that these guidelines are not ultimate standards but an important step in the evolution of generally acceptable international standards which complement, but do not substitute for, bilateral investment treaties,

therefore calls the attention of member countries to the following Guidelines as useful parameters in the admission and treatment of private foreign investment in their territories, without prejudice to the binding rules of international law at this stage of its development.

I

Scope of Application

1. These Guidelines may be applied by members of the World Bank Group institutions to private foreign investment in their respective territories, as a complement to applicable bilateral and multilateral treaties and other international instruments, to the extent that these Guidelines do not conflict with such treaties and binding instruments, and as a possible source on which national legislation governing the treatment of private foreign investment may draw. Reference to the "State" in these Guidelines, unless the context otherwise indicates, includes the State or any constituent subdivision, agency or instrumentality of the State and reference to "nationals" includes natural and juridical persons who enjoy the nationality of the State.

2. The application of these Guidelines extends to existing and new investments established and operating at all times as bona fide private foreign investments, in full conformity with the laws and regulations of the host State.

3. These Guidelines are based on the general premise that equal treatment of investors in similar circumstances and free competition among them are prerequisites of a positive investment environment. Nothing in these Guidelines therefore suggests that foreign investors should receive a privileged treatment denied to national investors in similar circumstances.

II

Admission

1. Each State will encourage nationals of other States to invest capital, technology and managerial skill in is territory and, to that end, is expected to admit such investments in accordance with the following provisions.

2. In furtherance of the foregoing principle, each State will: (a) facilitate the admission and establishment of investments by nationals of other States, and (b) avoid

making unduly cumbersome or complicated procedural regulations for, or imposing unnecessary conditions on, the admission of such investments.

3. Each State maintains the right to make regulations to govern the admission of private foreign investments. In the formulation and application of such regulations, States will note that experience suggests that certain performance requirements introduced as conditions of admission are often counterproductive and that open admission, possibly subject to a restricted list of investments (which are either prohibited or require screening and licensing), is a more effective approach. Such performance requirements often discourage foreign investors from initiating investment in the State concerned or encourage evasion and corruption. Under the restricted list approach, investments in nonlisted activities, which proceed without approval, remain subject to the laws and regulations applicable to investments in the State concerned.

4. Without prejudice to the general approach of free admission recommended in Section 3 above, a State may, as an exception, refuse admission to a proposed investment: (i) which is, in the considered opinion of the State, inconsistent with clearly defined requirements of national security; or (ii) which belongs to sectors reserved by the law of the State to its nationals on account of the State's economic development objectives or the strict exigencies of its national interest.

5. Restrictions applicable to national investment on account of public policy (*ordre public*), public health and the protection of the environment will equally apply to foreign investment.

6. Each State is encouraged to publish, in the form of a handbook or other medium easily accessible to other States and their investors, adequate and regularly updated information about its legislation, regulations and procedures relevant to foreign investment and other information relating to its investment policies including, *inter alia*, an indication of any classes of investment which it regards as falling under Sections 4 and 5 of this Guideline.

III

Treatment

1. For the promotion of international economic cooperation through the medium of private foreign investment, the establishment, operation, management, control, and exercise of rights in such an investment, as well as such other associated activities necessary therefor or incidental thereto, will be consistent with the following standards which are meant to apply simultaneously to all States without prejudice to the provisions of applicable international instruments, and to firmly established rules of customary international law.

2. Each State will extend to investments established in its territory by nationals of any other State fair and equitable treatment according to the standards recommended in these Guidelines.

3. (a) With respect to the protection and security of their person, property rights and interests, and to the granting of permits, import and export licenses and the

authorization to employ, and the issuance of the necessary entry and stay visas to their foreign personnel, and other legal matters relevant to the treatment of foreign investors as described in Section 1 above, such treatment will, subject to the requirement of fair and equitable treatment mentioned above, be as favorable as that accorded by the State to national investors in similar circumstances. In all cases, full protection and security will be accorded to the investor's rights regarding ownership, control and substantial benefits over his property, including intellectual property. (b) As concerns such other matters as are not relevant to national investors, treatment under the State's legislation and regulations will not discriminate among foreign investors on grounds of nationality.

4. Nothing in this Guideline will automatically entitle nationals of other States to the more favorable standards of treatment accorded to the nationals of certain States under any customs union or free trade area agreement.

5. Without restricting the generality of the foregoing, each State will: (a) promptly issue such licenses and permits and grant such concessions as may be necessary for the uninterrupted operation of the admitted investment; and (b) to the extent necessary for the efficient operation of the investment, authorize the employment of foreign personnel. While a State may require the foreign investor to reasonably establish his inability to recruit the required personnel locally, e.g., through local advertisement, before he resorts to the recruitment of foreign personnel, labor market flexibility in this and other areas is recognized as an important element in a positive investment environment. Of particular importance in this respect is the investor's freedom to employ top managers regardless of their nationality.

6. (1) Each State will, with respect to private investment in its territory by nationals of the other States: (a) freely allow regular periodic transfer of a reasonable part of the salaries and wages of foreign personnel; and, on liquidation of the investment or earlier termination of the employment, allow immediate transfer of all savings from such salaries and wages; (b) freely allow transfer of the net revenues realized from the investment; (c) allow the transfer of such sums as may be necessary for the payment of debts contracted, or the discharge of other contractual obligations incurred in connection with the investment as they fall due; (d) on liquidation or sale of the investment (whether covering the investment as a whole or a part thereof), allow the repatriation and transfer of the net proceeds of such liquidation or sale and all accretions thereto all at once; in the exceptional cases where the State faces foreign exchange stringencies, such transfer may as an exception be made in installments within a period which will be as short as possible and will not in any case exceed five years from the date of liquidation or sale, subject to interest as provided for in Section 6 (3) of this Guideline; and (e) allow the transfer of any other amounts to which the investor is entitled such as those which become due under the conditions provided for in Guidelines IV and V. (2) Such transfer as provided for in Section 6 (1) of this Guideline will be made (a) in the currency brought in by the investor where it remains convertible, in another currency designated as freely usable currency by the International Monetary Fund

or in any other currency accepted by the investor, and (b) at the applicable market rate of exchange at the time of the transfer. (3) In the case of transfers under Section 6 (1) of this Guideline, and without prejudice to Sections 7 and 8 of Guideline IV where they apply, any delay in effecting the transfers to be made through the central bank (or another authorized public authority) of the host State will be subject to interest at the normal rate applicable to the local currency involved in respect of any period intervening between the date on which such local currency has been provided to the central bank (or the other authorized public authority) for transfer and the date on which the transfer is actually effected. (4) The provisions set forth in this Guideline with regard to the transfer of capital will also apply to the transfer of any compensation for loss due to war, armed conflict, revolution or insurrection to the extent that such compensation may be due to the investor under applicable law.

7. Each State will permit and facilitate the reinvestment in its territory of the profits realized from existing investments and the proceeds of sale or liquidation of such investments.

8. Each State will take appropriate measures for the prevention and control of corrupt business practices and the promotion of accountability and transparency in its dealings with foreign investors, and will cooperate with other States in developing international procedures and mechanisms to ensure the same.

9. Nothing in this Guideline suggests that a State should provide foreign investors with tax exemptions or other fiscal incentives. Where such incentives are deemed to be justified by the State, they may to the extent possible be automatically granted, directly linked to the type of activity to be encouraged and equally extended to national investors in similar circumstances. Competition among States in providing such incentives, especially tax exemptions, is not recommended. Reasonable and stable tax rates are deemed to provide a better incentive than exemptions followed by uncertain or excessive rates.

10. Developed and capital surplus States will not obstruct flows of investment from their territories to developing States and are encouraged to adopt appropriate measures to facilitate such flows, including taxation agreements, investment guarantees, technical assistance and the provision of information. Fiscal incentives provided by some investors' governments for the purpose of encouraging investment in developing States are recognized in particular as a possibly effective element in promoting such investment.

IV

Expropriation and Unilateral Alterations or Termination of Contracts

1. A State may not expropriate or otherwise take in whole or in part a foreign private investment in its territory, or take measures which have similar effects, except where this is done in accordance with applicable legal procedures, in pursuance in good faith of a public purpose, without discrimination on the basis of nationality and against the payment of appropriate compensation.

2. Compensation for a specific investment taken by the State will, according to the details provided below, be deemed "appropriate" if it is adequate, effective and prompt.

3. Compensation will be deemed "adequate" if it is based on the fair market value of the taken asset as such value is determined immediately before the time at which the taking occurred or the decision to take the asset became publicly known.

4. Determination of the "fair market value" will be acceptable if conducted according to a method agreed by the State and the foreign investor (hereinafter referred to as the parties) or by a tribunal or another body designated by the parties.

5. In the absence of a determination agreed by, or based on the agreement of, the parties, the fair market value will be acceptable if determined by the State according to reasonable criteria related to the market value of the investment, i.e., in an amount that a willing buyer would normally pay to a willing seller after taking into account the nature of the investment, the circumstances in which it would operate in the future and its specific characteristics, including the period in which it has been in existence, the proportion of tangible assets in the total investment and other relevant factors pertinent to the specific circumstances of each case.

6. Without implying the exclusive validity of a single standard for the fairness by which compensation is to be determined and as an illustration of the reasonable determination by a State of the market value of the investment under Section 5 above, such determination will be deemed reasonable if conducted as follows: (i) for a going concern with a proven record of profitability, on the basis of the discounted cash flow value; (ii) for an enterprise which, not being a proven going concern, demonstrates lack of profitability, on the basis of the liquidation value; (iii) for other assets, on the basis of (a) the replacement value or (b) the book value in case such value has been recently assessed or has been determined as of the date of the taking and can therefore be deemed to represent a reasonable replacement value. For the purpose of this provision: -a "going concern" means an enterprise consisting of income-producing assets which has been in operation for a sufficient period of time to generate the data required for the calculation of future income and which could have been expected with reasonable certainty, if the taking had not occurred, to continue producing legitimate income over the course of its economic life in the general circumstances following the taking by the State; -"discounted cash flow value" means the cash receipts realistically expected from the enterprise in each future year of its economic life as reasonably projected minus that year's expected cash expenditure, after discounting this net cash flow for each year by a factor which reflects the time value of money, expected inflation, and the risk associated with such cash flow under realistic circumstances. Such discount rate may be measured by examining the rate of return available in the same market on alternative investments of comparable risk on the basis of their present value; -"liquidation value" means the amounts at which individual assets

comprising the enterprise or the entire assets of the enterprise could be sold under conditions of liquidation to a willing buyer less any liabilities which the enterprise has to meet; -"replacement value" means the cash amount required to replace the individual assets of the enterprise in their actual state as of the date of the taking; and -"book value" means the difference between the enterprise's assets and liabilities as recorded on its financial statements or the amount at which the taken tangible assets appear on the balance sheet of the enterprise, representing their cost after deducting accumulated depreciation in accordance with generally accepted accounting principles.

7. Compensation will be deemed "effective" if it is paid in the currency brought in by the investor where it remains convertible, in another currency designated as freely usable by the International Monetary Fund or in any other currency accepted by the investor.

8. Compensation will be deemed to be "prompt" in normal circumstances if paid without delay. In cases where the State faces exceptional circumstances, as reflected in an arrangement for the use of the resources of the International Monetary Fund or under similar objective circumstances of established foreign exchange stringencies, compensation in the currency designated under Section 7 above may be paid in installments within a period which will be as short as possible and which will not in any case exceed five years from the time of the taking, provided that reasonable, market-related interest applies to the deferred payments in the same currency.

9. Compensation according to the above criteria will not be due, or will be reduced in case the investment is taken by the State as a sanction against an investor who has violated the State's law and regulations which have been in force prior to the taking, as such violation is determined by a court of law. Further disputes regarding claims for compensation in such a case will be settled in accordance with the provisions of Guideline V.

10. In case of comprehensive non-discriminatory nationalizations effected in the process of large scale social reforms under exceptional circumstances of revolution, war and similar exigencies, the compensation may be determined through negotiations between the host State and the investors' home State and failing this, through international arbitration.

11. The provisions of Section I of this Guideline will apply with respect to the conditions under which a State may unilaterally terminate, amend or otherwise disclaim liability under a contract with a foreign private investor for other than commercial reasons, i.e., where the State acts as a sovereign and not as a contracting party. Compensation due to the investor in such cases will be determined in the light of the provisions of Sections 2 to 9 of this Guideline. Liability for repudiation of contract for commercial reasons, i.e., where the State acts as a contracting party, will be determined under the applicable law of the contract.

V

Settlement of Disputes

1. Disputes between private foreign investors and the host State will normally be settled through negotiations between them and failing this, through national courts or through other agreed mechanisms including conciliation and binding independent arbitration.

2. Independent arbitration for the purpose of this Guideline will include any ad hoc or institutional arbitration agreed upon in writing by the State and the investor or between the State and the investor's home State where the majority of the arbitrators are not solely appointed by one party to the dispute.

3. In case of agreement on independent arbitration, each State is encouraged to accept the settlement of such disputes through arbitration under the Convention establishing the International Centre for Settlement of Investment Disputes (ICSID) if it is a party to the ICSID Convention or through the "ICSID Additional Facility" if it is not a party to the ICSID Convention.

E. International Law Related to Political Risk

This section discusses the general principles of international law applicable to investors of one state when investing under the sovereign jurisdiction of another. Once such an investment has been made, the investment is subject to the domestic laws of the host state and is exposed to the public policy and political environment of the host country. Where equitable treatment is not believed to be available in the host country jurisdiction, the investor may also consider the possibility of recourse to public international law.

The reason these issues are important for investors is that international law plays an important role on the international commercial and political world stage. Although there is no international world sovereign or policeman to enforce principles of international law or to coerce rogue states into complying with international law [. . .] international law is, by and large, widely complied with, or at the least seriously considered by nations before choosing to flout it. [. . .]

Thus, although international law does not offer absolute guarantees, it is extremely significant for investors in its role in regulating and taming the conduct of states.

[. . .] a state's power within its border are not limitless under international law; a state will be held bound in certain circumstances, for certain promises it makes to another state or a national of another state. Although international law does not require a state to allow the establishment of foreign direct investment, once a state has made certain international agreements, they must, in general, be kept.[21] In a famous statement of this principle in the *Sapphire* case,[22] Judge Calvin stated:

"It is a fundamental principle of law, which is constantly being proclaimed by international Courts, that contractual undertakings must be respected. The rule "pacta sunt servanda" is the basis of every contractual relationship."[23]

a. Internationalization of Investor-State Contracts

[. . .] a state is not always liable under international law for breach of a contract with an investor. Many investor-state contracts, in fact, are governed by solely the law of the host state, and thus may be modified by the host state to the detriment of the investor. [. . .]

An alien investor who opens a restaurant and whose permit is later revoked by the state for health violations, for example, could not claim that the revocation of the permit was a breach of contract under international law.

A contract between a host state and a national of another state binds the state under international law when it is "internationalized". Internationalization of a contract occurs when the contract is made subject to international law (or international law in combination with domestic law), and the parties agree that to the extent that the law of the host state governs the contract, it will not be unilaterally modified by the state.[24] [. . .] Internationalization is accomplished by the inclusion of an international choice-of-law clause and a "stabilization clause" in the investor-state agreement. [. . .]

"Stabilization clauses incorporate in concession agreements not only express, but the specific concrete commitment on the part of the contracting State not to change the terms of the contractual relationship without the consent of the other contracting party. This commitment may make a difference from the point of view of international responsibility. The breach of the obligations contained in a stabilization clause may well be viewed as a circumstance aggravating the responsibility of the contracting State. The breach of any of the obligations emanating from the contractual relationship entails responsibility, but when there is a breach of an obligation involving an explicit State's promise to respect the agreement, the breach logically becomes a more serious act or omission, entailing a higher degree of responsibility.

---

21. Adeoye Akinsanya, *International Protection of Direct Foreign Investment in the Third World*, 36 Intl & Comp, L.Q. 58, 59 (1987).

22. *Sapphire International Petroleum Limited (Sapphire) v National Iranian Oil Co.*, 35 I.L.R 136 (1953).

23. *Sapphire*, 35 I.L.R. at 181.

24. Derek William Bowett, *State Contracts with Aliens: Contemporary Developments on Compensation for Termination or Breach*, 59 Br. Y.B. Int'l L. 49, 51–52 (1988).

It is also logical to think that the higher degree of responsibility will affect the measure of reparation."[25]

The effects of the "internationalization" of contracts has been affirmed by international tribunals. In *TOPCO*, Sole Arbitrator Dupuy found that one effect of internationalization of a contract is that the individuals acquire and can enforce certain rights against the state.[26]

[. . .] despite the fact that arbitral tribunals have consistently given effect to internationalized investor-state contracts, arguments persist that internationalization of a contract is contrary to international law. Many of these arguments confuse the issue of whether a state can be "bound" by its promises to investors by contract, and the consequences of breach of such contracts. [. . .] Just as a state is free to expropriate tangible property located within its territory upon the payment of full compensation, so a state may breach an internationalized contract, but must pay compensation. Judge Higgins of the International Court of Justice has made thus point, stating that "a state may still engage in what it sees as actions in the public good that violate contracts; but there is no reason why the foreign investor should underwrite thus exercise in state sovereignty."[27]

Professor Bowett argues against a state's ability to bind itself by an "internationalized" contract to a state. Arguing against the analogy that internationalization of a contract binds a state to the contract in the same manner that a state is bound to a treaty, Professor Bowett states "[. . .] for there is a world of difference between an agreement under international law between two equal, sovereign States and a contract between a State and a private party governed *prima facie* by the State's own law. Obviously, with a treaty one state cannot use its own municipal law to vary its treaty obligations towards another State. But it is by no means obvious why, with a private law contract, the State party should not assert that right."[28]

However, such a choice of law clause would not confer upon a private person competences comparable to those of a state but only certain capacities which enable him to act internationally in order to invoke the rights which result to him from an internationalized contract. For a claimant to make good their international law claims, they would have to establish that they have standing before a tribunal hearing such a case in relation to such claims. They must establish two things: (a) that the state may owe them duties under international law; (b) that they are themselves entitled to invoke the breach of such duties.

Very often the foreign investor is registered in the host state. In that event, it would be difficult for the corporation to meet the nationality requirements of

25. F.V. Garcia-Amador, State Responsibility in Case of "Stabilization" Clauses, 2. J. Transnat'l & Pol'y 23, 49–50 (1993).

26. *TOPCO* [*Texaco Overseas Petroleum Co. v. Libya*,] 17 I.L.M. 1 at para. 48 (1978).

27. Higgins, [Rosalyn Higgins, *Problems and Process: International Law and How We Use It* 78–79 (1994)] *at* 143.

28. Bowett, *supra* note [22], at 54.

customary international law such that it has standing to invoke it against the state. Customary international law has historically taken a very strict view of the nationality of corporations. The International Court of Justice held in *Barcelona Traction* that international law attributes the right to diplomatic protection of a corporate entity to the state under the laws of which it is incorporated.

1. The Doctrine of Restrictive Sovereign Immunity

© P.E. Comeaux and N.S. Kinsella, *Protecting Foreign Investment under International Law: Legal Aspects of Political Risk*, 1996, Oxford Publishing Limited (Academic). Reproduced with permission of the Licensor through PLSclear.

Sovereign immunity is a doctrine that prohibits one state from exercising jurisdiction over another state, or its agents or instrumentalities.[29] Judge Higgins has stated that:

[u]nder classical international law, states, including governments thereof, were granted immunity from the territorial jurisdiction of other states. Various reasons of policy have been suggested, all interrelated. First, the reason may be found in the doctrine of sovereign equality: *pari parim non habet imperium*, which means that no state could be expected to submit to the laws of another. Secondly, it has been said that it would offend the dignity of a state to submit to the jurisdiction of another.[30]

Before this century, this doctrine was often absolute—that is, a state would not subject another state to jurisdiction in its courts.

As states became increasingly involved in commercial activities in the 19th century, states began to question the doctrine of absolute immunity. [. . .]

European courts then began to develop the doctrine of "restrictive immunity", by which a state would not be immune to a suit based primarily on its commercial activities.[31] Under this doctrine, a distinction is made between *acta jure imperii*, which refers to acts of public authority for which there would be immunity, and *acte jure gestionis*, which refers to commercial acts for which states would not be granted immunity.[32] This is reflected in the European Convention on State Immunity, which, although it has not gained widespread acceptance, represents the view of many European states.

---

29. Troland S. Link, *Foreign Sovereign Immunity, Expropriation, Act of State, and Comity*, 703 PLI/Comm. L. & Prac. Handbook Series 183 (1994).

30. Higgins [Rosalyn Higgins, *Problems and Process: International Law and How We Use It* 78–79 (1994)], at 78-9. Isa Foighel has stated that "a state is competent, and solely competent, to do within its territory those acts which actually or potentially are done in the exercise of the governmental power of the state." Foighel, [Isa Foighel, *Nationalization: A Study in the Protection of Alien Property in International Law* 41 (1957)], at 42.

31. Link, *supra* note [27], at 183.

32. Higgins, *supra*, at 79.

In 1945, the United States recognized the doctrine of restrictive sovereign immunity, stating that immunity would be recognized "with regard to sovereign or public acts (jure imperii) of a state, but not with respect to private acts (jure gestionis)."[33] This recognition was codified in the Foreign Sovereign Immunities Act of 1976 (the "FSIA"),[34] [. . .] which sets forth criteria for determining whether a United States court may assume jurisdiction over a sovereign state or agency of a sovereign state, and provides procedures for service of process and attachment and execution of judgments. [. . .] and while Western states have generally accepted the doctrine of restrictive immunity, many states in the developing world have not.

a. Foreign Sovereign Immunities Act

The Foreign Sovereign Immunities Act of 1976 codified the restrictive theory of foreign sovereign immunity, which granted foreign sovereigns and their instrumentalities jurisdictional immunity in cases founded upon acts of a government, as opposed to commercial nature.

In *Dole Food Co. v. Patrickson*, 538 U.S. 468 (2003), the Court held that a majority of a foreign corporation's shares must be directly owned by a foreign sovereign in order for the corporation to qualify as a foreign government "instrumentality" and hence as a foreign state. The Court further held that instrumentality status is determined as at the time of the filing of the complaint.

Title 28, United States Code—Foreign Sovereign Immunities Act 1976

§ 1603. Definitions

For purposes of this chapter—

(a) A "foreign state", except as used in section 1608 of this title, includes a political subdivision of a foreign state or an agency or instrumentality of a foreign state as defined in subsection (b).

(b) An "agency or instrumentality of a foreign state" means any entity—

(1) which is a separate legal person, corporate or otherwise, and

(2) which is an organ of a foreign state or political subdivision thereof, or a majority of whose shares or other ownership interest is owned by a foreign state or political subdivision thereof, and

(3) which is neither a citizen of a State of the United States as defined in section 1332 (c) and (e) of this title, nor created under the laws of any third country.

(c) The "United States" includes all territory and waters, continental or insular, subject to the jurisdiction of the United States.

(d) A "commercial activity" means either a regular course of commercial conduct or a particular commercial transaction or act. The commercial character of an activity

33. Letter of Jack B. Tate, Acting Legal Advisor, to Acting Legal Attorney General, 26 Dept St. Bull. 984 (1952), *quoted* in link, *supra* note 109.

34. 28 U.S.C. §§ 1602–1611 (1988).

shall be determined by reference to the nature of the course of conduct or particular transaction or act, rather than by reference to its purpose.

(e) A "commercial activity carried on in the United States by a foreign state" means commercial activity carried on by such state and having substantial contact with the United States.

§ 1604. Immunity of a foreign state from jurisdiction

Subject to existing international agreements to which the United States is a party at the time of enactment of this Act a foreign state shall be immune from the jurisdiction of the courts of the United States and of the States except as provided in sections 1605 to 1607 of this chapter.

§ 1605—General exceptions to the jurisdictional immunity of a foreign state

(a) A foreign state shall not be immune from the jurisdiction of courts of the United States or of the States in any case—

(1) in which the foreign state has waived its immunity either explicitly or by implication, notwithstanding any withdrawal of the waiver which the foreign state may purport to effect except in accordance with the terms of the waiver;

(2) in which the action is based upon a commercial activity carried on in the United States by the foreign state; or upon an act performed in the United States in connection with a commercial activity of the foreign state elsewhere; or upon an act outside the territory of the United States in connection with a commercial activity of the foreign state elsewhere and that act causes a direct effect in the United States;

(3) in which rights in property taken in violation of international law are in issue and that property or any property exchanged for such property is present in the United States in connection with a commercial activity carried on in the United States by the foreign state; or that property or any property exchanged for such property is owned or operated by an agency or instrumentality of the foreign state and that agency or instrumentality is engaged in a commercial activity in the United States;

(4) in which rights in property in the United States acquired by succession or gift or rights in immovable property situated in the United States are in issue; or,

(5) not otherwise encompassed in paragraph (2) above, in which money damages are sought against a foreign state for personal injury or death, or damage to or loss of property, occurring in the United States and caused by the tortious act or omission of that foreign state or of any official or employee of that foreign state while acting within the scope of his office or employment; except this paragraph shall not apply to—

(A) any claim based upon the exercise or performance or the failure to exercise or perform a discretionary function regardless of whether the discretion be abused, or

(B) any claim arising out of malicious prosecution, abuse of process, libel, slander, misrepresentation, deceit, or interference with contract rights.

(b) A foreign state shall not be immune from the jurisdiction of Suit in admiralty, the courts of the United States in any case in which a suit in admiralty is brought to enforce a maritime lien against a vessel or cargo of the foreign state, which maritime lien is based upon a commercial activity of the foreign state: Provided That—

(1) notice of the suit is given by delivery of a copy of the summons and of the complaint to the person, or his agent, having possession of the vessel or cargo against which the maritime lien is asserted; but such notice shall not be deemed to have been delivered, nor may it thereafter be delivered, if the vessel or cargo is arrested pursuant to process obtained on behalf of the party bringing the suit—unless the party was unaware that the vessel or cargo of a foreign state was involved, in which event the service of process of arrest shall be deemed to constitute valid delivery of such notice; and

(2) notice to the foreign state of the commencement of suit as provided in section 1608 of this title is initiated within ten days either of the delivery of notice as provided in subsection (b) (1) of this section or, in the case of a party who was unaware that the vessel or cargo of a foreign state was involved, of the date such party determined the existence of the foreign state's interest.

Whenever notice is delivered under subsection (b) (1) of this section, the maritime lien shall thereafter be deemed to be an in personam claim against the foreign state which at that time owns the vessel or cargo involved: Provided That a court may not award judgment against the foreign state in an amount greater than the value of the vessel or cargo upon which the maritime lien arose, such value to be determined as of the time notice is served under subsection (b) (1) of this section.

[...]

§ 1607. Counterclaims

In any action brought by a foreign state, or in which a foreign state intervenes, in a court of the United States or of a State, the foreign state shall not be accorded immunity with respect to any counterclaim—

(a) for which a foreign state would not be entitled to immunity under section 1605 of this chapter had such claim been brought in a separate action against the foreign state; or

(b) arising out of the transaction or occurrence that is the subject matter of the claim of the foreign state; or

(c) to the extent that the counterclaim does not seek relief exceeding in amount or differing in kind from that sought by the foreign state.

[...]

§ 1609. Immunity from attachment and execution of property of a foreign state

Subject to existing international agreements to which the United States is a party at the time of enactment of this Act the property in the United States of a foreign state shall be immune from attachment arrest and execution except as provided in sections 1610 and 1611 of this chapter.

§ 1610. Exceptions to the immunity from attachment or execution

(a) The property in the United States of a foreign state, as defined in section 1603(a) of this chapter, used for a commercial activity in the United States, shall not be immune from attachment in aid of execution, or from execution, upon a judgment entered by a court of the United States or of a State after the effective date of this Act, if—

(1) the foreign state has waived its immunity from attachment in aid of execution or from execution either explicitly or by implication, notwithstanding any withdrawal of the waiver the foreign state may purport to effect except in accordance with the terms of the waiver, or

(2) the property is or was used for the commercial activity upon which the claim is based, or

(3) the execution relates to a judgment establishing rights in property which has been taken in violation of international law or which has been exchanged for property taken in violation of international law, or

(4) the execution relates to a judgment establishing rights in property—

(A) which is acquired by succession or gift, or

(B) which is immovable and situated in the United States: Provided that such property is not used for purposes of maintaining a diplomatic or consular mission or the residence of the Chief of such mission, or

(5) the property consists of any contractual obligation or any proceeds from such a contractual obligation to indemnify or hold harmless the foreign state or its employees under a policy of automobile or other liability or casualty insurance covering the claim which merged into the judgment.

(b) In addition to subsection (a), any property in the United States of an agency or instrumentality of a foreign state engaged in commercial activity in the United States shall not be immune from attachment in aid of execution, or from execution, upon a judgment entered by a court of the United States or of a State after the effective date of this Act, if—

(1) the agency or instrumentality has waived its immunity from attachment in aid of execution or from execution either explicitly or implicitly, notwithstanding any withdrawal of the waiver the agency or instrumentality may purport to effect except in accordance with the terms of the waiver, or

(2) the judgment relates to a claim for which the agency or instrumentality is not immune by virtue of section 1605(a) (2), (3), or (5), or 1605(b) of this chapter, regardless of whether the property is or was used for the activity upon which the claim is based.

(c) No attachment or execution referred to in subsections (a) and (b) of this section shall be permitted until the court has ordered such attachment and execution after having determined that a reasonable period of time has elapsed following the entry of judgment and the giving of any notice required under section 1608(e) of this chapter.

(d) The property of a foreign state, as defined in section 1603(a) of this chapter, used for a commercial activity in the United States, shall not be immune from attachment prior to the entry of judgment in any action brought in a court of the United States or of a State, or prior to the elapse of the period of time provided in subsection (c) of this section, if—

(1) the foreign state has explicitly waived its immunity from attachment prior to judgment, notwithstanding any withdrawal of the waiver the foreign state may purport to effect except in accordance with the terms of the waiver, and

(2) the purpose of the attachment is to secure satisfaction of a judgment that has been or may ultimately be entered against the foreign state, and not to obtain jurisdiction.

b. Exceptions to the Foreign Sovereign Immunities Act

In every action against a foreign state in a United States court, the court must first determine whether or not it has the jurisdiction over the foreign state based on one of the exceptions to the Foreign Sovereign Immunities Act.[35] The FSIA states that all "foreign states" are entitled to immunity from the jurisdiction of the courts of the United States,[36] then sets forth the exceptions to this rule.[37] In general, these exceptions deny immunity to sovereign states based on commercial activities of the state.

The exceptions of the FSIA set forth in the statute are exclusive.[38]

i. The Waiver of Immunity Exception

35. *Siderman de Blake v. Republic of Argentina*, 965 F.2d 699, 713 (9th Cir. 1992), *cert. den.*, 113 S. Ct. 1812 (1993). A United States court may only exercise jurisdiction over a foreign sovereign pursuant to the FSIA; the FSIA is the sole basis for jurisdiction over such actions. *Argentine Republic v. Amerada Hess Shipping Corp.*, 488 U.S. 428, 434–38 (1989).

36. 28 U.S.C. §§ 1604 1330(a), (b) (1988).

37. 28 U.S.C. § 1605 (1988).

38. 28 U.S.C. § 1602 (1988).

The most direct and effective way for an investor to ensure that a foreign sovereign will be subject to the jurisdiction of the US courts is to negotiate a waiver of sovereign immunity clause in the contract between the state and the investor. [. . .] or in an investment protection treaty.

Significantly, United States courts will not give effect to a subsequent withdrawal of a waiver of sovereign immunity, unless such withdrawal is pursuant to the terms of the waiver.[39]

Weltover, Inc. v. Republic of Argentina, 941 F.2d 145 (2d Cir. 1991).

Case Introduction

Since the 1970s, Argentina held significant public and private foreign debts. The peso and austral currency denominations were not accepted on the international markets, and this contributed to a severe devaluation of Argentina's local currency. Thus, Argentina relied on its reserve of United States dollars and other internationally recognized currencies in seeking to repay foreign debt.

In the early 1980s, Argentina's Ministry of Economy adopted severe austerity measures, and the Banco Central implemented the Republic's Foreign Exchange Insurance Contract ("FEIC") program. Specifically, the scheme provided the means for a private Argentine debtor to obtain US dollars at a pre-determined rate of local currency upon maturity of foreign debt. The exchange rate was calculated at the prevailing rate at the time the contract was executed, to lessen the impact of the devaluation of the local currency. FEIC contracts were not due until 1982, and so this financing bought Argentina some time for restructuring.

However, in 1982, Argentina found itself still in economic crisis and with an insufficient stock of U.S. dollars. Argentina and the Banco Central decided to refinance these obligations by issuing two forms of debt instruments: (1) bonds payable in U.S. dollars (Bonods), and (2) promissory notes. The Bonods provided for repayment in U.S. dollars through transfer on the market in one of several locations.

Subsequently, Argentina established that it lacked sufficient foreign exchange to retire the Bonods and unilaterally extended the time for payment, offering bondholders substitute instruments as a means of rescheduling the debts.

Two Panamanian corporations and a Swiss bank brought a breach-of-contract action in the Federal District Court.

Principal Points of the Judgment

McLaughlin, Circuit Judge

1. This appeal presents two issues of subject matter jurisdiction under the Foreign Sovereign Immunities Act of 1976 ("FSIA"). We must first determine whether the act of a foreign sovereign in issuing debt instruments to foreign creditors for the

---

39. 28 U.S.C. § 1605(a)(1).

stated purpose of controlling the nation's stock of foreign currency is "commercial activity" within the meaning of FSIA. If it is, we must then consider whether that action has a sufficient nexus with the United States to justify the exercise of subject matter jurisdiction over the foreign sovereign in an American court.

22. In *Letelier v. Republic of Chile* we stated that, for an act to be considered commercial, it must be the type that a private person could engage in. 748 F.2d at 797. We continued by stating that "the court must inquire whether the activity is of the type an individual *would customarily* carry on for profit." *Id.* (emphasis added). *Letelier* did not go so far as to require a profit motive on the part of the foreign sovereign. Such a requirement would eviscerate the "commercial activity" exception of the FSIA, because foreign sovereigns often act without a profit motive. Our decision in *Letelier* clearly did not intend such a result. Rather, *Letelier* instructs that where a private party would customarily engage in an activity for profit, there can be little question that that private party is engaging in commercial activity. When a foreign sovereign engages in the same conduct, that activity retains its commercial nature, even though the foreign sovereign acts without a profit motive.

23. In considering whether a private person could engage in the activity in question, and would normally conduct such activity for profit, we must isolate the specific conduct that underlies the suit, rather than focusing on "the broad program of policy of which the individual transaction is a part." *Rush-Presbyterian-St. Luke's Medical Center v. Hellenic Republic*, 877 F.2d at 580; see *Texas Trading & Milling Corp. v. Federal Republic of Nigeria*, 647 F.2d at 308 (court must identify particular conduct that is relevant). Were we to define the relevant conduct overbroadly, the activity would almost inevitably be characterized as sovereign in nature, rather than commercial. Foreign sovereigns constantly implement broad programs intended to stimulate their economy or to avoid economic catastrophe. Each of these programs, however, is implemented through numerous individual transactions. To imbue each transaction with a sovereign character simply because it is part of a broader governmental scheme would run afoul of the FSIA's restrictive theory of foreign sovereign immunity. See House Report at 6605 (immunity for foreign states restricted to public acts of the sovereign). Overbroad definition of the issue takes the Court perilously close to the shadowy line between the nature and the purpose of the activity in question. The FSIA clearly dictates that, in distinguishing commercial acts from sovereign acts, courts should refer to the nature of the activity, and not its purpose. 28 U.S.C. § 1603(d).

[. . .]

25. [. . .] Putting to one side defendants' attempts to cast this controversy in Keynesian terms as a response to Argentina's economic straits, we note that this case resolves around defendant's issuance of the Bonods as public debt, and the subsequent failure to retire that public debt upon maturity. The nature of this activity—the issuance of debt instruments—is clearly the type of activity that private persons can, and often do, engage in for profit. [. . .] Because defendant's issuance of public debt—the Bonods—immersed them in the stream of international commerce in

foreign currency, the nature of that act was commercial; there was nothing uniquely sovereign about this activity.

26. We decline defendant's implied invitation to characterize the conduct in issue as a governmental effort to conserve scare resources, i.e. U.S. dollars. Such an overbroad characterization goes to the purpose of the entire program, rather than to the nature of the transaction in issue. See *Rush-Presbyterian*, 877 F.2d at 580 (cautioning against overbroad definition of the relevant conduct); *Texas Trading*, 647 F.2d at 308. The nature of this particular transaction is clearly commercial, and, thus, we need look no further. [. . .]

28. We therefore hold that the relevant acts were commercial in nature, rather than sovereign, and we proceed to consider whether the requisite nexus with the United States is present.

29. [. . .] In *Texas Trading*, we expressly left open the question whether a foreign sovereign's nonpayment to a foreign plaintiff of a debt payable in the United States suffices to meet this statutorily-mandated nexus. *Texas Trading*, 647 F.2d at 312. This question now squarely confronts us. We hold that defendant's acts caused a direct effect in the United States. [. . .]

38. Public policy considerations compel the conclusion that Congress would have wanted an American court to entertain this action. New York, as a preeminent commercial center, has an interest in protecting those who rely upon that reputation to do business, whether through the banking industry or otherwise. See *Allied Bank v. Banco Credito Agricola de Cartago*, 757 F.2d at 521–22. If individuals or corporate entities become wary of their ability to protect their rights in business transactions conducted in New York they will look elsewhere. We think it clear that Congress, in enacting the "direct effects" clause of the commercial activity exception, intended American courts to entertain actions that promote the interest of forum jurisdictions in controlling conduct that occurs within their borders. Here, an assertion of subject matter jurisdiction fulfills that congressional intent.

Conclusion

39. We hold that defendants' issuance of the Bonods and subsequent breach of the agreements was "commercial activity" within the meaning of the FSIA. Furthermore, defendants' commercial acts caused a direct effect in the United States, thus providing the statutorily-mandated nexus. As such, defendants are stripped of sovereign immunity, and the district court has subject matter jurisdiction.

ii. The Commercial Activity Exception

The "Commercial Activity" exception to jurisdictional immunity, prescribed by Section 1605(a)(2), strips a foreign state of immunity when the action is based upon commercial activity carried on in the United States.[40]

40. The FSIA defines "commercial activity" as "either a regular course of commercial conduct or a particular commercial transaction or act." 28 U.S.C. § 1603(d).

Texas Trading and Milling Corp. v. Federal Republic of Nigeria interpreted this to mean that commercial activity of a state is any activity in which a private person could engage.

An example is *BP Chemicals v. Jiangsu Sopo Corp Ltd.*, 285 F. 3d 677 (8th Cir 2002). A Chinese company wholly owned by the government engaged another government owned corporation to procure sophisticated engineering products and equipment from American firms to further the construction of a Chinese chemical plant. The Court held that the principal was not entitled to jurisdictional immunity under the FSIA because, by employing an agent to procure the necessary equipment from American firms, it engaged in commercial activity and enjoyed substantial contact with the United States.

> To fall within the "commercial activities" exception to the FSIA, the activities of the foreign state must meet one of the following three requirements: the state undertakes commercial activity in the United States; the state performs an act in the United States in connection with commercial activity of the state elsewhere; or the state performs an act outside the United States in connection with a commercial activity of the elsewhere, and that act causes a direct effect in the United States.[41]

The Supreme Court held in *Republic of Arg. v. Weltover, Inc.*, 504 U.S. 607 (1992), that an effect is direct if it follows as an immediate consequence of the defendant's activity. In *Lyon v. Agusta S.p.A*, 252 F.3d 1078 (9th Cir. 2001), in a product liability situation, one should focus on whether there has been an intervening act that broke the chain of causation leading to the injury.[42]

In *Butters v. Vance Int'l, Inc.*, 225 F.3d 462 (4th Cir. 2000), the court held that a private agent of a foreign state, even one located in the United States, is entitled to derivative jurisdictional immunity under the FSIA when it is faithfully following the commands of a foreign state performing traditional state functions as opposed to a commercial activity. The holding of *Butters* was applied in *Velasco v. Government of Indonesia*, 370 F.3d 392 (4th Cir. 2004).

The US Supreme Court on February 27, 2019 delivered a major decision in *Jam v. Int'l Fin. Corp.*, 139 S. Ct. 759 (2018), on the question of whether the exceptions in the 1976 Foreign Sovereign Immunity Act apply to international organizations. The International Finance Corporation ("IFC") argued that the International Organizations Immunities Act of 1945 ("IOIA") entitles international organizations to virtually absolute immunity and does not incorporate subsequent developments in foreign immunity law that have restricted immunity for commercial acts.

---

41. 28 U.S.C. § 1605(a)(2).

42. Note that the scope of direct effect was also addressed in *Virtual Countries, Inc. v. Republic of South Africa*, 300 F.3d 230 (2d. Cir. 2002).

iii. Terrorism Exception

28 U.S. Code § 1605B—Responsibility of Foreign States for International Terrorism against the United States.

[. . .]

(b) Responsibility of foreign states.—A foreign state shall not be immune from the jurisdiction of the courts of the United States in any case in which money damages are sought against a foreign state for physical injury to a person or property or death occurring in the United States and caused by -

(1) an act of terrorism in the United States;

(2) a tortious act or acts of the foreign state, or of any official, employee, or agent of that foreign state, while acting with the scope of his or her office, employment, or agency, regardless where the tortious act or acts of the foreign state occurred.

(c) Claims by Nationals of the United States.—Notwithstanding section 2337(2) of title 18, a national of the United States may bring a claim against a foreign state in accordance with section 2333 of that title if the foreign state would not be immune under subsection (b).

On 27 September 2016, the United States Congress overrode the presidential veto to pass the Justice Against Sponsors of Terrorism Act (JASTA). Until JASTA, under the "terrorism exception" in the U.S. Foreign Sovereign Immunities Act, sovereign immunity could only be denied to foreign states officially designated by the U.S. as sponsors of terrorism at the time or as a result of the terrorist act. JASTA extends the scope of the terrorism exception to the jurisdictional immunity of foreign states so as to allow U.S. courts to exercise jurisdiction over civil claims regarding injuries, death or damages that occur inside the U.S. as result of a tort, including an act of terrorism, committed anywhere by a foreign state or official.

iv. Other Exceptions to the FSIA

In *Siderman de Blake v. Republic of Argentina*, the court held that a foreign state is not immune where property is taken in violation of international law. The case discusses the International Takings Exception, Existing Treaty Exception and other exceptions to the FSIA fully. In *Chuidian v. Philippine National Bank*, 912 F.2d 1095 (9th Cir. 1990), the Ninth Circuit refused to apply the expropriation exception of the FSIA where the plaintiff was a citizen of the defendant state at the time of the expropriation.

The courts have also held that absent an international agreement providing otherwise, FSIA affords jurisdictional immunity from the criminal jurisdiction of the courts of the United States.[43]

43. *Keller v. Central Bank of Nigeria*, 277 F.3d 811 (6th Cir. 2001).

Regarding arbitration and the FSIA, the Seventh Circuit found that by signing both the Inter-American Convention and the New York Convention on Foreign Arbitral Awards, Argentina had waived the prejudgment attachment protections afforded by the FSIA for its instrumentalities when one seeks to set aside or suspend an arbitral award.[44]

Siderman Blake v. Republic of Argentina, 965 F.2d 699 (1992).

Case Introduction

During the 1970s, the military in Argentina waged a war designed to purge the country of suspected subversive activity. In 1975, then-President Maria Estela Perón was prompted to declare a "state of siege," whereby she entrusted the Argentine Armed Forces with the responsibility of stifling acts of terrorism. President Perón's downfall came about on March 24, 1976, when the Argentine Armed Forces staged a successful coup d'etat and replaced her with a military junta.

Susana Siderman de Blake and Carlos, Jose and Lea Siderman (collectively, "the Sidermans") alleged that during that same night on March 24, 1976, sixty-five-year-old Jose Siderman was captured for seven days, beaten and tortured, as the captors howled anti-Semitic remarks. The Sidermans also alleged the expropriation of their physical property and the profits and revenue from their corporation, Inmobiliaria del Nor-Oeste, S.A. ("INOSA") by Argentine military officials. Susana, Carlos and Lea each owned 33% of INOSA, and Jose owned the remaining one percent. Its assets comprised numerous real estate holdings including a large hotel in Tucuman, the Hotel Gran Corona.

The district court dismissed the expropriation claims on the basis of the act of state doctrine, but granted a default judgment to Jose and Lea Siderman on the torture claims. Argentina then entered its first appearance in the case and moved for relief from judgment on the ground that the Foreign Sovereign Immunities Act rendered it immune from the Sidermans' action. The district court granted the motion and vacated the default judgment. The Sidermans now appeal.

Principal Points of the Judgment

Appeal from the United States District Court for the Central District of California.

Before: *Fletcher, Canby and Boochever, Circuit Judges.*

Fletcher, Circuit Judge:

[. . .] We reverse and remand for further proceedings.

[. . .]

11 Until 1952, foreign states and their agencies and instrumentalities enjoyed virtually absolute immunity from suit in the courts of the United States. See *Verlinden B.V. v. Central Bank of Nigeria*, 461 U.S. 480, 486, 103 S.Ct. 1962, 1967, 76 L.

44. *International Insurance Co. v. Caja Nacional de Ahorro y Seguro*, 293 F.3d 392 (7th Cir. 2002).

Ed.2d 81 (1983). Chief Justice John Marshall authored the seminal opinion that considered and recognized the immunity of a foreign state from suit in a United States court. In *The Schooner Exchange v. M'Faddon*, 11 U.S. (7 Cranch) 116, 3 L. Ed. 287 (1812), the Court upheld a French plea of immunity against an American citizen's assertion of title to an armed national vessel of France that had entered the territorial waters of the United States. In his opinion for the Court, Chief Justice Marshall first emphasized the "exclusive and absolute" nature of a nation's territorial jurisdiction, any exception to which could arise only from the consent or waiver of that nation. 11 U.S. (7 Cranch) at 136. He then explained:

> 12 The world being composed of distinct sovereignties, possessing equal rights and equal independence, . . . all sovereigns have consented to a relaxation in practice, in cases under certain peculiar circumstances, of that absolute and complete jurisdiction within their respective territories which sovereignty confers.

13 *Id.* Thus, Chief Justice Marshall announced that the common practice of nations forms the foundation for the doctrine of foreign sovereign immunity, while a given state's agreement to grant immunity in a particular case is a matter of grace, comity, and respect for the equality and independence of other sovereigns. See *Verlinden*, 461 U.S. at 486, 103 S.Ct. at 1967. Although *The Schooner Exchange* did not announce a rule of absolute sovereign immunity, in the following 140 years absolute immunity became the norm, principally because the courts practiced consistent deference to the Executive Branch, which "ordinarily requested immunity in all actions against friendly foreign sovereigns." *Id.*

14 In 1952, however, the Acting Legal Adviser of the State Department, Jack Tate, sent a letter to the Acting Attorney General announcing that the State Department was adopting the "restrictive" principle of foreign sovereign immunity. *Id.* at 487 & n. 9, 103 S.Ct. at 1968 & n. 9. Under the restrictive principle, as defined in the Tate Letter, "the immunity of the sovereign is recognized with regard to sovereign or public acts (*jure imperii*) of a state, but not with respect to private acts (*jure gestionis*)." 26 Dep't of State Bull. 984 (1952), reprinted in *Alfred Dunhill of London, Inc. v. Republic of Cuba*, 425 U.S. 682, 711, 96 S.Ct. 1854, 1869, 48 L.Ed.2d 301 (1976) (Appendix 2). With the issuance of the Tate Letter, the United States joined the emerging international consensus that private acts of a sovereign—commercial activities being the primary example—were not entitled to immunity. While the Tate Letter altered the Executive Branch's view of foreign sovereign immunity, it did not provide the courts with concrete legislative standards for determining whether to assert jurisdiction over actions against foreign states. Thus, the courts continued to defer to the Executive Branch. When the State Department issued a suggestion of immunity in a particular case, the court followed it; when the State Department remained silent, the court relied on prior suggestions for precedential assistance in determining immunity. *Verlinden*, 461 U.S. at 487, 103 S.Ct. at 1968.

15 With the enactment of the FSIA in 1976, Congress replaced the regime of deference to Executive suggestion with a comprehensive legislative framework "governing claims of immunity in every civil action against a foreign state or its political subdivisions, agencies, or instrumentalities." *Id.* at 488, 103 S.Ct. at 1968; H.R.Rep. No. 1487, 94th Cong., 2d Sess. 7, reprinted in 1976 U.S.Code Cong. & Admin.News 6604, 6606 ("A principal purpose of this bill is to transfer the determination of sovereign immunity from the executive branch to the judicial branch. . . ."). In essence, the FSIA codified the restrictive theory of sovereign immunity, which had become widely accepted in international law. See *Verlinden*, 461 U.S. at 487–88, 103 S.Ct. at 1968; H.R.Rep. No. 1487, 94th Cong., 2d Sess. 14, 1976 U.S.Code Cong. & Admin. News at 6613 (referring to international law and Tate Letter). Structurally, the FSIA sets forth the general rule that foreign states are immune from the jurisdiction of both federal and state courts in the United States, subject to certain exceptions. 28 U.S.C. §§ 1330(a) & 1604. A federal court lacks subject matter jurisdiction over a claim against a foreign state unless the claim falls within an exception to immunity under the FSIA. See 28 U.S.C. § 1330(a); *Verlinden*, 461 U.S. at 489, 103 S.Ct. at 1969; see also *Argentine Republic v. Amerada Hess Shipping Corp.*, 488 U.S. 428, 439, 109 S. Ct. 683, 690, 102 L.Ed.2d 818 (1989) (FSIA is the "sole basis for obtaining jurisdiction over a foreign state in federal court").

16 As a threshold matter, therefore, a court adjudicating a claim against a foreign state must determine whether the FSIA provides subject matter jurisdiction over the claim. *Liu v. Republic of China*, 892 F.2d 1419, 1424 (9th Cir.1989), cert. dismissed,—U.S.—, 111 S.Ct. 27, 111 L.Ed.2d 840 (1990). The existence of subject matter jurisdiction under the FSIA is a question of law subject to *de novo* review. *Id.* Where, as in the present case, a claim has been dismissed for lack of jurisdiction, we accept the allegations of the complaint as true. *Gerritsen v. de la Madrid Hurtado*, 819 F.2d 1511, 1513 (9th Cir.1987).

17 The parties and the district court have agreed that the Sidermans' claims fall into two categories: those relating to the expropriation of INOSA and those relating to the torture of Jose Siderman. The district court initially dismissed the expropriation claims on the basis of the act of state doctrine, while awarding a default judgment to the Sidermans on the torture claims. Only later did the court dismiss the torture claims and the Sidermans' entire action. Because the two categories of claims were dismissed at different stages of the suit, and for different reasons, we separately address each category.

I. Expropriation Claims

18 In its order of March 12, 1984, the district court dismissed the expropriation claims on the basis of the act of state doctrine; it did not consider whether it had subject matter jurisdiction over the claims pursuant to the FSIA. The district court erred in deciding the act of state issue without first considering the threshold issue of its subject matter jurisdiction. Because the federal courts lack jurisdiction over a claim against a foreign state that is immune under the FSIA, "[a]t the threshold

of every action in a district court against a foreign state . . . the court must satisfy itself that one of the [FSIA] exceptions applies." *Verlinden*, 461 U.S. at 493–94, 103 S. Ct. at 1971. The district court must address this issue "even if the foreign state does not enter an appearance to assert an immunity defense." *Id.* at 494 n. 20, 103 S.Ct. at 1971 n. 20. The court simply cannot proceed without subject matter jurisdiction.

19 In contrast to the jurisdictional nature of foreign sovereign immunity under the FSIA, "[t]he act of state doctrine is not a jurisdictional limit on courts." *Liu*, 892 F.2d at 1431. The doctrine reflects the prudential concern that the courts, if they question the validity of sovereign acts taken by foreign states, may be interfering with the conduct of American foreign policy by the Executive and Congress. *W.S. Kirkpatrick & Co. v. Environmental Tectonics Corp.*, 493 U.S. 400, 404, 110 S. Ct. 701, 704, 107 L.Ed.2d 816 (1990); Liu, 892 F.2d at 1431. The act of state doctrine is a principle or rule of decision that the courts apply in deciding cases within their jurisdiction. *Environmental Tectonics*, 493 U.S. at 406, 409, 110 S.Ct. at 705, 706–07, see also *West v. Multibanco Comermex, S.A.*, 807 F.2d 820, 827 (9th Cir.) (describing the act of state doctrine as "combination justiciability and abstention rule"), cert. denied, 482 U.S. 906, 107 S.Ct. 2483, 96 L.Ed.2d 375 (1987). In terms of the Federal Rules of Civil Procedure, the act of state doctrine does not bar an action for lack of subject matter jurisdiction, Fed.R.Civ.P.12(b)(1), but rather for failure to state a claim upon which relief can be granted, Fed.R.Civ.P.12(b)(6). See *Timberlane Lumber Co. v. Bank of America, N.T. & S.A.*, 549 F.2d 597, 602 (9th Cir. 1976). If a court lacks jurisdiction over a case involving a foreign state, the act of state doctrine never comes into play. "Because sovereign immunity is jurisdictional and the act of state doctrine is not, we must consider sovereign immunity before reaching the act of state doctrine." *De Sanchez v. Banco Central De Nicaragua*, 770 F.2d 1385, 1389 (5th Cir. 1985); see Liu, 892 F.2d at 1424 (first determining whether subject matter jurisdiction existed under FSIA before addressing the district court's act of state ruling).

20 Since the district court did not consider jurisdiction under the FSIA with regard to the expropriation claims, it made no findings of fact concerning jurisdiction. The record consists of the complaint and numerous declarations submitted by the Sidermans in support of their contention that certain of the FSIA exceptions apply, but includes no pleadings or evidence from Argentina, which had not yet entered an appearance in the case when the expropriation claims were dismissed. Argentina contends that the Sidermans' complaint and declarations fail to demonstrate that the expropriation claims fall within an FSIA exception, and asks us to affirm the district court's dismissal on that ground. We therefore review the record to determine whether the Sidermans have sustained their initial burden of alleging jurisdiction under the FSIA. If the allegations in the Sidermans' complaint, which we must accept as true, and the uncontroverted evidence presented by the Sidermans bring the claims within an FSIA exception, the burden then shifts to Argentina to prove that any relevant exceptions do not apply. "Once the plaintiff offers evidence that an FSIA exception to immunity applies, the party claiming immunity bears

the burden of proving by a preponderance of the evidence that the exception does not apply." *Schoenberg v. Exportadora de Sal, S.A. de C.V.*, 930 F.2d 777, 779 (9th Cir. 1991) (quoting *Joseph v. Office of the Consulate Gen'l of Nigeria*, 830 F.2d 1018, 1021 (9th Cir. 1987), cert. denied, 485 U.S. 905, 108 S.Ct. 1077, 99 L.Ed.2d 236 (1988)). If the Sidermans successfully have alleged that an exception to immunity under the FSIA applies to their claims, we must remand the claims in order to afford Argentina the opportunity to rebut the Siderman's evidence and sustain its burden of proof before the district court.

21 The Sidermans argue that two of the FSIA exceptions apply to their expropriation claims, the commercial activity exception, 28 U.S.C. § 1605(a)(2), and the international takings exception, 28 U.S.C. § 1605(a)(3). We consider each in turn.

Commercial Activity Exception

22 The commercial activity exception provides that a foreign state is not immune from jurisdiction where

> 23 [. . .] the action is based upon a commercial activity carried on in the United States by the foreign state; or upon an act performed in the United States in connection with a commercial activity of the foreign state elsewhere; or upon an act outside the territory of the United States in connection with a commercial activity of the foreign state elsewhere and that act causes a direct effect in the United States . . .

24 28 U.S.C. § 1605(a)(2). As the bracketed numbering indicates, section 1605(a)(2) contains three clauses. See *Schoenberg*, 930 F.2d at 779–80. We find that the Sidermans have presented sufficient allegations and evidence to demonstrate—at least at this stage of the proceedings—that their expropriation claims fall within the first and second clauses and may also fall within the third.

25 In order to come within the first clause of the exception, a claim against a foreign state must be "based upon a commercial activity carried on in the United States by the foreign state." Commercial activity "means either a regular course of commercial conduct or a particular commercial transaction or act." 28 U.S.C. § 1603(d). In determining whether an act or activity is commercial, we must look to its nature, not its purpose. 28 U.S.C. § 1603(d); *Schoenberg*, 930 F.2d at 780. Though activities that customarily are carried on for profit are certainly commercial, *Schoenberg*, 930 F.2d at 780, an activity need not be motivated by profit to be commercial, *Joseph*, 830 F.2d at 1024. The central question is "whether the activity is of a kind in which a private party might engage." *Id.* In light of the allegations and evidence submitted by the Sidermans, we have no doubt that the Sidermans' claims are based on commercial activity being conducted by Argentina. The activities that form the basis for the claims—Argentina's continuing management of INOSA, its operation of the Hotel Gran Corona, and its receipt of profits from the company's operations—are clearly activities "of a kind in which a private party might engage."

26 The more difficult question is whether this commercial activity is being "carried on in the United States." 28 U.S.C. § 1605(a)(2). As defined by the FSIA, "commercial activity carried on in the United States by a foreign state" means commercial activity carried on by such state and having substantial contact with the United States. 28 U.S.C. § 1603(e). Under this definition, the foreign state need not engage in commercial activity in the United States on a regular basis. *Shapiro v. Republic of Bolivia*, 930 F.2d 1013, 1018 (2d Cir. 1991). Instead, the critical inquiry is whether there is "a nexus between the defendant's commercial activity in the United States and the plaintiff's grievance." *America West Airlines, Inc. v. GPA Group, Ltd.*, 877 F.2d 793, 796 (9th Cir. 1989).

27 The Sidermans have alleged and put forward evidence that Argentina advertises the Hotel Gran Corona in the United States and solicits American guests through its U.S. agent, Aerolinas Argentinas, the national airline of Argentina. They have alleged further that numerous Americans have stayed at the Hotel, which accepts all the major American credit cards, including Mastercard, Visa, and American Express. On the present record, we believe that these allegations are sufficient to demonstrate that the commercial activities Argentina is conducting through INOSA have "substantial contact with the United States." The Sidermans' allegations also satisfy the nexus requirement established in *America West*. Several of the Sidermans' expropriation claims are directed toward the stream of revenue and benefits that Argentina is receiving through its operation of the Hotel. Argentina's continuing receipt of the profits and benefits that rightfully belong to the Sidermans—including those derived from U.S. sources—are some of the "specific acts that form the basis of the suit." *Id.* at 797 (quoting Joseph, 830 F.2d at 1023) (emphasis omitted). We conclude that the Sidermans' allegations and evidence bring their claims within clause one of the commercial activity exception.

28 Clause two of the exception applies to actions based "upon an act performed in the United States in connection with a commercial activity of the foreign state elsewhere." 28 U.S.C. § 1605(a)(2). As the few cases to address this clause have noted, it requires a "material connection . . . between the plaintiff's cause of action and the act performed in the United States." *Stena Rederi AB. v. Comision de Contratos del Comite Ejecutivo General*, 923 F.2d 380, 388 (5th Cir. 1991) (emphasis in original). A plaintiff must either demonstrate a causal connection between a sovereign's actions in the United States and those abroad giving rise to the plaintiff's claims, or the sovereign's acts in the United States must themselves represent an element in the plaintiff's cause of action. *Gilson v. Republic of Ireland*, 682 F.2d 1022, 1027 n. 22 (D.C. Cir. 1982); see also H.R.Rep. No. 1487, 94th Cong., 2d Sess. 19, reprinted in 1976 U.S.C.C.A.N. 6613, 6618.

29 The allegations and evidence set forth by the Sidermans that Argentina solicits its guests for the Hotel Gran Corona in the United States and presumably accepts payments for those reservations in this country, and that as a result numerous Americans stay at the Hotel, suffice to meet this test. Because of Argentina's acts in the United States—the solicitation and acceptance of reservations—Americans

spend money at the Hotel Gran Corona, money which the Sidermans claim rightfully belongs to them. The Sidermans' causes of action for conversion, constructive fraud, intentional interference with business relationships and breach of fiduciary duty directly relate, therefore, to Argentina's acts in this country. Argentina undertakes those acts, furthermore, in connection with commercial activity elsewhere, mainly its operation of the Hotel. The Sidermans' claims thus fall squarely within clause two of the commercial activity exception.

30 For the Sidermans' expropriation claims to satisfy clause three of the exception, the claims must be based "upon an act outside the territory of the United States in connection with a commercial activity of the foreign state elsewhere and that act [must] cause a direct effect in the United States." 28 U.S.C. § 1605(a)(2). The Sidermans base their claims on Argentina's seizure and continuing operation of INOSA, both of which constitute acts that Argentina has performed outside United States territory. It is equally clear that they have been performed in connection with the commercial activities of operating the Hotel Gran Corona and managing INOSA's real estate investments in Argentina. These activities are, as noted above, "of a kind in which a private party might engage." *Joseph*, 830 F.2d at 1024. The dispositive element in clause three for purposes of this case, therefore, is the requirement that the acts cause a direct effect in the United States.

31 Under the direct effect requirement, the "foreign sovereign's activities must cause an effect in the United States that is substantial and foreseeable in order to abrogate sovereign immunity." *America West*, 877 F.2d at 799. For example, in *America West*, an American airline sued an Irish national airline for damage sustained by an aircraft engine on which the Irish airline had performed faulty maintenance work. Finding that it was not foreseeable that the maintenance work performed in Ireland on an engine then owned by a Netherlands Antilles company would have an effect in the United States, we held that the direct effect requirement was unsatisfied. *Id.* at 800. The "purely fortuitous" fact that the plaintiff whose plane subsequently was fitted out with the engine was an American corporation was insufficient to create a direct effect. *Id.*; see also *Security Pacific Nat'l Bank v. Derderian*, 872 F.2d 281, 286 (9th Cir. 1989); *Martin v. Republic of S. Africa*, 836 F.2d 91, 94–95 (2d Cir. 1987) (finding no direct effect in United States where an African-American was denied medical treatment in South Africa).

32 As a general matter, therefore, "[m]ere financial loss" suffered by a person, whether individual or corporate, in the United States is not, in itself, sufficient to constitute a "direct effect." *America West*, 877 F.2d at 799–800. However, in cases where a plaintiff's claim is for breach of a contract providing that payment or performance must be made in the United States, the "direct effect" requirement has been deemed satisfied. For example, in *Meadows v. Dominican Republic*, 817 F.2d 517 (9th Cir. 1987), we considered an action brought by two U.S. residents to recover a loan commission they earned by obtaining a loan on behalf of a foreign government. Under the loan agreement, the commission was to be paid in the United States—through the plaintiffs' bank—and we found this to be a sufficiently direct effect to

permit jurisdiction under clause three. 817 F.2d at 523. See also *Gregorian v. Izvestia*, 871 F.2d 1515, 1527 (9th Cir. 1989) (discussing similar cases); *L'Europeenne de Banque v. La Republica de Venezuela*, 700 F.Supp. 114, 121 (S.D.N.Y. 1988) (extending the rule to encompass a foreign plaintiff).

33 As an owner and shareholder of INOSA, each of the Sidermans is entitled to a share of the profits earned by the corporation. If INOSA's articles of incorporation or by-laws (or the equivalent corporate documents under Argentine law) require INOSA to pay those dividends at the shareholder's place of residence, the United States, we believe in light of Meadows that the direct effect requirement would be satisfied. While the record before us does not reveal whether this is the case, it would be premature to hold that the Sidermans have failed to establish a direct effect. Since the Sidermans have alleged jurisdiction under clauses one and two, and we are remanding the expropriation claims on those grounds, on remand the Sidermans also may pursue jurisdiction under clause three and seek to cure any jurisdictional defects by amending their complaint or submitting additional evidence. See *Trentacosta v. Frontier Pac. Aircraft Indus.*, 813 F.2d 1553, 1561–62 (9th Cir. 1987); *In re Complaint of McLinn*, 744 F.2d 677, 685 (9th Cir. 1984).

B. International Takings Exception

34 The Sidermans argue that their claims also fall within the international takings exception to the FSIA's rule of immunity. That exception provides that a foreign state is not immune in an action

35 [. . .] in which rights in property taken in violation of international law are in issue and that property or any property exchanged for such property is present in the United States in connection with a commercial activity carried on in the United States by the foreign state; or that property or any property exchanged for such property is owned or operated by an agency or instrumentality of the foreign state and that agency or instrumentality is engaged in a commercial activity in the United States [. . .]

36 28 U.S.C. § 1605(a)(3). Though few courts have had the opportunity to consider the international takings exception, it is clear that Jose, Lea, and Carlos Siderman cannot assert a claim that comes within this exception. In *Chuidian v. Philippine Nat'l Bank*, 912 F.2d 1095, 1105 (9th Cir. 1990), we held that the exception does not apply where the plaintiff is a citizen of the defendant country at the time of the expropriation, because "[e]xpropriation by a sovereign state of the property of its own nationals does not implicate settled principles of international law." See also *De Sanchez v. Banco Central de Nicaragua*, 770 F.2d 1385, 1395 (5th Cir. 1985). However, Susana Siderman de Blake is eligible to invoke the international takings exception, and the Sidermans' allegations and evidence bring her claims within clause two of that exception.

37 Under that clause, the property at issue must have been taken in violation of international law. At the jurisdictional stage, we need not decide whether the taking actually violated international law; as long as a "claim is substantial and non-frivolous,

it provides a sufficient basis for the exercise of our jurisdiction." *West v. Multibanco Comermex, S.A.*, 807 F.2d 820, 826 (9th Cir.), cert. denied, 482 U.S. 906, 107 S.Ct. 2483, 96 L.Ed.2d 375 (1987). In *West*, we described three requisites under international law for a valid taking. First, "[v]alid expropriations must always serve a public purpose." 807 F.2d at 831. Second, "aliens [must] not be discriminated against or singled out for regulation by the state." *Id.* at 832. Finally, "[a]n otherwise valid taking is illegal without the payment of just compensation." *Id.* These well-established principles track the Restatement of Foreign Relations Law, which provides:

38 A state is responsible under international law for injury resulting from:

39 (1) a taking by the state of the property of a national of another state that

40 (a) is not for a public purpose, or

41 (b) is discriminatory, or

42 (c) is not accompanied by provision for just compensation. . . .

43 Restatement (Third) of the Foreign Relations Law of the United States § 712 (1987) [hereinafter "Restatement"]. The legislative history of the FSIA reveals a similar understanding of what constitutes a taking in violation of international law. See H.R.Rep. No. 1487, 94th Cong., 2d Sess. 19–20, reprinted in 1976 U.S.Code Cong. & Admin.News 6604, 6618 (taking violates international law if it is done "without payment of the prompt adequate and effective compensation required by international law" or is "arbitrary or discriminatory in nature"). If a taking violates any one of the aforementioned proscriptions, it violates international law.

44 Susana Siderman de Blake's claim that Argentina violated the international law of expropriation is substantial and non-frivolous. The complaint alleges that Argentina officials seized INOSA for their personal profit and not for any public purpose. The complaint also alleges that Argentina seized INOSA because the Siderman family is Jewish—a discriminatory motivation based on ethnicity. See Restatement § 712 Comment f (noting that "taking that singles out aliens generally, or aliens of a particular nationality, or particular aliens, would violate international law"). Finally, none of the Sidermans has received any compensation for the seizure, let alone just compensation. As in *West*, we have no difficulty concluding that the Sidermans' complaint contains "substantial and non-frivolous" allegations that INOSA was taken in violation of international law.

45 Beyond establishing that property has been taken in violation of international law, Susan Siderman de Blake must demonstrate that the expropriated property, or property exchanged for it, is owned or operated by an agency or instrumentality of Argentina and that the agency or instrumentality is engaged in commercial activity in the United States. The Sidermans' allegations establish that INOSA itself has become an agency or instrumentality of Argentina. As defined by the FSIA, an "agency or instrumentality"

46 means any entity—

47 (1) which is a separate legal person, corporate or otherwise, and

> 48 (2) which is an organ of a foreign state or political subdivision thereof [. . .] and
>
> 49 (3) which is neither a citizen of a State of the United States [. . .] nor created under the laws of any third country.

50 28 U.S.C. § 1603(b). As an Argentine corporation, INOSA satisfies the first and third elements of the above definition, and the Sidermans' basic allegation that Argentina has expropriated INOSA suffices as an allegation that INOSA is now an "organ" of Argentina or Tucuman. The Sidermans' allegations thus satisfy the "agency or instrumentality" definition. The final requirement under clause two—that the agency or instrumentality must be engaged in a commercial activity in the United States—is also met. The Sidermans' allegations concerning Argentina's solicitation and entertainment of American guests at the Hotel Gran Corona and the hotel's acceptance of American credit cards and traveler's checks are sufficient at this stage of the proceedings to show that Argentina is engaged in a commercial activity in the United States. The Sidermans' allegations bring Susana Siderman de Blake's expropriation claims within clause two of the international takings exception.

51 We hold that the Sidermans' complaint and declarations allege sufficient facts to bring their expropriation claims within both the commercial activity and international takings exceptions to the FSIA's grant of foreign sovereign immunity. We emphasize the preliminary nature of our holding; following further development of the factual record on remand, the district court ultimately must determine whether the FSIA exceptions do or do not apply to the expropriation claims. While the Sidermans have sustained their initial burden of alleging applicable exceptions to the FSIA, Argentina will have the opportunity on remand to challenge the evidence presented by the Sidermans and to present its own. Under the procedures our circuit has developed for considering jurisdiction under the FSIA, Argentina now bears the burden of proving by a preponderance of the evidence that none of the FSIA exceptions applies to the Sidermans' claims. *Schoenberg*, 930 F.2d at 779. To the extent that the jurisdictional facts are disputed on remand, the parties should be allowed to conduct discovery for the limited purpose of establishing jurisdictional facts before the claims can be dismissed. See *America West*, 877 F.2d at 801 ("[W]here pertinent facts bearing on the question of jurisdiction are in dispute, discovery should be allowed."); see also *Santos v. Compagnie Nationale Air France*, 934 F.2d 890, 892 n. 2 (7th Cir. 1991); *Filus v. LOT Polish Airlines*, 907 F.2d 1328, 1332 (2d Cir. 1990).

[. . .]

II. Torture Claims

53 The question of Argentina's immunity from the Sidermans' torture claims is squarely presented, without the procedural complications surrounding the district court's treatment of the expropriation claims. The district court dismissed the torture claims on the ground that they fell within no exception to immunity under the

FSIA. In defending the district court's decision on appeal, Argentina argues that the Sidermans' claims are foreclosed by the Supreme Court's opinion in *Argentine Republic v. Amerada Hess Shipping Corp.*, 488 U.S. 428, 109 S.Ct. 683, 102 L.Ed.2d 818 (1989). Since *Amerada Hess* represents the Court's most extensive treatment of the FSIA and its exceptions to immunity, we begin with a discussion of the case before turning to the Sidermans' arguments about why the case does not preclude their torture claims.

54 Amerada Hess involved a Liberian oil tanker that was attacked by Argentine military aircraft during the Falklands/Malvinas War between Great Britain and Argentina. The tanker's owner and its charterer each brought suit against Argentina, but the district court dismissed their actions for lack of subject matter jurisdiction under the FSIA. The court of appeals reversed, finding that subject matter jurisdiction existed under the Alien Tort Statute. The Supreme Court, reversing the court of appeals, held that the FSIA provides "the sole basis for obtaining jurisdiction over a foreign state in our courts," 488 U.S. at 434, 109 S.Ct. at 688, and found that none of the exceptions to the general FSIA rule of immunity encompassed the plaintiffs' claims. *Id.* at 439, 109 S.Ct. at 690.

55 In *Amerada Hess*, the plaintiffs relied primarily on the noncommercial tort exception to the FSIA's grant of immunity. That exception eliminates immunity in cases

> 56 [...] in which money damages are sought against a foreign state for personal injury or death, or damage to or loss of property, occurring in the United States and caused by the tortious act or omission of that foreign state or of any official or employee of that foreign state while acting within the scope of his office or employment....

57 28 U.S.C. § 1605(a)(5). The Court, limiting this exception to cases in which the damage to or loss of property occurred within the territorial jurisdiction of the United States, held that it did not encompass the plaintiffs' claims. 488 U.S. at 439–41, 109 S.Ct. at 690–91. Argentina has devoted the bulk of its argument in the present case to a discussion of the noncommercial tort exception and Amerada Hess's holding that the exception does not encompass tortious activity perpetrated outside the territorial jurisdiction of the United States. If the Sidermans were relying on section 1605(a)(5), their claims clearly would be barred under Amerada Hess. However, none of the three arguments they raise rests on that exception. Instead, the Sidermans contend that Argentina is precluded from asserting the defense of sovereign immunity by the international law principle of *jus cogens*, and by the FSIA's existing treaty (section 1604) and implied waiver (section 1605(a)(1)) exceptions. We consider each of these arguments in turn.

A. *Jus Cogens*

58 The Sidermans contend that Argentina does not enjoy sovereign immunity with respect to its violation of the *jus cogens* norm of international law condemning official torture. While we agree with the Sidermans that official acts of torture of the

sort they allege Argentina to have committed constitute a *jus cogens* violation, we conclude that Amerada Hess forecloses their attempt to posit a basis for jurisdiction not expressly countenanced by the FSIA.

[. . .]

60 While *jus cogens* and customary international law are related, they differ in one important respect. Customary international law, like international law defined by treaties and other international agreements, rests on the consent of states. A state that persistently objects to a norm of customary international law that other states accept is not bound by that norm, see Restatement § 102 Comment d, just as a state that is not party to an international agreement is not bound by the terms of that agreement. International agreements and customary international law create norms known as *jus dispositivum*, the category of international law that "consists of norms derived from the consent of states" and that is founded "on the self-interest of the participating states." Klein, A Theory for the Application of the Customary International Law of Human Rights by Domestic Courts, 13 Yale J. Int'l L. 332, 351 (1988) [hereinafter "Human Rights in Domestic Courts"]. *Jus dispositivum* binds only "those states consenting to be governed by it." *Id.*

61 In contrast, *jus cogens* "embraces customary laws considered binding on all nations," *id.* at 350–51, and "is derived from values taken to be fundamental by the international community, rather than from the fortuitous or self-interested choices of nations," *id.* at 351. Whereas customary international law derives solely from the consent of states, the fundamental and universal norms constituting *jus cogens* transcend such consent, as exemplified by the theories underlying the judgments of the Nuremberg tribunals following World War II. See Note, The Nuremberg Legacy: An Unfulfilled Promise, 63 S.Cal.L.Rev. 833, 868 (1990) [hereinafter "Nuremberg Legacy"] [. . .]

62 Because *jus cogens* norms do not depend solely on the consent of states for their binding force, they "enjoy the highest status within international law." [*Committee of U.S. Citizens Living in Nicaragua v. Reagan*, hereinafter:] *CUSCLIN*, 859 F.2d at 940 [(D.C. Cir. 1988)]. For example, a treaty that contravenes *jus cogens* is considered under international law to be void *ab initio.* See Vienna Convention, art. 53; Restatement § 102 Comment k. Indeed, the supremacy of *jus cogens* extends over all rules of international law; norms that have attained the status of *jus cogens* "prevail over and invalidate international agreements and other rules of international law in conflict with them." Restatement § 102 Comment k. A *jus cogens* norm is subject to modification or derogation only by a subsequent *jus cogens* norm. *Id.*

63 The Sidermans claim that the prohibition against official torture has attained the status of a *jus cogens* norm. There is no doubt that the prohibition against official torture is a norm of customary international law, as the Second Circuit recognized more than ten years ago in the landmark case of *Filartiga v. Pena-Irala*, 630 F.2d 876 (2d Cir. 1980). Dr. Filartiga and his daughter, citizens of Paraguay, brought suit against Paraguayan officials who had tortured Dr. Filartiga's son to

death. They alleged jurisdiction under the Alien Tort Statute, which grants the district courts "original jurisdiction of any civil action by an alien for a tort only, committed in violation of the law of nations or a treaty of the United States." 28 U.S.C. § 1350. Dr. Filartiga claimed that the defendants' torture of his son, perpetrated under color of official authority, violated a norm of customary international law prohibiting official torture, and the court agreed. Judge Kaufman, writing for the court, explained that "there are few, if any, issues in international law today on which opinion seems to be so united as the limitations on a state's power to torture persons held in its custody." 630 F.2d at 881. Judge Kaufman catalogued the evidence in support of this view, citing several declarations of the United Nations General Assembly and human rights conventions prohibiting torture, modern municipal law to the same effect, and the works of jurists, and finally concluded "that official torture is now prohibited by the law of nations." *Id.* at 884.

64 Other authorities have also recognized that official torture is prohibited by customary international law. In *Forti v. Suarez-Mason*, 672 F.Supp. 1531, 1541 (N.D.Cal. 1987), a suit predicated on atrocities committed by the same Argentine military government alleged to be responsible for the torture of Jose Siderman, the district court held that "official torture constitutes a cognizable violation of the law of nations," and described the prohibition against official torture as "universal, obligatory, and definable." Similarly, in *Tel-Oren v. Libyan Arab Republic*, 726 F.2d 774, 781 (D.C.Cir. 1984) (opinion of Edwards, J.), cert. denied, 470 U.S. 1003, 105 S.Ct. 1354, 84 L.Ed.2d 377 (1985), which involved an action against the Palestine Liberation Organization for its acts of terrorism, Judge Edwards identified torture as a violation of customary international law. Judge Bork, although raising considerable opposition to the application of customary international law in U.S. courts, see *id.* at 801–19 (opinion of Bork, J.), at the same time conceded that the international law prohibition against torture is not disputed. *Id.* at 820. The Restatement of Foreign Relations also holds to the view that customary international law prohibits official torture. Restatement § 702(d). Finally, the world now has an international agreement focused specifically on the prohibition against torture: The Convention Against Torture and Other Cruel, Inhuman or Degrading Treatment or Punishment, 39 U.N. GAOR Supp. (No. 51), 23 I.L.M. 1027 (1984) [hereinafter "Torture Convention"], which entered into force on June 26, 1987. The United States signed the Torture Convention in April 1988, the United States Senate gave its advice and consent in October 1988, see 136 Cong.Rec. S17486-92 (daily ed. October 27, 1990), and it now awaits the President's filing of the instrument of ratification with the Secretary-General of the United Nations.

65 In light of the unanimous view of these authoritative voices, it would be unthinkable to conclude other than that acts of official torture violate customary international law. And while not all customary international law carries with it the force of a *jus cogens* norm, the prohibition against official torture has attained that status. In *CUSCLIN*, 859 F.2d at 941–42, the D.C. Circuit announced that torture is one of a handful of acts that constitute violations of *jus cogens*. In *Filartiga*,

though the court was not explicitly considering *jus cogens*, Judge Kaufman's survey of the universal condemnation of torture provides much support for the view that torture violates *jus cogens*. In Judge Kaufman's words, "[a]mong the rights universally proclaimed by all nations, as we have noted, is the right to be free of physical torture." 630 F.2d at 890. Supporting this case law is the Restatement, which recognizes the prohibition against official torture as one of only a few *jus cogens* norms. Restatement § 702 Comment n (also identifying *jus cogens* norms prohibiting genocide, slavery, murder or causing disappearance of individuals, prolonged arbitrary detention, and systematic racial discrimination). Finally, there is widespread agreement among scholars that the prohibition against official torture has achieved the status of a *jus cogens* norm. See, e.g., Implied Waiver, *supra*, at 389, 393–94; Parker & Neylon, Jus Cogens: Compelling the Law of Human Rights, 12 Hastings Int'l & Comp.L.Rev. 411, 437–39 (1989); Human Rights in Domestic Courts, *supra*, at 354 n. 111; Randall, Universal Jurisdiction Under International Law, 66 Tex.L.Rev. 785, 830 (1988).

66 Given this extraordinary consensus, we conclude that the right to be free from official torture is fundamental and universal, a right deserving of the highest status under international law, a norm of *jus cogens*. The crack of the whip, the clamp of the thumb screw, the crush of the iron maiden, and, in these more efficient modern times, the shock of the electric cattle prod are forms of torture that the international order will not tolerate. To subject a person to such horrors is to commit one of the most egregious violations of the personal security and dignity of a human being. That states engage in official torture cannot be doubted, but all states believe it is wrong, all that engage in torture deny it, and no state claims a sovereign right to torture its own citizens. See *Filartiga*, 630 F.2d at 884 (noting that no contemporary state asserts "a right to torture its own or another nation's citizens"); *id.* at n. 15 ("The fact that the prohibition against torture is often honored in the breach does not diminish its binding effect as a norm of international law."). Under international law, any state that engages in official torture violates *jus cogens*.

67 The question in the present case is what flows from the Sidermans' allegation that Argentina tortured Jose Siderman and thereby violated a *jus cogens* norm. The Sidermans contend that when a foreign state's act violates *jus cogens*, the state is not entitled to sovereign immunity with respect to that act. This argument begins from the principle that *jus cogens* norms "enjoy the highest status within international law," *CUSCLIN*, 859 F.2d at 940, and thus "prevail over and invalidate . . . other rules of international law in conflict with them," Restatement § 102 Comment k. The Sidermans argue that since sovereign immunity itself is a principle of international law, it is trumped by *jus cogens*. In short, they argue that when a state violates *jus cogens*, the cloak of immunity provided by international law falls away, leaving the state amenable to suit.

68 As a matter of international law, the Sidermans' argument carries much force. We previously have recognized that "[s]overeign immunity is a principle of international law." *International Ass'n of Machinists & Aerospace Workers (IAM) v.*

Organization of Petroleum Exporting Countries (OPEC), 649 F.2d 1354, 1359 (9th Cir. 1981), cert. denied, 454 U.S. 1163, 102 S.Ct. 1036, 71 L.Ed.2d 319 (1982). Chief Justice Marshall identified the foundation of the doctrine of sovereign immunity as the "perfect equality and absolute independence of sovereigns," a state of affairs making it improper for one state to subject another to its jurisdiction. *The Schooner Exchange*, 11 U.S. (7 Cranch) at 137. As described by one scholar of international law, the doctrine of foreign sovereign immunity "is rooted in two bases of international law, the notion of sovereignty and the notion of the equality of sovereigns." Riesenfeld, Sovereign Immunity in Perspective, 19 Vand. J. Transnat'l L. 1 (1986). When Jack Tate, writing on behalf of the State Department, issued his famous letter in 1952, the United States was recognizing the trend in international law toward adoption of the restrictive principle of foreign sovereign immunity, under which states receive immunity for their sovereign acts (*jure imperii*) but not their private acts (*jure gestionis*). With the enactment of the FSIA, Congress explicitly adopted the restrictive principle, identifying its origin in international law. 28 U.S.C. § 1602 (findings and declaration of purpose); see also H.R.Rep. No. 1487, 94th Cong., 2d Sess. 7, reprinted in 1976 U.S.Code Cong. & Admin.News 6604, 6605 (FSIA "would codify the so-called 'restrictive' principle of sovereign immunity, as presently recognized in international law"); *id.* at 8, 1976 U.S.Code Cong. & Admin.News at 6606 ("Sovereign immunity is a doctrine of international law under which domestic courts, in appropriate cases, relinquish jurisdiction over a foreign state."); *id.* at 9, 1976 U.S.Code Cong. & Admin.News at 6608 ("[S]overeign immunity is a question of international law to be determined by the courts.").

69 The Sidermans posit that because sovereign immunity derives from international law, *jus cogens* supersedes it. "*Jus cogens* norms represent the fundamental duties incident to international life. They are an essential component of the modern law definition of sovereignty." Implied Waiver, *supra*, at 392. International law does not recognize an act that violates *jus cogens* as a sovereign act. A state's violation of the *jus cogens* norm prohibiting official torture therefore would not be entitled to the immunity afforded by international law.

70 Unfortunately, we do not write on a clean slate. We deal not only with customary international law, but with an affirmative Act of Congress, the FSIA. We must interpret the FSIA through the prism of *Amerada Hess*. Nothing in the text or legislative history of the FSIA explicitly addresses the effect violations of *jus cogens* might have on the FSIA's cloak of immunity. Argentina contends that the Supreme Court's statement in *Amerada Hess* that the FSIA grants immunity "in those cases involving alleged violations of international law that do not come within one of the FSIA's exceptions," 488 U.S. at 436, 109 S.Ct. at 688, precludes the Sidermans' reliance on *jus cogens* in this case. Clearly, the FSIA does not specifically provide for an exception to sovereign immunity based on *jus cogens*. In *Amerada Hess*, the Court had no occasion to consider acts of torture or other violations of the peremptory norms of international law, and such violations admittedly differ in kind from transgressions

of *jus dispositivum*, the norms derived from international agreements or customary international law with which the *Amerada Hess* Court dealt. However, the Court was so emphatic in its pronouncement "that immunity is granted in those cases involving alleged violations of international law that do not come within one of the FSIA's exceptions," *Amerada Hess*, 488 U.S. at 436, 109 S.Ct. at 688, and so specific in its formulation and method of approach, *id.* at 439, 109 S.Ct. at 690 ("Having determined that the FSIA provides the sole basis for obtaining jurisdiction over a foreign state in federal court, we turn to whether any of the exceptions enumerated in the Act apply here"), that we conclude that if violations of *jus cogens* committed outside the United States are to be exceptions to immunity, Congress must make them so. The fact that there has been a violation of *jus cogens* does not confer jurisdiction under the FSIA.

B. Existing Treaty Exception

71 The FSIA section establishing the general rule of foreign sovereign immunity in United States courts, 28 U.S.C. § 1604, provides that the rule of immunity is "[s] ubject to existing international agreements to which the United States is a party at the time of enactment of" the FSIA. In *Amerada Hess*, the plaintiffs argued that Argentina's immunity was subject to the Geneva Convention on the High Seas and the Pan American Maritime Neutrality Convention and that those treaties created an exception to FSIA immunity under section 1604. The Court rejected the argument, adopting a narrow view of section 1604:

> 72 This exception applies when international agreements expressly conflict with the immunity provisions of the FSIA, hardly the circumstances in this case. [The Geneva and Pan American Conventions] only set forth substantive rules of conduct and state that compensation shall be paid for certain wrongs. They do not create private rights of action for foreign corporations to recover compensation from foreign states in United States courts.

73 488 U.S. at 442, 109 S.Ct. at 692 (internal quotations, alterations, and citations omitted). Thus, the Court erected a serious obstacle to claims that, by subscribing to a treaty or other international agreement, a defendant state loses its immunity under the FSIA.

74 The Sidermans argue that Argentina's immunity under the FSIA is "subject to" the Universal Declaration of Human Rights, G.A. Res. 217A(III), U.N. Doc. A/810 (1948), and the United Nations Charter. Neither of these documents can support the weight the Sidermans place on them. The Universal Declaration of Human Rights is a resolution of the General Assembly of the United Nations. As such, it is a powerful and authoritative statement of the customary international law of human rights. See *Filartiga v. Pena-Irala*, 630 F.2d 876, 882–84 (2d Cir. 1980). However, it is not an "international agreement" within the meaning of section 1604. While the meaning of that term may not be restricted to treaties that the United States has ratified pursuant to Article II, Section 2 of the Constitution, see Restatement, Intro.

Note to Part III, at 146, the legislative history of the FSIA reveals that Congress intended the FSIA to be subject to enforceable agreements between the United States and other foreign states or international organizations. The House Report refers to several examples of "international agreements," including the NATO Status of Forces Agreement, and treaties of friendship, commerce and navigation. H.R.Rep. No. 1487, 94th Cong., 2d Sess. 17–18, reprinted in 1976 U.S.Code Cong. & Admin. News 6604, 6616. These international agreements, which are intended by the parties to be legally binding under international law, are categorically different from the Universal Declaration of Human Rights, which creates legal obligations only insofar as it represents evidence of customary international law. We see no indication in the FSIA or its legislative history that Congress intended the term "international agreements" to include non-binding resolutions of the General Assembly of the United Nations.

[...]

76 We hold that the Sidermans have failed to identify an international agreement to which the United States is a party that "expressly conflict[s] with the immunity provisions of the FSIA." *Amerada Hess*, 488 U.S. at 442, 109 S.Ct. at 692. The existing treaty exception of section 1604 does not apply to the torture claims.

C. Implied Waiver Exception

77 The FSIA provides that "[a] foreign state shall not be immune from the jurisdiction of courts of the United States or of the States in any case ... in which the foreign state has waived its immunity either explicitly or by implication, notwithstanding any withdrawal of the waiver which the foreign state may purport to effect except in accordance with the terms of the waiver." 28 U.S.C. § 1605(a)(1). The Sidermans contend that Argentina availed itself of our courts in its pursuit of Jose Siderman and, in doing so, implicitly waived its immunity defense with respect to their claims for torture and persecution. They assert that after the elder Siderman fled to this country, Argentina commenced malicious criminal proceedings against him in Argentina, and requested the assistance of the California state courts in obtaining jurisdiction over his person. The California courts, unaware of Argentina's true intentions, complied by effecting service of process.

78 Argentina did not controvert the Sidermans' implicit waiver argument in the district court. As is true with respect to the commercial activity and international takings clauses on which the Sidermans base jurisdiction for their expropriation claims, then, the only material before us on the subject of waiver is that presented by the Sidermans. We conclude that their allegations and evidence suffice to bring their claims for torture within section 1605(a)(1) of the FSIA. On remand, Argentina will have an opportunity to rebut the Sidermans' evidence. At this stage of the proceedings, however, we are unable to say that the Sidermans' arguments as to implied waiver are devoid of merit.

79 The FSIA's waiver exception "is narrowly construed." *Joseph v. Office of Consulate General of Nigeria*, 830 F.2d 1018, 1022 (9th Cir. 1987), cert. denied, 485 U.S. 905,

108 S.Ct. 1077, 99 L.Ed.2d 236 (1988). The House Report accompanying the passage of the FSIA gives three examples of an implied waiver:

> 80 With respect to implicit waivers, the courts have found such waivers in cases where a foreign state has agreed to arbitration in another country or where a foreign state has agreed that the law of a particular country should govern a contract. An implicit waiver would also include a situation where a foreign state has filed a responsive pleading in an action without raising the defense of sovereign immunity.

81 H.R.Rep. No. 1487, 94th Cong., 2d Sess. 18 (1976), reprinted in 1976 U.S.C.C.A.N. 6604, 6617. The House Report does not purport to provide an exclusive list of the circumstances giving rise to implied waivers, however, and we have not construed it in this fashion. Thus, while we stated in *Joseph* that implied waivers will "ordinarily [be] found" only in the three situations mentioned in the legislative history, 830 F.2d at 1022 (citing *Frolova v. Union of Soviet Socialist Republics*, 761 F.2d 370, 377 (7th Cir. 1985)), we went beyond those examples to establish the more general proposition that where a written agreement entered into by a foreign sovereign "contemplates adjudication of a dispute by the United States courts," we will find the sovereign to have waived its immunity. Joseph, 830 F.2d at 1023.

82 We concluded in *Joseph* that the Federal Republic of Nigeria, by signing a lease agreement which stated that the prevailing party in any court dispute arising out of its terms would be entitled to attorney's fees, had rendered itself susceptible to suit in our courts. The lease did not provide specifically for the adjudication of disputes in the United States. Nor did it state that United States law would govern such actions. Thus, it did not fall into one of the categories mentioned by the House Report. However, because the lease at issue concerned a house in San Francisco which Nigeria had rented as a consulate, we surmised that Nigeria must have had United States courts in mind when it agreed to its adjudicatory provisions. And since Nigeria could reasonably be said to have contemplated "participation of the United States courts in [its] disputes" with its landlord, 830 F.2d at 1023, we found it to have waived its immunity from a suit brought by that landlord.

83 Other courts have similarly focused on the question whether a sovereign defendant entering into a written agreement envisioned the involvement of United States courts in its dealings with another party. In *Maritime Int'l Nominees Establishment v. Republic of Guinea*, 693 F.2d 1094 (D.C.Cir. 1982), cert. denied, 464 U.S. 815, 104 S.Ct. 71, 78 L.Ed.2d 84 (1983), for example, the D.C. Circuit declined to find a waiver of immunity where the treaty on which the plaintiff premised its waiver argument "concededly did not foresee a role for the United States courts. . . ." *Id.* at 1104. Similarly, in *Frolova*, the Seventh Circuit held that the former Soviet Union had not waived its immunity in signing various international agreements where it could not have "anticipated . . . that American courts would be the means by which the documents' provisions would be enforced." And in *Liberian Eastern Timber Corp. v. Republic of Liberia*, 650 F.Supp. 73, 76 (S.D.N.Y. 1986), aff'd, 854 F.2d 1314 (2d Cir. 1987), Judge Weinfeld found that Liberia had waived its immunity from the

enforcement of an arbitration award by entering into a treaty which "clearly contemplated the involvement of the courts of any of the Contracting States, including the United States as a signatory to the Convention, in enforcing the pecuniary obligations of the award." Cf. *Amerada Hess*, 488 U.S. at 442–43, 109 S.Ct. at 692 (finding no basis for concluding that Argentina had waived its immunity, explicitly or implicitly, "by signing an international agreement that contains no mention of a waiver of immunity to suit in United States courts or even the availability of a cause of action in the United States.").

84 Thus, the essential inquiry in written agreement cases is whether a sovereign contemplated the involvement of United States courts in the affair in issue. Here, we confront a situation where Argentina apparently not only envisioned United States court participation in its persecution of the Sidermans, but by its actions deliberately implicated our courts in that persecution. The Sidermans have presented evidence that a year after Jose, Lea and Carlos Siderman fled Argentina in fear for their lives, the Argentine military authorities altered the Tucuman provincial land records to show that they had held title only to 127, as opposed to 127,000, acres of land in the Province, and that in their last-minute efforts to raise cash they had thus sold property which did not belong to them. The Tucuman Public Prosecutor then initiated criminal proceedings against Jose Siderman for this "fraudulent" sale, and had the Tucuman Supreme Court enlist the aid of our courts, via a letter rogatory, in serving him with process. The letter rogatory, dated May 11, 1980, informed the Presiding Judge of the Los Angeles Superior Court that criminal proceedings were pending against Jose Siderman in the Supreme Court of Tucuman. It requested the court's assistance in serving papers on Siderman, who was living in Los Angeles at the time. While the court complied with the request, the record is not clear as to the subsequent course of the lawsuit. In their papers in support of jurisdiction, the Sidermans suggest that the Argentine military authorities sought to obtain Jose's return to Argentina in order to further torture and perhaps even to kill him.

85 Shortly after the Los Angeles Superior Court received Argentina's letter rogatory, indeed, Argentina requested that the Italian authorities arrest Siderman, who had travelled to Italy for a wedding, and extradite him to Argentina for having allegedly forged certain travel documents. Siderman was detained in Italy for seven months, twenty-seven days of which time was spent in prison, before an Italian court dismissed the charges against him as pretextual and denied Argentina's extradition request.

86 We conclude that the Sidermans have presented evidence sufficient to support a finding that Argentina has implicitly waived its sovereign immunity with respect to their claims for torture. The evidence indicates that Argentina deliberately involved United States courts in its efforts to persecute Jose Siderman. If Argentina has engaged our courts in the very course of activity for which the Sidermans seek redress, it has waived its immunity as to that redress.

[. . .]

88 The district court erred in dismissing the Sidermans' torture claims.

Conclusion

89 The Sidermans' complaint and the evidence they have presented in support of their allegations paint a horrifying portrait of anti-Semitic, government-sponsored tyranny. The record that so far has been developed in this case reveals no ground for shielding Argentina from the Sidermans' claims that their family business was stolen from them by the military junta that took over the Argentine government in 1976. It further suggests that Argentina has implicitly waived its sovereign immunity with respect to the Sidermans' claims for torture.

90 We REVERSE and REMAND for further proceedings consistent with this opinion.

[. . .]

2. The Act of State Doctrine

The Act of State doctrine (the "AoS doctrine") is a judicial creation in the United States whereby a court will not inquire into the acts of a foreign state, because such inquiry may interfere with the foreign policy concerns of the executive branch.[45] The doctrine was originally based on principles of comity and sovereign immunity. In the United States Supreme Court case *Underhill v. Hernandez* in 1897, regarding the wrongful detention of a US citizen by the Government of Venezuela, the Court stated that "every sovereign state is bound to respect the independence of every other sovereign state, and the courts of one country will not sit in judgment on the acts of the government of another done within its own territory. Redress of grievances by reason of such acts must be obtained through the means open to be availed of by sovereign powers as between themselves."

In a case regarding the AoS doctrine 67 years later, *Banco Nacional de Cuba v. Sabbatino*, the Supreme Court de-emphasized the "sovereign immunity" reason for the AoS doctrine, and emphasized that the AoS doctrine was based on the U.S. doctrine of separation of powers: the court did not wish to interfere in matters that were primarily the responsibility of the executive or legislative branches of the government.

45. Danny Abir, *Suing a Foreign Government: A Note on Siderman v. Republic of Argentina*, 15 Whittier L. Rev. 575, 580 (1994).

Banco Nacional de Cuba v. Sabbatino, 376 U.S. 398 (1964).

Case Introduction

In 1960, Farr, Whitlock & Co ("Farr Whitlock"), an American commodity broker, contracted to purchase Cuban sugar from a wholly owned subsidiary of Compania Azucarera Vertientes-Camaguey de Cuba ("CAV"), a corporation organized under Cuban law whose capital stock was primarily owned by United States residents. It was agreed that Farr Whitlock would pay for the sugar in New York upon presentation of the shipping documents.

The summer of 1960 saw a number of trade restrictive measures and counter measures put in place between the United States and Cuba. This culminated in Cuban Law No. 851 giving the President and Prime Minister discretionary power to nationalize, by force if necessary, property or enterprises in which Americans had an interest. Some companies, including CAV, were, pursuant to Law No. 851, on the list for compulsory expropriation. In August 1960, the Farr Whitlock sugar was loaded on a Cuban ship, destined for Morocco. The consent of the Cuban government was needed before a ship carrying sugar for a named company could leave Cuban waters. For this reason, Farr Whitlock entered into an identical contract with the Banco Para el Comercio Exterior de Cuba ("Banco Exterior"), an instrument of the Cuban Government.

Banco Exterior assigned the bills of lading to the petitioner, Banco Nacional de Cuba ("Banco Nacional"), also an instrument of the Cuban government. Banco Nacional instructed its agent in New York, Societe Generale, to deliver the bills to Farr Whitlock in return for the payment sum of $175,250.69. Farr Whitlock was notified of CAV's claim of rightful ownership and initially refused the documents. Farr Whitlock subsequently accepted the shipping documents but refused to hand over the proceeds to Societe Generale.

Shortly after, Farr Whitlock was served an order of the New York Supreme Court, which had appointed Sabbatino as Temporary Receiver of CAV's New York assets. Farr Whitlock transferred the funds to Sabbatino.

Banco Nacional then introduced an action in the Federal District Court for the Southern District of New York, alleging conversion of the bills of lading and seeking the proceeds from Farr Whitlock.

The District Court held judgment against the petitioner. They found that the Cuban expropriation decree violated international law in three separate respects: it was motivated by a retaliatory and not a public purpose; it discriminated against American nationals; and it failed to provide adequate compensation. The District Court, "while acknowledging the continuing vitality of the act of state doctrine, [. . .] believed it inapplicable when the questioned foreign act is in violation of international law."

The Court of Appeals affirmed the decision. Although unwilling to declare the action of the Cuban government to be invalid under just one of the aspects outlined by the District Court, they concluded that in combination, the factors resulted in an expropriation invalid under international law. The case then proceeded to the Supreme Court.

Principal Points of the Judgment

Mr. Justice Harlan

421. [. . .] While historic notions of sovereign authority do bear upon the wisdom of employing the act of state doctrine, they do not dictate its existence.

423. [. . .] The traditional view of international law is that it establishes substantive principles for determining whether one country has wronged another. Because of its peculiar nation-to-nation character the usual method for an individual to seek relief is to exhaust local remedies and then repair to the executive authorities of his own state to persuade them to champion his claim in diplomacy or before an international tribunal. See *United States v. Diekelman*, 92 U.S. 520, 524. Although it is, of course, true that United States courts apply international law as a part of our own in appropriate circumstances, *Ware v. Hylton*, 3 U.S. (3 Dall.) 199, 281 (1976); *The Nereide*, 13 U.S. (9 Cranch) 388, 423 (1815); *The Paquete Habana*, 175 U.S. 677, 700 (1900), the public law of nations can hardly dictate to a country which is in theory wronged how to treat that wrong within its domestic borders.

[. . .] The text of the Constitution does not require the act of state doctrine; it does not irrevocably remove from the judiciary the capacity to review the validity of foreign acts of state.

The act of state doctrine does, however, have "constitutional" underpinnings. It arises out of the basic relationships between branches of government in a system of separation of powers.

428. If the act of state doctrine is a principle of decision binding on federal and state courts alike but compelled by neither international law nor the Constitution, its continuing vitality depends on its capacity to reflect the proper distribution of functions between the judicial and political branches of the Government on matters bearing upon foreign affairs. [. . .] It is also evident that some aspects of international law touch much more sharply on national nerves than do others; the less important the implications of an issue are for our foreign relations, the weaker the justification for exclusivity in the political branches. [. . .] Therefore, rather than laying down or reaffirming an inflexible and all-encompassing rule in this case, we decide only that the Judicial Branch will not examine the validity of a taking of property at the time of suit, in the absence of a treaty or other unambiguous agreement regarding controlling legal principles, even if the complaint alleges that the taking violates customary international law.

431. [. . .] Following an expropriation of any significance, the Executive engages in diplomacy aimed to assure that United States citizens who are harmed are compensated fairly. Representing all claimants of this country, it will often be able, either by bilateral or multilateral talks, by submission to the United Nations, or by the

employment of economic and political sanctions, to achieve some degree of general redress. Judicial determinations of invalidity of title can, on the other hand, have only an occasional impact, since they depend on the fortuitous circumstance of the property in question being brought into this country. Such decisions would, if the acts involved were declared invalid, often be likely to give offense to the expropriating country; since the concept of territorial sovereignty is so deep seated, any state may resent the refusal of the courts of another sovereign to accord validity to acts within its territorial borders. [. . .]

The dangers of such adjudication are present regardless of whether the State Department has, as it did in this case, asserted that the relevant act violated international law. If the Executive Branch has undertaken negotiations with an expropriating country, but has refrained from claims of violation of the law of nations, a determination to that effect by a court might be regarded as a serious insult, while a finding of compliance with international law, would greatly strengthen the bargaining hand of the other state with consequent detriment to American interests.

[. . .]

433. Respondents contend that, even if there is not agreement regarding general standards for determining the validity of expropriations, the alleged combination of retaliation, discrimination, and inadequate compensation makes it patently clear that this particular expropriation was in violation of international law. If this view is accurate, it would still be unwise for the courts so to determine. Such a decision now would require the drawing of more difficult lines in subsequent cases and these would involve the possibility of conflict with the Executive view. [. . .]

434. Another serious consequence of the exception pressed by respondents would be to render uncertain titles in foreign commerce, with the possible consequence of altering the flow of international trade. If the attitude of the United States courts were unclear, one buying expropriated goods would not know if he could safely import them into this country. [. . .]

Against the force of such considerations, we find respondents' countervailing arguments quite unpersuasive.

435. [. . .] The newly independent states are in need of continuing foreign investment; the creation of a climate unfavorable to such investment by wholesale confiscations may well work to their long-run economic disadvantage. Foreign aid given to many of these countries provides a powerful lever in the hands of the political branches to ensure fair treatment of United States nationals. Ultimately the sanctions of economic embargo and the freezing of assets in this country may be employed. Any country willing to brave any or all of these consequences is unlikely to be deterred by sporadic judicial decisions directly affecting only property brought to our shores. [. . .]

437. However offensive to public policy of this country and its constituent States an expropriation of this kind may be, we conclude that both the national interest

and progress toward the goal of establishing the rule of law among nations are best served by maintaining intact the act of state doctrine in this realm of its application.

439. Since the act of state doctrine proscribes a challenge to the validity of the Cuban expropriation decree in this case, any counterclaim based on asserted invalidity must fail. Whether a theory of conversion or breach of contract is the proper cause of action under New York law, the presumed validity of expropriation is unaffected. [. . .]

The judgment of the Court of Appeals is reversed and the case is remanded to the District Court for proceedings consistent with this opinion.

It is so ordered.

© P.E. Comeaux and N.S. Kinsella, *Protecting Foreign Investment under International Law: Legal Aspects of Political Risk*, 1996, Oxford Publishing Limited (Academic). Reproduced with permission of the Licensor through PLSclear.

It was [*Sabbatino*], in fact, that precipitated Congress' enacting of the Second Hickenlooper Amendment,[46] an exception to the AoS doctrine. [. . .] The AoS doctrine also does not apply if the expropriation violates a treaty between the United States and the expropriating state. In this case, a US court may grant relief.[47]

Another exception was created by the Hickenlooper Amendment,[48] enacted by Congress in reaction to the *Sabbatino* case. This Amendment requires US courts to adjudicate claims based on certain expropriations by a foreign state if the foreign states does not provide compensation for the property taken. It provides in part:

> [N]o court in the United States shall decline on the ground of the federal act of state doctrine to make a determination on the merits giving effect to the principles of international law in a case in which a claim of title or other right to property is asserted by any party including a foreign state [. . .] based upon (or traced through) a confiscation or other taking [. . .] by an act of that state in violation of the principles of international law.

Unfortunately, U.S. courts have read this exception narrowly to apply only to cases where the expropriated property has been brought into the United States.[49] In the *Hunt* case,[50] for example, the plaintiff, whose oil interests in Libya were nationalized, brought an action against a purchaser of such oil for conversion. To the claimant's arguments that the AoS Doctrine was not applicable under the Hickenlooper Amendment because the taking was illegal, the court responded that the Hicken-

46. 22 U.S.C. § 2370(e)(2) (1970).

47. *Kalamazoo Spice Ext. Co. v. Provisional Military Government of Socialist Ethiopia*, 729 F.2d 422 (6th Cir. 1984).

48. 22 U.S.C § 2370(e)(2) (1988).

49. *Empresa Cubana Exportadora, Inc v. Lamborn & Co.*, 652 F.2d 231 (2d. Cir. 1981).

50. *Hunt v. Coastal States Gas Producing Company*, 583 S.W.2d 322 (Tex. Civ. App. 1979).

looper Amendment only concerned the taking of a "title or other right in property", and in the present case, the state only expropriated contractual rights. [. . .]

Finally, a state cannot raise the AoS doctrine as a defense to a counterclaim to a suit originally brought by the state, except to the extent that the value of the counterclaim exceeds the value of the foreign state's claim.[51]

3. Alien Tort Statute

Argentine Republic v. Amerada Hess Shipping Corp., 488 U.S. 428 (1989).

Case Introduction

A crude oil tanker owned by United Carriers, Inc. ("United Carriers"), a Liberian corporation, was chartered to the respondent Amerada Hess Corp ("Amerada Hess"), also a Liberian corporation. The vessel was used to transport crude oil from Alaska to the United States Virgin Islands, and the contract was executed in New York City. During the war between Great Britain and the Argentine Republic over the Falkland Islands, the tanker was on its way from the Virgin Islands to Alaska when, without provocation, it was attacked three times by Argentine military aircraft in international waters and severely damaged.

Following unsuccessful attempts to obtain relief in Argentina, United Carriers and Amerada Hess brought separate actions against the petitioner in the United States District Court for the Southern District of New York, alleging violation of international law. Respondents invoked the District Court's jurisdiction under the Alien Tort Statute, 28 U.S.C. § 1350 ("ATS"), which provides that "[t]he district courts shall have original jurisdiction of any civil action by an alien for a tort only, committed in violation of the law of nations or a treaty of the United States." United Carriers sought $10 million in damages for the loss of the ship and Amerada Hess $1.9 million in damages for the fuel that went down with the ship. The District Court dismissed their complaints for lack of subject-matter jurisdiction, ruling their actions barred by the FSIA.

The Court of Appeals reversed, holding that the District Court had jurisdiction over the respondents' consolidated actions under the ATS. They reasoned that Congress' enactment of the FSIA was not meant to eliminate "existing remedies in United States courts for violation of international law" by foreign states under the ATS. The case then proceeded to the Supreme Court.

Principal Points of the Judgment

Chief Justice Rehnquist

Two Liberian corporations sued the Argentine Republic in a United States District Court to recover damages for a tort allegedly committed by its armed forces on the

51. *First National City Bank v. Banco Nacional de Cuba*, 406 U.S. 759 (1972).

high seas in violation of international law. We hold that the District Court correctly dismissed the action, because the Foreign Sovereign Immunities Act of 1976 (FSIA), 28 U.S.C. § 1330 et seq., does not authorize jurisdiction over a foreign state in this situation. [. . .]

We think that the text and structure of the FSIA demonstrate Congress' intention that the FSIA be the sole basis for obtaining jurisdiction over a foreign state in our courts. Sections 1604 and 1330(a) work in tandem: § 1604 bars federal and state courts from exercising jurisdiction when a foreign state is entitled to immunity, and § 1330(a) confers jurisdiction on district courts to hear suits brought by United States citizens and by aliens when a foreign state is not entitled to immunity. As we said in *Verlinden*, the FSIA "must be applied by the district courts in every action against a foreign sovereign, since subject matter jurisdiction in any such action depends on the existence of one of the specified exceptions to foreign sovereign immunity." *Verlinden B. V. v. Central Bank of Nigeria*, 461 U.S. 480, 493 (1983).

[. . .]

Congress had violations of international law by foreign states in mind when it enacted the FSIA. For example, the FSIA specifically denies foreign states immunity in suits "in which rights in property taken in violation of international law are in issue." 28 U.S.C. § 1605(a)(3). Congress also rested the FSIA in part on its power under Art. I, § 8, cl. 10, of the Constitution "[t]o define and punish Piracies and Felonies committed on the high Seas, and Offenses against the Law of Nations." *See* H.R.Rep. at 12; S.Rep. at 12. From Congress' decision to deny immunity to foreign states in the class of cases just mentioned we draw the plain implication that immunity is granted in those cases involving alleged violations of international law that do not come within one of the FSIA's exceptions.

In this Court, respondents argue that cases were brought under the Alien Tort Statute against foreign states for the unlawful taking of a prize during wartime. The Alien Tort Statute makes no mention of prize jurisdiction, and § 1333(2) now grants federal district courts exclusive jurisdiction over "all proceedings for the condemnation of property taken as a prize." In *The Santissima Trinidad*, (7 Wheat.) 283, 20 U.S. 353–354 (1822), we held that foreign states were not immune from the jurisdiction of United States courts in prize proceedings. That case, however, was not brought under the Alien Tort Statute, but rather as a libel in admiralty. Thus there is a distinctly hypothetical cast to the Court of Appeals' reliance on Congress' failure to repeal the Alien Tort Statute, and respondents' arguments in this Court based on the principle of statutory construction that repeals by implication are disfavored.

[. . .]

For similar reasons we are not persuaded by respondents' arguments based upon the rule of statutory construction under which repeals by implication are disfavored. This case does not involve two statutes that readily could be seen as supplementing one another, See *Wood v. United States*, (16 Pet.) 342, 41 U.S. 363 (1842), nor is it a case where a more general statute is claimed to have repealed by implication an earlier statute dealing with a narrower subject. *See Morton v. Mancari,* 417 U. S. 535, 549–551 (1974). We think that Congress' decision to deal comprehensively with the subject of foreign sovereign immunity in the FSIA, and the express provision in § 1604 that "a foreign state shall be immune from the jurisdiction of the courts of the United States and of the States except as provided in sections 1605–1607" preclude a construction of the Alien Tort Statute that permits the instant suit. *See Red Rock v. Henry,* 106 U. S. 596, 601–602 (1883); *United States v. Tynen,* (11 Wall.) 88, 78 U.S. 92 (1871). The Alien Tort Statute, by its terms, does not distinguish among classes of defendants, and it of course has the same effect after the passage of the FSIA as before with respect to defendants other than foreign states.

[. . .]

Having determined that the FSIA provides the sole basis for obtaining jurisdiction over a foreign state in federal court, we turn to whether any of the exceptions enumerated in the Act apply here. These exceptions include cases involving the waiver of immunity, § 1605(a)(1), commercial activities occurring in the United States or causing a direct effect in this country, § 1605(a)(2), property expropriated in violation of international law, § 1605(a)(3), inherited, gift, or immovable property located in the United States, § 1605(a)(4), noncommercial torts occurring in the United States, § 1605(a)(5), and maritime liens, § 1605(b). We agree with the District Court that none of the FSIA's exceptions applies on these facts.

Respondents assert that the FSIA exception for noncommercial torts, § 1605(a)(5), is most in point. [. . .]

In this case, the injury to respondents' ship occurred on the high seas some 5,000 miles off the nearest shores of the United States. Despite these telling facts, respondents nonetheless claim that the tortious attack on the Hercules occurred "in the United States." They point out that the FSIA defines "United States" as including all "territory and waters, continental and insular, subject to the jurisdiction of the United States," § 1603(c), and that their injury occurred on the high seas, which is within the admiralty jurisdiction of the United States, See *The Plymouth,* (3 Wall.) 20, 36 (1866). They reason, therefore, that, "by statutory definition," petitioner's attack occurred in the United States.

We find this logic unpersuasive. We construe the modifying phrase "continental and insular" to restrict the definition of United States to the continental United States and those islands that are part of the United States or its possessions; any other reading would render this phrase nugatory. Likewise, the term "waters" in § 1603(c) cannot reasonably be read to cover all waters over which United States courts might exercise jurisdiction. When it desires to do so, Congress knows how to place the high seas within the jurisdictional reach of a statute. We thus apply "[t]he canon of construction which teaches that legislation of Congress, unless contrary intent appears, is meant to apply only within the territorial jurisdiction of the United States." *Foley Bros., Inc. v. Filardo,* 336 U.S. 281, 285 (1949); *see also*

Weinberger v. Rossi, 456 U.S. 25, 32 (1982). Because respondents' injury unquestionably occurred well outside the 3-mile limit then in effect for the territorial waters of the United States, the exception for noncommercial torts cannot apply.

The result in this case is not altered by the fact that petitioner's alleged tort may have had effects in the United States. Respondents state, for example, that the Hercules was transporting oil intended for use in this country, and that the loss of the ship disrupted contractual payments due in New York. Brief for Respondents 51. Under the commercial activity exception to the FSIA, § 1605(a)(2), a foreign state may be liable for its commercial activities "outside the territory of the United States" having a "direct effect" inside the United States. But the noncommercial tort exception, § 1605(a)(5), upon which respondents rely, makes no mention of "territory outside the United States" or of "direct effects" in the United States. Congress' decision to use explicit language in § 1605(a)(2), and not to do so in § 1605(a)(5), indicates that the exception in § 1605(a)(5) covers only torts occurring within the territorial jurisdiction of the United States. Respondents do not claim that § 1605(a)(2) covers these facts.

We also disagree with respondents' claim that certain international agreements entered into by petitioner and by the United States create an exception to the FSIA here. [. . .] this exception applies when international agreements "expressly conflict" with the immunity provisions of the FSIA, hardly the circumstances in this case.

We hold that the FSIA provides the sole basis for obtaining jurisdiction over a foreign state in the courts of this country, and that none of the enumerated exceptions to the Act apply to the facts of the case. The judgment of the Court of Appeals is therefore reversed.

Jesner v. Arab Bank, PLC, 138 S. Ct. 1386 (2018).

Case Introduction

Jesner, et al. ("Petitioners") sought compensation under the Alien Tort Statute ("ATS"), based on terrorist acts committed abroad. They alleged that those acts were in part facilitated by Arab Bank ("Respondent"), a Jordanian institution with a New York branch. Petitioners alleged that Arab Bank maintained bank accounts for terrorists and their front groups and allowed the accounts to be used to pay the families of suicide bombers. Although most of Petitioner's allegations involved conduct that occurred in the Middle East, Petitioners claimed that the New York branch was used to clear dollar-denominated transactions that benefited terrorists through the Clearing House Interbank Payments System (CHIPS) and to launder money for the Holy Land Foundation for Relief and Development ("HLF"), a Texas-based charity allegedly affiliated with Hamas and other terrorist groups. Petitioners sought to impose liability on the bank for the conduct of its human agents, including high-ranking bank officials.

The Second Circuit and Supreme Court affirmed the dismissal of the case. Foreign corporations may not be defendants in suits brought under the ATS, which is "strictly jurisdictional" and does not provide or define a cause of action for international law violations.

Principal Points of the Judgment

Justice Kennedy delivered the opinion of the Court, in which *The Chief Justice* and *Justice Thomas* join.

[. . .]

Petitioners contend that international and domestic laws impose responsibility and liability on a corporation if its human agents use the corporation to commit crimes in violation of international laws that protect human rights. The question here is whether the Judiciary has the authority, in an ATS action, to make that determination and then to enforce that liability in ATS suits, all without any explicit authorization from Congress to do so.

The answer turns upon the proper interpretation and implementation of the ATS. The statute provides: "The district courts shall have original jurisdiction of any civil action by an alien for a tort only, committed in violation of the law of nations or a treaty of the United States." 28 U.S.C. § 1350. The Court must first ask whether the law of nations imposes liability on corporations for human-rights violations committed by its employees. [. . .]

During the pendency of this litigation, there was an unrelated case that also implicated the issue whether the ATS is applicable to suits in this country against foreign corporations. See *Kiobel v. Royal Dutch Petroleum Co.*, 621 F.3d 111 (CA2 2010). That suit worked its way through the trial court and the Court of Appeals for the Second Circuit. The *Kiobel* litigation did not involve banking transactions. Its allegations were that holding companies incorporated in the Netherlands and the United Kingdom had, through a Nigerian subsidiary, aided and abetted the Nigerian Government in human-rights abuses. *Id.*, at 123. In *Kiobel*, the Court of Appeals held that the ATS does not extend to suits against corporations. *Id.*, at 120. This Court granted certiorari in *Kiobel*. 565 U.S. 961 (2011).

[. . .] The Court ruled that "all the relevant conduct took place outside the United States." *Id.*, at 124. Dismissal of the action was required based on the presumption against extraterritorial application of statutes. *Kiobel v. Royal Dutch Petroleum Co.*, 569 U. S. 108, 114, 124–125 (2013). So while this Court in *Kiobel* affirmed the ruling that the action there could not be maintained, it did not address the broader holding of the Court of Appeals that dismissal was required because corporations may not be sued under the ATS. [. . .]

The majority opinion in *Kiobel*, written by Judge Cabranes, held that the ATS does not apply to alleged international-law violations by a corporation. [. . .]

Under the Articles of Confederation, the Continental Congress lacked authority to "cause infractions of treaties, or of the law of nations to be punished." *Sosa v.*

Alvarez-Machain, 542 U.S. 692, 716 (2004) (quoting J. Madison, Journal of the Constitutional Convention 60 (E. Scott ed. 1893)). The Continental Congress urged the States to authorize suits for damages sustained by foreign citizens as a result of violations of international law; but the state courts' vindication of the law of nations remained unsatisfactory. Concerns with the consequent international-relations tensions "persisted through the time of the Constitutional Convention." 542 U.S., at 717.

Under the Articles of Confederation, the inability of the central government to ensure adequate remedies for foreign citizens caused substantial foreign-relations problems. In 1784, the French Minister lodged a protest with the Continental Congress after a French adventurer, the Chevalier de Longchamps, assaulted the Secretary of the French Legation in Philadelphia. See *Kiobel*, 569 U.S., at 120. A few years later, a New York constable caused an international incident when he entered the house of the Dutch Ambassador and arrested one of his servants. *Ibid.* Under the Articles of Confederation, there was no national forum available to resolve disputes like these under any binding laws that were or could be enacted or enforced by a central government.

The Framers addressed these matters at the 1787 Philadelphia Convention; and, as a result, Article III of the Constitution extends the federal judicial power to "all cases affecting ambassadors, other public ministers and consuls," and "to controversies . . . between a state, or the citizens thereof, and foreign states, citizens, or subjects." § 2. The First Congress passed a statute to implement these provisions: The Judiciary Act of 1789 authorized federal jurisdiction over suits involving disputes between aliens and United States citizens and suits involving diplomats. §§ 9, 11, 1 Stat. 76–79.

The Judiciary Act also included what is now the statute known as the ATS. § 9, *id.*, at 76. As noted, the ATS is central to this case and its brief text bears repeating. Its full text is: "The district courts shall have original jurisdiction of any civil action by an alien for a tort only, committed in violation of the law of nations or a treaty of the United States." 28 U.S.C. § 1350.

The ATS is "strictly jurisdictional" and does not by its own terms provide or delineate the definition of a cause of action for violations of international law. *Sosa*, 542 U.S., at 713–714. But the statute was not enacted to sit on a shelf awaiting further legislation. *Id.*, at 714. Rather, Congress enacted it against the backdrop of the general common law, which in 1789 recognized a limited category of "torts in violation of the law of nations." *Ibid.* [. . .]

This history teaches that Congress drafted the ATS "to furnish jurisdiction for a relatively modest set of actions alleging violations of the law of nations." *Id.*, at 720. The principal objective of the statute, when first enacted, was to avoid foreign entanglements by ensuring the availability of a federal forum where the failure to provide one might cause another nation to hold the United States responsible for an injury to a foreign citizen. See *id.*, at 715–719; *Kiobel*, 569 U.S., at 123–124.

[. . .]

The question whether foreign corporations are subject to liability under the ATS should be addressed; for, if there is no liability for Arab Bank, the lengthy and costly litigation concerning whether corporate contacts like those alleged here suffice to impose liability would be pointless. In addition, a remand to the Court of Appeals would require prolonging litigation that already has caused significant diplomatic tensions with Jordan for more than a decade. So it is proper for this Court to decide whether corporations, or at least foreign corporations, are subject to liability in an ATS suit filed in a United States district court.

Before recognizing a common-law action under the ATS, federal courts must apply the test announced in *Sosa*. An initial, threshold question is whether a plaintiff can demonstrate that the alleged violation is "of a norm that is specific, universal, and obligatory." 542 U.S., at 732. And even assuming that, under international law, there is a specific norm that can be controlling, it must be determined further whether allowing this case to proceed under the ATS is a proper exercise of judicial discretion, or instead whether caution requires the political branches to grant specific authority before corporate liability can be imposed. See *id*., at 732–733, and nn. 20–21. "[T]he potential implications for the foreign relations of the United States of recognizing such causes should make courts particularly wary of impinging on the discretion of the Legislative and Executive Branches in managing foreign affairs." *Id*., at 727.

It must be said that some of the considerations that pertain to determining whether there is a specific, universal, and obligatory norm that is established under international law are applicable as well in determining whether deference must be given to the political branches. For instance, the fact that the charters of some international tribunals and the provisions of some congressional statutes addressing international human-rights violations are specifically limited to individual wrongdoers, and thus foreclose corporate liability, has significant bearing both on the content of the norm being asserted and the question whether courts should defer to Congress. The two inquiries inform each other and are, to that extent, not altogether discrete.

With that introduction, it is proper now to turn first to the question whether there is an international-law norm imposing liability on corporations for acts of their employees that contravene fundamental human rights.

A

Petitioners and Arab Bank disagree as to whether corporate liability is a question of international law or only a question of judicial authority and discretion under domestic law. The dispute centers on a footnote in *Sosa*. In the course of holding that international norms must be "sufficiently definite to support a cause of action," the Court in *Sosa* noted that a "related consideration is whether international law extends the scope of liability for a violation of a given norm to the perpetrator being sued, if the defendant is a private actor such as a corporation or individual." *Id*., at 732, and n. 20.

In the Court of Appeals' decision in *Kiobel*, the majority opinion by Judge Cabranes interpreted footnote 20 to mean that corporate defendants may be held liable under the ATS only if there is a specific, universal, and obligatory norm that corporations are liable for violations of international law. 621 F.3d, at 127. In Judge Cabranes' view, "[i]nternational law is not silent on the question of the subjects of international law—that is, those that, to varying extents, have legal status, personality, rights, and duties under international law," "[n]or does international law leave to individual States the responsibility of defining those subjects." *Id.*, at 126 (internal quotation marks omitted). There is considerable force and weight to the position articulated by Judge Cabranes. And, assuming the Court of Appeals was correct that under *Sosa* corporate liability is a question of international law, there is an equally strong argument that petitioners cannot satisfy the high bar of demonstrating a specific, universal, and obligatory norm of liability for corporations. Indeed, Judge Leval agreed with the conclusion that international law does "not provide for any form of liability of corporations." *Kiobel*, 621 F. 3d, at 186.

1

In modern times, there is no doubt, of course, that "the international community has come to recognize the common danger posed by the flagrant disregard of basic human rights," leading "the nations of the world to recognize that respect for fundamental human rights is in their individual and collective interest." *Filartiga*, 630 F.2d, at 890. That principle and commitment support the conclusion that human-rights norms must bind the individual men and women responsible for committing humanity's most terrible crimes, not just nation-states in their interactions with one another. "The singular achievement of international law since the Second World War has come in the area of human rights," where international law now imposes duties on individuals as well as nation-states. *Kiobel*, 621 F. 3d, at 118.

It does not follow, however, that current principles of international law extend liability—civil or criminal—for human-rights violations to corporations or other artificial entities. This is confirmed by the fact that the charters of respective international criminal tribunals often exclude corporations from their jurisdictional reach.

[...]

The jurisdictional reach of more recent international tribunals also has been limited to "natural persons." See Statute of the International Criminal Tribunal for the Former Yugoslavia, S.C. Res. 827 (May 25, 1993), adopting U.N. Secretary-General Rep. Pursuant to Paragraph 2 of Security Council Resolution 808, Art. 6, U. N. Doc. S/25704 (May 3, 1993) [...] The drafters of the Rome Statute considered, but rejected, a proposal to give the International Criminal Court jurisdiction over corporations. Eser, Individual Criminal Responsibility, in 1 Rome Statute of the International Criminal Court 767, 778–779 (A. Cassese et al. eds. 2002).

2

In light of the sources just discussed, the sources petitioners rely on to support their contention that liability for corporations is well established as a matter of international law lend weak support to their position.

Petitioners first point to the International Convention for the Suppression of the Financing of Terrorism.[52] This Convention imposes an obligation on "Each State Party" "to enable a legal entity located in its territory or organized under its laws to be held liable when a person responsible for the management or control of that legal entity has, in that capacity," violated the Convention.

But by its terms the Convention imposes its obligations only on nation-states "to enable" corporations to be held liable in certain circumstances under domestic law. The United States and other nations, including Jordan, may fulfill their obligations under the Convention by adopting detailed regulatory regimes governing financial institutions. See, e.g., 18 U.S.C. § 2333(a) (private right of action under the Anti-Terrorism Act); 31 U.S.C. § 5311 et seq. (Bank Secrecy Act); 31 CFR pt. 595 (2017) (Terrorism Sanctions Regulations); Brief for Central Bank of Jordan as Amicus Curiae 5 (describing Jordan's "comprehensive approach to preventing money laundering and terrorist financing"). The Convention neither requires nor authorizes courts, without congressional authorization, to displace those detailed regulatory regimes by allowing common-law actions under the ATS. And nothing in the Convention's text requires signatories to hold corporations liable in common-law tort actions raising claims under international law.

In addition, petitioners and their amici cite a few cases from other nations and the Special Tribunal for Lebanon that, according to petitioners, are examples of corporations being held liable for violations of international law. E.g., Brief for Petitioners 50–51. Yet even assuming that these cases are relevant examples, at most they demonstrate that corporate liability might be permissible under international law in some circumstances. That falls far short of establishing a specific, universal, and obligatory norm of corporate liability.

It must be remembered that international law is distinct from domestic law in its domain as well as its objectives. International human-rights norms prohibit acts repugnant to all civilized peoples—crimes like genocide, torture, and slavery, that make their perpetrators "enem[ies] of all mankind." *Sosa*, 542 U.S., at 732 (internal quotation marks omitted). In the American legal system, of course, corporations are often subject to liability for the conduct of their human employees, and so it may seem necessary and natural that corporate entities are liable for violations of international law under the ATS. It is true, furthermore, that the enormity of the offenses that can be committed against persons in violation of international human-rights protections can be cited to show that corporations should be subject

52. Dec. 9, 1999, S. Treaty Doc. No. 106–49, 2178 U.N.T.S. 232.

to liability for the crimes of their human agents. But the international community has not yet taken that step, at least in the specific, universal, and obligatory manner required by *Sosa*. Indeed, there is precedent to the contrary in the statement during the Nuremberg proceedings that "[c]rimes against international law are committed by men, not by abstract entities, and only by punishing individuals who commit such crimes can the provisions of international law be enforced." *The Nuremberg Trial*, 6 F.R.D. 69, 110 (1946).

[. . .]

The political branches, not the Judiciary, have the responsibility and institutional capacity to weigh foreign-policy concerns. See *Kiobel*, 569 U.S., at 116–117. That the ATS implicates foreign relations "is itself a reason for a high bar to new private causes of action for violating international law." *Sosa*, *supra*, at 727. In *Sosa*, the Court emphasized that federal courts must exercise "great caution" before recognizing new forms of liability under the ATS. 542 U.S., at 728. In light of the foreign-policy and separation-of-powers concerns inherent in ATS litigation, there is an argument that a proper application of *Sosa* would preclude courts from ever recognizing any new causes of action under the ATS. But the Court need not resolve that question in this case. Either way, absent further action from Congress it would be inappropriate for courts to extend ATS liability to foreign corporations.

[. . .]

If, moreover, the Court were to hold that foreign corporations may be held liable under the ATS, that precedent setting principle "would imply that other nations, also applying the law of nations, could hale our [corporations] into their courts for alleged violations of the law of nations." *Kiobel*, 569 U.S., at 124. This judicially mandated doctrine, in turn, could subject American corporations to an immediate, constant risk of claims seeking to impose massive liability for the alleged conduct of their employees and subsidiaries around the world, all as determined in foreign courts, thereby "hinder[ing] global investment in developing economies, where it is most needed." Brief for United States as Amicus Curiae in *American Isuzu Motors, Inc. v. Ntsebeza*, O.T. 2007, No. 07–919, p. 20.

In other words, allowing plaintiffs to sue foreign corporations under the ATS could establish a precedent that discourages American corporations from investing abroad, including in developing economies where the host government might have a history of alleged human-rights violations, or where judicial systems might lack the safeguards of United States courts. And, in consequence, that often might deter the active corporate investment that contributes to the economic development that so often is an essential foundation for human rights.

It is also true, of course, that natural persons can and do use corporations for sinister purposes, including conduct that violates international law. That the corporate form can be an instrument for inflicting grave harm and suffering poses serious and complex questions both for the international community and for Congress. So there are strong arguments for permitting the victims to seek relief from corporations themselves. Yet the urgency and complexity of this problem make it all the more important that Congress determine whether victims of human-rights abuses may sue foreign corporations in federal courts in the United States. Congress, not the Judiciary, is the branch with "the facilities necessary to make fairly such an important policy decision where the possibilities of international discord are so evident and retaliative action so certain." *Kiobel*, 569 U.S., at 116. As noted further below, there are many delicate and important considerations that Congress is in a better position to examine in determining whether and how best to impose corporate liability. And, as the TVPA illustrates, Congress is well aware of the necessity of clarifying the proper scope of liability under the ATS in a timely way.

[. . .]

The ATS was intended to promote harmony in international relations by ensuring foreign plaintiffs a remedy for international-law violations in circumstances where the absence of such a remedy might provoke foreign nations to hold the United States accountable. Brief for United States as Amicus Curiae 7. But here, and in similar cases, the opposite is occurring. Petitioners are foreign nationals seeking hundreds of millions of dollars in damages from a major Jordanian financial institution for injuries suffered in attacks by foreign terrorists in the Middle East. The only alleged connections to the United States are the CHIPS transactions in Arab Bank's New York branch and a brief allegation regarding a charity in Texas. The Court of Appeals did not address, and the Court need not now decide, whether these allegations are sufficient to "touch and concern" the United States under *Kiobel*. See 569 U.S., at 124–125. At a minimum, the relatively minor connection between the terrorist attacks at issue in this case and the alleged conduct in the United States well illustrates the perils of extending the scope of ATS liability to foreign multinational corporations like Arab Bank. For 13 years, this litigation has "caused significant diplomatic tensions" with Jordan, a critical ally in one of the world's most sensitive regions.

[. . .]

For these reasons, judicial deference requires that any imposition of corporate liability on foreign corporations for violations of international law must be determined in the first instance by the political branches of the Government. The judgment of the Court of Appeals is affirmed.

It is so ordered.

Justice Sotomayor, with whom *Justice Ginsburg*, *Justice Breyer*, and *Justice Kagan* join, dissenting.

The Court today holds that the Alien Tort Statute (ATS), 28 U.S.C. § 1350, categorically forecloses foreign corporate liability. In so doing, it absolves corporations from responsibility under the ATS for conscience-shocking behavior. I disagree both with the Court's conclusion and its analytic approach. The text, history, and purpose of the ATS, as well as the long and consistent history of corporate liability in tort, confirm that tort claims for law of nations violations may be brought against corporations under the ATS. Nothing about the corporate form in itself raises foreign policy concerns that require the Court, as a matter of common-law discretion, to immunize all foreign corporations from liability under the ATS, regardless of the specific law-of-nations violations alleged. I respectfully dissent.

I

The plurality assumes without deciding that whether corporations can be permissible defendants under the ATS turns on the first step of the two-part inquiry set out in *Sosa v. Alvarez-Machain*, 542 U.S. 692 (2004). But by asking whether there is "a specific, universal, and obligatory norm of liability for corporations" in international law, *ante*, at 13, the plurality fundamentally misconceives how international law works and so misapplies the first step of *Sosa*.

A

In *Sosa*, the Court considered whether a Mexican citizen could recover under the ATS for a claim of arbitrary detention by a Mexican national who had been hired by the Drug Enforcement Administration to seize and transport him to the United States. See 542 U.S., at 697–698. The Court held that the ATS permits federal courts to "recognize private causes of action for certain torts in violation of the law of nations," *id*., at 724, without the need for any "further congressional action," *id*., at 712. The Court then articulated a two-step framework to guide that inquiry. First, a court must determine whether the particular international-law norm alleged to have been violated is "accepted by the civilized world and defined with a specificity comparable to the features of the 18th-century paradigms," i.e., "violation of safe conducts, infringement of the rights of ambassadors, and piracy." *Id*., at 724–725. Only if the norm is "'specific, universal, and obligatory'" may federal courts recognize a cause of action for its violation. *Kiobel v. Royal Dutch Petroleum Co*., 569 U.S. 108, 117 (2013) (quoting *Sosa*, 542 U.S., at 732). Second, if that threshold hurdle is satisfied, a court should consider whether allowing a particular case to proceed is an appropriate exercise of judicial discretion. *Sosa*, 542 U.S., at 727–728, 732–733, 738. Applying that framework, *Sosa* held that the alleged arbitrary detention claim at issue failed at step one because "a single illegal detention of less than a day, followed by the transfer of custody to lawful authorities and a prompt arraignment, violates no norm of customary international law so well defined as to support the creation of a federal remedy." *Id*., at 738.

Sosa's norm-specific first step is inapposite to the categorical question whether corporations may be sued under the ATS as a general matter. International law imposes certain obligations that are intended to govern the behavior of states and private actors. See *id*., at 714–715; 1 Restatement (Third) of Foreign Relations Law of the United States, pt. II, Introductory Note, pp. 70–71 (1987) (Restatement). Among those obligations are substantive prohibitions on certain conduct thought to violate human rights, such as genocide, slavery, extrajudicial killing, and torture. See 2 Restatement § 702. Substantive prohibitions like these are the norms at which *Sosa*'s step-one inquiry is aimed and for which *Sosa* requires that there be sufficient international consensus.

Sosa does not, however, demand that there be sufficient international consensus with regard to the mechanisms of enforcing these norms, for enforcement is not a question with which customary international law is concerned. Although international law determines what substantive conduct violates the law of nations, it leaves the specific rules of how to enforce international-law norms and remedy their violation to states, which may act to impose liability collectively through treaties or independently via their domestic legal systems. [. . .]

C

Instead of asking whether there exists a specific, universal, and obligatory norm of corporate liability under international law, the relevant inquiry in response to the question presented here is whether there is any reason—under either international law or our domestic law—to distinguish between a corporation and a natural person who is alleged to have violated the law of nations under the ATS. As explained above, international law provides no such reason. See *Kiobel*, 621 F.3d, at 175 (Leval, J., concurring in judgment) ("[T]he answer international law furnishes is that it takes no position on the question"). Nor does domestic law. The text, history, and purpose of the ATS plainly support the conclusion that corporations may be held liable.

Beginning "with the language of the statute itself," *United States v. Ron Pair Enterprises*, Inc., 489 U.S. 235, 241 (1989), two aspects of the text of the ATS make clear that the statute allows corporate liability. First, the text confers jurisdiction on federal district courts to hear "civil action[s]" for "tort[s]." 28 U.S.C. § 1350. Where Congress uses a term of art like tort, "it presumably knows and adopts the cluster of ideas that were attached to [the] borrowed word in the body of learning from which it was taken and the meaning its use will convey to the judicial mind unless otherwise instructed." *Morissette v. United States*, 342 U. S. 246, 263 (1952).

Corporations have long been held liable in tort under the federal common law. See *Philadelphia, Wilmington, & Balt. R.R v. Quigley*, 62 U.S. (21 How.) 202, 210–211 (1859) ("At a very early period, it was decided in Great Britain, as well as in the United States, that actions might be maintained against corporations for torts; and instances may be found, in the judicial annals of both countries, of suits for torts arising from the acts of their agents, of nearly every variety"); *Chestnut Hill & Spring House Turnpike Co. v. Rutter*, 4 Serg. & Rawle 6, 17 (Pa. 1818) ("[F]rom the earliest times to the present, corporations have been held liable for torts"). This Court "has assumed that, when Congress creates a tort action, it legislates against a legal background of ordinary tort-related . . . rules and consequently intends its legislation to incorporate those rules." *Meyer v. Holley*, 537 U.S. 280, 285 (2003). The presumption, then, is that, in providing for "tort" liability, the ATS provides for corporate liability. Second, whereas the ATS expressly limits the class of permissible plaintiffs to "alien[s]," § 1350, it "does not distinguish among classes of defendants," *Argentine Republic v. Amerada Hess Shipping Corp.*, 488 U.S. 428, 438 (1989). That silence as to defendants cannot be presumed to be inadvertent.

That is because in the same section of the Judiciary Act of 1789 as what is now the ATS, Congress provided the federal district courts with jurisdiction over "all suits against consuls or vice-consuls." § 9, 1 Stat. 76–77. Where Congress wanted to limit the range of permissible defendants, then, it clearly knew how to do so. *Russello v. United States*, 464 U.S. 16, 23 (1983) ("[W]here Congress includes particular language in one section of a statute but omits it in another section of the same Act, it is generally presumed that Congress acts intentionally and purposely in the disparate inclusion or exclusion".

Nothing about the historical background against which the ATS was enacted rebuts the presumption that the statute incorporated the accepted principle of corporate liability for tortious conduct. Under the Articles of Confederation, the Continental Congress was unable to provide redress to foreign citizens for violations of treaties or the law of nations, which threatened to undermine the United States' relationships with other nations. See *Kiobel*, 569 U.S., at 123. The First Congress responded with, inter alia, the ATS. Although the two incidents that highlighted the need to provide foreign citizens with a federal forum in which to pursue their grievances involved conflicts between natural persons, see *ante*, at 7 (majority opinion) (describing the assault by a French adventurer on the Secretary of the French Legation and the arrest of one of the Dutch Ambassador's servants by a New York constable), there is "no reason to conclude that the First Congress was supremely concerned with the risk that natural persons would cause the United States to be drawn into foreign entanglements, but was content to allow formal legal associations of individuals, i.e., corporations, to do so," *Doe v. Exxon Mobil Corp.*, 654 F.3d 11, 47 (CADC 2011), vacated on other grounds, 527 Fed. Appx. 7 (CADC 2013); see also Brief for United States as Amicus Curiae 6 ("The ATS was enacted to ensure a private damages remedy for incidents with the potential for serious diplomatic consequences, and Congress had no good reason to limit the set of possible defendants in such actions to potentially judgment-proof individuals"). Indeed, foreclosing corporations from liability under the ATS would have been at odds with the contemporaneous practice of imposing liability for piracy on ships, juridical entities. See, e.g., *Skinner v. East India Co.*, 6 State Trials 710, 711 (1666); *The Marianna Flora*, 24 U.S. (11 Wheat.) 1, 40–41 (1826); *Harmony v. United States* (*The Malek Adhel*), 43 U.S. (2 How.) 210, 233 (1844).

Finally, the conclusion that corporations may be held liable under the ATS for violations of the law of nations is not of recent vintage. More than a century ago, the Attorney General acknowledged that corporations could be held liable under the ATS. See 26 Op. Att'y. Gen. 250, 252 (1907) (stating that citizens of Mexico could bring a claim under the ATS against a corporation, the American Rio Grande Land and Irrigation Company, for violating provisions of a treaty between the United States and Mexico).

[. . .]

II

At its second step, *Sosa* cautions that courts should consider whether permitting a case to proceed is an appropriate exercise of judicial discretion in light of potential foreign-policy implications. See 542 U.S., at 727–728, 732–733, 738. The plurality only assumes without deciding that international law does not impose liability on corporations, so it necessarily proceeds to *Sosa*'s second step. Here, too, its analysis is flawed.

A

Nothing about the corporate form in itself justifies categorically foreclosing corporate liability in all ATS actions. Each source of diplomatic friction that respondent Arab Bank and the plurality identify can be addressed with a tool more tailored to the source of the problem than a blanket ban on corporate liability. Arab Bank contends that foreign citizens should not be able "to sue a Jordanian corporation in New York for events taking place in the Middle East." Brief for Respondent 42. The heart of that qualm was already addressed in *Kiobel*, which held that the presumption against extraterritoriality applies to the ATS. 569 U.S., at 124. Only where the claims "touch and concern the territory of the United States . . . with sufficient force" can the presumption be displaced. *Id.*, at 124–125. "[M]ere corporate presence" does not suffice. *Id.*, at 125. Thus, contrary to the majority's contention, "the relatively minor connection between the terrorist attacks at issue in this case and the alleged conduct in the United States" does not "well illustrat[e] the perils of extending the scope of ATS liability to foreign multinational corporations," *ante*, at 25, but merely illustrates the risks of extending the scope of ATS liability extraterritorially absent sufficient connection to the United States.

[. . .]

B

1

The Court urges that "[t]he political branches, not the Judiciary, have the responsibility and institutional capacity to weigh foreign-policy concerns." *Ante*, at 19. I agree that the political branches are well poised to assess the foreign-policy concerns attending ATS litigation, which is why I give significant weight to the fact that the Executive Branch, in briefs signed by the Solicitor General and State Department Legal Advisor, has twice urged the Court to reach exactly the opposite conclusion of the one embraced by the majority. See Brief for United States as Amicus Curiae 5 ("This Court should vacate the decision below, which rests on the mistaken premise that a federal common law claim under the ATS may never be brought against a corporation"); Brief for United States as Amicus Curiae in *Kiobel v. Royal Dutch Petroleum Co.*, O.T. 2012, No. 10–1491, p. 7 ("Courts may recognize corporate liability in actions under the ATS as a matter of federal common law. . . . *Sosa*'s cautionary admonitions provide no reason to depart from the common law on this issue"). At oral argument in this case, the United States told the Court that it saw no "sound reason to categorically exclude corporate liability." Tr. of Oral Arg. 29. It explained that another country would hold the United States accountable for not providing a remedy against a corporate defendant in a "classic" ATS case, such as one involving a "foreign officia[l] injured in the United States," *id.*, at 32–33, and suggested that foreclosing the ability to recover from a corporation actually would raise "the possibility of friction," *id.*, at 33. Notably, the Government's position that categorically barring corporate liability under the ATS is wrong has been consistent across two administrations led by Presidents of different political parties.

Likewise, when Members of Congress have weighed in on the question whether corporations can be proper defendants in an ATS suit, it has been to advise the Court against the rule it now adopts. *See*, Brief for Sen. Sheldon Whitehouse et al. as Amici Curiae 7–11; Brief for Former Sen. Arlen Specter et al. as Amici Curiae in *Kiobel v. Royal Dutch Petroleum Co.*, O.T. 2012, No. 10–1491, pp. 17–18. Congress has also never seen it necessary to immunize corporations from ATS liability even though corporations have been named as defendants in ATS suits for years. See *Monessen Southwestern R. Co. v. Morgan*, 486 U.S. 330, 338 (1988) ("Congress' failure to disturb a consistent judicial interpretation of a statute may provide some indication that 'Congress at least acquiesces in, and apparently affirms, that [interpretation]'" (quoting *Cannon v. University of Chicago*, 441 U.S. 677, 703 (1979))).

Given the deference to the political branches that *Sosa* encourages, I find it puzzling that the Court so eagerly departs from the express assessment of the Executive Branch and Members of Congress that corporations can be defendants in ATS actions.

[. . .]

Furthermore, holding corporations accountable for violating the human rights of foreign citizens when those violations touch and concern the United States may well be necessary to avoid the international tension with which the First Congress was concerned. Consider again the assault on the Secretary of the French Legation in Philadelphia by a French adventurer. See *supra*, at 14; *ante*, at 7 (majority opinion). Would the diplomatic strife that followed really have been any less charged if a corporation had sent its agent to accost the Secretary? Or, consider piracy. If a corporation owned a fleet of vessels and directed them to seize other ships in U.S. waters, there no doubt would be calls to hold the corporation to account. See *Kiobel*, 621 F.3d, at 156, and n. 10 (observing that "Somali pirates essentially operate as limited partnerships"). Finally, take, for example, a corporation posing as a job-placement agency that actually traffics in persons, forcibly transporting foreign nationals to the United States for exploitation and profiting from their abuse. Not only are the individual employees of that business less likely to be able fully to compensate successful ATS plaintiffs, but holding only individual employees liable does not impose accountability for the institution-wide disregard for human rights. Absent a corporate sanction, that harm will persist unremedied. Immunizing the corporation from suit under the ATS merely because it is a corporation, even though the violations stemmed directly from corporate policy and practice, might cause serious diplomatic friction.

[. . .]

In sum, international law establishes what conduct violates the law of nations, and specifies whether, to constitute a law-of-nations violation, the alleged conduct must be undertaken by a particular type of actor. But it is federal common law that determines whether corporations may, as a general matter, be held liable in tort for law-of-nations violations. Applying that framework here, I would hold that the ATS does not categorically foreclose corporate liability. Tort actions against corporations have long been available under federal common law. Whatever the majority might think of the value of modern-day ATS litigation, it has identified nothing to support its conclusion that "foreign corporate defendants create unique problems" that necessitate a categorical rule barring all foreign corporate liability. *Ante*, at 26. Absent any reason to believe that the corporate form in itself raises serious foreign-policy concerns, and given the repeated urging from the Executive Branch and Members of Congress that the Court need not and should not foreclose corporate liability, I would reverse the decision of the Court of Appeals for the Second Circuit and remand for further proceedings, including whether the allegations here sufficiently touch and concern the United States, see *Kiobel*, 569 U.S., at 124–125, and whether the international law norms alleged to have been violated by Arab Bank—the prohibitions on genocide, crimes against humanity, and financing of terrorism—are of sufficiently definite content and universal acceptance to give rise to a cause of action under the ATS.

III

In categorically barring all suits against foreign corporations under the ATS, the Court ensures that foreign corporations—entities capable of wrongdoing under our domestic law—remain immune from liability for human rights abuses, however egregious they may be. Corporations can be and often are a force for innovation and growth. Many of their contributions to society should be celebrated. But the unique power that corporations wield can be used both for good and for bad. Just as corporations can increase the capacity for production, so, too, some can increase the capacity for suffering. Consider the genocide that took upwards of 800,000 lives in Rwanda in 1994, which was fueled by incendiary rhetoric delivered via a private radio station, the Radio Télévision Libre des Mille Collines (RTLM). Men spoke the hateful words, but the RTLM made their widespread influence possible. There can be, and sometimes is, a profit motive for these types of abuses. Although the market does not price all externalities, the law does. We recognize as much when we permit a civil suit to proceed against a paint company that long knew its product contained lead yet continued to sell it to families, or against an oil company that failed to undertake the requisite safety checks on a pipeline that subsequently burst. There is no reason why a different approach should obtain in the human rights context. Immunizing corporations that violate human rights from liability under the ATS undermines the system of accountability for law-of-nations violations that the First

Congress endeavored to impose. It allows these entities to take advantage of the significant benefits of the corporate form and enjoy fundamental rights, see, e.g., *Citizens United v. Federal Election Comm'n*, 558 U.S. 310 (2010); *Burwell v. Hobby Lobby Stores*, Inc., 573 U.S. ___ (2014), without having to shoulder attendant fundamental responsibilities.

I respectfully dissent.

Chapter 3

Investment Insurance, Features, Concepts

7. OPIC and the Tucker Act (28 U.S.C. § 1491)
   Optiperu, SA v. Overseas Private Inv. Corp., 640 F. Supp. 420 (D.D.C. 1986)
   Solaria Corp. v. United States, 123 Fed. Cl. 105 (2015)

D. United States International Development Finance Corporation

A. Globalizing the Investment Insurance Approach to Development

Foreign direct investment can have significant benefits for host country development. These generally include input of financial resources, managerial skills and know-how, and a material contribution to economic growth. Importantly, foreign direct investment does not create debt for the host country. Furthermore, foreign direct investment can stimulate local entrepreneurship by providing increased competition and opportunities for subcontracting by local suppliers.

Foreign direct investment implies acquisition of a lasting interest in a host country, with powers of management and control. This, as distinct from an international sales transaction, means that the investors are more involved and have more exposure to the public policy and political environment of the host country. As this may introduce significant risks for the foreign investor, the availability of political risk insurance through various schemes can be an important factor in the decision to go ahead with an investment.

© Gordon, K. *Investment Guarantees and Political Risk Insurance: Institutions, Incentives and Development*, OECD Investment Policy Perspectives (2008).[53]

Most OECD governments and many non-OECD governments provide investment guarantees and political risk insurance designed to meet the needs of international investors. Private insurers also provide such services. Typically, international investment projects for which such insurance is sought are located in developing countries. [. . .]

Political Risk Insurance [PRI] is of particular relevance for the international policy co-operation undertaken by the investment policy community. This is because of its focus on developing countries and its potential for altering the behavior of both international investors and of host country political actors. Understanding its characteristics and functioning will help the international policy in several areas: investment for development (does the investment facilitated by these programs contribute to improved economic, social and environmental performance in host countries); international investment agreements (how do PRI and international

53. Republished with permission of OECD, from OECD Investment Policy Perspectives 2008; permission conveyed through Copyright Clearance Center, Inc.

investment agreements interact to promote investment protection and international investment) and responsible business conduct (how do governments use investment guarantee programs to promote legal compliance and observance of internationally-agreed standards for business conduct). [. . .]

"Insurable risk" [. . .] conditions under which the insurance industry will be able, over the long run, to profitably provide insurance that clients will want to buy. The technical conditions that make a risk insurable are, according to the OECD Insurance Committee: "assessability (probability and severity of losses should be quantifiable); randomness (the time at which the insured event occurs should be unpredictable when the policy is underwritten, and the occurrence itself must be independent of the will of the insured); mutuality (numerous persons exposed to a given hazard should be able to join together to form a risk community within which the risk is shared and diversified)".

Political risks deviate in important ways from the concept of insurable risk. For example, insured political events may [. . .] partially under the control of and not "independent of the will of the insured" [. . .]. Furthermore, political risks tend to be quite idiosyncratic (they are influenced by the specifics of the host country's political environment, the sector and the investor-state relationship). [. . .] Political events can unfold over many months or years, they take place within a relationship between investor and host country officials and reasonable people can [. . .] disagree about whether or not an insurable event has taken place—thus, at times, political risk is not easily assessable. Finally, the perception in the industry is that political risks are cross-correlated (so that insurers are likely to face multiple claims at the same time).

1. Political Risk Insurance (PRI): Institutions, Incentives and Development

Insurance schemes for this purpose are divided into private insurers, country specific schemes such as OPIC in the U.S. and the Treuarbeit in Germany, or multilateral schemes. All such insurance schemes are designed to cover non-business risks and may either be available to all investors regardless of national origin (as in the case of the Multilateral Investment Guarantee Agency (MIGA)), or to investors from a specific country only (as with OPIC).

© Gordon, K. *Investment Guarantees and Political Risk Insurance: Institutions, Incentives and Development*, OECD Investment Policy Perspectives (2008).[54]

Private PRI providers

The private sector is also active in the provision of political risk insurance. [Gordon sets out her methodology of fact-finding comparisons between private and public

54. Republished with permission of OECD, from OECD Investment Policy Perspectives 2008; permission conveyed through Copyright Clearance Center, Inc.

insurers. She bases her sample on the directory of private political risk insurers provided on MIGA's PRI Centre website].

[. . .] The range of risks covered by the private sector is essentially identical to those covered by the publicly-sponsored programs: 1) currency inconvertibility and transfer restrictions; 2) confiscation, expropriation, nationalization; 3) political violence; 4) default on obligations such as loans, arbitral claims, and contracts.

The private insurers also adapts its contracting practices in order to deal with the difficulties of PRI contracting. [. . .]

The breakdown of activities in the private sector between brokerage, underwriting, insurance and reinsurance is typical for a private insurance sector. Brokerage and agents act as intermediates between the client and the underwriters and their role is to help the client find a good match between its needs and the available insurance products. This marketing function is absent in publicly sponsored programs, presumably because they can rely on their visibility as sole public providers to attract customers. 23 of the 63 companies in the sample describe themselves as underwriters. The underwriter accepts the obligation to pay or indemnify the insured—thus, underwriting is the process which defines the terms by which the insured shifts his risk onto the underwriter. [. . .] Reinsurance [is] important in the PRI market because, as noted earlier, risks in the market are cross-correlated (thus, insurers are likely to receive many claims all at once). [. . .]

The prominent role of business expertise and advisory services in the positioning of private PRI providers [. . .] call attention to the value of their information. [. . .] They position themselves to take advantage of synergies between PRI provision and their political, sectoral and managerial expertise. [. . .] Often, expertise is sectoral, geographical and/or by risk category—[. . .] frequently cited include petrochemicals, aviation, maritime transport, construction and electricity.

Private PRI insurers only rarely cite their capacities for advocacy and recovery as being important competitive strengths. [. . .] advocacy involves intervention with host country political actors with a view to forestalling an event that could result in a PRI claim. [. . .] it is an important part of public PRI provision. Only one private PRI insurer mentions that it engages with host country officials in this way. [. . .] Thus, judging from their websites, private insurers do not attempt to position themselves as having competitive advantage in advocacy and recovery.

Relationship with International Investment Agreements

[. . .] The goals of IIAs and PRI are essentially identical—both seek to promote international investment by lowering political risks. The political events they cover—expropriation, conflict, currency inconvertibility, and breach of host government commitments—are very similar. [. . .] however, while IIAs are treaties between sovereign governments, public PRI are generally based on contracts linking public PRI agencies and private investors. Another difference is that, while many governments are reluctant to include texts on environment, labor, anti-corruption or human rights into their investment agreements, international standards in these areas are promoted by nearly all of the OECD investment guarantee programs in the survey.

The multilateral political risk insurance provider MIGA is discussed first.

B. The World Bank Group's Multilateral Investment Guarantee Agency (MIGA)

The Multilateral Investment Guarantee Agency (MIGA) was established in 1988 by international convention as the newest member of the World Bank Group. MIGA's original 29 members included the United States and the United Kingdom. MIGA Corporation is a worldwide scheme and possesses juridical personality at international law. MIGA is legally and financially independent and now has wide international membership.

The principal purpose and objective of MIGA is to encourage the flow of investment to and among developing countries by means of investment guarantees. The insurance scheme is designed to eliminate non-commercial risks for the investor attributable to government.

The functions of MIGA are set out in the founding Convention. The structure covers insurable risks, eligibility of investors and eligibility of investments. MIGA also provides for dispute settlement on a self-contained basis, and this provides the guarantee of enforcement which has become a key component of MIGA's success.

Additionally, the Convention sets out a powerful mechanism of subrogation, that is, to enforce the rights of the insured against a third party. This provides a strong guarantee for MIGA and, it is argued, helps to makes MIGA more attractive and successful than a private insurer or country specific schemes. Country specific schemes such as OPIC, which will be discussed later, depend on the United States being able to negotiate such rights with the individual country of destination through Bilateral or Multilateral Investment Treaties. In the absence of such treaty provisions, the investor would be obliged to rely on customary international law only.

In the event of a state dealing with MIGA, the state has few options in terms of escaping from a MIGA claim, i.e., a state can't sue MIGA directly, MIGA's rights are valid everywhere, and its property cannot be seized before the delivery of the final judgment or award against the Agency. Thus, the host state has strong incentives to conform to protection of MIGA backed investment.

1. MIGA's Convention

CONVENTION ESTABLISHING THE MULTILATERAL INVESTMENT GUARANTEE AGENCY

CHAPTER I Establishment, Status, Purposes and Definitions

Article 1. Establishment and Status of the Agency

(a) There is hereby established the Multilateral Investment Guarantee Agency (hereinafter called the Agency).

(b) The Agency shall possess full juridical personality and, in particular, the capacity to:

(i) contract;

(ii) acquire and dispose of movable and immovable property; and

(iii) institute legal proceedings.

Article 2. Objective and Purposes

The objective of the Agency shall be to encourage the flow of investments for productive purposes among member countries, and in particular to develop member countries, thus supplementing the activities of the International Bank for Reconstruction and Development (hereinafter referred to as the Bank), the International Finance Corporation and other international development finance institutions.

To serve its objective, the Agency shall:

(a) issue guarantees, including coinsurance and reinsurance, against non-commercial risks in respect of investments in a member country which flow from other member countries;

(b) carry out appropriate complementary activities to promote the flow of investments to and among developing member countries; and

(c) exercise such other incidental powers as shall be necessary or desirable in the furtherance of its objective.

The Agency shall be guided in all its decisions by the provisions of this Article.

Article 3. Definitions

For the purposes of this Convention:

(a) "Member" means a State with respect to which this Convention has entered into force in accordance with Article 61.

(b) "Host country" or "host government" means a member, its government, or any public authority of a member in whose territories, as defined in Article 66, an investment which has been guaranteed or reinsured, or is considered for guarantee or reinsurance, by the Agency is to be located.

(c) A "developing member country" means a member which is listed as such in Schedule A hereto as this Schedule may be amended from time to time by the Council of Governors referred to in Article 30 (hereinafter called the Council).

(d) A "special majority" means an affirmative vote of not less than two-thirds of the total voting power representing not less than fifty-five percent of the subscribed shares of the capital stock of the Agency.

(e) A "freely usable currency" means (i) any currency designated as such by the International Monetary Fund from time to time and (ii) any other freely available and effectively usable currency which the Board of Directors referred to in Article 30 (hereinafter called the Board) may designate for the purposes of this Convention after consultation with the International Monetary Fund and with the approval of the country of such currency.

CHAPTER III Operations

Article 11. Covered Risks

(a) Subject to the provisions of Sections (b) and (c) below, the Agency may guarantee eligible investments against a loss resulting from one or more of the following types of risk:

(i) Currency Transfer

any introduction attributable to the host government of restrictions on the transfer outside the host country of its currency into a freely usable currency or another currency acceptable to the holder of the guarantee, including a failure of the host government to act within a reasonable period of time on an application by such holder for such transfer;

(ii) Expropriation and Similar Measures

any legislative action or administrative action or omission attributable to the host government which has the effect of depriving the holder of a guarantee of his ownership or control of, or a substantial benefit from, his investment, with the exception of non-discriminatory measures of general application which the governments normally take for the purpose of regulating economic activity in their territories;

(iii) Breach of Contract

any repudiation or breach by the host government of a contract with the holder of a guarantee, when (a) the holder of a guarantee does not have recourse to a judicial or arbitral forum to determine the claim of repudiation or breach, or (b) a decision by such forum is not rendered within such reasonable period of time as shall be prescribed in the contracts of guarantee pursuant to the Agency's regulations, or (c) such a decision cannot be enforced; and

(iv) War and Civil Disturbance

any military action or civil disturbance in any territory of the host country to which this Convention shall be applicable as provided in Article 66.

(b) In addition, the Board, by special majority, may approve the extension of coverage under this Article to specific non-commercial risks other than those referred to in Section (a) above, but in no case to the risk of devaluation or depreciation of currency.

(c) Losses resulting from the following shall not be covered:

(i) any host government action or omission to which the holder of the guarantee has agreed or for which he has been responsible; and

(ii) any host government action or omission or any other event occurring before the conclusion of the contract of guarantee.

Article 12. Eligible Investments

(a) Eligible investments shall include equity interest, including medium- or long-term loans made or guaranteed by holders of equity in the enterprise concerned, and such forms of direct investment as may be determined by the Board.

(b) Loans other than those mentioned in Section (a) above may be eligible for coverage

(i) if they are made to finance or are otherwise related to a specific investment or project in which some other form of direct investment is present, whether or not guaranteed by the Agency and regardless of when such other investment was made, or

(ii) as may be otherwise approved by the Board by special majority.

(c) The Board, by special majority, may extend eligibility to any other medium- or long-term form of investment.

(d) Guarantees shall generally be restricted to investments the implementation of which begins subsequent to the registration of the application for the guarantee by the Agency or receipt by the Agency of other satisfactory evidence of investor intent to obtain guarantees from the Agency. Such investments may include:

(i) a transfer of foreign exchange made to modernize, expand, or develop an existing investment, in which case both the original investment and the additional investment may be considered eligible for coverage;

(ii) the use of earnings from existing investments which could otherwise be transferred outside the host country;

(iii) the acquisition of an existing investment by a new eligible investor;

(iv) existing investments where an eligible investor is seeking to insure a pool of existing and new investments;

(v) existing investments owned by an eligible investor where there is an improvement or enhancement of the underlying project or the investor otherwise demonstrates medium-or long-term commitment to the project, and the Agency is satisfied that the project continues to have a high developmental impact in the host country; and

(vi) such other investments as may be approved by the Board by special majority.

(e) In guaranteeing an investment, the Agency shall satisfy itself as to:

(i) the economic soundness of the investment and its contribution to the development of the host country;

(ii) compliance of the investment with the host country's laws and regulations;

(iii) consistency of the investment with the declared development objectives and priorities of the host country; and

(iv) the investment conditions in the host country, including the availability of fair and equitable treatment and legal protection for the investment.

Article 13. Eligible Investors

(a) Any natural person and any juridical person may be eligible to receive the Agency's guarantee provided that:

(i) such natural person is a national of a member other than the host country;

(ii) such juridical person is incorporated and has its principal place of business in a member or the majority of its capital is owned by a member or members or nationals thereof, provided that such member is not the host country in any of the above cases; and

(iii) such juridical person, whether or not it is privately owned, operates on a commercial basis.

(b) In case the investor has more than one nationality, for the purposes of Section (a) above the nationality of a member shall prevail over the nationality of a non-member, and the nationality of the host country shall prevail over the nationality of any other member.

(c) Upon the joint application of the investor and the host country, the Board, by special majority, may extend eligibility to a natural person who is a national of the host country or a juridical person which is incorporated in the host country or the majority of whose capital is owned by its nationals, provided that the assets invested are transferred from outside the host country.

Article 18. Subrogation

(a) Upon paying or agreeing to pay compensation to a holder of a guarantee, the Agency shall be subrogated to such rights or claims related to the guaranteed investment as the holder of a guarantee may have had against the host country and other obligors. The contract of guarantee shall provide the terms and conditions of such subrogation.

(b) The rights of the Agency pursuant to Section (a) above shall be recognized by all members.

(c) Amounts in the currency of the host country acquired by the Agency as subrogee pursuant to Section (a) above shall be accorded, with respect to use and conversion, treatment by the host country as favorable as the treatment to which such funds would be entitled in the hands of the holder of the guarantee. In any case, such amounts may be used by the Agency for the payment of its administrative expenditures and other costs.

CHAPTER VII Privileges and Immunities

Article 44. Legal Process

Actions other than those within the scope of Articles 57 and 58 may be brought against the Agency only in a court of competent jurisdiction in the territories of a member in which the Agency has an office or has appointed an agent for the purpose of accepting service or notice of process. No such action against the Agency shall be brought:

(i) by members or persons acting for or deriving claims from members or

(ii) in respect of personnel matters.

The property and assets of the Agency shall, wherever located and by whomsoever held, be immune from all forms of seizure, attachment or execution before the delivery of the final judgment or award against the Agency.

Article 45. Assets

(a) The property and assets of the Agency, wherever located and by whomsoever held, shall be immune from search, requisition, confiscation, expropriation or any other form of seizure by executive or legislative action.

(b) To the extent necessary to carry out its operations under this Convention, all property and assets of the Agency shall be free from restrictions, regulations, controls and moratoria of any nature; provided that property and assets acquired by the Agency as successor to or subrogee of a holder of a guarantee, a reinsured entity or an investor insured by a reinsured entity shall be free from applicable foreign exchange restrictions, regulations and controls in force in the territories of the member concerned to the extent that the holder, entity or investor to whom the Agency was subrogated was entitled to such treatment.

(c) For purposes of this Chapter, the term "assets" shall include the assets of the Sponsorship Trust Fund referred to in Annex I to this Convention and other assets administered by the Agency in furtherance of its objective.

2. MIGA Structure and Functions

MIGA was established as affiliate of the World Bank Group Institutions to increase and promote the flow of investment among member countries and, in particular, private investment from capital-exporting to capital-importing countries. To this end, the Agency is authorised under the MIGA Convention to issue guarantees to such investment against non-commercial risks and to carry out co-operative, consultative and advisory activities beneficial to these countries and investors.

Eligible Risks

Currency Transfer Risk

Under Article 11(a)(i) of the Convention, the MIGA Underwriting Authority may provide coverage for losses from such risk arising from any introduction attributable to the government of the host country of restrictions on the transfer outside the host country of either the local currency or the foreign currency into which the local currency was converted, and/or restrictions on the conversion of local currency into a freely usable currency or into another currency acceptable to the guarantee holder. Such restrictions must be introduced after the date of issuance of the contract of guarantee [. . .].

These restrictions may take both active and passive forms or either. An active restriction is a decision of the host government denying conversion and/or transfer of local currency [. . .] or authorising [. . .] at an exchange rate less favourable than the lowest exchange rate determined under the contract of guarantee. [. . .]

A passive restriction is a failure of the host country's exchange authority to act on conversion and/or transfer within 90 days from the date on which the guarantee holder applies or such other period as the contract of guarantee provides. In order for the guarantee holder to be entitled to claim coverage, the following contractual obligations must be performed. The guarantee holder must apply for conversion and/or transfer in accordance with the laws of the host country and seek appropriate administrative remedies to obtain such conversion and/or transfer. The guarantee holder or the project enterprise must carry out instructions of the Agency, including instructions to transfer to the Agency rights to the local currency covered by the guarantee as a condition for or on receipt of payment from it, or to deposit such currency in an account of the Agency or any person designated by the Agency.

Risk of Expropriation and Similar Measures

Article 11(a)(ii) [. . .] provides for certain criteria in determining whether the measure is attributable to the host government. Covered measures must be any legislative action, administrative action or omission. [. . .]

Measures attributable to the host government must have any of the following effects. First, the effects of depriving the guarantee holder of his ownership or control of, or a substantial benefit from his investment. [. . .] Second, the effects of preventing the guarantee holder from exercising his rights of ownership or control over his investment, or from using his funds or enforcing claims against debtors in the host country. [. . .] In the case of non-equity direct investments, such rights may take the form of claims against the project enterprise for agreed payment, the right to transfer such claims to third parties and the right of participation in the management of the investment project.

Article 11(a)(ii) of the Convention provides for a clear exception to the abovementioned covered measures in order to enable the host country to exercise its regulatory powers. Measures taken by the host government which are non-discretionary, of general application, in the public interest and for the purpose of regulating economic activity in its territory shall not be eligible for coverage. [. . .] These four criteria must all be complied with by the host government in order to establish that the measure is ineligible for cover. However, a series of measures by the host government which in their combined effect are expropriatory shall be regarded as covered measures even if each individual measure, taken alone, would appear to satisfy all these criteria. In applying these criteria, the Agency must ensure that it does not prejudice the rights of a member country or of investors under bilateral investment treaties, other treaties and international law.

Breach of Contract Risk

In accordance with Article 11(a)(iii) of the Convention, [. . .]

(1) [. . .] a juridical or arbitral forum shall be any competent court or arbitral tribunal which is independent from the executive branch of the host government, acts judicially and is authorized to make a final and binding decision. The guarantee holder is deemed to lack recourse to such a forum where access to it is denied because, for example, the host government has established unreasonable impediments.

(2) [. . .] reasonable period of time [. . .] must not be less than two years from the initiation of a proceeding by the guarantee holder and the final decision by forum.

(3) [. . .] a decision shall be deemed unenforceable where the measures to be taken by the guarantee holder as specified in the contract of guarantee have not resulted in enforcement after 90 days from the date of the initiation of such measures or such other period as may be provided in the contract. If such measures appear to be futile in the judgment of the Agency, the Agency need not insist that they must be taken by the guarantee holder.

War and Civil Disturbance

The concept of 'military action' implies war or hostilities between armed forces of rival governments in the host country [. . .] 'Civil disturbance' must be organized violence directed against the host government which has the objective of the overthrow of such government or its ousting from a specific region. [. . .] Civil disturbance may include revolutions, rebellions, insurrections and coup d'état, and may also take the form of riot and civil commotion. Riot is an assemblage of individuals who commit public acts of violence in defiance of lawful authority. [. . .] Therefore, acts undertaken to further labour, student or other specific interests and acts of terrorism, kidnapping or similar acts directed against the guarantee holder shall not qualify for coverage as civil disturbance. However, if such acts are politically motivated, they shall be covered if the Board of Directors by special majority, so decides under Article 11(b) of the Convention.

As to the place of covered events, although Article 11(a)(iv) of the Convention stipulates that it is 'in any territory of the host country', paragraph 1.50 of the Operational

Regulations does not define the term to covered events occurring inside such territory but also outside it.

[. . .]

The scope of covered losses arising from the risk of war and civil disturbance is subject to the discretionary power of the MIGA Underwriting Authority and must be specified in the contract of guarantee. The MIGA Underwriting Authority may confine covered loss either to goods essential to the operation of the investment project, or to a total destruction of the project or such substantial damage as would render impossible the project's continued profitability, or losses calculated on the basis of the historical cost of the damage or destroyed assets of the investment project. [. . .] the calculation of the losses on the basis of historical cost can be regarded as unfair and discouraging to foreign investors, because the amount of payment which shall be made to such investors is the actual cost of purchasing the assets purchased in the past. Such amount may not enable the indemnified investor to set up his investment.

Other Non-Commercial Risks and Exclusions

Article 11(b) provides that other specific non-commercial risks [. . .] shall be covered at the joint request of the investor and the host country if the Board so approves by special majority. [. . .]

However, Article 11(b) and (c) of the Convention provides for certain types of risks and losses which are excluded from coverage. First, the risk of devaluation or depreciation of currency. Second, losses arising from any action or omission of the host country to which the guarantee holder agreed [. . .] or has been responsible. Finally, losses arising from any host government action or omission or other event occurring before the conclusion of the contract of guarantee. However, the last exclusion shall not affect the validity of the contract of guarantee in cases of events or circumstances unknown to both the agency and the investor at the time of the conclusion of the contract which led only thereafter to the occurrence of a specific covered event giving rise to a covered loss.

Underwriting Guidelines

Even though Paragraph 3.01 of the Operational Regulations provides that the underwriting decisions are by their nature business decisions as distinguished from legal determinations, one should consider them as being both legal and business in nature. They are taken in the light of and in implementation of general principles established under the Convention [set out in Article 12(d)], namely, the economic soundness of the investment project, its contribution to the development of the host country, its compliance with the laws and regulations of the host country and its consistency with the declared development objectives and priorities of the host country [. . .] The Underwriting Authority is required to assess the investment project, the risks to be covered by the proposed guarantee, and the effect of such guarantee on the Agency's guarantee capacity and risk portfolio.

Guidelines on Project Assessment

In determining [the economic soundness of the investment project], the Underwriting Authority must assess the investment's project's technical feasibility and its financial and economic viability over the proposed period of guarantee. Moreover, it shall assess all relevant economic factors, including the need for a reasonable economic rate of return (profit) regardless of external factors such as trade concessions or subsidies. In determining [its contribution to the development of the host country], the Authority shall have regard to the following factors:

(1) [. . .] potential to generate revenues for the host country, its contributions to maximizing production, producing exports or import substitutes and reducing vulnerability to external economic changes;

(2) the extent to which the project will diversify economic activities, expand employment opportunities and improve income distribution;

(3) the degree to which the project will transfer knowledge and skills to the host country;

(4) its effects on the social infrastructure and the environment of the host country.

Investments of a military or highly speculative nature or in legally prohibited activities such as narcotics shall not be covered. [. . .]

These guidelines are open to criticism. The Underwriting Authority is not required to consider the environmental effects of the investment project on a country contiguous to the host country and whether or not the environmental law thereof is compatible with international minimum standards. Moreover, it is not prevented from terminating the contract of guarantee if it was notified by the host country that the guaranteed investment was financed with funds transferred from such country in violation of its laws. Under the Convention and the Operational Regulations, the guarantee holder does not have the right to prevent the Agency from terminating the contract, whereas the host country has the right to make such notification before or after the outset of the investment. It is suggested that these guidelines should be modified to the effect that once the host country has approved the investment and the investment has been set up, it must not have the right to make such notification even if there was an error on the part of the host country or the Underwriting Authority.

Guidelines on Risk Assessment

[. . .] In the assessment of all non-commercial risks to which the proposed investment project may be exposed, the Underwriting Authority shall take into account certain factors relating to such project. [. . .] Under Article 12(d)(iv) of the Convention, the host country must prove that fair and equitable treatment and adequate legal protection for foreign investment are available. Such requirements must be deemed to have been satisfied if a bilateral or multilateral treaty is in force between the host country and the home country of the investor, or the host country's laws are consistent with international law. However, in case of inconsistency, the assessment of the Underwriting Authority must be conducted in strict confidentiality and its outcome must be shared only with the government of the host country concerned with a view to enabling it to improve its laws and the investment conditions therein. In this case, the Underwriting Authority must not issue coverage unless the Agency has concluded an agreement with the host country. Such agreement must assure that the proposed investment project guaranteed by the Agency has treatment at least as favourable as that agreed by the member concerned for the most favoured investment guarantee Agency or state in an investment agreement.[55] It is clear that the ultimate objective of the assessment is neither to deny coverage nor to discourage investment. It is rather to protect and reconcile the interests of the host country, investors and the Agency.

The MIGA Underwriting Authority is also required to take into account factors relevant to specific non-commercial risks covered under the Convention. [. . .]

It must be emphasized that the relationship between factors relating to the host country and those relating to the proposed investment project must be recognised. A currency transfer risk might be acceptable despite the unfavourable foreign exchange position of the host country if the investment project has the potential to earn freely useable currency through export. A risk of expropriation or breach of investment contract might also be acceptable despite the unfavourable record of the host country, if the host country has arrangements with the investor to accept international arbitration or has an interest in continuing cooperation with the investor. A risk of existing insurgency or war might also be acceptable if the investment project is or will be located in a region sufficiently protected by the host government forces, or has no strategy to the belligerent parties. Risk assessment should not be restricted to the above factors. The Operational Regulations do not prohibit the Underwriting Authority from developing and adding to such factors.

Subrogation by the Guarantee Holder

Subrogation, a generally accepted principle of insurance law, is incorporated in Article 18(a) of the Convention under which the guarantee holder is under contractual obligation to subrogate to the Agency his rights or claims related to the guaranteed investment which he may have had against the host country or other obligators. [. . .] Such subrogated rights are to be recognised by all member countries including the host county whose approvals are not required. [. . .] The language of Article 18(a) of the Convention simply provides for the right of the Agency to such subrogation on paying or agreeing to pay compensation. Neither the Convention nor the Operational Regulations specify whether or not the guarantee holder has the right to decline to make such subrogation in cases where the Agency and the guarantee holder disagree on the amount of compensation. They should, it is suggested, have provided that in such cases the guarantee holder should have the right to subrogate

55. Article 23(b)(ii) of the Convention.

to the Agency such right and claims in proportion to the amount of compensation agreed between them.

[. . .] The Agency has the discretion to insure up to 90 percent of the value of the investment project. Therefore, the Agency must only be assigned by the guarantee holder to such rights, claims and interest as correspond to the portion of the investment which is covered by the Agency's guarantee. As to the remaining uncovered portion of the investment project which could be more than 10 percent thereof, the Agency has the discretion to agree with the guarantee holder and/or coinsurers as the case may be to be assigned to such portion in order to pursue it for the account of the guarantee holder and/or coinsurers if the host country approves such assignment. [. . .] If the Agency recovered from the host country any amount in excess of the Agency's payment made to the guarantee holder for the subrogated and assigned rights, the Agency is required to pay him any such excess recovery less expenses.[56]

3. MIGA and Dispute Settlement

CONVENTION ESTABLISHING THE MULTILATERAL INVESTMENT GUARANTEE AGENCY

CHAPTER IX Settlement of Disputes

Article 56. Interpretation and Application of the Convention

(a) Any question of interpretation or application of the provisions of this Convention arising between any member of the Agency and the Agency or among members of the Agency shall be submitted to the Board for its decision. Any member which is particularly affected by the question and which is not otherwise represented by a national in the Board may send a representative to attend any meeting of the Board at which such question is considered.

(b) In any case where the Board has given a decision under Section (a) above, any member may require that the question be referred to the Council, whose decision shall be final. Pending the result of the referral to the Council, the Agency may, so far as it deems necessary, act on the basis of the decision of the Board.

Article 57. Disputes between the Agency and Members

(a) Without prejudice to the provisions of Article 56 and of Section (b) of this Article, any dispute between the Agency and a member or an agency thereof and any dispute between the Agency and a country (or agency thereof) which has ceased to be a member, shall be settled in accordance with the procedure set out in Annex II to this Convention.

(b) Disputes concerning claims of the Agency acting as subrogee of an investor shall be settled in accordance with either

(i) the procedure set out in Annex II to this Convention, or

56. Paragraphs 4.18 and 4.19 of the Operational Regulations.

(ii) an agreement to be entered into between the Agency and the member concerned on an alternative method or methods for the settlement of such disputes.

In the latter case, Annex II to this Convention shall serve as a basis for such an agreement which shall, in each case, be approved by the Board by special majority prior to the undertaking by the Agency of operations in the territories of the member concerned. [. . .]

ANNEX II Settlement of Disputes Between A Member and the Agency Under Article 57

Article 1. Application of the Annex

All disputes within the Scope of Article 57 of this Convention shall be settled in accordance with the procedure set out in this Annex, except in the cases where the Agency has entered into an agreement with a member pursuant to Section (b) (ii) of Article 57.

Article 2. Negotiation

The parties to a dispute within the scope of this Annex shall attempt to settle such dispute by negotiation before seeking conciliation or arbitration. Negotiations shall be deemed to have been exhausted if the parties fail to reach a settlement within a period of one hundred and twenty days from the date of the request to enter into negotiation.

Article 3. Conciliation

(a) If the dispute is not resolved through negotiation, either party may submit the dispute to arbitration in accordance with the provisions of Article 4 of this Annex, unless the parties, by mutual consent, have decided to resort first to the conciliation procedure provided for in this Article.

[. . .]

Article 4. Arbitration

(a) Arbitration proceedings shall be instituted by means of a notice by the party seeking arbitration (the claimant) addressed to the other party or parties to the dispute (the respondent). The notice shall specify the nature of the dispute, the relief sought and the name of the arbitrator appointed by the claimant. The respondent shall, within thirty days after the date of receipt of the notice, notify the claimant of the name of the arbitrator appointed by it. The two parties shall, within a period of thirty days from the date of appointment of the second arbitrator, select a third arbitrator, who shall act as President of the Arbitral Tribunal (the Tribunal).

(b) If the Tribunal shall not have been constituted within sixty days from the date of the notice, the arbitrator not yet appointed or the President not yet selected shall be appointed, at the joint request of the parties, by the Secretary-General of ICSID. If there is no such joint request, or if the Secretary-General shall fail to make the appointment within thirty days of the request, either party may request the President of the International Court of Justice to make the appointment.

(c) No party shall have the rights to change the arbitrator appointed by it once the hearing of the dispute has commenced. In case any arbitrator (including the President of the Tribunal) shall resign, die, or become incapacitated, a successor shall be appointed in the manner followed in the appointment of his predecessor and such successor shall have the same powers and duties of the arbitrator he succeeds.

(d) The Tribunal shall convene first at such time and place as shall be determined by the President. Thereafter, the Tribunal shall determine the place and dates of its meetings.

(e) Unless otherwise provided in this Annex or agreed upon by the parties, the Tribunal shall determine its procedure and shall be guided in this regard by the arbitration rules adopted pursuant to the Convention on the Settlement of Investment Disputes between States and Nationals of Other States.

(f) The Tribunal shall be the judge of its own competence except that, if any objection is raised before the Tribunal to the effect that the dispute falls within the jurisdiction of the Board or the Council under Article 56 or within the jurisdiction of a judicial or arbitral body designated in an agreement under Article 1 of this Annex and the Tribunal is satisfied that the objection is genuine, the objection shall be referred by the Tribunal to the Board or the Council or the designated body, as the case may be, and the arbitration proceedings shall be stayed until a decision has been reached on the matter, which shall be binding upon the Tribunal.

(g) The Tribunal shall, in any dispute within the scope of this Annex, apply the provisions of this Convention, any relevant agreement between the parties to the dispute, the Agency's by-laws and regulations, the applicable rules of international law, the domestic law of the member concerned as well as the applicable provisions of the investment contract, if any. Without prejudice to the provisions of this Convention, the Tribunal may decide a dispute *ex aequo et bono* if the Agency and the member concerned so agree. The Tribunal may not bring a finding of *non liquet* on the ground of silence or obscurity of the law.

(h) The Tribunal shall afford a fair hearing to all the parties. All decisions of the Tribunal shall be taken by a majority vote and shall state the reasons on which they are based. The award of the Tribunal shall be in writing, and shall be signed by at least two arbitrators and a copy thereof shall be transmitted to each party. The award shall be final and binding upon the parties and shall not be subject to appeal, annulment or revision.

(i) If any dispute shall arise between the Parties as to the meaning or scope of an award, either party may, within sixty days after the award was rendered, request interpretation of the award by an application in writing to the President of the Tribunal which rendered the award. The President shall, if possible, submit the request to the Tribunal which rendered the award and shall convene such Tribunal within sixty days after receipt of the application. If this shall not be possible, a new Tribunal shall be constituted in accordance with the provisions of Sections (a) to (d) above. The Tribunal may stay enforcement of the award pending its decision on the requested interpretation.

(j) Each member shall recognize an award rendered pursuant to this Article as binding and enforceable within its territories as if it were a final judgment of a court in that member. Execution of the award shall be governed by the laws concerning the execution of judgments in force in the State in whose territories such execution is sought and shall not derogate from the law in force relating to immunity from execution.

(k) Unless the parties shall agree otherwise, the fees and remuneration payable to the arbitrators shall be determined on the basis of the rates applicable to ICSID arbitration. Each party shall defray its own costs associated with the arbitration proceedings. The costs of the Tribunal shall be borne by the parties in equal proportion unless the Tribunal decides otherwise. Any question concerning the division of the Cost of the Tribunal or the procedure for payment of such costs shall be decided by the Tribunal.

© Ossman, G., *Legal and Institutional Aspects of the Multilateral Investment Guarantee Agency as the Fifth Affiliate of the World Bank Group*, Journal of International Banking Law, Sweet and Maxwell, London (1996). Reproduced with permission of the Licensor through PLSclear.

Disputes between the Guarantee Holder and the Agency

Article 58 of the Convention provides a guarantee holder, reinsurer and the Agency with the right to submit any dispute arising under a contract of guarantee or reinsurance to an arbitral tribunal of one or more arbitrators whose award is final and binding. Each member country regardless of whether or not it was a party to such dispute is obliged to recognize the finality and binding nature of the award. The arbitral tribunal is required to determine such dispute in accordance with such rules as may be provided in the contract of guarantee or reinsurance. Contracts of guarantee must refer to the Institution and Arbitration Rules of the International Centre for Settlement of Investment Disputes ('ICSID') and any such modifications thereof as the parties agree. The Secretary-General of the Permanent Court of Arbitration at the Hague shall be the appointing authority of the arbitrator or arbitrators who are not otherwise appointed under the ICSID, and that of arbitrators whose names are not on the ICSID's Panel of Arbitrators. As to the applicable law, the arbitral tribunal must apply the principles and rules specified in the contract of guarantee and the Convention to issues covered thereby. It must also apply general principles of law to the extent that issues in dispute are not covered by the contract of guarantee or the Convention.[57]

57. Paragraphs 2.16 and 2.17 of the Operational Regulations.

4. MIGA and Development

Berger, Klaus Peter, *The New Multilateral Investment Guarantee Agency: Globalizing the Investment Insurance Approach Towards Development*, 15 Syr. J. Int'l L. & Com. 1988, at 13 et seq.

The Role of FDI In the Development Process

While there are some undisputed benefits of FDI for multinationals and their home countries (establishing or securing a monopoly in international trade, exploring new attractive markets and resources), there is some controversy on the question of relative costs and benefits of FDI to developing countries. However, several advantages of FDI are generally accepted and may have a long term beneficial impact on the development process. First and foremost, FDI insulates host countries,[58] to a certain extent, from unanticipated external payment difficulties. Because FDI is not a debt creating instrument requiring regular payments and generating continuous demands on the host countries' balance of payments, only when the investment earns a profit are payments implied, thereby placing part of the risk on the foreign investor.[59] Despite the lack of reliable key information, there appears to be a positive correlation between the annual rate of return on FDI and the annual growth of the GNP in the host country.[60] [. . .] FDI is also often substantially involved with import substituting and export industries so the foreign trade performance of enterprises based on direct investment can have a significant impact on their host's balance of payments.[61] [. . .] These countries need to increase domestic resource mobilization and stimulate export oriented industries to reduce their debt-service ratio,[62] improve their balance of payment and restore their credit worthiness, which has suffered heavily from the debt crisis. [. . .] FDI can also help these economies to improve their long term growth prospects, [. . .] permanent input of financial resources, managerial skills, technical know how and marketing connections [. . .]

---

58. The term "host country" means the country where the investment takes place, whereas "home country" refers to the origin of the investor.

59. Shihata, *Factors Influencing the Flow of Foreign Investment and the Relevance of a Multilateral Investment Guarantee Scheme*, 21 Int'l L. 671, 673 (1987).

60. IMF Occasional Paper, [IMF, Foreign Private Investment in Developing Countries 28 (Occasional Paper No. 33, 1985)], at 23 (chart 3). The study points out that for 28 countries which rescheduled debt during 1983, the stock of FDI accounted for an average of only 14 percent of their total external liabilities, compared to an average of 24 percent for those 24 LDCs that did not reschedule debt, obviously not facing severe payment problems.

61. *Ibid.* at 11. However, the paper also hints at the danger of multinational corporations being engaged mainly in intrafirm transactions which makes them less responsive to relative price changes than companies engaged in arms length market transactions which have no reason to be concerned with the effects of their transactions on other affiliates.

62. The debt-service ratio is a primary indicator of creditworthiness of debtor countries and reflects the ratio of external debt payments to exports. Financial authorities regard a ratio of 20 percent as prudent. *See*, Barnett, et al., *On Third World Debt*, 25 Harv. Int'l L.J. 83, 89 n.18 (Winter 1982).

FDI also stimulates local entrepreneurship by providing increased competition and opportunities for subcontracting by local suppliers. [. . .]

[. . .] Many developing countries have been extremely concerned with the behavior of multinational enterprises and the loss of autonomy caused by investment that is connected with a substantial degree of overseas managerial control by large transnational corporations.[63] This was regarded as perpetuating the economic dependence of the Third World[64] and as being inconsistent with the Principle of Permanent Sovereignty over Natural Resources as developed in several UN Resolutions.[65] [. . .] In the past decade, however; due to an increasing willingness of home countries to accept economic and social objectives of host countries and the fruitful negotiations on the UN Code of Conduct on Transnational Corporations,[66] host countries have gained increasing confidence in the role of FDI in development.[67] [. . .]

The Agency's Acceptability of the Investment Community

[. . .] The concerns connected with the OECD proposal, that the Agency may not appear as financially safe, since it is not backed by government budgetary resources (OPIC's obligations are entitled to the "full faith and credit" of the U.S. government)[68] and will therefore be less appealing to investors,[69] seems unwarranted in view of MIGA's capital reserve requirements and commitment to prudent management.

MIGA's Relation to Existing Guarantee Schemes

- MIGA and National Investment Guarantee Programs

To date, most of the investment protection and promotion between North and South takes place on a national or bilateral basis. Apart from bilateral investment treaties, most Development Assistance Committee (DAC) member countries and Korea and India operate national investment guarantee programs, the most important being

63. These concerns ultimately led to a wave of nationalizations and expropriations in the 1970s. e.g. the nationalization of British Petrol's and Milton Bunker Hunt's oil interests in Libya in 1973, [. . .] the expropriation of Kennecott's and Anaconda's copper mines in Chile in 1971 with a book value [of over $318 million]. Deduction of "excess profits", i.e. alleged amount of injury caused to national interests by these enterprises, led to a denial of compensation and the resulting claims of over $360 million against OPIC, which exceeded its insurance reserves.

64. Rubin, *Transnational Corporations and International Codes of Conduct: A Study of the Relationship Between International Legal Cooperation and Economic Development*, 30 AM. U.L. REV. 903, 912 (1981).

65. [. . .] stating that each state has the right "to nationalize, expropriate or transfer ownership of foreign property".

66. See Code of Conduct on Transnational Corporations: Outstanding Issues in the Draft Code of Conduct, U.N. Doc. CE/C.10/1985/S/2.

67. Moran [Moran, *Shaping a Future for Foreign Direct Investment in the Third World*, 11 THE WASH. Q. 119, 128 (Winter 1988)], at 119. "There has been a fundamental shift from the overwhelming criticism of multinational corporations to a pervasive enthusiasm about it." *Id.*

68. OPIC ANNUAL REPORT 1987, at 39.

69. Martin, [*Multilateral Investment Insurance: The OECD Proposal*, 8 HARV. INT'L L.J. 281, 282 (1967)], at 327; Brewer, [*The Proposal for Investment Guarantees by an International Agency*, 58 A.J.I.L. 62, 72 (1964)], at 76.

(in order of size) the Japanese Export Insurance Division, Ministry of International Trade and Industry (EID/MITI), the U.S. Overseas Private Investment Corporation (OPIC) and the German program administered by the Treuarbeit AG in Hamburg.[70] Like FDI itself, the purpose of these programs is twofold, promotion of development and of domestic industries.[71]

- MIGA and International Protection and Promotion Schemes
- [. . .] The Guaranteed Recovery of Investment Principal (GRIP) Program in particular, which goes further than MIGA since it covers all risks, not just non-commercial risks,[72] is, like MIGA, expected to increase additionality the development process and promote multilateralization of investment standards.

ICSID provides not only a unique dispute settlement scheme for investment conflicts, but is also designed to increase the availability of information, knowledge, and expertise related to investment by processing and carrying out research, and disseminating pertinent information.[73] MIGA will primarily try to avoid investment disputes and contribute a great deal to their "depoliticization" as a necessary by-product of its day to day activities, limiting decision making and problem resolution to wholly legal and economic criteria.

C. Overseas Private Investment Corporation (OPIC)

The Overseas Private Investment Corporation (OPIC) was founded by the Foreign Assistance Act (FAA) 1971 and is a profit based agency of the U.S. government. OPIC's objective is to promote American investments and free markets in the world economy. Its roots lie in the Marshall Plan of 1948, and prior to the establishment of OPIC, the comparable tasks were administered by the Agency for International Development (USAID). However, USAID was concerned more with government-to-government matters, and OPIC was created as a separate business-orientated agency for U.S. entities investing abroad. Typically, international investment projects for which such insurance or financing is sought are in developing and post-conflict

70. These institutions have to be distinguished from national export insurance agencies which often times cover the same non-commercial, political risks such as the U.S. Commodity Credit Corporations Export Guarantee Program, based on the Commodity Credit Charter Act, and the German Hermes Kreditversicherungs AG.

71. Seidl-Hohenveldern, *General Course on Public International Law*, 3 Recueil Des Cours 13, 190 (1986).

72. In the GRIP Program the IFC invests the funds provided by the investor in its own name. At the end of an agreed period, the investor has the option to become the full legal and beneficial owner of the shares of the company in which the investment has been made or to be paid back its original investment. *See*, Silkenat, GRIP: Guaranteed Recovery of Investment Principle 7 Int'l Fin. L. Rev. 39 (March 1988).

73. Shihata, *Towards a Greater Depoliticization of Investment Disputes: The Roles of ICSID and MIGA*, 1 ICSID Rev., Foreign Investment L.J. 1, 22 (1986), at 4.

countries,[74] with the highest commitments in 2016 reported in the Sub-Saharan African and Asian regions.[75]

OPIC is a country-based political risk insurance and project financing scheme for U.S. investors. It only offers coverage for projects that support the development needs of the host country and don't negatively impact on the U.S. economy or employment. It addresses four main areas of political risk: political violence, war damage, expropriation and currency inconvertibility. Since 1971, OPIC has made 295 insurance claim settlements totaling $976.8 million.[76] These settlements have been structured either as cash settlements to investors or as OPIC arrangements guarantying host government obligations. Of these, a significant majority of the compensation claims considered have been for expropriation and inconvertibility.

OPIC obligations are supported from its own substantial reserves, but it is also further fully backed by the U.S. government. The Board of Directors consists of eight members from the private sector and seven from the U.S. government. The President of the United States nominates the private sector board members, and they must be confirmed by the United States Senate.

© Gordon, K., *Investment Guarantees and Political Risk Insurance: Institutions, Incentives and Development*, OECD Investment Policy Perspectives (2008).[77]

Public versus Private Provision

Government's competitive strengths as PRI insurers [. . .] would stem primarily from governments' ability to use their diplomatic networks as risk management and asset recovery tools. [. . .] One example of how this might work can be found in recovery of claims for currency inconvertibility. OPIC's CEO explains "[. . .] OPIC obtains special arrangements for recovering salvage when it pays inconvertibility claims. Under these arrangements, OPIC makes inconvertible local currency available for other U.S. government uses, in exchange for dollars that would have been spent, for example, by a U.S. embassy for its local currency expenses. Through this mechanism, which is not available to private sector insurers, OPIC has been able to obtain excellent salvage on currency inconvertibility claims."

Another major difference between public and private PRI providers is that publicly-sponsored providers position themselves as platforms for promoting responsible business conduct at the same time investment is being promoted. The survey shows that the private insurance sector is not involved in such promotion. This is in marked contrast to the OECD-based public agencies surveyed, which frequently use

74. OPIC is authorized to do business in more than 160 developing and post-conflict countries. OPIC has suspended consideration of any new financing and insurance transactions in Russia and Venezuela.

75. OPIC 2016 Annual Report.

76. OPIC Annual Claims Report 2014.

77. Republished with permission of OECD, from OECD Investment Policy Perspectives 2008; permission conveyed through Copyright Clearance Center, Inc.

and promote relevant international standards (especially environmental standards under the OECD Common Understanding, the OECD Convention against Bribery of Foreign Public Officials and the OECD Guidelines for Multinational Enterprises) and/or monitor clients' observance of these standards.

The survey shows that, viewed as a whole, investment guarantee programs do not view their mission as being one of contributing to host country development. [. . .] only one (U.S. OPIC) has host country development as its primary mission. [. . .] The main non-business and non-executive directors are trade union representatives. Thus membership in governing bodies seems to reflect the statutory focus of these agencies on home country economic growth, employment creation and competitiveness goals. [. . .] [Furthermore], performance reporting practices [seem] not generally geared to holding the programs accountable for their host country development impacts.

It could be argued that the fact that these investment guarantee programs make possible investment in developing countries that would not otherwise have occurred is, in itself, a development benefit. [. . .] as pointed out in the OECD Policy Framework for Investment the "benefits of investment do not necessarily accrue automatically or evenly across countries, sectors and local communities. Countries' continuous efforts to strengthen national policies and public institutions, and international co-operation, to create sound investment environments matter most."

1. OPIC Eligibility

The Foreign Assistance Act of 1961 determines eligibility criteria for coverage by OPIC's investment insurance.

FOREIGN ASSISTANCE ACT (FAA) 1961

Title IV — Overseas Private Investment Corporation

Sec. 231. Creation, Purpose and Policy. — To mobilize and facilitate the participation of United States private capital and skills in the economic and social development of less developed countries and areas, and countries in transition from nonmarket to market economies, thereby complementing the development assistance objectives of the United States, there is hereby created the Overseas Private Investment Corporation (hereinafter called the "Corporation"), which shall be an agency of the United States under the policy guidance of the Secretary of State. The Corporation, in determining whether to provide insurance, financing, or reinsurance for a project, shall especially — [. . .]

In carrying out its purpose, the Corporation, utilizing broad criteria, shall undertake —

(i) to conduct its activities in consonance with the activities of the agency primarily responsible for administering part I and the international trade, investment, and financial policies of the United States Government, and to seek to support those developmental projects having positive trade benefits for the United States;

Sec. 234. Investment Insurance and Other Programs.— The Corporation is hereby authorized to do the following: (a) INVESTMENT INSURANCE.— (1) To issue insurance, upon such terms and conditions as the Corporation may determine, to eligible investors assuring protection in whole or in part against any or all of the following risks with respect to projects which the Corporation has approved—(A) inability to convert into United States dollars other currencies, or credits in such currencies, received as earnings or profits from the approved project, as repayment or return of the investment therein, in whole or in part, or as compensation for the sale or disposition of all or any part thereof; (B) loss of investment, in whole or in part, in the approved project due to expropriation or confiscation by action of a foreign government or any political subdivision thereof; (C) loss due to war, revolution, insurrection or civil strife; and (D) loss due to business interruption caused by any of the risks set forth in **subparagraphs** (A), (B), and (C). [. . .]

Sec. 238(c). the term "eligible investor" means: (1) United States citizens; (2) corporations, partnerships, or other associations including nonprofit associations, created under the laws of the United States any State or territory thereof, or the District of Columbia, and substantially beneficially owned by United States citizens; and (3) foreign corporations, partnerships, or other associations wholly owned by one or more such United States citizens, corporations, partnerships, or other associations: Provided however, that the eligibility of such foreign corporation shall be determined without regard to any shares, in aggregate less than 5 per centum of the total issued and subscribed share capital, held by other than the United States owners: Provided further, that in the case of any loan investment a final determination of eligibility may be made at the time the insurance or guaranty is issued; in all other cases, the investor must be eligible at the time a claim arises as well at the time the insurance or guaranty is issued; [. . .]

© Pablo M. Zylberglait, *OPIC's Investment Insurance: The Platypus of Governmental Programs and its Jurisprudence*, 25 Law & Pol'y Int'l Bus. 359, 361 (1993). Reprinted with permission of Georgetown Journal of International Law.

[. . .] When OPIC makes an insurance contract decision, the agency draws mainly from canons of contractual interpretation. However, many of its decisions also reflect an effort by the agency to carry out its congressionally mandated duties; that is, to foster international commerce and to aid projects that will eventually benefit the economy of the United States. Hence, the agency has developed a double personality. While it is contractually strict in some instances, it is unusually flexible as necessary to promote certain beneficial commercial ventures.

Availability and Extent of Coverage and Premiums

The term of an insurance policy may extend a maximum of twenty years. [. . .] OPIC will only insure and pay claims on ninety percent of a loss.[78] [. . .] The maximum amount of coverage available for any one project is $100 million. However, if the investment takes place in a country where OPIC has a high portfolio concentration or highly sensitive projects, the agency may further limit coverage.[79]

OPIC calculates premiums for most equity investments based on the amount of investment at risk during a given year. For other investment types, premiums are computed on the basis of a contractually stipulated Maximum Insured Amount (MIA) and Current Insured Amount (CIA), which may, within the limits of the contract, be elected by the investor, normally on a yearly basis. The CIA represents the insurance actually in force during any contract year. The difference between the CIA and the MIA is called the standby amount. For expropriation and political violence coverage, the insured must maintain current coverage (CIA) at a level equal to the amount of investment at risk. OPIC sets base rates that may be increased or decreased, usually by not more than one-third, depending on the risk profile of the specific project.

OPIC Versus Other Insurers

OPIC [. . .] does not keep any actuarial tables. According to Frederick Jenney, Senior Commercial Counsel, the base rates are quite inelastic. For example, if the risk of war in one country is ten times greater than in another, OPIC will not charge ten times the base rate.[80] But this inelastic rate variation does not mean that OPIC is out to lose money. As a matter of fact, OPIC has been profitable every year since its inception. OPIC's healthy financial situation is likely due to two factors. First, from an actuarial point of view, OPIC is ahead of the investor. Second, those investors who pay the highest premiums contribute enough to subsidize the least risky contracts.

OPIC's Investment Insurance and International Law

One important reason that OPIC offers political risk insurance coverage is to help insulate private investors from the controversy among states as to what customary international compensation law is or should be. Companies insured by OPIC need not face the uncertainties of international law and the potential obstacles that

---

78. OPIC's statute requires that investors bear the risk of loss of the remaining ten percent. This statutory requirement functions as a form of co-insurance. Interview with Frederick Jenney, OPIC Senior Commercial Counsel (Jan. 3, 1993).

79. Investors are required to register projects with OPIC before the investment has been made or irrevocably committed. Registration is free of charge and treated as privileged business information.

80. OPIC is bound to continue coverage regardless of changes in risk, which is more than private insurers can offer.

the doctrines of sovereign immunity and act of state raise.[81] Avoiding the expense, delay, and inconvenience of prosecuting claims against foreign states for these kinds of losses may justify the purchase of this type of insurance.

Adoption of the New Contract

OPIC's jurisprudence is the jurisprudence of contractual interpretation. OPIC's contracts attempt to reflect the policies and objectives of the agency, and its agreements must be interpreted accordingly. In 1985, OPIC adopted [a new] contract form [. . .] Perhaps the very simplicity that frightens some attorneys allows OPIC to implement its legislatively mandated policies through a "flexible contract compliance" approach. [. . .] the new contract represents a change in language more than a change in policy or substance. [. . .]

Despite the advent of this new contract, OPIC's rulings on cases under the old contract are highly illustrative, since the underlying policies of the agency have not changed. These rulings are the most important source of OPIC's private claim jurisprudence, as there have been no significant adjudications under the new contract.[82]

2. OPIC Cases — Governmental Nexus

In the following cases of investors seeking recovery of losses from USAID/OPIC, it can be seen that a high threshold is set for causation attributable to government action.

Webster Publishing Co., Contract No. 894, Determination of Claim (AID Sept. 2, 1966).

Case Introduction

Webster Publishing Company ("Webster") held an equity investment in Sherkat-Sahami Iran-Webster ("Webster-Iran"). The main business of the company in Iran was the sale of books to schools. After the Iranian Revolution in 1976, the new government established a government agency to publish all textbooks for Iranian schools. Webster claimed the Government's actions amounted to expropriation of a large part of its market in Iran. USAID denied Webster's claim, finding that the restructuring of the textbook supply system was a legitimate regulatory scheme.

Principal Points of the Judgment

[. . .] After reviewing the facts and law in this matter, AID concludes that there was no expropriation as that term is defined by Contract of Guaranty No. 894. The acts in question appear an ordinary and reasonable exercise of governmental authority, "essentially regulatory" in the guaranty contract's terminology, and there

81. Vance R. Koven, *Expropriation and the "Jurisprudence" of OPIC*, 22 Harv. Int'l L.J. 269, 270 (1981).

82. A contract entered into in 1985 will be effective until the year 2025.

has been no indication that they were issued with primary object of divesting the Investor or any other persons of their share of ownership or control of the Foreign Enterprise.

Neither the Investor not the Foreign Enterprise had any inherent or contractual right to continue in the publication of primary and secondary textbooks for the governmental schools in Iran, and, in any event, the authority of the Iranian Government to regulate its own purchase of textbooks for those schools brings this situation within the stated exceptions to the definition of Expropriation in the Investor's Contract of Guaranty. Because consideration was received and the sale was not compelled, the transfer of textbooks following the decrees is found not to be expropriation, nationalization or confiscation as defined in the Guaranty Contract. [. . .]

Central Soya Co. Inc., Contract Nos. 5128 and 5129, Action Memorandum (AID Sept. 21, 1967).

Case Introduction

For about five days, employees in Venezuela took control of a mill and hatchery jointly owned by Central Soya Co. Inc. ("Central Soya"), Incubation Tropical and Alimentos Agro. The seizure was intended to prevent entry by creditors until overdue wages had been paid. All shipments of merchandise and feed were prevented, chickens starved and profits lost. There was no solid evidence that the seizure was linked to the government of Venezuela. USAID considered that the employers often dealt with employee disturbances, the seizure was not politically inspired and a claim would only be entertained if police had been there and done nothing. Accordingly, the claim on USAID was rejected. It was held that although the workers had damaged the factory, this was attributable to riots and not to causation by the government. The disturbances were caused by labor disputes over unpaid wages, and this was a business risk not insured by USAID.

Principal Points of the Judgment

[. . .] While the evidence presented indicates that the laborers took over Central Soya's property, it does not indicate that such action was "taken, ratified or condoned" by the government within the meaning of the contract. The conclusion is that the action of the laborers grew out of insolvency or creditors' proceedings against the Foreign Enterprise which are specifically exempted from coverage by Subsection (5) Section 1.15 of the General Terms and Conditions. In other words, the difficulties were, at best, a labor dispute over unpaid wages and therefore a business risk not insured by AID. Finally, there is insufficient evidence to show efforts to take all reasonable measures, including proceeding under available administrative and judicial procedures in the project country, to prevent or postpone such action.

For the above reasons, it is concluded that the action complained of was not Expropriatory under Contracts of Guaranty Nos. 5128 and 5129, and recommend that you deny said claim and sign the attached letter.

W.E. Belcher Lumber Co., Contract No. 5759, Action Memorandum (AID Feb. 17, 1971).

Case Introduction

W.E. Belcher Lumber Company ("Belcher") held equity and debt investment in Forestal Centroamericano S.A. ("Foreca"), a Costa Rican lumber-cutting corporation. In June 1969, Forestal tried to obtain an export permit, but the Government of Costa Rica delayed the process. By the time the export permit was approved in October 1969, 45% of the logs had deteriorated and were unusable. The investor claim on OPIC was denied for failure to establish a causal relationship between the government action and the investor's loss. Bad storage, bad weather and inability to obtain transportation were considered overriding contributing factors.

Principal Points of the Judgment

[. . .] As a result of a dispute between Belcher and the government concerning payment of a stumpage fee, however, no export license was issued until October 31, 1969. Rough seas and a lack of vessels then prevented the timber from being shipped until the following spring, by which time many of the logs had rotted and were valueless.

In its claim to OPIC, Belcher argued that the Costa Rican government's failure to issue the export permit was "expropriatory action" because it not only violated the concession agreement, but also frustrated the object of the investment by preventing the export of the timber.

OPIC denied the claim on two grounds. First, it found that Costa Rica's refusal to issue the permit did not last the requisite one year. Second, OPIC determined that the real cause of Belcher's loss was bad weather and the inability to obtain transportation, not Costa Rica's refusal to issue an export permit. Thus, Belcher's claim was denied for failure to establish a causal relationship between the government action and the investor's loss.[83]

3. OPIC Cases—Inconvertibility

Caterpillar Fin. Servs. Corp., Memorandum of Determinations (Venezuela Aug. 21, 2006).

Case Introduction

Caterpillar Financial Services Corporation (the "Insured") is a Delaware corporation wholly-owned by Caterpillar, Inc., also a Delaware corporation, which is listed on the New York Stock Exchange. By letters dated May 24, 2006, the Insured filled Applications for Compensation (the "Applications") concerning OPIC Contracts

83. Vance R. Koven, *Expropriation and the "Jurisprudence" of OPIC*, 22 Harv. Int'l L.J. 269, 283–284 (1981).

of Insurance Nos. F107 and F314 related to investment in a passenger ferry in Venezuela.

These claims were brought for the inconvertibility of scheduled payments of principal and interest with respect to (a) the F107 loan agreement dated March 29, 2000 and a subsequent Promissory Note dated April 11, 2000, in the original principal amount of $29,280,307 and (b) the F314 loan agreement dated May 30, 2002 and subsequent Promissory Note dated October 9, 2002 in the original principal amount of $26,805,020. The amount claimed under the F107 Contract was $1,302,917.36 for a payment due September 15, 2005, and the amount claimed under the F314 Contract was $1,342,071.79 for a payment due October 15, 2005. These two claims for payment are collectively referred to as the "Claims".

OPIC found the Claims to be valid and that the Insured was entitled to compensation in the aggregate amount of $2,644,989.15 in exchange for the eligible local currency Venezuelan Bolivars.

Principal Points of the Judgment

The Memorandum of Determinations

II Background

The F107 Contract was issued and became effective on April 11, 2000; the F314 Contract was issued and became effective on July 30, 2002. The Contracts were based on OPIC's Standard Form 234 KGT 5- 73 PL, Contract of Institutional Lenders Insurance Against Inconvertibility, Expropriation, and Political Violence, amended to include certain special terms and conditions.

Under Venezuelan law, foreign investors are entitled to convert and transfer abroad the proceeds of their investments. However, the Law of the Central Bank of Venezuela No. 37,296 of October 2, 2001, as amended, contemplates the possibility of imposing restrictions to convertibility in certain circumstances.

After a steep decline in the value of the national currency (the Bolivar) following a two-month general strike that brought oil production to a near standstill, the Central Bank of Venezuela halted trade in Bolivars on January 21, 2003.

On February 5, 2003, the National Executive, acting through the Minister of Finance, and the Central Bank of Venezuela entered into an agreement imposing exchange controls. Simultaneously, by Presidential Decree, President Chavez announced the creation of an Exchange Administration Board, the Comision de Administracion de Divisas ("CADIVI") on February 5, 2003 to regulate the purchase and sale of foreign currency.

The new regime adopts currency controls, restricts access to foreign exchange at the fixed official rate, and requires prior authorization for most purchases from CADIVI. [. . .]

[. . .] In the spirit of cooperation with CADIVI established in 2003, OPIC encouraged its insured parties, including the Insured, to continue to process payments through the CADIVI process. These payments were generally eventually approved but with some delays, often extending past the waiting period in the Contracts.

Thus, since 2003, OPIC has received three claims from the Insured for payments under the Contracts, each of which was withdrawn when the payment was belatedly obtained through the CADIVI process. In particular, OPIC received claims applications from the Insured in September 2003 that were withdrawn in January 2004, applications in May 2004 that were withdrawn in August 2004, and, in September 2004 applications that were withdrawn later the same month. OPIC continued to use advocacy efforts to speed up the process with CADIVI, including setting up a meeting between CADIVI and the Foreign Enterprise in December 2003, meetings with the Venezuelan embassy in 2003 and 2004, and various calls with the Insured and the Foreign Enterprise throughout 2005 to assist with delays in the process. In early 2005, the Insured reported that payments were being approved, albeit slowly, and no claims were filed that year.

III Determinations Under the Contracts

A. The local currency is deemed inconvertible in accordance with Section 2.01 of the Contracts.

Section 2.01 of the Contracts set forth the following requirements for inconvertibility coverage: "(1) the Insured or the foreign enterprise is unable legally to convert local currency [. . .] (2) held by or for the account of the foreign enterprise for conversion into U.S. dollars to discharge a scheduled payment (or part thereof) into United States dollars (3) through any customary legal channels for transactions of the type contemplated in the loan agreement on any business day (4) during the 60 successive days following a scheduled payment date. [. . .]" OPIC finds that each of these requirements has been met.

1. The Foreign Enterprise is unable legally to convert local currency.

The Foreign Enterprise has been unable legally to convert local currency in Venezuela through the official channel. On November 9, 2005 the Foreign Enterprise submitted a completed application to CADIVI for both Loans in accordance with the official procedures. The Insured stated in the Applications that it has "exhausted all known solutions for obtaining payment from CADIVI." The Insured arranged for a meeting between CADIVI and the Foreign Enterprise in February 2006. OPIC's local counsel also attended the meeting and reported that the Legal and Financial Departments of CADIVI acknowledged general delays in the processing of authorizations for the payment of debt due to the new requirements, including that each authorization be unanimously approved by the members of the Commission.

Since the request for authorization was submitted in its entirety over nine months ago and has still not been granted, nor has it been rejected, it is clear that the Foreign Enterprise, using the official legal channel, is unable to convert local currency.

[. . . .]

B. Section 2.02 Exclusions and 3.03 Limitations.

The duty to pay compensation by OPIC is subject to the limitations and exclusions in Sections 2.02 and 3.03 of the Contracts. None of the exclusions apply to this claim.

1. Pre-existing Restrictions.

No compensation is payable if, on the date of execution of the Contracts, a lender or the Foreign Enterprise would in comparable circumstances have been unable legally to convert local currency into United States dollars. The Contracts became effective on April 11, 2000, and the foreign exchange restrictions were put into place in February 2003. Therefore, on the date of execution of the Contracts, the Insured or the Foreign Enterprise would have been able legally to convert local currency into United States dollars, and this exclusion does not apply.

Furthermore, no compensation is payable if the Insured knew or should have known about the restriction. Again, since the exchange control regime was put into place several years after the Contracts were in place, this exclusion also does not apply.

2. Insured Diligence.

No compensation is payable unless the Insured has made all reasonable efforts to convert or cause the Foreign Enterprise to convert the local currency into United States dollars [. . .] through all customary legal channels [. . .] Therefore, OPIC finds that for the Claims at hand, this exclusion does not apply.

C. Other Provisions of the Contracts.

5. Ownership and Eligibility.

[. . .] Where shares of stock of a U.S. corporation with widely dispersed public ownership are held in the names of trustees or nominees (including stock brokerage firms) with addresses in the United States, such shares may be deemed to be owned by United States citizens unless the Insured has knowledge to the contrary. The Insured's legal counsel confirmed to OPIC that the Insured is approximately 98% owned by U.S. citizens. Therefore, the ownership and eligibility criterion of Section 9.01.2 of the Contracts is met.

4. OPIC Cases—Expropriation

Actions that are not openly expropriatory but are calculated to significantly disrupt the operations of a foreign enterprise or industry may be examples of "creeping" expropriation and can be considered by OPIC for compensation. Government action is compensable as a total expropriation only if it has the effect of directly depriving the investor of fundamental rights in the insured investment. Rights are "fundamental" if their denial substantially deprives the investor of the benefits of the investment. This includes measures such as forcing an enterprise into bankruptcy or an unfavorable settlement with authorities designed to achieve indirect nationalization.

Many such claims involve alleged violations of concession or development contracts, where these are arbitrarily canceled and then awarded to a third party, usually a government insider. Other claims arise from construction agreements, especially where these represent the substance of the investment. OPIC requires that a loss suffered by a construction enterprise constitutes a substantial impediment to its ability to proceed at all with the project.

Generally, the amount of compensation is based on the net book value of the insured investment. OPIC determines book value by relying on financial statements maintained and translated into dollars by the investor in accordance with U.S. generally accepted accounting principles (GAAP).

Northern Indiana Brass Co., Contract No. 6360, Action Memorandum (OPIC Jan. 22, 1973).

Case Introduction

The Northern Indiana Brass Company (NIBCO) held a 50 percent interest and management control of a Chilean subsidiary, NIBCO SGM Sudamerica Ltd (NIBSA), that manufactured brass plumbing fittings for housing and industrial markets in Chile. On August 1, 1969, AID extended insurance coverage to NIBCO, Contract of Guaranty No. 6360, covering its equity investment in NIBSA.

In 1970, the Marxist Salvador Allende was democratically elected President of Chile. The economy began to disintegrate, and NIBSA's principal market, the housing industry, collapsed. Severe operating restrictions and labor controls were enacted, whereby NIBSA was required to maintain full employment, with the result that it built up a large inventory at the expense of its liquid assets.

The Government of Chile (GOC) and government-backed labor unions increasingly intervened in the plant management. The General Manager, Mr. Hyams, made extensive efforts to save the company from bankruptcy, but in 1970 he shut down the manufacturing plant. The GOC quickly expelled him from Chile and sought to acquire NIBCO's interest in NIBSA, so that it would have full control of the plant.

CORFO (the GOC development agency) purchased NIBCO's 50 percent interest in NIBSA for $300,000 in cash and the release of NIBCO's guaranty on a $75,000 loan to NIBSA from CORFO. The purchase price was somewhat less than the value of NIBCO's investment for insurance purposes. OPIC and NIBCO agreed to a procedure for computing the value of NIBCO's Net Investment in NIBSA on the Date of Expropriation. Under this agreement, OPIC and NIBCO each appointed a certified public accountant to audit the books. If the accountants were not able to agree on the value of the Net Investment, they would appoint a third accountant, who would assist in resolving any differences.

The accountants were not able to agree, but an agreement was finally reached whereby OPIC paid NIBCO an additional $110,000.

Principal Points of the Judgment

Determinations under Contract of Guaranty No. 6360.

That the Government of Chile has taken Expropriatory Action contrary to Section 1.15 of Contract of Guaranty [. . .] NIBCO alleges that NIBCO was permanently prohibited from exercising its fundamental rights acquired through ownership of NIBSA equity shares. The rights involved primarily were those of exercising effective control over the management of NIBSA. At the time of intervention, the General Manager was acting with authority granted to him by a resolution of NIDSA's Board of Directors and under a contract for his services. [. . .]

Although a full year did not pass from the date of intervention before NIBCO signed the compensation agreement with CORFO, the events that occurred during that period confirmed that the GOC was preventing NIBCO from exercising control over NIBSA [. . .]

Exception (1) of Section 1.15 cannot be sustained on the basis of information available to OPIC. Although the intervention by the GOC on November 12, 1970, was purportedly made pursuant to the laws of Chile which on their face appear to fall within the scope of exception (1), the manner in which the intervention was conducted, particularly in light of the action by NIBSA's unions, the economic and political situation existing in Chile at the time, and the battle being waged in the Chilean press against NIBCO, manifested an intent on the part of the GOC to strip NIBCO of the ownership right to control NIBSA, and vest it in the workers. Application of labor laws in this manner was clearly unreasonable.

Exception (2) of Section 1.15 is not applicable in this claim because NIBCO's efforts to prevent or postpone the GOC's action were rendered moot by the compensation agreement which provided a reasonable settlement to the dispute and to which OPIC did not object. Prior to that agreement, NIBCO had contributed with both United States and local counsel and had initiated various actions designed to protest the action and obtain the return of the project. The struggle led to a GOC newspaper campaign against NIBCO and Mr. Hyams, and his personal safety was threatened. Ultimately a compensation agreement was possible only through the offices of a mediator and Mr. Hyams was allowed to leave Chile only through the intercession of the United States Ambassador.

[. . .] If OPIC were to deny the claim based on the failure of Mr. Hyams to obtain permission of the GOC before closing the plant, there is a substantial probability that the decision would be reversed in arbitration. Although GOC labor laws could be interpreted to require NIPSA to obtain GOC permission before temporarily suspending operations, the failure of the GOC to give its consent under the circumstances of this case was unreasonable. [. . .]

[. . .] The difference between the Net Investment as asserted by NIBCO and as calculated by OPIC's accountants arises from the method of recording the amount of $75,562 due for certain technical services provided to NIBSA. NIBCO recorded these as accounts receivable but now asserts that they should be treated as part of NIBCO's Investment under the Contract of Guarantee.

Although we believe that NIBCO's assertion in regard to the Net Investment is not in accord with the definition of Net Investment contained in Section 1.28 of the General Terms and Conditions of the Contract (GT&C) and would be rejected by an arbitration panel, we believe that there is a substantial likelihood that an arbitration panel would interpret our letter of April 30, 1971 and the terms of Section 18.01 of the GT&C to require that the $300,000 payment from CORFO be apportioned between Net Investment and Total Capital Investment, the latter including the adjusted value of the technical services of $75,562. Thus, the Net Investment of $380,408 calculated by OPIC's accountants would be reduced not by $300,000 but by only $258,409.50, yielding a compensable loss of $121,996.50. [. . .]

In settlement negotiations with OPIC however, NIBCO agreed to accept an even lower value of $110,000 based on an apparently pessimistic estimate of their chances of prevailing in arbitration coupled with a desire to reach a prompt conclusion to the case. NIBCO also agreed to assign to OPIC any right NIBCO still had to collect the $75,562 in accounts receivable. NIBCO apparently did not assign the account receivable to CORFO under the compensation settlement, but as a practical matter, the chances of collection are poor. [. . .]

Fearn Foods International Incorporated, Contracts Nos. 5969 and 6159 (Somalia; Nov. 1973).

Case Introduction

Fearn Foods International Incorporated ("Fearn") held a 49 percent investment of debt and equity in PRODMA Ltd. ("PRODMA"), with Contract of Guaranty No. 5969 issued by AID on March 14, 1968 covering these investments. PRODMA was a Somali company engaged in the business of catching, processing, freezing and selling shell fish. Contract No. 6159 was issued by AID on September 15, 1968 for the construction and operation of a petroleum products depot (owned by PRODMA but leased to a Shell Oil subsidiary) to service vessels using the Port of Kismayo.

In October 1969, when a military coup occurred in Somalia, a series of repeated and continuous hostile acts by the Government of Somalia ("GSDR") personnel were directed against PRODMA and its employees. This included harassment, arrest and deportation of PRODMA's personnel; unreasonable restrictions on the use of PRODMA's aircraft; infringements on PRODMA's fishing concession; and the nationalization of PRODMA's petroleum depot, making it impossible for PRODMA to conduct normal business operations. Fearn made the decision to close the PRODMA plant on or around August 18, 1970.

OPIC and Fearn discussed selling PRODMA to the Somali government or to a private third party but could not find a private entity investor willing to engage on reasonable commercial terms. Fearn did not believe it was in a position to negotiate directly with the Somalia government, as its local partners had been arrested.

OPIC sent a representative to visit the Somalia government and explore the possibility of the purchase of PRODMA by the government. An agreement was reached both with respect to the fishing operation and the petroleum depot. The agreed price was USD 375,000 but only after PRODMA had been liquidated and the assets distributed to its creditors. A total of USD 345,713 was received by OPIC on account of this claim.

Determinations under Contracts of Guaranty Nos. 5969 and 6159.

Section 1.15—That Expropriatory Action has occurred within the definition of Section 1.15.

[. . . .] the Foreign Enterprise was prevented from exercising effective control over the use or disposition of its property [or from constructing the project] or from operating the same. [. . .] OPIC asked the US Embassy in Mogadishu whether Fearn's description of the acts of harassment were an accurate reflection of what occurred. In a cabled response, the embassy said that Fearn's written submission reflected "the facts situation as Embassy understood them with remarkable objectivity." [. . .]

[. . .] I conclude that Expropriatory Action did occur within the definition of Section 1.15(d). Moreover, on the basis of information available, or likely to become available to OPIC, there do not appear to be any grounds to raise any of the exceptions to Expropriatory Action set forth in Section 1.15.

Section 1.12—That the Date of Expropriation within meaning of Section 1.12 was August 18, 1970.

In its letter of January 13, 1971, Fearn took the position that August 18, 1970 was the Date of Expropriation. On that date "conditions had become so acute" that Fearn was forced to conclude that the conduct of further business operations by PRODMA was impossible. It is not possible in the case of Expropriatory Action based upon continued acts of harassment to designate with great precision when the cumulative effect of these acts was such as to constitute an expropriatory act. Nevertheless, it can be said that the total effect of the actions complained of by Fearn did constitute Expropriatory Action by August 18, 1970, the date Fearn caused PRODMA to cease operations. As noted above, our Embassy took the position that a private profit-seeking operation could not be reasonably expected to continue to operate.

[. . .]

Ponderosa Assets, L.P. Argentina, Contract of Insurance No. D733, 2005.

Case Introduction

On August 12, 2002, Ponderosa Assets, L.P ("Ponderosa" or "Investor") filed an application under OPIC Insurance Contract No. D733 for recovery of losses from the expropriation of its equity investment in the privatization, acquisition and operation of Transportadora de Gas del Sur ("TGS"), a gas pipeline company located in southern Argentina (the "Project"). The Investor sought compensation in the amount of $50,000,000 (the "Application").

Enron Corp. ("Enron") was the entity that initially applied for political risk insurance with OPIC for coverage of the Project. On June 1, 1993, OPIC and Enron executed the OPIC Contract, which provided coverage against the risks of inconvertibility, expropriation, and political violence. On December 18, 1998, Enron entered into an Assumption and Consent Agreement with OPIC and Ponderosa (the "Assignment"), whereby Enron transferred all of its interests in the OPIC Contract to Ponderosa, and OPIC consented to such assignment.

In the matter before OPIC, it was found that an expropriation within the meaning of the OPIC Contract had occurred. This finding was based upon OPIC's determination that, even if enactment of the Emergency Laws could be justified in general, the actions of the Government of Argentina constituted repudiation of their contract with Ponderosa, motivated by noncommercial considerations. The Government of Argentina did not pay compensatory damages for expropriation, and this was in direct violation of the Government of Argentina's responsibilities to a foreign investor under international law. OPIC provided full compensation in the amount of $50,000,000.

Principal Points of the Judgment

[. . .]

As part of the privatization of its gas industry, Argentina divided and sold its state gas company, Gas del Estado, into numerous smaller companies, including TGS, one of two transportation companies that was formed and privatized. CIESA acquired 70% of TGS capital stock. In turn, 25% of the CIESA's shares were owned by each of the four investors, giving each, indirectly, a 17.5% interest in TGS. As described above, Enron acquired an additional 25% interest in CIESA in 1996 and amended the OPIC Contract accordingly, increasing its indirect equity interest in TGS to 35%.

The government of Argentina (the "GOA") granted TGS its rights to transport gas through a gas transportation license (the "License") dated December 18, 1992 with a term of thirty-five years. The License allows TGS to collect revenues for transporting gas through tariffs set by GOA. However, the License specifies that the tariffs will be calculated in U.S. dollars and expressed in Argentine pesos and that the tariffs shall be adjustable every six months in accordance with variations in the US Producer Price Index ("PPI"). These provisions were meant to protect the Investor against the respective risks of devaluation of the peso and of inflation in Argentina. TGS's main source of revenue is the tariffs.

The GOA enacted the Public Emergency and Exchange Regime Reform Law No. 25,561 (the "Emergency Law") on January 6, 2002. Article 8 of the Emergency Law provides that "in contracts entered into by the public administration and subject to public law, including contracts for works and public services, dollar adjustment clauses and indexation clauses based on the price indexes of other countries, as well as any other indexation mechanisms shall no longer be effective. The prices and rates resulting from such clauses shall be fixed in pesos at a ONE PESO ($1) = ONE DOLLAR (US$I) exchange rate.

As a result of the enactment of the Emergency Law, TGS' revenues have been (1) frozen at the January 2000 rate and an adjustment to the PPI index has not been permitted; and (2) limited to the peso equivalent of the U.S. dollar amount which should have been paid. These two elements have resulted in a decrease in the revenues of TGS so great that it justified a total writeoff by the Investor of its investment in TGS.

Beginning in 2000, the GOA attempted through various other measures to limit TGS's rights to adjust the tariff, culminating in the Emergency Law. In January 2000, according to Ponderosa, the GOA "pressured" TGS to defer the PPI-linked tariff increase for the six-month period from January-June 2000. Then, in July 2000, it further pressured TGS to enter into another such agreement, providing for 30% of the previous tariff adjustment and postponing any further adjustments until October 2000. [. . .] Ponderosa stated in the April Letter that its sole basis for the claim is the passing of the Emergency Law.

IV. Determinations Under the OPIC Contract

A. The actions taken by the GOA with respect to Ponderosa's insured investment in TGS constitute total expropriation within the meaning of Section 4.01 of the OPIC Contract.

Four issues are presented by Section 4.01 of the OPIC Contract, which sets forth the requirements for total expropriation coverage: (1) whether the acts were attributable to a foreign governing authority in de facto control of the part of the country where the Project is located; (2) whether the acts constituted a violation of international law or a material breach of local law; (3) whether Ponderosa was deprived of fundamental rights in the insured investment, and if so, whether the stated acts directly caused such loss; and (4) whether the expropriatory effect has continued for the requisite six-month period.

[. . . .] the main expropriatory action, and the action on which the claim is based,[84] consists of the enactment of the Emergency Law, which resulted in a change in tariff treatment in violation of the GOA's contractual obligation under the License to allow tariff payments in dollars and with a PPI-indexed adjustment. The enactment of the Emergency Law was authorized and implemented by the GOA.

84. The April letter states that "the sole basis of the claim is the Emergency Law."

The acts are violations of international law (without regard to the availability of local remedies).

[. . . .] If, according to these principles, the GOA bears state responsibility for injury resulting from the Emergency Law, then this provision of the OPIC Contract has been satisfied.

We take no position as to whether the GOA's enactment of the Emergency Law constitutes a "taking" by the state of the Investor's property.

One ground for determining whether the enactment of the Emergency Law was a violation of international law above is that the action constitutes a "taking." Although traditional interpretations of expropriation deal with "taking" as actions which force the foreign entity to abandon operations entirely or where legal title is actually lost, the theory of indirect expropriation recognizes that a government may deprive an investor of the economic value of its investment and that such deprivation is tantamount to a "taking". [. . .]

The Iran-U.S. Claims Tribunal found takings in Iran's deprivation of fundamental property or contract rights of several American companies notwithstanding the lack of a formal decree of nationalization. In numerous cases, the tribunal recognized that interference by a state with the foreign national's use of the property or enjoyment of its benefits may constitute a compensable expropriation, even where legal title was not affected.[85] In one of these cases in particular, the tribunal ruled that the government of Iran's enactment of legislation requiring the foreign national's land to be used for a particular purpose constituted an impairment of the foreign national's right to use his property "that prevents, unreasonably interferes with, or unduly delays, effective enjoyment" of such property, thereby constituting a taking. In this case, the main asset of TGS, and of Ponderosa's investment, is the License, and the GOA is preventing TGS from enjoying the benefits of its "property", i.e. charging a tariff to its customers paid in dollars and adjusted via the PPI index.

The deprivation of property is a violation of international law if prompt, adequate, and effective compensation is not paid.[86] The GOA has failed to pay or offer to pay any compensation to the Investor. Furthermore, GOA has, through another provision of the Emergency Law, prevented the Investor from suspending compliance with its own obligations, thereby forcing it to endure ongoing losses.[87] [. . .]

The theory that certain contractual breaches may constitute expropriation has other bases in law. International arbitral tribunals have recognized that rights

85. See, e.g., *Jahangir Mohtadi, et al. v. Iran*, Iran Award 573-271-3, Case No. 271 (1996) ("It is firmly established in the Tribunal's jurisprudence that liability for interference with property rights may be found even where the formal legal title to property has not been affected.").

86. *See*, O'Connell, 2 International Law 776-77 (2d. ed. 1970).

87. *See*, Article 10 of the Emergency Law: "The provisions of Articles 8 and 9 of this Law shall under no circumstances authorize utility providers or contractors to suspend or alter compliance with their obligations."

under contracts are property subject to expropriation. Furthermore, in its definition of expropriation in the United States Code, Congress has explicitly included impairment by a government of a contract with a foreign investor.[88] The elements of the Code, which, although reflecting U.S. law, can be seen as well as indicative of customary international law, are all met here: the enactment of the Emergency Law constituted a repudiation of GOA's contractual obligation under Section 4.5 of the License, the repudiation was not caused by the Investor's fault or misconduct, and the repudiation, by limiting the Investor's right to collect revenues from TGS' operations, materially and adversely affected the continued operation of the Project, and ultimately caused a write-off of the Investor's investment in TGS.

We need not decide whether the repudiation or breach of the License by GOA was discriminatory.

A state is responsible for a repudiation or breach of contract where the repudiation or breach is "discriminatory."[89] Although the Emergency Law was nondiscriminatory on its face in as much as it applied to Argentine as well as foreign holders of dollar-denominated obligations, its impact on specific groups of people must be further examined in order to determine whether it was discriminatory in substance.

Since the discriminatory nature of the act is just one of two conditions, either of which must be met in order to constitute an international law violation, and the other of which (as shown below) has been met, it is not necessary to decide this question for purposes of our determination.

The contractual repudiation was motivated by noncommercial reasons, and compensatory damages were not paid, giving rise to state responsibility for contract repudiation under international law.

International law prohibits "a repudiation or breach by the state of a contract with a national of another state (a) where the repudiation or breach is . . . (ii) motivated by noncommercial considerations, and compensatory damages are not paid." OPIC finds that the GOA's repudiation of the License was motivated by noncommercial considerations. [. . .]

[. . .] Because there is a fine line between commercial and policy motives where a governmental contract is concerned, this provision should be examined in light of the actual motive of the GOA in enacting the Emergency Law. In this case, the Emergency Law was purportedly enacted for public policy reasons, specifically to curb the risk of inflation and devaluation and to control the flight of foreign exchange from Argentina. The Emergency Law itself begins with GOA declaring a state of emergency and sets as its goal "to rearrange the financial, banking and

88. *Libyan Am. Oil Co. v. Libyan Arab Republic*, 20 I.L.M. 1, 60 (I.C.J. 1977); German Interests in *Polish Upper Silesia* 1926 P.C.I.J., Ser. A, No. 7 at 14045 (Judgment of May 25, 1926); *Norwegian Shipowner's Case*, 1 R. Int'l Arb. Awards 307 (1922); *See also*, O'Connell, 2 International Law 763-68 (2d. ed. 1970).

89. Restatement (Third) of Foreign Relations Law of the United States 5712 (1987), Part (2)(a)(i).

exchange market system" and "to relaunch the economy. If the GOA acted "essentially on governmental motives" i.e., the public policy motive of curbing the risk of inflation and easing the effect of the state's severe devaluation, it cannot have been acting in its commercial capacity. The same consideration that might relieve GOA of state responsibility for a "taking" for public policy purposes gives rise to state responsibility for abrogation or repudiation of contract. [. . .]

The acts deprived the Investor of fundamental rights in the insured investment.

[. . .] not all of the investor's rights with respect to the insured investment need be affected for an Investor to be fundamentally deprived of the benefits of its investment. In determining whether total expropriation has occurred, OPIC will examine the significance of the rights in question in the context of the overall investment.

Ponderosa, together with its fellow consortium members, retains full control of the assets of TGS, including the License. However, the revenue stream of TGS has been reduced so drastically as a result of the provisions of the Emergency Law that it resulted in the total write off of the investment under the equity method of accounting. [. . .]

In the context of an investment, the right to recover its economic value in accordance with the terms governing that investment is a fundamental right of the investor. In this case, the most important asset of TGS, the License, has been dramatically altered, depriving Ponderosa of its right to collect revenues via the tariffs. [. . .]

B. Section 4.03 Exclusions and 5.04 Limitations.

The duty to pay compensation by OPIC is subject to the limitations and exclusions in Section 4.03 and 5.04 of the OPIC Contract. None of the exclusions apply to this claim.

Provocation. No compensation is payable if "the preponderant cause is unreasonable action attributable to the Investor, including corrupt practices."

[. . .] Although Ponderosa did agree to defer the PPI-indexed increase in 2000, thereby arguably allowing for the loss for this period, the action was reasonable under the circumstance, and the subsequent enactment of the Emergency Law cannot be attributed to this concession.

Government Action. No compensation is payable if "the action is taken by the foreign governing authority in its capacity or through its powers as a purchaser, supplier, creditor, shareholder, director or manager of the project company."

When the License was originally granted, GOA retained a 30% interest in TGS, but this interest was subsequently sold to TGS employees and the general public; therefore, GOA is not a shareholder of the TGS. Furthermore, GOA entered into the License as a regulator and not as a purchaser or supplier of natural gas. GOA is not a purchaser, supplier, creditor, shareholder, director or manager of TGS.

[. . .] While the original request by GOA to defer the PPI-indexed tariff was made in its capacity as a contracting party, the same cannot be said for the enactment of the Emergency Law. The Emergency Law was undertaken by the GOA acting in its sovereign capacity, as it was a legislative act. [. . .]

Active Amount. Compensation is limited to "the Active Amount on the date the expropriatory effect commences"

According to the executed Election of Political Risk Insurance Coverage for the period from October 22, 2001 through January 21, 2002, the Active Amount (as defined in the OPIC Contract) was $50,000,000 on January 6, 2002 which is when the Emergency Law was enacted. Since the enactment of the Emergency Law has been determined to be the expropriatory event, and the claim is for the Active Amount as of the date of such expropriatory event, a limitation of $50,000,000 applies. [. . .]

5. OPIC Cases — Political Violence

Sector Resources, Ltd., Contract of Insurance No. F030 (OPIC 2012).

Case Introduction

Sector Resources Ltd ("Insured"), a U.S. owned Cayman Island Company, invested in a project involving the acquisition and expansion of the Las Animas underground quartz, gold and silver mine ("Las Animas") in the State of Tolima, Colombia. Sector Resources made up to a $3.5 million investment in its Colombian branch ("Sector Resources Colombia"), as well as a $2 million equipment lease to its Colombian branch through one of its U.S. affiliates, Sector Capital Corporation ("Sector Capital"). Contract of Insurance No. F030 (the "Contract") was issued by OPIC effective August 18, 1999, to cover Sector's $3.5 million equity investment in the Project.

By letters dated November 29, 2005 and February 2, 2007, and further supplemented on March 29, 2007 and April 3, 2007, the Insured filed political violence claims under their OPIC insurance contracts. These contracts included provisions for "Political Violence-Scope of Coverage" and "Political Violence-Amount of Compensation".

The alleged incidents of political violence occurred on a road between the minerals mine and the mine offices, all of which were located southwest of Bogota. The first incident was on November 28, 2005, when members of the National Liberation Army ("ELN") stopped a truck owned by the Insured, forcibly removed the driver and seized the Insured's property (the "First Incident"). Nearly a year later, on November 8, 2006, members of the Revolutionary Armed Forces of Columbia ("FARC") allegedly hijacked a truck and similarly removed the Insured's property (the "Second Incident"). OPIC agreed to pay compensation to the Insured for losses sustained.

Principal Points of the Judgment

[. . .]

V. Determinations Under the Contract

A determination under an OPIC insurance contract addresses three categories of issues: (1) whether the acts complained of satisfy all the elements required to bring them within the scope of coverage; (2) the amount of compensation payable; and (3) whether the insured fulfilled its duties under the insurance contracts.

Political violence was the direct and immediate cause of the permanent loss of tangible property of the foreign enterprise used for the Project.

According to Sector, two shipments of gold concentrate were hijacked while enroute from the mine to company headquarters. The issue is whether this constitutes political violence or ordinary highway robbery. Sector has provided certifications by the Colombian army attributing the First Incident to specific units of the ELN and ERP and the Second Incident to the same unit of the FARC that was held responsible for the acts of political violence that formed the basis of eight prior claims that OPIC found valid.

"Political violence" is defined in Section 6.01 of the Contract as a violent act undertaken with the primary intent of achieving a political objective, including insurrection and terrorism.

The organizations to which responsibility for the incident has been attributed have generally been described as insurgent groups and terrorist organizations. They are known to have engaged in hijackings and other criminal acts, both to finance other activities and as means of destabilizing Colombia's economy while striking at its political and military institutions and attacking foreign investments.

In light of all these factors, OPIC determines that political violence was the direct and immediate cause of the loss.

[. . .]

Compensation is payable in the aggregate amount of $75,548 on the basis of the adjusted cost of the lost property.

The Contract (Section 7.01) provides two possible bases for compensation in the event of asset loss, namely adjusted cost and replacement cost. Considering the nature of the property lost (gold concentrate from the mine), replacement cost would be meaningless. The contract provides three possible measures of adjusted cost, i.e. original cost, fair market value and reasonable cost of repair. Again, considering the nature of the property lost, only fair market value is appropriate.

Sector has provided documentation supporting a fair market value for the lost property in the aggregate amount of $75,548. The documentation consists of laboratory records establishing the metallurgical content of the concentrate in each shipment, shipping records showing the weight of the concentrate, and evidence of the market price of gold on each date of loss. Together, these documents establish the fair market value of the property that was lost. Sector calculated the fair market value of the concentrate by determining its gold content in troy ounces through laboratory analysis of samples that were milled on the dates of loss and determining the fair market value by reference to the published London PM fix on the dates of loss.

Thus, the loss on November 25, 2005 amounted to 87.6 troy ounces of gold, valued at $496 each, resulting in a claim for $43,449.60. Following the same method, Sector established the compensation due for the loss on November 8, 2006 at $32,097.92 (55.505 troy ounces of gold at $623.20 each).

None of the Limitations applies.

Section 7.03 of the contract provides three possible limitations upon compensation for loss of assets, none of which applies.

The Active Amounts (Section 8.06) on the dates of the First Incident and the Second Incident exceeded the claimed compensation as of each date (Sec. 703(a)). The Insured still retains the risk of loss of at least 10% of the book value of its interest in the foreign enterprise (Sec. 703. (a), Sec. 901.3).

The amounts of compensation that have been determined to be payable do not exceed the book value of the insured investment at the time of loss. Based on the balance sheets of the foreign enterprise for 2005 and 2006, OPIC has confirmed that the amounts of compensation do not exceed the book value of the insured investment (Section 7.04) as of the date of the First Incident and as of the date of the Second Incident. None of the adjustments described in Section 7.04(b) is required in this instance.

[. . .]

6. Contract Renegotiation: The Dabhol Power Project in India

Bechtel Ents. Int'l (Bermuda) Ltd.; Ben Dabhol Holdings, Ltd.; and Capital India Power Mauritius I, v. Overseas Private Inv. Corp., AAA Case No. 50 T195 00509 02 (Sept. 25, 2003).

Case Introduction

In the early 1990s, the Government of India announced legislation that would allow private investors, including foreign project investors, to participate in the expansion of the Indian power sector. In 1992, United States investors Enron Power Corporation, Bechtel Enterprises International (Bermuda) Ltd and General Electric (the "Sponsors"), signed a Memorandum of Understanding for a power generation project and formed the Dabhol Power Company ("DPC"). DPC is a company established under Indian law for the purpose of constructing and operating a power station, a related liquid natural gas regasification facility and associated services. Accordingly, DPC is a "project financed" entity.

The Sponsors set up the project in the Indian state of Maharashtra, near the village of Dabhol. Maharashtra was the second largest state in India in terms of population and had a healthy economy and advantageous geographical location for the construction of the project. The government was stable, having been controlled by the centrist Congress Party since Independence. The Sponsors' customer was the Maharashtra State Electricity Board ("MSEB"), an administrative subdivision closely controlled by the Government of Maharashtra ("GOM"). The GOM coordinated all of its agencies' activities with respect to the project. After construction began on the project, the Sponsors obtained financing and political risk insurance from the Overseas Private Investment Corporation ("OPIC").

Public opposition to the Dabhol Power Project grew as construction activity proceeded. Political opposition mounted, and the opposition Bharatiya Janata Party ("BJP") made opposition to the Dabhol Project a centerpiece in their state election campaigns. Subsequently, after a series of actions taken by the Government of India ("GOI"), the GOM and the MSEB, the project was shut down and put in the hands of a court-appointed receiver.

In agreeing to provide financing for the project, OPIC joined a large number of banks and credit agencies, including both India-based financial institutions ("IFIs") and non-Indian Lenders (the "Offshore Lenders"), collectively the "Lenders". The Lenders committed approximately U.S. $2 billion to the Project, and the equity sponsors committed a total of approximately US $1 billion.

The equity owners of the DPC were Capital India Power Mauritius I ("CIPM I"), Bechtel Enterprises International (Bermuda) Ltd. and Ben Dabhol Holdings, Ltd ("Bechtel") ("Claimants"). These Claimants also insured their investments via OPIC Contracts of Insurance and initiated arbitration at the American Arbitration Association International Centre for Dispute Resolution under the provisions of their insurance policies with OPIC.

The insurance contracts at issue in this arbitration were OPIC Contract of Insurance No. E418 between OPIC and Bechtel, effective August 1, 1995; OPIC Contract of Insurance No. E839 between OPIC and Dabhol, effective February 21, 1997 (collectively the "Bechtel Insurance Contracts"); and OPIC Contract of Insurance No. F153 between OPIC and CIPM I, effective August 1, 1999 (the "GE Insurance Contract"). These are collectively referred to as the "Insurance Contracts". OPIC, in concluding that the project would deliver substantial benefits for both the United States and India and was consistent with OPIC's mandate to facilitate U.S. capital investment in developing economies, agreed to provide $200 million in political risk insurance for the project and a further $160 million in loan guarantees.

OPIC's standard policy form was attached to the OPIC Commitment Letter, thereby providing insurance for expropriation, including "creeping" expropriation, political violence and currency inconvertibility. It also provided for insurance coverage if claimants were denied recourse to their arbitral rights under the Project Agreements.

In spring 1995, the GOM attempted to cancel the Project for political reasons, acting on the advice of a project specific government panel known as the "Munde Committee". As detailed policy discussions were still underway between OPIC and

Claimants, the standard OPIC policy was the only version provided to the Sponsors until July 12, 1995. These policy discussions focused principally on OPIC's potential liability regarding the Munde Committee, and on a revision of the OPIC standard exclusion for acts taken by a host government in its capacity as a commercial actor. OPIC was concerned with obligations resulting from losses due to the Munde Committee, while the Sponsors wanted to amend the exclusion for acts taken by the host government as a commercial actor because MSEB was guaranteed by GOM and GOI.

On July 12, 1995, OPIC proposed two changes to deal with these concerns. The first was a "Munde Carve Out" to cover expropriatory acts taken by GOM in response to the Munde Committee. The second was an exception to the exclusion for acts taken by government acting in a commercial capacity.

The arbitral proceedings concluded that OPIC should compensate the Claimants for losses incurred.

Principal Points of the Judgment

Findings of Fact

12. An important Project Agreement was the Power Purchase Agreement between DPC and MSEB ("PPA"), originally executed in 1993. It was the principal asset of DPC. The PPA obligated DPC to generate power sufficient to meet MSEB's demands, and MSEB to purchase power from DPC at rates specifically defined in the PPA. The PPA provided that disputes arising under it would be resolved by international arbitration. The PPA also gave Claimants the right to terminate the agreement upon MSEB's nonperformance of its obligations and thereby require MSEB to purchase the Project for a sum defined as the "Transfer Amount". [. . .]

31. OPIC's July 12, 1995 draft also included several other provisions, including para 10.05/10.07,[90] that had never been discussed among the parties. According to an OPIC memorandum written contemporaneously with the execution of the Policies, the purpose of para 10.05/10.07 was to ensure that "no compensation [would] be payable under expropriation coverage unless DPC [had] exhausted its available remedies under the project agreements . . ." [. . .] the Sponsors fully intended to exercise the remedies referenced in para 10.05/10.07 in the event that MSEB were to breach the PPA. [. . .]

33. The Sponsors never contemplated that the only risk OPIC assumed under the policies was the risk of nonpayment of an arbitral award confirmed by an Indian court of last resort. The parties had no discussion to that effect. [. . .] Mr. XXX testified that, in part, para 10.05/10.07 had been inserted to assist OPIC, in the event it was required to pay claims under the policies and then proceeded to seek recovery of these amounts from the Indian government, pursuant to the Investment Incentive

90. Para 10.05 and 10.07 are identical—the former is on the GE policy, the earlier is in the Bechtel policy.

Agreement between the Government of the United States and the Government of India ("the IIA"). [. . .]

35. In August 1995, OPIC and the Sponsors executed final versions of the insurance contracts, with effective dates of August 1, 1995. [. . .]

40. In 1997, OPIC amended the policies to delete the Munde Carve Out, effective March 15, 1997. According to OPIC, the amendment was warranted in light of "recent project developments, including the conclusion of arbitral proceedings in favor of [DPC] on December 17, 1996."

41. GE sought to clarify certain terms of its Policy upon the Policy's renewal in 1999. In a number of meetings, telephone conversations and other communications, GE's representative, XXX, inquired of OPIC whether certain events would be considered expropriatory under the policy even if they did not lead to a termination of the PPA. OPIC representatives confirmed to Mr. XXX that OPIC's policy covered "creeping expropriation" but they never addressed Mr. XXX's particular inquiries.

42. In the course of the 1999 renewal discussions, the OPIC representatives did not tell Mr. XXX that OPIC interpreted the expropriation coverage of the Policy to mean that OPIC had assumed only the risk of nonpayment by the Indian government of a confirmed arbitration award. Mr. XXX would not have recommended that GE renew its policy in 1999 if OPIC had informed him that the Policy was so limited.

43. When GE and OPIC negotiated the 1999 renewal of GE's policy, neither GE nor OPIC foresaw the possibility that Indian regulators or courts would enjoin DPC from pursuing international arbitration under the Project Agreements. In addition, the possibility that the Indian courts would affirm an injunction issued by Indian regulatory agencies was not contemplated by OPIC and did not enter into the Parties' discussions. [. . .]

45. Pursuant to the Electricity Regulatory Commission Act ("ERC"), Maharashtra created the Maharashtra Electricity Regulatory Commission ("MERC") in 1999, more than three years after the renegotiated Project Agreements and the Policies has been executed. MERC is an administrative subdivision of the GOM that regulates the Maharashtra power section and sets tariffs charged to power consumers by MSEB. The GOM is in control of MERC.

46. MSEB failed to make timely payments for power from the Project beginning in October 2000 and stopped payment altogether in early 2001. DPC began the formal process of terminating the PPA because of the MSEB's untimely payments and breaches of the PPA by issuing two Preliminary Termination Notices to MSEB on May 19, 2001. The Lenders consented to the issuance of the Preliminary Termination Notices, which OPIC supported.

47. On May 23, 2001, following directions from the GOM, MSEB purported to rescind the PPA. Two days later, MSEB filed an action before MERC seeking an

injunction to prevent DPC from pursuing arbitration against MSEB under the PPA for nonpayment, and to prevent DPC from exercising its rights to an Escrow Agreement with MSEB. On May 29, 2001, MSEB announced it would cease purchasing power from DPC.

48. MSEB's motivations for failing to pay for power, repudiating the PPA and petitioning MERC for an injunction were political. To the extent MSEB was experiencing financial hardship, it was caused solely and directly by political choices. In particular, the GOM and MSEB engaged in a program of politically motivated subsidies, handouts and favors to large power-consuming constituencies [. . .]

49. On May 29, 2001, two business days after MSEB filed its petition with MERC, MERC issued an order enjoining DPC from (a) exercising its right to seek redress through international arbitration pursuant to the dispute resolution clause of the PPA and (b) activating the escrow arrangements under the Escrow Agreement. The Bombay High Court and Indian Supreme Court subsequently continued the injunction. [. . .]

51. DPC demanded payment from the GOM under the GOM Guarantee in February and March 2001 for power payments that MSEB had refused to make. The GOM failed to pay on its Guarantee.

52. The GOM's decision not to pay DPC was a political choice: GOM politicians wanted to "scrap" the politically unpopular PPA. The decision was not due to the GOM's lack of financial resources.

53. DPC demanded payment from the GOI under the GOI Guarantee on March 7, 2001, after the GOM had failed to pay DPC. On advice from the GOM, the GOI declined to pay as well. The GOI had the ability to honor the GOI Guarantee, but chose not to for political reasons. [. . .]

57. [. . .] Pursuant to the termination procedures contained in the PPA, on October 15, 2001, DPC circulated a consent request letter to the Lenders, including OPIC, seeking permission to issue a Final Termination Notice. The Final Termination Notice was a necessary step to transfer the Project to the Indian government in exchange for the Transfer Amount.

58. [. . .] OPIC had the power to grant consent unilaterally, and if OPIC had timely consented to DPC's request, DPC would have been in a position to issue a Final Termination Notice immediately. [. . .]

59. Although some within OPIC supported the issuance of a Final Termination Notice, OPIC did not grant its consent in light of the "calculated risk" OPIC perceived. OPIC refused DPC's request for consent to issue the Final Termination Notice at least in part to avoid paying an expropriation claim under the Policies. OPIC internal documents from the period demonstrate this:

- "OPIC believes that project renegotiations offer the best chance for OPIC Finance to recover its loans, while reducing the risk of OPIC Insurance making a claim payment."

- "OPIC recognizes that the termination and transfer option has serious shortcomings. First, there is a greater risk that OPIC insurance might pay a claim."

[. . .]

61. On November 9, 2001, the Bombay High Court, at the request of the IFIs, enjoined DPC from issuing a Final Termination Notice under the PPA. The injunction made it impossible for DPC to go forward with the termination procedures provided for in the PPA or initiate the process of complying with para 10.05/10.07 of the Policies. [. . .]

63. On March 21, 2002, the Bombay High Court, at the request of the IFIs, appointed a receiver for DPC's physical assets and accounts. As a result, Claimants currently do not exercise control over the Project or any of its assets. MPDCL, a subsidiary of MSEB and shareholder of DPC, has also taken steps to prevent the Project Sponsors, including Claimants, from exercising their rights as shareholders of DPC pursuant to Indian company law.

64. From its inception to the present day, the Project has been a political lightning rod. Its existence has been defined by the push and pull of Indian politics. The expropriatory events were the sole and direct consequence of political decisions and competing political forces within Maharashtra and India. [. . .]

72. Claimants eventually learned that OPIC had no intention of paying their insurance claims. [. . .] In November 2002, Claimants consented to OPIC's request to consolidate their claims against OPIC into the present action. [. . .]

77. The damages suffered by Claimants exceed the policy limits of their respective insurance notices with OPIC.

Conclusions of Law

1. A Total Expropriation Within the Meaning of Section 4.01 of the OPIC Policies Has Taken Place.

Article IV of the Bechtel and GE policies set out four elements, subject to the exclusions provided for in Sec. 4.03 and limitations of Sec. 5.04, that must be present for an act or series of acts to constitute a total expropriation. We recite these elements followed by our findings as to each of them:

1.a. The acts are attributable to a foreign governing authority which is in de facto control of the part of the country in which the project is located. [. . .]

1.b. The acts are violations of international law without regard to the availability of local remedies or material breaches of local law.

The evidence makes clear that MSEB, the GOM, and the GOI violated each of (a) the PPA, (b) the GOM and GOI guarantees and (c) the State Support Agreements, for political reasons and without any legal justification. MERC, MSEB, the IFIs and the Indian courts have enjoined and otherwise taken away Claimant's international arbitration remedies under PPA, all in violation of established principles of international law, in disregard of India's commitments under the UN Convention as well as the Indian Arbitration Act.[. . .] OPIC has publicly acknowledged that the concerned acts of the lenders with the GOM and GOI have effectively destroyed the investment of Claimants in the DPC, all in violation of international and local law.

1.c. The acts directly deprive the Investor of fundamental rights in the insured investment (Rights are "fundamental" if without them the Investor is substantially deprived of the benefits of the investment);

There is no doubt that [. . .] the GOM and GOI refused to honor their respective guarantees, [. . .] and in this process deprived DPC of its international arbitral remedies under the Project Agreements that were the essential vehicle by which Claimants might have been able to recoup their investment in the Project.

1.d. The violations of law are not remedied and the expropriatory effect continues for six months. [. . .]

2. The exclusion under Section 4.03(b) does not apply here [. . .]

3. All of the acts undertaken, [. . .] were, openly political, and not commercially, motivated, thus eliminating the Section 4.03(b) exclusion. [. . .]

5. Claimants Complied With para 10.05/10.07 of The Policies.

Section 10.05/10.07 of the Policies provides for procedures which have to be followed in order for the investors to be entitled to receive compensation. [. . .] as the evidence was far from clear as to what Claimants or OPIC understood the insertion of para 10.05/10.07 to mean, the Panel has applied certain fundamental rules of insurance contract construction to para 10.05/10.07 and its impact on the contract.

6. In the event of uncertainty or ambiguity, insurance contracts are generally interpreted and construed against the drafting party. [. . .]

7. The evidence indicated that neither party had anticipated that the Indian courts would grant injunctions making it impracticable to comply with the provisions in the agreements that triggered computation of the Transfer Amount as contemplated under the contracts. Moreover, neither party at the hearing could produce any evidence which showed there was any precedent for the Indian courts issuing such an injunction. [. . .] The issuance of the injunction by the Indian courts rendered compliance with the provisions of para 10.05/10.07 by Claimants to be, at the very least, impracticable, if not impossible, without violating the terms of the court's injunction. [. . .]

9. [. . .] the panel is cognizant that to enforce compliance with the provisions of para 10.05/10.07 by claimants, when the reason for non-compliance was the unforeseen action of a party beyond the control of either Claimants or OPIC, namely MERC and the Indian Courts, would result in forfeiture of Claimant's rights under the insurance agreements.

10. For the reasons set forth above, the Panel finds that Claimants were discharged of their obligation to comply with the provisions para 10.05/10.07 as the result of the action of MERC and the Indian courts.

11. OPIC must pay Bechtel Enterprises International (Bermuda) Ltd. and Ben Dabhol Holdings, Ltd. a total of twenty-eight million five hundred and seventy thousand ($28,570,000).

12. OPIC must pay Capital India Power Mauritius I, the sum of twenty-eight million five hundred and seventy thousand ($28,570,000).

7. OPIC and the Tucker Act (28 U.S.C. § 1491)

Optiperu, SA v. Overseas Private Inv. Corp., 640 F. Supp. 420 (D.D.C. 1986).

Case Introduction

Optiperu, S.A. ("Optiperu"), a corporation organized under the laws of Peru, filed a breach of contract action in the United States District Court, District of Columbia seeking damages for the alleged breach by Overseas Private Investment Corporation ("OPIC") of a loan commitment of up to $275,000 to Optiperu for an eyeglass-lens manufacturing project in Peru. Optiperu seeks reliance damages in the amount of $75,000 and lost profits damages totaling more than $1,000,000 from OPIC.

The matter before the U.S. District Court concerns the defendant's motion to dismiss for lack of subject matter jurisdiction under Rule 12(b)(1) of the Federal Rules of Civil Procedure. Under the Tucker Act, subject matter jurisdiction for Optiperu's contract claim lies appropriately in the Court of Federal Claims.

Principal Points of the Judgment

I. The Complaint's Jurisdictional Contention: 22 U.S.C. § 2199(d)

In its complaint, Optiperu asserts that the Court has jurisdiction over Optiperu's contract claim under 22 U.S.C. § 2199(d). Section 2199(d) identifies the general corporate powers granted to OPIC by Congress. OPIC is authorized, inter alia, "to sue and be sued in its corporate name . . . ." Although this "sue and be sued clause" clearly represents a waiver of sovereign immunity as to OPIC, Section 2199(d) contains no express grant of jurisdiction to this or any other court to entertain an action brought by or against OPIC for an alleged breach of contract.

In *Portsmouth Redevelopment and Housing Authority v. Pierce*, 706 F.2d 471 (4th Cir.), cert. denied, 464 U.S. 960, 104 S. Ct. 392, 78 L. Ed. 2d 336 (1983), the Fourth Circuit held that a "sue and be sued clause," standing alone, merely waived sovereign immunity but did not confer subject matter jurisdiction on the district courts. [. . .] In *Van Drasek v. Lehman*, 762 F.2d 1065, 1071 n.10 (D.C.Cir. 1985), the United States Court of Appeals for the District of Columbia Circuit cited approvingly the "sue and be sued" analysis of the Fourth Circuit in *Portsmouth*.

In the present case, therefore, because 22 U.S.C. § 2199(d) authorizes OPIC only "to sue and be sued" in its corporate name, but fails to prescribe that suits brought by or against OPIC may be brought "in any court of competent jurisdiction, State or

Federal," the Court holds that Section 2199(d) represents merely a waiver of sovereign immunity as to OPIC and not a grant of subject matter jurisdiction to district courts to entertain contract actions naming OPIC as plaintiff or defendant. Cf. *Breitback v. United States*, 205 Ct.Cl. 208, 500 F.2d 556, 557-58 & 560 n.2 (1974) (Saint Lawrence Seaway Development Corporation, which "may sue and be sued in its corporate name," amenable to Claims Court jurisdiction and perhaps to jurisdiction of specific district court, where, under 33 U.S.C. § 984(a)(6), corporation "shall be held to be an inhabitant and resident of the northern judicial district of New York within the meaning of the laws of the United States relating to the venue of civil suits"). Moreover, Optiperu has failed in its complaint to name any other statutory provision specifically regarding OPIC, See 22 U.S.C. §§ 2191-2200b (1982 and Supp.1985), which could be so construed. Accordingly, because Optiperu, as plaintiff, bears the burden of establishing jurisdiction, and the basis of jurisdiction must appear on the face of the complaint, Optiperu's complaint shall be dismissed. *Tavoulareas v. Comnas*, 720 F.2d 192, 195 (D.C.Cir. 1983); Fed.R.Civ.P. 8(a)(1).

II. The "Tucker Act" vis-a-vis 28 U.S.C. § 1349.

In its motion to dismiss, OPIC not only argues correctly that 22 U.S.C. § 2199(d) does not confer jurisdiction on the Court over Optiperu's claim, OPIC contends that Optiperu's contract action falls under the Tucker Act, 28 U.S.C. §§ 1346(a) and 1491, so that this case belongs properly before the United States Claims Court. In its opposition to the motion to dismiss, however, Optiperu contests OPIC's Tucker Act contention by raising a second ground for this Court's jurisdiction, 28 U.S.C. § 1349, which provides as follows: "The district courts shall not have jurisdiction of any civil action by or against any corporation upon the ground that it was *incorporated by or under an Act of Congress, unless the United States is the owner of more than one-half of its capital stock*." (Emphasis added.)

Although Optiperu raises Section 1349 in its opposition, it has failed to cite this ground for jurisdiction in its complaint or to move to amend the same to include this new ground. Rather than order Optiperu to amend its complaint and thereby delay resolution of the subject matter jurisdiction question, however, the Court has evaluated the merits of the Tucker Act/Section 1349 debate. After due consideration of the arguments raised and briefed by the parties in this regard, the Court concludes both that the Tucker Act applies to Optiperu's contract claim against OPIC, and that Section 1349 does not represent a manifestation of Congress' intent to establish this Court as an alternative forum to the Claims Court for the adjudication of Optiperu's contract action for more than $10,000 against OPIC. Therefore, jurisdiction over Optiperu's claim shall lie in the Claims Court.

A. The Tucker Act: Claims for Money Damages against the United States

The Tucker Act consists of Sections 1346(a) and 1491 of Title 28 of the United States Code. 28 U.S.C. § 1346(a) provides in pertinent part as follows: "The district courts shall have original jurisdiction, concurrent with the United States Claims Court of: *** (2) Any ... civil action or claim *against the United States, not exceeding*

$10,000 in amount founded . . . upon any express or implied contract with the United States. . . ." (Emphasis added.) 28 U.S.C. § 1491(a)(1) provides in relevant part as follows: "The United States Claims Court shall have jurisdiction to render judgment upon any claim *against the United States founded . . . upon any express or implied contract with the United States. . . .*" (Emphasis added.) Thus, for money claims against the federal government up to and including $10,000, the Tucker Act grants concurrent jurisdiction to the district courts and the Claims Court. If a contract claim is for more than $10,000, however, this Circuit and others have held that exclusive jurisdiction lies in the Claims Court under Section 1491. See, e.g., *Doe v. United States Department of Justice*, 753 F.2d 1092, 1101 (D.C.Cir. 1985); *Graham v. Henegar*, 640 F.2d 732, 734 n. 5 (5th Cir. 1981); *Marcus Garvey Square, Inc. v. Winston Burnett Construction Co.*, 595 F.2d 1126, 1132 (9th Cir. 1979).

Although federal courts have thus generally characterized contract actions brought against the federal government according to the amount of damages in controversy, this simple bifurcation does not comprehensively delineate the jurisdictional framework of the Tucker Act. As made clear by this Circuit just last year:

> "*the jurisdiction of the Court of Claims for suits claiming more than $10,000 is not exclusive*; rather, there is rarely any statute available that waives sovereign immunity for suits in the district court, other than the Tucker Act with its $10,000 limit." The proper inquiry, then, is *whether the statute or statutes relied upon by the plaintiff manifest a congressional intent to consent to suits for money claims against the United States in the district courts notwithstanding the limitations found in the Tucker Act.*"

Van Drasek, 762 F.2d at 1071 n. 10 (quoting *Ghent v. Lynn*, 392 F. Supp. 879, 881 (D.Conn. 1975)). There is clearly more than $10,000 in controversy in Optiperu's contract action against OPIC. Therefore, if the Tucker Act applies to this case (see *infra* Part II. B.), and if 28 U.S.C. § 1349, the jurisdictional statute cited by Optiperu in its opposition, does not demonstrate a specific exception to the $10,000 limit rule (see *infra* Part II. C.), jurisdiction for this action lies exclusively in the Claims Court. See *Spectrum Leasing Corp. v. United States*, 764 F.2d 891, 895 n. 8 (D.C.Cir. 1985).

B. Applicability of the Tucker Act

28 U.S.C. § 1491, which defendant OPIC relies on, grants jurisdiction to the Claims Court over contract claims brought "against the United States," where the plaintiff seeks more than $10,000 in money damages. Thus, for a contract claim to be based upon the Tucker Act here, upon Section 1491(a)(1) it must be founded upon a contract that "'can fairly be interpreted as mandating compensation by the Federal government for the damages sustained.'" *Van Drasek*, 762 F.2d at 1070 (quoting *United States v. Mitchell*, 463 U.S. 206, 103 S. Ct. 2961, 77 L. Ed. 2d 580 (1983)). "The existence of a substantive right to recovery against the United States is a *jurisdictional* prerequisite to suit under the Tucker Act." 762 F.2d at 1070 n. 7 (emphasis in original). If Optiperu's contract claim for more than $10,000 against OPIC, a

corporation owned wholly by the United States, is properly characterized as a claim that would require, if prosecuted successfully, compensation from the federal government, Optiperu's claim falls under the Tucker Act.

The Claims Court has held that a contract action under the Tucker Act "is not precluded by the mere fact that the entity is a wholly-owned federal corporation." *Breitback*, 500 F.2d at 558 (discussing *Butz Engineering Corp. v. United States*, 204 Ct.Cl. 561, 499 F.2d 619 (1974)). The analysis required is two-tiered: A contract claim for more than $10,000 against such a corporation is subject to 28 U.S.C. § 1491 and, thereunder, the jurisdiction of the Claims Court, if, first, the defendant organization is "*functioning as an instrumentality of the Federal government*"; and, second, the party asserting district court jurisdiction cannot "*demonstrate some special reason*" why the Claims Court is without jurisdiction even though the agency is a federal instrumentality. 500 F.2d at 558 (emphasis added). See *infra* Part II. C.

After careful evaluation of the statutory provisions pertinent to OPIC's creation and operation, 22 U.S.C. §§ 2191-2200b (1982 and Supp.1985), the Court concludes that OPIC is an "instrumentality" of the federal government, and, accordingly, that the Tucker Act applies to Optiperu's contract claim.

OPIC's authority to issue the loan commitment at issue in this case is found in the mandate of Congress that established OPIC in order "[t]o mobilize and facilitate the participation of United States private capital and skills in the economic and social development of less developed friendly countries and areas, thereby *complementing the development assistance objectives of the United States* [. . .]." *Id.* § 2191 (emphasis added). Thus, OPIC was expressly created by Congress as "*an agency of the United States under the policy guidance of the Secretary of State.*" *Id.* (emphasis added). Furthermore, although OPIC is authorized by Congress to carry out commercial activities that can be characterized as private in nature, OPIC's transactions must further the policy interests of the federal government. See, e.g., *id.* § 2191(e)(1) & (2) (OPIC to give preferential consideration to projects sponsored by or involving "United States small business"); *id.* § 2191(h) (OPIC to further to "greatest degree possible [. . .] the balance of payments and employment objectives of the United States"); and, *id.* § 2191(i) (OPIC to conduct "activities in consonance with [. . .] [the] activities of [. . .] [the] agency primarily responsible for administering [. . .] international trade, investment, and financial policies of the United States Government, and to seek to support projects having positive trade benefits for the United States").

Nonetheless, even though OPIC is clothed with all of the trappings of a federal "instrumentality," Optiperu argues that, because of the nature of the transaction at issue i.e., the loan commitment negotiations, OPIC is not entitled to an instrumentality characterization by the Court.

In evaluating Optiperu's argument, the Court notes initially that OPIC is empowered by Congress to participate in three primary types of transactions: First, OPIC may "*issue insurance*" to eligible investors, *id.* § 2194(a)(1); second, OPIC *may issue* "*guaranties of loans*," *id.* § 2194(b); and third, OPIC may "*make loans* [. . .] to firms privately owned or of mixed private and public ownership upon such terms and conditions as [OPIC] may determine [. . .]" *id.* § 2194(c) (emphasis added). The loan commitment negotiations at issue fall under the last of these provisions.

Where insurance and guaranties are concerned, "Congress, in considering the budget programs transmitted by the President for [OPIC], may limit the obligations and contingent liabilities to be undertaken [. . .] as well as the use of funds for operating and administrative expenses." *Id.* § 2195(a)(4). Moreover, "[t]here shall be established in the Treasury of the United States an insurance and guaranty fund, which shall have separate accounts to be known as the Insurance Reserve and the Guaranty Reserve, which reserves shall be available for discharge of liabilities." *Id.* § 2195(c).

On the other hand, Congress apparently possesses no corresponding power of limitation over "obligations and contingent liabilities to be undertaken" by OPIC where direct investment loans are concerned. In addition, as Optiperu points out, "[t]here shall be established *a revolving fund, known as the Direct Investment Fund, to be held by [OPIC]. Such fund* [. . .] *shall be available for [loans]* authorized under [22 U.S.C. § 2194(c)]" *Id.* § 2195(b). Finally, "*all revenues and income* transferred to or earned by [OPIC], from whatever source derived, *shall be held by [OPIC]* and shall be available to carry out its purposes, including without limitation—(a) *payment of all expenses of [OPIC]*." *Id.* § 2196 (emphasis added.) Optiperu maintains that "expenses" payable by OPIC under Section 2196(a) would include satisfaction of a judgment arising from a successful breach of contract action against OPIC.

In sum, Optiperu argues that the Court may not properly characterize OPIC as an instrumentality of the federal government, because Congress retains no express power of limitation over the obligations and contingent liabilities to be undertaken by OPIC in a loan context, because OPIC holds the Direct Investment Fund from which loans are made available, and because a judgment against OPIC would be payable as an expense out of the revenues and income held by OPIC. Optiperu concludes, therefore, that this contract action against OPIC for more than $10,000 is not subject to the Tucker Act: as an entity that can "sue and be sued" in its corporate name under 22 U.S.C. § 2199(d), OPIC's legal identity is wholly separate from that of the federal government; and, accordingly, recovery would not come from the United States Treasury.

Although impressive analytically, Optiperu's argument proves merely to highlight distinctions without differences. First, although it is true that no express provision prescribes for Congress a power of limitation over obligations and contingent liabilities to be undertaken by OPIC in a loan context (vis-a-vis, insurance or guaranty contexts), OPIC, a designated "agency of the United States" under 22 U.S.C. § 2191, is subject to the express congressional proscription that "[l]oans may be made [. . .] *only for projects that are sponsored by or significantly involve United States small business or cooperatives*." *Id.* § 2194(c) (2) (emphasis added). Thus, Congress has, in fact, by statute restricted OPIC's authority to extend loans to achieve a single legislative purpose. Whenever OPIC enters into loan commitment negotiations with a firm such as Optiperu, it acts, necessarily, as an agent of the federal government.

Second, the fact that the funding for direct investment loans is held by OPIC while the reserve accounts for insurance and guaranties are established in the United States Treasury is readily justifiable in practical terms, and in no way weakens OPIC's status as an instrumentality of the federal government. In an insurance or guaranty context, OPIC becomes liable to a qualified investor only if that investor suffers losses that result from the materialization of risks originally contemplated in the pertinent insurance or guaranty agreement. OPIC never uses this funding unless and until it is needed; and, in the meantime, the respective reserve accounts are more appropriately retained and managed by the Treasury. In contrast, in order for OPIC to operate efficiently as an agency that extends loans for projects that are sponsored by or significantly involve United States small business or cooperatives, OPIC must have available funding directly in hand. It is difficult, if not impossible, for the Court to conceive of how OPIC could effectively manage its congressionally mandated loan program if Congress had required OPIC to turn to the Treasury Department each and every time OPIC approved a loan application submitted by a qualified business firm. Although the funding mechanism prescribed by Congress for OPIC's insurance and guaranty programs differs from the mechanism prescribed for OPIC's loan program, the Court will not deny OPIC an instrumentality characterization under the Tucker Act on this basis.

Finally, Optiperu's contention that any judgment secured by it in this contract action would be satisfied out of OPIC's own funds, because under 22 U.S.C. § 2196(a) all of OPIC's "expenses" are to be satisfied out of the revenue and income held solely by OPIC, does not require the Court to eradicate OPIC's status as a federal instrumentality. If Optiperu prevails ultimately on its claim, OPIC may very well prove to satisfy the resulting judgment out of its own revenues and income. Nevertheless, as OPIC, through its counsel, the United States Attorney for the District of Columbia, concedes readily in its motion to dismiss (at 3-4 & n. 13), where an agency is functioning as an instrumentality of the federal government, and that agency has the power to sue or be sued in its own name, the concurrent liability of the United States as a principal is not necessarily nullified. *Butz Engineering*, 499 F.2d at 625. Thus, the United States would be jointly or severally liable for any money damages obtained by Optiperu in the appropriate forum. Optiperu may be required, therefore, to name the United States as a defendant. See *Gibbons v. Republic of Ireland*, 532 F. Supp. 668, 671 & n. 3 (D.D.C. 1982) (Gesell, J.) (although immunity of United States is not abrogated when Congress provides merely that an agency or instrumentality may sue or be sued, "United States may be proper party defendant" where action arises from conduct of agency with power to sue and be sued and independent waiver of immunity of United States such as Tucker Act is applicable to action in question).

The Court concludes that, because Optiperu's contract claim for more than $10,000 against OPIC is a claim for money damages against the United States, Optiperu's action falls under the Tucker Act.

C. 28 U.S.C. § 1349

Where the Tucker Act applies, jurisdiction over a claim for money damages against the United States in excess of $10,000 lies exclusively in the Claims Court, unless the party seeking district court jurisdiction can demonstrate "some special reason" why the Claims Court lacks jurisdiction. *Breitback*, 500 F.2d at 558. More specifically, the "question turns solely on whether Congress has manifested an intent to provide an alternative forum for adjudication of claims that would otherwise fall under the Tucker Act." *Spectrum Leasing*, 764 F.2d at 895 n. 8. In its opposition to OPIC's motion to dismiss ("Opp."), Optiperu asserts that 28 U.S.C. § 1349 represents such a manifestation of congressional intent for contract claims brought against OPIC.

Section 1349, a "special federal question" provision, provides as follows: "The district courts shall not have jurisdiction of any civil action by or against any corporation upon the ground that it was incorporated by or under an Act of Congress, *unless the United States is the owner of more than one-half of its capital stock.*" (Emphasis added.) Optiperu asserts that "[t]he implication fairly drawn from Section 1349 is that a corporation that is more than 50% owned by the U.S. Government and is created by an act of Congress (both of which requirements are met by OPIC) is amenable to the jurisdiction of [this] court." Opp. at 3. Thus, without having amended its complaint to include Section 1349, Optiperu contends that this section confers jurisdiction on the Court to entertain Optiperu's contract claim.

Optiperu relies, however, too heavily on this simple reading of Section 1349. In *Graham*, 640 F.2d at 734, the Fifth Circuit held that neither 28 U.S.C. § 1331 (general federal question jurisdiction) nor 28 U.S.C. § 1337 (commerce clause jurisdiction) could be used to override the exclusive jurisdiction of the Claims Court over contract claims against the United States in excess of $10,000 as enunciated by the Tucker Act. As the Graham panel made clear:

> Because adjudication in a federal district court of a lawsuit that falls within the exclusive jurisdiction of the Court of Claims would seriously undermine the purposes of the Tucker Act, courts confronting the issue have consistently held that *the Court of Claims is the sole forum for the adjudication of such a claim, even though the claim would otherwise fall within the coverage of some other statute [e.g., 28 U.S.C. § 1349] conferring jurisdiction on the district court.*

640 F.2d at 734 (emphasis added). The law of this Circuit is consistent with the analysis of *Graham*. As both *Spectrum Leasing*, 764 F.2d at 895 n. 8, and *Van Drasek*, 762 F.2d at 1071 n. 10 make clear, Congress must have manifested a clear intent to provide an alternative forum e.g., the district courts for the adjudication of a claim that would otherwise lie within the exclusive jurisdiction of the Claims Court under 28 U.S.C. § 1491. Even though Optiperu contends that "[t]here is an abundance of law involving governmentally-owned corporations ...," apart from the Tucker Act and under 28 U.S.C. § 1349, it fails to cite and the Court has failed to

locate a single case, in this or any other Circuit, that has specifically held that Congress intended Section 1349 to override Section 1491 where OPIC is the defendant in a breach of contract action for more than $10,000. The Court refuses, therefore, to give Section 1349 the broad reading Optiperu requests in the present case, and Optiperu's claim, a claim falling under the Tucker Act, shall be dismissed for want of this Court's jurisdiction. See *Breitback*, 500 F.2d at 560.

[. . .]

ORDER

In accordance with the Court's Memorandum Opinion issued contemporaneously herewith, it is by the Court this 21st day of April, 1986, hereby

ORDERED that defendant's motion to dismiss the complaint pursuant to Fed. R. Civ. P. 12(b)(1) is GRANTED; and it is

FURTHER ORDERED that the above-captioned action is dismissed.

Solaria Corp. v. United States, 123 Fed. Cl. 105 (2015).

Case Introduction

In 2010, Solaria Corporation, a Delaware Corporation doing business in California, and Solaria India Private Limited (collectively herein "Solaria") developed a business plan to increase production of solar panels in India ("the India Project"). Solaria Corporation manufactures and sells solar panels; Solaria India Private Limited is a subsidiary that produces solar panels in India.

Between October 2010 and April 2011, Solaria and the Overseas Private Investment Corporation ("OPIC") discussed financing for the India Project. In April 2011, Solaria began negotiating a commitment letter for OPIC to provide $30 million in debt financing for the India Project that OPIC allegedly represented would be available in late 2011 or early 2012. Between May and September 2011, OPIC conducted due diligence on the India Project. In May 2011, an OPIC team visited Solaria's office in Fremont, California for several days. During this visit, OPIC's Managing Director stated that "the results were among the smoothest and strongest OPIC had ever had from a due diligence investigation" and that she would recommend approval of the India Project and Solaria could expect financing within two months of the commitment letter's execution.

On September 29, 2011, the parties executed a Commitment Letter that provided a loan facility in the aggregate principal amount of up to US$30,000,000. In December 2011, Solaria elected not to pursue additional sources of debt financing.

On April 5, 2012, OPIC senior management advised Solaria officials that "the deal was done," and added that "it was a matter of completing the paperwork and formalities" and apologized for the delay. On September 16, 2012, OPIC informed Solaria that it was withdrawing its loan commitment and cited continuing dramatic deterioration in panel prices that appeared to make it very challenging for Solaria to stay on the business plan that was the basis for OPICs credit approval.

On December 3, 2013, Solaria filed a Complaint in the United States Court of Federal Claims, alleging eight counts including breach of contract, tort of fraud, breach of good faith and fair dealing and seeking $28,673,236.81 in damages.

Principal Points of the Judgment

[. . .]

A. Jurisdiction.

The United States Court of Federal Claims has jurisdiction under the Tucker Act, 28 U.S.C. § 1491, "to render judgment upon any claim against the United States founded either upon the Constitution, or any Act of Congress or any regulation of an executive department, or upon any express or implied contract with the United States, or for liquidated or unliquidated damages in cases not sounding in tort." 28 U.S.C. § 1491(a)(1). The Tucker Act, however, is "a jurisdictional statute; it does not create any substantive right enforceable against the United States for money damages [. . . .] [T]he Act merely confers jurisdiction upon [the United States Court of Federal Claims] whenever the substantive right exists." *United States v. Testan*, 424 U.S. 392, 398 (1976).

To pursue a substantive right under the Tucker Act, a plaintiff must identify and plead an independent contractual relationship, Constitutional provision, federal statute, and/or executive agency regulation that provides a substantive right to money damages. See *Todd v. United States*, 386 F.3d 1091, 1094 (Fed. Cir. 2004) ("[J]urisdiction under the Tucker Act requires the litigant to identify a substantive right for money damages against the United States separate from the Tucker Act[.]"); see also *Fisher v. United States*, 402 F.3d 1167, 1172 (Fed. Cir. 2005) (en banc) ("The Tucker Act [. . .] does not create a substantive cause of action; . . . a plaintiff must identify a separate source of substantive law that creates the right to money damages. [T]hat source must be 'money-mandating.'"). Specifically, a plaintiff must demonstrate that the source of substantive law upon which he relies "can fairly be interpreted as mandating compensation by the Federal Government[.]" *Testan*, 424 U.S. at 400. And, the plaintiff bears the burden of establishing jurisdiction by a preponderance of the evidence. See *Reynolds v. Army & Air Force Exch. Serv.*, 846 F.2d 746, 748 (Fed. Cir. 1988) ("[O]nce the [trial] court's subject matter jurisdiction [is] put in question [the plaintiff] bears the burden of establishing subject matter jurisdiction by a preponderance of the evidence."). [. . .]

[. . .] Plaintiffs suffered monetary injury that is concrete, particularized, and fairly traceable to OPIC's actions. Any financial injury established by Plaintiffs also can be redressed by a monetary award. For these reasons, the court has determined that Plaintiffs have standing to seek adjudication of the claims alleged in the December 3, 2013 Complaint.

[. . .]

Count III — Breach of Contract.

The Government's Argument.

[. . .]

The September 29, 2011 Commitment Letter "allows OPIC to withdraw from its commitment for a number of reasons." Gov't Mot. at 24 (citing Compl. Ex. A at 4) "OPIC may, at any time, terminate its obligations hereunder and pursue any rights and remedies then available to OPIC upon the occurrence of any of the following: (a) the Sponsor or the Borrower fails or refuses to comply in a timely manner with any of the terms, provisions, or conditions of this Commitment Letter; (b) OPIC, in its sole judgment, determines that a material adverse change has occurred or is reasonably likely to occur [. . .]; or (e) OPIC, in its sole judgment, is not satisfied with the results of its due diligence investigation."; see also Gov't Reply at 8 ("[W]hether [Plaintiffs] complied with the terms of the [C]ommitment [L]etter or not, OPIC, in its sole discretion, had the right to terminate the [C]ommitment [L]etter."). As such, Plaintiffs "assumed the risk" that OPIC would withdraw. Gov't Reply at 8; *see* also Gov't Reply at 9 ("Even though [Plaintiffs] contend[] that economic conditions were still favorable for the [India P]roject's potential success at the time OPIC cancelled the commitment, this, too, was for OPIC, not [Plaintiffs], to decide.").

[. . .]

Plaintiffs' Response.

Plaintiffs respond that the September 29, 2011 Commitment Letter is a binding contract, because a meeting of the minds occurred. Pl. Resp. at 14. "All agreements have some degree of indefiniteness and some degree of uncertainty." Pl. Resp. at 15 (citing Restatement (Second) of Contracts § 33 cmt. a ("[T]he actions of the parties may show conclusively that they have intended to conclude a binding agreement, even though one or more terms are missing or are left to be agreed upon. In such cases courts endeavor, if possible, to attach a sufficiently definite meaning to the bargain.")). And, "OPIC [. . .] has not managed to point to a single term that would be in the final loan agreement that the parties have a disagreement about or that is unclear in the Commitment Letter." Pl. Resp. at 15–16. As such, "discovery [will] demonstrate that OPIC was fabricating its concerns in order to end the loan for political reasons," not due to a "dispute about how to interpret or implement a term in the Commitment Letter loan agreement[.]"

In sum, Plaintiffs fulfilled all of the conditions in the September 29, 2011 Commitment Letter. Pl. Resp. at 18. "No reason exists for OPIC to have found either a material adverse change or unsatisfactory due diligence." Pl. Resp. at 19. And, even if OPIC identified a material change, the specific terms of agreement would govern over the more general language granting OPIC discretion to withdraw. Pl. Resp. at 20. As such, OPIC "fail[ed] to negotiate in good faith," constituting a breach of contract. Pl. Resp. at 19.

The Court's Resolution.

As a preliminary matter, the court must determine whether the September 29, 2011 Commitment Letter was a contract. "The elements necessary to determine that a contract exists are [. . .] (1) mutuality of intent to contract; (2) consideration; and

(3) lack of ambiguity in offer and acceptance." *D & N Bank v. United States*, 331 F.3d 1374, 1378 (Fed. Cir. 2003). And, "[w]hen the United States is a party, a fourth requirement is added: the [G]overnment representative whose conduct is relied upon must have actual authority to bind the [G]overnment in contract." *Id.* In this case, the parties agree that the September 29, 2011 Commitment Letter is a contract. See Gov't Reply at 8 (stating that the September 29, 2011 Commitment Letter "is a binding contract to *consider* making a loan") (emphasis in original); Pl. Resp. at 14 (stating that the September 29, 2011 Commitment Letter represented a "meeting of the minds"). The September 29, 2011 Commitment Letter evidences the four necessary elements of a Government contract, because the parties demonstrated: (1) mutuality of intent to contract by agreeing that the September 29, 2011 Commitment Letter "shall constitute an effective and legally binding agreement among [the parties]" and signing thereto (Compl. Ex. A at 6); (2) consideration by "OPIC's commitment to provide . . . a loan facility" and Plaintiffs' agreement to repay the loan, including interest and fees (Compl. Ex. A at 2–3); (3) lack of ambiguity in offer and acceptance by stating that "OPIC is willing to provide the Credit Facility" and that "the Borrower confirms that it is willing to borrow a loan or loans" (Compl. Ex. A at 2); and (4) authority to bind the Government by having Ms. Tabernacki, OPIC's Managing Director, sign the September 29, 2011 Commitment Letter (Compl. Ex. A at 6).

Next, the court must determine whether OPIC breached the September 29, 2011 Commitment Letter. "A breach of contract claim requires two components: (1) an obligation or duty arising out of the contract and (2) factual allegations sufficient to support the conclusion that there has been a breach of the identified contractual duty." *Bell/Heery v. United States*, 739 F.3d 1324, 1330 (Fed. Cir. 2014) (citing *San Carlos Irrigation & Drainage Dist. v. United States*, 877 F.2d 957, 959 (Fed. Cir. 1989) ("To recover for breach of contract, a party must allege and establish: (1) a valid contract between the parties, (2) an obligation or duty arising out of the contract, (3) a breach of that duty, and (4) damages caused by the breach.")).

First, to identify the "obligation or duty arising out of the contract," the court must interpret the September 29, 2011 Commitment Letter. "In interpreting a contract, [the court] begin[s] with the plain language," and "interpret[s] the contract in a manner that gives meaning to all of its provisions and makes sense." *Massie v. United States*, 166 F.3d 1184, 1189 (Fed. Cir. 1999) (citations omitted). The plain language of the September 29, 2011 Commitment Letter expressly provides that it is not a loan agreement but only provides the terms if an agreement is reached. Compl. Ex. A at 4 ("If for any reason the Loan Agreement is not executed and delivered on or before [December 31, 2012], OPIC's obligations hereunder shall terminate."); Compl. Ex A at 8 (entitling the term sheet as "Indicative Terms and Conditions for the Proposed Direct Loan Transaction") (emphasis added); Compl. Ex. A at 13 ("The terms and conditions of the Loan shall be set forth in a definitive loan agreement between OPIC and the Borrower ('the Loan Agreement')[.]"). In addition, OPIC's obligation to make the loan was subject to OPIC's "sole" determination that Plaintiffs fulfilled certain conditions prior to December 31, 2012. Compl. Ex. A at 4. Therefore, the September 29, 2011 Commitment Letter only bound OPIC to negotiate a potential loan agreement, subject to Plaintiffs' fulfillment of certain conditions to OPIC's satisfaction and the execution of a loan agreement prior to a specific date.

Second, as to the "factual allegations sufficient to support the conclusion that there has been a breach of the identified contractual duty," the court must determine whether Plaintiffs alleged sufficient facts to support a claim that OPIC breached its duty. See [*Bell. Atl. Corp. v.*] *Twombly*, 550 U.S. at 555 (holding that the plaintiff's factual allegations, making all reasonable inferences in the plaintiff's favor, must be substantial enough to raise the right to relief "above the speculative level"). This requires consideration of OPIC's discretion to terminate the September 29, 2011 Commitment Letter and the reasons proffered by OPIC provided for termination.

[. . .]

Therefore, OPIC properly exercised its discretion to "terminate its obligations" under the September 29, 2011 Commitment Letter, because OPIC determined, "in its sole judgment, [that it was] not satisfied with the results of its due diligence investigation."

Equally important is the fact that the September 29, 2011 Commitment Letter provided that "[i]f for any reason the Loan Agreement is not executed and delivered on or before March 30, 2012, OPIC's obligations hereunder shall terminate." ("On March 28, 2012, the parties mutually agreed that the Commitment letter would expire on 31 December 2012 rather than 30 March 2012."). It is undisputed that the loan agreement was never executed. Therefore, "OPIC's obligations [. . .] terminate[d]." Compl. Ex. A at 4.

For these reasons, the court has determined that Count III of the December 3, 2013 Complaint does not allege sufficient facts of OPIC's alleged breach of the September 29, 2011 Commitment Letter to raise the right to relief "above the speculative level." *Twombly*, 550 U.S. at 555. As such, Count III is dismissed "for failure to state a claim upon which relief can be granted [.]" RCFC 12(b)(6).

[. . .]

Count VI—Breach of Duty of Good Faith and Fair Dealing and Count VIII—Bad Faith Denial.

The Government's Argument.

[. . .]

"[A]lthough couched in terms of a breach of the implied duty of good faith and fair dealing, the allegations really charge OPIC with bad faith termination. This however, requires a specific intent by OPIC to injure [Plaintiffs]." Gov't Mot. at 35 (citing *Kalvar Corp. v. United States*, 211 Ct. Cl. 192, 199 (1976) ("[S]pecific intent to injure the plaintiff" is required to demonstrate a breach of the duty of good faith and fair dealing.)). The December 3, 2013 Complaint, however, does not allege specific intent to injure Plaintiffs but instead alleges that OPIC's actions constitute bad faith. Gov't Mot. at 36–38.

Again, the September 29, 2011 Commitment Letter only obligated OPIC to negotiate towards a loan agreement, so "OPIC's 'refusal' to provide [Plaintiffs] with $30 million of public money is not sufficient evidence to establish a breach of the covenant of good faith and fair dealing." Gov't Mot. at 36 (citing *Metcalf Constr. Co. v. United States*, 742 F.3d 984, 991 (Fed. Cir. 2013) (holding that "the duty's focus [is] on 'faithfulness to an agreed upon common purpose and consistency with the justified expectations of the other party")). [. . .] In addition, OPIC was not responsible for ensuring that Plaintiffs did not invest the potential loan funds prior to closing, since Plaintiffs were aware that OPIC might decide not to make the loan. Gov't Reply at 16. "OPIC simply exercised an express right in the [C]ommitment [L]etter." Gov't Reply at 16.

Plaintiffs' Response.

Plaintiffs respond that OPIC violated the duty of good faith and fair dealing "[b]y having [Plaintiffs] spend $30 million to change to a tier one manufacturer, implement a marketing program, begin production and meet control requirements[.]" Pl. Resp. at 29. Although OPIC had discretion to terminate the September 29, 2011 Commitment Letter, "it was implicit that OPIC would exercise its sole discretion in a manner consistent with the purpose of the commitment." Pl. Resp. at 28. Instead, OPIC's actions "frustrated the purpose of the commitment." Pl. Resp. at 28. In particular, OPIC "contrive[d] various excuses to cancel the loan rather than informing [Plaintiffs] that OPIC had changed its mind." Pl. Resp. at 29. And, OPIC misrepresented the applicable law by stating that New York law did not apply. Pl. Resp. at 27.

In addition, OPIC's November 9, 2012 letter demonstrates specific intent to injure Plaintiffs, because "OPIC cancelled the loan for reasons outside the purview of the Commitment Letter—political embarrassment[.]" Pl. Resp. at 31. "OPIC did not want the circumstances of the loan to be publicized, but rather contrived false reasons to end the loan." Pl. Resp. at 32. Therefore, OPIC acted in bad faith. Pl. Resp. at 30.

The Court's Resolution.

As a matter of law, the covenant of good faith and fair dealing "imposes obligations on both contracting parties that include the duty not to interfere with the other party's performance and not to act so as to destroy the reasonable expectations of the other party regarding the fruits of the contract." *Centex Corp. v. United States*, 395 F.3d 1283, 1304 (Fed. Cir. 2005). Both the "duty not to hinder and the duty to cooperate are aspects of the implied duty of good faith and fair dealing." *Precision Pine & Timber, Inc. v. United States*, 596 F.3d 817, 820 n.1 (Fed. Cir. 2010). "What is promised or disclaimed in a contract helps define what constitutes 'lack of diligence and interference with or failure to cooperate in the other party's performance.'" *Metcalf*, 742 F.3d at 991 (quoting *Malone v. United States*, 849 F.2d 1441, 1445 (Fed. Cir. 1988)).

[...]

For these reasons, the court has determined that the December 3, 2013 Complaint does not allege sufficient facts of OPIC's alleged breach of the implied duty of good faith and fair dealing to raise the right to relief "above the speculative level." *Twombly*, 550 U.S. at 555.[10] As such, Counts VI and VIII are dismissed for "failure to state a claim upon which relief can be granted[.]" RCFC 12(b)(6).

Whether the Court Has Jurisdiction to Adjudicate Counts I, II, V, and VII of the December 3, 2013 Complaint.

Count I—Failure to Pay Appropriate Termination for Convenience Costs.

The Government's Argument

The Government argues that the court does not have jurisdiction to adjudicate Count I, concerning failure to pay costs for a termination for convenience. Gov't Mot. at 16–18. The loan "OPIC contemplated making to [Plaintiffs] is not subject to the [Contracts Disputes Act ('CDA')], because a loan is not a procurement of property or services." Gov't Mot. at 17 (citing 41 U.S.C. §7102(a)[11]; see also *New Era Constr. v. United States*, 890 F.2d 1152, 1157 (Fed. Cir. 1989) (explaining that "procurement" is the "acquisition by purchase, lease or barter, of property or services for the *direct benefit* or use of the Federal Government") (emphasis in original); *Laudes Corp. v. United States*, 86 Fed. Cl. 152, 161 (2009) (stating that the CDA "extends only to the *procurement* of services by the Government and not the *provision* of such services") (emphasis in original)). Here, "OPIC did not procure a service but, instead, provided a service, namely offering the loan for [Plaintiffs] to invest in its facility in India." Gov't Reply at 5.

[...]

Plaintiffs' Response.

Plaintiffs respond that "none of the cases quoted by [the Government] address the question [of] whether the interest paid to the Government under a loan contract constitutes 'property or services for the direct benefit or use of the Federal Government'—the key CDA language." Pl. Resp. at 9. The September 29, 2011 Commitment Letter "provides for large interest payments to be made to the U[nited] S[tates] Government," and OPIC "generated $426 million in profits last year" from these payments. Pl. Resp. at 10. Thus, the court must determine "whether interest payments paid to OPIC constitute property for the direct benefit of the Government." Pl. Resp. at 10. And, the interest payments are clearly property. Pl. Resp. at 10–11.[12]

The Court's Resolution.

Section 7102(a) of the CDA applies to "(1) the procurement of property, other than real property in being; (2) the procurement of services; (3) the procurement of construction, alteration, repair, or maintenance of real property; or (4) the disposal of personal property." 41 U.S.C. §7102(a) (emphases added). A procurement is characterized by "the acquisition by purchase, lease or barter, of property or services for the *direct benefit or use* of the Federal Government[.]" *New Era*, 890 F.2d at 1157 (citation omitted) (emphasis in original); see also *Delta S.S. Lines, Inc. v. United States*, 3 Cl. Ct. 559, 569 (1983) ("It is [. . .] the conventional contract for the direct procurement of property, services and construction, to be used directly by the Government, which is the type of Government contract covered by the Act.").

Again, in this case, OPIC was neither procuring services nor receiving any direct benefit from Plaintiffs. Instead, if Plaintiffs were approved, OPIC would provide Plaintiffs with a loan commitment, but Plaintiffs would be required to reimburse OPIC for the loan, as well as the associated interest and fees. Compl. Ex. A at 1. Therefore, the December 3, 2013 Complaint does not allege a claim under the CDA. See 41 U.S.C. 7102(a); see also *New Era*, 890 F.2d at 1157.

For these reasons, the court has determined that it does not have jurisdiction under the CDA to adjudicate Count I of the December 3, 2013 Complaint. As such, Count I is dismissed. See RCFC 12(b)(1). [. . .]

D. United States International Development Finance Corporation

In February 2018, in the U.S. Senate, Senator Bob Corker introduced the Better Utilization of Investments Leading to Development Act of 2018 or the BUILD Act. It was incorporated into House bill FAA Reauthorization Act of 2018 and passed the House in September 2018, the Senate in October 2018, and was signed by President Trump on October 5, 2018. This bipartisan legislation replaces the Overseas Private Investment Corporation ("OPIC") with the United States International Development Finance Corporation ("IDFC"), a wholly owned government corporation.

This self-sustaining development finance corporation will facilitate the participation of private sector capital and skills in the economic development of countries with low- or lower-middle-income economies and countries transitioning from nonmarket to market economies. The IDFC loan liability cap, which stands at $60 billion, is twice the OPIC cap of $29 billion. This will double the total U.S. development finance portfolio to $60 billion. In an apparent move to counter Chinese-backed investments globally, this new U.S. agency would itself issue direct loans, including local currency loans, and invest and lend capital for projects, no longer relying solely on the private sector. The IDFC would not provide assistance to a country whose government has repeatedly supported acts of international terrorism, or a private sector entity that is engaged in monopolistic practices.

The Act prescribes transitional provisions, including transferring to the corporation the functions, personnel, assets, and liabilities of the Overseas Private Investment Corporation (which is subsequently terminated) and specified elements of the U.S. Agency for International Development (USAID).

As with the House bill, the amended Senate text incorporated changes to address conservative criticism, starting with shortening the authorization to seven years versus twenty years in the previous version.

The final text removes a specific instruction for the USIDFC to "develop appropriate policies and guidelines" with regard to state-owned enterprises ("SOE") and sovereign wealth funds. It does not prohibit the USIDFC from supporting or investing in SOEs owned by foreign governments. The prohibition on support to monopolies was also removed from the original bill.[91]

Division F—Build Act of 2018.

SEC. 1401. SHORT TITLE.

This division may be cited as the "Better Utilization of Investments Leading to Development Act of 2018" or the "BUILD Act of 2018".

SEC. 1402. DEFINITIONS.

In this division:

[. . .]

(2) LESS DEVELOPED COUNTRY.—The term "less developed country" means a country with a low-income economy, lower-middle-income economy, or upper-middle-income economy, as defined by the International Bank for Reconstruction and Development and the International Development Association (collectively referred to as the "World Bank").

[. . .]

TITLE I—ESTABLISHMENT

SEC. 1411. STATEMENT OF POLICY.

It is the policy of the United States to facilitate market-based private sector development and economic growth in less developed countries through the provision of credit, capital, and other financial support—

(1) to mobilize private capital in support of sustainable, broad-based economic growth, poverty reduction, and development through demand-driven partnerships with the private sector that further the foreign policy interests of the United States;

(2) to finance development in a way that builds and strengthens civic institutions, promotes competition, provides for public accountability and transparency;

(3) to help private sector actors overcome identifiable market gaps and inefficiencies without distorting markets;

(4) to achieve clearly defined economic and social development outcomes;

91. Sec. 505. Market displacement by state-owned enterprises and monopolies. (b)—The Corporation may not provide support under title II to private sector entities engaged in monopolistic practices.

(5) to coordinate with institutions with purposes similar to the purposes of the Corporation to leverage resources of those institutions to produce the greatest impact;

(6) to help countries currently receiving United States assistance to graduate from their status as recipients of assistance;

(7) to leverage the private sector and innovative development tools as a means to lessen the reliance of the United States on traditional forms of foreign assistance over time; and

(8) to complement and be guided by overall United States foreign policy and development objectives, taking into account the policies of countries receiving support.

SEC. 1412. UNITED STATES INTERNATIONAL DEVELOPMENT FINANCE CORPORATION.

(a) Establishment.—There is established in the Executive branch the United States International Development Finance Corporation (in this Act referred to as the "Corporation"), which shall be a wholly owned Government corporation (as defined in section 9101 of title 31, United States Code).

(b) Purpose.—The purpose of the Corporation shall be to mobilize and facilitate the participation of private sector capital and skills in the economic development of less developed countries, as described in subsection (c), and countries in transition from nonmarket to market economies, in order to complement the development assistance objectives, and advance the foreign policy interests, of the United States. In carrying out its purpose, the Corporation, utilizing broad criteria, shall take into account in its financing operations the economic and financial soundness of projects for which it provides support under title II.

(c) Less Developed Economy Focus.—

(1) IN GENERAL.—The Corporation shall prioritize the provision of support under title II in countries with low-income economies or lower-middle-income economies, as defined by the World Bank.

(2) SUPPORT IN COUNTRIES WITH UPPER-MIDDLE-INCOME ECONOMIES.—The Corporation shall restrict the provision of support under title II in a country with an upper-middle-income economy, as defined by the World Bank, unless—

(A) the President determines such support furthers the national economic or foreign policy interests of the United States; and

(B) such support is likely to be highly developmental or provide developmental benefits to the poorest population of that country.

SEC. 1413. MANAGEMENT OF CORPORATION.

(a) STRUCTURE OF CORPORATION.—There shall be in the Corporation a Board of Directors (in this division referred to as the "Board"), a Chief Executive Officer, a Deputy Chief Executive Officer, a Chief Risk Officer, a Chief Development Officer, and such other officers as the Board may determine.

(b) BOARD OF DIRECTORS. [. . .]

(c) PUBLIC HEARINGS.—The Board shall hold at least 2 public hearings each year in order to afford an opportunity for any person to present views with respect to whether—

(1) the Corporation is carrying out its activities in accordance with this division; and

(2) any support provided by the Corporation under title II in any country should be suspended, expanded, or extended.

[. . .]

(d) CHIEF EXECUTIVE OFFICER.—There shall be in the Corporation a Chief Executive Officer, who shall be appointed by the President, by and with the advice and consent of the Senate, and who shall serve at the pleasure of the President.

[. . .]

SEC. 1421. AUTHORITIES RELATING TO PROVISION OF SUPPORT.

[. . .]

(b) Lending And Guaranties.—

(1) IN GENERAL.—The Corporation may make loans or guarantee loans upon such terms and conditions as the Corporation may determine.

(2) DENOMINATION.—Loans and guaranties issued under paragraph (1) may be denominated and repayable in United States dollars or foreign currencies. Foreign currency denominated loans and guaranties should only be provided if the Board determines there is a substantive policy rationale for such loans and guaranties.

[. . .]

(c) Equity Investments.—

(1) IN GENERAL.—The Corporation may, as a minority investor, support projects with funds or use other mechanisms for the purpose of purchasing, and may make and fund commitments to purchase, invest in, make pledges in respect of, or otherwise acquire, equity or quasi-equity securities or shares or financial interests of any entity, including as a limited partner or other investor in investment funds, upon such terms and conditions as the Corporation may determine.

(2) DENOMINATION.—Support provided under paragraph (1) may be denominated and repayable in United States dollars or foreign currency.

(3) GUIDELINES AND CRITERIA.—The Corporation shall develop guidelines and criteria to require that the use of the authority provided by paragraph (1) with respect to a project has a clearly defined development rationale, taking into account the following factors:

(A) The support for the project would be more likely than not to substantially reduce or overcome the effect of an identified market failure in the country in which the project is carried out.

(B) The project would not have proceeded or would have been substantially delayed without the support.

(C) The support will meaningfully contribute to transforming local conditions to promote the development of markets.

(D) The support can be shown to be aligned with commercial partner incentives.

(E) The support can be shown to have significant developmental impact and will contribute to long-term commercial sustainability.

(4) LIMITATIONS ON EQUITY INVESTMENTS.—

(A) PER PROJECT LIMIT.—The aggregate amount of support provided under this subsection with respect to any project shall not exceed 20 percent of the aggregate amount of all equity investment made from any source to the project at the time that the Corporation approves support of the project.

(B) TOTAL LIMIT.—Support provided pursuant to this subsection shall be limited to not more than 35 percent of the Corporation's aggregate exposure on the date that such support is provided. [. . .]

(d) Insurance And Reinsurance.—The Corporation may issue insurance or reinsurance, upon such terms and conditions as the Corporation may determine, to private sector entities and qualifying sovereign entities assuring protection of their investments in whole or in part against any or all political risks such as currency inconvertibility and transfer restrictions, expropriation, war, terrorism, and civil disturbance, breach of contract, or non-honoring of financial obligations.

(e) Promotion Of And Support For Private Investment Opportunities.—

(1) IN GENERAL.—The Corporation may initiate and support, through financial participation, incentive grant, or otherwise, and on such terms and conditions as the Corporation may determine, feasibility studies for the planning, development, and management of, and procurement for, bilateral and multilateral development projects, including training activities undertaken in connection with such projects, for the purpose of promoting investment in such projects and the identification, assessment, surveying, and promotion of private investment opportunities, utilizing wherever feasible and effective, the facilities of private investors.

(2) CONTRIBUTIONS TO COSTS.—The Corporation shall, to the maximum extent practicable, require any person receiving funds under the authorities of this subsection to—

(A) share the costs of feasibility studies and other project planning services funded under this subsection; and

(B) reimburse the Corporation those funds provided under this section, if the person succeeds in project implementation.

(f) Special Projects And Programs.—The Corporation may administer and manage special projects and programs, including programs of financial and advisory support that provide private technical, professional, or managerial assistance in the development of human resources, skills, technology, capital savings, and intermediate financial and investment institutions and cooperatives and including the initiation of incentives, grants, and studies for renewable energy, microenterprise households, and other small business activities.

(g) ENTERPRISE FUNDS.—

[. . .]

(3) PURPOSES FOR WHICH SUPPORT MAY BE PROVIDED.—The Corporation, subject to the approval of the Board, may designate private, nonprofit organizations as eligible to receive support under this subsection for the following purposes:

(A) To promote development of economic freedom and private sectors, including small- and medium-sized businesses and joint ventures with the United States and host country participants.

(B) To facilitate access to the credit to small- and medium-sized businesses with sound business plans in countries where there is limited means of accessing credit on market terms.

(C) To promote policies and practices conducive to economic freedom and private sector development.

(D) To attract foreign direct investment capital to further promote private sector development and economic freedom.

(E) To complement the work of the United States Agency for International Development and other donors to improve the overall business-enabling environment, financing the creation and expansion of the private business sector.

(F) To make financially sustainable investments designed to generate measurable social benefits and build technical capacity in addition to financial returns.

[. . .]

(7) REPORTS.—Not later than one year after the date of the establishment of an enterprise fund under this subsection, and annually thereafter until the enterprise fund terminates in accordance with paragraph (10), the Board of Directors of the enterprise fund shall—

(A) submit to the appropriate congressional committees a report—

(i) detailing the administrative expenses of the enterprise fund during the year preceding the submission of the report;

(ii) describing the operations, activities, financial condition, and accomplishments of the enterprise fund during that year; and

(iii) describing the results of the audit conducted under paragraph (8) during that year; and

(iv) describing how audits conducted under paragraph (8) are informing the operations and activities of the enterprise fund; and

(B) publish, on a publicly available internet website of the enterprise fund, each report required by subparagraph (A).

(8) OVERSIGHT.—

(A) INSPECTOR GENERAL PERFORMANCE AUDITS.—

(i) IN GENERAL.—The Inspector General of the Corporation shall conduct periodic audits of the activities of each enterprise fund established under this subsection.

(ii) CONSIDERATION.—In conducting an audit under clause (i), the Inspector General shall assess whether the activities of the enterprise fund—

(I) support the purposes described in paragraph (3);

(II) result in profitable private sector investing; and

(III) generate measurable social benefits.

(B) RECORDKEEPING REQUIREMENTS.—The Corporation shall ensure that each enterprise fund receiving support under this subsection—

(i) keeps separate accounts with respect to such support; and

(ii) maintains such records as may be reasonably necessary to facilitate effective audits under this paragraph.

(9) RETURN OF FUNDS TO TREASURY.—Any funds resulting from any liquidation, dissolution, or winding up of an enterprise fund, in whole or in part, shall be returned to the Treasury of the United States.

[. . .]

TITLE III—ADMINISTRATIVE AND GENERAL PROVISIONS

SEC. 1431. OPERATIONS.

(a) Bilateral Agreements.—The Corporation may provide support under title II in connection with projects in any country the government of which has entered into an agreement with the United States authorizing the Corporation to provide such support in that country.

[. . .]

SEC. 1433. MAXIMUM CONTINGENT LIABILITY.

The maximum contingent liability of the Corporation outstanding at any one time shall not exceed in the aggregate $60,000,000,000.

[. . .]

SEC. 1464. TERMINATION OF OVERSEAS PRIVATE INVESTMENT CORPORATION AND OTHER SUPERCEDED AUTHORITIES.

Effective at the end of the transition period—

(1) the Overseas Private Investment Corporation is terminated; and

(2) title IV of chapter 2 of part I of the Foreign Assistance Act of 1961 (22 U.S.C. 2191 et seq.) (other than subsections (g), (l), and (n) of section 237 of that Act) is repealed.

[. . .]

SEC. 1465. TRANSITIONAL AUTHORITIES.

[. . .]

(c) Acting Officials.—

(2) RULE OF CONSTRUCTION.—Nothing in this division shall be construed to require the advice and consent of the Senate to the appointment by the President to a position in the Corporation of any officer whose agency is transferred to the Corporation pursuant to this title and whose duties following such transfer are germane to those performed before such transfer.

(d) Transfer Of Personnel, Assets, Obligations, And Functions.—Upon the transfer of an agency to the Corporation under section 1463—

(1) the personnel, assets, and obligations held by or available in connection with the agency shall be transferred to the Corporation for appropriate allocation, subject to the approval of the Director of the Office of Management and Budget and in accordance with section 1531(a)(2) of title 31, United States Code; and

(2) the Corporation shall have all functions—

(A) relating to the agency that any other official could by law exercise in relation to the agency immediately before such transfer; and

(B) vested in the Corporation by this division or other law. [. . .]

Chapter 4

The Protection of Investments through Bilateral Treaties

A. The Legal Status of Bilateral Investment Treaties

The latest figures show 2912 Bilateral Investment Treaties (BITs) in existence worldwide.[92] A significant majority of these include the capital exporting countries, such as Germany, China, the United Kingdom, France and the United States. In 2019, nine BITs were signed, including the Hong Kong, China SAR–United Arab Emirates BIT and the Brazil-Morocco BIT, but these have not yet entered in to force.[93]

For the counterparty, BITs are a signal that a country is open to foreign investments.[94] They are designed to encourage investment and to establish reciprocal rules governing investments, through setting rules for treatment of firms and the protection of investment related risks. BITs generally cover only non-commercial risks, most usually political risks such as protection against expropriation in countries with unstable or potentially hostile political regimes. In this context BITs provide clarity of legal norms and expectations with the agreement of both parties.

What Do BITs Do in Terms of the law?

The legal status of BITs is clear and undisputed. BITs are treaties between two countries, and treaty law is international law governed by the Vienna Convention. Once a BIT is in place between countries, it becomes a major source of substantive law, and an investor can rely on it as a source of law for the resolution of disputes. It is in this way that BITs are said to vary customary international law norms.

In the event of disputes, companies can look to the dispute resolution options open to them under BITs. These treaties typically deal with such issues as protection of investment, repatriation of profits and non-discriminatory treatment of investments, and provide for dispute resolution and arbitration proceedings on a state-to-state basis. An investor will normally need to establish that there is a wider policy issue at stake, or be able to demonstrate that many companies are affected, in order for a national government to take up at state-to-state level.

More recent BITs may, in addition, include a provision for direct investor-to-state arbitration under the conditions set out in the Treaty. Where such a provision is in place, it presents the opportunity for a foreign investor to bring a case in its own right against the state concerned. Under these provisions, the investor may typically choose to submit the case to the International Centre for Settlement of Investment Disputes (ICSID), or to an ad-hoc tribunal established under the Arbitration Rules of the United Nations Commission on International Trade Law (UNCITRAL).

---

92. UNCTAD: International Investment Agreements (as of 2, October 2019), http://investmentpolicyhub.unctad.org/IIA.

93. Most Recent IIAs (as of 2, October 2019), http://investmentpolicyhub.unctad.org/IIA/MostRecentTreaties#iiaInnerMenu.

94. *See* Rudolf Dolzer & Margrete Stevens, *Bilateral Investment Treaties* (1995) ICSID, 12.

It is also increasingly common for U.S. trading partners to seek to include comprehensive investment chapters in their negotiation of Free Trade Agreements (FTAs) with the U.S.[95] Such investment chapters are generally similar in content to BITs but differ in the process through which the U.S. ratifies and implements the pact.

BITs as Tools for Globalization and Economic Liberalization

Bilateral Investment Treaties (BITs) are treaties establishing the terms and conditions for private investment by nationals and companies of one state in another state with recourse to international arbitration for enforcement. While states are the primary subjects of international law, the emergence of BITs has created an additional level of protection for investors in terms of the standard of protection and dispute settlement of investor/state disputes. The first generation of these treaties were Friendship, Commerce and Navigation Treaties (FCN), which required the host state to treat foreign investments on the same level as investments from any other country, including in some instances, treatment that was as favourable as the host nation's treatment of its own national investors. FCNs also established the terms of trade and shipping between the parties, and the rights of foreigners to conduct business and own property in the host state. The second generation of these treaties is referred to as BITs.

The world's first BIT was signed on 25 November 1959 between Pakistan and Germany. As observed by the United Nations Conference on Trade and Development (UNCTAD), the 1990s saw a rapid increase in the number of BITs and, by the end of the decade, the universe of these treaties looked dramatically different from that of previous decades.

As Basedow points out, in the 1990s, the United States (U.S.), followed by Canada, Japan, the European Union (EU) and more recently China, started to negotiate new types of BITs. These BITs did not only comprise post-establishment treatment and investment provisions like the traditional BITs, but also contain substantive investment liberalization commitments.[96] They grant foreign investors national and most favoured nation treatment at the pre-establishment state. BITs have become the dominant international vehicle through which investment is regulated and protected. They have become a tool for the diffusion of legal ideals and an attempt to create a unique legal regime distinct yet complementary to customary international law on foreign direct investment. Developing countries are most of the time encouraged by global economic development agencies like the International Monetary Fund (IMF) and the World Bank to sign BITs as a means of attracting foreign investment into their economies.[97] The reality of today's economic legal landscape is that BITs have become ubiquitous.

---

95. Paraguay-United States TIFA (2017).

96. Robert Basedow, *Preferential Investment Liberalization under Bilateral Investment Treaties: How to Ensure Compliance with WTO Law?* (2015) Columbia FDI Perspectives No.162.

97. According to the report of UNCTAD, countries continue to use international investment agreements (IIAs) as a tool for international investment policy making. The year 2014 saw the

Undoubtedly, then, BITs have increased dramatically by leveraging within the context of the general world-wide acceptance of the role of the private sector in growth and development. It also appears to have tacitly endorsed the capacity of private investments to shape norms governing settlement of disputes. However, this is a ground of contestation in the field. Thus, since the 1980s, developing countries have become much more open to foreign direct investment. Equally, since the 1990s, many transition economies have joined in this trend as a means to achieving sustainable economic growth triggered by foreign direct investment. It is significant to note that, previously, corporations were perceived as part of the problem of underdevelopment by both capital exporting countries and developing/transitional economies. Today, these corporations are now seen as part of the solution to underdevelopment. They are seen as providing the much needed capital to stimulate growth and development as well as potential sources of technology and skills transfer to foreign markets, thus creating/enhancing employment.[98]

Be that as it may, BITs are principally developed by capital-exporting countries to promote investment and protect their nationals in capital-importing countries. They are intended to put in place a comprehensive, specific, timely, and largely uncontested set of rules with recourse to international tribunals for enforcement. BITs essentially displace the relevant domestic laws in many important respects. BITs may also have an impact in creating or shaping law outside of their specific texts. In ratifying a BIT, a country makes the treaty part of its legal system. In order to meet the demands of both the letter and intent of a BIT, a country may modify internal legislation affecting investment. With capital flowing predominantly from more advanced countries to developing countries, the bulk of these BITs have traditionally been concluded between developed states and developing countries. The rise of emerging states like China, India, Malaysia, and South Korea has caused the trend to adjust. There is now an increasing number of BITs being concluded by China and India.

BITs are instruments designed to open a domestic market to foreign investors and enhance the role of the private sector in the economy. BITs consciously seek to approximate in the developing, capital-importing state the minimal legal, administrative and regulatory framework that fosters and sustains investment in industrialized capital-exporting states with open markets. Indeed, BITs have been used as tools for promoting free markets and globalization and for stimulating local economies by various states around the world.[99] Globalization leads to an increase in the cross-border flows of goods, services, capital and know-how. Globalization and free markets require a legal system to underpin them, and BITs are one of the instruments that provide the legal infrastructure to enable investors to expand their

---

conclusion of 27 IIAS, which amounts to one every other week. *See* UNCTAD, IIA Issues Note (No. 1 February 2015) at 1.

98. UNCTAD, Role of International Investment, at 11.

99. UNCTAD, Role of International Investment, at 20.

operations in foreign markets. As stated earlier, BITs can also be seen as a mechanism to extend the scope of the standard of treatment available to foreign investors under customary international law. Most BITs provide greater protection to foreign investors than is available under international law. However, BITs do not confine themselves to codifying the rules of customary international law (for example, rules on compensation, NT and MFN).

Although BITs are designed to create a bilateral set of obligations between the contracting parties, the risk is that these obligations can become in effect obligations *erga omnes* (that is, binding against all) for a number of reasons. These reasons include broad interpretation of the principles contained in them such as the MFN principle. BITs also tend to change the standard of compensation in nationalization. Regardless of the negotiating position taken by various states on international platforms, when it comes to negotiating BITs, the host states have, by and large, accepted the Hull formula as favored by the US BIT model.[100] Individual BITs can also allow the contracting parties to deviate from the standards of treatment accorded in customary law such as those concerning the standard of compensation. A major feature of BITs is to allow foreign investors access to international investment tribunals, such as ICSID, for the resolution of disputes between the investor and the host state. This is a major concession. Before the establishment of ICSID, investors had to rely on espousal by their home state before an action could be brought before an international tribunal. BITs sometimes also specify the applicable law. The most common approach is to state that the applicable law is the host state's law and principles of international law.

B. The Reach of Bilateral Investment Treaties

The provision for direct investor-to-state arbitration, under the conditions set out in the BITs, is central to overcoming the issues raised in *Barcelona Traction.*

Barcelona Traction, Light, and Power Co., Ltd. (*Belg. v. Spain*), 1970 I.C.J. Rep. 3 (Feb. 5).

Principal Points of the Judgment

Edited by: E. Lauterpracht Q.C.

30. The States which the present case principally concerns are Belgium, the national State of the alleged shareholders, Spain, the State whose organs are alleged to have committed the unlawful acts complained of, and Canada, the State under whose

---

100. US Model BIT, at 6. The "Hull formula" refers to a letter from Secretary of State Cordell Hull to the Mexican government insisting that compensation for expropriation be "prompt, adequate, and effective".

laws Barcelona Traction was incorporated and in whose territory it has its registered office ("head office" in the terms of the by-laws of Barcelona Traction).

31. Thus the Court has to deal with a series of problems arising out of a triangular relationship involving the State whose nationals are shareholders in a company incorporated under the laws of another State, in whose territory it has its registered office; the State whose organs are alleged to have committed against the company unlawful acts prejudicial to both it and its shareholders; and the State under whose laws the company is incorporated, and in whose territory it has its registered office.

32. In these circumstances it is logical that the Court should first address itself to [. . .] the question of the right of Belgium to exercise diplomatic protection of Belgian shareholders in a company which is a juristic entity incorporated in Canada, the measures complained of having been taken in relation not to any Belgian national but to the company itself.

33. [. . .] In particular, an essential distinction should be drawn between the obligations of a State towards the international community as a whole, and those arising vis-à-vis another State in the field of diplomatic protection. By their very nature the former are the concern of all States. [. . .]

34. Such obligations derive, for example, in contemporary international law, from the outlawing of acts of aggression, and of genocide, as also from the principles and rules concerning the basic rights of the human person, including protection from slavery and racial discrimination. [. . .]

35. Obligations the performance of which is the subject of diplomatic protection are not of the same category. [. . .] In order to bring a claim in respect of the breach of such an obligation, a State must first establish its right to do so. [. . .] In the present case it is therefore essential to establish whether the losses allegedly suffered by Belgian shareholders in Barcelona Traction were the consequences of the violation of obligations of which they were the beneficiaries.

36. [. . .] In the absence of any treaty on the subject between the Parties, this essential issue has to be decided in the light of the general rules of diplomatic protection.

38. [. . .] International law has to recognize the corporate entity as an institution created by States in a domain essentially within their domestic jurisdiction. This in turn requires that, whenever legal issues arise concerning the rights of States with regard to the treatment of companies and shareholders, as to which rights international law has not established its own rules, it has to refer to the relevant rules of municipal law.

41. [. . .] The concept and structure of the company are founded on and determined by a firm distinction between the separate entity of the company and that of the shareholder, each with a distinct set of rights. The separation of property rights as between company and shareholder is an important manifestation of this distinction. So long as the company is in existence the shareholder has no right to the corporate assets.

42. [. . .] no individual shareholder can take legal steps, either in the name of the company or in his own name. If the shareholders disagree with the decisions taken on behalf of the company they may, in accordance with its articles or the relevant provisions of the law, change them or replace its officers, or take such action as is provided by law. [. . .] Nonetheless the shareholder's rights in relation to the company and its assets remain limited, this being, moreover, a corollary of the limited nature of their liability.

44. Notwithstanding the separate corporate personality, a wrong done to the company frequently causes prejudice to its shareholders. But the mere fact that damage is sustained by both company and shareholder does not imply that both are entitled to claim compensation. Thus no legal conclusion can be drawn from the fact that the same event caused damage simultaneously affecting several natural or juristic persons [. . .] Thus whenever a shareholder's interests are harmed by an act done to the company, it is to the latter that he must look to institute appropriate action; for although two separate entities may have suffered from the same wrong, it is only one entity whose rights have been infringed.

46. It has also been contended that the measures complained of, although taken with respect to Barcelona Traction and causing it direct damage, constituted an unlawful act vis-à-vis Belgium, because they also, though indirectly, caused damage to the Belgian shareholders in Barcelona Traction. This again is merely a different way of presenting the distinction between injury in respect of a right and injury to a simple interest. But, as the Court has indicated, evidence that damage was suffered does not *ipso facto* justify a diplomatic claim [. . .] Not a mere interest affected, but solely a right infringed involves responsibility, so that an act directed against and infringing only the company's rights does not involve responsibility towards the shareholders, even if their interests are affected.

47. The situation is different if the act complained of is aimed at the direct rights of the shareholder as such. It is well known that there are rights which municipal law confers upon the latter distinct from those of the company, including the right to any declared dividend, the right to attend and vote at general meetings, the right to share in the residual assets of the company on liquidation. Whenever one of his direct rights is infringed, the shareholder has an independent right of action. On this there is no disagreement between the Parties. But a distinction must be drawn between a direct infringement of the shareholder's rights, and difficulties or financial losses to which he may be exposed as the result of the situation of the company.

48. The Belgian Government claims that shareholders of Belgian nationality suffered damage in consequence of unlawful acts of the Spanish authorities and, in particular, that the Barcelona Traction shares, though they did not cease to exist, were emptied of all real economic content. It accordingly contends that the shareholders had an independent right to redress, notwithstanding the fact that the acts complained of were directed against the company as such. Thus the legal issue is reducible to the question of whether it is legitimate to identify an attack on

company rights, resulting in damage to shareholders, with the violation of their direct rights.

49. The Court has noted, [. . .] that the Belgian Government did not base its claim on an infringement of the direct rights of the shareholders. Thus it is not open to the Court to go beyond the claim as formulated by the Belgian Government and it will not pursue its examination of this point any further.

50. [. . .] If the Court were to decide the case in disregard of the relevant institutions of municipal law it would, without justification, invite serious legal difficulties. [. . .] Thus the Court has, as indicated, not only to take cognizance of municipal law but also to refer to it. It is to rules generally accepted by municipal legal systems which recognize the limited company whose capital is represented by shares, and not to the municipal law of a particular State, that international law refers. In referring to such rules, the Court cannot modify, still less deform them.

51. On the international plane, the Belgian Government has advanced the proposition that it is inadmissible to deny the shareholder's national State a right of diplomatic protection merely on the ground that another State possesses a corresponding right in respect of the company itself [. . .] In fact the Belgian government has repeatedly stressed that there exists no rule of international law which would deny the national State of the shareholders the right of diplomatic protection for the purpose of seeking redress pursuant to unlawful acts committed by another State against the company in which they hold shares.

52. International law may not, in some fields, provide specific rules in particular cases. [. . .] As to the shareholder, while he has certain rights expressly provided for him by municipal law as referred to in paragraph 42 above, appeal can, in the circumstances of the present case, only be made to the silence of international law. Such silence scarcely admits of interpretation in favour of the shareholder.

56. [. . .] The law has recognized that the independent existence of the legal entity cannot be treated as an absolute. It is in this context that the process of "lifting the corporate veil" or "disregarding the legal entity" has been found justified and equitable in certain circumstances or for certain purposes.

57. Hence the lifting of the veil is more frequently employed from without, in the interest of those dealing with the corporate entity. However, it has also been operated from within, in the interest of—among others—the shareholders, but only in exceptional circumstances.

58. [. . .] It follows that on the international plane also there may in principle be special circumstances which justify the lifting of the veil in the interest of shareholders.

65. [. . .] Barcelona Traction has lost all its assets in Spain, and was placed in receivership in Canada, a receiver and manager having been appointed. It is common ground that from the economic viewpoint the company has been entirely paralyzed. It has been deprived of all its Spanish sources of income, and the Belgian

Government has asserted that the company could no longer find the funds for its legal defence, so that these had to be supplied by the shareholders.

66. It cannot however, be contended that the corporate entity of the company has ceased to exist, or that it has lost its capacity to take corporate action. It was free to exercise such capacity in the Spanish courts and did in fact do so. It has not become incapable in law of defending its own rights and the interests of the shareholders. In particular, a precarious financial situation cannot be equated with the demise of the corporate entity, which is the hypothesis under consideration: the company's status in law is alone relevant, and not its economic condition, nor even the possibility of its being "practically defunct"—a description on which argument has been based but which lacks all legal precision. Only in the event of the legal demise of the company are the shareholders deprived of the possibility of a remedy available through the company; it is only if they became deprived of all such possibility that an independent right of action for them and their government could arise.

67. [. . .] Though in receivership, the company continues to exist. Moreover, it is a matter of public record that the company's shares were quoted on the stock-market at a recent date.

68. [. . .] Thus, even if the company is limited in its activity after being placed in receivership, there can be no doubt that it has retained its legal capacity and that the power to exercise it is vested in the manager appointed by the Canadian courts.

70. [. . .] Indeed, it has been the practice of some States to give a company incorporated under their law diplomatic protection solely when it has its seat (*siege social*) or management or centre of control in their territory, or when a majority or a substantial proportion of the shares has been owned by nationals of the State concerned. [. . .] However, in the particular field of the diplomatic protection of corporate entities, no absolute test of the "genuine connection" has found general acceptance. [. . .] In this connection reference has been made to the *Nottebohm* case [(*Liech. v. Guat.*) 1955 I.C.J. Rep. 4 (Apr. 6)]. [. . .] However, given both the legal and factual aspects of protection in the present case the Court is of the opinion that there can be no analogy with the issues raised or the decisions given in that case.

71. [. . .] The incorporation of the company under the law of Canada was an act of free choice. Not only did the founders of the company seek its incorporation under Canadian law but it has remained under that law for a period of over 50 years. [. . .] Thus a close and permanent connection has been established, fortified by the passage of over half a century. This connection is in no way weakened by the fact that the company engaged from the very outset in commercial activities outside Canada.

85. The Court will now examine the Belgian claim from a different point of view, disregarding municipal law and relying on the rule that in inter-State relations, whether claims are made on behalf of a State's national or on behalf of the State itself, they are always the claims of the State.

86. Hence the Belgian Government would be entitled to bring a claim if it could show that one of its rights had been infringed and that the acts complained of involved the breach of an international obligation arising out of a treaty or a general rule of law. [. . .]

87. [. . .] When a State admits into its territory foreign investments or foreign nationals it is, [. . .] bound to extend to them the protection of the law. [. . .] The real question is whether a right has been violated, which right could only be the right of the State to have its nationals enjoy a certain treatment guaranteed by general international law, in the absence of a treaty applicable to the particular case.

88. It follows from what has already been stated above that, where it is a question of an unlawful act committed against a company representing foreign capital, the general rule of international law authorizes the national State of the company alone to make a claim.

90. Thus, in the present state of the law, the protection of shareholders requires that recourse be had to treaty stipulations or special agreements directly concluded between the private investor and the State in which the investment is placed. States ever more frequently provide for such protection, in both bilateral and multilateral relations, either by means of special instruments or within the framework of wider economic arrangements. [. . .] The instruments in question contain provisions as to jurisdiction and procedure in case of disputes concerning the treatment of investing companies by the States in which they invest capital. Sometimes companies are themselves vested with a direct right to defend their interests against States through prescribed procedures. No such instrument is in force between the Parties to the present case.

92. [. . .] A theory has been developed to the effect that the State of the shareholders has a right of diplomatic protection when the State whose responsibility is invoked is the national State of the company. Whatever the validity of this theory may be, it is certainly not applicable to the present case, since Spain is not the national State of Barcelona Traction.

95. The Belgian Government, it is true, has also contended that as high a proportion as 88 percent of the shares in Barcelona Traction belonged to natural or juristic persons of Belgian nationality, and it has used this argument for the purpose not only of determining the amount of the damages which it claims, but also of establishing its right of action on behalf of the Belgian shareholders. [. . .]

96. The Court considers that the adoption of the theory of diplomatic protection of shareholders as such, by opening the door to competing diplomatic claims, could create an atmosphere of confusion and insecurity in international economic relations. The danger would be all the greater in as much as the shares of companies whose activity is international are widely scattered and frequently change hands.

100. [. . .] As far as appeared to the Court, there was nothing to prevent Canada from continuing to grant its diplomatic protection to Barcelona Traction if it had considered that it should do so.

102. [. . .] Since no *jus standi* before the Court has been established, it is not for the Court in its judgment to pronounce upon any other aspect of the case, on which it should take a decision only if the Belgian Government had a right of protection in respect of its nationals, shareholders in Barcelona Traction.

C. Treaty Violation — Use of BITs to overcome *Barcelona*

Elettronica Sicula S.p.A. (ELSI) (U.S. v. It.), 1989 I.C.J. Rep 15 (July 20).

Case Introduction

The United States initiated proceedings in the ICJ, claiming that Italy had violated its international legal obligations under the bilateral Treaty of Friendship, Commerce and Navigation ("the FCN Treaty"). This was alleged in the context of Italy's acts concerning the treatment of two United States corporations, the Raytheon Company ("Raytheon") and Machlett Laboratories Incorporated ("Machlett"), in relation to the Italian corporation, Raytheon-Elsi S.p.A. (previously Elettronica Sicula S.P.A. ("ELSI")), which was wholly owned by the two US corporations.

In the mid-1960s, ELSI fell into financial difficulties. Its accumulated losses exceeded one-third of the company's share capital, and Italian law required it to reduce its equity. Meetings were held to find ELSI an Italian partner and explore governmental support. In the hope of improvement, ELSI decided to dismiss some 300 employees, but it soon became apparent that the discussions with Italian officials would not lead to an arrangement. As a consequence, Raytheon and Machlett began serious plans for closure of ELSI, to minimize their losses, and in early 1968, detailed plans were consolidated for liquidation. On 29 March 1968, letters of dismissal were mailed to the employees of ELSI. These gave rise to strikes and local public and press support for the employees.

On 1 April 1968, the Mayor of the Municipality of Palermo, where the plant was located, issued an order, effective immediately, seizing ELSI's plant and related assets for a period of six months. ELSI claimed the requisition was illegal and expressed its intention to take all legal steps to have it revoked and damages awarded. The Mayor did not respond, and ELSI brought an administrative appeal against the decision of the local government. On 25 April 1968, referring to the requisition order as the cause, the ELSI Board of Directors filed a voluntary petition to bankruptcy. Meanwhile, negotiations were being carried on for a takeover of the plant by Italian industrialists (IRI), and a series of auctions were held.

ELSI filed an administrative appeal in April 1968, and this was decided in August 1969. In the meantime, the requisition was not formally prolonged and ceased to have legal effect after six months. The ELSI appeal was upheld, and the court annulled the requisition order made by the Mayor of Palermo.

In the meantime, the trustee in bankruptcy had brought proceedings in the Court of Palermo against the Minister of the Interior of Italy and the Mayor of Palermo for damages resulting from the requisition. On appeal, the Court of Appeal of Palermo upheld the conclusion of the lower court regarding no entitlement to damages for the alleged decrease in value of the plant and equipment. However, the Appeal Court reversed the finding on the second part of the claim for damages, finding the trustee was entitled to compensation from the Minister of Interior for loss of use and possession of ELSI's plant and assets during the six months requisition period.

Jurisdiction for the case at the International Court of Justice ("ICJ") arises out of Article XXVI of the FCN Treaty between Italy and the United States, which provides for disputes not resolved via diplomacy to be submitted to the ICJ, unless other means are agreed. The core claims were brought by the United States, based on the requisition order of the Mayor of Palermo and its effects on the liquidation process for ELSI. Italy denied violation of the FCN Treaty and contended that no injury was caused for which indemnity payments would be justified.

Principal Points of the Judgment

Exhaustion of Local Remedies

49. While the jurisdiction of the chamber is not in doubt, an objection to the admissibility of the present case was entered by Italy in its Counter-Memorial, on the ground of an alleged failure of the two United States corporations, Raytheon and Machlett, on whose behalf the United States claim is brought, to exhaust the local remedies available to them in Italy. This objection, which the Parties agreed should be heard and determined in the framework of the merits, must, therefore, be considered at the outset.

50. The United States questioned whether the rule of the exhaustion of local remedies could apply at all to a case brought under Article XXVI of the FCN Treaty. That Article, it was pointed out, is categorical in its terms, and unqualified by a reference to the local remedies rule; and it seemed right, therefore, to conclude that the Parties to the FCN Treaty, had they intended the jurisdiction conferred upon the Court to be qualified by the local remedies rule in cases of diplomatic protection, would have used express words to that effect; as was done in an Economic Co-operation Agreement between Italy and the United States of America also concluded in 1948. The Chamber has no doubt that the parties to a treaty can therein either agree that the local remedies rule shall not apply to claims based on alleged breaches of that treaty; or confirm that it shall apply. Yet the Chamber finds itself unable to accept that an important principle of customary international law should be held to have been tacitly dispensed with, in the absence of any words making clear an intention

to do so. This part of the United States response to the Italian objection must therefore be rejected.

52. Moreover, when the Court was, in the *Interhandel* case, faced with a not dissimilar argument by Switzerland that in that case its "principal submission" was in respect of a "direct breach of international law" and therefore not subject to the local remedies rule, the Court, having analyzed that "principal submission", found that it was bound up with the diplomatic protection claim, and that the Applicant's arguments "do not deprive the dispute . . . of the character of a dispute in which the Swiss Government appears as having adopted the cause of its national . . ." (*Interhandel*, Judgment, I.C.J. Reports 1959, p.28). In the present case, likewise, the Chamber has no doubt that the matter which colours and pervades the United States claim as a whole, is the alleged damage to Raytheon and Machlett, said to have resulted from the actions of the Respondent. Accordingly, the Chamber rejects the argument that in the present case there is a part of the Applicant's claim which can be severed so as to render the local remedies rule inapplicable to that part.

53. [. . .] In the "Memorandum of Law" elaborating the United States claim on the diplomatic plane, transmitted to the Italian Government by Note Verbale of 7 February 1974, one finds that the whole of Part VI (pp. 133 et seq.) deals generally and at some length with the "Exhaustion of Local Remedies". [. . .] The Memorandum concluded that Raytheon and Machlett had indeed exhausted "every meaningful remedy available to them in Italy". In view of this evidence that the United States was very much aware that it must satisfy the local remedies rule, that it evidently believed that the rule had been satisfied, and that it had been advised that the shareholders of ELSI had no direct action against the Italian Government under Italian law, it was argued by the Applicant that Italy, if it was indeed at that time of the opinion that the local remedies had not been exhausted, should have apprised the United States of its opinion. According to the United States, however, at no time until the filing of the Respondent's Counter-Memorial in the present proceedings did Italy suggest that Raytheon and Machlett should sue in the Italian courts on the basis of the Treaty.

54. It was argued by the Applicant that this absence of riposte from Italy amounts to an estoppel. [. . .] although it cannot be excluded that an estoppel could in certain circumstances arise from a silence when something ought to have been said, there are obvious difficulties in constructing an estoppel from a mere failure to mention a matter at a particular point in somewhat desultory diplomatic exchanges.

55. On the basis that the local remedies rule does apply in this case, this Judgment may now turn to the question whether local remedies were, or were not, exhausted by Raytheon and Machlett.

59. With such a deal of litigation in the municipal courts about what is in substance the claim now before the Chamber, it was for Italy to demonstrate that there was nevertheless some local remedy that had not been tried; or at least, not exhausted.

60. The question, therefore, reduces itself to this: ought Raytheon and Machlett, suing in their own right, as United States corporations allegedly injured by the requisition of property of an Italian company whose shares they held, have brought an action in the Italian courts, within the general limitation period (five years), alleging violation of certain provisions of the FCN Treaty between Italy and the United States.

61. Italy contends that Raytheon and Machlett could have based such an action before the Italian courts on Article 2043 of the Italian Civil Code, which provides that

> "Any act committed either willfully or through fault which causes wrongful damages to another person implies that the wrongdoer is under an obligation to pay compensation for those damages".

According to Italy, this provision is frequently invoked by individuals against the Italian State, and substantial sums have been awarded to claimants where appropriate.

62. However, those decisions were not based on Article 2043 of the Italian Civil Code; and the treaty provisions applied were given effect in conjunction with municipal legislation or the provisions of other treaties, through the mechanism of a most-favoured-nation provision. In none of the cases cited was the FCN Treaty provision relied on to establish the wrongfulness of conduct of Italian public officials. When in 1971 Raytheon consulted two Italian jurists on the question of local remedies for the purposes of a diplomatic claim, it apparently did not occur to either of them to refer even as a possibility to action under Article 2043 in conjunction with the FCN Treaty. [. . .] Where the determination of a question of municipal law is essential to the Court's decision in a case, the Court will have to weigh the jurisprudence of the municipal courts, and "If this is uncertain or divided, it will rest with the Court to select the interpretation which it considers most in conformity with the law" (*Brazilian Loans*, P.C.I.J., Series A, Nos. 20/21, p. 124). In the present case, however, it was for Italy to show, as a matter of fact, the existence of a remedy which was open to the United States stockholders and which they failed to employ. The Chamber does not consider that Italy has discharged that burden.

Protection and Security of Nationals

64. [. . .] it will be kept in mind that although the stated purposes of the FCN Treaty were those normally to be found in treaties of that kind, nevertheless a purpose of the Supplementary Agreement, which is to "constitute an integral part" of the FCN Treaty, was to give "added encouragement to investments of the one country in useful undertakings in the other country".

66. The most important of [. . .] acts of Respondent which the Applicant claims to have been in violation of the FCN Treaty is the requisition of the ELSI plant by the Mayor on 1 April 1968, which is claimed to have frustrated the plan for what the Applicant terms an "orderly liquidation" of the company[. . .].

68. [. . .] Paragraph 2 of Article III is important for the Applicant's claim; it provides:

> "The nationals, corporations and associations of either High Contracting Party shall be permitted, in conformity with the applicable laws and regulations within the territories of the other High Contracting Party, to organize, control and manage corporations and associations of such other High Contracting Party for engaging in commercial, manufacturing, processing, mining, educational, philanthropic, religious and scientific activities.[. . .]"

69. [. . .] The claim of the United States focusses on the right to "control and manage". Is there, then, a violation of this Article if, as the United States alleges, the requisition had the effect of depriving ELSI of both the right and practical possibility of selling off its plant and assets for satisfaction of its liabilities to its creditors and satisfaction of its shareholders?

70. [. . .] It was objected by Italy that the requisition in no way affected "control by the shareholders over the company", but merely concerned the management by the company of property belonging to the company. [. . .] It is however also undeniable that this requisition, which remained in effect until 30 September 1968, was issued to avoid the closure of ELSI's plant, the dismissal of its workforce, and as a consequence the probable dispersal of its assets, all of which were integral to ELSI's plan for orderly liquidation. Since the requisition thus had the design of preventing Raytheon from exercising, for six critical months, what was at that time a most important part of its right to control and manage ELSI, there exists a question whether the requisition was in conformity with the requirements of Article III, paragraph 2, of the FCN Treaty.

73. [. . .] What is a breach of treaty may be lawful in the municipal law and what is unlawful in the municipal law may be wholly innocent of violation of a treaty provision. Even had the Prefect held the requisition to be entirely justified in Italian law, this would not exclude the possibility that it was a violation of the FCN Treaty.

76. There remains however a crucial question to be considered. According to the Respondent, Raytheon and Machlett were, because of ELSI's financial position, already naked of those very rights of control and management of which they claim to have been deprived.

77. [. . .] This plan for an orderly liquidation was however very much bound up with the financial state of ELSI, and the two need to be considered together.

80. On 7 March 1968, Raytheon formally notified ELSI of its decision that Raytheon would not provide any further capital, whether in the form of subscribing to new stock or guaranteeing additional loans. [. . .] The plan for an orderly liquidation, as conceived by the ELSI management, was to be managed by them.

83. [. . .] That plan, as already conceived, contemplated that the disposal of plant and assets might produce enough to pay all creditors 100 per cent of their dues, with a modest residue for the shareholders. [. . .] This must have seemed a reasonable aim, for the "book value" may well have been a conservative figure.

84. Nevertheless since no new investment capital was forthcoming, the possibility of paying creditors in full depended upon putting the orderly liquidation plan into operation in good time. This was running out because money was running out. As the position worsened daily, the moment might at any time arrive when liabilities exceeded assets, or default resulted from lack of liquidity.

86. First, [. . .] the creditors had to be asked to give the company time. If ELSI had been confident of continuing to meet all its obligations promptly and regularly while seeking a buyer for its assets, no negotiations with creditors, and no elaborate calculations of division of the proceeds, on different hypotheses, such as have been produced to the Chamber, would have been needed.

87. Secondly, the management were by no means certain that the sale of the assets would realize enough to pay all creditors in full; in fact, the existence of the calculation of a "quick-sale value" suggests perhaps more than uncertainty.

89. Thirdly, [. . .] according to the evidence, when in late March 1968 ELSI started using funds made available by Raytheon to pay off the small creditors in full, "the banks intervened and said that they did not want that to happen as that was showing preference".

92. All of these factors point toward a conclusion that the feasibility at 31 March 1968 of a plan of orderly liquidation, an essential link in the chain of reasoning upon which the United States claim rests, has not been sufficiently established.

93. Finally, [. . .] the position in Italian bankruptcy law [. . .] provides that "an entrepreneur who is in a state of insolvency shall be declared bankrupt".

> "The state of insolvency, moreover, becomes apparent not only by default but also by other external acts which show that the debtor is no longer in a position regularly to discharge his obligations."

"Regular" payment apparently refers to payment in full at the due time.

94. If however ELSI was in a state of legal insolvency at 31 March 1968, and if, as contended by Italy, a state of insolvency entailed an obligation on the company to petition for its own bankruptcy, then the relevant rights of control and management would not have existed to be protected by the FCN Treaty.

101. If, therefore, the management of ELSI, at the material time, had no practical possibility of carrying out successfully a scheme of orderly liquidation under its own management, and may indeed already have forfeited any right to do so under Italian law, it cannot be said that it was the requisition that deprived it of this faculty of control and management. [. . .] There were several causes acting together that led to the disaster at ELSI. No doubt the effects of the requisition might have been one of the actors involved. But the underlying cause was ELSI's headlong course towards insolvency; which state of affairs it seems to have attained even prior to the requisition. [. . .] In short, the possibility of that solution of orderly liquidation,

which Raytheon and Machlett claim to have been deprived of as a result of the requisition, is purely a matter of speculation.

102. There are two claims of the Applicant based upon Article V of the FCN Treaty [. . .] concerned with protection and security of nationals and their property;

> "1. The national of each High Contracting Party shall receive, within the territories of the other High Contracting Party, the most constant protection and security for their persons and property, and shall enjoy in this respect the full protection and security required by international law.[. . .] In so far as the term 'nationals' were used in this paragraph is applicable in relations to property it shall be construed to include corporations and associations."

Paragraph 3 provides as follows:

> "3. [. . .] no less than the protection and security which is or may hereafter be accorded to the nationals, corporations and associations of such other High Contracting Party and no less than that which is or may hereafter be accorded to the nationals, corporations and associations of any third country."

105. It is the contention of the United States that once the plant had been requisitioned, ELSI's employees began an occupation of the premises [. . .] and that this occupation had the tacit approval of local authorities. [. . .] To this occupation the United States attributes as injurious consequences, first a deterioration of the plant and related material and equipment, and secondly that it impeded the efforts of the trustee in bankruptcy to dispose of the plant.

108. The reference in Article V to the provision of "constant protection and security" cannot be construed as the giving of warranty that property shall never in any circumstances be occupied or disturbed. The dismissal of some 800 workers could not reasonably be expected to pass without some protest. [. . .] In any event, considering that it is not established that any deterioration in the plant and machinery was due to the presence of the workers, and that the authorities were able not merely to protect the plant but even in some measure to continue production, the protection provided by the authorities could not be regarded as falling below "the full protection and security required by international law"; or indeed as less than the national or third-State standards.

109. The Applicant sees a further breach of Article V, paragraphs 1 and 3, of the FCN Treaty, in the time taken—16 months—before the Prefect rules on ELSI's administrative appeal against the Mayor's requisition order. [. . .] The time taken by the Prefect was undoubtedly long; and the Chamber was not entirely convinced by the Respondent's suggestion that such lengthy delays by Prefects were quite usual.

110. Counsel for the Applicant has referred to this delay as "a denial of the level of procedural justice accorded by international law". [. . .] First, it is said, the bankruptcy of ELSI could have been avoided; the Chamber is unable to accept this argument, for the reasons already explained. [. . .] Secondly, it is contended that once

the requisition occurred, the Respondent had an obligation to protect ELSI from its deleterious effects, and one of the ways in which it fell short of this obligation was by failing to provide an adequate method of overturning the requisition.

112. [. . .] The Chamber [. . .] is not satisfied that a "national standard" of more rapid determination of administrative appeals has been shown to have existed. The Chamber is therefore unable to see in this delay a violation of paragraphs 1 and 3 of Article V of the FCN Treaty.

Expropriation

113. The Chamber now turns to the United States claim based on Article V, paragraph 2, of the FCN Treaty, which provides as follows:

> "2. The property of nationals, corporations and associations of either High Contracting Party shall not be taken within the territories of the other High Contracting Party without due process of law and without the prompt payment of just and effective compensation."

[. . .] In the contention of the United States, both the Respondent's act of requisitioning the ELSI plant and its subsequent acts in acquiring the plant, assets, and work in progress, singly and in combination, constitute takings of property without due process of law and just compensation. [. . .] In international law a "taking" is not merely outright expropriation of property, but also unreasonable interference with its use, enjoyment or disposal. Secondly, the United States claims that the Respondent, after the requisition and before the Prefect rules on the administrative appeal, proceeded through ELTEL to acquire the ELSI plant and assets for less than fair market value.

115. [. . .] Having requisitioned the plant and caused ELSI's bankruptcy, the Government of Italy discouraged private bidders at the auctions held to dispose of ELSI's assets, by informing the public at large that the Government would be taking over ELSI's facilities.

116. [. . .] What is thus alleged by the Applicant, if not an overt expropriation, might be regarded as a disguised expropriation; because, at the end of the process, it is indeed title to property itself that is at stake.

118. The argument that there was a "taking" involving transfer of title gives rise to a number of difficulties. [. . .] a question whether the paragraph can be extended to include even a "taking" of an Italian corporation in Italy, of which, strictly speaking, Raytheon and Machlett only held the shares. [. . .] The English text of this provision suggests that it was designed precisely to resolve the doubts just described. The interests of shareholders in the assets of a company, and in their residuary value on liquidation, would appear to fall in the category of the "interests" to be protected by Article V, paragraph 2, and the Protocol. Italy has however drawn attention to the use in the Italian text—which is equally authentic—of the narrower term "*diritti*" (rights), and has argued that, on the basis of the principle expressed in Article 33, paragraph 4, of the Vienna Convention on the Law of Treaties, the

correct interpretation of the Protocol must be in the more restrictive sense of the Italian text.

Even if it were possible to see the requisition as having been designed to bring about bankruptcy, as a step towards disguised expropriation, then, if ELSI was already under an obligation to file a petition of bankruptcy, or in such a financial state that such a petition could not be long delayed, the requisition was an act of supererogation. [. . .] this requisition [. . .] being by its terms for a limited period, and liable to be overturned by administrative appeal, could not, in the Chamber's view, amount to a "taking" contrary to Article V. [. . .] In fact the bankruptcy of ELSI transformed the situation less than a month after requisition. The requisition could therefore only be regarded as significant for this purpose if it caused or triggered the bankruptcy.

120. Article I of the Supplementary Agreement to the FCN Treaty, which confers rights not qualified by national or most-favoured-nation standards, provides as follows:

> "The nationals, corporations and associations of either High Contracting Party shall not be subjected to arbitrary or discriminatory measures within the territories of the other High Contracting Party resulting particularly in: (a) preventing their effective control and management of enterprises which they have been permitted to establish or acquire therein; or (b) impairing their other legally acquired rights and interests in such enterprises or in the investments which they have made, whether in the form of funds (loans, shares or otherwise), materials, equipment, services, processes, patents, techniques or otherwise.

121. [. . .] The requisition, it is said, clearly prevented Raytheon and Machlett from exercising their control and management of ELSI and also resulted in an impairment of their legally acquired rights and interests in ELSI, inasmuch as it prevented the voluntary liquidation of ELSI and caused it to file for bankruptcy. To the claim as it is presented in those terms, however, the Chamber has already given its answer: the absence of a sufficiently palpable connection between the effects of the requisition and the failure of ELSI to carry out its planned orderly liquidation. [. . .]

122. [. . .] But the United States claims that there was "discrimination" in favour of IRI, an entity controlled by Italy; and this was, in the view of the United States, contrary to the FCN Treaty and Supplementary Agreement. However, the requisition order in itself did not serve any interest of IRI.

123. In order to show that the requisition order was an "arbitrary" act in the sense of the Supplementary Agreement to the FCN Treaty, the Applicant has relied (*inter alia*) upon the status of that order in Italian law.

Relationship between Domestic and International Law

124. Yet it must be borne in mind that the fact that an act of a public authority may have been unlawful in municipal law does not necessarily mean that that act was

unlawful in international law, as a breach of treaty or otherwise. A finding of the local courts that an act was unlawful may well be relevant to an argument that it was also arbitrary, but by itself, and without more, unlawfulness cannot be said to amount to arbitrariness.

128. Arbitrariness is not so much something opposed to a rule of law, as something opposed to the rule of law. This idea was expressed by the Court in the *Asylum* case, when it spoke of "arbitrary action" being "substituted for the rule of law". (*Asylum Judgment*, I.C.J. Reports 1950, p. 284). It is a willful disregard of due process of law, an act which shocks, or at least surprises, a sense of juridical propriety. Nothing in the decision of the Prefect, or in the judgment of the Court of Appeal of Palermo, conveys any indication that the requisition order of the Mayor was to be regarded in that light.

129. United States counsel felt able to describe the requisition generally as being an "unreasonable or capricious exercise of authority". [. . .] with the threatened sudden unemployment of some 800 workers at one factory. It cannot be said to have been unreasonable or merely capricious for the Mayor to seek to use the powers conferred on him by the law in an attempt to do something about a difficult and distressing situation. [. . .] although later annulled by the Prefect because "the intended purpose of the requisition could not in practice be achieved by the order itself", it was nonetheless within the competence of the Mayor of Palermo. [. . .] Furthermore, here was an act belonging to a category of public acts from which appeal on juridical grounds was provided in law (and indeed in the event used, not without success).

136. Having found that the Respondent has not violated the FCN Treaty in the manner asserted by the Applicant, it follows that the Chamber rejects also the claim for reparation made in the Submissions of the Applicant. (Unanimously, by four votes to one.)

Dissenting Opinion of Judge Schwebel

[. . .] The claims of the United States in this case have not been sustained, but that is not because the Chamber has found against the United States on the law of the Treaty; it has found against the United States on the practical and legal significance to be attached to the facts of the case. [. . .]

[. . .] The Court of Appeal held that "damages" were due for the period in which the plant and its equipment were not available to ELSI or its representative but were operationally unavailable by reason of the requisition. Thus the Court of Appeal imported that ELSI or its representative continued as of the date of the requisition and thereafter to have possessory rights in ELSI's plant and equipment of which they had been deprived before the requisition took place. If the Court of Appeal saw ELSI as deprived of no right by the requisition because such right had been dissolved by the prior fact of insolvency and its effects in Italian law, how could it have awarded what it described as "damages" deriving from the requisition? [. . .]

[. . .] ELSI's financial difficulties came to a head when Raytheon informed it that it was no longer prepared to invest capital in ELSI. [. . .] But that is not at all to say that Raytheon was not ready and willing to advance such further sums as might be required to permit an orderly liquidation of ELSI's assets. [. . .] In my view, it is unpersuasive for the Chamber to say, in effect, that ELSI would have gone into bankruptcy later if not sooner, and accordingly that the requisition did not matter. [. . .] Was it consistent with "the principles of equitable treatment" which the Preamble to the Supplementary Agreement describes the Treaty as containing? [. . .] Did it respect "the guaranty against political risks" which the Treaty as a whole was designed to provide? Not in my view.

The weightiest reason advanced by the Chamber in support of its conclusion that the requisition was not arbitrary may be that it was reviewed administratively and judicially. [. . .] To be sure, the Prefect's decision was seriously and unjustifiably delayed, and that delay was materially prejudicial to the interests of ELSI and its creditors. Nevertheless it remains the fact that, in this case, Italian administrative and judicial processes functioned. [. . .] The Prefect would have had to have acted almost immediately—as other Prefects in some other requisition cases had been shown to have acted—if the requisition was to have been lifted before ELSI was forced into bankruptcy. [. . .]

It may of course be maintained that, even in the absence of the requisition, ELSI would have gone bankrupt. That indeed is the essential conclusion of the Italian courts and of this Chamber. But this conclusion does not take account of the fact—or of what is believed to have been shown in this Opinion to be the fact—that, if the requisition had not been imposed when it was imposed, ELSI would have been enabled to realize materially more from its assets than in fact was realized, even if, at some point, ELSI might have been obliged to go into bankruptcy.

It accordingly follows that ELSI was not placed in the position it would have been in had there been no requisition. The equivalent result was not attained by Italian administrative and judicial processes, however estimable they were. Thus, in my view, those processes do not absolve Italy of having committed an arbitrary act within the meaning of the Treaty's Supplementary Agreement.

Sumitomo Shoji America, Inc. v. Avagliano, 457 U.S. 176 (1982).

Case Introduction

A class action was brought by a group of twelve past and present female secretarial employees of Sumitomo Shoji America, Inc, ("Sumitomo"). Sumitomo is incorporated in the United States and is a wholly owned subsidiary of Sumitomo Shoji Kabushiki Kaisha, a Japanese general trading company.

The plaintiffs were all, except one, United States citizens. The exception was a Japanese citizen living in the United States. The class action claimed that Sumitomo's practice of hiring only male Japanese for executive, managerial and sales positions violated Title VII of the Civil Rights Act 1964, which provides against discrimination on the basis of gender and national origin. Sumitomo moved to dismiss the complaint on the ground that its practices were protected under Art. VIII(1) of the Friendship, Commerce and Navigation Treaty ("FCN Treaty") between the United States and Japan. They alleged that the wording "of their choice" in Art.VIII(1) immunized them from the language of Title VII.

Relying on Article XXII(3) of the FCN Treaty, the District Court held that a company must be established under Japanese law to be considered a Japanese company for treaty purposes. It follows that Sumitomo America "is a domestic corporation and as such has neither standing nor need to invoke the aegis of the Treaty."[101] Thus, Sumitomo's American subsidiary could not claim immunity from United States law, including Title VII.

The Court of Appeals held that Art. VIII(1) intended to cover locally incorporated subsidiaries of foreign companies but that the Treaty language did not protect Sumitomo's employment practices from Title VII scrutiny.

© Pauline C. Reich: *After Avagliano v. Sumitomo Shoji America, Inc.: What Standard of Title VII Will Apply to Foreign-Owned U.S. Subsidiaries and Branches?* 10 B.C. Third World L.J. 259 (1990).

[. . .] The *Avagliano* case is currently the benchmark decision involving non-discrimination in the employment of Americans by foreign-owned U.S. companies. [. . .] As the Japanese equivalent of the Fortune 500 have set up subsidiaries, branches, and manufacturing plants abroad, in many instances they have exported Japanese-style labor relations practices. These practices are characterized by harmonious relations between paternalistic management and workers pleased with their work environment. [. . .] Other Japanese practices are less adaptable to American labor law and social norms. [. . .]

American courts must decide whether to permit foreign-owned U.S.-incorporated subsidiaries, considered by the Supreme Court to be companies of the United States, the privilege to be subject to modification of standards applied to domestic companies. The courts' decisions may be influenced by the policy consideration that these subsidiaries bring investments into the U.S. economy. A further question is whether branches of foreign parent companies should be exempt from civil rights laws because the FCN Treaty's provisions supersede domestic law. These difficult problems occur in other host countries dealing with the phenomenon of investment by multinational enterprises. [. . .]

While reducing regulation may be possible from a government policy standpoint, it may not be possible in the United States, where case law holds that a treaty does not supplant domestic law, and the EEOC has promulgated policy upholding the *Avagliano* decision. The Supreme Court's view that a locally incorporated subsidiary

101. *Avagliano v. Sumitomo Shoji America, Inc.*, 473 F. Supp. 506 (S.D.N.Y. 1979).

is an American company indicates that subsidiaries will continue to be treated as domestic corporations with respect to employment practices. Whether holdings such as *Avagliano* are remnants of a former, more affluent period of American legal history or are immutable will be left to the courts and legislators to decide with respect to the exact standards to be applied to employees at various levels of the U.S. organization for purposes of hiring and promotion.

Principal Points of the Judgment

Chief Justice Burger delivered the opinion of the Court

We granted certiorari to decide whether Article VIII(1) of the Friendship, Commerce and Navigation Treaty between the United States and Japan provides a defense to a Title VII employment discrimination suit against an American subsidiary of a Japanese company.

II

Interpretation of the Friendship, Commerce and Navigation Treaty between Japan and the United States must, of course, begin with the language of the Treaty itself. The clear import of treaty language controls unless "application of the words of the treaty according to their obvious meaning effects a result inconsistent with the intent or expectations of its signatories." *Maximov v. United States*, 373 U.S. 49, 54, 83 S.Ct. 1054, 10 L.Ed.2d 184 (1963).

Article VIII(1) of the Treaty provides in pertinent part:

> "[C]ompanies of either Party shall be permitted to engage, within the territories of the other Party, accountants and other technical experts, executive personnel, attorneys, agents and other specialists of their choice." [. . .]

Both the Ministry of Foreign Affairs of Japan and the United States Department of State agree that a United States corporation, even when wholly owned by a Japanese company, is not a company of Japan under the Treaty, and is therefore not covered by Article VIII(1). [. . .]

A series of Treaties negotiated before World War II gave corporations legal status and access to foreign courts, but it was not until the postwar Friendship, Commerce and Navigation Treaties that United States corporations gained the right to conduct business in other countries. The purpose of the Treaties was [. . .] to assure them the right to conduct business on an equal basis without suffering discrimination based on their alienage.

The Treaties accomplished their purpose by granting foreign corporations "national treatment" in most respects and by allowing foreign individuals and companies to form locally incorporated subsidiaries. [. . .]

D. Causation and Compensation

Asian Agric. Prod. Limited v. Republic of Sri Lanka, ICSID Case No. ARB/87/3, Award (June 27, 1990).

Case Introduction

Asian Agricultural Products Ltd ("AAPL"), a Hong Kong company, held a 48.2% share of Serendib Seafoods Ltd ("Serendib"), a Sri Lankan joint venture that was formed to cultivate and export shrimp to Japan. Its principal facility was a shrimp farm located in eastern Sri Lanka, an area which had come under control of Tamil insurgents during a major insurrection. In January 1987, during a counter-insurgency operation of the Sri-Lankan Security Forces, this key shrimp farm was destroyed. Serendib soon went out of business, and AAPL lost its investment.

In July 1987, AAPL brought a dispute before an ICSID Tribunal claiming violations by Sri Lanka of the 1980 Sri Lanka-UK BIT (extended to Hong Kong). AAPL argued that Sri Lanka had failed to comply with its general BIT obligation to accord "full protection and security" to foreign investments (BIT Article 2) and that this was a standard of "strict liability" without any need to prove that the damages were attributable to the state or its agents. Additionally, they pointed to BIT Article 4 on rules of compensation for losses suffered due to war or other armed conflict. Based on their ownership, AAPL requested $8 million in compensation.

Significance of Case

At the time of the case, it was unique in many respects. First, it raised the issue of jurisdiction as regards the right of a third party to rely on the provisions of a bilateral investment treaty to make a claim against a state. Second, it illustrated the extent arbitral tribunals are ready to go to protect foreign investors and investment even in situations of insurgency that may demand extraordinary measures from host states. Third, it also showed the difficulty this could create for sovereign states in taking steps that they consider best for protecting the larger interests of states.

Principal Points of the Judgment

[. . .]

45. The Claimant's primary submission—as previously explained (*supra*, § 26)—is based on the assumption that the "full protection and security" provision of Article 2(2) created a "strict liability" which renders the Sri Lankan Government liable for any destruction of the investment, even if caused by persons whose acts are not attributable to the Government and under circumstances beyond the State's control. For sustaining this construction introducing a new type of objective absolute responsibility called "without fault", the Claimant's main argument relies on the existence in the text of the Treaty of two terms: "enjoy" and "full". According to the Claimant, this combination confirms, that the Parties intended to provide the Investor with a "guarantee" against all losses suffered due to the destruction of the Investment, for whatever reason and without any need to establish the person

that caused the damage. In other words, the Parties substituted the "due diligence" standard of general international law by a new obligation creating an obligation to achieve a result ("obligation de resultat"), effectively providing the foreign investor with a form of "insurance" against the risk of having his investment destroyed under whatever circumstances.

46. The Tribunal is of the opinion that the Claimant's construction of Article 2(2) as explained herein-above cannot be justified under any of the canons of interpretation previously stated (*supra*, § 40).

47. In conformity with Rule (B), the words "shall enjoy full protection and security" have to be construed according to the "common use which custom has affixed" to them, their "*usus loqueni*", "natural and obvious sense", and "fair meaning."

In fact, similar expressions, or even stronger wordings like the "most constant protection", were utilized since last century in a number of bilateral treaties concluded to encourage the flow of international economic exchanges and to provide the citizens and national companies established on the territory of the other Contracting Party with adequate treatment for them as well as to their property. [. . .]

48. The Arbitral Tribunal is not aware of any case in which the obligation assumed by the host State to provide the nationals of the other Contracting State with "full protection and security" was construed as an absolute obligation which guarantees that no damages will be suffered, in the sense that any violation thereof creates automatically a "strict liability" on behalf of the host State. *Sambiaggio* case [(It. v. Venez.), 10 R.I.A.A. 499 (Ven. Arb. 1903),] seems to be the only reported case in which such argument was voiced, but without success. The Italian Commissioner AGNOLI, referred in his Report to:

> The protection and security . . . which the Venezuelan Government explicitly guarantees by Article 4 of the Treaty of 1861 to Italians residing in Venezuela (U.N. Reports, op. cit., p. 502—underlining added).

The Venezuelan Commissioner ZULOAGA responded by indicating that:

> Governments are constituted to afford protection, not to guarantee it (*Ibid.*, p. 511).

The Umpire RALSTON put an end to the Italian allegation by emphasizing that:

> If it had been the contract between Italy and Venezuela, understood and consented by both, that the latter should be held liable for the acts of revolutionists something in derogation of the general principles of international law—this agreement would naturally have found direct expression in the protocol itself and would not have been left to doubtful interpretation (*Ibid.*, p. 521).

49. In the recent case concerning *Eleittvnica Sicula S.P.A. (ELSI)* between the U.S.A. and Italy adjudicated by a Chamber of the International Court of Justice, the U.S.A. Government invoked Article V(1) of the Bilateral Treaty which established an obligation to provide "the most constant protection and security", but without claiming that this obligation constitutes a "guarantee" involving the emergence of a "strict

liability" (Section 2, Chapter V of the U.S.A. Memorial dated May 15, 1987, where reference is made, on the contrary at page 135 to the: "One well-established aspect of the international standard of treatment . . . that States must use "due diligence" to prevent wrongful injuries to the person or property of aliens within their territory").

In its Judgment of July 20. 1989, the ICJ Chamber clearly stated that:

> The reference in Article V to the provision of "constant protection and security" cannot be construed as the giving of a warranty that property shall never in any circumstances be occupied or disturbed (I.C.J., Recueil, 1989, 108, p. 65).

Consequently, both the oldest reported arbitral precedent and the latest I.C.J. ruling confirms that the language imposing on the host State an obligation to provide "protection and security" or "full protection and security required by international law" (the other expression included in the same Article V) could not be construed according to the natural and ordinary sense of the words as creating a "strict liability". The rule remains that:

> The State into which an alien has entered . . . is not an insurer or a guarantor of his security . . . It does not, and could hardly be asked to, accept an absolute responsibility for all injuries to foreigners (Alwyn V. Freeman, *Responsibility of States for Unlawful Acts of Their Armed Forces*, Sijthoff, Leiden, 1957, p.14)

This conclusion arrived at more than three decades ago, still reflects in the Tribunal's opinion—the present status of International Law Investment Standards as reflected in "the worldwide BIT network" (K.S. Gudgeon, "Valuation of Nationalized Property Under United States and other Bilateral Investment Treaties". Chapter III, in the *Valuation of Nationalized Property in International Law*, Ed. by Richard B. Lillich, vol. 1V, (1987), p. 120).

50. In the opinion of the present Arbitral Tribunal, the addition of words like "constant" or "full" to strengthen the required standards of "protection and security" could justifiably indicate the Parties' intention to require within their treaty relationship a standard of "due diligence" higher than the "minimum standard" of general international law. But, the nature of both the obligation and ensuring responsibility remain unchanged, since the added words "constant" or "full" are by themselves not sufficient to establish that the Parties intended to transform their mutual obligation into a "strict liability".

51. The Tribunal's opinion arrived at in applying the established rule, according to which the words contained in a treaty provision have to be given the natural and fair meaning affixed to them by the common usage, is further supported by recourse to the other canons of interpretation.

According to Rule (C) (*supra*, § 40), proper interpretation has to take into account the realization of the Treaty's general spirit and objectives, which is clearly in the present case the encouragement of investment through securing an adequate environment of legal protection. But, in the absence of travaux preparatoires in the proper sense, it would be almost impossible to ascertain whether Sri Lanka and the United Kingdom had contemplated during their negotiations the necessity of disregarding the common habitual pattern adopted by the previous treaties, and to establish a "strict liability" in favour of the foreign investor as one of the objectives of their treaty protection.

Equally, none among the authors referred to by the Parties claimed in his commentary that the Sri Lanka–U.K. Treaty or similar Bilateral Investment Treaties had the effect of increasing the customary international law standards of protection to the extent of imposing "strict liability" on the host State in cases where the investment suffers losses due to property destruction.

Accordingly, recourse to the spirit of the Treaty and its objectives would not alter the conclusion arrived at by the Tribunal in refusing to consider that the Sri Lanka–U.K. Treaty imposed by Article 2.(2) a "strict liability" in the event of failure to provide "full protection and security".

52. Moreover, both Rules (D) and (E) confirm the Tribunal's opinion, as Article 2(2) should not be taken separately out of the Treaty's global context. The Claimant's contention that Article 2(2) adopted a standard of "strict liability" would lead logically to the inevitable conclusion that Article 4 in its entirety becomes superfluous, in the sense that according to the Claimant's interpretation the Parties were not serious in adding to their Treaty two provisions which are not susceptible of getting any application in practice. Such an interpretation has to be rejected in application of Rule (E) which requires that Article 2(2) be interpreted in a manner that does not deprive Article 4 from having any meaning or scope of applicability. Such an unaccepted result could have been easily avoided if the Claimant had not disregarded Rule (D) according to which the rules of general international law have to be taken into consideration by necessary implication, and not to be deemed totally excluded as alleged by the Claimant.

In the Tribunal's opinion the non-reference to international law in Article 2(2) of the Sri Lanka–U.K. Treaty should not be taken as implying the Parties' intention to avoid its application under any aspect, including its role as supplementary source providing guidance in the process of interpretation. [. . .]

53. Finally, it has to be recalled that in reliance upon Rule (F) the precedents established by the Arbitral Tribunal in the *Sambiaggio* case (1903) and by the ICJ Chamber in the *Elettronia Sicula* case (1989), both previously referred to (*supra*, §48-49) are categoric in supporting the Tribunal's refusal to construe the words "full protection and security" as imposing a "strict liability" on the host State for whatever losses suffered due to the destruction of the investment protected under the treaty.

Therefore, and taking into consideration all the reasons stated in the previous paragraphs (*supra*, 45-52), the Tribunal declares unfounded the Claimant's main plea aiming to consider the Government of Sri Lanka assuming strict liability under Article 2(2) of the Bilateral Investment Treaty, without any need to prove that the damages suffered were attributable to the State or its agents, and to establish the State's responsibility for not acting with "due diligence".

54. For the same reasons, the Tribunal rejects the Claimant's argument based on the most-favored-nation clause contained in Article 3 of the Sri Lanka–U.K. Bilateral Investment Treaty. By invoking the absence in the Sri Lanka–Switzerland Treaty of a text similar to Article 4 providing for a "war clause" or "civil disturbance" exemption from the full protection and security standard, the Claimant based his argument on two implicit assumptions:

(i)—that the Sri Lanka–Switzerland Treaty provides equally for a "strict liability" standard of protection in case of losses suffered due to property destruction; and

(ii)—that the rules of general international law are totally excluded and replaced exclusively by the Treaty's "strict liability" standard.

Both assumptions are unfounded, as the Tribunal has no reasons to believe that the Sri Lanka–Switzerland Treaty adopted a "strict liability" standard, and the Tribunal is convinced that, in the absence of a specific rule provided for in the Treaty itself as lex specialis, the general international law rules have to assume their role as lex generalis. Accordingly, it is not proven that the Sri Lanka–Switzerland Treaty contains rules more favorable than those provided for under the Sri Lanka–U.K. Treaty, and hence, Article 3 of the latter Treaty cannot be justifiably invoked in the present case.

[. . .]

67. Consequently, it could be safely ascertained that the Bilateral Investment Treaty, through the above-stated renvoi technique, had not left the host State totally immune from any responsibility in case the foreign investor suffers losses due to the destruction of his investment which occurs during a counter-insurgency action undertaken by the governmental security forces.

In implementation of Article 4(1), the host State could find itself in such a situation bound to bear a certain degree of responsibility to be determined in implementation of the renvoi contained in that Article 4(1). Once failure to provide "full protection and security" has been proven (under Article 2(2) of the Sri Lanka/U.K. Treaty or under a similar provision existing in other bilateral Investment Treaties extending the same standard to nationals of a third State), the host State's responsibility is established, and compensation is due according to the general international law rules and standards previously developed with regard to the State's failure to comply with its "due diligence" obligation under the minimum standard of customary international law.

[. . .]

72. It is a generally accepted rule of International Law, clearly stated in international arbitral awards and in the writings of the doctrinal authorities, that:

(i)—A State on whose territory an insurrection occurs is not responsible for loss or damage sustained by foreign investors unless it can be shown that the Government of that state failed to provide the standard of protection required, either by treaty, or under general customary law, as the case may be; and (ii)—Failure to provide the standard of protection required entails the state's international responsibility for laws suffered, regardless of whether the damages occurred during an insurgents' derisive act or resulting from governmental counter-insurgency activities.

[. . .]

88. Both Parties are equally in agreement about the principle, according to which, in case of property destruction, the amount of the compensation due has to be calculated in a manner that adequately reflects the full value of the investment lost as a result of said destruction and the damages incurred as a result thereof. [. . .]

Thus, the task of the Tribunal in the present case has to focus on the determination of the "value" of the Claimant's right which suffered losses due to the destruction that took place on January 28, 1987, and throughout the following days during which Serendib's farm remained under governmental temporary occupation (unjustifiably characterized by the Claimant as de facto "requisition", since it has not been proven that the Government used the farm to promote its own military interests and to benefit thereof).

[. . .]

95. In deciding on the issues under consideration which are subject to disagreement among the Parties, the Tribunal has primarily to indicate that AAPL is entitled in the present arbitration case to claim compensation under the Sri Lanka–U.K. Bilateral Investment Treaty, on the legal grounds previously described in Part II of this award due to the fact that the Claimant's "investment" in Sri Lanka "suffered losses" owing to events falling under one or more of the circumstances enumerated by Article 4(1) of the Treaty ("revolution, state of national emergence, revolt, insurrection", etc . . .).

The undisputed "investments" effected since 1985 by AAPL in Sri Lanka are in the form of acquiring shares in Serendib Company, which has been incorporated in Sri Lanka under the domestic Companies Law.

Accordingly, the Treaty protection provides no direct coverage with regard to Serendib's physical assets as such ("farm structures and equipment", "shrimp stock in ponds", cost of "training the technical staff', etc.), or to the intangible assets of Serendib if any ("good will", "future profitability", etc [. . .]). The scope of the international law protection granted to the foreign investor in the present case is limited to a single item: the value of his share-holding in the joint-venture entity (Serendib Company).

96. In the absence of a stock market at which the price for Serendib's shares were quoted on January 27, 1987 (the day preceding the events which led to the destruction of the value of AAPL's investment in Serendib's capital), the evaluation of the shares owned by AAPL in Serendib has to be established by the alternative method of determining what was the reasonable price a willing purchaser would have offered to AAPL to acquire its shareholding in Serendib. [. . .]

E. Definition of Investment: An Example— *Mr. Saba Fakes v. Turkey* (ICSID Case No. ARB/07/20)

Mr. Saba Fakes v. Republic of Turkey, ICSID Case No. ARB/07/20, Award (July 14, 2010).

Case Introduction

This case involves application of the Netherlands-Turkey Bilateral Investment Treaty ("BIT"), which entered into force on November 1, 1989. Mr. Saba Fakes was of Jordanian and Dutch nationality.

The Uzan family, prominent in Turkey, maintained a large group of companies and owned 67% of Telsim Mobil Telekomunikayson Hizmetleri A.S. ("Telsim"), a leading Turkish mobile phone company. The Uzans held these shares indirectly through Standard Telekomunikasyon Biligisayar Hizmetleri AS ("Standard Telekom").

Mr. Fakes claimed that on July 3, 2003, he became legal owner of 66.96% of Telsim shares, this legal ownership resulting from the transfer of temporary Telsim share certificates from Standard Telekom to Masoud International Trading Establishment ("Masoud"), a company incorporated in Jordan and then transferred to himself. Mr. Fakes paid the amount of US$3,800 in cash for the temporary share certificates, immediately payable upon the execution of the transfer Agreements. It was agreed that a total of US$17,668,000 would be due and payable upon certain timings described in the Agreements. An oral agreement between Mr. Fakes and Mr. Hakan Uzan concluded in 2003, declared that beneficial ownership of these shares remains with Mr. Uzan.

Mr. Fakes further claimed that in July 2003, Turkey commenced a series of actions to freeze Telsim assets and subsequently sold the whole of Telsim to Vodafone for approximately US$4.5 billion. In parallel, criminal proceedings had been brought in Turkey against Uzan family members for alleged fraud and money laundering.

Mr. Fakes brought his claim against Turkey for alleged expropriation and failure to ensure fair and equitable treatment. The claimant assessed the damages suffered at US$19 million.

Turkey responded that Mr. Fakes was "serving as a front" or "dummy shareholder" for the Uzans who, being Turkish, could not bring a claim in their own right against Turkey before the International Centre for Settlement of Investment Disputes ("ICSID").

Principal Points of the Award

V. Jurisdictional Issues

51. The Respondent's jurisdictional objections may be summarized as follows:

- The Claimant lacks effective Dutch nationality which is necessary for him to qualify as an investor under Article 1(a)(i) of the Netherlands-Turkey BIT and Article 25(2)(a) of the ICSID Convention.

- The Claimant did not make an "investment" within the meaning of Article 25(1) of the ICSID Convention and Article 1 of the Netherlands-Turkey BIT. The Claimant holds, at best, an assigned claim belonging to third parties, namely the Uzan family, and has engaged in abusive treaty shopping prohibited under general principles of international law; and
- The Claimant's alleged investment was made in violation of the laws and regulations of the Republic of Turkey and, thus, does not qualify as a protected investment under Articles 2(1) and (2) of the Netherlands-Turkey BIT.

Nationality under ICSID Convention

A. Does the Claimant satisfy the Nationality Requirement under Article 25(2)(a) of the ICSID Convention and Article 1(a)(i) of the Netherlands-Turkey BIT?

1) The Parties' Respective Positions

54. The Respondent accepts that the Claimant holds both Jordanian and Dutch nationalities. The Respondent contends, however, that in order to bring ICSID arbitration under the Netherlands-Turkey BIT, it does not suffice to hold Dutch nationality. Such nationality must be effective. The Respondent submits that the effective nationality test, as established in the *Nottebohm* case [(*Liech. v. Guat.*) 1955 I.C.J. Rep. 4 (Apr. 6),] by the ICJ, is one of international law without limitations to any particular forum. The Respondent maintains that the Claimant did not submit any evidence of the effectiveness of his Dutch nationality. To the contrary, according to the Respondent, the evidence before the Tribunal suggests that the Claimant holds an effective Jordanian nationality, and should be precluded from relying on the provisions of the Netherlands-Turkey BIT.

55. The Claimant argues that the question of his effective nationality is irrelevant in the context of ICSID arbitration. The Claimant submits that while he is a dual national, such dual nationality does not concern the nationality of the Respondent State. To the extent that he is a national of a Contracting Party within the meaning of Article 1(a)(i) of the Netherlands-Turkey BIT and Article 25(2)(a) of the ICSID Convention. Furthermore, the Claimant disputes the contention that he does not have effective Dutch nationality and submits that he has a substantial bond to the Netherlands. The Claimant emphasizes that he has always maintained a genuine link with the Netherlands (he was born to a Dutch mother and a Jordanian father who acquired Dutch nationality when the Claimant was eight years of age), and that his Dutch nationality is effective.

2) The Tribunal's Decision

56. [. . .] the Tribunal is not convinced by the Respondent's arguments that the Claimant should be precluded from submitting his claims to the present Tribunal due to the alleged lack of effectiveness of his Dutch nationality.

59. The wording of Article 25(2)(a) of the ICSID Convention expressly excludes from the Centre's jurisdiction any natural person who holds the nationality of a Contracting State party to the dispute.

61. The explicit exclusion from the Centre's jurisdiction of dual nationals who hold the nationality of the host State is the only jurisdictional bar relating to a natural person's nationality that was contemplated by the drafters of the Convention. It is significant, in the Tribunal's opinion, that this bar is not subject to the test of the effectiveness of the host State's nationality.

62. On the other hand, the Contracting Parties to the ICSID Convention did not exclude claims of dual nationals *per se*, in circumstances when such dual nationals (i) hold the nationality of at least one Contracting State and (ii) do not hold the nationality of the host State. This is precisely the case here, since the Claimant holds the nationality of an ICSID Contracting Party (the Netherlands) and does not hold the nationality of the Respondent State.

64. [. . .] Pursuant to Article 1(a)(i) of the Netherlands-Turkey BIT, for the purposes of this BIT *"investor" means: (i) "a natural person who is a national of a Contracting Party under its applicable law."* It clearly results from this definition that the Netherlands-Turkey BIT does not require an investor's nationality to be effective for him or her to bring a claim against the host State on the basis of the BIT. [. . .]

65. The Netherlands-Turkey BIT therefore does not exclude dual nationals from the protection extended by the BIT, to the effect that Mr. Fakes may file a claim against the Republic of Turkey as a Dutch national regardless of the fact that he also holds Jordanian nationality.

66. [. . .] The Respondent suggests that the Claimant's nationality should meet the effective nationality test as set forth in the *Nottebohm* case.

68. While the *Nottebohm* case set forth a requirement of a "genuine link" *with the State of nationality*, that requirement was applied in the context of diplomatic protection of nationals by way of claims filed by the State whose nationality they hold. The issue in that case was not one of dual *nationality* and its consequences, if any, on an individual's right to bring a direct claim against a third State, but whether a State could exercise diplomatic protection *on behalf of* an individual who had no "genuine link" with that State.

69. The Tribunal notes that treaties for the promotion and protection of investments, as well as the ICSID Convention, establish a separate mechanism of direct recourse to international arbitration against the host State. Pursuant to Article 27(1) of the ICSID Convention, Contracting Parties have waived their right to grant diplomatic protection to, or bring an international claim on behalf of, their nationals who pursue arbitration under the auspices of the Centre. The rules of customary international law applicable in the context of diplomatic protection do not apply as such to investor-State arbitration. [. . .] *"This is a manifestation of the very scheme of ICSID, which 'firmly establishes the capacity of a private individual or a corporation to proceed directly against a State in an international forum', and renders an award binding on both State and investor."* [A. Sinclair, "ICSID"s Nationality Requirement", in TJ Grierson Weiler (ed.), *Investment Treaty Arbitration and International Law* (2008), at pp. 86-87.]

70. [. . .] Had the Contracting Parties intended to set additional limitations as regards jurisdiction *ratione personae*, no doubt they would have expressly stated such limitations in the text of the BIT.

73. [. . .] the Tribunal notes that previous ICSID decisions and awards specifically excluded the application of the effective nationality test in the context of investor-State arbitration. Indeed, when previous ICSID tribunals made references to *Nottebohm* case it was to rule that those decisions found no application in the context of the ICSID Convention. Specifically, the majority in the *Siag* case stated: "*While it may be asserted that if this were a diplomatic protection case it could be argued differently, the parties have consented to have their dispute resolved under the ICSID Convention and it sets out a particular regime for the determination of jurisdiction. Under Article 9(3) of the BIT the avenue of diplomatic protection is specifically excluded while the arbitration is in progress.*" [*Waguih Elie George Siag and Clorinda Vecchi v. Egypt* (ICSID Case No. ARB/05/15), Decision on Jurisdiction, April 11, 2007, para 198.]

75. [. . .] The Respondent submits that the effective nationality test is distinct and should not be "*confused*" with the question of dual nationality dealt with in Article 25(2)(a) of the ICSID Convention.

76. The Tribunal cannot side with this interpretation [. . .]. The language of Article 25(2)(a) of the ICSID Convention is clear and does not require any further clarification. Pursuant to the generally accepted rules of treaty interpretation, as codified in Article 31 of the Vienna Convention on the Law of Treaties, the Tribunal is precluded from elaborating any interpretation that would run counter to this clear language, in particular any interpretation that would result in establishing additional limitations to the Centre's jurisdiction where no such limitations were provided by the Contracting Parties.

77. This is not to say that the effective nationality test never has any bearing in the context of ICSID arbitration.

78. Thus, one might argue that a nationality of convenience, acquired "*in exceptional circumstances of speed and accommodation*", for the purposes of bringing a claim before the Centre should not be considered to satisfy the nationality requirements of a BIT and Article 25(2)(a) of the Convention.[102] [. . .] Mr. Fakes acquired his Dutch nationality as a youngster, while living in the Netherlands with his parents, and there is certainly nothing exceptional in such acquisition. His nationality is not one of convenience, obtained for the purposes of bringing his claim against the Respondent.

81. In view of the foregoing, the Respondent's jurisdictional objection based on the Claimant's nationality is rejected and the Tribunal finds that it has jurisdiction *ratione personae* over the Claimant.

---

102. *See*, for instance, A. Sinclair, ICSID's Nationality Requirement, in TJ Grierson Weiler (ed.), *Investment Treaty Arbitration and International Law* (2008), at p.101, Exhibit R-97.

Investment under Turkish Law

B. Did the Claimant Make an Investment in the Republic of Turkey?

1) The Parties' Respective Positions

82. The Respondent argues that the Claimant's alleged holding of shares in Telsim does not constitute a protected investment within the meaning of Article 25(1) of the ICSID Convention and Article 1 of the Netherlands-Turkey BIT. The Respondent submits that the definition of an investment is contingent on the fulfilment of the requirements of both the ICSID Convention and the relevant BIT.

83. The Respondent invites the Tribunal to follow the so-called *Salini* test [*Salini Constuttori SPA and Italstrade SPA v. Kingdom of Morocco* (ICSID Case No. ARB/00/4), Decision on Jurisdiction, July 23, 2001,] when examining whether there is an investment within the meaning of Article 25(1) of the ICSID Convention, namely the fulfilment of the following four requirements: (i) a contribution, (ii) a certain duration, (iii) an element of risk, and (iv) a contribution to the host State's economic development or, at the very minimum, a contribution to the economy of the host State.

84. According to the Respondent, the Claimant's payment of US$3,800 in cash cannot amount to a contribution reasonably expected under the ICSID Convention and the Netherlands-Turkey BIT. Likewise, the duration criterion is lacking, since the Claimant never intended to retain the shares in his ownership and for his benefit, but pursued an objective of facilitating the transfer of those shares to a third party. [. . .] Moreover, by entering into an "arrangement" with Mr. Uzan, the Claimant did not assume any risk distinctive of an investment under the ICSID Convention. [. . .] the Claimant did not carry out any economic activity and did not contribute to any flow of international capital or technology into the Republic of Turkey.

85. Furthermore, relying on the *Phoenix Action v. The Czech Republic* award of April 15, 2009,[103] the Respondent submits that an operation made in violation of the principle of good faith cannot qualify as an investment protected under the ICSID Convention and the relevant BIT. The Respondent contends that Mr. Fakes' arrangement violated the principle of good faith, as it was aimed at artificially transforming a domestic dispute between Turkish nationals, namely the Uzans, and the Turkish State into an international dispute involving a foreign national fronting the claims of Turkish nationals.

86. Finally, the Respondent submits that the Claimant's operation constitutes [. . .] an abusive treaty shopping which violates the "investment" requirement of both the ICSID Convention and the Netherlands-Turkey BIT.

87. [. . .] The Claimant submits that the definition of an investment agreed upon in the relevant BIT should prevail over the interpretation of the ICSID Convention in

103. *Phoenix Action, Ltd v. The Czech Republic* (ICSID Case No. ARB/06/5), Award, April 15, 2009.

circumstances where the Convention's drafters have explicitly left the term "investment" to be defined further by the Contracting Parties in their respective BITs.

2) The Tribunal's Decision

92. Article 1(b) of the Netherlands-Turkey BIT provides for its part:

> "For the purposes of the present Agreement:
>
> (b) 'investment' means every kind of asset such as equity, debt, claims and service and investment contracts and includes:
>
> (ii) shares of stock or other interests in a company or interests in the assets thereof; [. . .]"

93. While the ownership of shares by a Dutch national in a company incorporated in the Republic of Turkey falls within the definition of an investment provided in Article 1(b)(ii) of the Netherlands-Turkey BIT, this general conclusion does not suffice to address fully the Respondent's jurisdictional objection.

(i) ***The definition of 'investment' within the meaning of Article 25(1) of the ICSID Convention***

96. The Tribunal is not bound by the decisions adopted by previous ICSID tribunals. At the same time, it believes that it should pay due regard to earlier decisions of such tribunals. [. . .]

97. As far as the definition of 'investment' is concerned, however, the Tribunal observes that, while a number of ICSID tribunals have dealt with this notion, no unanimous approach has emerged so far from the existing case law. The proposed solutions are inconsistent, if not conflicting, and do not provide any clear guidance to future arbitral tribunals.

109. [. . .] the Tribunal agrees with the Tribunal in *Joy Mining v. Egypt* case, which emphasized that the "*Convention itself, in resorting to the concept of investment in connection with jurisdiction, establishes a framework to this effect: jurisdiction cannot be based on something different or entirely unrelated . . . The parties to the dispute cannot by contract or treaty define as investment, for the purposes of ICSID jurisdiction, something which does not satisfy the objective requirements of Article 25 of the Convention.*"[104]

110. Second, the present Tribunal considers that the criteria of (i) a contribution, (ii) a certain duration, and (iii) an element of risk, are necessary and sufficient to define an investment within the framework of the ICSID Convention. [. . .] These three criteria derive from the ordinary meaning of the word "investment", be it in the context of a complex international transaction or that of the education of one's child.

---

104. *Joy Mining v. Egypt* (ICSID Case No. ARB/03/11), Award on Jurisdiction, August 6, 2004, paras 49-50.

111. The Tribunal is not convinced, on the other hand, that a contribution to the host State's economic development constitutes a criterion of an investment within the framework of the ICSID Convention. Those tribunals that have considered this element as a separate requirement for the definition of an investment, such as the *Salini* Tribunal, have mainly relied on the preamble to the ICSID Convention to support their conclusions. The present Tribunal observes that while the preamble refers to the "*need for international cooperation for economic development*", it would be excessive to attribute to this reference a meaning and function that is not obviously apparent from its wording. [. . .] this objective is not in and of itself an independent criterion for the definition of an investment.

112. Likewise, the principles of good faith and legality cannot be incorporated into the definition of Article 25(1) of the ICSID Convention without doing violence to the language of the ICSID Convention: an investment might be "legal" or "illegal", made in "good faith" or not, it nonetheless remains an investment.

113. While a treaty should be interpreted and applied in good faith, this is a general requirement under treaty law, from which an additional criterion of "good faith" for the definition of investments, which was not contemplated by the text of the ICSID Convention, cannot be derived.

Legality

(ii) The legality requirement of the Netherlands-Turkey BIT

115. Article 2(2) of the Netherlands-Turkey BIT provides that: "*[t]he present Agreement shall apply to investments owned or controlled by investors of one Contracting Party in the territory of the other Contracting Party which are established in accordance with the laws and regulations in force in the latter Contracting Party's territory at the time the investment was made.*" This provision plainly states that the BIT protection shall not apply to investments which have not been established in conformity with the Respondent's laws and regulations, the term 'investment' having been defined in Article 1(b) of the BIT. If this condition is not satisfied, the BIT does not apply. As a result, the Contracting Party cannot be deemed to have given its consent to arbitrate the dispute under Article 8(3) of the BIT and there would therefore be no consent to the Centre's jurisdiction within the meaning of Article 25(1) of the ICSID Convention.

119. [. . .] As to the nature of the rules contemplated in Article 2(2) of the Netherlands-Turkey BIT, it is the Tribunal's view that the legality requirement contained therein concerns the question of compliance with the host State's domestic laws governing the admission of investments in the host State. [. . .] The Tribunal also considers that it would run counter to the object and purpose of investment protection treaties to deny substantive protection to those investments that would violate domestic laws that are unrelated to the very nature of investment regulation.

120. In the present case, the Respondent alleges that the Claimant's transaction was made in breach of the Republic of Turkey's legislation relating to the encouragement of foreign investment, the regulation of the telecommunication sector, as well

as Turkish competition law. The first violation, if demonstrated, might be covered by the legality requirement of Article 2(2) of the Netherlands-Turkey BIT. [. . .] On the other hand, the Tribunal believes that a violation of the regulations in the telecommunication sector or of competition law requirements would not trigger the application of the legality requirement in Article 2(2) of the BIT.

Protection of Investment and Conclusion

(iii) Is there an investment within the meaning of Article 25(1) of the ICSID Convention and Article 1(b) of the BIT and, if so, is the investment made in accordance with Turkish law pursuant to Article 2(2) of the Netherlands-Turkey BIT?

123. According to the Claimant, his legal ownership of Telsim's shares results from the transfer of Telsim's temporary share certificates from Standard Telekom to Masoud and, subsequently, from Masoud to the Claimant.

(a) Are the temporary share certificates valid under Turkish law?

126. [. . .] The Respondent filed a Legal Opinion by Professor Bahtiyar in support of its proposition that this provision also governs the form of the temporary share certificates, and that a joint signature is a prerequisite for the validity of these temporary certificates under Turkish law. To the extent that the temporary share certificates bear only the signature of Mr. Hakan Uzan, the Respondent argues that these certificates are not valid under Turkish law.

129. To the extent that there appears to be no case law or legal provision in Turkish law requiring a double signature on a temporary share certificate, the Tribunal considers that in the present case the Respondent did not meet the burden of proof of the compulsory nature of such requirement in Turkish law. [. . .] However, the question remains as to whether these temporary share certificates transferred any rights to the Claimant that would warrant the corresponding shareholding to qualify as an investment within the meaning of Article 25(1) of the ICSID Convention and Article 1(b) of the Netherlands-Turkey BIT.

133. [. . .] According to the Claimant, pursuant to the Uzan-Fakes oral agreement, which was concluded prior to the signing of the Masoud-Fakes Agreements, the Claimant holds legal title to Telsim's shares and Mr. Uzan has the beneficial ownership of such shares. Furthermore, the Claimant "*would vote [his] shares as instructed by Mr. Uzan, and Mr. Uzan would make any final decision as to when and to whom the shares in Telsim would be sold.*"[105]

134. [. . .] The separation of legal title and beneficial ownership rights does not deprive such ownership of the characteristics of an investment within the meaning of the ICSID Convention or the Netherlands-Turkey BIT.

135. However, upon careful examination of the evidence before it, the Tribunal reached the conclusion that the Claimant does not hold legal title over the share

105. Fakes Witness Statement II, para 5.

certificates in Telsim and, thus, does not have an investment within the meaning of Article 25(1) of the ICSID Convention and Article 1(b) of the Netherlands-Turkey BIT.

136. In the Tribunal's opinion, the Claimant's statements unequivocally indicate that the parties to the Masoud-Fakes and the Uzan-Fakes transactions never had any intention to transfer any rights to the Claimant in relation to Telsim's shares, nor did they actually transfer such rights.

137. [. . .] When questioned by the tribunal, Mr. Fakes conceded that the name of the beneficial owner would have to be disclosed to potential buyers in order for any negotiations to proceed further.

139. The lack of any meaningful role played by the Claimant within the structure explains, in the Tribunal's opinion, the very low purchase price requested of the Claimant at the time of the transfer of shares between Masoud and Mr. Fakes. Had the Claimant acquired any genuine legal rights in the transactions, no doubt he would have been expected to make a contribution (either financial or managerial) beyond the US$3,800 cash payment allegedly made in July 2003. Such figure cannot be reconciled with the significance of the underlying business of the Claimant's valuation of his alleged shareholding at US$19 billion for the purposes of his claim in this arbitration.

140. [. . .] While the Masoud-Fakes Agreements provided for a further total payment of US$17.6 million, no such payment was made by the Claimant within the stipulated 5-year period from the date of the transfer of shares. [. . .] the tribunal is convinced that he was never expected (nor did he expect) to make any payments beyond the initial US$3,800, even assuming that this initial down payment has actually been made.

141. It results from the Claimant's explanations [. . .] that Mr. Fakes never actually came into possession of those shares following their endorsement by Masoud. [. . .] The Tribunal is of the opinion that Mr. Fakes was at no point put in a position to exercise his alleged "legal ownership" over Telsim's shares as he had no independent access to those shares.

147. In light of the foregoing, the Tribunal concludes that the parties to the Uzan-Masoud-Fakes "arrangement" never intended to give effect to the alleged transfer of shares from Masoud to Mr. Fakes and, instead, agreed to implement an agreement which did not transfer even the legal ownership of the share certificates in Telsim to Mr. Fakes. [. . .] In other words, Mr. Fakes has not made any investment in Telsim which would satisfy any of the three criteria for an investment to exist within the meaning of Article 25(1) of the ICSID Convention.

148. To the extent that Mr. Fakes does not hold an investment in the present case, there is no need for this Tribunal to consider whether Mr. Fakes' transaction was conducted in accordance with the Respondent's laws and regulations relating to the admission of investments on Turkey and, thus, satisfied the requirement of legality set forth by the BIT to qualify as an investment protected by that instrument.

149. It results from the foregoing that the present dispute brought by Mr. Saba Fakes against the Republic of Turkey is not within the jurisdiction of the Centre and of this Tribunal.

C. Allocation of Costs

153. [. . .] the Tribunal considers it appropriate that the Claimant bear in full his legal fees and expenses, as well as the arbitration costs which are estimated to US$365,000.

154. The Tribunal also considers it appropriate that the Claimant bear the Respondent's legal fees and expenses. A party pursuing a claim which is clearly outside the scope of the Centre's jurisdiction should not be encouraged, and should bear the risk of paying the full costs of such frivolous proceedings.

F. Rationale, Elements and Expanding Scope of BITs

The rationale behind BITs is that, by offering investors enhanced security and protection through guaranteeing protections beyond those that are provided by the laws of the host state and customary international law, the host nations will attract more foreign direct investment.[106] However, an interplay of factors influence the flow of foreign direct investment other than solely signing a BIT.[107] These factors include political stability, availability of well-trained cheap labor, markets, government efficiency, low levels of corruption, availability of raw materials, and the rule of law.

Broadly speaking, BITs are comprised of the following elements: (a) definitions of what constitutes investment thereby establishing what the treaty covers. The general goal is to construe the term "investment" broadly, so as to cover as many situations as possible[108] and other conditions and criteria for exercising protection other than nationality alone and thereby obviate the limitations of the law as established in the *Barcelona Traction* case; (b) set out substantive obligations for host countries,

106. JL Tobin & M Busch, *A BIT is Better Than a Lot: Bilateral Investment Treaties and Preferential Trade Agreements* (2010) 62 World Politics 1 at 31. A contrary view is presented by Lauge Skovgaard Poulsen, *Bilateral Investment Treaties and Preferential Agreements: Is a BIT Really Better than a Lot?* Investment Treaty News (14 January 2016) online: www.iisd.org/in2010/09/23.

107. E Neumayer & L Spess, *Do Bilateral Investment Treaties Increase Foreign Direct Investment to Developing Countries?* (2005) 33 World Development 1567; K Gallagher and MBL Birch, *Do Investment Agreements Attract Investment?* (2006) J World Investment & Trade 7; JB Yackee, *Conceptual Difficulties in the Empirical Study of Bilateral Investment Treaties*, Brook. J. Int'l L. 33 (2008).

108. *FedEx v. Venezuela* (1998) ILM 1378. This is an interesting case in which the domestic holders of promissory notes, who were not entitled to any protection, transferred them to foreign citizens of a state with an investment treaty, who then became entitled to claim against the state on the basis that the treaty protected portfolio investments. The case illustrates the problems that can attend the inclusion of portfolio investments in investment treaties.

which include, non-discrimination principles, fair and equitable treatment, and most favored nation treatment; (c) protection of investments against expropriation and; (d) provisions on settlement of investment disputes that provide for international arbitration under a western based institutional arbitration center or the International Center for the Settlement of Investment Disputes (ICSID).

BITs provide foreign investors with a number of basic benefits. Under BITs, investors and their covered investments are entitled to be treated as favorably as the host nation treats its own investors and investors from any third country. The BITs generally afford national treatment (NT) or most favored nation (MFN) treatment for the full life cycle of the investment—from its establishment or acquisition, through its management, operation to its disposition. BITs establish clear limits on the expropriation of investments and provide for the payment of prompt, adequate and effective compensation when expropriation takes place. BITs provide for transferability of funds into and out of the host country without delay. BITs strictly limit the circumstances in which performance requirements can be imposed. For example, the performance requirements prohibitions apply to circumstances that would require covered investments to adopt local content requirements as a condition of establishment, acquisition, expansion, management, conduct, or operation. BITs often also give investors the right to engage the top managerial personnel of their choice regardless of nationality. It does away with what is generally referred to as "local content" in the affairs of the investor.

The distinctive feature of many BITs is that they allow for an alternative dispute resolution mechanism, where an investor whose rights under the BIT is allegedly violated can have recourse to international arbitration, usually under the auspices of the International Chamber of Commerce, the London Court of Arbitration, and the Stockholm Chamber of Commerce. Increasingly, the forum of choice is the International Centre for Settlement of Investment Disputes ("ICSID"), rather than suing the host state in its courts. There is typically no requirement to use the country's domestic courts. ICSID arbitration is considered the preferred option, as it is a self-contained regime, with its own enforcement mechanism, and its awards can be enforced in all ICSID member states.[109]

1. The Impact of BITs on Domestic Policy Space

The lack of exhaustion of local remedies requirements in most arbitration processes frustrates development of the rule of law in the host state by diverting cases from the domestic public justice system to the international system. BITs do not make a distinction between performance requirements that are designed to extract concessions from foreign investors and performance requirements used to promote

109. *See* Convention on the Settlement of Investment Disputes between States and Nationals of Other States, art, 53(1)(2). *See also* Chapter 8.

economic development objectives or to address particular economic, social, or environmental problems.

Another weak area involving BITs is that they tend to promote the idea of rights without responsibilities. For example, most BITs do not include obligations relating to environmental protections, combating corruption, good governance, human rights, illicit payment, corporate governance, disclosure requirements, and marketing rules for products. Arbitration tribunals are quick to decline jurisdiction on matters concerning these subjects on grounds that they are not included in the definition of investment.

Things are this way because of power imbalance during BIT negotiations. Some BITs have started to include provisions on the environment and labor standards. For example, the Model BIT, discussed below, falls short of establishing such explicit obligations, as it does in the provisions relating to the protection of property in cases of nationalization, minimum standards of treatment, reparation of profits and in arrangements for dispute settlement. In Articles 12 and 13 dealing with environment and labor respectively, there is a strong reliance on respect for domestic law. The domestic law is referred to, but there is no adoption of binding norms.

In 2015, South Africa enacted the Protection of Investment Act. In place of BITs, the purpose of the Act is to protect investment in accordance with and subject to the South African Constitution, in a manner which balances the public interest and the rights and obligations of investors. Opponents of the Act argue that unlike treaties, the Act could be changed unilaterally by parliament, while treaty protected investments are secure for the duration of the treaty.

Many developing countries are reviewing their positions with regard to BITs because of their perceived limitations and unbalanced protection of international corporations.

2. Exhaustion of Local Remedies

In 2013, the United States Supreme Court heard its first ever case concerning an international arbitration award rendered pursuant to an investment treaty dispute. The United Kingdom-Argentina BIT in question provides for final, binding resolution of disputes by international arbitration but is silent on where arbitration should be held. The BIT contains a clause requiring litigation of disputes in the host-country's courts prior to international arbitration.[110]

BG Group PLC v. Republic of Argentina, 572 U.S. 25 (2014).

Case Introduction

BG Group PLC ("BG Group") requested arbitration under the BIT against the host country, claiming the Argentine government had expropriated BG Group's

110. Article 8(2) of the BIT.

investments in response to a currency crisis. Neither BG Group nor Argentina litigated the dispute in the Argentine courts prior to BG Group's request for arbitration. The parties selected the United States as the seat of arbitration. Argentina contended that the investment treaty expressly provided for exhaustion of local litigation prior to arbitration, and that the arbitrators exceeded their authority in determining that the provision did not apply to the arbitration. The Supreme Court ruled 7–2 against Argentina, concluding that arbitrators acted within their power when they concluded that a British firm was not required to file suit in Argentina's courts before seeking arbitration.

Principal Points of the Judgment

Justice Breyer delivered the opinion of the Court.

[. . .] In late December 2007, the arbitration panel reached a final decision. It began by determining that it had "jurisdiction" to consider the merits of the dispute. In support of that determination, the tribunal concluded that BG Group was an "investor," that its interest in MetroGAS amounted to a Treaty-protected "investment," and that Argentina's own conduct had waived, or excused, BG Group's failure to comply with Article 8's local litigation requirement. [App. to Pet. for Cert.] at 99a, 145a, 161a, 171a. The panel pointed out that in 2002, the President of Argentina had issued a decree staying for 180 days the execution of its courts' final judgments (and injunctions) in suits claiming harm as a result of the new economic measures. *Id.*, at 166a-167a. In addition, Argentina had established a "renegotiation process" for public service contracts, such as its contract with MetroGAS, to alleviate the negative impact of the new economic measures. *Id.*, at 129a, 131a. But Argentina had simultaneously barred from participation in that "process" firms that were litigating against Argentina in court or in arbitration. *Id.*, at 168a-171a. These measures, while not making litigation in Argentina's courts literally impossible, nonetheless "hindered" recourse "to the domestic judiciary" to the point where the Treaty implicitly excused compliance with the local litigation requirement. *Id.*, at 165. Requiring a private party in such circumstances to seek relief in Argentina's courts for 18 months, the panel concluded, would lead to "absurd and unreasonable result[s]." *Id.*, at 166a. On the merits, the arbitration panel agreed with Argentina that it had not "expropriate[d]" BG Group's investment, but also found that Argentina had denied BG Group "fair and equitable treatment." *Id.*, at 222a-223a, 240a-242a. It awarded BG Group $185 million in damages. *Id.*, at 297a. [. . .]

[. . .] A treaty may contain evidence that shows the parties had an intent contrary to our ordinary presumptions about who should decide threshold issues related to arbitration. But the treaty before us does not show any such contrary intention. We concede that the local litigation requirement appears in ¶(1) of Article 8, while the Article does not mention arbitration until the subsequent paragraph, ¶(2). Moreover, a requirement that a party exhaust its remedies in a country's domestic courts before seeking to arbitrate may seem particularly important to a country offering protections to foreign investors. And the placing of an important matter prior to any mention of arbitration at least arguably suggests an intent by Argentina, the

United Kingdom, or both, to have courts rather than arbitrators apply the litigation requirement. [. . .]

3. Key Provisions and Areas of Discussion in the 2012 U.S. Model Bilateral Investment Treaty

a. Comprehensive Definition of Investment

Section A Article 1: Definitions

"investment" means every asset that an investor owns or controls, directly or indirectly, that has the characteristics of an investment, including such characteristics as the commitment of capital or other resources, the expectation of gain or profit, or the assumption of risk. Forms that an investment may take include:

(a) an enterprise;

(b) shares, stock, and other forms of equity participation in an enterprise;

(c) bonds, debentures, other debt instruments, and loans;[111]

(d) futures, options, and other derivatives;

(e) turnkey, construction, management, production, concession, revenue-sharing, and other similar contracts;

(f) intellectual property rights;

(g) licenses, authorizations, permits, and similar rights conferred pursuant to domestic law;[112] and

(h) other tangible or intangible, movable or immovable property, and related property rights, such as leases, mortgages, liens, and pledges.

There is no agreed definition of investment in international law. All BITs contain definitions of the term investment. It is the gem of all bilateral investment treaties, and is therefore very important. The interpretation and application of the term in the context of a particular BIT depends to a large extent on what is included in

111. Some forms of debt, such as bonds, debentures, and long-term notes, are more likely to have the characteristics of an investment, while other forms of debt, such as claims to payment that are immediately due and result from the sale of goods or services, are less likely to have such characteristics.

112. Whether a particular type of license, authorization, permit, or similar instrument (including a concession, to the extent that it has the nature of such an instrument) has the characteristics of an investment depends on such factors as the nature and extent of the rights that the holder has under the law of the Party. Among the licenses, authorizations, permits, and similar instruments that do not have the characteristics of an investment are those that do not create any rights protected under domestic law. For greater certainty, the foregoing is without prejudice to whether any asset associated with the license, authorization, permit, or similar instrument has the characteristics of an investment.

the illustrative list accompanying the definition. The term "investment" is often defined as broadly as possible in order to cover a large number of various types of assets. This is largely to dispel any lingering doubts that may still exist from earlier ideas that intangible property is not property that is protected by international law. Early definitions of the term contained the idea that the intangible property of an alien is incapable of protection under international law, presumably because the creation of intangible property is dependent on the laws of the host state.

However, it has increasingly been accepted that the protection of intangible rights is central to investment protection. BITs include intangible assets within the definition of property and often spell out the types of intangible assets protected by the treaty. For example, the U.S. Model BIT includes licenses and permits as assets covered by investments. The inclusion of these public law rights will in effect mean that rights that are granted in connection with the exploitation of natural resources cannot later be withdrawn without violating the BIT. The absolute protection of concession agreements could be said to be inconsistent with the notion of permanent sovereignty over natural resources.

The *Barcelona Traction* case approach, that the nationality of a company is based on its place of incorporation, has led investors to shop for home states by incorporating their businesses or parent organizations in such countries as Canada and Netherlands, which have a large number of BITs with a large number of countries in order to enjoy the full rights, remedies, and benefits arising from the liberal definition of investments.[113] These broad, open-ended definitions of investment make for uncertainty whenever disputes occur. As UNCTAD has noted, in recognition of the problems posed by such a broad definition of investment in a globalizing world characterized by rapidly increasing transnational investment flows, recent treaty practice is witnessing new approaches that aim to narrow the definition. Within the host country, the existence of a bilateral investment treaty creates two regimes of law covering investments. One group of investments will be governed by treaty law due to the fact that the home country has entered into a BIT with the host state, and the other group of investments will be governed by general norms of international investment law and domestic law due to the absence of a BIT agreement.

b. National Treatment—Addressing Discrimination on the Basis of Nationality of Ownership of an Investment

Article 3: National Treatment

1. Each Party shall accord to investors of the other Party treatment no less favorable than that it accords, in like circumstances, to its own investors with respect to the

113. *See Lao Holding NV v. Lao People's Democratic Republic*, ICSID Case No. ARB (AF)/12/6. It was argued by the government of Laos, the respondent in the case, that the claimant was incorporated in the Netherlands as a device to escape a new tax policy introduced by the government and enjoy the remedies and rights provided by the Laos-Netherlands BIT.

establishment, acquisition, expansion, management, conduct, operation, and sale or other disposition of investments in its territory.

2. Each Party shall accord to covered investments treatment no less favorable than that it accords, in like circumstances, to investments in its territory of its own investors with respect to the establishment, acquisition, expansion, management, conduct, operation, and sale or other disposition of investments.

3. The treatment to be accorded by a Party under paragraphs 1 and 2 means, with respect to a regional level of government, treatment no less favorable than the treatment accorded, in like circumstances, by that regional level of government to natural persons resident in and enterprises constituted under the laws of other regional levels of government of the Party of which it forms a part, and to their respective investments.

c. Most Favored Nation Treatment—Preventing Competitive Disadvantage

Article 4: Most-Favored-Nation Treatment

1. Each Party shall accord to investors of the other Party treatment no less favorable than that it accords, in like circumstances, to investors of any non-Party with respect to the establishment, acquisition, expansion, management, conduct, operation, and sale or other disposition of investments in its territory.

2. Each Party shall accord to covered investments treatment no less favorable than that it accords, in like circumstances, to investments in its territory of investors of any non-Party with respect to the establishment, acquisition, expansion, management, conduct, operation, and sale or other disposition of investments.

d. Minimum Standard of Treatment—Fair and Equitable Treatment Provisions

Article 5: Minimum Standard of Treatment[114]

1. Each Party shall accord to covered investments treatment in accordance with customary international law, including fair and equitable treatment and full protection and security.

2. For greater certainty, paragraph 1 prescribes the customary international law minimum standard of treatment of aliens as the minimum standard of treatment to be afforded to covered investments. The concepts of "fair and equitable treatment" and "full protection and security" do not require treatment in addition to or beyond that which is required by that standard, and do not create additional substantive rights. The obligation in paragraph 1 to provide:

---

114. Article 5 [Minimum Standard of Treatment] shall be interpreted in accordance with Annex A.

(a) "fair and equitable treatment" includes the obligation not to deny justice in criminal, civil, or administrative adjudicatory proceedings in accordance with the principle of due process embodied in the principal legal systems of the world; and

(b) "full protection and security" requires each Party to provide the level of police protection required under customary international law.

[. . .]

The fair and equitable treatment provision has dominated as the principal ground of liability at issue in many investment treaty arbitration claims. A similar approach is found in the China-Korea FTA and the Canadian model BIT. Based on the elements of fairness and equity, the concept is deeply rooted in customary international law. However, the concept of fair and equitable treatment is tricky to define and leaves itself open to different interpretations. In *Noble Ventures v. Romania*, it is defined as a more "general standard". *Noble Ventures* also discusses the limited approach to interpreting "full protection and security". This requires a standard not broader than the general customary international law duty to provide protection and security through state provision of due diligence.

Noble Venture Inc. v. Romania, ICSID Case No. ARB/01/11, Award (Oct. 12, 2005).

Case Introduction

The dispute arises in the context of a bilateral investment treaty (BIT) between Romania and the U.S. of May 28, 1992, which entered into force on January 15, 1994.

Noble Ventures, Inc. ("Noble Ventures") is an American company, incorporated under the laws of the State of Maryland, U.S. Noble Ventures provides business consulting services for steel companies in Eastern Europe. The dispute at hand arose out of a privatization agreement concerning the acquisition, management and operation of a substantial steel mill, Combinatul Siderurgic Resita (CSR), located in Resita, Romania. The agreement was made between Noble Ventures and the Romanian State Ownership Fund (SOF), which was responsible for the privatization of Romanian state-owned enterprises. Completion of the agreement took place on August 16, 2000, when Noble Ventures paid SOF the initial installment of the purchase price and SOF transferred to Noble Ventures its shareholding in CSR which comprised almost CSR's entire equity share capital. At the time of its acquisition by Noble Ventures, CSR had a significant amount of debt owing to other governmental entities.

The privatization contract was terminated in December 2002, based on one of its clauses setting forth that the privatization was subject to cancellation in the event of failure by the investor to pay two consecutive installments.

Principal Points of the Award

ARTICLE II 2. (a) Investment shall at all times be accorded fair and equitable treatment, shall enjoy full protection and security and shall in no case be accorded treatment less than that required by international law.

164. With regard to the Claimant's argument that the Respondent breached Art. II (2)(a) of the BIT which stipulates that the "Investment shall . . . enjoy full protection and security", the Tribunal notes: that it seems doubtful whether that provision can be understood as being wider in scope than the general duty to provide for protection and security of foreign nationals found in the customary international law of aliens. The latter is not a strict standard, but one requiring due diligence to be exercised by the State. Questions concerning the content of the standards of protection have already been discussed to some extent by inter alia ICSID Tribunals in *Asian Agricultural Products Ltd. v. Republic of Sri Lanka*, (ICSID Case No. ARB/87/3, Award of 27 June 1990, 4 ICSID Reports, p. 246, 278 et seq.) and in *American Manufacturing & Trading, Inc. v. Republic of Zaire*, (ICSID Case No. ARB/93/1, Award of 21 February 1997, 5 ICSID Reports, p. 14, 30) although the facts in those cases were quite different from those in the present case.

165. However, in its *ELSI* judgment (ICJ Reports 1989, p. 15 et seq.), the ICJ had to deal with a situation not so different from that in the present case. In *ELSI* the Court was concerned with the occupation of a plant by its employees and with an alleged breach of a protection standard provided for in a Treaty of Friendship, Commerce and Navigation concluded between the United States and Italy in 1948. The Court found that the protection provided by Italy could not be regarded as falling below the full protection and security required by international law which, considering the facts of that case, indicates that violations of protection standards are not easily established. Comparing the facts of the *ELSI* case with the situation in the present case, it is difficult to see in what respect the conduct of the Respondent in the present case was more harmful than that of Italy in the *ELSI* case, so as to justify a different result.

166. However, it does not seem to be necessary to enter into a detailed examination with regard to the claimed violation of Art. II (2)(a) of the BIT. Even assuming the correctness of the Claimant's factual allegations, it is difficult to identify any specific failure by the Respondent to exercise due diligence in protecting the Claimant. And even if one concluded that there was a certain failure on the side of the Respondent sufficiently grave to regard it as a violation, it has not been established that non-compliance with the obligation prejudiced the Claimant, to a material degree. The Claimant has failed to prove that its alleged injuries and losses could have been prevented had the Respondent exercised due diligence in this regard, nor has it established any specific value of the losses.

[. . .]

180. The Tribunal now turns to the question of whether the proceedings were discriminatory. The parties have not provided the Tribunal with any information that

comparable proceedings have been initiated against investors from other countries or in particular against U.S. investors. But that in itself does not exclude the possibility that the proceedings constituted a discriminatory measure because it is possible for a single measure to be discriminatory if proof to that effect is given. As one cannot rely on objective criteria in such situations, the Claimant has to demonstrate that a certain measure was directed specifically against a certain investor by reason of his, her or its nationality. As demonstrated above, the judicial proceedings against CSR were in no way arbitrary but on the contrary were well founded. And there was no indication whatsoever that the measure was specifically directed against the Claimant as a U.S. company. Furthermore, the Claimant failed to prove that other investors with debt problems not being subjected to judicial proceedings were in fact in a situation as grave as that of CSR. Equally the Claimant did not demonstrate that other investors were left unaffected by judicial proceedings although they were in similar situations. The Tribunal accordingly concludes that the measure was not discriminatory and that therefore no violation of Art. II(2)(b) has been established.

181. The Tribunal will now address the question whether the Respondent complied with the duty to accord fair and equitable treatment to the Claimant. Here the Tribunal is confronted with two notions which are particularly difficult to define. Although in this respect Art. II(2)(a) mirrors standard clauses in BITs and other international instruments and courts and tribunals have been concerned with violations of fair and equitable treatment standards, the question whether those standards have been violated has to be considered in the light of the circumstances of each case.

182. Considering the place of the fair and equitable treatment standard at the very beginning of Art. II(2), one can consider this to be a more general standard which finds its specific application in *inter alia* the duty to provide full protection and security, the prohibition of arbitrary and discriminatory measures and the obligation to observe contractual obligations towards the investor. [. . .]

e. Expropriation and Compensation

Article 6: Expropriation and Compensation[115]

1. Neither Party may expropriate or nationalize a covered investment either directly or indirectly through measures equivalent to expropriation or nationalization ("expropriation"), except:

(a) for a public purpose;

(b) in a non-discriminatory manner;

(c) on payment of prompt, adequate, and effective compensation; and

(d) in accordance with due process of law and Article 5 [Minimum Standard of Treatment] (1) through (3).

115. Article 6 [Expropriation] shall be interpreted in accordance with Annexes A and B.

2. The compensation referred to in paragraph 1(c) shall:

(a) be paid without delay;

(b) be equivalent to the fair market value of the expropriated investment immediately before the expropriation took place ("the date of expropriation");

(c) not reflect any change in value occurring because the intended expropriation had become known earlier; and

(d) be fully realizable and freely transferable.

[. . .]

Unless carefully interpreted, BIT provisions (or subsequent claims) that deal with creeping, regulatory and/or indirect expropriation are likely to conflict with policy making, because they generally refer to regulatory actions by the state. In Article 7, it provides that each party shall permit all transfers relating to a covered investment to be made freely and without delay into and out of its territory. The model BIT also provides that each party shall permit transfers relating to a covered investment to be made in a freely usable currency at the market rate of exchange prevailing at the time of transfer sale or disposition of the investment of an investor of a party in its territory. Article 8 deals with performance requirements. It prohibits either party from mandating or enforcing specified performance requirements as a condition for the establishment, acquisition, expansion, management, conduct, or operation of a covered investment.

The list of prohibited requirements is exhaustive and covers domestic content requirements and domestic purchase preferences, the balancing of imports or sales in relation to exports or foreign exchange earnings, requirements to export products or services, technology transfer requirements, and requirements relating to the conduct of research and development in the host country. In Article 9, the U.S. Model BIT states that "neither party may require that an enterprise of that party that is a covered investment appoint to senior management positions natural persons of any particular nationality." Article 23 deals with dispute settlement. The Model BIT provides that in the event that an investment dispute cannot be settled amicably, the investor may submit the dispute to ICSID arbitration. The Model BIT also provides for binding arbitration of disputes between the U.S. investors and a host state.

The dispute settlement system advocated by BITs allows investors to circumvent domestic courts and bring claims against host governments directly before an international arbitral tribunal. The treaties invariably do not require the exhaustion of local remedies before accessing international tribunals. This is a huge contrast to customary international law and human rights treaties,[116] which require the exhaustion

---

116. *Valasquez v. Honduras*, Inter-Am. Ct. H.R. (ser.C) No. 4 (1988).

of local remedies. This is a critical factor that has led to a host of arbitration awards against host states. Indeed, investor versus state arbitrations have become the nightmare of many developing economies which, despite whatever best intentions they have, must kneel before investors or pay dearly before arbitration panels.

f. Transfers of Profits and Dividends

Article 7: Transfers

1. Each Party shall permit all transfers relating to a covered investment to be made freely and without delay into and out of its territory. Such transfers include:

(a) contributions to capital;

(b) profits, dividends, capital gains, and proceeds from the sale of all or any part of the covered investment or from the partial or complete liquidation of the covered investment;

(c) interest, royalty payments, management fees, and technical assistance and other fees;

(d) payments made under a contract, including a loan agreement;

(e) payments made pursuant to Article 5 [Minimum Standard of Treatment] (4) and (5) and Article 6 [Expropriation and Compensation]; and

(f) payments arising out of a dispute.

[...]

g. Questions of Management

Article 9: Senior Management and Boards of Directors

1. Neither Party may require that an enterprise of that Party that is a covered investment appoint to senior management positions natural persons of any particular nationality.

2. A Party may require that a majority of the board of directors, or any committee thereof, of an enterprise of that Party that is a covered investment, be of a particular nationality, or resident in the territory of the Party, provided that the requirement does not materially impair the ability of the investor to exercise control over its investment.

h. Environment and Labor

Article 12: Investment and Environment

1. The Parties recognize that their respective environmental laws and policies, and multilateral environmental agreements to which they are both party, play an important role in protecting the environment.

2. The Parties recognize that it is inappropriate to encourage investment by weakening or reducing the protections afforded in domestic environmental laws. Accordingly,

each Party shall ensure that it does not waive or otherwise derogate from or offer to waive or otherwise derogate from its environmental laws in a manner that weakens or reduces the protections afforded in those laws, or fail to effectively enforce those laws through a sustained or recurring course of action or inaction, as an encouragement for the establishment, acquisition, expansion, or retention of an investment in its territory.

3. The Parties recognize that each Party retains the right to exercise discretion with respect to regulatory, compliance, investigatory, and prosecutorial matters, and to make decisions regarding the allocation of resources to enforcement with respect to other environmental matters determined to have higher priorities. Accordingly, the Parties understand that a Party is in compliance with paragraph 2 where a course of action or inaction reflects a reasonable exercise of such discretion, or results from a bona fide decision regarding the allocation of resources.

4. For purposes of this Article, "environmental law" means each Party's statutes or regulations, or provisions thereof, the primary purpose of which is the protection of the environment, or the prevention of a danger to human, animal, or plant life or health, through the:

(a) prevention, abatement, or control of the release, discharge, or emission of pollutants or environmental contaminants;

(b) control of environmentally hazardous or toxic chemicals, substances, materials, and wastes, and the dissemination of information related thereto; or

(c) protection or conservation of wild flora or fauna, including endangered species, their habitat, and specially protected natural areas,

in the Party's territory, but does not include any statute or regulation, or provision thereof, directly related to worker safety or health.

[. . .]

Article 13: Investment and Labor

1. The Parties reaffirm their respective obligations as members of the International Labor Organization ("ILO") and their commitments under the ILO Declaration on Fundamental Principles and Rights at Work and its Follow-Up.

2. The Parties recognize that it is inappropriate to encourage investment by weakening or reducing the protections afforded in domestic labor laws. Accordingly, each Party shall ensure that it does not waive or otherwise derogate from or offer to waive or otherwise derogate from its labor laws where the waiver or derogation would be inconsistent with the labor rights referred to in subparagraphs (a) through (e) of paragraph 3, or fail to effectively enforce its labor laws through a sustained or recurring course of action or inaction, as an encouragement for the establishment, acquisition, expansion, or retention of an investment in its territory.

3. For purposes of this Article, "labor laws" means each Party's statutes or regulations, or provisions thereof that are directly related to the following:

(a) freedom of association;

(b) the effective recognition of the right to collective bargaining;

(c) the elimination of all forms of forced or compulsory labor;

(d) the effective abolition of child labor and a prohibition on the worst forms of child labor;

(e) the elimination of discrimination in respect of employment and occupation; and

(f) acceptable conditions of work with respect to minimum wages, hours of work, and occupational safety and health.

[. . .]

i. Dispute Settlement

Section B

Article 23: Consultation and Negotiation

In the event of an investment dispute, the claimant and the respondent should initially seek to resolve the dispute through consultation and negotiation, which may include the use of nonbinding, third-party procedures.

Article 24: Submission of a Claim to Arbitration

1. In the event that a disputing party considers that an investment dispute cannot be settled by consultation and negotiation:

(a) the claimant, on its own behalf, may submit to arbitration under this Section a claim

(i) that the respondent has breached

(A) an obligation under Articles 3 through 10,

(B) an investment authorization, or

(C) an investment agreement; and

(ii) that the claimant has incurred loss or damage by reason of, or arising out of, that breach; and

(b) the claimant, on behalf of an enterprise of the respondent that is a juridical person that the claimant owns or controls directly or indirectly, may submit to arbitration under this Section a claim

(i) that the respondent has breached

(A) an obligation under Articles 3 through 10,

(B) an investment authorization, or

(C) an investment agreement;

and

(ii) that the enterprise has incurred loss or damage by reason of, or arising out of, that breach, provided that a claimant may submit pursuant to subparagraph (a)(i)(C) or (b)(i)(C) a claim for breach of an investment agreement only if the subject matter of the claim and the claimed damages directly relate to the covered investment that was established or acquired, or sought to be established or acquired, in reliance on the relevant investment agreement.

2. At least 90 days before submitting any claim to arbitration under this Section, a claimant shall deliver to the respondent a written notice of its intention to submit the claim to arbitration ("notice of intent"). The notice shall specify:

(a) the name and address of the claimant and, where a claim is submitted on behalf of an enterprise, the name, address, and place of incorporation of the enterprise;

(b) for each claim, the provision of this Treaty, investment authorization, or investment agreement alleged to have been breached and any other relevant provisions;

(c) the legal and factual basis for each claim; and

(d) the relief sought and the approximate amount of damages claimed.

3. Provided that six months have elapsed since the events giving rise to the claim, a claimant may submit a claim referred to in paragraph 1:

(a) under the ICSID Convention and the ICSID Rules of Procedure for Arbitration Proceedings, provided that both the respondent and the non-disputing Party are parties to the ICSID Convention;

(b) under the ICSID Additional Facility Rules, provided that either the respondent or the non-disputing Party is a party to the ICSID Convention;

(c) under the UNCITRAL Arbitration Rules; or

(d) if the claimant and respondent agree, to any other arbitration institution or under any other arbitration rules.

4. A claim shall be deemed submitted to arbitration under this Section when the claimant's notice of or request for arbitration ("notice of arbitration"):

(a) referred to in paragraph 1 of Article 36 of the ICSID Convention is received by the Secretary-General;

(b) referred to in Article 2 of Schedule C of the ICSID Additional Facility Rules is received by the Secretary-General;

(c) referred to in Article 3 of the UNCITRAL Arbitration Rules, together with the statement of claim referred to in Article 20 of the UNCITRAL Arbitration Rules, are received by the respondent; or

(d) referred to under any arbitral institution or arbitral rules selected under paragraph 3(d) is received by the respondent.

A claim asserted by the claimant for the first time after such notice of arbitration is submitted shall be deemed submitted to arbitration under this Section on the date of its receipt under the applicable arbitral rules.

5. The arbitration rules applicable under paragraph 3, and in effect on the date the claim or claims were submitted to arbitration under this Section, shall govern the arbitration except to the extent modified by this Treaty.

6. The claimant shall provide with the notice of arbitration:

(a) the name of the arbitrator that the claimant appoints; or

(b) the claimant's written consent for the Secretary-General to appoint that arbitrator.

Article 25: Consent of Each Party to Arbitration

1. Each Party consents to the submission of a claim to arbitration under this Section in accordance with this Treaty.

2. The consent under paragraph 1 and the submission of a claim to arbitration under this Section shall satisfy the requirements of:

(a) Chapter II of the ICSID Convention (Jurisdiction of the Centre) and the ICSID Additional Facility Rules for written consent of the parties to the dispute; [and]

(b) Article II of the New York Convention for an "agreement in writing[."] [;" and

(c) Article I of the Inter-American Convention for an "agreement."]

Section C

Article 37: State-State Dispute Settlement

1. Subject to paragraph 5, any dispute between the Parties concerning the interpretation or application of this Treaty, that is not resolved through consultations or other diplomatic channels, shall be submitted on the request of either Party to arbitration for a binding decision or award by a tribunal in accordance with applicable rules of international law. In the absence of an agreement by the Parties to the contrary, the UNCITRAL Arbitration Rules shall govern, except as modified by the Parties or this Treaty.

2. Unless the Parties otherwise agree, the tribunal shall comprise three arbitrators, one arbitrator appointed by each Party and the third, who shall be the presiding arbitrator, appointed by agreement of the Parties. If a tribunal has not been constituted within 75 days from the date that a claim is submitted to arbitration under this Section, the Secretary-General, on the request of either Party, shall appoint, in his or her discretion, the arbitrator or arbitrators not yet appointed.

3. Expenses incurred by the arbitrators, and other costs of the proceedings, shall be paid for equally by the Parties. However, the tribunal may, in its discretion, direct that a higher proportion of the costs be paid by one of the Parties.

4. Articles 28(3) [Amicus Curiae Submissions], 29 [Investor-State Transparency], 30(1) and (3) [Governing Law], and 31 [Interpretation of Annexes] shall apply *mutatis mutandis* to arbitrations under this Article.

5. Paragraphs 1 through 4 shall not apply to a matter arising under Article 12 or Article 13.

G. Internal Investment Protection Violates EU Law: The Case of the Slovakia-Netherlands Treaty

The European Court of Justice ruled that a private arbitration clause in the Slovakia-Netherlands investment treaty is incompatible with EU law. The Court found that, by concluding the BIT, Slovakia and the Netherlands established a mechanism for settling disputes which is not capable of ensuring that those disputes will be decided by a court within the judicial system of the EU. Only such a court is able to ensure the full effectiveness of EU law. In those circumstances, the Court concluded that the arbitration clause in the BIT has an adverse effect on the autonomy of EU law, and is therefore incompatible with EU law.

This is a win to the European Commission, which has been urging EU countries to annul some 195 similar investment protection treaties. The case describes the investor-state dispute settlement clause, which allows foreign investors from one EU country to sue another state for financial compensation in cases of alleged discrimination, as having an adverse effect on the autonomy of EU law.

The case had been referred to the European Court of Justice after Slovakia contested a decision by the treaty's arbitration tribunal, which had ordered Bratislava to pay about €22 million to the Dutch insurance company Achmea for partly revoking the liberalization of the Slovakian sickness insurance market.

The ruling deals a blow to Germany, France, the Netherlands, Austria and Finland, which have been arguing that such private arbitration clauses in all 196 investment treaties between EU countries are in line with EU law. The Commission requested in 2015 that EU countries terminate those treaties and launched infringement procedures against some countries in 2016. The ruling has no effect on investment protection in external EU treaties.

In January 2019, EU countries signed a declaration agreeing to terminate their roughly 200 intra-EU investment treaties no later than December 2019.[117]

---

117. Declaration of the Representatives of the Governments of the Member States: Of the Legal Consequences of the Judgment of the Court of Justice in *Achmea* and on Investment Protection in the European Union (01/15/19). https://ec.europa.eu/info/sites/info/files/business_economy_euro/banking_and_finance/documents/190117-bilateral-investment-treaties_en.pdf?utm_source=POLITICO.EU&utm_campaign=e92a8afd57-EMAIL_CAMPAIGN_2019_01_17_12_00&utm_medium=email&utm_term=0_10959edeb5-e92a8afd57-189512373

Judgment of the Court (Grand Chamber) of 6 March 2018 (request for a preliminary ruling from the Bundesgerichtshof—Germany)—*Slowakische Republik v. Achmea BV* (Case C-284/16).

1 This request for a preliminary ruling concerns the interpretation of Articles 18, 267 and 344 TFEU. [. . .]

Legal context

The BIT

[. . .]

4 Article 8 of the BIT provides:

> '1. All disputes between one Contracting Party and an investor of the other Contracting Party concerning an investment of the latter shall if, possible, be settled amicably.
>
> 2. Each Contracting Party hereby consents to submit a dispute referred to in paragraph 1 of this Article to an arbitral tribunal, if the dispute has not been settled amicably within a period of six months from the date on which either party to the dispute requested amicable settlement.
>
> 3. The arbitral tribunal referred to in paragraph 2 of this Article will be constituted for each individual case in the following way: each party to the dispute appoints one member of the tribunal and the two members thus appointed shall select a national of a third State as Chairman of the tribunal. Each party to the dispute shall appoint its member of the tribunal within two months, and the Chairman shall be appointed within three months from the date on which the investor has notified the other Contracting Party of his decision to submit the dispute to the arbitral tribunal.
>
> 4. If the appointments have not been made in the abovementioned periods, either party to the dispute may invite the President of the Arbitration Institute of the Chamber of Commerce of Stockholm to make the necessary appointments. If the President is a national of either Contracting Party or if he is otherwise prevented from discharging the said function, the Vice-President shall be invited to make the necessary appointments. If the Vice-President is a national of either Contracting Party or if he too is prevented from discharging the said function, the most senior member of the Arbitration Institute who is not a national of either Contracting Party shall be invited to make the necessary appointments.
>
> 5. The arbitration tribunal shall determine its own procedure applying the United Nations Commission on International Trade Law (UNCITRAL) arbitration rules.
>
> 6. The arbitral tribunal shall decide on the basis of the law, taking into account in particular though not exclusively:

— the law in force of the Contracting Party concerned;

— the provisions of this Agreement, and other relevant agreements between the Contracting Parties;

— the provisions of special agreements relating to the investment;

— the general principles of international law.

7. The tribunal takes its decision by majority of votes; such decision shall be final and binding upon the parties to the dispute.'

German law

5 Under Paragraph 1059(2) of the Zivilprozessordnung (Code of Civil Procedure), an arbitral award can be set aside only if one of the grounds set out in that provision is present, which include the arbitration agreement being invalid under the law to which the parties have subjected it, and the recognition or enforcement of the arbitral award being contrary to public policy.

The dispute in the main proceedings and the questions referred for a preliminary ruling

6 On 1 January 1993 the Slovak Republic, as a successor State to the Czech and Slovak Federative Republic, succeeded to the rights and obligations of that State under the BIT, and on 1 May 2004 it acceded to the European Union.

7 As part of a reform of its health system, the Slovak Republic opened the Slovak market in 2004 to national operators and those of other Member States offering private sickness insurance services. Achmea, an undertaking belonging to a Netherlands insurance group, after obtaining authorisation as a sickness insurance institution, set up a subsidiary in Slovakia to which it contributed capital and through which it offered private sickness insurance services on the Slovak market.

8 In 2006 the Slovak Republic partly reversed the liberalisation of the private sickness insurance market. In particular, by a law of 25 October 2007, it prohibited the distribution of profits generated by private sickness insurance activities. Subsequently, after the Ústavný súd Slovenskej republiky (Constitutional Court of the Slovak Republic) held in a judgment of 26 January 2011 that the prohibition was contrary to the Slovak constitution, the Slovak Republic, by a law which entered into force on 1 August 2011, once more allowed the distribution of the profits in question.

9 Since it considered that the legislative measures of the Slovak Republic had caused it damage, Achmea brought arbitration proceedings against the Slovak Republic in October 2008 pursuant to Article 8 of the BIT.

10 As Frankfurt am Main (Germany) was chosen as the place of arbitration, German law applies to the arbitration proceedings concerned.

11 In those arbitration proceedings the Slovak Republic raised an objection of lack of jurisdiction of the arbitral tribunal. It submitted in that respect that, as a result of its accession to the European Union, recourse to an arbitral tribunal provided

for in Article 8(2) of the BIT was incompatible with EU law. By an interlocutory arbitral award of 26 October 2010, the arbitral tribunal dismissed the objection. The applications for that award to be set aside brought by the Slovak Republic before the German courts were unsuccessful at first instance and on appeal.

12 By arbitral award of 7 December 2012, the arbitral tribunal ordered the Slovak Republic to pay Achmea damages in the principal amount of EUR 22.1 million. The Slovak Republic brought an action to set aside that arbitral award before the Oberlandesgericht Frankfurt am Main (Higher Regional Court, Frankfurt am Main, Germany). When that court dismissed the action, the Slovak Republic appealed on a point of law against the dismissal to the Bundesgerichtshof (Federal Court of Justice, Germany).

13 The referring court notes that, since the accession of the Slovak Republic to the European Union on 1 May 2004, the BIT has constituted an agreement between Member States, so that in the event of conflict the provisions of EU law take precedence, in the matters governed by them, over the provisions of the BIT.

14 The Slovak Republic expressed doubts as to the compatibility of the arbitration clause in Article 8 of the BIT with Articles 18, 267 and 344 TFEU. Although the referring court does not share those doubts, it nonetheless considered that, since the Court has not yet ruled on those questions and the questions are of considerable importance because of the numerous bilateral investment treaties still in force between Member States which contain similar arbitration clauses, it was necessary to make the present reference to the Court in order to decide the case before it.

15 In the first place, the referring court doubts that Article 344 TFEU is even applicable. To begin with, the subject matter and purpose of that provision show that, even if its wording does not make this clearly apparent, it does not concern disputes between an individual and a Member State.

16 Next, the subject matter of Article 344 TFEU is confined to disputes relating to the interpretation and application of the Treaties. The dispute in the main proceedings is not such a case, however, as the arbitral award of 7 December 2012 was made on the basis of the BIT alone.

17 Finally, the purpose of Article 344 TFEU is to safeguard the allocation of powers laid down by the Treaties, and hence the autonomy of the EU legal system, observance of which is ensured by the Court, and at the same time it is a specific manifestation of the duty of the Member States to cooperate with the Court within the meaning of Article 4(3) TEU. It cannot, however, be concluded from that that Article 344 TFEU safeguards the jurisdiction of the Court with respect to any dispute in which EU law may be applied or interpreted. That provision in fact protects the exclusive jurisdiction of the Court only to the extent that the Member States have to make use of the procedures before the Court laid down by the Treaties. Yet a dispute such as that in the main proceedings cannot be resolved in proceedings before the EU judicature. The Treaties make no provision for any judicial

procedure in which an investor such as Achmea can bring a claim, before the EU judicature, for compensation from a Member State under a bilateral investment treaty such as the BIT.

18 In the second place, the referring court questions whether Article 267 TFEU precludes an arbitration clause such as that at issue in the main proceedings.

19 It observes, first, that the arbitration procedure is not in itself capable of ensuring the uniform application of EU law that Article 267 TFEU aims to guarantee. Even though, under Article 8(6) of the BIT, the arbitral tribunal had to comply with EU law and, in the event of conflict, apply it in priority, it would not have the possibility of making a reference to the Court for a preliminary ruling, however, since it could not be regarded as a 'court or tribunal' within the meaning of Article 267 TFEU.

20 The referring court considers, next, that the uniform interpretation of EU law could nonetheless be regarded as being ensured in the present case, in that, prior to enforcement of the arbitral award, a court of the State may be called on to review the compatibility of the arbitral award with EU law, and can make a reference to the Court if need be. Further, in accordance with Paragraph 1059(2)(2)(b) of the Code of Civil Procedure, one of the grounds for setting aside an arbitral award is that its recognition or enforcement would be contrary to public policy. In line with the Court's rulings on arbitral awards deciding disputes between individuals, the national courts' power of review of an arbitral award concerning a dispute between an individual and a Member State can validly be limited solely to breaches of fundamental provisions of EU law. That circumstance should not lead to an arbitration clause such as that at issue in the main proceedings being contrary to Article 267 TFEU.

21 The referring court adds, finally, that the Court has previously held that an international agreement providing for the establishment outside the institutional and judicial framework of the EU of a special court responsible for the interpretation and application of the provisions of that agreement is compatible with EU law in so far as there is no adverse effect on the autonomy of the EU legal order. The Court has not expressed reservations as to the creation of a judicial system that is designed, in essence, to resolve disputes relating to the interpretation or application of the actual provisions of the international agreement concerned and does not affect the powers of the courts and tribunals of the Member States in relation to the interpretation and application of EU law, nor the power, or indeed the obligation, of those courts and tribunals to request a preliminary ruling from the Court. The arbitral tribunal at issue in the main proceedings is called on precisely to rule on an infringement of the provisions of the BIT, which it must interpret in the light of EU law, in particular the provisions governing the free movement of capital.

22 In the third place, the referring court notes that, unlike Netherlands or Slovak investors, those from Member States other than the Kingdom of the Netherlands

and the Slovak Republic are unable to bring proceedings before an arbitral tribunal instead of a court of the State, which represents a considerable disadvantage which may constitute discrimination contrary to Article 18 TFEU. However, the restriction by an intra-EU bilateral agreement of an advantage to nationals of the contracting Member States is discriminatory only if the nationals of other Member States who do not enjoy that advantage are in an objectively comparable situation. That is not so in the present case, since the fact that the reciprocal rights and obligations apply only to nationals of the two contracting Member States is a consequence that is inherent in the bilateral agreements concluded between them.

23 Having regard to the above considerations, the Bundesgerichtshof (Federal Court of Justice) decided to stay the proceedings and to refer the following questions to the Court for a preliminary ruling:

(1) Does Article 344 TFEU preclude the application of a provision in a bilateral investment protection agreement between Member States of the European Union (a so-called intra-EU BIT) under which an investor of a Contracting State, in the event of a dispute concerning investments in the other Contracting State, may bring proceedings against the latter State before an arbitral tribunal where the investment protection agreement was concluded before one of the Contracting States acceded to the European Union but the arbitral proceedings are not to be brought until after that date?

If Question 1 is to be answered in the negative:

(2) Does Article 267 TFEU preclude the application of such a provision?

If Questions 1 and 2 are to be answered in the negative:

(3) Does the first paragraph of Article 18 TFEU preclude the application of such a provision under the circumstances described in Question 1 [. . .]

Consideration of the questions referred

Questions 1 and 2

31 By its first and second questions, which should be taken together, the referring court essentially asks whether Articles 267 and 344 TFEU must be interpreted as precluding a provision in an international agreement concluded between Member States, such as Article 8 of the BIT, under which an investor from one of those Member States may, in the event of a dispute concerning investments in the other Member State, bring proceedings against the latter Member State before an arbitral tribunal whose jurisdiction that Member State has undertaken to accept.

32 In order to answer those questions, it should be recalled that, according to settled case-law of the Court, an international agreement cannot affect the allocation of powers fixed by the Treaties or, consequently, the autonomy of the EU legal system, observance of which is ensured by the Court. That principle is enshrined in particular in Article 344 TFEU, under which the Member States undertake not to submit

a dispute concerning the interpretation or application of the Treaties to any method of settlement other than those provided for in the Treaties (Opinion 2/13 (Accession of the EU to the ECHR) of 18 December 2014, EU:C:2014:2454, paragraph 201 and the case-law cited).

33 Also according to settled case-law of the Court, the autonomy of EU law with respect both to the law of the Member States and to international law is justified by the essential characteristics of the EU and its law, relating in particular to the constitutional structure of the EU and the very nature of that law. EU law is characterised by the fact that it stems from an independent source of law, the Treaties, by its primacy over the laws of the Member States, and by the direct effect of a whole series of provisions which are applicable to their nationals and to the Member States themselves. Those characteristics have given rise to a structured network of principles, rules and mutually interdependent legal relations binding the EU and its Member States reciprocally and binding its Member States to each other (see, to that effect, Opinion 2/13 (Accession of the EU to the ECHR) of 18 December 2014, EU:C:2014:2454, paragraphs 165 to 167 and the case-law cited).

34 EU law is thus based on the fundamental premise that each Member State shares with all the other Member States, and recognises that they share with it, a set of common values on which the EU is founded, as stated in Article 2 TEU. That premise implies and justifies the existence of mutual trust between the Member States that those values will be recognised, and therefore that the law of the EU that implements them will be respected. It is precisely in that context that the Member States are obliged, by reason *inter alia* of the principle of sincere cooperation set out in the first subparagraph of Article 4(3) TEU, to ensure in their respective territories the application of and respect for EU law, and to take for those purposes any appropriate measure, whether general or particular, to ensure fulfilment of the obligations arising out of the Treaties or resulting from the acts of the institutions of the EU (Opinion 2/13 (Accession of the EU to the ECHR) of 18 December 2014, EU:C:2014:2454, paragraphs 168 and 173 and the case-law cited).

35 In order to ensure that the specific characteristics and the autonomy of the EU legal order are preserved, the Treaties have established a judicial system intended to ensure consistency and uniformity in the interpretation of EU law (Opinion 2/13 (Accession of the EU to the ECHR) of 18 December 2014, EU:C:2014:2454, paragraph 174).

36 In that context, in accordance with Article 19 TEU, it is for the national courts and tribunals and the Court of Justice to ensure the full application of EU law in all Member States and to ensure judicial protection of the rights of individuals under that law (see, to that effect, Opinion 1/09 (Agreement creating a unified patent litigation system) of 8 March 2011, EU:C:2011:123, paragraph 68; Opinion 2/13 (Accession of the EU to the ECHR) of 18 December 2014, EU:C:2014:2454, paragraph 175; and judgment of 27 February 2018, Associação Sindical dos Juízes Portugueses, C-64/16, EU:C:2018:117, paragraph 33).

37 In particular, the judicial system as thus conceived has as its keystone the preliminary ruling procedure provided for in Article 267 TFEU, which, by setting up a dialogue between one court and another, specifically between the Court of Justice and the courts and tribunals of the Member States, has the object of securing uniform interpretation of EU law, thereby serving to ensure its consistency, its full effect and its autonomy as well as, ultimately, the particular nature of the law established by the Treaties (Opinion 2/13 (Accession of the EU to the ECHR) of 18 December 2014, EU:C:2014:2454, paragraph 176 and the case-law cited). [. . .]

40 Even if, as Achmea in particular contends, that tribunal, despite the very broad wording of Article 8(1) of the BIT, is called on to rule only on possible infringements of the BIT, the fact remains that in order to do so it must, in accordance with Article 8(6) of the BIT, take account in particular of the law in force of the contracting party concerned and other relevant agreements between the contracting parties.

41 Given the nature and characteristics of EU law mentioned in paragraph 33 above, that law must be regarded both as forming part of the law in force in every Member State and as deriving from an international agreement between the Member States. [. . .]

43 It must therefore be ascertained, secondly, whether an arbitral tribunal such as that referred to in Article 8 of the BIT is situated within the judicial system of the EU, and in particular whether it can be regarded as a court or tribunal of a Member State within the meaning of Article 267 TFEU. The consequence of a tribunal set up by Member States being situated within the EU judicial system is that its decisions are subject to mechanisms capable of ensuring the full effectiveness of the rules of the EU (see, to that effect, Opinion 1/09 (Agreement creating a unified patent litigation system) of 8 March 2011, EU:C:2011:123, paragraph 82 and the case-law cited). [. . .]

45 In the case in the main proceedings, the arbitral tribunal is not part of the judicial system of the Netherlands or Slovakia. Indeed, it is precisely the exceptional nature of the tribunal's jurisdiction compared with that of the courts of those two Member States that is one of the principal reasons for the existence of Article 8 of the BIT.

46 That characteristic of the arbitral tribunal at issue in the main proceedings means that it cannot in any event be classified as a court or tribunal 'of a Member State' within the meaning of Article 267 TFEU. [. . .]

49 It follows that a tribunal such as that referred to in Article 8 of the BIT cannot be regarded as a 'court or tribunal of a Member State' within the meaning of Article 267 TFEU, and is not therefore entitled to make a reference to the Court for a preliminary ruling.

50 In those circumstances, it remains to be ascertained, thirdly, whether an arbitral award made by such a tribunal is, in accordance with Article 19 TEU in particular,

subject to review by a court of a Member State, ensuring that the questions of EU law which the tribunal may have to address can be submitted to the Court by means of a reference for a preliminary ruling.

51 It should be noted that under Article 8(7) of the BIT the decision of the arbitral tribunal provided for in that article is final. Moreover, pursuant to Article 8(5) of the BIT, the arbitral tribunal is to determine its own procedure applying the UNCITRAL arbitration rules and, in particular, is itself to choose its seat and consequently the law applicable to the procedure governing judicial review of the validity of the award by which it puts an end to the dispute before it.

52 In the present case, the arbitral tribunal applied to by Achmea chose to sit in Frankfurt am Main, which made German law applicable to the procedure governing judicial review of the validity of the arbitral award made by the tribunal on 7 December 2012. It was thus that choice which enabled the Slovak Republic, as a party to the dispute, to seek judicial review of the arbitral award, in accordance with German law, by bringing proceedings to that end before the competent German court. [. . .]

54 It is true that, in relation to commercial arbitration, the Court has held that the requirements of efficient arbitration proceedings justify the review of arbitral awards by the courts of the Member States being limited in scope, provided that the fundamental provisions of EU law can be examined in the course of that review and, if necessary, be the subject of a reference to the Court for a preliminary ruling (see, to that effect, judgments of 1 June 1999, Eco Swiss, C-126/97, EU:C:1999:269, paragraphs 35, 36 and 40, and of 26 October 2006, Mostaza Claro, C-168/05, EU:C:2006:675, paragraphs 34 to 39).

55 However, arbitration proceedings such as those referred to in Article 8 of the BIT are different from commercial arbitration proceedings. While the latter originate in the freely expressed wishes of the parties, the former derive from a treaty by which Member States agree to remove from the jurisdiction of their own courts, and hence from the system of judicial remedies which the second subparagraph of Article 19(1) TEU requires them to establish in the fields covered by EU law (see, to that effect, judgment of 27 February 2018, Associação Sindical dos Juízes Portugueses, C-64/16, EU:C:2018:117, paragraph 34), disputes which may concern the application or interpretation of EU law. In those circumstances, the considerations set out in the preceding paragraph relating to commercial arbitration cannot be applied to arbitration proceedings such as those referred to in Article 8 of the BIT.

56 Consequently, having regard to all the characteristics of the arbitral tribunal mentioned in Article 8 of the BIT and set out in paragraphs 39 to 55 above, it must be considered that, by concluding the BIT, the Member States parties to it established a mechanism for settling disputes between an investor and a Member State which could prevent those disputes from being resolved in a manner that ensures the full effectiveness of EU law, even though they might concern the interpretation or application of that law.

57 It is true that, according to settled case-law of the Court, an international agreement providing for the establishment of a court responsible for the interpretation of its provisions and whose decisions are binding on the institutions, including the Court of Justice, is not in principle incompatible with EU law. The competence of the EU in the field of international relations and its capacity to conclude international agreements necessarily entail the power to submit to the decisions of a court which is created or designated by such agreements as regards the interpretation and application of their provisions, provided that the autonomy of the EU and its legal order is respected (see, to that effect, Opinion 1/91 (EEA Agreement—I) of 14 December 1991, EU:C:1991:490, paragraphs 40 and 70; Opinion 1/09 (Agreement creating a unified patent litigation system) of 8 March 2011, EU:C:2011:123, paragraphs 74 and 76; and Opinion 2/13 (Accession of the EU to the ECHR) of 18 December 2014, EU:C:2014:2454, paragraphs 182 and 183).

58 In the present case, however, apart from the fact that the disputes falling within the jurisdiction of the arbitral tribunal referred to in Article 8 of the BIT may relate to the interpretation both of that agreement and of EU law, the possibility of submitting those disputes to a body which is not part of the judicial system of the EU is provided for by an agreement which was concluded not by the EU but by Member States. Article 8 of the BIT is such as to call into question not only the principle of mutual trust between the Member States but also the preservation of the particular nature of the law established by the Treaties, ensured by the preliminary ruling procedure provided for in Article 267 TFEU, and is not therefore compatible with the principle of sincere cooperation referred to in paragraph 34 above.

59 In those circumstances, Article 8 of the BIT has an adverse effect on the autonomy of EU law.

60 Consequently, the answer to Questions 1 and 2 is that Articles 267 and 344 TFEU must be interpreted as precluding a provision in an international agreement concluded between Member States, such as Article 8 of the BIT, under which an investor from one of those Member States may, in the event of a dispute concerning investments in the other Member State, bring proceedings against the latter Member State before an arbitral tribunal whose jurisdiction that Member State has undertaken to accept. [. . .]

On those grounds, the Court (Grand Chamber) hereby rules:

Articles 267 and 344 TFEU must be interpreted as precluding a provision in an international agreement concluded between Member States, such as Article 8 of the Agreement on encouragement and reciprocal protection of investments between the Kingdom of the Netherlands and the Czech and Slovak Federative Republic, under which an investor from one of those Member States may, in the event of a dispute concerning investments in the other Member State, bring proceedings against the latter Member State before an arbitral tribunal whose jurisdiction that Member State has undertaken to accept.

H. A Move Towards "Next Generation" Bilateral Investment Treaties

1. Morocco-Nigeria BIT 2016

Institutional Provisions

The treaty establishes a Joint Committee composed of representatives of both Parties.

Article 4 Institutional Governance

1) For the purpose of this agreement, the Parties hereby establish a Joint Committee for the administration of this Agreement (hereinafter referred to as "Joint Committee").

2) The Joint Committee shall be composed of representatives as designated by both Parties.

3) The Joint Committee shall meet at such times, in such places and through such means as the Parties may agree. Meetings shall be held, whenever it is necessary, with alternating Chair between the Parties.

4) The joint Committee shall have the following responsibilities:

a) Monitor the implementation and execution of this Agreement;

b) Debate and share opportunities for the expansion of mutual Investment;

c) Request and welcome the participation of the private sector and civil society, when applicable, on specific issues related to the work of the Joint Committee; and

d) Seek to resolve any issues or disputes concerning Parties' investment in an amicable manner.

5) The joint Committee shall not replace or impair in any way, any other agreement or the diplomatic channels existing between the Parties.

Sustainable Development

Sustainability is a key theme of the BIT. Sustainable development is referenced four times in the Preamble, and this emphasis is continued throughout the agreement. The following provisions point towards a more socially responsible form of investment promotion. The BIT strikes an interesting balance between investor protection and state sovereignty. The drafting of the state's right to regulate is relatively broad, by reference to sustainable development and "other legitimate social and economic policy objectives" in Article 23(1). However, in Article 23(2), it is confirmed that the state's right to regulate is not absolute and lies within the broader framework of the balance of rights and obligations contained in the BIT.

Article 1 Definitions

3) [. . .]

"Investment" Investment means an enterprise within the territory of one State established, acquired, expanded or operated, in good faith, by an investor of the other State in accordance with law of the Party in whose territory the investment is made taken together with the asset of the enterprise which contribute sustainable development of that Party and has the characteristics of an investment involving a commitment of capital or other similar resources, pending profit, risk-taking and certain duration. [. . .]

Article 13 Investment and Environment

[. . .]

4) Nothing in this Agreement shall be constructed to prevent a Party from adopting maintaining, or enforcing, in a non-discriminatory manner, any measure otherwise consistent with this Agreement that it considers appropriate to ensure that investment activity in its territory is undertaken in a manner sensitive to environmental and social concerns.

Article 23 Right of State to Regulate

1) In accordance with customary international law and other general principles of international law, the Host State has the right to take regulatory or other measures to ensure that development in its territory is consistent with the goals and principles of sustainable development, and with other legitimate social and economic policy objectives.

2) Except where the rights of Host State are expressly stated as an exception to the obligation of this Agreement, a Host State's pursuit of its rights to regulate shall be understood as embodied within a balance of the rights and obligations of Investors and Investments and Host States, as set out in the Agreement.

[. . .]

Article 24 Corporate Social Responsibiuty

[. . .] investors and their investments should strive to make the maximum feasible contributions to the sustainable development of the Host State and local community through high levels of socially responsible practices.

Obligations for Foreign Investors

As compared to traditional investment treaties, the treaty between Morocco and Nigeria introduces a series of obligations upon investors.

Article 14 Impact Assessment

1) Investors or the investment shall comply with environmental assessment screening and assessment processes applicable to their proposed investments prior to their establishment, as required by the laws of the Host State for such an investment or

the laws of the home state for such an investment, whichever is more rigorous in relation to the investment in question.

2) Investors or the investment shall conduct a social impact assessment of the potential investment. The Parties shall adopt standards for this purpose at the meeting of the Joint Committee.

3) Investors, their investment and Host State authorities shall apply the precautionary principle to their environmental impact assessment and to decisions taken in relation to a proposed investment, including any necessary mitigation or alternative approaches of the precautionary principle by investors and investments shall be described in the environmental impact assessment they undertake.

Article 17 Anti-Corruption

1) Each Contracting Party shall ensure that measures and efforts are undertaken to prevent and combat corruption regarding matters covered by this Agreement in accordance with its laws and regulations.

2) Investors and their Investments shall not, prior to the establishment of an Investment or afterwards, offer, promise or give any undue pecuniary or other advantage, whether directly or through intermediaries, to a public official of the Host State, or a member of an official's family or business associate or other person in close proximity to an official, for that official or for a third party, in order that the official or third party act or refrain from acting in relation to the performance of official duties, in order to achieve any favour in relation to a proposed investment or any licences, permits, contracts or other rights in relations to an investment.

3) Investors and their Investments shall not be complicit in any act described in Paragraph 1 above, including incitement, aiding and abetting, and conspiracy to commit of authorization of such acts.

4) A breach of this article by an investor or an investment is deemed to constitute a breach of the domestic law of the Host State Party concerning the establishment and operation of an investment.

5) The States Parties to this Agreement, consistent with their applicable law, shall prosecute and where convicted penalize persons that have breached the applicable law implementing this obligation.

Article 18 Post-Establishment Obligations

1) Investments shall, in keeping with good practice requirements relating to the size and nature of the investment, maintain an environmental management system. Companies in areas of resource exploitation and high-risk industrial enterprises shall maintain a current certification to ISO 14001 or an equivalent environmental management standard.

2) Investments shall uphold human rights in the host state.

3) Investors and investments shall act in accordance with core labour standards as required by the ILO Declaration on Fundamental Principles and Rights of Work, 1998.

4) Investors and investments shall not manage or operate the investments in a manner that circumvents international environmental, labour and human rights obligations to which the Host State and/or Home State are Parties.

Dispute Settlement

The treaty contains an innovative yet problematic section entitled "Disputes Prevention".

Although Article 26(1) seems to expressly refer to disputes between the "Parties" (being the two State signatories), the provisions that follow suggest that the requirement may apply equally to investor-state disputes. The uncertainty arising from this drafting is problematic in a provision of key jurisdictional importance. It will no doubt be tested in future investor-state arbitrations.

Compulsory consultation on the part of the Joint Committee may risk contamination of the negotiation process with political motives, particularly given that the referral of a dispute is in the hands of the home state. If the effect of the drafting is to require the state of the investor to submit any dispute to the Joint Committee before the investor may initiate arbitration proceedings, this introduces a significant political hurdle to the commencement of Investor-State proceedings.

Article 26 Disputes Prevention

1) Before initiating an eventual arbitration procedure, any dispute between the Parties shall be assessed through consultations and negotiations by the Joint Committee. [. . .]

4) The meeting of the Joint Committee and all documentation, as well as steps taken in the context of the mechanism established in this Article, shall remain confidential, except for the submitted reports.

5) If the dispute cannot be resolved within six (6) months from the date of the written request for consultations and negotiations, the investor may, after the exhaustion of local remedies or the domestic courts of the Host State, resort to international arbitration mechanisms.

2. Model Text for the Indian Bilateral Investment Treaty (2015)

The Indian Model BIT 2015 states the definition of investment as:

Article 1.6

1.6 **"Investment"** means an Enterprise in the Host State, constituted, organized and operated in compliance with the law of the Host State and owned and controlled in good faith by an investor.

1.6.1 For the purposes of this Treaty, an Enterprise will be considered as:

(i) **"Controlled"** by the Investor, if such Investor has the right to appoint a majority of the directors or senior management officials or to control the management or policy decisions of such Enterprise, including by virtue of their shareholding, management, partnership or other legal rights or by virtue of shareholders agreements or voting agreements or partnership agreements or any other agreements of similar nature.

(ii) **"Owned"**, by the Investor, if more than 50% of the capital or funds or contribution in the Enterprise is directly or beneficially owned by such Investor, or by other companies or entities which are ultimately owned and controlled by the Investor.

1.7 For greater clarity, Investment does not include the following assets of an Enterprise: (i) any interest in debt securities issued by a government or government-owned or controlled enterprise, or loans to a government or government owned or controlled enterprise; (ii) any pre-operational expenditure relating to admission, establishment, acquisition or expansion of the Enterprise that is incurred before the commencement of substantial and real business operations of the Enterprise in the Host State; (iii) portfolio investments; (iv) claims to money that arise solely from commercial contracts for the sale of goods or services; (v) Goodwill, brand value, market share or similar intangible rights; (vi) claims to money that arise solely from the extension of credit in connection with any commercial transaction referred to in (v) above; (vii) an order or judgment sought or entered in any judicial, regulatory, administrative, or arbitral proceeding; (viii) any other claims to money that do not involve the kind of interests or operations set out in the definition of Investment in this Treaty.

1.8 For the purposes of this Treaty, a holding company or an investment company shall not be considered an Investment nor shall such companies be considered as protected assets of an Investment.

It defines an enterprise as:

1.2 **"Enterprise"** means: (i) any legal entity constituted, organized and operated in compliance with the law of the Host State, including any company, corporation, limited liability partnership or a joint venture (ii) having its management and real and substantial business operations in the territory of the Host State.

Article 13 Home State Obligations

13.1 Without prejudice to the jurisdiction of the Courts located in the Host State, Investors and its Investments shall be subject to civil actions for liability in the judicial process of their Home State for the acts, decisions or omissions made in the Home State in relation to the Investment where such acts, decisions or omissions lead to significant damage, personal injuries or loss of life in the Host State.

13.2 The Home State shall ensure that their legal systems and rules allow for, or do not prevent or unduly restrict, the bringing of court actions on their merits before their domestic courts relating to the civil liability of Investors and Investments for damages resulting from alleged acts, decisions or omissions made by Investments or Investors in relation to their Investments in the territory of the Host State.

I. Protection under Regional Trade and Investment Treaties

This topic will be discussed at greater length in Chapter 10 (emerging issues). Topics will include protection and promotion of investment under the sectoral, but multilateral, Energy Charter Treaty; current negotiations on investment protection under the now Comprehensive and Progressive Agreement for Trans-Pacific Partnership (CPTPP), and to what extent there is the potential for an eventual global comprehensive treaty on foreign investment.

© Surya P. Subedi, 2008, *International Investment Law: Reconciling Policy and Principle*, 2nd Edition, Hart Publishing, Bloomsbury Publishing Plc.

In the absence of a global treaty on foreign investment, both BITs and regional treaties have sought to fill this vacuum and lead the way in terms of protection of investment. This is especially the case with NAFTA. At the time of adoption, the provisions of this regional treaty provided far more protection to foreign investors than accorded hitherto in customary international law. Appleton states that '[p]lurilateral treaties such as NAFTA go even further than customary international law'.[118] Thus, NAFTA set the trend throughout the 1990s for significantly improved protection of foreign investment, whether through BITs, the TRIMS agreement of the WTO, or other regional treaties. In this respect, Jackson, Davey and Skyes observed that:

> If global progress on investment issues has been slow, more dramatic developments are visible at the regional level. NAFTA incorporates broad rules on investment within the region, including general obligations to afford MFN and national treatment to NAFTA investors. The 'investor rights' provisions of NAFTA are particularly remarkable in that they create private rights of action to enforce their terms (unlike most of the provisions of NAFTA, which can only be enforced by member nations), including a private right of action for damages in the event of "expropriation", a concept that has proved elusive.[119]

The NAFTA provisions on the treatment of foreign investors are by far the most favorable ones for foreign investors. They offer greater protection to foreign investment than does the TRIMS agreement. The main NAFTA provision on foreign investment protection reads, in Article 1110(1), as follows:

> No Party may directly or indirectly nationalize or expropriate an investment of an investor of another Party in its territory or take measure tantamount to nationalization or expropriation of such investment ('expropriation') except:

118. *See*, the remarks of B Appleton under the title 'Investment Disputes and NAFTA Chapter 11' in ASIL Proceedings, 2001, footnote 6, 197.

119. JH Jackson, WJ Davey and AO Sykes, Jr, *Legal Problems of International Economic Relations: Cases, Materials and Text* 1137 (St. Paul, MN., West Group, 4th ed. 2002).

(a) for public purpose

(b) on a non-discriminatory basis

(c) in accordance with due process of law and Article 1105(1)

(d) on payment of compensation in accordance with paragraphs 2 through 6

Article 1105 (1) provides for additional protection for foreign investors:

> Each Party shall accord to investments of investors of another Party treatment in accordance with international law, including fair and equitable treatment and full protection and security.

Thus, this provision implies that the protection of foreign investment under customary international law is as broad as that provided in NAFTA, as if the NAFTA provisions were mere codification of customary international law. It is doubtful whether the protection afforded to foreign investors under customary international law goes as far as that afforded under NAFTA. This provision of NAFTA represents an attempt to broaden the scope of customary international law and expand its reach beyond the limits generally accepted in international law.

Indeed, Article 1110(1) and 1105(1) add the following three new concepts to the regime of protection available to foreign investors:

(a) the due process of law

(b) fair and equitable treatment, and

(c) full protection and security.

Of course, there can be little doubt that these three new elements derive from customary international law on the subject matter. The problem, however, lies in the interpretation of the meaning, nature and scope of these concepts, as there have been tendencies on the part of the various NAFTA tribunals to stretch the meaning of these concepts beyond the limits generally understood in customary international law. It is doubtful whether the idea of the minimum international standard of treatment of foreign investment accepted in traditional international law encompasses all of the new elements embodied in the NAFTA regime under the heading *Minimum Standard of Treatment.*

Traditionally, BITs were designed to extend the national, non-discriminatory and MFN treatment to foreign investors and to protect their property against acts of expropriation. Thus, BITs sought to accord greater protection to foreign investors than that provided under customary international law. However, the NAFTA provisions imply that the projections enjoyed by foreign investors under BITs are also available under customary international law, which is, perhaps, not the case. What is more, neither customary law nor BITs have ever provided free and unhindered opportunities for investment in any given country; there have always been some restrictions on foreign investment, either in terms of the areas of economic activity or geographical regions of the country concerned.

Unlike other investment treaties, NAFTA includes provisions relating to the method according to which compensation has to be paid against expropriation. It provides for the award of monetary damages with interest. It also requires that compensation must be equivalent to the fair market value of the expropriated investment immediately before the expropriation took place. The treaty goes on to outline the valuation criteria of the assets expropriated:

> The valuation criteria shall include going concern value, asset value including the declared tax value of tangible property, and other criteria, as appropriate, to determine fair market value.[120]

The Energy Charter Treaty of 1994 includes equally greater protection for foreign investment than that accorded under customary international law. Article 10(1) on Promotion, Protection and Treatment of Investments provides that

> Each Contracting Party shall, in accordance with the provisions of this Treaty, encourage and create stable, equitable, favourable and transparent conditions for Investors of other Contracting Parties to make Investments in its Area. Such conditions shall include a commitment to accord at all times to Investments of Investors of other Contracting Parties fair and equitable treatment. Such Investments shall also enjoy the most constant protection and security and no Contracting Party shall in any way impair by unreasonable or discriminatory measures their management, maintenance, use, enjoyment or disposal. In no case shall such Investments be accorded treatment less favourable than that required by international law, including treaty obligations. Each Contracting Party shall observe any obligations it has entered into with an Investor or an Investment of an Investor of any other Contracting Party.

Conceived initially as the European Energy Charter, the 1994 Treaty has been ratified not only by western and eastern European States, including Russia, but also by the other members of the CIS, as well as by Japan, Mongolia and Australia. The protections accorded to foreign investors are enforceable by international arbitration. The protection accorded to foreign investors under principles of national treatment and MFN treatment is also extended to the 'related activities including management, maintenance, use, enjoyment or disposal.'[121]

---

120. Art 1135(1)(a) of NAFTA.
121. Art 10(1) of the Energy Charter Treaty.

Chapter 5

Nationalization, Investment Protection and Compensation

S.D. Myers, Inc. v. Gov't Canada, UNCITRAL (NAFTA), Partial Award (Merits) (Nov. 13, 2000)
Marvin Feldman v. United Mexican States, ICSID Case No. ARB(AF)/99/1, Award (Dec. 3, 2002), 5 ICSID Rep. 212 (2002)

A. Legality in the Context of International Law

Case Concerning the Factory at Chorzów (Ger. v. Pol.), Claim for Indemnity: Jurisdictional, 1927 P.C.I.J. (ser. A) No. 8 (July 26).

Case Introduction

In 1915, the German Chancellery and the Bavarian company Bayerische Stickstoffwerke A-G (Stickstoffwerke) contracted for the construction of a nitrate factory in Chorzów, now in Southern Poland but then located in the German Empire. In 1920, Stickstoffwerke was entered in the Chorzów land register as owner of the nitrate factory property. Following the defeat of Germany in the First World War, sovereignty over the part of Upper Silesia including Chorzów was transferred to the newly established Polish state. On July 1, 1922, the Stickstoffwerke registration was voided, and the property rights were registered in the name of the Polish Treasury. Subsequently, full powers to take charge of the factory at Chorzów were delegated by a Polish ministerial decree to a new owner of their choice.

In May 1925, Germany filed an Application in the Permanent Court of International Justice that the Polish law constituted a liquidation of the property involved, and that this was not in conformity with Articles 92 (property rights) and 297 (liquidation rules) of the Peace Treaty of Versailles (1919). Article 92 also provided for a Mixed Arbitral Tribunal to examine the conditions of transfer of German property to Poland and, at its discretion, to award the owner equitable compensation to be paid by the Polish Government.

Germany also alleged the transfer of ownership was contrary to the relevant Articles of the German-Polish Convention (Geneva Convention) of 1922. Under Articles 7 to 23 of the Convention, expropriation of German property in Polish Upper Silesia, as provided for under Article 6 of the Convention, was subject to stipulations prohibiting, with certain exceptions, the expropriation of industrial undertakings in Polish Upper Silesia for a period of fifteen years.

Poland responded with a preliminary objection, asking the Court to hold either that it had no jurisdiction of the suit, or that the Application could not be entertained until after the judgment of the German-Polish Mixed Arbitral Tribunal at Paris.

The Court, invoking Article 23 of the Geneva Convention, overruled the preliminary objection raised. It held that it had jurisdiction and this was not affected by the rights claimed under Article 6 to 22 of the Geneva Convention or other treaties. In international law, a breach of responsibility imposes an obligation to make satisfactory reparation for the injury sustained, including failure to apply the Articles in question. Furthermore, the pending Mixed Arbitral Tribunal at Paris did not prevent the Court from exercising its jurisdiction under Article 23 of the Geneva Convention.

Principal Points of the Judgment

[53] The position of the Polish Government is mainly based on the two following contentions:

1. that Article 23, paragraph 1, of the Geneva Convention, which gives the Court jurisdiction for "differences of opinion, resulting from the interpretation and the application of Articles 6 to 22", which may arise between the German Government and the Polish Government, does not contemplate differences in regard to reparations claimed for violation of those articles;

2. that the Geneva Convention has instituted special jurisdictions for claims which private persons might assert in the event of the suppression or diminution of their rights, and that the existence of these jurisdictions would affect that of the Court even if Article 23, paragraph 1, of the Geneva Convention could be construed as including differences of opinion in regard to reparations amongst those relating to the application of Articles 6 to 22; therefore, the interested Parties should themselves have recourse to the jurisdictions in question.

[54] In the first place, the meaning and scope of paragraph 1 of Article 23 must be considered, for it is upon this clause—and upon this clause only—that the Court's jurisdiction in the present case rests.

[55] [. . .] It is a principle of international law that the breach of an engagement involves an obligation to make reparation in an adequate form. Reparation therefore is the indispensable complement of a failure to apply a convention and there is no necessity for this to be stated in the convention itself. Differences relating to reparations, which may be due by reason of failure to apply a convention, are consequently differences relating to its application.

[56] Now, Poland maintains that the words "differences of opinion, resulting from . . . the application" in Article 23 cannot have the meaning just indicated, but that they must be construed as covering merely the question whether, in a given case, the application of Articles 6 to 22 is or is not correct, to the exclusion of any differences in regard to reparations.

[57] In this connection, the Polish Government, in support of its contention that paragraph I of Article 23 of the Geneva Convention should be restrictively construed, has traced the development of general treaties of arbitration during the last fifty years, comprising (1) the so-called *la clause compromissoire* (arbitration clause) introduced into commercial and other treaties during the last twenty-five years of the XIXth century and subsequently, by which the contracting Parties agreed to submit to arbitration any differences as to the interpretation or application of the

particular treaties; (2) general treaties for the compulsory arbitration of certain specified categories of disputes, concluded since 1900, and (3) treaties and clauses for the arbitration of pecuniary claims. It is needless to say that paragraph 1 of Article 23 is an example of the first of these three classes of agreements.

[. . .]

[84] There is, moreover, another reason which the Court feels called upon to invoke in order to show that the jurisdiction of the Mixed Arbitral Tribunal cannot be urged in this case in opposition to the jurisdiction conferred on the Court by Article 23 of the Geneva Convention.

[85] [. . .] one of the fundamental principles [. . .] as regards procedure, is that no dispossession may be effected without previous notice to the real or apparent owner, affording him an opportunity of being heard before the competent tribunal. [. . .] in this case such a procedure has not been adopted [. . .] Consequently, the Polish Government cannot in this particular case require the interested Parties to look for redress of the injury sustained by them to the tribunals which might have been open to them if the Convention had been applied. [. . .]

[87] It is, moreover, a principle generally accepted in the jurisprudence of international arbitration, as well as by municipal courts, that one Party cannot avail himself of the fact that the other has not fulfilled some obligation or has not had recourse to some means of redress, if the former Party has, by some illegal act, prevented the latter from fulfilling the obligation in question, or from having recourse to the tribunal which would have been open, to him.

[. . .]

It follows from the foregoing considerations that the Court affirms its jurisdiction and reserves the suit for judgment on the merits [. . .].

Norwegian Shipowners' Claims (Norway v. United States), 1 R.I.A.A. 307 (Perm. Ct. Arb. 1922).

Case Introduction

During the First World War, a number of shipbuilding contracts were placed by Norwegian nationals with U.S. shipyards. Following its declaration of war on Germany on April 6, 1917, the United States Shipping Board Emergency Fleet Corporation was formed and seized these ships for its own use. Norway brought suit before the Permanent Court of Arbitration, which in its ruling, noted it was not bound by U.S. law.

Principal Points of the Award of the Tribunal—The Law Governing the Arbitration

It is common ground between the parties to this arbitration that the fifteen claims against the United States are presented by the Government of the Kingdom of Norway, which Government, and not the individual claimants, "is the sole claimant before this Tribunal". [. . .]

IV. The Parties have disagreed also as regards the question whether this Tribunal is bound by the municipal law of the United States, [. . .] The special agreement of June 30, 1921, Article I provides that "The Tribunal shall examine and decide the aforesaid claims in accordance with the principles of law and equity". The United States, [. . .] has advanced the contention that the Tribunal should not fail to give effect to the municipal law of the United States, regarding any matters within the jurisdiction of the United States [. . .] The Kingdom of Norway, on the other hand, has maintained that, in the absence of an express agreement to the contrary, arbitration of differences between nations is governed by international law, and that no arbitral tribunal is bound by the municipal law of any of the States which are Parties to the arbitration. [. . .]

As regards private law this Tribunal has not the power to modify, correct or improve the contracts agreed between citizens of the two countries, nor to modify their consequences. It may have to resolve certain conflicts of private law in the absence of contract. [. . .] But should the public law of one of the Parties seem contrary to international public policy ("Ordre Public International"), an International Tribunal is not bound by the municipal law of the States which are Parties to the arbitration. [. . .]

"If no special principles are prescribed to the arbitrator, he must doubtless decide in the first place in accordance with international law to be applied from both sources of this science, not only from treaties, but also from customary law, and the practice of judges in other international courts." [. . .] The words "law and equity" used in the special agreement of 1921 [. . .] The majority of international lawyers seem to agree that these words are to be understood to mean general principles of justice as distinguished from any particular system of jurisprudence or the municipal law of any State.

It must also be borne in mind that this Tribunal has been instituted in a general arbitration convention between United States and Norway, which has expressly provided that: "Differences which may arise of a legal nature or relating to the interpretation of principles existing between the two contracting Parties, and which it may not have been possible to settle by diplomacy, shall be referred to arbitration in the way which has been followed in this case."

This Tribunal is therefore a regular legal institution, which possesses by consent of the two Parties a compulsory jurisdiction, independent of the national courts of the Parties. Both Parties come before the Tribunal on a footing of perfect equality. [. . .]

The Tribunal cannot agree, therefore, with the contention of Norway that it should be entirely free to disregard the municipal law of the United States, when this has been implicitly accepted by Norwegian citizens in their dealings with American citizens, although this law may be less favourable to their present claims than the municipal laws of certain other civilised countries.

But the Tribunal cannot agree, on the other hand, with the contention of the United States that it should be governed by American Statutes whenever the United States claims jurisdiction.

This Tribunal is at liberty to examine if these Statutes are consistent with the equality of the two Contracting Parties, with Treaties passed by the United States, or with well established principles of international law, including the customary law and the practice of judges in other international courts.

After careful examination of the Constitution of the United States, of the American jurisprudence quoted by both parties, and of the American legislation passed by Congress from 1916 onwards [. . .], the Tribunal agrees with the contention of the United States that there was nothing in this emergency legislation, under the special circumstances, that was contrary to international law. [. . .]

The Tribunal is further of the opinion that the present arbitration is not due to possible defects in this legislation or in Presidential Orders, but to the action of some of the officials of the United States Shipping Board and Shipping Board Emergency Fleet Corporation.

[. . .]

It is common ground that, in the absence of any treaty, the Norwegian owners of these contracts were protected by the Fifth Amendment of the Constitution of the United States against any expropriation not necessary for public use, and that they are entitled to just compensation if expropriation occurs. It has been proved that the claimants lost the use and possession of their property through an exercise by the United States of their power of eminent domain. [. . .] this action of the United States is equivalent to the taking of private property as defined in the Fifth Amendment of their Constitution.

Whether the action of the United States was lawful or not, just compensation is due to the claimants under the municipal law of the United States, as well as under the international law, based upon the respect for private property.

But, as it is common ground that such compensation is measured not only by:

(a) the fair actual value of the property taken, but also

(b) at the time and place it was taken, and

(c) in view of all the surrounding circumstances,

It is necessary to examine, first, these surrounding circumstances, and to see:

I. Whether the claimants' property was taken and withheld for public use,

II. Whether the taking for title and the keeping of the title without a sufficient emergency or after the emergency had passed, was necessary. [. . .]

[. . .] in order to assess the amount of just compensation, and to justify liberal compensation, it is necessary to say this: In fact, the United States have not proved that the Shipping Board, nor the Fleet Corporation, acted in conformity with the liberal spirit of the municipal law of the United States, on which they rely in the present arbitration. Especially they have not proved:

(a) That the keeping for title to the claimants' property was needed for public use after July 1st, 1919 [. . .]

(b) That neither war emergency nor public needs forced them to act as they did, towards the claimants in July 1919, after the signature of the Treaty of Versailles. On the other hand, making due allowance for the circumstances, and especially for war conditions, it may be said that discrimination against the claimants has not been sufficiently arbitrary to justify any special claim for damages by the Kingdom of Norway, apart from damages for use, for the time of war, as far as the taking and keeping for title during that time was concerned.

It is necessary to mention here that, while the Norwegian claimants might have *bona fide* believed themselves to be entitled to privileged treatment under the Treaty between the Parties, it was agreed on June 30th, 1921 between the Parties not to apply such Treaty in the present arbitration. The Tribunal has acted according to this agreement. The Norwegian claimants are entitled, however, to the perfect equality of treatment which is provided for them under the Constitution of the United States. [. . .]

It must be admitted, in favor of the present claimants, that the American War legislation gave a large discretionary power to the Shipping Board and to the Emergency Fleet Corporation, and that some officials do not seem, as regards the claimants, to have always used their power in the true spirit of the American Constitution, or of the Congressional Acts, or for instance of Presidential Orders of 1917 and 1918. As has already been stated, the national peril was not such as to free them from the obligation of making the necessary inventory and valuation of all the property taken for the purpose of determining and paying "just compensation". This was not a case of "requisition of neutral property" in the special meaning of that term in the laws and customs of war. [. . .]

Just compensation implies a complete restitution of the status quo ante, based, not upon future gains of the United States or other powers, but upon the loss of profits of the Norwegian owners as compared with other owners of similar property. [. . .]

No State can exercise towards the citizens of another civilized State the "power of eminent domain" without respecting the property of such foreign citizens or without paying just compensation as determined by an impartial tribunal, if necessary. [. . .] the claims made on August 11th, 1922 amounted to a total of $13,223,185 and that in addition to this sum the Kingdom of Norway claimed interest for a period of more than five years at the rate of 7 cent per annum, compounded semi-annually, from the dates of the progress payments made to the shipbuilders up to and including September 1st, 1922. On this basis the total amount claimed by the Kingdom of Norway would have amounted, at the present date, to a sum exceeding $18,000,000. [. . .]

The United States is responsible for having thus made a discriminating use of the power of eminent domain towards citizens of a friendly nation, and they are liable for the damaging action of their officials and agents towards these citizens of the Kingdom of Norway. [. . .]

Anglo-Iranian Oil Co. Case (United Kingdom v. Iran), Preliminary Objection, 1952 I.C.J. Rep. 93 (July 22, 1952).

Case Introduction

In April 1933, a concessionary agreement for the exploration and exploitation of oil in Iran was concluded between the Government of Iran and the Anglo-Iranian Oil Company (now BP). In 1951, Iran passed a series of laws pronouncing the nationalization of the oil industry and the accompanying procedures for enforcement. The United Kingdom adopted the cause for the British Anglo-Iranian Oil Company before the International Court of Justice, claiming its right of diplomatic protection of a UK interest. Iran disputed the Court's jurisdiction.

Principal Points of the Judgment

[. . .] in the present case the jurisdiction depends on the Declarations accepting the compulsory jurisdiction of the Court made by Iran and by the United Kingdom under Article 36, paragraph 2, of the Statute. [. . .]

According to this Declaration, the Court has jurisdiction only when a dispute relates to the application of a treaty or convention accepted by Iran. But Iran maintains that, according to the actual wording of the text, the jurisdiction is limited to treaties subsequent to the Declaration. The United Kingdom maintains, on the contrary, that earlier treaties may also come into consideration. [. . .] the Court cannot base itself on a purely grammatical interpretation: it must seek the interpretation which is in harmony with a natural and reasonable way of reading the text, having due regard to the intention of Iran at the time when it formulated the Declaration. [. . .] leads to the conclusion that only treaties subsequent to the ratification come into consideration. [. . .] it may be admitted that Iran had special reasons for drafting her Declaration in a very restrictive manner, and for excluding the earlier treaties. [. . .] Moreover, the Iranian law by which the Najlis approved and adopted the Declaration, before it was ratified, provides a decisive confirmation of Iran's intention, for it states that the treaties and conventions which come into consideration are those which "the Government will have accepted after the ratification".

The earlier treaties are thus excluded by the Declaration, and the United Kingdom cannot therefore rely on them. [. . .]

The United Kingdom maintains that [. . .] the agreement signed in 1933 between the United Kingdom and the Company had a double character: being at once a concessionary contract and a treaty between the two States. In the view of the Court, that it not the case. The United Kingdom is not a party to the contract, which does not constitute a link between the two Governments or in any way regulate the relations between them. [. . .]

Thus the Court arrives at the conclusion that it lacks jurisdiction.

B. History and Sources of the Law of Expropriation

Expropriation and Standards of Compensation Prior to World War II

International arbitral decisions that did address expropriation routinely held [. . .] that states have the right to "appropriate private property for public use", but upon such expropriation, the State had an obligation to pay full compensation. In fact, this principle was so well settled that in treaties among European countries, compensation for expropriated property was rarely mentioned—it was taken for granted. [. . .]

International arbitrations both prior to and following the *Chorzów Factory* case support the proposition that the proper level of compensation following an expropriation is the full value of the property taken. Early twentieth-century cases in which full compensation was ordered include [. . .] the *Norwegian Shipowners' Claim* [. . .]. The principle of full compensation for expropriation has long been established as a fundamental rule of customary international law. [. . .]

The United States first precisely articulated the principle of full compensation in 1938, when Secretary of State Cordell Hull, in a letter to the Mexican government regarding the nationalization of certain agricultural and oil-related properties, insisted that expropriation of foreign owned property must be assisted by "prompt, adequate, and effective" compensation. This phrasing has now come to be known as he "Hull formula", and it has been interpreted to require compensation in the amount of the full fair market value of an investment as a going concern. [. . .] not only did traditional international law require that an alien be fully compensated for the taking of its property, but it also permitted the use of force by the alien's home State to protect such rights.

a. Latin American States

As early as the 19th century, a number of Latin American States challenged the international law standards [. . .] arguing that (1) aliens whose property was expropriated were entitled only to treatment equivalent to that granted by the expropriating State to its own nationals, and no more (and that the national treatment might well be that no compensation is required at all); and (2) that States were not obligated to recognize any international claims in relation to expropriation.

As an expression of their view of international law, many of these countries insisted upon the inclusion of a so-called "Calvo clause" [Brownlies Calvo clause doctrine opine] in investment contracts, by which the investor agreed to renounce the right to diplomatic protection, and to submit all disputes to the jurisdiction of the host State's courts. These [. . .] have declined in prominence in recent decades, as Latin American states increasingly accept the standard of full compensation following expropriation and the settlement of investment disputes through international arbitration.

b. Nationalization in the Twentieth Century

Many states nationalized the property of both their own citizens and foreign investors without compensation in the early twentieth century, often following revolutions that wrought radical changes in political and economic structures. [. . .] Both the Soviet Union and Cuba, for example, after their respective revolutions of 1917 and 1959, attempted to abolish the institution of private property, and refused to pay any compensation to foreign businesses that had suffered the confiscation of assets. [. . .]

Expropriations triggered by political change continued into the 1970s. [. . .]

[. . .] nationalization programs were also implemented by the newly independent and newly prosperous states of the Middle East, Asia and Africa, usually involving the expropriation of petroleum rights from multinational corporations operating under the auspices of concession agreements. These takings often resulted not so much from socialist ideological inspiration as from the desire of these States to enjoy a greater share in the profits derived from their petroleum reserves.

[. . .] the expropriations by Libya that gave rise to the British Petroleum, TOPCO and LIAMCO arbitrations were triggered in part by the UK's refusal to react to Iran's occupation of three islands in the Persian Gulf, which were then nominally under British protection.

c. Justifications for Expropriation and the UN Resolutions on Permanent Sovereignty

[. . .] Some, especially in the Middle East and Africa, argued that they were tied to long-term contracts that had been concluded between foreign investors and former colonial authorities, and that the continuation of these arrangements despite de-colonialization deprived them of essential control over their ostensibly independent economies. [. . .] gave foreign interests the power to dispose of their natural resources. [. . .]

These views are reflected in a series of United Nations General Assembly Resolutions endorsed, for the most part, by developing states. The first of these resolutions, and the only one that received broad support from States in both the developed and developing world, was General Assembly Resolution 1803 (XVII) of 1962, the Declaration on Permanent Sovereignty Over Natural Resources.

General Assembly resolution 1803 (XVII) of 14 December 1962, "Permanent sovereignty over natural resources"

> 4. Nationalization, expropriation or requisitioning shall be based on grounds or reasons of public utility, security or the national interest which are recognized as overriding purely individual or private interests, both domestic and foreign.

> In such cases the owner shall be paid appropriate compensation, in accordance with the rules in force in the State taking such measures in the exercise of its sovereignty and in accordance with international law. In any case where the question of compensation gives rise to a controversy, the national jurisdiction of the State taking such measures shall be exhausted. However, upon agreement by sovereign States and other parties concerned, settlement of the dispute should be made through arbitration or international adjudication.

[. . .] it sparked widespread debate over the meaning of the phrase "appropriate compensation". The United States voted in favor of Resolution 1803 because, in its view, the term "appropriate" compensation was equivalent to "prompt, adequate, and effective" compensation. Many developing states disagreed, arguing that the "appropriate compensation" standard allowed them to pay less than full compensation following an expropriation. [. . .]

Treaties as Evidence of Customary International law

[. . .] Most bilateral investment treaties ("BITs") in effect today provide that full compensation should be paid following an expropriation. [. . .] Some have argued that these treaties, and the protections that they offer to foreign investment are evidence of customary international law. Professor Brownlie opines that:

> It is a fact that a very considerable number of hosts to foreign capital are willing to conclude treaties for the protection of investments which contain a provision for the payment of "prompt, adequate and effective" compensation in cases of expropriation or, more frequently, "just compensation". While these are negotiated deals, the pattern of agreements surely constitutes evidence of an international standard based upon the principle of compensation."[122]

F.A. Mann also believed that "these treaties establish and accept and thus enlarge the force of traditional conceptions of the law of state responsibly for foreign investment."[123] Mann argued that States cannot credibly insist on the one hand that customary international law allows them to set the level of compensation following expropriation, and on the other hand accept the principle of full compensation in the BITs that they sign.[124]

Negotiated Settlements

Many twentieth-century expropriation claims were settled by lump sum payments from the expropriating State to the home State of the foreign individuals and corporations whose property was taken. In these cases, the two governments negotiated to arrive at a total compensation amount for all outstanding claims, and then the

---

122. Ian Brownlie, *Principles of Public International Law* (6th ed. 2003).

123. F.A. Mann, *British Treaties for the Promotion and Protection of Investment*, 52 Brit. Y.B. Int'l L. 241, 249 (1981).

124. *Id.* For a contrary opinion, *see*, Bernard Kishoiyian, *The Utility of Bilateral Investment Treaties in the Formulation of Customary International Law*, 14 N.W. J. Int'l L. & Bus. 327 (1994).

receiving State distributed payments to individual investors (normally on a pro-rate basis). In many of these settlements, the States involved agreed to an amount less than full compensation for the property expropriated. [. . .]

Some commentators have argued that the results of these lump sum settlement negotiations between States (i.e., the payment of less than full compensation) create international custom, which constitutes one source of international law,[125] and should therefore be viewed as evidence of a corresponding customary international law norm.

The *Khemco* tribunal took issue with this position, concluding that the existence of lump sum settlements for less than full value of property taken cannot be seen in and of themselves as evidence of any underlying legal principle. "As a rule, a State practice as reflected in settlement agreements cannot be considered as giving birth to customary rules of international law, unless it presents specific features which demonstrate the conviction of the State's parties that they were acting in application of what they consider to be settled law. The provisions of such an agreement, indeed, are the outcome of negotiations in which many motivations other than legal ones may have prevailed. This is especially true here, where certain commercial advantages given to companies (even if they were not expressly detailed in the agreements) produced the concessions that they accepted on the standard of compensation."

[. . .]

Thus, for the purposes of international law formation, there may be an important distinction between negotiations that were clearly based upon perceptions of customary law and those based primarily upon economic and political considerations. Since almost all lump sum settlement agreements have been concluded on the basis of a variety of interests, it is difficult to draw any general conclusions about the extent to which such negotiations reflect customary international law.

C. Customary International Law and Breach of State Contracts

Upton Case, Mixed Claims Commission (U.S. v. Venez.), Int'l Arb. Award., 9 R.I.A.A. 234 (1903).

Case Introduction

The Government of Venezuela granted a concession ($1 million) to Jose Madriz and on the following day assigned the same contract and concession to another person, Jose Ricart. A United States citizen ("Claimant") bought the same concession from Ricart with all its rights and privileges granted therein. The Claimant asked that the

125. Statute of the International Court of Justice, art. 38(1) (1945).

Mixed Claims Commission, as a preliminary item of his claim, establish as a record that the Government of Venezuela make acknowledgment upon its official records of his compliance with the terms of the contract. This was clearly not a "claim", and the Commission agreed that it had no jurisdiction to do so.

A further two claims made by the Claimant in front of the Commission referred to damage incurred in Venezuela to the steam boat "Protector". This was used by the Government of Venezuela to fend off revolutionaries when the Claimant was in the United States. While being transported by railway, the boat was badly damaged by careless or inefficient handling and rendered useless. It could not be repaired, and the Claimant sought compensation of $3,500.

In addition, a duplicate steel hull with boiler was used by the Venezuelan military authorities to resist an attack by revolutionaries. In doing so, they filled the hull with stones, rocks and sand of great weight. It was discovered later that this had seriously damaged the hull, and without the hull, the boiler was completely lost. The Claimant sought compensation of $4,002.25.

Compensation was also sought for other items lost, such as sacks of coffee, chattels and money.

Principal Points of the Judgment

[. . .] It appears from the evidence that the Government paid the expenses of removing the launch from the streets of Puerto Cabello to a vacant lot where, it is alleged, the boat has remained absolutely useless ever since.

The seizure of the launch may have been justified by the necessities of the State, but it was a taking of private property for public use and involved the obligation of just compensation to the owner. The evidence is sufficient as to the fact of the taking of the boat and that as a result thereof it was rendered useless. But as the launch appears to have some value, and as it still remains the property of the claimant, an award of $3,000, with interest thereon at 3 per cent per annum from October 1st, 1900 to December 31st, 1903, is hereby made as compensation for the loss or damage sustained by the claimant upon this item. [. . .]

[. . .] the hull [. . .] the same principle is applicable here as in the foregoing item. The right of the State, under the stress of necessity, to appropriate private property for public use is unquestionable, but always with the corresponding obligation to make just compensation to the owner thereof.

It is believed, however, from all the evidence here presented, that the sum of $2,000, with interest thereon at 3 per cent per annum from July 15th, 1902 to December 31st, 1903 will fully compensate Mr. Upton for whatever loss or damage he has sustained on this item of his claim.

As to the remaining items of this claim it is evident from the claimant's own statement that the losses set forth in his memorial arose from the disturbed condition of the country, due to the civil war then existing in Venezuela, and not from any acts of the Venezuelan Government or its agents, specially directed against the claimant or his property. Under these circumstances the claimant's privileges and immunities were not different from those of other inhabitants of the country. He must be held, in going into a foreign country, to have voluntarily assumed the risks as well as the advantages of his residence there. Neither claimant nor his property can be exempted from the evils incident to a state of war to which all other persons and property within the same territory were exposed. As to these items, therefore, the claim must be disallowed.

Walter Fletcher Smith Claim (Cuba v. U.S.), 2 R.I.A.A 915 (1929).

Case Introduction

Captain Walter Fletcher Smith ("Captain Smith"), an American citizen, lived in Cuba for about twenty-eight years prior to the events at issue. Captain Smith owned all the stocks of the Marianao Beach Company. Prior to 1919, Captain Smith sold all the Marianao Beach Company stock to the Playa Company for the sum of $240,000. The contract of sale passed all title to Playa Company except for two lots of land (approx. $4000m^2$), which were excluded from the transfer of title because they stood in the name of Captain Smith personally, and not in that of the company.

Captain Smith's home was on his land, and the contract of sale provided specifically that the view to the water-front should not be obstructed. Around May 1919, the municipality of Marianao granted the Playa Company a concession for the purpose of urbanizing the area around the beach, which included the lands bought by the company from Captain Smith and also Smith's private land. It was expected that Smith's land could be bought, but a price was never agreed. Captain Smith received threats to destroy his property if he did not sell it and consequently wrote to the Government of Cuba requesting protection.

The Mayor of Marianao, for the benefit of the Playa Company, instituted proceedings for Captain Smith's land at the Court of First Instance of Marianao. The court gave "preliminary" possession for the houses to be demolished and land possessed. The team carrying out the demolition were said to have been acting under the supervision of Congressman Carlos de Cruz, attorney for the Playa Company. It is claimed that Captain Smith did not know of the petition until the houses had been partially demolished. He immediately applied to the court to prevent further destruction.

Captain Smith contested the expropriation in the Cuban courts and later acquired a judgment that the proceedings in the lower court were illegal. He applied to the lower court for restoration of possession. Captain Smith's petition was denied, and he appealed this decision. The matter was taken up by the United States Government with the Government of Cuba through diplomatic channels. These efforts were unsuccessful, and it was agreed to arbitrate the question before a sole arbitrator.

Principal Points of the Judgment

The learned counsel for the defendant contend that the expropriation proceedings were conducted in strict compliance with the constitution and laws of the Republic of Cuba [. . .] that these proceedings were for the "urbanization of the property" and "solely for purposes of public utility".

Article 32 of the Constitution of Cuba requires:

> No one shall be deprived of his property except by competent authority upon the justified proof that the condemnation is required by public utility and previous indemnification. If the indemnification is not previously paid, the judges and the courts shall protect the owners and, if needed, restore to them the property.

From a careful examination of the testimony and of the records, the Arbitrator is impressed that the attempted expropriation of the claimant's property was not in compliance with the constitution, nor with the laws of the Republic; that the expropriation proceedings were not, in good faith, for the purpose of public utility. [. . .]

While the proceedings were municipal in form, the properties seized were turned over immediately to the defendant company, ostensibly for public purposes, but, in fact, to be used by the defendant for purposes of amusement and private profit, without any reference to public utility. [. . .]

[. . .] No reflection is to be made upon the character of the courts of Cuba. [. . .]

While believing, as hereinbefore indicated, that the defendant company has acquired no clear title to the premises in question, the Arbitrator is of the opinion that it is for the best interests of the parties, and of the public, that the award be made under item "c" of the Agreement of Arbitration: "That, if the land is not to be restored, the Arbitrator should consider what Smith is entitled to receive in complete settlement", and the Arbitrator decides accordingly.

[. . .] the Arbitrator finds that, as compensation for the value of the land, of the buildings and personal effects contained therein, also the deprivation of the use of the property and in consideration of his expense in defending his rights, he should receive in complete settlement $190,000. [. . .]

Marquerite de Joly de Sabla (U.S. v. Pan.), 6 R.I.A.A 358 (1933).

Case Introduction

After the death of her husband, Mrs. T.J. de Sabla ("Sabla") immediately became the private owner of his 3,180 hectares land in Panama. Despite this, officials of the Government of Panama treated the land as if it were public, conveying to grantees full title through adjudications and granting numerous farmers' licenses to others, thereby rendering the land worthless for its owner. Panama asserted that its laws provided for all grants to be filed unless opposition was made and that the system provided claimants an adequate means of defending themselves. Thus, the actions were not confiscatory by international standards. The United States contended that those laws imposed so unreasonable a burden on private landowners as to fall below international standards.

Panama also maintained that Mrs. Sabla could not claim for damages arising out of acts occurring prior to her ownership of the land. However, on reference to the General Claims Commission (U.S. and Panama), the Commission found that acts committed during the life of Mr. Sabla were sufficient for the United States to raise a claim. The claim did not lapse on the death of Mr. Sabla, and this allowed the United States to present on behalf of Mr. Sabla's executrix.

Principal Points of the Judgment

[. . .] Since the land laws by their terms contemplated the adjudication only of public lands, and since the result of granting adjudications on private property was to deprive the owner of his property without compensation, the burden of persuasion on this issue is clearly on Panama. She has failed to sustain it. The Commission finds that the legislative intent to have applications for known private lands refused by the authorities of their own accord, is established. [. . .]

(a) All the land laws, beginning in 1907, contemplated the making of a national land map, to demarcate public from private lands. The clear inference from this requirement is that, once such maps were made, adjudications of lands shown thereon to be private, were to be denied. Otherwise, if private owners had to oppose each application even after the map was made, the making of the map, an expensive task, would have been useless and superfluous. The legislative intent clearly was, not that private owners should have to protect their rights by constant oppositions, but that adjudications should be made only on lands shown to be public on the map [. . .].

(b) Pursuant to the plan for a general land map, the laws [. . .] directed the Land Commissions to conduct proceedings to demarcate public from private lands. [. . .] The purpose of such demarcation proceedings clearly was to inform the commission as to what land was public and adjudicable. It follows from this, as from the map project, that the intent of the legislature was that, when the commissions thus got the information as to what was public land, no private land should thereafter be adjudicated, without the necessity of oppositions by private owners. [. . .]

(c) Article 6 of decree No. 23 of 1913 admonished the Administrators of Lands that law 20 of 1913 could not destroy vested rights. If the intent of this law had been to put the onus of defending private titles on the owners, through opposition proceedings, as asserted by Panama, this admonition would be pointless.

[. . .]

Thus, the most important protection held out to private owners by the law was denied to claimant, and was denied through the fault of government officials, the Provincial Administrators. [. . .]

It is by no means clear that, under a fair construction of the land laws prior to 1917, the opposition procedure was open to the claimant at all. [. . .]

The opposition procedure was designed, not to accomplish the primary step of preventing private lands from being adjudicated, but to settle disputes where two individuals claimed the right to be adjudicated the same piece of public land. [. . .]

The United States contends that the opposition procedure was no real protection. This contention is based on three grounds: first, that the notice provided by the law was in fact inadequate; second, that the period allowed for opposition was unreasonably short when the protection of private property was in question; and third, that to be required to oppose every petition is an unreasonable hardship, particularly in a case where applications were as multifarious as in this one. [. . .] although the edictos were both posted and published, [. . .] as described in the applications and consequently in the edictos, were customarily so vague that a landowner could not tell whether the land applied for was on his property or not. [. . .]

In view of the fact that the result of an adjudication on private land might be the uncompensated loss of private property, the period allowed for opposition by the laws, 15 days after a 30-day posting of the edicto, also seems unreasonably brief. [. . .]

The Commission therefore finds that the machinery of opposition, as actually administered, did not constitute an adequate remedy to the claimant for the protection of her property. [. . .]

As to the adequacy of the remedy of opposition to the licenses, the claimant's case is even stronger than with respect to adjudications. No publication of applications for licenses was required by law. As a result, the first knowledge that licenses had been granted came from actual discovery of the licensees on the land. [. . .] The cumbersomeness of a system which required the claimant to oppose 123 applications for cultivator's licenses, after discovering the licensees on her land prior to planting, and gave her no general remedy, is obvious.

The Commission therefore finds that the authorities should have afforded the owners of Bernardino protection, by denying applications for grants and licenses thereon, and that Panama cannot avoid liability because of the claimant's failure to oppose each application. [. . .]

The Commission concludes that the adjudications and licenses granted by the authorities on Bernardino constituted wrongful acts for which the Government of Panama is responsible internationally. It is axiomatic that acts of a government in depriving an alien of his property without compensation impose international responsibility. [. . .]

It remains only to determine the question of the damages caused to the claimant by the adjudications and licenses. [. . .] As to this portion, the Commission holds that the proper measure of damages arising from adjudications is to determine the total number of hectares on Bernardino which have been adjudicated, and the value of Bernardino lands per hectare, from the evidence before the Commission, and to award to the claimant the full value of the number of hectares of her property which have been adjudicated. [. . .]

We turn now from the adjudications to the matter of cultivator's licenses. The evidence indicates that the bulk of the licenses were on the central and southern part of the property, while most of the adjudications were in the northern part. [. . .]

The licenses were all temporary, usually for two years, but there is evidence that the licensees often did not leave at the end of the term and did not observe the proper limitations as to area. There is also evidence that these numerous licenses encouraged trespassers to come on the property. There is evidence also that the licensees destroyed the timber and denuded the soil by improper cultivation. The claimant asserts a constructive total loss of the property because the breaking up of the continuity of the estate by adjudications, coupled with the damage done to forests and soil by the licensees, have rendered impracticable any development of the land. [. . .]

D. Quantification of Compensation for Expropriation—Approaches

Norwegian Shipowners' Claims (Norway v. United States), 1 R.I.A.A. 307 (Perm. Ct. Arb. 1922).

Principal Points of the Award of the Tribunal—The Amount of Compensation

It is common ground between the Parties that just compensation, as it is understood in the United States, should be liberally awarded, and that it should be based upon the net value of the property taken. [. . .]

As a rule, abnormal circumstances, speculative prices, etc., cannot form the legal basis of compensation in condemnation awards. [. . .] the Tribunal is not bound by [US law], in so far as these provisions restricted the right of the claimants to receive immediate and full compensation, with interest from the day on which the compensation should have been fully paid *ex aequo et bono.*

Just compensation should have been paid to the Claimants or arranged with them on the basis of the net value of the property taken:

1. On the October 6th, 1917, for use, during the war (whenever such use was possible without destroying the property, according to the contract, state of completion of ship, etc.), and

2. At the latest on the July 1st, 1919 as damages for the unlawful retaining of the title and use of the ships after all emergency ceased;

Or

On the October 6th, 1917 as full compensation for the destruction of the Norwegian property. [. . .]

In assessing the net amount of compensation, the Tribunal has taken into consideration in each case all the circumstances pertaining to the net value of the property requisitioned or taken by the United States and especially the following: the date of each contract or sub-contract between shipbuilder and shipowner; the technical characteristics and qualities of each contract [. . .]; the legal value of the contract, namely the liens, rights and interests in each original contract, etc.; the original contract (or sub-contract) price; the progress (and brokerage) payments made by each of the parties on the original contract price; the date of delivery promised in the contract; the date of delivery which was expected at or about the date of the general requisition order and about the date of the effective requisition of each contract as far as these can be ascertained; the various elements pertaining to the value and degree of completion of the tangible objects of completion as: for instance, the percentage of materials ordered, and the percentage of materials on hand; the date at which the keel was laid, before or after the general requisition; and the date when the ship was launched; [. . .]

Case Concerning the Factory at Chorzów (*Ger. v. Pol.*), Judgment, Claim for Indemnity, Merits, 1928 P.C.I.J. (ser. A) No. 13 (Sept. 13).

Principal Points of the Judgment

[54] The Court's Judgment No. 7 was given on May 25th, 1926. This judgment was the source of developments tending in two different directions.

[56] On the one hand, at the initiative of the German Government, it formed the starting point for direct negotiations between the two Governments concerned. In regard to these negotiations, it is only necessary here to note that, on January 14th, 1927, the German Government had recognized that the factory could no longer be restored in kind and that consequently the reparation due must, in principle, take the form of the payment of compensation, a statement which is moreover formally repeated in the Case. [. . .]The failure of the negotiations resulted in the institution of the present proceedings. [. . .]

The Law.

I.

[62] In the application the Court is asked:

(1) to declare that the Polish Government, by reason of its attitude in respect of the Oberschlesische and Bayerische Companies, which attitude the Court had declared not to be in conformity with the Geneva Convention, is under an obligation to make good the consequent damage sustained by those Companies;

(2) to award compensation, the amount of which is indicated in the application, for the damage caused to each of the respective Companies;

(3) to fix the method of payment, and amongst other things to order the payments to be made by the Polish Government to be effected to the account of the two Companies with the Deutsche Bank at Berlin.

[63] In the course of the oral proceedings, a difference of opinion between the two Parties became apparent as to the nature and scope of the application. The Agent for the German Government argued in his address to the Court that a government may content itself with reparation in any form which it may consider proper, and that reparation need not necessarily consist in the compensation of the individuals concerned. The following passage should especially be noted:

[Translation.]

> "It is in fact a question of the German Government's own rights. The German Government has not brought this suit as representative of the individuals who have suffered injury, but it may estimate the damage for which it claims reparation on its own behalf, according to the measure provided by the losses suffered by the companies whose case it has taken up. The German Government may claim the payment of this compensation at any locus solution is which it may think fit in this case, whether it be a public or a private office."

The present dispute is therefore a dispute between governments and nothing but a dispute between governments. It is very clearly differentiated from an ordinary action for damages, brought by private persons before a civil court, as the Polish Government has said in its Rejoinder.

[. . .]

[68] It is a principle of international law that the reparation of a wrong may consist in an indemnity corresponding to the damage which the nationals of the injured State have suffered as a result of the act which is contrary to international law. This is even the most usual form of reparation; it is the form selected by Germany in this case and the admissibility of it has not been disputed. The reparation due by one State to another does not however change its character by reason of the fact that it takes the form of an indemnity for the calculation of which the damage suffered by a private person is taken as the measure. The rules of law governing the reparation are the rules of international law in force between the two States concerned, and not the law governing relations between the State which has committed a wrongful act and the individual who has suffered damage. Rights or interests of an individual the violation of which rights causes damage are always in a different plane to rights belonging to a State, which rights may also be infringed by the same act. The damage suffered by an individual is never therefore identical in kind with that which will be suffered by a State; it can only afford a convenient scale for the calculation of the reparation due to the State.

[69] International law does not prevent one State from granting to another the right to have recourse to international arbitral tribunals in order to obtain the direct award to nationals of the latter State of compensation for damage suffered by them as a result of infractions of international law by the first State. But there is nothing—either in the terms of Article 23 or in the relation between this provision and certain others of a jurisdictional character included in the Geneva Convention—which tends to show that the jurisdiction established by Article 23 extends to reparation other than that due by one of the contracting Parties to the other in consequence of an infraction of Articles 6 to 22, duly recognized as such by the Court.

[. . .]

[72] It follows from the foregoing that the application is designed to obtain, in favour of Germany, reparation the amount of which is determined by the damage suffered by the Oberschlesische and Bayerische. Three fundamental questions arise:

(1) The existence of the obligation to make reparation.

(2) The existence of the damage which must serve as a basis for the calculation of the amount of the indemnity.

(3) The extent of this damage.

[73] As regards [the existence of the obligation to make reparation], the Court observes that it is a principle of international law, that any breach of an engagement involves an obligation to make reparation. In Judgment No. 8 [. . .] the Court has already said that reparation is the indispensable complement of a failure to apply a convention, and there is no necessity for this to be states in the convention itself. The existence of the principle establishing the obligation to make reparation, as an element of positive international law, has moreover never been disputed in the course of the proceedings in the various cases concerning the Chorzów factory.

[74] The obligation to make reparation being in principle recognized, it remains to be ascertained whether a breach of an international engagement has in fact taken place in the case under consideration. Now this point is *res judicata*. The nonconformity of Poland's attitude in respect of the two Companies with Article 6 and the following articles of the Geneva Convention is established by No. 2 of the operative provisions of Judgment No. 7. The application of the principle to the present case is therefore evident.

III.

[122] The existence of a damage to be made good being recognized by the respondent Party as regards the Bayerische, and the objections raised by the same Party against the existence of any damage that would justify compensation to the Oberschlesische being set aside, the Court must now lay down the guiding principles according to which the amount of compensation due may be determined.

[123] The action of Poland which the Court has judged to be contrary to the Geneva Convention is not an expropriation—to render which lawful only the payment of fair compensation would have been wanting; it is a seizure of property, rights and interests which could not be expropriated even against compensation, save under the exceptional conditions fixed by Article 7 of the said Convention. As the Court has expressly declared in Judgment No. 8, reparation is in this case the consequence not of the application of Articles 6 to 22 of the Geneva Convention, but of acts contrary to those articles.

[124] It follows that the compensation due to the German Government is not necessarily limited to the value of the undertaking at the moment of dispossession, plus interest to the day of payment. This limitation would only be admissible if the Polish Government had had the right to expropriate, and if its wrongful act consisted merely in not having paid to the two Companies the just price of what was expropriated; in the present case, such a limitation might result in placing Germany and the interests protected by the Geneva Convention, on behalf of which interests the German Government is acting, in a situation more unfavourable than that in which Germany and

these interests would have been if Poland had respected the said Convention. Such a consequence would not only be unjust, but also and above all incompatible with the aim of Article 6 and following articles of the Convention—that is to say, the prohibition, in principle, of the liquidation of the property, rights and interests of German nationals and of companies controlled by German nationals in Upper Silesia—since it would be tantamount to rendering lawful liquidation and unlawful dispossession indistinguishable in so far as their financial results are concerned.

[125] The essential principle contained in the actual notion of an illegal act—a principle which seems to be established by international practice and in particular by the decisions of arbitral tribunals—is that reparation must, as far as possible, wipe out all the consequences of the illegal act and re-establish the situation which would, in all probability, have existed if that act had not been committed. Restitution in kind, or, if this is not possible, payment of a sum corresponding to the value which a restitution in kind would bear; the award, if need be, of damages for loss sustained which would not be covered by restitution in kind or payment in place of it such are the principles which should serve to determine the amount of compensation due for an act contrary to international law. [. . .]

[. . .]

[181] For these reasons,

The Court,
having heard both Parties,
by nine votes to three,

[. . .]

(7) gives judgment to the effect that the compensation to be paid by the Polish Government to the German Government shall be fixed as a lump sum;

(8) reserves the fixing of the amount of this compensation for a future judgment, to be given after receiving the report of experts to be appointed by the Court for the purpose of enlightening it on the questions set out in the present judgment and after hearing the Parties on the subject of this report;

(9) also reserves for this future judgment the conditions and methods for the payment of the compensation in so far as concerns points not decided by the present judgment.

Gov't of the State of Kuwait v. American Independent Oil Co. (AMINOIL) (Kuwait v. U.S.), 21 I.L.M. 976 (1982).

Case Introduction

In 1948, the Government of Kuwait granted the American Independent Oil Company ("Aminoil") a 60-year oil concession. In 1961, Kuwait and Aminoil amended the fixed-royalties principle of the Concession Agreement with a 50/50 profit-sharing arrangement. After the declaration of Kuwait's independence in the early 1960s, the Aminoil concession continued. However, in 1973, the parties agreed on another set of changes to the Concession Agreement that further increased Kuwait's profit share. Subsequently, Kuwait demanded a further increase in its profit share, in line with the "Abu Dhabi formula" agreed to by the OPEC countries. Aminoil did not consent, and in 1977, Kuwait, by Decree Law No. 124, terminated Aminoil's concession, seized Aminoil's assets in Kuwait and stated that "fair" compensation should be paid to Aminoil.

On the basis of a separate arbitration agreement, Aminoil initiated arbitration proceedings, contesting the nationalization as contrary to the stabilization clause in the Concession Agreement and claiming damages.

Principal Points of the Judgment

87. [. . .] In 1977 nationalization was not extended to both of the Companies then operating in concessionaries, Aminoil and the "Arabian Oil Company" (AOC). The latter was spared. The question accordingly arises whether the nationalization of Aminoil was not thereby tainted with discrimination, and whether this differentiation does not show that the Decree Law had other objects than that of realizing a program of economic development. The Tribunal does not think so. First of all, it has never for a single moment been suggested that it was because of the American nationality of the Company that the Decree Law applied to Aminoil's Concession. Next, and above all, there were adequate reasons for not nationalizing Arabian oil. The Minister for Oil had touched upon this question and had given the following reasons for the non-nationalization of AOC—which there is no difficulty in finding convincing: "AOC's" high-cost off-shore production operations are such as to give it a special position which requires a high degree of expertise. At the same time, it is working within the framework of a concession granted by both Kuwait and Saudi Arabia, so its position is completely different. Any modification of the concession must be agreed to by both countries (Am Vol. VII, Exh.3).

88. [. . .] these clauses combined, but especially Article 17, constituted what are sometimes called the "stabilization" clauses of the contract. A straight-forward and direct reading of them can lead to the conclusion that they prohibit any nationalization. [. . .]

89. [. . .] In the present case, as Aminoil has pointed out, [. . .] the fact that one of the Parties, being a State, had available to it all the powers of a public Authority and, by using them, could take those steps against which it was the very object of these clauses to protect the concessionaire.

Secondly, according to an initial Government contention, these provisions had a "colonial" character and were imposed upon Kuwait at a time when that State was still under British protectorate, and not in possession of its full sovereign powers. On this basis the stabilization clauses were devoid of value. However, quite apart from any attempt to enquire into the factual circumstances in which these clauses were adopted, this contention cannot be upheld, for they were expressly confirmed on the occasion of the 1961 revision of the Concession after the attainment of complete independence by Kuwait, and again in 1973 when the text of the "1973 Agreement" was put into operation.

90. [. . .] on the public international law plane it has been claimed that permanent sovereignty over natural resources has become an imperative rule of *jus cogens* prohibiting States from affording, by contract or by treaty, guarantees of any kind against the exercise of the public authority in regard to all matters relating to natural riches. This contention lacks all foundation. [. . .]

143. The most general formulation of the rules applicable for a lawful nationalization was contained in the United Nations General Assembly Resolution n. 1803 (XVII) of 14 December, 1962 on Permanent Sovereignty over Natural Resources, Article 4 of which provides that:

> "Nationalization, expropriation or requisitioning shall be based on grounds or reasons of public utility, security or the national interest which are recognized as overriding purely individual or private interests, both domestic and foreign. In such cases the owner shall be paid appropriate compensation, in accordance with the rules in force in the State taking such measures in the exercise of its sovereignty and in accordance with international law".

[. . .]

144. The Tribunal considers that the determination of the amount of an award of "appropriate" compensation is better carried out by means of an enquiry into all the circumstances relevant to the particular concrete case, than through abstract theoretical discussion. [. . .]

146. [. . .] in the case of the present dispute there is no room for rules of compensation that would make nonsense of foreign investment.

148. Both parties to the present litigation have invoked the notion of "legitimate expectations" for deciding on compensation. That formula is well-advised, and justifiably brings to mind the fact that, with reference to every long-term contract, especially such as involve an important investment, there must necessarily be economic calculations, and the weighing up of rights and obligation, of chances and risks, constituting the contractual equilibrium. [. . .] It is in this fundamental equilibrium that the very essence of the contract consists.

149. For assessment of that equilibrium itself, and of the legitimate expectations to which it gives rise, it is above all the text of the contract that signifies, and it is of moment that this text should be precise and exhaustive [. . .].

151. [. . .] the most important of these was Article 13 of 1948 which provided that at the expiry of the Concession, the entire undertaking should be "handed over to the Shaikh"—i.e. the Government—"free of cost"—that is, without compensation. [. . .]

154. [. . .] the Tribunal cannot accept the projections as to the future of the petroleum industry based on the consultations of experts that the Company has relied upon. [. . .] It is because the Tribunal thinks that in the present case, as will be shown later, the Parties adopted a different conception in the course of their relations and negotiations—namely that of the reasonable rate of return. [. . .]

155. On behalf of the Government, it was maintained that the only compensation Aminoil was entitled to claim must be determined by precedents resulting from a series of transnational negotiations and agreements about compensation. These precedents, so it was said, had instituted a particular rule, of an international and customary character, specific to the oil industry.

159. To start with, as was mentioned earlier in connection with Aminoil's nationalization, whereas the contract of concession did not forbid nationalization, the stabilization clauses inserted in it were nevertheless not devoid of all consequence, for they prohibited any measures that would have had a confiscatory character. These clauses created for the concessionaire a legitimate expectation that must be taken into account. [. . .] The persistent desideratum of its representatives was to see the prospect of retaining for it a reasonable rate of return. It was on this note that it opened the negotiations of 1967-77, and in the light of this expectation that appropriate compensation has now to be assessed. [. . .]

164. [. . .] As the Tribunal has stated earlier, it considers it to be just and reasonable to take some measure of account of all the elements of the undertaking. This leads to a separate appraisal of the value, on the one hand of the undertaking itself, as a source of profit, and on the other of the totality of the assets, and adding together the results obtained.

165. As regards deciding on a method for valuing the physical assets, it is not possible to postulate any absolute rule. Doubtless it is necessary in all cases to consider the value of the assets as at the date of transfer, taking due account of the depreciation they have undergone by reason of wear and tear and obsolescence. But in general, only values for accounting or taxation purposes can be utilized. [. . .]

178. (2) [. . .] as regards the fixed assets, the "net book value" used as a basis merely gives a formal accounting figure which, in the present case, cannot be considered adequate. [. . .] (4) [. . .] the sum total of the amount due to Aminoil as at September 19th, 1977, comes to $206,041,000 less the liabilities of $123,041,000 that is to say $83,000,000. [. . .] (5) in order to establish what is due in 1982, account must be taken both of the reasonable rate of interest, which could be put at 7.5%, and of a level of inflation which the Tribunal fixes at an overall rate of 10%,—that is to say at a total annual increase of 17.5% in the amount due, over the amount due for the preceding year.

179. For these reasons, THE TRIBUNAL, unanimously, [. . .] AWARDS to Aminoil, the sum of $179,750,764.

AGIP Co. S.p.A. v. People's Republic of the Congo, ICSID Case No. ARB/77/1, Award (Nov. 30, 1979), 21 I.L.M. 726 (1982).

Case Introduction

In 1962, AGIP established AGIP S.A. ("the Company") in the People's Republic of the Congo (Brazzaville) under Congolese law. AGIP held 90% of the shares in the Company, and Hydrocarbons International Holding Company ("Hydrocarbons"), a Swiss company, held the remaining 10%. In 1965, the Company began its oil distribution activities.

On January 12, 1974, the oil products distribution sector in the Congo was nationalized by Law No. 1/74, transferring the assets of nationalized companies to the Hydro-Congo State Corporation ("Hydro-Congo"). This nationalization did not affect AGIP, as they had signed a protocol agreement ("the Agreement") with the Congolese Government ten days prior to the introduction of the new legislation. This Agreement provided that AGIP sell shares representing 50% of the Company's capital to the Government, while retaining the status of a limited liability company under private law.

In November 1968, AGIP signed a "finished products purchase agreement" with the Societe Gabonnaise de Raffinage (SOGARA), providing for the supply of finished products to the Company in exchange for guaranteed payments. In January 1975, Hydro-Congo agreed with SOGARA to purchase the products required to meet the needs of the Company for that year. Despite this agreement, Hydro-Congo did not fulfill their obligations, and the Company was obliged to close its installations. Soon after, the President of the Republic declared the nationalization of the Company under Order No. 6/75, which included the provision in Article 2 that "this decision creates no right to any compensation." Subsequent to this order, the Company offices were occupied by the army, and the Company lost all ability to manage its affairs.

In 1977, the Chairman of AGIP wrote to the Minister of Energy advising of its intention to proceed to arbitration as provided for in the Agreement. All Government proposed negotiations failed, and the parties proceeded with ICSID arbitration.

Principal Points of the Judgment

72. Congolese law consists on the one hand of constitutional rules and on the other of civil and commercial law rules. From the point of view of constitutional law, the fact that private property is guaranteed by Article 33 of the Constitution cannot be regarded as depriving the Congolese State of the right that it possesses as a sovereign State to nationalize, since the same Article stipulates that "limitation of ownership may when the general interest so requires be determined by an act of Government," while Article 55 of the Constitution adds: "within the domain of the law are ... nationalizations of companies and transfers of company property."

73. Since the measures taken [...] against the Company were put into effect through an Order ratified by Law, [...] there can be no doubt that they are in accordance with the forms required by Congolese constitutional law.

74. Nevertheless, AGIP maintained that the nationalization was irregular since it did not satisfy the basic condition laid down by the Constitution, namely that it was required by the national interest. [. . .]

75. The Tribunal does not feel that it can accept the distinction AGIP makes between the general interest and the private interest of the State acting as shareholder. [. . .]

76. However, though the Government could consider that its interest as a shareholder might basically coincide with the general interest, it does not necessarily follow that in the present case the latter could only be satisfied by recourse to nationalization. [. . .]

88. [. . .] The reference to international law is enough to demonstrate the irregular nature, under this law, of the act of nationalization which occurred in this case. Consequently, the Government must compensate AGIP for the damage it suffered from the nationalization, particularly in respect of the value of its share of the Company's capital and the amount paid by AGIP [. . .]

89. The Tribunal notes that the principle of this compensation was indeed accepted by the Government, which in 1978 published Order No. 5/78 revoking the refusal to pay compensation contained in Article 2 of Law 6/75, and which on several occasions, [. . .] recognized the said principle. [. . .]

95. Application has been made to the Tribunal by AGIP not only for compensation for nationalization of the Company but also for damages for losses resulting from all the contractual obligations not performed by the Government. [. . .]

98. As regards compensation for material losses, according to the basic rules of Article 1149 of the French Civil Code both the loss suffered (*damnum emergens*) and the loss of profits (*lucrum cessans*) must be taken into account.

99. This principle of full compensation for losses is limited in certain circumstances, which in the Tribunal's opinion do not apply in this case. [. . .]

103. Article 1 of the Agreement provides that the Government and AGIP confirm their intention to pursue in the conduct of the Company's affairs a policy of development and of paying dividends, and undertake that all the Company's annual profits should be applied to this purpose, except as otherwise required by law.

104. In the Tribunal's opinion, if the contract between the parties had not been broken by the Government, as indicated above, AGIP could have made a reasonable profit in this connection, at least for a time.

Metalclad Corp. v. United Mexican States, ICSID Case No. ARB(AF)/97/1, Award (Aug. 30, 2000).

Case Introduction

This case deals with compensation for expropriation in the context of the North American Free Trade Agreement ("NAFTA"). In 1990, the federal government of

Mexico authorized Mexican company Confinamiento Tecnico de Residuos Industriales, S.A. de C.V. ("COTERIN") to construct a hazardous waste landfill. In 1993, the National Ecological Institute ("INE"), an independent sub-agency of the Federal Secretariat of the Mexican Environment, granted COTERIN a permit for this construction.

Metalclad Corporation ("Metalclad") entered into a 6-month option agreement to purchase COTERIN for the sole purpose of developing and operating the hazardous waste landfill in the Mexican Municipality of Guadalcázar, located in the Mexican State of San Luis Potosí ("SLP"). Shortly after, the government of SLP granted COTERIN a state land use permit to construct the landfill. One month later, Metalclad met with the Governor of SLP and obtained his support for the project. Metalclad asserted that the President of INE also confirmed that all necessary permits had been issued, with the exception of the federal permit for operation of the landfill. In August 1993, COTERIN was granted the federal permit for operation of the landfill, and Metalclad exercised its option and acquired COTERIN, the landfill site and the associated permits. Metalclad stressed that it would not have exercised its COTERIN purchase option but for the apparent approval and support of the project by federal and state officials.

Metalclad started construction openly and without interruption until October 1994, when officials inspected the construction site. Metalclad was assured by federal officials that it had all the necessary authority to construct and operate the landfill. However, on October 26, 1994, the Municipality stated that Metalclad had no municipal construction permit and ordered the closure of all building activities. Construction was abruptly terminated. On November 15, 1994, Metalclad applied for a municipal construction permit and resumed construction.

Metalclad completed construction in March 1995 and held their "inauguration ceremony" at the landfill. The project was not popular with local people, and demonstrators impeded the event, blocked entries and intimidated Metalclad employees. Metalclad asserted that the demonstrations were organized, at least in part, by the Mexican state and local governments, and pointed out that the Governor of SLP had already embarked on public campaigns to denounce operation of the landfill. The effect was to prevent Metalclad from operating the landfill.

In December 1995, thirteen months after Metalclad's application for the municipal construction permit, the application was formally denied. The Municipality noted the "impropriety" of Metalclad's construction of the landfill prior to receiving a municipal construction permit. Metalclad pointed out that there was no evidence that the Municipality had ever required or issued a municipal construction permit for any other construction projects, and there was no evidence of an established administrative process for issuance of municipal construction permits in the Municipality of Guadalcázar.

From May until December 1996, Metalclad and SLP attempted to resolve the matter through informal discussions. However, these efforts failed, and on January 2, 1997,

Metalclad initiated arbitral proceedings against the United Mexican States ("Mexico") under Chapter Eleven of NAFTA.

In September 1997, three days before the expiry of his term, the Governor of SLP issued an Ecological Decree declaring a Natural Area for the protection of rare cactus. This area encompassed the area of the landfill and effectively and permanently precluded the operation of the landfill. The landfill remained dormant, and Metalclad did not sell or transfer any portion of it.

In bringing the matter to arbitration, Metalclad asserted that Mexico, through its federal and local government structures, interfered with and precluded its operation of the landfill. These actions violated the Chapter Eleven investment provisions of NAFTA, including the requirement for "fair and equitable treatment" and "full protection and security", as well as constituting "direct or indirect expropriation". Mexico denied these allegations.

Principal Points of the Judgment

27. As permitted by NAFTA, Article 1128, the United States made a written submission to the Tribunal on November 9th, 1999. Although the United States does not have any specific commercial interest in the dispute in this case, the submission set forth the United States' position that the actions of local governments, including municipalities, are subject to NAFTA standards. The United States also submitted that the NAFTA, Article 1110, term "tantamount to expropriation" addressed both measures that directly expropriate and measures tantamount to expropriation that thereby indirectly expropriate investments. The United States rejected the suggestion that the term "tantamount to expropriation" was intended to create a new category of expropriation not previously recognized in customary international law. [. . .]

VI. Applicable Law

70. A Tribunal established pursuant to NAFTA Chapter Eleven, Section B must decide the issues in dispute in accordance with NAFTA and applicable rules of international law. (NAFTA Article 1131(1)). In addition, NAFTA Article 102(2) provides that the Agreement must be interpreted and applied in the light of its stated objectives and in accordance with applicable rules of international law. These objectives specifically include transparency and the substantial increase in investment opportunities in the territories of the Parties. (NAFTA Article 102(1)(c)). The Vienna Convention on the Law of Treaties, Article 31(1) provides that a treaty is to be interpreted in good faith in accordance with the ordinary meaning to be given to the terms of the treaty in their context and in the light of the treaty's object and purpose. The context for the purpose of the interpretation of a treaty shall comprise, in addition to the text, including its preamble and annexes, any agreement relating to the treaty which was made between all the parties in connection with the conclusion of the treaty. (*Id.*, Article 31(2)(a)). There shall also be taken into account, together with the context, any relevant rules of international law applicable in the relations between the parties. (*Id.*, Article 31(3)). Every treaty in force is binding

upon the parties to it and must be performed by them in good faith. (*Id.*, Article 26). A State party to a treaty may not invoke the provisions of its internal law as justification for its failure to perform the treaty. (*Id.*, Article 27). [. . .]

73. [. . .] [Mexico] was, and remains, prepared to proceed on the assumption that the normal rule of state responsibility applies; that is, that the Respondent can be internationally responsible for the acts of state organs at all three levels of government." [. . .]

74. NAFTA Article 1105(1) provides that "each Party shall accord to investments of investors of another Party treatment in accordance with international law, including fair and equitable treatment and full protection and security." For the reasons set out below, the Tribunal finds that Metalclad's investment was not accorded fair and equitable treatment in accordance with international law, and that Mexico has violated NAFTA Article 1105(1). [. . .]

78. The Government of Mexico issued federal construction and operating permits for the landfill prior to Metalclad's purchase of COTERIN, and the Government of SLP likewise issued a state operating permit which implied its political support for the landfill project. [. . .]

80. When Metalclad inquired, prior to its purchase of COTERIN, as to the necessity for municipal permits, federal officials assured it that it had all that was needed to undertake the landfill project. [. . .]

85. Metalclad was led to believe, and did believe, that the federal and state permits allowed for the construction and operation of the landfill. Metalclad argues that in all hazardous waste matters, the Municipality has no authority. However, Mexico argues that constitutionally and lawfully the Municipality has the authority to issue construction permits.

86. Even if Mexico is correct that a municipal construction permit was required, the evidence also shows that, as to hazardous waste evaluations and assessments, the federal authority's jurisdiction was controlling and the authority of the municipality only extended to appropriate construction considerations. Consequently, the denial of the permit by the Municipality by reference to environmental impact considerations in the case of what was basically a hazardous waste disposal landfill, was improper, as was the municipality's denial of the permit for any reason other than those related to the physical construction or defects in the site. [. . .]

88. [. . .] The absence of a clear rule as to the requirement or not of a municipal construction permit, as well as the absence of any established practice or procedure as to the manner of handling applications for a municipal construction permit, amounts to a failure on the part of Mexico to ensure the transparency required by NAFTA.[. . .]

91. Moreover, the permit was denied at a meeting of the Municipal Town Council of which Metalclad received no notice, to which it received no invitation, and at which it was given no opportunity to appear. [. . .]

96. In 1997 SLP re-entered the scene and issued an Ecological Decree in 1997 which effectively and permanently prevented the use by Metalclad of its investment. [. . .]

99. Mexico failed to ensure a transparent and predictable framework for Metalclad's business planning and investment. [. . .]

100. Moreover, the acts of the State and the Municipality—and therefore the acts of Mexico—fail to comply with or adhere to the requirements of NAFTA, Article 1105(1) that each Party accord to investments of investors of another Party treatment in accordance with international law, including fair and equitable treatment. This is so particularly in light of the governing principle that internal law (such as the Municipality's stated permit requirements) does not justify failure to perform a treaty. (Vienna Convention on the Law of Treaties, Arts. 26, 27).

101. The Tribunal therefore holds that Metalclad was not treated fairly or equitably under the NAFTA and succeeds on its claim under Article 1105.

102. NAFTA Article 1110 provides that "[n]o party shall directly or indirectly . . . expropriate an investment . . . or take a measure tantamount to . . . expropriation . . . except: (a) for a public purpose; (b) on a nondiscriminatory basis; (c) in accordance with due process of law and Article 1105(1); and (d) on payment of compensation . . . ." "A measure" is defined in Article 201(1) as including "any law, regulation, procedure, requirement or practice."

103. Thus, expropriation under NAFTA includes not only open, deliberate and acknowledged takings of property, such as outright seizure or formal or obligatory transfer of title in favour of the host State, but also covert or incidental interference with the use of property which has the effect of depriving the owner, in whole or in significant part, of the use or reasonably-to-be-expected economic benefit of property even if not necessarily to the obvious benefit of the host State. [. . .]

107. These measures, taken together with the representations of the Mexican federal government, on which Metalclad relied, and the absence of a timely, orderly or substantive basis for the denial by the Municipality of the local construction permit, amount to an indirect expropriation.

108. The present case resembles in a number of pertinent respects that of *Biloune, et al. v. Ghana Investment Centre, et al.*, 95 I.L.R.183, 207–10 (1993) (Judge Schwebel, President; Wallace and Leigh, Arbitrators). In that case, a private investor was renovating and expanding a resort restaurant in Ghana. As with Metalclad, the investor, basing itself on the representations of a government affiliated entity, began construction before applying for a building permit. As with Metalclad, a stop work order was issued after a substantial amount of work had been completed. The order was based on the absence of a building permit. An application was submitted, but although it was not expressly denied, a permit was never issued. The Tribunal found that an indirect expropriation had taken place because the totality of the circumstances had the effect of causing the irreparable cessation of work on the project. The Tribunal paid particular regard to the investor's justified reliance on the government's representations regarding the permit, the fact that government authorities knew of the

construction for more than one year before issuing the stop work order, the fact that permits had not been required for other projects and the fact that no procedure was in place for dealing with building permit applications. Although the decision in *Biloune* does not bind this Tribunal, it is a persuasive authority and the Tribunal is in agreement with its analysis and its conclusion.

109. Although not strictly necessary for its conclusion, the Tribunal also identifies as a further ground for a finding of expropriation the Ecological Decree issued by the Governor of SLP on September 20th, 1997. [. . .] This Decree had the effect of barring forever the operation of the landfill. [. . .]

111. [. . .] Indeed, a finding of expropriation on the basis of the Ecological Decree is not essential to the Tribunal's finding of a violation of NAFTA Article 1110. However, the Tribunal considers that the implementation of the Ecological Decree would, in and of itself, constitute an act tantamount to expropriation.

112. In conclusion, the Tribunal holds that Mexico has indirectly expropriated Metalclad's investment without providing compensation to Metalclad for the expropriation. Mexico has violated Article 1110 of the NAFTA.

VIII. Quantification of Damages or Compensation

A. Basic Elements of Valuation

113. In this instance, the damages arising under NAFTA, Article 1105 and the compensation due under NAFTA, Article 1110 would be the same since both situations involve the complete frustration of the operation of the landfill and negate the possibility of any meaningful return on Metalclad's investment. In other words, Metalclad has completely lost its investment.

114. Metalclad has proposed two alternative methods for calculating damages: the first is to use a discounted cash flow analysis of future profits to establish the fair market value of the investment (approximately $90 million); the second is to value Metalclad's actual investment in the landfill (approximately $20–25 million). [. . .]

116. Mexico asserts that a discounted cash flow analysis is inappropriate where the expropriated entity is not a going concern. Mexico offers an alternative calculation of fair market value based on COTERIN's "market capitalization". Mexico's "market capitalization" calculations show a loss to Metalclad of $13–15 million.

117. Mexico also suggests a direct investment value approach to damages. Mexico estimates Metalclad's direct investment value, or loss, to be approximately $3–4 million.

118. NAFTA, Article 1135(1)(a), provides for the award of monetary damages and applicable interest where a Party is found to have violated a Chapter Eleven provision. With respect to expropriation, NAFTA, Article 1110(2), specifically requires compensation to be equivalent to the fair market value of the expropriated investment immediately before the expropriation took place. [. . .]

120. However, where the enterprise has not operated for a sufficiently long time to establish a performance record or where it has failed to make a profit, future profits

cannot be used to determine going concern or fair market value. [. . .] in *Asian Agricultural Products v. Sri Lanka* (4 ICSID Reports 246 (1990) at 292), another ICSID Tribunal observed, in dealing with the comparable problem of the assessment of the value of good will, that its ascertainment "requires the prior presence on the market for at least two or three years, which is the minimum period needed in order to establish continuing business connections".

121. The Tribunal agrees with Mexico that a discounted cash flow analysis is inappropriate in the present case because the landfill was never operative and any award based on future profits would be wholly speculative.

122. Rather, the Tribunal agrees with the parties that fair market value is best arrived at in this case by reference to Metalclad's actual investment in the project. Thus, in *Phelps Dodge Corp. v. Iran* (10 Iran-U.S. C.T.R. 121 (1986)), the Iran--U.S. Claims Tribunal concluded that the value of the expropriated property was the value of claimant's investment in that property. In reaching this conclusion, the Tribunal considered that the property's future profits were so dependent on as yet unobtained preferential treatment from the government that any prediction of them would be entirely speculative. (*Id.* at 132-33). Similarly, in the *Biloune* case (see above), the Tribunal concluded that the value of the expropriated property was the value of the claimant's investment in that property. While the Tribunal recognized the validity of the principle that lost profits should be considered in the valuation of expropriated property, the Tribunal did not award lost profits because the claimants could not provide any realistic estimate of them. In that case, as in the present one, the expropriation occurred when the project was not yet in operation and had yet to generate revenue. (*Biloune*, 95 I.L.R. at 228-229). The award to Metalclad of the cost of its investment in the landfill is consistent with the principles set forth in *Chorzów Factory (Claim for Indemnity)(Merits), Germany v. Poland*, P.C.I.J. Ser. A., No. 17 (1928) at p.47, namely, that where the state has acted contrary to its obligations, any award to the claimant should, as far as is possible, wipe out all the consequences of the illegal act and reestablish the situation which would in all probability have existed if that act had not been committed (the status quo ante).

123. Metalclad asserts that it invested $20,474,528.00 in the landfill project, basing its value on its United States Federal Income Tax Returns and Auditors' Workpapers of Capitalized Costs for the Landfill [. . .]

125. The Tribunal agrees, however, with Mexico's position that costs incurred prior to the year in which Metalclad purchased COTERIN are too far removed from the investment for which damages are claimed. The Tribunal will reduce the Award by the amount of the costs claimed for 1991 and 1992. [. . .]

128. The question arises whether any interest is payable on the amount of the compensation. In providing in Article 1135(1) that a Tribunal may award "monetary damages and any applicable interest", NAFTA clearly contemplates the inclusion of interest in an award. On the basis of a review of the authorities, the tribunal in

Asian Agricultural Products v. Sri Lanka (4 ICSID Reports 245) held that "interest becomes an integral part of the compensation itself, and should run consequently from the date when the State's international responsibility became engaged" (*ibid.* p.294, para. 114). The Tribunal sees no reason to depart from this view. As has been shown above, Mexico's international responsibility is founded upon an accumulation of a number of factors. In the circumstances, the Tribunal considers that of the various possible dates at which it might be possible to fix the engagement of Mexico's responsibility, it is reasonable to select the date on which the Municipality of Guadalcázar wrongly denied Metalclad's application for a construction permit. The Tribunal therefore concludes that interest should be awarded from that date until the date 45 days from that on which this Award is made. So as to restore the Claimant to a reasonable approximation of the position in which it would have been if the wrongful act had not taken place, interest has been calculated at 6% p.a., compounded annually. [. . .]

130. [. . .] equitable in this matter for each party to bear its own costs and fees, as well as half the advance payments made to ICSID.

131. [. . .] Respondent shall, within 45 days from the date on which this Award is rendered, pay to Metalclad the amount of $16,685,000.00.

Noble Ventures, Inc. v. Romania (*U.S. v. Rom.*), ICSID Case No. ARB/01/11, Award (Oct. 12, 2005).

Case Introduction

This dispute arose in the context of a bilateral investment treaty (BIT) between Romania and the U.S. of May 28, 1992, which entered into force on January 15, 1994.

Noble Ventures, Inc. ("Noble Ventures"), an American company incorporated under the laws of the State of Maryland, provided business consulting services for steel companies in Eastern Europe. The dispute arose out of a privatization agreement concerning the acquisition, management and operation of a substantial steel mill, Combinatul Siderurgic Resita ("CSR"), located in Resita, Romania. The agreement was made between Noble Ventures and the Romanian State Ownership Fund ("SOF"), which was responsible for the privatization of Romanian state-owned enterprises. Completion of the agreement took place on August 16, 2000, when Noble Ventures paid SOF the initial installment of the purchase price and SOF transferred to Noble Ventures its shareholding in CSR, which comprised almost CSR's entire equity share capital. At the time of its acquisition by Noble Ventures, CSR had a significant amount of debt owing to other governmental entities.

The privatization contract was terminated in December 2002, based on a clause providing that the privatization would be subject to cancellation in the event of failure by the investor to pay two consecutive installments of the purchase price.

Principal Points of the Judgment

H.X. Considerations Concerning Damages

224. [. . .] the Tribunal considers that, in order to put on record the economic relevance of the case for the parties, this should be reflected in this Award in spite of the conclusions of the Tribunal regarding liability. [. . .]

225. The Claimant proposes [. . .]

> "88. A DCF valuation is simply the calculation of projected revenues less projected costs and the application of a discount rate to reflect the value of those future cash flows at a present date. When asked about the projected revenues in Mr. Rosen's calculations, Mr. Kaczmarek declined to describe them as 'speculative'. Instead, he said this was a matter to be left to the respective industry experts. [. . .]"
>
> "89. [. . .] Mr. Trendell provides a highly reliable forecast of future sales volumes. The capacity of CSR to produce these volumes is confirmed by the evidence of Mr. Ciurel of IPROLAM and Mr. Perian, a former CSR director. The prices at which these volumes would be sold is a matter of public record, as steel is a traded commodity."
>
> "90. Given CSR's long track record of production, the forecast of its costs is simply an exercise of cost accounting."
>
> "96. The use of hindsight is a legal issue and not one to be determined by the valuation experts. The legal issue was settled in the *Chorzów Factory* case which held that compensation must 'wipe out the consequences' of Romania's illegal acts. In that case, the majority referred the valuation of Germany's damages to a team of experts and directed them to use hindsight."
>
> "99. The Tribunal should not adopt an amounts invested approach in this case as such an approach does not provide any compensation for lost profits. [. . .]"

227. With regard to the compensation model presented by the Claimant [. . .] for the calculation of damages, the Respondent made the following further submission. "Additionally, Romania objects to Claimant's new compensation model. Romania's objections to this most recent model are contained in the Addendum attached hereto." [. . .]

228. The Addendum referred to reads as follows:

1. CSR Was Not A Going Concern

> "1 . . . The new model contains three methods of calculating compensation: a Discounted Cash Flow ("DCF") methodology, a transaction-based methodology, and an amounts invested approach. As with Claimant's previous models, the new model contains baseless assumptions and is otherwise plagued with methodological and technical problems that make it unreliable and unusable. The amounts invested approach, as calculated by Romania, provides the only proper, non-speculative basis for measuring compensation (assuming that liability were to be established)."

"2. The first question in the model is whether the Tribunal believes that a DCF methodology should be used. [. . .] The Tribunal instead must first determine several threshold issues, including: (1) whether CSR was a going concern; (2) whether Noble Ventures could have successfully implemented its entire business plan; and (3) whether Claimant has proven what CSR's financial performance would have been from the privatization to the alleged expropriation had CSR's debts been restructured as Claimant allegedly expected. [. . .] As summarized below, the answer to these questions is negative, rendering Claimant's DCF methodology speculative and unreliable."

"3. Under international law, an enterprise may be considered a going concern only if it has a recent history of profitability from which to project future profits with a reasonable degree of certainty. Thus, in deciding whether CSR was a going concern, the Tribunal must consider its actual performance in the years just prior to the alleged expropriation."

[. . .]

"6. Moreover, it is clear that Claimant itself was never a going concern; Claimant did not have any history of operating or reviving steel mills under plans similar to the one it prepared for CSR."

2. Noble Ventures Could Not Have Successfully Implemented Its Business Plan

"8. [. . .] Claimant's business plan assumed unreasonably that all of CSR's debts would be restructured immediately. [. . .]"

"9. [. . .] Claimant's business plan assumed an immediate refinancing of all of CSR's un-restructured ROL denominated debt into USD denominated debt. [. . .] The model also does not show how each debt would be refinanced over time, or the effect of such relief."

"10. [. . .] Claimant's CD-ROM fails to address the likelihood that CSR would not succeed at all, let alone immediately. [. . .] Claimant has produced no evidence that it could have funded its investment program even if CSR's debts had been restructured."

3. Claimant's Model Does Not Explain How CSR Would Have Performed Under Claimant's Ownership Had CSR's Debts Been Restructured

"11. [. . .] An analysis of this time period is critical [. . .] Claimant begins its DCF analysis on the date of the alleged expropriation, July 31st, 2001, and simply assumes that the projections in its business plan would have come to pass. [. . .]"

"12. [. . .] any use of the Claimant's DCF model—or any other DCF model—is inherently speculative."

"15. [. . .] Romania considers the 'amounts invested' approach as calculated by Navigant to be the only proper, non-speculative measure of compensation in this case should liability and causation be established.

ADC Affiliate Ltd. and ADC & ADMC Mgmt. Ltd. v. Republic of Hungary, ICSID Case No. ARB/03/16, Award (Oct. 2, 2006).

Case Introduction

In 1995, the Claimants, ADC Affiliate Limited ("ADC") and ADC & ADMC Management Limited ("ADC/ADMC"), both companies incorporated under the laws of the Republic of Cyprus but owned by Canadian investors, contracted with a Hungarian state agency ("ATAA") to renovate, construct and operate two terminals of Budapest Ferenc Liszt International Airport in Hungary.

In December 2001, the Minister of Transport of Hungary issued a Decree, resulting in the takeover from the Claimants of all the activities related to the operation of the Airport.

In 2003, ADC and ADC/ADMC initiated arbitration proceedings against Hungary under the Cyprus-Hungary Bilateral Investment Treaty (1989), claiming that their investments had been expropriated and requesting compensation.

In accordance with Article 42(1) of the ICSID Convention, the Tribunal applied the rules chosen by the parties in accordance with the provisions of the Cyprus-Hungary BIT. As no specific provisions were made in the BIT for compensation payable in the event of unlawful expropriation, the Tribunal concluded that it was required to apply the default standard contained in customary international law.

Principal Points of the Judgment

423. The Tribunal cannot accept the Respondent's position that the actions taken by it against the Claimants were merely an exercise of its rights under international law to regulate its domestic economic and legal affairs. It is the Tribunal's understanding of the basic international law principles that while a sovereign State possesses the inherent right to regulate its domestic affairs, the exercise of such right is not unlimited and must have its boundaries. As rightly pointed out by the Claimants, the rule of law, which includes treaty obligations, provides such boundaries. Therefore, when a State enters into a bilateral investment treaty like the one in this case, it becomes bound by it and the investment protection obligations it undertook therein must be honoured rather than be ignored by a later argument of the State's right to regulate. [. . .]

432. In the Tribunal's opinion, a treaty requirement for "public interest" requires some genuine interest of the public. If mere reference to "public interest" can magically put such interest into existence and therefore satisfy this requirement, then this requirement would be rendered meaningless since the Tribunal can imagine no situation where this requirement would not have been met.

434. The Tribunal concludes that the taking was not under due process of law as required by Article 4 of the BIT.

435. The Tribunal agrees with the Claimants that "due process of law", in the expropriation context, demands an actual and substantive legal procedure for a foreign investor to raise its claims against the depriving actions already taken or about to be taken against it. Some basic legal mechanisms, such as reasonable advance notice, a fair hearing and an unbiased and impartial adjudicator to assess the actions in dispute, are expected to be readily available and accessible to the investor to make such legal procedure meaningful. In general, the legal procedure must be of a nature to grant an affected investor a reasonable chance within a reasonable time to claim its legitimate rights and have its claims heard. If no legal procedure of such nature exists at all, the argument that "the actions are taken under due process of law" rings hollow. And that is exactly what the Tribunal finds in the present case. [. . .]

441. The Tribunal cannot accept the Respondent's argument that as the only foreign parties involved in the operation of the Airport, the Claimants are not in a position to raise any claims of being treated discriminately.

442. It is correct for the Respondent to point out that in order for a discrimination to exist, particularly in an expropriation scenario, there must be different treatments to different parties. However and unfortunately, the Respondent misses the point because the comparison of different treatments is made here between that received by the Respondent appointed operator and that received by foreign investors as a whole.

443. The Tribunal therefore rejects the contentions made by the Respondent and concludes that the actions taken by the Respondent against the Claimants are discriminatory.

444. It is abundantly obvious to the Tribunal that no just compensation was provided by the Respondent to the Claimants and feels no need to expand its discussion here. [. . .]

479. The applicable standard for assessing damages has given rise to considerable debate between the Parties.

480. The principal issue is whether the BIT standard is to be applied or the standard of customary international law. The Claimants argue that the Respondent's deprivation of its investments was a breach of the BIT and as an internationally wrongful act is subject to the customary international law standard as set out in *Chorzów Factory (Claim for Indemnity) (Merits), Germany v. Poland,* P.C.I.J. Ser. A., No. 17 (1928). The Respondent contends that the BIT standard is a *lex specialis* which comes in lieu of the customary international law standard.

481. There is general authority for the view that a BIT can be considered as a *lex specialis* whose provisions will prevail over rules of customary international law (see, e.g., *Phillips Petroleum Co. Iran v. Iran*, 21 Iran-U.S. Cl. Trib. Rep. at 121). But in the present case the BIT does not stipulate any rules relating to damages payable in the case of an unlawful expropriation. The BIT only stipulates the standard of

compensation that is payable in the case of a lawful expropriation, and these cannot be used to determine the issue of damages payable in the case of an unlawful expropriation since this would be to conflate compensation for a lawful expropriation with damages for an unlawful expropriation. This would have been possible if the BIT expressly provided for such a position, but this does not exist in the present case.

482. The standard set forth in Article 4(1)(a) of the BIT refers to "just compensation." Article 4 further provides:

> "2. The amount of compensation must correspond to the market value of the expropriated investments at the moment of the expropriation.
>
> 3. The amount of this compensation may be estimated according to the laws and regulations of the country where the expropriation is made."

The latter refers to Hungarian law in the present case. Section 132 of the Hungarian Constitution provides that expropriation of ownership must be accompanied by "full, unconditional and prompt compensation" (Respondent's Counter-Memorial at para.584).

483. Since the BIT does not contain any *lex specialis* rules that govern the issue of the standard for assessing damages in the case of an unlawful expropriation, the Tribunal is required to apply the default standard contained in customary international law in the present case.

484. The customary international law standard for the assessment of damages resulting from an unlawful act is set out in the decision of the PCIJ in the *Chorzów Factory* case at page 47 of the Judgment which reads:

> "reparation must, as far as possible, wipe out all the consequences of the illegal act and re-establish the situation which would, in all probability, have existed if that act had not been committed."

In the same case at page 21, the PCIJ also pointed out that "reparation therefore is the indispensable complement of a failure to apply a convention." [. . .]

486. This statement of the customary international law standard has subsequently been affirmed and applied in a number of international arbitrations relating to the expropriation of foreign owned property. Due to the considerable disagreement between the Parties on the continued existence of this standard it is necessary to recite the authorities in this area in some detail.

487. In *S.D. Myers, Inc. v. Canada*, UNICTRAL (NAFTA) Award (Merits), 13 November 2000, the Tribunal stated at para.311: "The principle of international law stated in the *Chorzów Factory (Indemnity)* case is still recognised as authoritative on the matter of general principle."

488. The Tribunal in *Metalclad Corporation v. Mexico*, ICSID Case No. ARB(AF)/97/1, Award, 30 August 2000, held at paragraph 122 of its Award that: "[t]he award to Metalclad of the cost of its investment in the landfill is consistent with the

principles set forth in *Chorzów* [. . .] namely, that where the state has acted contrary to its obligations, any award to the claimant should, as far as is possible, wipe out all the consequences of the illegal act and reestablish the situation which would in all probability have existed if that act had not been committed (the status quo ante)." [. . .]

493. Finally, the International Court of Justice itself, the PCIJ's successor, in recent years repeatedly has reconfirmed the validity, indeed the primacy, of *Chorzów Factory* as the standard of compensation for acts by States unlawful under international law. [. . .]

495. The remaining issue is what consequence does application of this customary international law standard have for the present case. It is clear that actual restitution cannot take place and so it is, in the words of the *Chorzów Factory* decision, "payment of a sum corresponding to the value which a restitution in kind would bear," which is the matter to be decided.

496. The present case is almost unique among decided cases concerning the expropriation by States of foreign owned property, since the value of the investment after the date of expropriation (January 1st, 2002) has risen very considerably, while other arbitrations that apply the *Chorzów Factory* standard all invariably involve scenarios where there has been a decline in the value of the investment after regulatory interference. It is for this reason that application of the restitution standard by various arbitration tribunals has led to use of the date of the expropriation as the date for the valuation of damages.

497. However, in the present, *sui generis*, type of case the application of the *Chorzów Factory* standard requires that the date of valuation should be the date of the Award and not the date of expropriation, since this is what is necessary to put the Claimants in the same position as if the expropriation had not been committed. This kind of approach is not without support. The PCIJ in the *Chorzów Factory* case stated that damages are "not necessarily limited to the value of the undertaking at the moment of dispossession." [. . .]

499. Based on the foregoing reasons, the Tribunal concludes that it must assess the compensation to be paid by the Respondent to the Claimants in accordance with the Chorzów *Factory* standard, i.e., the Claimants should be compensated the market value of the expropriated investments as at the date of this Award, which the Tribunal takes as of September 30th, 2006.

E. Creeping Expropriation and NAFTA Cases

1. Business Venture Risks

The following cases illustrate how risks ordinarily related to a business venture may not amount to an expropriation.

The Oscar Chinn Case (*U.K. v. Belg.*), 1934 P.C.I.J. (ser. A/B) No. 63 (Dec. 12, 1934).

Case Introduction

Before the First World War and afterwards until 1925, transport services on the Congo were operated by the Belgian Government, but this did not exclude private enterprises. Belgian company "Sonatra" combined with private company "Citas" and became Union Nationale des Transports Fluviaux "UNATRA". According to UNATRA more than half of their shares were owned by Belgians.

In 1929, Mr. Chinn, a British subject, established a river transport and ship building/repair business on the Congo. Mr. Chinn was the only other river transporter in the Belgian Congo who at the same time did not carry on business as a merchant or producer.

During the Great Depression of the 1930s, trade in the Congo colony was seriously affected. As part of an order to temporarily relieve the critical state of trade, the Belgium Minister for the Colonies granted significant subsidies to the Belgian company, UNATRA, under the 1931 Colony Agreement. Mr. Chinn could not compete and had to suspend all his business. Mr. Chinn's vessels were laid up. The Government of the United Kingdom took up the claim, and after negotiations with the Belgian government proved fruitless, the Governments agreed to submit the case to the Permanent Court of International Justice.

Referring to the Convention of Saint-Germain-en-Laye (1919), which provided for freedom of fluvial transport on the African lakes and river systems, the UK claimed reparation of the damage suffered by Mr. Chinn as a result of the 1931 Colony Agreement, as it did not afford to him the benefits of the treatment extended to UNATRA. In effect, the Colony Agreement had established a UNATRA monopoly of the river transport business.

Principal Points of the Judgment

[. . .] It is evident that the fundamental issue in the present suit is the lawfulness or otherwise under international law of the measures taken in 1931. [. . .]

The action of the Minister appears as a governmental act, applying to several companies engaged in transport and in particular to Unatra; in the case of the latter enterprise, this act constituted a kind of [. . .] supervision which the Government retained over that Company; [. . .]

[. . .] the Belgian Government's action had in view-as has been shown-a substantial reduction in the transport tariffs on certain native products; it is not a measure applying especially to the Unatra Company, since it also affects certain land transport concerns under State supervision. On the other hand, to compensate for the expenses and losses which it imposes, it provides for a refund to each of the enterprises concerned, subject however to the condition that the profit and loss account of that particular enterprise, as a whole, reveals a deficit. These reimbursements are, moreover, recoverable by the State [. . .]

[. . .] the Unatra Company was in form a private Company; but it was charged, [. . .] the supervision therein reserved to the State [. . .]

[. . .] the circumstance which, according to the Belgian Government, was the determining cause of the measure which it took on June 30th, 1931, was the general economic depression and the necessity of assisting trade, [. . .] and of warding off the danger which threatened to involve the whole colony in a common disaster.

The Belgian Government was the sole judge of this critical situation and of the remedies that it called for-subject of course to its duty of respecting its international obligations.

3. As regards the international obligations of the Belgian Government towards the Government of the United Kingdom, these have been clearly indicated by the Parties in their written Memorials and in the course of the pleadings. They are, in the first place, the obligations arising from the international régime of the Congo Basin, under the Convention of Saint-Germain-en-Laye of September 10th, 1919, and in the second place the obligations resulting from the general principles of international law. [. . .]

[. . .] the Government of the United Kingdom relies on the obligation incumbent upon all States to respect the vested rights of foreigners in their territories, and that it is this obligation which the Belgian Government is alleged to have infringed in regard to Mr. Chinn.

In considering, [. . .] whether the impugned measures were or were not in conflict with the international obligations of the Belgian Government, the Court, [. . .] will examine the arguments advanced by the Government of the United Kingdom [. . .].

In the first place, it is alleged that the Belgian Government, [. . .] enabled the Unatra Company to exercise a de facto monopoly which-in the view of the Government of the United Kingdom-is incompatible with the Belgian Government's obligation to maintain commercial freedom and equality, and also with the obligation arising out of Article 5 of the Convention of Saint-Germain, which applies those principles to fluvial navigation. [. . .]

Alternatively, it is alleged that the Belgian Government, [. . .] was practising a discrimination, contrary to the equality of treatment stipulated in the Convention of Saint-Germain.

Lastly, in case the Court should not find that the measures taken in 1931 constituted a breach of the said Convention, [. . .] by making it commercially impossible for Mr. Chinn, a British subject, to carry on his business, these measures constituted—it is alleged—a violation of vested rights, protected by the general principles of international law.

[. . .] the Belgian Government submits [. . .]

The measures which it adopted became necessary in order to safeguard the interests of the community [. . .] it never formed part of the intentions of the Belgian

Government to create a monopoly of any kind [. . .] The measures that it took were lawful from the standpoint of international law, whether conventional or customary.

The Belgian Government further maintains that a distinction must be drawn between the sphere of navigation and that of the management of national shipping. Whereas, in the former—sphere, the riparian State is forbidden to encroach on freedom of navigation, its freedom of action in the latter sphere is not subject to restriction.

[. . .] no injury has been caused to already existing vested rights [. . .]

The idea of freedom of trade has not, however, disappeared from the Convention of Saint-Germain. Its first Article is devoted to the principle of commercial equality, and the latter in itself presupposes in principle, freedom of trade. [. . .]

Freedom of trade does not mean the abolition of commercial competition; it presupposes the existence of such competition. Every undertaking freely carrying on its commercial activities may find itself confronted with obstacles placed in its way by rival concerns which are perhaps its superiors in capital or organization. [. . .]

The Court must therefore consider whether the alleged concentration of transport business in the hands of Unatra, of which the Government of the United Kingdom complains, and the fact that, because of this concentration, it was commercially impossible for Mr. Chinn to carry on his business, are inconsistent with the conception of freedom of trade [. . .]

A concentration of business of this kind will only infringe freedom of commerce if [. . .] a "monopoly" is established which others are bound to respect. [. . .]

In what the Government of the United Kingdom describes in this case as a "de facto monopoly," the Court, however, sees only a natural consequence of the situation of the services under State supervision as compared with private concerns. The Court also sees therein, in some respects, a possible effect of commercial competition; but it cannot be argued from this that the freedom of trade and the freedom of navigation, provided for by the Convention of Saint-Germain, imply an obligation incumbent on the Belgian Government to guarantee the success of each individual concern. [. . .]

On the other hand, the Court is unable to accept the general proposition of the Belgian Government regarding its conception of "the management of national shipping". However legitimate and unfettered governmental action in connection with the management and subsidizing of national shipping may be, it is clear that this does not authorize a State to evade on this account its international obligations.

(b) [. . .] alleging discrimination inconsistent with the equality of treatment provided for in the Convention of Saint-Germain [. . .] equality of treatment is only guaranteed by the Convention to the nationals of Powers which are parties to the Convention or of Powers adhering to it. [. . .]

The form of discrimination which is forbidden is therefore discrimination based upon nationality and involving differential treatment by reason of their nationality as between persons belonging to different national groups.

It should be recalled in this connection that the treatment accorded to Unatra was based on the special position of that Company, as a Company under the supervision of the Belgian Government. [. . .] The inequality of treatment could only have amounted to a discrimination forbidden by the Convention if it had applied to concerns in the same position as Unatra, and this was not the case.

[. . .] there is no justification for supposing, that it was owing to his status as a British national that Mr. Chinn was not given the benefit of the arrangement accorded to the Belgian Company Unatra. In this respect, the position of the British national Mr. Chinn was not, as such, either better or worse than that of the other concerns not under State supervision; these included, according to the evidence produced, Belgian concerns and a French concern. The Court therefore is equally unable to accept the alternative plea as to an alleged discrimination.

(c) It remains to consider [. . .] by depriving indirectly Mr. Chinn of any prospect of carrying on his business profitably, constituted a breach of the general principles of international law, and in particular of respect for vested rights.

[. . .] Favourable business conditions and goodwill are transient circumstances, subject to inevitable changes; the interests of transport undertakings may well have suffered as a result of the general trade depression and the measures taken to combat it.

No enterprise, least of all a commercial or transport enterprise, the success of which is dependent on the fluctuating level of prices and rates-can escape from the chances and hazards resulting from general economic conditions. [. . .] exposed to the danger of ruin or extinction if circumstances change. Where this is the case, no vested rights are violated by the State.

[. . .]

The Court, by six votes to five, decides:

that the measures taken and applied in the month of June 1931 and subsequently thereto by the Belgian Government in connection with the limited liability Company Union Nationale Des Transports Fluviaux (commonly known as UNATRA) and in relation to fluvial transport on the waterways of the Belgian Congo, are not, having regard to all the circumstances of the case, in conflict with the international obligations of the Belgian Government towards the Government of the United Kingdom.

2. NAFTA Cases

S.D. Myers, Inc. v. Gov't Canada, UNCITRAL (NAFTA), Partial Award (Merits) (Nov. 13, 2000).

Case Introduction

Mr. Stanley Myers ("Myers") founded his business S.D. Myers, Inc. ("SDMI") in Tallmadge, Ohio in 1965. Tallmadge is approximately 100 kilometers from the US/Canadian border. In due course, the business thrived (annual turnover of $25 million) and became one of the two largest employers in Tallmadge. Myers later handed over ownership of the business to his four sons, leaving the eldest, Dana, with 51% of the share capital of the principal company within the group.

SDMI's interest in Canada developed in the 1990s as the US market declined. The main business of the Canadian corporation was to obtain PCB hazardous waste for treatment by SDMI in its US facility.

When Canada banned the export of PCB wastes to the United States in late 1995, SDMI claimed that Canada had violated Articles 1102 (National Treatment), 1105 (Minimum Level of Treatment), 1106 (Performance Requirements) and 1110 (Expropriation and Indemnification) of NAFTA. The losses suffered or expected as a result of Canada's breaches of its obligations under NAFTA included lost sales and profits since the date of introduction of the measures; loss of its investment in its joint venture with Myers Canada; and the cost of reducing operations in Canada.

Principal Points of the Judgment

162. The evidence establishes that CANADA's policy was shaped to a very great extent by the desire and intent to protect and promote the market share of enterprises that would carry out the destruction of PCBs in CANADA and that were owned by Canadian nationals. Other factors were considered, particularly at the bureaucratic level, but the protectionist intent of the lead minister in this matter was reflected in decision-making at every stage that led to the ban. [. . .]

222. [. . .] It is a claim by SDMI itself as an "investor" on its own behalf. It is a dispute in relation to SDMI's alleged investment in CANADA and is for damages arising out of the alleged breach by CANADA of its obligations under Section A of Chapter 11. SDMI asserts that it . . . has suffered economic harm to its Investment through interference with its operations, lost contracts and opportunities in CANADA. [. . .]

230. The uncontradicted evidence before the Tribunal was that Mr. Stanley Myers had transferred his business to his sons so that it remained wholly within the family and that he had chosen his son Mr. Dana Myers to be the controlling person in respect of the entirety of the Myers family's business interests.

231. On the evidence and on the basis of its interpretation of the NAFTA, the Tribunal concludes that SDMI was an "investor" for the purposes of Chapter 11 of the NAFTA and that Myers Canada was an "investment".

250. The Tribunal considers that the interpretation of the phrase "like circumstances" in Article 1102 must take into account the general principles that emerge from the legal context of the NAFTA, including both its concern with the environment and the need to avoid trade distortions that are not justified by environmental concerns. The assessment of "like circumstances" must also take into account circumstances that would justify governmental regulations that treat them differently in order to protect the public interest. The concept of "like circumstances" invites

an examination of whether a non-national investor complaining of less favourable treatment is in the same "sector" as the national investor. The Tribunal takes the view that the word "sector" has a wide connotation that includes the concepts of "economic sector" and "business sector".

251. From the business perspective, it is clear that SDMI and Myers Canada were in "like circumstances" with Canadian operators such as Chem-Security and Cintec. [. . .] It was precisely because SDMI was in a position to take business away from its Canadian competitors that Chem-Security and Cintec lobbied the Minister of the Environment to ban exports when the U.S. authorities opened the border.

254. Intent is important, but protectionist intent is not necessarily decisive on its own. The existence of an intent to favour nationals over non-nationals would not give rise to a breach of Chapter 1102 of the NAFTA if the measure in question were to produce no adverse effect on the non-national complainant. The word "treatment" suggests that practical impact is required to produce a breach of Article 1102, not merely a motive or intent that is in violation of Chapter 11.

255. CANADA was concerned to ensure the economic strength of the Canadian industry, in part, because it wanted to maintain the ability to process PCBs within Canada in the future. This was a legitimate goal, consistent with the policy objectives of the Basel Convention. There were a number of legitimate ways by which CANADA could have achieved it, but preventing SDMI from exporting PCBs for processing in the USA by the use of the Interim Order and the Final Order was not one of them. The indirect motive was understandable, but the method contravened CANADA's international commitments under the NAFTA. [. . .]

256. The Tribunal concludes that the issuance of the Interim Order and the Final Order was a breach of Article 1102 of the NAFTA. [. . .]

259. The minimum standard of treatment provision of the NAFTA is similar to clauses contained in BITs.

261. When interpreting and applying the "minimum standard", a Chapter 11 tribunal does not have an open-ended mandate to second-guess government decision-making. [. . .]

263. The Tribunal considers that a breach of Article 1105 occurs only when it is shown that an investor has been treated in such an unjust or arbitrary manner that the treatment rises to the level that is unacceptable from the international perspective.

268. By a majority, the Tribunal determines that the issuance of the Interim and Final Orders was a breach of Article 1105 of the NAFTA. The Tribunal's decision in this respect makes it unnecessary to review SDMI's other submissions in relation to Article 1105.

280. The term "expropriation" in Article 1110 must be interpreted in light of the whole body of state practice, treaties and judicial interpretations of that term in

international law cases. In general, the term "expropriation" carries with it the connotation of a "taking" by a governmental-type authority of a person's "property" with a view to transferring ownership of that property to another person, usually the authority that exercised its de jure or de facto power to do the "taking".

283. An expropriation usually amounts to a lasting removal of the ability of an owner to make use of its economic rights [. . .].

284. In this case the closure of the border was temporary. SDMI's venture into the Canadian market was postponed for approximately eighteen months. Mr. Dana Myers testified that this delay had the effect of eliminating SDMI's competitive advantage. This may have significance in assessing the compensation to be awarded in relation to CANADA's violations of Articles 1102 and 1105, but it does not support the proposition on the facts of this case that the measure should be characterized as an expropriation within the terms of Article 1110.

286. The Tribunal agrees with the conclusion in the Interim Award of the *Pope & Talbot* Arbitral Tribunal [*Pope & Talbot Inc. v. Gov't of Canada*, UNCITRAL (NAFTA), Arb. Trib. (2000–2002),] that something that is "equivalent" to something else cannot logically encompass more. In common with the *Pope & Talbot* Tribunal, this Tribunal considers that the drafters of the NAFTA intended the word "tantamount" to embrace the concept of so-called "creeping expropriation", rather than to expand the internationally accepted scope of the term expropriation.

287. In this case, the Interim Order and the Final Order were designed to, and did, curb SDMI's initiative, but only for a time. CANADA realized no benefit from the measure. The evidence does not support a transfer of property or benefit directly to others. An opportunity was delayed.

288. The Tribunal concludes that this is not an "expropriation" case.

Marvin Feldman v. United Mexican States, ICSID Case No. ARB(AF)/99/1, Award (Dec. 3, 2002), 5 ICSID Rep. 212 (2002).

Case Introduction

The Claimant, Mr. Marvin Roy Feldman Karpa ("Feldman"), as the sole investor on behalf of Corporación de Exportaciones Mexicanas, S.A. De C.V. ("CEMSA"), sued the United Mexican States ("Mexico") on the basis that the application of certain tax laws to the export of CEMSA tobacco products by the Mexican authorities constituted a breach of Mexico's obligations under Chapter 11, Section A of the North American Free Trade Agreement ("NAFTA"). The claim referred, in particular, to a tax imposed by Mexico on the production and sale of cigarettes in the domestic market under the Impuesto Especial Sobre Producción y Servicios ("IEPS") law.

Mr. Feldman alleged violations of NAFTA Articles 1102 (National Treatment), 1105 (Minimum Level of Treatment), and 1110 (Expropriation and Indemnification). Mexico denied these allegations.

Principal Points of the Judgment

89. In this proceeding, the Claimant's key contention is that the various actions of Mexican authorities, particularly SHCP [Secretaría de Hacienda y Crédito Público, hereinafter "SHCP"], in denying the IEPS rebates on cigarette exports to CEMSA, resulted in an indirect or "creeping" expropriation of the Claimant's investment and were tantamount to expropriation under Article 1110. [. . .] Nor does the Claimant believe that the Mexican government policy of limiting cigarette exports is justified by public policy concerns, particularly in light of the stated purpose of the IEPS law in 1980, which was to encourage Mexican exports.

90. In particular, the Claimant asserts that the 1993 Supreme Court *Amparo* decision required Mexican officials not only to provide CEMSA with the 0% excise tax rate on exports, but also to permit CEMSA to obtain rebates of the tax amounts included in the price CEMSA paid its suppliers, Walmart and Sam's Club. [. . .] In seeking the rebates, the Claimant asserts that he reasonably relied on a series of letters from SHCP officials, oral assurances from those officials, and their actions in granting the rebates during some periods (1992 and April 1996 to September 1997). [. . .]

91. It is the Claimant's view, however, that the Mexican government did not comply with the *Amparo* decision, despite the oral agreement to afford the Claimant the rebates. Rather, Mexican government officials sought return of the rebates that had been granted between April 1996 and September 1997, and ultimately denied the Claimant's rebates for October and November 1997, effectively preventing the Claimant from exporting cigarettes. [. . .] SHCP's actions effectively drove CEMSA out of the cigarette export business, in violation of Article 1110. [. . .] The Claimant concludes that the fact that tax laws are applied in such a way as to accomplish the expropriation does not convert an expropriation into valid regulation.

96. A threshold question is whether there is an "investment" that is covered by NAFTA. The term "investment" is defined in Article 1139, in exceedingly broad terms. It covers almost every type of financial interest, direct or indirect, except certain claims to money. The first listed item under "investment" is "an enterprise." There is no disagreement among the parties that CEMSA is a corporate entity organized under the laws of Mexico, essentially wholly owned by the American citizen investor, Marvin Roy Feldman Karpa [. . .].

97. Expropriation under Chapter 11 is governed by NAFTA Article 1110, although NAFTA lacks a precise definition of expropriation. That provision reads in pertinent part as follows:

> 1. No Party may *directly* or *indirectly* nationalize or expropriate an investment of an investor of another Party in its territory or *take a measure tantamount to nationalization or expropriation* of such an investment ("expropriation"), except:
>
> (a) for a public purpose;
>
> (b) on a non-discriminatory basis;

(c) in accordance with due process of law and article 1105(1); and

(d) on payment of compensation in accordance with paragraphs 2 through 6.[126]

The key issue, in general and in the instant case, is whether the Respondent's actions constitute an expropriation.

98. [. . .] In the Tribunal's view, the essential determination is whether the actions of the Mexican government constitute an expropriation or nationalization, or are valid governmental activity. [. . .] If there is a finding of expropriation, compensation is required, even if the taking is for a public purpose, non-discriminatory and in accordance with due process of law and Article 1105(1). [. . .]

100. Most significantly with regard to this case, Article 1110 deals not only with direct takings, but indirect expropriation and measures "tantamount to expropriation," which potentially encompass a variety of government regulatory activity that may significantly interfere with an investor's property rights. [. . .] it is much less clear when governmental action that interferes with broadly-defined property rights—an "investment" under NAFTA, Article 1139—crosses the line from valid regulation to a compensable taking, and it is fair to say that no one has come up with a fully satisfactory means of drawing this line. [. . .]

103. [. . .] In the past, confiscatory taxation, denial of access to infrastructure or necessary raw materials, imposition of unreasonable regulatory regimes, among others, have been considered to be expropriatory actions. At the same time, governments must be free to act in the broader public interest through protection of the environment, new or modified tax regimes, the granting or withdrawal of government subsidies, reductions or increases in tariff levels, imposition of zoning restrictions and the like. Reasonable governmental regulation of this type cannot be achieved if any business that is adversely affected may seek compensation, and it is safe to say that customary international law recognizes this. [. . .]

104. Drawing the line between expropriation and regulation has proved difficult both in the pre-NAFTA context and for the handful of NAFTA Chapter 11 tribunals that have considered the issue. [. . .]

110. No one can seriously question that in some circumstances government regulatory activity can be a violation of Article 1110. For example, in *Pope & Talbot* [*Pope & Talbot Inc. v. Gov't of Canada*, UNCITRAL (NAFTA), Arb. Trib. (2000–2002),] Canada argued that "mere interference is not expropriation; rather, a significant degree of deprivation of fundamental rights of ownership is required." That tribunal rejected this approach: Regulations can indeed be characterized in a way that would constitute creeping expropriation. [. . .] Indeed, much creeping expropriation could be conducted by regulation, and a blanket exception for regulatory

126. Emphasis added. Paras, 2-6 provide for compensation "equivalent to the fair market value of the expropriated investment immediately before the expropriation took place;" that compensation be paid without delay and be fully realizable; include interest in a hard currency; and be freely transferable. *Id.* Article 1110(1) (2-6).

measures would create a gaping loophole in international protection against expropriation (*Id.*, para. 99.).

However, the *Pope & Talbot* tribunal failed to find a violation of Article 1110 in that case. This Tribunal finds the legal arguments against a finding of expropriation more persuasive, for reasons described in detail below, and reaches the same conclusion on facts very different from those in *Pope & Talbot*.

111. This Tribunal's rationale for declining to find a violation of Article 1110 can be summarized as follows: (1) As *Azinian* suggests [*Azinian v. United Mexican States*, ICSID Case No. ARB(AF)/97/2, Award (Nov. 1, 1999), 5 ICSID Rep. 416], not every business problem experienced by a foreign investor is an expropriation under Article 1110; (2) NAFTA and principles of customary international law do not require a state to permit "gray market" exports of cigarettes; (3) at no relevant time has the IEPS law, as written, afforded Mexican cigarette resellers such as CEMSA a "right" to export cigarettes (due primarily to technical/legal requirements for invoices stating tax amounts separately and to their status as non-taxpayers); and (4) the Claimant's "investment," the exporting business known as CEMSA, as far as this Tribunal can determine, remains under the complete control of the Claimant, in business with the apparent right to engage in the exportation of alcoholic beverages, photographic supplies, contact lenses, powdered milk and other Mexican products—any product that it can purchase upon receipt of invoices stating the tax amounts—and to receive rebates of any applicable taxes under the IEPS law. While none of these factors alone is necessarily conclusive, in the Tribunal's view taken together they tip the expropriation/regulation balance away from a finding of expropriation.

Many Business Problems Are Not Expropriations

112. [. . .] To paraphrase *Azinian*, not all government regulatory activity that makes it difficult or impossible for an investor to carry out a particular business, change in the law or change in the application of existing laws that makes it uneconomical to continue a particular business, is an expropriation under Article 1110. Governments, in their exercise of regulatory power, frequently change their laws and regulations in response to changing economic circumstances or changing political, economic or social considerations. Those changes may well make certain activities less profitable or even uneconomic to continue.

113. Here, it is undeniable that the Claimant has experienced great difficulties in dealing with SHCP officials, and in some respects has been treated in a less than reasonable manner, but that treatment under the circumstances of this case does not rise to the level of a violation of international law under Article 1110. [. . .]

114. [. . .] Despite the legal uncertainties of the issues upon which the success of his business depended, the Claimant asked for clarification of the legal issues under Article 4 of the IEPS law only when effectively forced to do so, in April 1998 after SHCP denied the Claimant's request for tax rebates for the October 1997-January 1998 exports, and in March 1999 when as a result of a tax audit

SHCP demanded return of rebates, plus interest, inflation adjustment and penalties, for rebates earlier received in 1996 and 1997 [. . .].

Gray Market Exports and International Law

115. [. . .] A prohibition to this effect may rely on objective reasons. Such reasons include discouragement of smuggling [. . .] which may deprive a government of substantial amounts of tax revenue, maintenance of high cigarette taxes to discourage smoking [. . .] assisting producers in complying with trademark licensing [. . .].

116. The conclusion that neither NAFTA nor rules of customary international law require a state to permit gray market cigarette exports is to some extent reinforced by the determination of the U.S. Competent Authority that Mexico's action in enacting legislation effective January 1, 1998, which restricted the availability of rebates of excise taxes to those who purchase cigarettes in the "first sale" within Mexico (i.e., the sale from the producer to the producer's customer, but not any subsequent resales) was not an expropriation under Article 1110 of NAFTA. [. . .] At minimum, it suggests that tax law and policy changes are intended to be given relatively broad leeway under NAFTA, even if their effect is to make it impractical for certain business activities to continue.

Continuing Requirements of Article 4(III) of IEPS Law

118. [. . .] Thus, it appears to the Tribunal that the Claimant never really possessed a "right" to obtain tax rebates upon exportation of cigarettes, but only a right to the 0% tax rate. This is important, because as far as the Tribunal can determine, the only significant asset of the investment, the enterprise known as CEMSA, is its alleged right to receive IEPS tax rebates upon exportation of cigarettes, and to profit from that business. [. . .] The Claimant relies, [. . .] on the alleged refusal of Mexican authorities to comply with the 1993 *Amparo* decision and the alleged subsequent agreement between the Claimant and SHCP officials that the Claimant would be permitted the rebates despite the absence of invoices stating the tax amounts separately.

119. The key contentious issue here is whether the denial of IEPS rebates for failure to meet with the invoice requirement constituted expropriation of the Claimant's investment (a right to export cigarettes) under Article 1110. [. . .] it is important to observe that the invoice requirements of the IEPS law were not new, and had not been changed by Mexican officials (except to the extent or non-extent of enforcement) to the detriment of the Claimant. [. . .]

120. [. . .] If the *Amparo* decision resolves only the 0% tax rate, but the Claimant cannot satisfy the other requirements of the IEPS law, including Article 4 regarding invoices, there is no possibility of CEMSA's benefiting from that decision with regard to cigarette exports, as the company is still prevented from carrying on its cigarette export business.

121. The problem for the Claimant is that a careful reading of the *Amparo* Supreme Court decision reveals no mention of Article 4 [. . .] In this respect, even the

Claimant admits that the court in the *Amparo* case did not review the mechanics of IEPS [. . .]

126. Unfortunately for the Claimant, however, even if there was some sort of oral understanding, there is little persuasive evidence as to its scope, i.e., whether it was limited to assuring the availability of the 0% tax rate as required by the 1993 Amparo Supreme Court decision, or whether it also authorized the Claimant to obtain rebates notwithstanding the lack of invoices stating the tax amounts separately, or even authorized the Claimant to obtain rebate amounts in excess of those otherwise permitted. Not only has no written document from SHCP been made available to the Tribunal, but apparently neither the Claimant nor his counsel prepared any contemporaneous memoranda reflecting such an agreement, despite the many meetings with SHCP officials. [. . .]

128. As noted above, a finding of expropriation here depends in significant part on whether under the circumstances the Article 4 invoice requirements are inconsistent with the Claimant's rights under NAFTA Article 1110. On the basis of the evidence presented to the Tribunal, the Tribunal is not persuaded that they are. [. . .]

131. It is inconceivable to the Tribunal that even if SHCP officials were prepared to forego the invoice requirement informally during some periods, as appears to be the case, they would have given the Claimant or any other taxpayer carte blanche to over-estimate the amount of the rebates, in flagrant violation of the IEPS law.

132. [. . .] The various written and oral communications from SHCP to the Claimant are at best ambiguous and misleading, perhaps intentionally so in some instances, as were SHCP's actions in permitting rebates during some periods and denying them in others. However, a reasonable person, given the complex and exacting nature of tax laws and regulations, and the ambiguity of statements by and correspondence with SHCP officials, should have sought expert tax counsel if it was not already available to him. [. . .]

133. While the transparency in some of the actions of SHCP may be questioned, it is doubtful that lack of transparency alone rises to the level of violation of NAFTA and international law, particularly given the complexities not only of Mexican but most other tax laws. [. . .]

Public Purpose

135. [. . .] the Tribunal is reluctant to give excessive weight to the public purpose, non-discrimination and due process criteria in Article 1110(1). [. . .] the Tribunal believes that they do not contradict an otherwise negative finding. [. . .]

136. [. . .] the Tribunal has already indicated its view that there are rational public purposes for this policy. These include, inter alia, discouraging "grey" market exports and seeking to control illegal re-exportation of Mexican cigarettes into Mexico. [. . .] there are valid public policy reasons for requiring invoices that separately state the IEPS tax amounts as a condition of receiving the refunds, i.e., to prevent inaccurate or excessive claims for rebates.

Non-Discrimination

137. The Chapter 11 scheme establishes a right to national treatment for investors (and damages for breach thereof) that is distinct from the right to damages from acts of expropriation. [. . .]

Due Process/Fair and Equitable Treatment/Denial of Justice

139. In this instance, the allegations of denial of due process or denial of justice are weakened by several factors. [. . .] *Azinian* states that "A governmental authority surely cannot be faulted for acting in a manner validated by its own courts unless the courts themselves are disavowed at the international level." *Azinian* further suggests that there must be a showing that the court decision itself is a violation of NAFTA, or that the relevant courts have not accepted the suit, or there is "a clear and malicious misapplication of the law".

140. [. . .] NAFTA does not require a claimant to exhaust local court remedies before submitting a claim to arbitration. [. . .]

Other NAFTA Decisions

148. [. . .] The assurances received by the investor from the Mexican government in *Metalclad* were definitive, unambiguous and repeated, in stating that the federal government had the authority to authorize construction and operation of hazardous waste landfills, and that Metalclad had obtained all necessary federal and other permits for the facility. [. . .] Finally, Metalclad was deprived of all beneficial use of its property, which was incorporated into an "ecological preserve."

149. In contrast, in the present case, the Mexican government essentially opposed the Claimant's business activities at every step of the way, notwithstanding a few periods when the rebates were granted. [. . .]

150. *S.D. Myers v. Canada* involved a government action barring exports (hazardous waste). There, the tribunal noted that expropriation normally constitutes a taking of "property" with a view toward transfer of ownership, a situation that did not occur in that case or in this one. No expropriation was found in *S.D. Myers*, although the Tribunal did find violations of Articles 1102, 1105 and 1106.

151. [. . .] *Pope & Talbot* again focused on the alleged denial of a right to export, in this instance, softwood lumber.[127] [. . .] The Tribunal suggested further that in determining "whether a particular interference with business activities amounts to an expropriation, the test is whether that interference is sufficiently restrictive to support a conclusion that the property has been 'taken' from its owner."

---

127. The Claimant had argued that the Canadian lumber export control regime had "deprived the Investment of its ordinary ability to alienate its product to its traditional and natural market," and that by reducing the claimant's quota of lumber that could be exported to the United States without paying a fee, Canada violated Article 1110. *Pope & Talbot v. Government of Canada*, Interim Award, June 26, 2000, para. 81, http://www.state.gov/documents/organization/3989.pdf.

152. Given that the Claimant here has lost the effective ability to export cigarettes, and any profits derived therefrom, application of the *Pope & Talbot* standard might suggest the possibility of an expropriation. However, as with *S.D. Myers*, it may be questioned as to whether the Claimant ever possessed a "right" to export that has been "taken" by the Mexican government. Also, here, as in *Pope & Talbot*, the regulatory action (enforcement of longstanding provisions of Mexican law) has not deprived the Claimant of control of the investment, CEMSA, interfered directly in the internal operations of CEMSA or displaced the Claimant as the controlling shareholder. The Claimant is free to pursue other continuing lines of export trading, such as exporting alcoholic beverages, photographic supplies, or other products for which he can obtain from Mexico the invoices required under Article 4, although he is effectively precluded from exporting cigarettes. Thus, this Tribunal believes there has been no "taking" under this standard articulated in *Pope & Talbot*, in the present case.

Chapter 6

Intellectual Property Protection and Transfer of Technology to Developing Countries

A. General Introduction

Intellectual property moves across borders with international trade or investment. The protection of intellectual property is consequently a crucial issue for all companies engaged in international business. Protection for intellectual property is available under international law, and this can be of particular importance in the context of foreign direct investment, where intellectual property embedded in a foreign investment may be exposed to particular risk of appropriation in the territory of the investment.

The principal international agency for the protection of intellectual property is the World Intellectual Property Organization (WIPO). This is a specialized agency of the United Nations and hosts the International Patent System, the International Trademark System and the International Design System. It maintains a register of patents and is the home of the Paris Convention for the Protection of Industrial Property (1883). The Paris Convention was subsequently incorporated into and supplemented by the WTO Trade-Related Aspects of Intellectual Property Rights (TRIPS) Agreement (1994).[128] This chapter describes and assesses the development and application of these protections and their application to foreign direct investment.

B. WIPO Paris Convention for the Protection of Industrial Property (1883)

This is the original and oldest international agreement on the protection of intellectual property. The U.S. is a party to the Convention.

1. Protection Entitlement under the Paris Convention

a. Concept of Priority

The concept of priority is central to intellectual property rights. If a discovery has already been registered, it is protected. In practice, many of the disputes that arise are related to the priority rule and the timings of discovery and registration.

---

128. Along with the Berne Convention for the Protection of Literary and Artistic Works (1886).

PARIS CONVENTION

Article 4
A to I. Patents, Utility Models, Industrial Designs, Marks, Inventors' Certificates: Right of Priority
G. Patents: Division of the Application

A.—

(1) Any person who has duly filed an application for a patent, or for the registration of a utility model, or of an industrial design, or of a trademark, in one of the countries of the Union, or his successor in title, shall enjoy, for the purpose of filing in the other countries, a right of priority during the periods hereinafter fixed.

(2) Any filing that is equivalent to a regular national filing under the domestic legislation of any country of the Union or under bilateral or multilateral treaties concluded between countries of the Union shall be recognized as giving rise to the right of priority.

(3) By a regular national filing is meant any filing that is adequate to establish the date on which the application was filed in the country concerned, whatever may be the subsequent fate of the application.

b. National Treatment

PARIS CONVENTION

Article 2 National Treatment for Nationals of Countries of the Union

(1) Nationals of any country of the Union shall, as regards the protection of industrial property, enjoy in all the other countries of the Union the advantages that their respective laws now grant, or may hereafter grant, to nationals; all without prejudice to the rights specially provided for by this Convention. Consequently, they shall have the same protection as the latter, and the same legal remedy against any infringement of their rights, provided that the conditions and formalities imposed upon nationals are complied with.

(2) However, no requirement as to domicile or establishment in the country where protection is claimed may be imposed upon nationals of countries of the Union for the enjoyment of any industrial property rights.

(3) The provisions of the laws of each of the countries of the Union relating to judicial and administrative procedure and to jurisdiction, and to the designation of an address for service or the appointment of an agent, which may be required by the laws on industrial property are expressly reserved.

2. Compulsory Working/Licensing under Paris Convention

The concept of compulsory working is applicable in any field of technology, although often a particular issue in pharmaceuticals. Under compulsory working, a state may instruct a patent holder to make the intellectual property available for use by another party in that country, although ownership of the intellectual property remains with the patent holder.

The Paris Convention recognizes compulsory working and provides that each country can make its own rules with respect to compulsory working. As the Paris Convention is based on the principle of National Treatment, rights with respect to compulsory working are determined under domestic law. This is crucial to understanding the limitations of the Paris approach and the subsequent transition to multilateral rights and obligations as set out under TRIPS.

PARIS CONVENTION

Article 5

A. Patents: Importation of Articles; Failure to Work or Insufficient Working; Compulsory Licenses

A.—

(1) Importation by the patentee into the country where the patent has been granted of articles manufactured in any of the countries of the Union shall not entail forfeiture of the patent.

(2) Each country of the Union shall have the right to take legislative measures providing for the grant of compulsory licenses to prevent the abuses which might result from the exercise of the exclusive rights conferred by the patent, for example, failure to work.

(3) Forfeiture of the patent shall not be provided for except in cases where the grant of compulsory licenses would not have been sufficient to prevent the said abuses. No proceedings for the forfeiture or revocation of a patent may be instituted before the expiration of two years from the grant of the first compulsory license.

(4) A compulsory license may not be applied for on the ground of failure to work or insufficient working before the expiration of a period of four years from the date of filing of the patent application or three years from the date of the grant of the patent, whichever period expires last; it shall be refused if the patentee justifies his inaction by legitimate reasons. Such a compulsory license shall be non-exclusive and shall not be transferable, even in the form of the grant of a sub-license, except with that part of the enterprise or goodwill which exploits such license.

(5) The foregoing provisions shall be applicable, mutatis mutandis, to utility models.

3. Madrid Convention Concerning the International Registration of Marks (1891)

The Madrid Convention was an early attempt to provide international trademark protection through facilitating a "bundled" approach in multiple jurisdictions.

However, many important countries, including the United States, the United Kingdom and Japan, never acceded to the Madrid system. A key reason was that registrations under different national rules, for example, under "first to file" without investigation as to the "true inventor", would apply multilaterally and put U.S. inventors (for example) at a disadvantage.

The Madrid Protocol to the Madrid Agreement (1989) sought to address this and other difficulties and has now been adopted by 97 members, including the United States and European Union.

4. United States Patent Reform: Leahy-Smith America Invents Act (2011)

The Leahy-Smith America Invents Act (AIA) is a United States federal statute passed by Congress and signed into law by President Barack Obama on September 16, 2011. The Act brought significant changes to the Patent Act of 1952. The new Act switched the U.S. from a "first to invent" approach, whereby the first individual to conceive of an invention and reduce it to practice received the patent, to a "first inventor to file" system. The law also expands the definition of "prior art" used in determining patentability. Proponents believe the changes simplify the application process and bring the U.S. patent law closer to that of other countries, most of which operate on a "first to file" system.

The constitutionality of the "first inventor to file" provisions of the AIA, and by extension the whole of the AIA, were challenged under the Copyright Clause of the United States Constitution[129] in the case of *MadStad Engineering, Inc. v. USPTO*, 756 F.3d 1366 (Fed. Cir. 2014). The court ruled MadStad had no standing in court without concrete proof of an injury and dismissed the case.

Leahy-Smith America Invents Act.

SEC. 3. FIRST INVENTOR TO FILE.

(b) CONDITIONS FOR PATENTABILITY.—

(1) IN GENERAL.—Section 102 of title 35, United States Code, is amended to read as follows:

[. . .] "§ 102. Conditions for patentability; novelty

"(a) NOVELTY; PRIOR ART.—A person shall be entitled to a patent unless—

"(1) the claimed invention was patented, described in a printed publication, or in public use, on sale, or otherwise available to the public before the effective filing date of the claimed invention; or

129. United States Constitution: Article I, Section 8, Clause 8.

"(2) the claimed invention was described in a patent issued under section 151, or in an application for patent published or deemed published under section 122(b), in which the patent or application, as the case may be, names another inventor and was effectively filed before the effective filing date of the claimed invention.

"(b) EXCEPTIONS.—

"(1) DISCLOSURES MADE 1 YEAR OR LESS BEFORE THE EFFECTIVE FILING DATE OF THE CLAIMED INVENTION.—A disclosure made 1 year or less before the effective filing date of a claimed invention shall not be prior art to the claimed invention under subsection (a)(1) if—

"(A) the disclosure was made by the inventor or joint inventor or by another who obtained the subject matter disclosed directly or indirectly from the inventor or a joint inventor; or

"(B) the subject matter disclosed had, before such disclosure, been publicly disclosed by the inventor or a joint inventor or another who obtained the subject matter disclosed directly or indirectly from the inventor or a joint inventor.

"(2) DISCLOSURES APPEARING IN APPLICATIONS AND PATENTS.—A disclosure shall not be prior art to a claimed invention under subsection (a)(2) if—

"(A) the subject matter disclosed was obtained directly or indirectly from the inventor or a joint inventor;

"(B) the subject matter disclosed had, before such subject matter was effectively filed under subsection (a)(2), been publicly disclosed by the inventor or a joint inventor or another who obtained the subject matter disclosed directly or indirectly from the inventor or a joint inventor; or

"(C) the subject matter disclosed and the claimed invention, not later than the effective filing date of the claimed invention, were owned by the same person or subject to an obligation of assignment to the same person.

"(c) COMMON OWNERSHIP UNDER JOINT RESEARCH AGREEMENTS.—Subject matter disclosed and a claimed invention shall be deemed to have been owned by the same person or subject to an obligation of assignment to the same person in applying the provisions of subsection (b)(2)(C) if—

"(1) the subject matter disclosed was developed and the claimed invention was made by, or on behalf of, 1 or more parties to a joint research agreement that was in effect on or before the effective filing date of the claimed invention;

"(2) the claimed invention was made as a result of activities undertaken within the scope of the joint research agreement; and

"(3) the application for patent for the claimed invention discloses or is amended to disclose the names of the parties to the joint research agreement.

"(d) PATENTS AND PUBLISHED APPLICATIONS EFFECTIVE AS PRIOR ART.—For purposes of determining whether a patent or application for patent is prior art to a claimed invention under subsection (a)(2), such patent or application shall be considered to have been effectively filed, with respect to any subject matter described in the patent or application—

"(1) if paragraph (2) does not apply, as of the actual filing date of the patent or the application for patent; or "(2) if the patent or application for patent is entitled to claim a right of priority under section 119, 365(a), or 365(b), or to claim the benefit of an earlier filing date under section 120, 121, or 365(c), based upon 1 or more prior filed applications for patent, as of the filing date of the earliest such application that describes the subject matter.".

(2) CONTINUITY OF INTENT UNDER THE CREATE ACT.—The enactment of section 102(c) of title 35, United States Code, under paragraph (1) of this subsection is done with the same intent to promote joint research activities that was expressed, including in the legislative history, through the enactment of the Cooperative Research and Technology Enhancement Act of 2004 (Public Law 108–453; the "CREATE Act"), the amendments of which are stricken by subsection (c) of this section. The United States Patent and Trademark Office shall administer section 102(c) of title 35, United States Code, in a manner consistent with the legislative history of the CREATE Act that was relevant to its administration by the United States Patent and Trademark Office.

[...]

C. Limitations of Paris Convention and Motivation for the TRIPS Agreement

1. Diversity of Laws, Reliance on National Legislation and Weaknesses of the Paris Convention

The Paris Convention provides formal procedures for multi-jurisdictional registration and requires National Treatment to be applied. However, it does not deal with the substantive law of intellectual property rights, which remain subject to tremendous national diversity. In addition, problems may arise in terms of enforcement, which is wholly dependent on national provisions. The Convention is silent on compensation and does not set specific procedures or standards.

Under national legislation, countries generally have the right in certain circumstances, to order the compulsory working of a patent or trademark. This may arise, for example, where the owner of the patent has failed to work the patent in that country, raising the public policy concern that a firm has registered the patent in order to prevent local production, that may be cheaper for consumers and increase local employment.

2. Importance of an International Arrangement in the Context of Patents

The need for an agreed international arrangement for intellectual property protection is illustrated in the *McDonald's v. Joburgers* case.

McDonald's Corp. v. Joburgers Drive-Inn Restaurant (Pty), Case No. 547/95 (S. Afr. 1996).

Case Introduction

The appellant McDonald's had registered its patents and 52 trademarks in South Africa, such that every aspect of the business was comprehensively covered. Joburgers Drive-Inn Restaurant (Pty) Limited ("Joburgers") was a South African company engaged in the fast food industry. Its Managing Director. Mr. George Sombonos, registered a company called Golden Fried Chicken (Pty) Limited ("Chicken Licken") in 1979, in which he held 90% of the shares.

During 1992, Mr. Sombonos, on behalf of Joburgers, decided to establish fast food outlets and restaurants using the trade marks McDONALD'S, BIG MAC and the golden arches design. In 1993, Mr. Sombonos applied for the registration of these and some other McDonald's marks. At the same time, he applied to have McDonald's registrations expired, on the grounds that they were not working their registrations in South Africa. McDonald's opposed these applications and filed its counter-statements in expungement applications during August 1993. During the same period, McDonald's applied again for the registration of all the trade marks in its name.

Up to that point, McDonald's had not opened a single shop in South Africa and was not trading in the country at all.

Significance of Case

The lower court judgment on this case in the latter half of 1995 threw South African trade-mark law into turmoil.

© Oh Dean, *McDonald's Turns the Tables on Trade-Mark Hijackers,* SA Mercantile Law Journal (SAMercLJ), Vol 8, 1996, p408–423 (1996). Printed with permission from the author and copyright holder.

Southwood J held in the Transvaal Provincial Division of the Supreme Court of South Africa that the trademark McDONALD'S in respect of hamburgers and other fast foods, which is one of the top five trade marks in the world, was not a well-known foreign trade mark in South Africa and that a portfolio of more than 50 registered trademarks belonging to McDonald's Corporation ('MC') must be cancelled on the grounds of non-use.

This decision was greeted with incredulity in trademark legal and business circles around the world, particularly in the United States. It had far-reaching and significant legal, political, and commercial implications, and gave rise to the contention that South African trade mark law does not comply with international standards for protecting foreign trademarks. Pressure to amend the law was brought to bear against the country in international circles. American and other foreign trademark proprietors interpreted the judgment to mean that South Africa does not adequately protect foreign trademarks, which was seen as a disincentive to extending business and investment in South Africa, when the country was earnestly seeking such foreign participation in its economy. Ironically, the judgment came at a time when MC had begun to invest and open McDONALD'S restaurants in South Africa.

An appeal against the judgment of the lower court, which proceeded on an expedited basis, brought about a reversal of the judgment of the lower court. The judgment of the Appellate Division found that the trademark McDONALD'S is a well-known international trademark in South Africa. The appeal court also declined to cancel McDONALD'S registered trademarks on the grounds of non-use.

The approach of EM Grosskopf JA, with whom the other four judges of appeal concurred, was diametrically opposed to the approach adopted by the lower court. When one considers the two judgments, it is difficult to comprehend how the two courts could have reached such contrasting judgments on the same facts and law.

Principal Points of the Judgment

EM Grosskopf, JA

[. . .] For convenience I start with the well-known marks application. Sec 35 of the new act reads as follows: [. . .]

> (3) "The proprietor of a trade mark which is entitled to protection under the Paris Convention as a well-known trade mark is entitled to restrain the use in the Republic of a trade mark which constitutes, or the essential part of which constitutes, a reproduction, imitation or translation of the well-known trade mark in relation to goods or services which are identical or similar to the goods or services in respect of which the trade mark is well known and where the use is likely to cause deception or confusion." [. . .]

Section 35 of the new act was intended to provide a practical solution to the problems of foreign businessmen whose marks were known in South Africa but who did not have a business here. The South African population is a diverse one in many respects. There are wide differences in income, education, cultural values, interests, tastes, personal life styles, recreational activities, etc. This was obviously known to the legislature when it passed the new act. If protection is granted only to marks which are known (not to say well-known) to every segment of the population (or even to most segments of the population) there must be very few marks, if any, which could pass the test. [. . .] I consider therefore that a mark is well-known in the Republic if it is well-known to persons interested in the goods or services to which the mark relates.

The next question then is: how well should it be known to such persons? [. . .] In the present context the important practical question is not whether a few people know the mark well but rather whether sufficient persons know it well enough to entitle it to protection against deception or confusion. [. . .]

The legislature intended to extend the protection of a passing off action to foreign businessmen who did not have a business or enjoy a goodwill inside the country provided their marks were well-known in the Republic. It seems logical to accept that the degree of knowledge of the marks that is required would be similar to that protected in the existing law of passing off.[130] The concept of a substantial number of persons is well established. It provides a practical and flexible criterion which is consistent with the terms of the statute. No feasible alternative has been suggested.

[. . .]

Mr Paul R Duncan, the vice president and general counsel of McDonald's, stated on affidavit that, in view of the vast scale of his organization's operations, the McDonald's trade marks are in all probability some of the best known trade marks in the world. [. . .] The conduct of Joburgers and Dax in the present case confirms the reputation attaching to the McDonald's marks. Intrinsically the word McDonald has no attractive force. It is a fairly common surname. Had it not been for the reputation it has acquired over the years nobody would wish to appropriate it. [. . .] During September 1993 Mr Corder was instructed to conduct a market survey on behalf of McDonald's.

[. . .] The results indicate that the majority of white adults, aged 16 and over, living in households in higher income suburbs of Johannesburg and Pretoria are aware of the McDonald's brand name, and associate McDonald's with hamburgers. [. . .] The results indicate that the majority of white adults, aged 16 and over, living in the higher income Durban suburbs of Broadway, Essenwood, Morningside and Musgrave are aware of the McDonald's brand name, and associate McDonald's with hamburgers.

As I have said above, I consider that it would be enough for McDonald's to show that its marks are known to a substantial number of persons who are interested in the goods or services provided by it. On behalf of McDonald's it was contended, correctly in my view, that there are two categories of such persons—potential customers and potential franchisees. Potential customers would cover a wide field. It would include all persons who like fast food of this type and have the money to buy it.

[. . .]

130. UK common law.

The evidence adduced by McDonald's leads, in my view, to the inference that its marks, and particularly the mark McDonald's, are well known amongst the more affluent people in the country. [. . .]

Potential franchisees, I consider, would be the type of persons who would almost without exception have heard of McDonald's and know its marks. [. . .]

I consider therefore that at least a substantial portion of persons who would be interested in the goods or services provided by McDonald's know its name, which is also its principal trade mark. At least this mark is in my view well-known for the purposes of sec. 35 of the new act. Since McDonald's has not in fact carried on business in South Africa, people who know its mark will also know it as a foreign (and, more particularly, American) business. It almost goes without saying that if the McDonald's mark is used as contemplated by Joburgers and Dax in relation to the same type of fast food business as that conducted by McDonald's, it would cause deception or confusion within the meaning of sec 35 (3) of the new act. In the result McDonald's has in my view satisfied all the requirements of this sub-section.

D. WTO Agreement on Trade Related Aspects of Intellectual Property Rights (TRIPS)

1. Substantive Law Standards

The TRIPS Agreement of 1994 was the first time that an Intellectual Property Agreement was negotiated under the WTO framework. TRIPS sets in place agreed international standards for intellectual property protection, as opposed to dependence on domestic law as provided in the Paris Convention. The extent and duration of intellectual property protection is determined under the Agreement. However, registration is not dealt with under TRIPS, so the Paris and Berne (protection of literary and artistic works) systems are still important for this purpose.

In all respects, TRIPS represents a major shift from the Paris Convention, by calling on countries to enforce comprehensive minimum standards of IP protection on a non-discriminatory basis. The TRIPS agreement incorporates the Paris and Berne Conventions by reference and thereby universalizes them. This has legal consequences, in that if a country is a member of the WTO but has never acceded to the Paris Convention, TRIPS in any case brings the country under the jurisdiction of the Paris Convention.

Recognition of the onerous provisions of TRIPS led to different timeframes being allowed for developing countries to begin to comply with TRIPS, i.e. 2005 for developed and 2016 for least developed countries.

The TRIPS Agreement recognizes that intellectual property rights should contribute to the promotion of technological innovation and the transfer and dissemination of technology. TRIPS introduces standards (substantive law and enforcement mechanisms) which require states to revise their domestic laws so that they meet the standards of TRIPS. States can only deviate from these standards only by giving better protection and must comply with the specific rights conferred on patent owners under Article 28 of the Agreement.

AGREEMENT ON TRADE RELATED ASPECTS OF INTELLECTUAL PROPERTY RIGHTS

Article 2
Intellectual Property Conventions

1. In respect of Parts II, III and IV of this Agreement, Members shall comply with Articles 1 through 12, and Article 19, of the Paris Convention (1967).

2. Nothing in Parts I to IV of this Agreement shall derogate from existing obligations that Members may have to each other under the Paris Convention, the Berne Convention, the Rome Convention and the Treaty on Intellectual Property in Respect of Integrated Circuits.

Article 7
Objectives

The protection and enforcement of intellectual property rights should contribute to the promotion of technological innovation and to the transfer and dissemination of technology, to the mutual advantage of producers and users of technological knowledge and in a manner conducive to social and economic welfare, and to a balance of rights and obligations.

Article 26
Protection

1. The owner of a protected industrial design shall have the right to prevent third parties not having the owner's consent from making, selling or importing articles bearing or embodying a design which is a copy, or substantially a copy, of the protected design, when such acts are undertaken for commercial purposes.

2. Members may provide limited exceptions to the protection of industrial designs, provided that such exceptions do not unreasonably conflict with the normal exploitation of protected industrial designs and do not unreasonably prejudice the legitimate interests of the owner of the protected design, taking account of the legitimate interests of third parties.

3. The duration of protection available shall amount to at least 10 years.

Article 28
Rights Conferred

1. A patent shall confer on its owner the following exclusive rights:

(a) where the subject matter of a patent is a product, to prevent third parties not having the owner's consent from the acts of: making, using, offering for sale, selling, or importing for these purposes that product;

(b) where the subject matter of a patent is a process, to prevent third parties not having the owner's consent from the act of using the process, and from the acts of: using, offering for sale, selling, or importing for these purposes at least the product obtained directly by that process.

2. Patent owners shall also have the right to assign, or transfer by succession, the patent and to conclude licensing contracts.

2. Enforcement Standards

Article 41

1. Members shall ensure that enforcement procedures as specified in this Part are available under their law so as to permit effective action against any act of infringement of intellectual property rights covered by this Agreement, including expeditious remedies to prevent infringements and remedies which constitute a deterrent to further infringements. These procedures shall be applied in such a manner as to avoid the creation of barriers to legitimate trade and to provide for safeguards against their abuse.

2. Procedures concerning the enforcement of intellectual property rights shall be fair and equitable. They shall not be unnecessarily complicated or costly, or entail unreasonable time-limits or unwarranted delays.

3. Decisions on the merits of a case shall preferably be in writing and reasoned. They shall be made available at least to the parties to the proceeding without undue delay. Decisions on the merits of a case shall be based only on evidence in respect of which parties were offered the opportunity to be heard.

4. Parties to a proceeding shall have an opportunity for review by a judicial authority of final administrative decisions and, subject to jurisdictional provisions in a Member's law concerning the importance of a case, of at least the legal aspects of initial judicial decisions on the merits of a case. However, there shall be no obligation to provide an opportunity for review of acquittals in criminal cases.

5. It is understood that this Part does not create any obligation to put in place a judicial system for the enforcement of intellectual property rights distinct from that for the enforcement of law in general, nor does it affect the capacity of Members to enforce their law in general. Nothing in this Part creates any obligation with respect to the distribution of resources as between enforcement of intellectual property rights and the enforcement of law in general.

Article 45
Damages

1. The judicial authorities shall have the authority to order the infringer to pay the right holder damages adequate to compensate for the injury the right holder has suffered because of an infringement of that person's intellectual property right by an infringer who knowingly, or with reasonable grounds to know, engaged in infringing activity.

2. The judicial authorities shall also have the authority to order the infringer to pay the right holder expenses, which may include appropriate attorney's fees. In appropriate cases, Members may authorize the judicial authorities to order recovery of profits and/or payment of pre-established damages even where the infringer did not knowingly, or with reasonable grounds to know, engage in infringing activity.

3. Subject to WTO Dispute Settlement Mechanisms

Disputes arising with respect to TRIPS rights and obligations are subject to the WTO dispute settlement mechanisms.

Article 64
Dispute Settlement

1. The provisions of Articles XXII and XXIII of GATT 1994 as elaborated and applied by the Dispute Settlement Understanding shall apply to consultations and the settlement of disputes under this Agreement except as otherwise specifically provided herein.

2. Subparagraphs 1(b) and 1(c) of Article XXIII of GATT 1994 shall not apply to the settlement of disputes under this Agreement for a period of five years from the date of entry into force of the WTO Agreement.

3. During the time period referred to in paragraph 2, the Council for TRIPS shall examine the scope and modalities for complaints of the type provided for under subparagraphs 1(b) and 1(c) of Article XXIII of GATT 1994 made pursuant to this Agreement, and submit its recommendations to the Ministerial Conference for approval. Any decision of the Ministerial Conference to approve such recommendations or to extend the period in paragraph 2 shall be made only by consensus, and approved recommendations shall be effective for all Members without further formal acceptance process.

E. Pharmaceutical Innovation in Developing Economies

1. The Implications of Article 31 of TRIPS

Article 31 of TRIPS regulates the circumstances under which a country may order compulsory working and the conditions applicable to compulsory working. It leaves relatively little room for discretion by the state concerned.

Article 31
Other Use Without Authorization of the Right Holder

Where the law of a Member allows for other use (7) of the subject matter of a patent without the authorization of the right holder, including use by the government or third parties authorized by the government, the following provisions shall be respected:

[(*footnote original*) 7 "Other use" refers to use other than that allowed under Article 30.]

(a) authorization of such use shall be considered on its individual merits;

(b) such use may only be permitted if, prior to such use, the proposed user has made efforts to obtain authorization from the right holder on reasonable commercial terms and conditions and that such efforts have not been successful within a reasonable period of time. This requirement may be waived by a Member in the case of a national emergency or other circumstances of extreme urgency or in cases of public noncommercial use. In situations of national emergency or other circumstances of extreme urgency, the right holder shall, nevertheless, be notified as soon as reasonably practicable. In the case of public noncommercial use, where the government or contractor, without making a patent search, knows or has demonstrable grounds to know that a valid patent is or will be used by or for the government, the right holder shall be informed promptly;

(c) the scope and duration of such use shall be limited to the purpose for which it was authorized, and in the case of semi-conductor technology shall only be for public non-commercial use or to remedy a practice determined after judicial or administrative process to be anti-competitive;

(d) such use shall be non-exclusive;

(e) such use shall be non-assignable, except with that part of the enterprise or goodwill which enjoys such use;

(f) any such use shall be authorized predominantly for the supply of the domestic market of the Member authorizing such use;

(g) authorization for such use shall be liable, subject to adequate protection of the legitimate interests of the persons so authorized, to be terminated if and when the circumstances which led to it cease to exist and are unlikely to recur. The competent authority shall have the authority to review, upon motivated request, the continued existence of these circumstances;

(h) the right holder shall be paid adequate remuneration in the circumstances of each case, taking into account the economic value of the authorization;

(i) the legal validity of any decision relating to the authorization of such use shall be subject to judicial review or other independent review by a distinct higher authority in that Member;

(j) any decision relating to the remuneration provided in respect of such use shall be subject to judicial review or other independent review by a distinct higher authority in that Member;

(k) Members are not obliged to apply the conditions set forth in subparagraphs (b) and (f) where such use is permitted to remedy a practice determined after judicial or administrative process to be anti-competitive. The need to correct anti-competitive practices may be taken into account in determining the amount of remuneration in such cases. Competent authorities shall have the authority to refuse termination of authorization if and when the conditions which led to such authorization are likely to recur;

(l) where such use is authorized to permit the exploitation of a patent ("the second patent") which cannot be exploited without infringing another patent ("the first patent"), the following additional conditions shall apply:

(i) the invention claimed in the second patent shall involve an important technical advance of considerable economic significance in relation to the invention claimed in the first patent;

(ii) the owner of the first patent shall be entitled to a cross-license on reasonable terms to use the invention claimed in the second patent; and

(iii) the use authorized in respect of the first patent shall be non-assignable except with the assignment of the second patent.

2. Conditions Applicable to Compulsory Working

There is a vigorous public policy debate surrounding TRIPS Article 31, and Article 31(f) in particular, stemming from a perception that the provisions are too strict and may have the effect of preventing countries from helping others to obtain important medical supplies. The public policy and commercial significance of this debate is illustrated in the following case regarding compulsory licensing of a pharmaceutical product in India.

Natco Pharma Ltd. v. Bayer Corp., C.L.A. No. 1/2011 (Controller of Patents, Mumbai Mar. 9, 2012).

Case Introduction

In 2008, the international drug manufacturing corporation Bayer ("Bayer") received regulatory approval as patentee for import and marketing of a life extending drug for the treatment of kidney and liver cancer (trade name Nexavar) and launched the product in India. Bayer registered a patent in India. Indian pharmaceutical company Natco Pharma Limited ("Natco") filed an application with Bayer for the voluntary license to manufacture and sell the drug, but this request was denied. Natco proposed to sell the drug at a price of Rs.8800 (USD 135.96) for one month therapy, compared to the price of about Rs.280,423 (USD 4332.43), which was being charged by Bayer at the time.

India had joined TRIPS and the deadline for complying with TRIPS obligations was January 1, 2005.

In 2011, Natco filed an application under Section 84(1) of the Patents Act 1970 before the Controller of Patents Court in Mumbai, for grant of a compulsory license. The WTO states that compulsory licensing is "when a government allows someone else to produce the patented product or process without the consent of the patent owner". A compulsory license was granted for manufacturing of the drug in bulk by Natco. The hearings were concluded on 28th February 2012.

Significance of Case

The case brings into focus the fine balance between patent holders' rights and national health care and access to medicines requirements.

Principal Points of the Judgment

2. [. . .] Present case is the first of its kind in the history of Patents Act, 1970, wherein the provisions of Section 84 have been invoked by the Applicant herein for seeking the grant of a compulsory license. As such, there is no precedent to guide this tribunal. [. . .]

10. Reasonable requirements of the public

Section 84 of the Act states as follows:

> "**84. Compulsory licenses.**—
>
> (1) At any time after the expiration of three years from the date of the grant of a patent, any person interested may make an application to the Controller for grant of compulsory license on patent on any of the following grounds, namely—
>
> (a) that the reasonable requirements of the public with respect to the patented invention have not been satisfied . . ."
>
> [. . .]

Applicant's submissions

b. Patentee imports and sells the drug in India and has not taken adequate steps to manufacture the product in India to make full use of the invention. The drug is exorbitantly priced and out of reach of most of the people. The product is available only in limited quantities. It is available in pharmacies attached to certain hospitals and that too only in metro cities such as Mumbai, Chennai, Kolkata and Delhi. The product in question is not a luxury item but a lifesaving drug and it is highly important that substantial part of the demand be met strictly. In the present case, even 1% of the public does not derive benefit of the patented drug. [. . .]

c. [. . .] [Figures] show that although the Patentee has fully developed and launched the product in various parts of the world and reported sales at least since 2006, and despite the fact that the Patentee had filed its application in India in 2000, the Patentee clearly neglected India and did not launch until 2009.[. . .]

d. The Patentee only imports the drug into the Indian market and does not manufacture the drug by itself in India, though it does manufacture and sell other products in India. [. . .]

e. [. . .] If the terms are unreasonable such as high cost of Rs 280,000/-, availability is meaningless.

f. [. . .] The number of patients and the actual demand for the drug far exceeds the supply thereof by the patentee.

[. . .] In view of the above, the reasonable requirements of the public with respect to the patented invention have not been satisfied and this makes out a fit case for the grant of Compulsory License.

Patentee's submissions

b. [. . .] the following procedure is followed by the Patentee to ensure that the drug is available wherever it is required:

i. Distributors supply to hospitals, pharmacies, retailers and patients.

ii. Distributors supply to outstation towns, cities where the drug is required.

iii. For outstation patients, supply is done through courier.

c. Further, the treatment with the drug should be supervised by Doctors who have experience of anticancer treatments (Oncologists). Hence, the allegation of the Applicant that it is not available in villages is of no consequence as it has to be made available in cancer hospitals and institutes, which duty the Patentee has duly performed.[. . .]

e. [. . .] access to a patented invention is not identical to affordability thereof and cannot be on the identical footing. [. . .] The aforesaid submission is further strengthened by the fact that the Patents Act provides two different/specific grounds Section 84(1)(a) [lack of accessibility] and Section 84(1)(b) [lack of affordability] for the grant of Compulsory License. [. . .] the two grounds cannot be mixed as has been done by the Applicant in the present case. [. . .]

Decision

[. . .] I am accordingly of the view that the number of patients requiring treatment by this drug will be much higher than the figure derived by the Patentee. [. . .]

[. . .] the Patentee's conduct of not making the drug available as per the requirements of public policy in India during four years, since the grant of Patent, is not at all justifiable. This is in spite of the fact that the Patentee was already marketing the drug in other parts of the world from 2006 onwards. It is not the case of the Patentee that he had to develop the drug before launching the same in the Indian market or had no means to market the drug. The Patentee has a considerable Field Force and Distributors, being an old and established force in the Indian market. [. . .]

It is also pertinent to refer to Section 84(7) of the Act, which states as follows:

[. . .]

(a)(ii) the demand for the patented article has not been met to an adequate extent or on reasonable terms; or . . ."

[. . .] invoked beyond doubt. Accordingly, I hold that the reasonable requirements of the public with respect to the patented invention have not been satisfied in this case and consequently a compulsory license be issued to the Applicant under Section 84 of the Act.

11. Reasonably affordable price

Section 84 of the Act states as follows:

> "**84. Compulsory licenses**—
>
> (1) At any time after the expiration of three years from the date of the grant of a patent, any person interested may make an application to the Controller for grant of compulsory license on patent on any of the following grounds, namely—
>
> [. . .]
>
> (b) that the patented invention is not available to the public at a reasonably affordable price . . ."

Applicant's submissions

[. . .] The Applicant submitted through the affidavit of Sh. C. Rammanohar Reddy, the Editor of Economic and Political Weekly that there are a number of ways for determining the affordability of a drug.[. . .]

i. Shanti Mendis et al, "The availability and affordability of selected essential medicines for chronic diseases in six-low and middle income countries" [Bulletin of the World Health Organization, April 2007, 85(4)]:

> As per this approach, the number of days a lowest paid government worker would be required to work to purchase from the public sector, a month's course of medicine at the standard or common dose, has to be considered. It has been argued that in the case of the present drug such a Government Worker would have to work for three and a half years to be able to purchase the drug at a price of Rs. 280,000. [. . .]

ii. Laurens M. Niens et al., "Quantifying the Impoverishing Effects of Purchasing Medicines: A Cross-Country Comparison of the Affordability of Medicines in the Developing World," PLOS Medicine, August 2010, Volume 7, Issue 8:

> [. . .] the percentage that would be pushed below a certain income level when having to purchase the medicine. [. . .] a medicine that costs Rs.280,000 a month will push a large proportion of the population into poverty. [. . .]

Patentee's submissions

It was submitted that innovation based products cost a price over generics, but this price pays for the pipeline (i.e. the future innovation) and competition. [. . .] it also involves the Research and Development (R&D) cost of innovators as against the Applicant who merely copies the drug discovered by the patentee thereby taking advantage of the R&D carried out by the Patentee. [. . .] the marketed product must pay not only for its own R&D cost but also for the cost of the underlying failed R&D, and further must underwrite the additional R&D for the next generation of innovations. [. . .] It is important to understand that R&D on a new drug does not all stop when the drug is launched in the market but actually continues with considerable investments. In conclusion, it is neither possible nor—if it were somehow possible—would it be reasonable to look at past R&D expenditure for a launched product to decide whether its current price is reasonable. [. . .] Balance needs to be created. Therefore, the cost of R&D and the cost of manufacture, both have to be taken into account while determining "reasonable affordable price". [. . .]

"Treating unequal as equal" is discriminatory and is not permissible under law. Placing "the rich class" and "the lower class" in one category at the expense of the patentee is unreasonable and cannot be the intention of the legislature. In case of a drug, if R&D is not to be killed, this device has to be implemented. [. . .]

Decision

[. . .] Patentee also submitted that affordable to public is required to be considered as affordable to different classes/sections of public. On this point, I fully agree with the Patentee. I only wonder why the Patentee did not execute this concept by offering differential pricing for different classes/sections of the public in India. [. . .] I am of the view that reasonably affordable price has to be construed predominately with reference to the public. [. . .]

It stands to common logic that a patented article like the drug in this case was not bought by the public due to only one reason, i.e. its price was not reasonably affordable to them. Hence, I conclude beyond doubt that the patented invention was not available to the public at a reasonably affordable price and that Section 84(1)(b) of the Patents Act, 1970 is invoked in this case. Consequently, a compulsory license be issued to the Applicant under Section 84 of the Act.

12. Patented invention not worked in the territory of India

Section 84 of the Act states as follows:

> "**84. Compulsory licenses**—
>
> (1) At any time after the expiration of three years from the date of the grant of a patent, any person interested may make an application to the Controller for grant of compulsory license on patent on any of the following grounds, namely—
>
> [. . .]
>
> (c) that the patented invention is not worked in the territory of India"

Applicant's submissions

[. . .] As per the Act, the law expects the Patentee to work the invention in the country to the fullest extent possible. [. . .] It is pertinent to note that Patentee has been working the Patent in other countries since 2006; however, the Patent has not been exploited in India and no reason has been ascribed for such neglect. This is especially in view of the fact that the Patentee claims to have manufacturing facilities in India for several products, including Oncology products. As such there is no hurdle preventing the Patentee from working the Patent in India.

Patentee's submissions

[. . .] An attempt to impose local working requirements—in the sense of local manufacturing—on patents granted in India would be beyond the scope of the Patents Act and against the intent of the legislature. [. . .] Manufacturing of the drug requires huge investment in terms of infrastructure and logistics. [. . .] Patentee made a strategic decision to consolidate [. . .] bulk production of the product covered by the Subject Patent within its manufacturing facilities in Germany. [. . .] In addition, production in Germany allows for taking advantage of good infrastructure for supplying global markets as good downstream and upstream industries ensure a smooth supply chain process. The quantities required in India do not economically justify setting up a manufacturing facility by Bayer in India. [. . .]

Decision

[. . .] The term 'worked in the territory of India' has not been defined in the Act. Hence, one has to seek its meaning from various International Conventions and Agreements on intellectual property, provisions contained in the Patents Act, 1970, the context in which this concept appears, and also the legislative history. [. . .] certain key terms relating to TRIPS obligations are not defined in the Agreement itself, which leaves considerable discretion to WTO Members as to how to apply the criteria within their national laws.[. . .]

Section 83(b) states that Patents are not granted merely to enable patentees to enjoy a monopoly for importation of the patented article. Upon a reading of this provision, it becomes amply clear to me that mere importation cannot amount to working of a patented invention. [. . .]

[. . .] 'worked in the territory of India' implies manufactured in India to a reasonable extent so that the principles enumerated in Section 83 can be brought into effect. [. . .]

Another indication is provided by Section 84(6) [. . .]

> **Section 84(6)**
>
> 'In considering the application filed under this section, the Controller shall take into account—
>
> [. . .]
>
> (ii) the ability of the applicant to work the invention to the public advantage;

[. . .]

The term 'work the invention' does not include imports as a compulsory license holder has to necessarily work the patent by manufacturing the patented invention in India. If the licensee cannot import the product into India, for working the invention under the terms of the License, barring exceptional circumstances mentioned in Section 90(3) of the Act, then this implies that importing cannot amount to working for a licensee. A combined reading of these provisions implies that the same logic must apply with respect to the Patentee as well. [. . .] I am therefore convinced that 'worked in the territory of India' means 'manufactured to a reasonable extent in India'.

[. . .] However, even after the lapse of four years from the date of the grant of the patent, the Patentee failed to do so. The Patentee has also failed to grant a voluntary license on reasonable terms to anyone including the Applicant herein to work the invention within the territory of India. Accordingly, I hold that Section 84(1)(c) is attracted in this case and consequently a compulsory license be issued to the Applicant under Section 84 of the Act.

3. WTO Declaration on TRIPS Agreement and Public Health, Adopted on 14 November 2001

The Doha Declaration on the TRIPS Agreement and Public Health sought to address the public policy and humanitarian case for medicines to be made available to address epidemic disease in developing and least-developed countries.

DOHA WTO MINISTERIAL 2001: TRIPS

WT/MIN(01)/DEC/2
20 November 2001
Declaration on the TRIPS agreement and public health

Adopted on 14 November 2001

1. We recognize the gravity of the public health problems afflicting many developing and least-developed countries, especially those resulting from HIV/AIDS, tuberculosis, malaria and other epidemics.

2. We stress the need for the WTO Agreement on Trade-Related Aspects of Intellectual Property Rights (TRIPS Agreement) to be part of the wider national and international action to address these problems.

3. We recognize that intellectual property protection is important for the development of new medicines. We also recognize the concerns about its effects on prices.

4. We agree that the TRIPS Agreement does not and should not prevent members from taking measures to protect public health. Accordingly, while reiterating our

commitment to the TRIPS Agreement, we affirm that the Agreement can and should be interpreted and implemented in a manner supportive of WTO members' right to protect public health and, in particular, to promote access to medicines for all.

In this connection, we reaffirm the right of WTO members to use, to the full, the provisions in the TRIPS Agreement, which provide flexibility for this purpose.

5. Accordingly and in the light of paragraph 4 above, while maintaining our commitments in the TRIPS Agreement, we recognize that these flexibilities include:

a. In applying the customary rules of interpretation of public international law, each provision of the TRIPS Agreement shall be read in the light of the object and purpose of the Agreement as expressed, in particular, in its objectives and principles.

b. Each member has the right to grant compulsory licences and the freedom to determine the grounds upon which such licences are granted.

c. Each member has the right to determine what constitutes a national emergency or other circumstances of extreme urgency, it being understood that public health crises, including those relating to HIV/AIDS, tuberculosis, malaria and other epidemics, can represent a national emergency or other circumstances of extreme urgency.

d. The effect of the provisions in the TRIPS Agreement that are relevant to the exhaustion of intellectual property rights is to leave each member free to establish its own regime for such exhaustion without challenge, subject to the MFN and national treatment provisions of Articles 3 and 4.

6. We recognize that WTO members with insufficient or no manufacturing capacities in the pharmaceutical sector could face difficulties in making effective use of compulsory licensing under the TRIPS Agreement. We instruct the Council for TRIPS to find an expeditious solution to this problem and to report to the General Council before the end of 2002.

7. We reaffirm the commitment of developed-country members to provide incentives to their enterprises and institutions to promote and encourage technology transfer to least-developed country members pursuant to Article 66.2. We also agree that the least-developed country members will not be obliged, with respect to pharmaceutical products, to implement or apply Sections 5 and 7 of Part II of the TRIPS Agreement or to enforce rights provided for under these Sections until 1 January 2016, without prejudice to the right of least-developed country members to seek other extensions of the transition periods as provided for in Article 66.1 of the TRIPS Agreement. We instruct the Council for TRIPS to take the necessary action to give effect to this pursuant to Article 66.1 of the TRIPS Agreement.

4. The Main Proposed Solutions in Comparison

Option	Steps to achieve	Conditions	Considerations	Considerations
(a) To amend Article 31(f) to carve out an exception for exports under CL, or to remove limitations on export entirely.	a. Agreement to reopen TRIPS and approval of amendment b. Changes in national laws c. Grant of CL	a. Criteria to ensure importing countries face serious public health problems b. Safeguards against re-exportation of CL product c. Reporting of action to trading partners	Requires granting of two CLs Requires compensation in exporting and importing countries Changes in CL legislation in importing countries may be required	Would require exporting country to assess "capacity" of importing country Subject to pressures both in importing and exporting Granting of licence case-by-case.
(b) To interpret limited exceptions clause of Article 30 to allow production for export to countries with no or inefficient manufacturing capacity	a. Authoriative interpretation (3/4 vote) b. Change in national laws of exporting countries c. Change in CL legislation in importing countries may be required	a. Entirety of the product must be exported to countries with the public health problem b. Prohibition of re-export	Export country not required to do a case-by-case decision No amendment of TRIPS needed Compensation payable only in importing country	Any party can invoke the exception, at any time, in exporting country
(c) Moratorium on WTO complaints/disputes	Ministerial Conference/Amendment	Criteria to be established	Not a solution; as such, it is only temporary The criteria could be disputable even if mechanism is not	

CL = Compulsory license

5. Implementation of Paragraph 6 of the Doha Declaration on the TRIPS Agreement and Public Health — Decision of the General Council of 30 August 2003

The WTO General Council Decision implemented Paragraph 6 of the Doha Declaration on the TRIPS Agreement and Public Health through provision of a waiver on the obligations of the exporting country under TRIPS Article 31(f) and subject to the conditions set out in the Decision.

GENERAL COUNCIL

WT/L/540 and Corr.1
1 September 2003
Implementation of paragraph 6 of the Doha Declaration on the TRIPS Agreement and public health

Decision of the General Council of 30 August 2003

The General Council,

Having regard to paragraphs 1, 3 and 4 of Article IX of the Marrakesh Agreement Establishing the World Trade Organization ("the WTO Agreement");

Conducting the functions of the Ministerial Conference in the interval between meetings pursuant to paragraph 2 of Article IV of the WTO Agreement;

Noting the Declaration on the TRIPS Agreement and Public Health (WT/MIN(01)/DEC/2) (the "Declaration") and, in particular, the instruction of the Ministerial Conference to the Council for TRIPS contained in paragraph 6 of the Declaration to find an expeditious solution to the problem of the difficulties that WTO Members with insufficient or no manufacturing capacities in the pharmaceutical sector could face in making effective use of compulsory licensing under the TRIPS Agreement and to report to the General Council before the end of 2002;

Recognizing, where eligible importing Members seek to obtain supplies under the system set out in this Decision, the importance of a rapid response to those needs consistent with the provisions of this Decision;

Noting that, in the light of the foregoing, exceptional circumstances exist justifying waivers from the obligations set out in paragraphs (f) and (h) of Article 31 of the TRIPS Agreement with respect to pharmaceutical products;

Decides as follows:

1. For the purposes of this Decision:

(a) "pharmaceutical product" means any patented product, or product manufactured through a patented process, of the pharmaceutical sector needed to address the public health problems as recognized in paragraph 1 of the Declaration. It is understood that active ingredients necessary for its manufacture and diagnostic kits needed for its use would be included; (1)

(b) "eligible importing Member" means any least-developed country Member, and any other Member that has made a notification (2) to the Council for TRIPS of its intention to use the system as an importer, it being understood that a Member may notify at any time that it will use the system in whole or in a limited way, for example only in the case of a national emergency or other circumstances of extreme urgency or in cases of public non-commercial use. It is noted that some Members will not use the system set out in this Decision as importing Members (3) and that some other Members have stated that, if they use the system, it would be in no more than situations of national emergency or other circumstances of extreme urgency;

(c) "exporting Member" means a Member using the system set out in this Decision to produce pharmaceutical products for, and export them to, an eligible importing Member.

2. The obligations of an exporting Member under Article 31(f) of the TRIPS Agreement shall be waived with respect to the grant by it of a compulsory licence to the extent necessary for the purposes of production of a pharmaceutical product(s) and its export to an eligible importing Member(s) in accordance with the terms set out below in this paragraph:

(a) the eligible importing Member(s) (4) has made a notification (2) to the Council for TRIPS, that:

(i) specifies the names and expected quantities of the product(s) needed (5);

(ii) confirms that the eligible importing Member in question, other than a least developed country Member, has established that it has insufficient or no manufacturing capacities in the pharmaceutical sector for the product(s) in question in one of the ways set out in the Annex to this Decision; and

(iii) confirms that, where a pharmaceutical product is patented in its territory, it has granted or intends to grant a compulsory licence in accordance with Article 31 of the TRIPS Agreement and the provisions of this Decision (6);

(b) the compulsory licence issued by the exporting Member under this Decision shall contain the following conditions:

(i) only the amount necessary to meet the needs of the eligible importing Member(s) may be manufactured under the licence and the entirety of this production shall be exported to the Member(s) which has notified its needs to the Council for TRIPS;

(ii) products produced under the licence shall be clearly identified as being produced under the system set out in this Decision through specific labelling or marking. Suppliers should distinguish such products through special packaging and/or special colouring/shaping of the products themselves, provided that such distinction is feasible and does not have a significant impact on price; and

(iii) before shipment begins, the licensee shall post on a website (7) the following information:

—the quantities being supplied to each destination as referred to in indent (i) above; and

—the distinguishing features of the product(s) referred to in indent (ii) above;

(c) the exporting Member shall notify (8) the Council for TRIPS of the grant of the licence, including the conditions attached to it (9). The information provided shall include the name and address of the licensee, the product(s) for which the licence has been granted, the quantity(ies) for which it has been granted, the country(ies) to which the product(s) is (are) to be supplied and the duration of the licence. The notification shall also indicate the address of the website referred to in subparagraph (b)(iii) above.

3. Where a compulsory licence is granted by an exporting Member under the system set out in this Decision, adequate remuneration pursuant to Article 31(h) of the TRIPS Agreement shall be paid in that Member taking into account the economic value to the importing Member of the use that has been authorized in the exporting Member. Where a compulsory licence is granted for the same products in the eligible importing Member, the obligation of that Member under Article 31(h) shall be waived in respect of those products for which remuneration in accordance with the first sentence of this paragraph is paid in the exporting Member.

[. . .]

a. Waiver with Conditions

The effectiveness of the waiver with conditions as a means of implementing Paragraph 6 of the Doha Declaration on TRIPS and Public Health is discussed by experts.[131] Core considerations are:

- The simple and expeditious review process in the TRIPS Council.
- Short time-frame and requirements for a waiver can be defined in advance.
- Article IX: 3 of the WTO Agreement provides for a three-fourths majority of the Members.
- Although the decision to grant a waiver must state the date on which the waiver will terminate, the duration of a waiver is not limited (Article IX: 4 of the WTO Agreement). Members can decide to extend the initial period.

The question of Members' qualification is twofold. First, which Members facing public health crises would qualify for importing these products, and second, which Members would qualify for exporting these products.

---

131. Jacques H.J. Bourgeois & Thaddeus J. Burns, *Implementing Paragraph 6 of the Doha Declaration on TRIPS and Public Health: The Waiver Solution*, Journal of World Intellectual Property (2005); Paul Vandoren Jean & Charles Van Eeckhaute, *The WTO Decision on Paragraph 6 of the Doha Declaration on the Trips Agreement and Public Health: Making it Work*, Journal of World Intellectual Property (2005).

The Council for Trade-Related Aspects of Intellectual Property Rights, *Paragraph 6 of the Ministerial Declaration on the TRIPS Agreement and Public Health*, IP/C/W/355, 24 June 2002.

II. THE PROBLEM RECOGNIZED IN PARAGRAPH 6 OF THE MINISTERIAL DECLARATION ON TRIPS AND PUBLIC HEALTH

4. Any WTO Member could face difficulties in making effective use of compulsory licenses due to insufficient or no manufacturing capacities in the pharmaceutical sector. Therefore, the solution to be considered by the TRIPs Council needs not and should not be limited to a specific category of countries—although developing countries, in particular least-developed countries, might figure among its main beneficiaries. Obstacles to granting compulsory licenses for the supply of the local market may result from a number of factors. The lack of adequate manufacturing facilities present within the country, for instance, may result from a failure to fulfil the objective of transfer of technology of the TRIPs Agreement. A country with insufficient or no manufacturing capacities may also lack potential licensees that are willing or capable of manufacturing locally. In some countries, capacity to manufacture public health-related products may be owned or controlled by the same companies that hold local patents, and there would be no enterprises interested in taking the role of a compulsory license supplier. Even in cases where technology may be available, there may be no potential licensees due to lack of economies of scale or other conditions for a viable economic manufacturing. Least-developed country Members generally face particularly dire difficulties in this respect, as there may be no pharmaceutical manufacturing capacities at all in their territories. In light of the above, each Member shall have the right to determine whether it is in a situation of insufficient or no manufacturing capacities in the pharmaceutical sector.

© Jacques H.J. Bourgeois & Thaddeus J. Burns, *Implementing Paragraph 6 of the Doha Declaration on TRIPS and Public Health: The Waiver Solution*, Journal of World Intellectual Property (2005). Printed with permission of John Wiley and Sons and Copyright Clearance Center.

Multilateral trade negotiations are not the exclusive prerogative of lawyers, and the WTO is still an instrument of diplomacy. Both the Article 30 authoritative interpretation and the moratorium on disputes are strictly rejected by key major players of the multilateral trading system. Also, if a procedure to amend the TRIPS Agreement were initiated, no one could anticipate the consequences of the re-opening of Pandora's Box, and the time such negotiations would take. Thus, a waiver is not only the best solution from a legal perspective, but also from an economic and political standpoint.

Finally, it is important to recall that a waiver, or any other solution eventually agreed upon, is not intended to be a miracle cure for all public health problems. It is only a response to the challenge identified in Paragraph 6, namely, how to exercise a compulsory license in those developing and least-developing countries with insufficient or no manufacturing capacities in the pharmaceutical sector. Meeting the mandate of Paragraph 6 of the Doha Declaration on the TRIPS Agreement and Public Health should not slow down other initiatives aimed at pharmaceutical innovation, investment and technology transfer in developing countries—or, for that matter, broader public health and development priorities. Political will and massive efforts such as the Global Fund for AIDS, Tuberculosis and Malaria go to the roots of the problem: adequate financing of the health systems and the development of stable health infrastructures. The TRIPS Agreement is not the problem, but part of the solution.

6. Noncompliance with TRIPS

Although India fought TRIPS mandating comprehensive intellectual property rights and insisted that patent protection be tailored to a country's level of economic development, it eventually submitted to signing TRIPS as a condition of joining the WTO, "fearing restrictions on its exports" if it refused.[132] India did, however, negotiate a transition period in which it did not have to bring its patent laws into full compliance with TRIPS until January 1, 2005. Under the "mailbox" system, patent applicants could submit applications ahead of time, which the Indian patent office would review when India became TRIPS compliant in 2005.

Accordingly, the Novartis AG litigation[133] took place during a transitional period in Indian patent law—between the enactments of the Patents Act of 1970, an era that prohibited granting patents for drugs and the enactment of TRIPS, an era that permitted it. By prohibiting the grant of pharmaceutical product patents, competition among drug producers increased, and important drugs could be made available to the general public at the lowest possible cost. Power in the Indian pharmaceutical market was held by indigenous producers, leading to a dramatic increase in the production of bulk drugs. As India's domestic pharmaceutical industry grew stronger, however, changes at the international level profoundly affected India's patent law. In 1995, TRIPS was enacted, which required all WTO member nations to grant patent protection for pharmaceutical products.

To comply with its international obligations, the Indian parliament contentiously passed the 2005 Amendment, which brought India's intellectual property law into harmony with other WTO nations. Although the 2005 Amendment authorized the patenting of pharmaceutical products, it did not do so without imposing

132. Janice M. Mueller, *The Tiger Awakens: The Tumultuous Transformation of India's Patent System and the Rise of Indian Pharmaceutical Innovation*, 68 U. Pitt. L. Rev. 491, 495, 536–37 (2007) ("India has been a net exporter of drugs since 1988-89 . . .").

133. *Novartis AG v. Union of India*, A.I.R. 2013 S.C. 1311, at 2 (India), available at http://supremecourtofindia.nic.in/outtoday/patent.pdf.

restrictions on the grant of such patents—specifically, through the implementation of Section 3(d).

Novartis AG v. Union of India and Ors. (2013) 6 SCC 1, Civil Appeal Nos. 2706–2716 of 2013.

Case Introduction

Scientist Jurg Zimmermann created many derivatives of N-phenyl-2-pyrimidine-amine, one of which was termed Imatinib by the World Health Organization. Imatinib was the subject matter of this case. It was capable of inhibiting tumors in warm blooded animals and could be used in the preparation of pharmaceutical drugs used to treat tumors and atherosclerosis. A patent for Imatinib was granted by the US patent office on May 28, 1996, and subsequently, a European patent was granted as well. Novartis marketed this pharmaceutical drug under the brand name Gleevec in both the US and India.

Novartis claimed that it developed/invented a beta crystalline form of Imatinib Mesylate in a two-step process. It filed an application for the grant of a patent for Imatinib Mesylate in its beta crystalline form with the Chennai Patent office on July 17 1998, claiming that the new crystal has:

(i) More beneficial flow properties;

(ii) Better thermodynamic stability; and

(iii) Lower hygroscopicity than the alpha crystal form of Imatinib Mesylate.

Novartis argued that, by way of the aforesaid properties, the invention was "new".

At the time that Novartis applied for the patent in Switzerland (18 July 1997), Indian law regarding product patent was in a transitional stage and its application lay dormant for a significant period of time under the "mailbox procedure". During the pendency of its application, Novartis applied for the exclusive marketing rights of the invention, which were granted to it on November 10, 2003, by the Patent Office.

Procedural History of the Case

The Assistant Controller of Patents and Designs rejected the application for grant of patent on various grounds including:

a. The invention was anticipated by prior publication of the Zimmermann patent (Imatinib);

b. The invention was obvious to a person skilled in the art because of the disclosures in the Zimmermann patent;

c. Patentability disallowed by Section 3(d) of the Indian Patent Act; and

d. July 18, 1997, the Swiss priority date, was incorrectly claimed as the priority date for the application in India and hence the invention was already anticipated by the specification made in the application submitted in Switzerland.

Novartis filed writ petitions challenging Section 3(d) of the Indian Patent Act as a violation of Article 14 of the Constitution of India (which enshrines the Fundamental Right to Equality) and not being in compliance with TRIPS, which were dismissed by the Madras High Court and never challenged further. Its appeals against the non-granting of the patent were transferred to the Intellectual Property Appellate Board ("IPAB") after the IPAB's formation and were dismissed by the IPAB on June 26, 2009. While the IPAB reversed the findings on anticipation and obviousness, it held that the patentability of the product was barred by Section 3(d) of the Patent Act, observing that:

> Since India is having a requirement of higher standard of inventive step by introducing the amended section 3(d) of the Act, what is patentable in other countries will not be patentable in India. As we see, the object of amended section 3(d) of the Act is nothing but a requirement of higher standard of inventive step in the law particularly for the drug/pharmaceutical substances.

The IPAB did however grant a process patent to Novartis for the preparation of Imatinib Mesylate in its beta crystal form. Novartis approached the Supreme Court of India against the IPAB's order. The Supreme Court dismissed the appeal, affirming and reversing parts of the IPAB's order. It found that the crystalline form of Imatinib Mesylate failed both the tests of invention and patentability under the Indian Patent Act.

Principal Points of the Judgment

Aftab Alam, J.

[...]

18. The IPAB also referred to the judgment of the Madras High Court, dismissing the appellant's writ petitions challenging the constitutional validity of section 3(d) where the High Court had observed:

> "We have borne in mind the object which the amending Act wanted to achieve namely, to prevent evergreening; to provide easy access to the citizens of the country to life saving drugs and to discharge their constitutional obligation of providing good health care to its citizens."

19. In light of the High Court's observation, the IPAB also referred to the pricing of the drug Gleevec by the appellant while it enjoyed EMR over it, and held that the patentability of the subject product would also be barred by section 3(b) of the Act and in this regard observed as follows:

> "We are fully conscious of the Appellant's benevolent GIPAP program for free distribution of GLEEVEC to certain cancer patients. But as per information furnished in its written counter-argument by R 3 that when the Appellant was holding the right as EMR on GLEEVEC it used to charge Rs.1,20,000/- per month for a required dose of the drug from a cancer patient, not disputed by the Appellant, which in our view is too unaffordable to the poor cancer patients in India. Thus, we also observe that a grant of product patent on this application

> can create havoc to the lives of poor people and their families affected with the cancer for which this drug is effective. This will have disastrous effect on the society as well. Considering all the circumstances of the appeals before us, we observe that the Appellant's alleged invention won't be worthy of a reward of any product patent on the basis of its impugned application for not only for not satisfying the requirement of section 3(d) of the Act, but also for its possible disastrous consequences on such grant as stated above, which also is being attracted by the provisions of section 3(b) of the Act which prohibits grant of patent on inventions, exploitation of which could create public disorder among other things (Sic .) We, therefore, uphold the decision of R 8 on section 3(d) of the Act to the extent that product patent cannot be made available to the Appellant . . ." [. . .]

65. In the course of the hearing, we were told that the Doha Declaration effectively reflected and addressed the deep disquiet of the developing and the least-developed countries regarding their obligation under TRIPS to grant patent protection for pharmaceutical and agricultural chemical products and the likelihood of its highly adverse consequence on public-health. Dr. Dhawan, appearing for Cipla (one of the Objectors), was particularly severe in his criticism of the TRIPS Agreement and called it a "predatory and coercive" agreement. The other counsel, though, appearing for the different Objectors, were more muted in their criticism of the TRIPS Agreement. Mr. Kuhad, the learned Additional Solicitor General appearing for the Union of India, and Mr. Grover, Senior Advocate, appearing on behalf of the M/s. Cancer Patients Aid Association (one of the Objectors), especially adapted their submissions, taking the TRIPS Agreement as a fact that cannot be simply wished away. However, all the counsel representing the Union of India and the different Objectors unanimously took the stand that the TRIPS Agreement has sufficient flexibility (vide Articles 7, 8 and 27), which was further reaffirmed by the Doha Declaration (in paragraphs 4 to 6), to enable the member States to control the patent rights in a manner as to avoid any adverse impact on public-health. It was contended on behalf of the Union of India and the Objectors that the TRIPS Agreement coupled with the Doha Declaration leaves it open to the member States to adjust their respective patent systems by regulating the grant of patents and to set up higher standards for patent protection for pharmaceutical and agricultural chemical products. The Union of India and all the Objectors maintained that the patent law in India, as it stands today after major changes were brought about in the Patents Act, 1970 in 2005, is fully TRIPS compliant. But they insisted that the Indian law must be judged and interpreted on its own terms, and not on the basis of standards of patentability prescribed in some countries of the western world.

66. We have referred to the TRIPS Agreement and certain developments arising from it not to comment upon the fairness or otherwise of the Agreement nor to examine the correctness and wisdom of the decision of the Government of India to subscribe to the Agreement. That is farthest from our mind. We have referred to the Agreement as being the main reason behind the basic changes brought about in the

patent law of the country by legislative action. We have also referred to the Agreement as being the cause of a good deal of concern not only in this country but also (as we shall see presently) in other parts of the world; the concern being that patent protection to pharmaceutical and agricultural chemical products might have the effect of putting life-saving medicines beyond the reach of a very large section of people. In the following lines we shall see how the Indian legislature addressed this concern and, while harmonizing the patent law in the country with the provisions of the TRIPS Agreement, strove to balance its obligations under the international treaty and its commitment to protect and promote public health considerations, not only of its own people but in many other parts of the world (particularly in the Developing Countries and the Least Developed Countries).

67. We have seen above that, simultaneously with the TRIPS coming into force, the Government of India had brought an Ordinance to comply with the provisions of Article 70 (8) and (9), but the Ordinance lapsed without being replaced by any enactment. Complaints were then filed on which pronouncements were made against India. On the complaint filed by the USA, the decision of the Appellate Body was rendered on December 19, 1997; and on the complaint filed by the European Communities, the report of the Panel came on August 24, 1998. Thus faced with the threat of trade sanctions, Parliament passed the Patents (Amendment) Act 1999 (Act No. 17 of 1999) on March 26, 1999, which amended the provisions of the Patents Act 1970 retrospectively, with effect from January 1, 1995, the date when the TRIPS Agreement came into force. By the Amendment Act of 1999, section 5 of the Parent Act was amended to provide for making "a claim for patent of an invention for a substance itself intended for use or capable of being used, as medicine or drug". The Amendment Act further incorporated in the Parent Act, Chapter IVA, which contained provisions for grant of exclusive marketing rights in respect of pharmaceutical substances for which a claim for patent was made under section 5 of the Act. The Amendment Act of 1999 thus complied with Article 70(8) and (9) of the TRIPS Agreement.

68. Three years later the Patents (Amendment) Act, 2002 (Act No. 38 of 2002) came to be enacted on June 25, 2002. It brought large scale amendments in the Patents Act, 1970. The Statement of Objects and Reasons for the Amendment Act of 2002 is stated as under:

> "Amendment Act 38 of 2002—Statement of Objects and Reasons.—The law relating to patents is contained in the Patents Act, 1970 which came into force on the 20th April, 1972. The Act was last amended in March, 1999 to meet India's obligations under the Agreement on Trade Related Aspects of Intellectual Property Rights (TRIPS) which forms part of the Agreement establishing the World Trade Organisation (WTO). . . . Development of technological capability in India, coupled with the need for integrating the intellectual property system with international practices and intellectual property regimes, requires that the Act be modified into a modern, harmonised and user-friendly piece of legislation to adequately protect national and public interests while simultaneously

meeting India's international obligations under the TRIPS Agreement which are to be fulfilled by 31st December, 1999.

2. xxx

3. While considering amendment to the Act, efforts have been made to make the law not only TRIPS complaint (sic) but also to provide therein necessary and adequate safeguards for protection of public interest, national security, bio-diversity, traditional knowledge, etc. Opportunity is also proposed to be availed for harmonising the procedure for grant of patents in accordance with international practices and to make the system more user friendly.

4. Some of the salient features of the Bill are as under:—

(a) to define the term "invention" in consonance with international practices and consistent with TRIPS Agreement;

(b) to modify section 3 of the present Act to include exclusions permitted by TRIPS Agreement and also subject-matters like discovery of any living or non-living substances occurring in nature in the list of exclusions which in general do not constitute patentable invention;

(c) to align rights of patentee as per article 28 of the TRIPS Agreement;

[. . .]

(l) to amend several provisions of the Act with a view to simplifying and rationalising the procedures aimed at benefiting users."

69. The Amendment Act of 2002 greatly expanded the definition clause in section 2 of the Parent Act by including a number of new expressions and terms and redefining some earlier terms.

70. "Invention" was defined in the Parent Act as under:

"Section 2(1)(j) "Invention" means any new and useful(i) art, process, method or manner of manufacture; (ii) machine, apparatus or other article; (iii) substance produced by manufacture, and includes any new and useful improvement of any of them, and an alleged invention."

71. "Invention" was re-defined by the Amendment Act of 2002 as under:

"Section 2(1)(j) "invention" means a new product or process involving an inventive step and capable of industrial application."

72. The expressions "capable of industrial application" and "inventive step" were separately defined in clauses (ac) and (ja) respectively which are as under:

"Section 2(1)(ac) "capable of industrial application", in relation to an invention, means that the invention is capable of being made or used in an industry.

Section 2(1)(ja) "inventive step" means a feature that makes the invention not obvious to a person skilled in the art."

73. Section 3 of the Parent Act, which provided for exclusions from patentability, was recast. In section 5 of the Parent Act, an Explanation was added after sub-section (2). Chapter XVI was substituted with the Chapter Heading "Working of Patents, Compulsory Licenses and Revocation". Section 83 in this Chapter laid down the general principles applicable to working of patented inventions; section 84 provided for compulsory licenses; and section 85 for revocation of patents for non-working. Here, it may not be out of place to take note of section 83 which provided as under:

> "Section 83: General principles applicable to working of patented inventions.— Without prejudice to the other provisions contained in this Act, in exercising the powers conferred by this Chapter, regard shall be had to the following general considerations, namely:—
>
> (a) that patents are granted to encourage inventions and to secure that the inventions are worked in India on a commercial scale and to the fullest extent that is reasonably practicable without undue delay;
>
> (b) that they are not granted merely to enable patentees to enjoy a monopoly for the importation of the patented article;
>
> (c) that the protection and enforcement of patent rights contribute to the promotion of technological innovation and to the transfer and dissemination of technology, to the mutual advantage of producers and users of technological knowledge and in a manner conducive to social and economic welfare, and to a balance of rights and obligations;
>
> (d) that patents granted do not impede protection of public health and nutrition and should act as instruments to promote public interest specially in sectors of vital importance for socio-economic and technological development of India;
>
> (e) that patents granted do not in any way prohibit Central Government in taking measures to protect public health;
>
> (f) that the patent right is not abused by the patentee or person deriving title or interest on patent from the patentee, and the patentee or a person deriving title or interest on patent from the patentee does not resort to practices which unreasonably restrain trade or adversely affect the international transfer of technology; and
>
> (g) that patents are granted to make the benefit of the patented invention available at reasonably affordable prices to the public." [. . .]

88. Section 2(1)(j) requires a product to satisfy three conditions to qualify as an invention.

(i) It must be "new", that is to say it must not have been anticipated;

(ii) Its coming into being must involve an "inventive step"; and

(iii) It must be "capable of industrial application", that is to say it must be capable of being made or used in an industry [section 2(1)(ac)].

89. "Inventive step" is separately defined in section 2(j)(a) to mean a feature of an invention that involves technical advance as compared to the existing knowledge, or having economic significance or both and that makes the invention not obvious to a person skilled in the art. To paraphrase, the invention that creates the product must have a feature that involves technical advance as compared to the existing knowledge or having economic significance or both and this feature should be such as to make the invention not obvious to a person skilled in the art.

90. On a combined reading of causes (j), (a)(c) and (j)(a) of section 2(1), in order to qualify as "invention", a product must, therefore, satisfy the following tests:

(i) It must be "new";

(ii) It must be "capable of being made or used in an industry"

(iii) It must come into being as a result of an invention which has a feature that:

(a) entails technical advance over existing knowledge;

Or

(b) has an economic significance

And

(c) makes the invention not obvious to a person skilled in the art.

91. We have seen the meaning of "invention"; we have also seen earlier that the Patents Act, 1970, dealt with "invention" and "patentability" as two distinctly separate concepts. The duality of the two concepts is best illustrated by section 4 of the Act, which prohibits the grant of patent (either process or product) "in respect of inventions relating to atomic energy falling within sub-section (1) of section 20 of the Atomic Energy Act, 1962", and which has not undergone any change since inception. It is, therefore, fundamental that for grant of patent the subject must satisfy the twin tests of "invention" and "patentability". Something may be an "invention" as the term is generally understood and yet it may not qualify as an "invention" for the purposes of the Act. Further, something may even qualify as an "invention" as defined under the Act and yet may be denied patent for other larger considerations as may be stipulated in the Act. Having, therefore, seen the meaning of "invention", we may now advert to section 3 as it stands after the amendment of the Act in 2005. [. . .]

99. In regard to section 3(d) both Mr. Andhyarujina and Mr. Subramanium, learned counsel appearing for the appellant, strenuously argued that section 3(d) is not meant to be an exception to clauses (j) and (ja) of section 2(1) of the Act. Both the learned counsel insisted that section 3(d) has no application to the case of the subject product. The subject product, having satisfied the tests of invention as provided in clauses (j) and (ja) of section 2(1), cannot be denied patent for allegedly failing to satisfy the tests under section 3(d). Mr. Andhyarujina submitted that section 3(d) is a provision put in *ex abundanti cautela non nocet* to remove all doubts.

100. Mr. Subramanium submitted that section 3(d) is *ex majore cautela*. The learned counsel submitted that the primary purpose of section 3(d), as is evidenced from the legislative history, is to prevent "evergreening" and yet to encourage incremental inventions. "Evergreening" is a term used to label practices that have developed in certain jurisdictions wherein a trifling change is made to an existing product, and claimed as a new invention. The coverage/protection afforded by the alleged new invention is then used to extend the patentee's exclusive rights over the product, preventing competition. Mr. Subramanium submitted that, by definition, a trifling change, or in the words of the section "a mere discovery of a new form of a known substance", can never ordinarily meet the threshold of novelty and inventive step under clauses (j) and (ja) of section 2(1). An invention cannot be characterized by the word "mere". The word "invention" is distinct from the word "discovery". He, therefore, submitted that section 3(d) operates only as *ex majore cautela*, ensuring that mere discoveries can never, by an effort at interpretation of clauses (j) and (ja) of section 2(1), be considered inventions.

101. In regard to the concerns about public health issues and the flexibility of the TRIPS Agreement coupled with the Doha Declaration, allowing the scope to address the issues of public health, Mr. Subramanium submitted that those concerns are addressed in the Act, in provisions relating to compulsory licensing for opposition to the grant of patent.

102. The submission may appear plausible if the scrutiny of the law is confined only to the Act as it stands today after undergoing the amendments in 2005. But examined in the larger perspective of the development of the law of patent over the past 100 years and especially keeping in mind the debates in the Parliament preceding the 2005 amendment, it would appear completely unacceptable. We find no force in this submission that section 3(d) is a provision *ex majore cautela*. To our mind, the submission completely misses the vital distinction between the concepts of invention and patentability—a distinction that was at the heart of the Patents Act as it was framed in 1970, and which is reinforced by the 2005 amendment in section 3(d).

103. We are clearly of the view that the importance of the amendment made in section 3(d), that is, the addition of the opening words in the substantive provision and the insertion of explanation to the substantive provision, cannot be underestimated. It is seen above that, in course of the Parliamentary debates, the amendment in section 3(d) was the only provision cited by the Government to allay the fears of the Opposition members concerning the abuses to which a product patent in medicines may be vulnerable. We have, therefore, no doubt that the amendment/addition made in section 3(d) is meant especially to deal with chemical substances, and more particularly pharmaceutical products. The amended portion of section 3(d) clearly sets up a second tier of qualifying standards for chemical substances/pharmaceutical products in order to leave the door open for true and genuine inventions but, at the same time, to check any attempt at repetitive patenting or extension of the patent term on spurious grounds.

104. We have so far seen section 3(d) as representing "patentability", a concept distinct and separate from "invention". But if clause (d) is isolated from the rest of section 3, and the legislative history behind the incorporation of Chapter II in the Patents act, 1970, is disregarded, then it is possible to see section 3(d) as an extension of the definition of "invention" and to link section 3(d) with clauses (j) and (ja) of section 2(1). In that case, on reading clauses (j) and (ja) of section 2(1) with section 3(d) it would appear that the Act sets different standards for qualifying as "inventions" things belonging to different classes, and for medicines and drugs and other chemical substances, the Act sets the invention threshold further higher, by virtue of the amendments made in section 3(d) in the year 2005. [. . .]

125. Further, Natco Pharma Ltd., one of the Objectors to the grant of patent to the appellant in this country, had marketed a drug called VEENAT 100 (capsules) in the UK. A legal notice on behalf of the appellant was given to Natco Pharma Ltd. on February 13, 2004. The notice stated that the appellant was the proprietor of European patent EP-A0 564 409 (the Zimmermann patent) and that this patent claimed, among other things, the compound Imatinib and acid addition salts of that compound such as the Mesylate salt. In the notice it was pointed out that Natco Pharma Ltd. was selling, in the UK market, VEENAT 100 capsules, the active pharmaceutical ingredient of which was Imatinib Mesylate as claimed in the Zimmermann patent. The importation, sale and offer to sell VEENAT 100 capsules in the UK market infringed the Zimmermann patent and Natco Pharma Ltd. was therefore warned to immediately cease the importation, sale and promotion of VEENAT 100 capsules and other pharmaceutical substances containing "Imatinib". The matter was finally settled out of court, we are told, at considerable expense to Natco Pharma Ltd. which of course had to stop marketing its drug VEENAT 100 capsules in the UK.

126. From the above discussion it would be clear that the drug Gleevec directly emanates from the Zimmermann patent and comes to the market for commercial sale. Since the grant of the Zimmermann patent, the appellant has maintained that Gleevec (that is, Imatinib Mesylate) is part of the Zimmermann patent. It obtained drug approval for Gleevec on that basis. It claimed extension of the term of the Zimmermann patent for the period of regulatory review for Gleevec, and it successfully stopped Natco Pharma Ltd. from marketing its drug in the UK on the basis of the Zimmermann patent. Not only the appellant but the US Board of Patent Appeals, in its judgment granting patent for beta crystalline form of Imatinib Mesylate, proceeded on the basis that though the beta crystal form might not have been covered by the Zimmermann patent, the Zimmermann patent had the teaching for the making of Imatinib Mesylate from Imatinib, and for its use in a pharmacological compositions for treating tumours or in a method of treating warmblooded animals suffering from a tumoral disease. This finding was recorded by the US Board of Patent Appeals, in the case of the appellant itself, on the very same issue that is now under consideration. The appellant is, therefore, fully bound by the finding and cannot be heard to take any contrary plea. [. . .]

156. However, before leaving Hogan and proceeding further, we would like to say that in this country the law of patent, after the introduction of product patent for all kinds of substances in the patent regime, is in its infancy. We certainly do not wish the law of patent in this country to develop on lines where there may be a vast gap between the coverage and the disclosure under the patent; where the scope of the patent is determined not on the intrinsic worth of the invention but by the artful drafting of its claims by skillful lawyers, and where patents are traded as a commodity not for production and marketing of the patented products but to search for someone who may be sued for infringement of the patent.

157. In light of the discussions made above, we firmly reject the appellant's case that Imatinib Mesylate is a new product and the outcome of an invention beyond the Zimmermann patent. We hold and find that Imatinib Mesylate is a known substance from the Zimmermann patent itself. Not only is Imatinib Mesylate known as a substance in the Zimmermann patent, but its pharmacological properties are also known in the Zimmermann patent and in the article published in the Cancer Research journal referred to above. The consequential finding, therefore, is that Imatinib Mesylate does not qualify the test of "invention" as laid down in section 2(1)(j) and section 2(1)(ja) of the Patents Act, 1970. [. . .]

164. It may also be stated here that while going through the Zimmermann patent one cannot but feel that it relates to some very serious, important and valuable researches. The subject patent application, on the other hand, appears to be a loosely assembled, cut-and paste job, drawing heavily upon the Zimmermann patent. As a matter of fact, Mr. Kuhad, learned Additional Solicitor General, submitted before us a tabular chart showing over a dozen statements and averments made in the subject application that are either lifted from the Zimmermann patent or are very similar to corresponding statements in the Zimmermann patent. The aforesaid chart is appended at the end of the judgment as Appendix II.

165. It further needs to be noted that, on the issue of section 3(d), there appears to be a major weakness in the case of the appellant. There is no clarity at all as to what is the substance immediately preceding the subject product, the beta crystalline form of Imatinib Mesylate. In course of the hearing, the counsel appearing for the appellant greatly stressed that, in terms of invention, the beta crystalline form of Imatinib Mesylate is two stages removed from Imatinib in free base form. The same is said in the written notes of submissions filed on behalf of the appellant. But this position is not reflected in the subject application, in which all the references are only to Imatinib in free base form (or to the alpha crystalline form of Imatinib Mesylate in respect of flow properties, thermodynamic stability and lower hygroscopicity). Going through the subject application, the impression one gets is that the beta crystalline form of Imatinib Mesylate is derived directly from Imatinib free base. This may, perhaps, be because once the beta crystalline form of the methanesulfonic acid salt of Imatinib came into being, the Imatinib free base got seeded with the nuclei of Imatinib Mesylate beta crystalline form and, as a result, starting from Imatinib one would inevitably arrive directly at the beta

crystalline form of Imatinib Mesylate. But all this is nowhere said in the subject application. [. . .]

176. The way in which the case is presented by Mr. Subramanium is an entirely new case made before this Court for the first time. Nevertheless, let us consider the case of the appellant as presented by Mr. Subramanium.

177. The portion added in section 3(d) by the 2005 amendment reads as under:

> The mere discovery of a new form of a known substance which does not result in the enhancement of the known efficacy of that substance . . . [is not inventions within the meaning of the Act].

178. The Explanation to section 3(d) also added by the 2005 amendment provides as under:

> "Explanation.—For the purposes of this clause, salts, esters, ethers, polymorphs, metabolites, pure form, particle size, isomers, mixtures of isomers, complexes, combinations and other derivatives of known substance shall be considered to be the same substance, unless they differ significantly in properties with regard to efficacy."

179. It may be seen that the word "efficacy" is used both in the text added to the substantive provision as also in the explanation added to the provision. 180. What is "efficacy"? Efficacy means "the ability to produce a desired or intended result". Hence, the test of efficacy in the context of section 3(d) would be different, depending upon the result the product under consideration is desired or intended to produce. In other words, the test of efficacy would depend upon the function, utility or the purpose of the product under consideration. Therefore, in the case of a medicine that claims to cure a disease, the test of efficacy can only be "therapeutic efficacy". The question then arises, what would be the parameter of therapeutic efficacy and what are the advantages and benefits that may be taken into account for determining the enhancement of therapeutic efficacy? With regard to the genesis of section 3(d), and more particularly the circumstances in which section 3(d) was amended to make it even more constrictive than before, we have no doubt that the "therapeutic efficacy" of a medicine must be judged strictly and narrowly. Our inference that the test of enhanced efficacy in case of chemical substances, especially medicine, should receive a narrow and strict interpretation is based not only on external factors but there are sufficient internal evidence that leads to the same view. It may be noted that the text added to section 3(d) by the 2005 amendment lays down the condition of "enhancement of the known efficacy". Further, the explanation requires the derivative to "differ significantly in properties with regard to efficacy". What is evident, therefore, is that not all advantageous or beneficial properties are relevant, but only such properties that directly relate to efficacy, which in case of medicine, as seen above, is its therapeutic efficacy. [. . .]

192. Section 2(1)(j) defines "invention" to mean, "a new product or . . .", but the new product in chemicals and especially pharmaceuticals may not necessarily mean something altogether new or completely unfamiliar or strange or not existing

before. It may mean something "different from a recent previous" or "one regarded as better than what went before" or "in addition to another or others of the same kind". However, in case of chemicals and especially pharmaceuticals if the product for which patent protection is claimed is a new form of a known substance with known efficacy, then the subject product must pass, in addition to clauses (j) and (ja) of section 2(1), the test of enhanced efficacy as provided in section 3(d) read with its explanation.

193. Coming back to the case of the appellant, there is yet another angle to the matter. It is seen above that in the US the drug Gleevec came to the market in 2001. It is beyond doubt that what was marketed then was Imatinib Mesylate and not the subject product, Imatinib Mesylate in beta crystal form. It is also seen above that even while the appellant's application for grant of patent lay in the "mailbox" awaiting amendments in the law of patent in India, the appellant was granted Exclusive Marketing Rights on November 10, 2003, following which Gleevec was marketed in India as well. On its package, the drug was described as "Imatinib Mesylate Tablets 100 mg" and it was further stated that "each film coated tablet contains: 100 mg Imatinib (as Mesylate)". On the package there is no reference at all to Imatinib Mesylate in beta crystalline form. What appears, therefore, is that what was sold as Gleevec was Imatinib Mesylate and not the subject product, the beta crystalline form of Imatinib Mesylate.

194. If that be so, then the case of the appellant appears in rather poor light and the claim for patent for beta crystalline form of Imatinib Mesylate would only appear as an attempt to obtain patent for Imatinib Mesylate, which would otherwise not be permissible in this country.

195. In view of the findings that the patent product, the beta crystalline form of Imatinib Mesylate, fails in both the tests of invention and patentability as provided under clauses (j), (ja) of section 2(1) and section 3(d) respectively, the appeals filed by Novartis AG fail and are dismissed with cost. The other two appeals are allowed.

7. The Future of the Doha Negotiations — Recent Developments

6 November 2015

PRESS STATEMENT

Decision taken by the WTO's Council for Trade-Related Aspects of Intellectual Property Rights (TRIPS)

WTO members agree to extend drug patent exemption for poorest members

"Least-developed country" (LDC) members of the WTO will be allowed to maintain maximum flexibility in their approach to patenting pharmaceutical products until at least 2033, following a decision taken by the WTO's Council for Trade-Related Aspects of Intellectual Property Rights (TRIPS) on 6 November.

The Council's decision extends until January 2033 the period during which key provisions of the WTO's intellectual property agreement, the TRIPS Agreement, do not apply to pharmaceutical products in LDCs. This means LDCs can choose whether or not to protect pharmaceutical patents and clinical trial data before 2033. The decision also keeps open the option for further extensions beyond that date.

The latest extension, the second specifically applied to pharmaceutical products for LDCs, is in line with directions set by WTO ministers in the 2001 Doha Declaration on the TRIPS Agreement and Public Health. It also follows the adoption of the new UN Sustainable Development Goals(SDGs), which affirm the right of developing countries to utilize TRIPS Agreement flexibilities to ensure access to medicines for all.

WTO Director-General Roberto Azevêdo hailed the TRIPS Council's decision.

"This decision by the TRIPS Council represents a clear and unambiguous signal that WTO members are committed to addressing the needs of the organization's poorest members. With the concerns of least developed countries at centre stage next month at our Nairobi Ministerial Conference, now is the time for WTO to build upon this momentum in other areas of our work," said Director-General Azevêdo.

WTO members, speaking in the TRIPS Council, unanimously welcomed the decision. A wide spectrum of members recalled the benefits of this extension for public health outcomes in LDCs, in light of the continuing challenges faced by these countries.

Ambassador Shameem Ahsan of Bangladesh, coordinator of the LDC group in the WTO, described the decision as "historic," adding that it "will assure the LDCs the necessary legal certainty to procure or to produce generic medicines for those who need it most but do not have any access."

This step, responding to a request tabled by LDC members of the WTO (IP/C/W/605), comes just a month after the UN General Assembly adopted the SDGs as a framework for global action up to 2030.

SDG Goal 3 on ensuring healthy lives and promoting well-being for all at all ages includes the target of providing "access to affordable essential medicines and vaccines", and in that context recalls the affirmation in the Doha Declaration on the right of developing countries to use to the full the provisions in the TRIPS Agreement regarding flexibilities to protect public health, and, in particular, provide access to medicines for all.

The need to take full account of the special needs and circumstances of the LDCs is recognized expressly in the TRIPS Agreement itself, and this recognition runs through many areas of the WTO's work. LDC members are already exempted from applying all substantive TRIPS standards until 2021, a period that may also be extended.'

[. . .]

F. International Technology Transfer Contracts

Manufacturing and services in many countries across the world are moving increasingly into higher value-added sectors such as pharmaceuticals and IT.

China, for instance, has initiated a policy of indigenous innovation to encourage its own companies to climb the value-added chain. A range of policies is also in place requiring the transfer of technology by foreign companies selling products or services to Chinese companies in higher technology sectors. However, foreign investors often express deep concerns about technology transfer and the protection of their intellectual property, and many companies are still reluctant to commit their core intellectual property capability to the Chinese market.

In this context, it is not surprising that litigation concerning protection of intellectual property rights and technology transfer is relatively common in China. Issues can arise in areas such as misappropriation or infringement of intellectual property, stealing of technology, breaching of intellectual property rights and counterfeit. There are sophisticated rules in China to protect intellectual and creative inventions in China, but enforcement may not be ideal.

Furthermore, the character of intellectual property disputes has changed over time. In the past, the most frequent issue tended to be copying of products on a local, entrepreneurial basis. However, as the Chinese economy has become more sophisticated and luxury goods more widely available, smaller entrepreneurs are having proportionately less impact, and foreign firms are less concerned about this type of pirating.

Of more concern to foreign investors is "forced" technology transfer. Although there is usually prior agreement with the foreign company regarding the technologies to be transferred, the pressure can increase over time for more technology to be included. This may result from a deliberate government policy intention to accelerate the transfer of certain types of technology. Where the foreign investment is through a joint venture or minority holding, there can be particular risk of handing over more technical information than planned, without appropriate compensation through licensing or similar agreements. This appears to be a particular issue in sectors such as automobiles, telecoms, aerospace, computer software and green technologies.

1. Provisions and Conditions for Transferring

International technology transfer (ITT) is predominately driven by national policies and is difficult to regulate effectively at international level. For example, when a company from country X invests in a manufacturing plant in country Y, provisions for the transfer of technology will often be requested by country Y. In this case, the investor has to be comfortable that national patent protection is sufficient. Often, the parties will enter into a contract with a specific focus on transfer of technology, as this is important to both the host and investor.

Contract terms to be addressed in the area of technology transfer may include: Description of Technology; Conditions Restricting Technology Transfers; Payment for Technology; Guarantees; Claims by Third Persons; and issues common to provision of know-how such as i) Confidentiality, ii) Training of Personnel, and iii) Supply of Documentation.

In drafting these types of contracts, issues related to technology know-how, industry related research, applicable law in both the home and host state, and prohibited and mandatory provisions, will need to be considered. For example, the following Philippine Law on Technology Transfer Arrangements includes several clauses which, if violated, may lead to the state breaking the contract.

PHILIPPINE LAW ON TECHNOLOGY TRANSFER ARRANGEMENTS

June 6, 1997; January 1, 1998

REPUBLIC ACT NO. 8293

AN ACT PRESCRIBING THE INTELLECTUAL PROPERTY CODE AND ESTABLISHING THE INTELLECTUAL PROPERTY OFFICE, PROVIDING FOR ITS POWERS AND FUNCTIONS, AND FOR OTHER PURPOSES

PART I—The Intellectual Property Office

[. . .]

SECTION 2. Declaration of State Policy.—The State recognizes that an effective intellectual and industrial property system is vital to the development of domestic and creative activity, facilitates transfer of technology, attracts foreign investments, and ensures market access for our products. It shall protect and secure the exclusive rights of scientists, inventors, artists and other gifted citizens to their intellectual property and creations, particularly when beneficial to the people, for such periods as provided in this Act. [. . .]

SECTION 4. Definitions.—

4.2. The term "technology transfer arrangements" refers to contracts or agreements involving the transfer of systematic knowledge for the manufacture of a product, the application of a process, or rendering of a service including management contracts; and the transfer, assignment or licensing of all forms of intellectual property rights, including licensing of computer software except computer software developed for mass market.

[. . .]

CHAPTER IX Voluntary Licensing

SECTION 87. Prohibited Clauses.—Except in cases under Section 91, the following provisions shall be deemed prima facie to have an adverse effect on competition and trade:

87.1. Those which impose upon the licensee the obligation to acquire from a specific source capital goods, intermediate products, raw materials, and other technologies, or of permanently employing personnel indicated by the licensor;

87.2. Those pursuant to which the licensor reserves the right to fix the sale or resale prices of the products manufactured on the basis of the license;

87.3. Those that contain restrictions regarding the volume and structure of production;

87.4. Those that prohibit the use of competitive technologies in a nonexclusive technology transfer agreement;

87.5. Those that establish a full or partial purchase option in favor of the licensor;

87.6. Those that obligate the licensee to transfer for free to the licensor the inventions or improvements that may be obtained through the use of the licensed technology;

87.7. Those that require payment of royalties to the owners of patents for patents which are not used;

87.8. Those that prohibit the licensee to export the licensed product unless justified for the protection of the legitimate interest of the licensor such as exports to countries where exclusive licenses to manufacture and/or distribute the licensed product(s) have already been granted;

87.9. Those which restrict the use of the technology supplied after the expiration of the technology transfer arrangement, except in cases of early termination of the technology transfer arrangement due to reason(s) attributable to the licensee;

87.10. Those which require payments for patents and other industrial property rights after their expiration, termination arrangement;

87.11. Those which require that the technology recipient shall not contest the validity of any of the patents of the technology supplier;

87.12. Those which restrict the research and development activities of the licensee designed to absorb and adapt the transferred technology to local conditions or to initiate research and development programs in connection with new products, processes or equipment;

87.13. Those which prevent the licensee from adapting the imported technology to local conditions, or introducing innovation to it, as long as it does not impair the quality standards prescribed by the licensor;

87.14. Those which exempt the licensor for liability for non-fulfilment of his responsibilities under the technology transfer arrangement and/or liability arising from third party suits brought about by the use of the licensed product or the licensed technology; and

87.15. Other clauses with equivalent effects. (Sec. 33-C (2), RA 165a)

SECTION 88. Mandatory Provisions.—The following provisions shall be included in voluntary license contracts:

88.1. That the laws of the Philippines shall govern the interpretation of the same and in the event of litigation, the venue shall be the proper court in the place where the licensee has its principal office;

88.2. Continued access to improvements in techniques and processes related to the technology shall be made available during the period of the technology transfer arrangement;

88.3. In the event the technology transfer arrangement shall provide for arbitration, the Procedure of Arbitration of the Arbitration Law of the Philippines or the Arbitration Rules of the United Nations Commission on International Trade Law (UNCITRAL) or the Rules of Conciliation and Arbitration of the International Chamber of Commerce (ICC) shall apply and the venue of arbitration shall be the Philippines or any neutral country; and

88.4. The Philippine taxes on all payments relating to the technology transfer arrangement shall be borne by the licensor. (n)

[. . .]

CHAPTER X Compulsory Licensing

SECTION 93. Grounds for Compulsory Licensing.—The Director of Legal Affairs may grant a license to exploit a patented invention, even without the agreement of the patent owner, in favor of any person who has shown his capability to exploit the invention, under any of the following circumstances:

93.1. National emergency or other circumstances of extreme urgency;

93.2. Where the public interest, in particular, national security, nutrition, health or the development of other vital sectors of the national economy as determined by the appropriate agency of the Government, so requires; or

93.3. Where a judicial or administrative body has determined that the manner of exploitation by the owner of the patent or his licensee is anti-competitive; or

93.4. In case of public non-commercial use of the patent by the patentee, without satisfactory reason;

93.5. If the patented invention is not being worked in the Philippines on a commercial scale, although capable of being worked, without satisfactory reason: Provided, that the importation of the patented article shall constitute working or using the patent. (Secs. 34, 34-A, 34-B, R.A. No. 165(a)).

[. . .]

SECTION 95. Requirement to Obtain a License on Reasonable Commercial Terms.—

95.1. The license will only be granted after the petitioner has made efforts to obtain authorization from the patent owner on reasonable commercial terms and conditions but such efforts have not been successful within a reasonable period of time.

95.2. The requirement under Subsection 95.1 shall not apply in the following cases: a. Where the petition for compulsory license seeks to remedy a practice determined after judicial or administrative process to be anti-competitive; b. In situations of national emergency or other circumstances of extreme urgency; c. In cases of public non-commercial use.

95.3. In situations of national emergency or other circumstances of extreme urgency, the right holder shall be notified as soon as reasonably practicable.

95.4. In the case of public non-commercial use, where the government or contractor, without making a patent search, knows or has demonstrable grounds to know that a valid patent is or will be used by or for the government, the right holder shall be informed promptly. (n)

SECTION 96. Compulsory Licensing of Patents Involving Semi-Conductor Technology.—In the case of compulsory licensing of patents involving semiconductor technology, the license may only be granted in case of public noncommercial use or to remedy a practice determined after judicial or administrative process to be anti-competitive. (n)

[. . .]

SECTION 98. Form and Contents of Petition.—The petition for compulsory licensing must be in writing, verified by the petitioner and accompanied by payment of the required filing fee. It shall contain the name and address of the petitioner as well as those of the respondents, the number and date of issue of the patent in connection with which compulsory license is sought, the name of the patentee, the title of the invention, the statutory grounds upon which compulsory license is sought, the ultimate facts constituting the petitioner's cause of action, and the relief prayed for. (Sec. 34-D, R.A. No. 165)

[. . .]

SECTION 100. Terms and Conditions of Compulsory License.—The basic terms and conditions including the rate of royalties of a compulsory license shall be fixed by the Director of Legal Affairs subject to the following conditions:

100.1. The scope and duration of such license shall be limited to the purpose for which it was authorized;

100.2. The license shall be non-exclusive;

100.3. The license shall be non-assignable, except with that part of the enterprise or business with which the invention is being exploited;

100.4. Use of the subject matter of the license shall be devoted predominantly for the supply of the Philippine market: Provided, That this limitation shall not apply where the grant of the license is based on the ground that the patentee's manner of exploiting the patent is determined by judicial or administrative process, to be anticompetitive.

100.5. The license may be terminated upon proper showing that circumstances which led to its grant have ceased to exist and are unlikely to recur: Provided, That adequate protection shall be afforded to the legitimate interest of the licensee; and

100.6. The patentee shall be paid adequate remuneration taking into account the economic value of the grant or authorization, except that in cases where the license was granted to remedy a practice which was determined after judicial or administrative process, to be anticompetitive, the need to correct the anti-competitive practice may be taken into account in fixing the amount of remuneration. (Sec. 35-B, R.A. No. 165(a)).

SECTION 101. Amendment, Cancellation, Surrender of Compulsory License.—

101.1. Upon the request of the patentee or the licensee, the Director of Legal Affairs may amend the decision granting the compulsory license, upon proper showing of new facts or circumstances justifying such amendment.

101.2. Upon the request of the patentee, the said Director may cancel the compulsory license: a. If the ground for the grant of the compulsory license no longer exists and is unlikely to recur; b. If the licensee has neither begun to supply the domestic market nor made serious preparation therefore; c. If the licensee has not complied with the prescribed terms of the license;

101.3. The licensee may surrender the license by a written declaration submitted to the Office.

101.4. The said Director shall cause the amendment, surrender, or cancellation in the Register, notify the patentee, and/or the licensee, and cause notice thereof to be published in the IPO Gazette. (Sec. 35-D, R.A. No. 165(a)).

[. . .]

2. Fostering Technology Transfer for Economic Development

This article further explores the public policy issues related to technology transfer and economic development.

Keith E. Maskus; *Using the International Trading System to Foster Technology Transfer for Economic Development*, 2005 Mich. St. L. Rev. 219.

Development of new technologies continues to reside overwhelmingly in the advanced industrial economies. [. . .]

[. . .] history suggests it is difficult to regulate ITT effectively at the international level. Technology owners are unlikely to transfer knowledge without an adequate and reasonably certain return, while there are significant problems in monitoring compliance with any rules that might be imposed. Thus, ITT flows are predominately influenced by national policies rather than by international disciplines. [. . .]

In the 1990s, multilateral disciplines on ITT-related policies began to deepen. The WTO Agreement on Trade-Related Aspects of Intellectual Property Rights (TRIPS) calls on countries to enforce comprehensive minimum standards of intellectual property rights (IPRs) protection on a nondiscriminatory basis. [. . .]

In 2001, WTO members established a Working Group on Trade and Technology Transfer to examine relationships between trade and the transfer of technology and explore what could be done to increase ITT in developing countries. [. . .]

I. TRIPS and International Technology Transfer

Discussion over whether TRIPS will increase or decrease ITT flows is polarized. [. . .]

Critics see TRIPS as a mechanism for enhancing the global market power of information developers, permitting them to act in monopolistic and abusive ways that slow down ITT, especially to the poorest countries.[134] Many developing countries consider the agreement to be unbalanced in this regard [. . .].

ITT is a complex and multi-varied process and the expected impacts of a trade agreement cannot be characterized so easily. [. . .] Among the more important factors are the local investment climate, market competition, governance policies, openness, proximity to markets, human capital and skills, and efficiency of labor markets.[135]

[. . .] enforceable IPRs are neither necessary nor sufficient to establish robust inflows of technology. [. . .] It is useful, therefore, to overview the main features of TRIPS that could affect incentives for ITT.

A. General TRIPS Provisions

The preamble of TRIPS [. . .] recognizes both that technological development is an IPR-related policy objective of all nations and that the least-developed countries (LDCs) have particular needs in terms of creating a technological foundation. [. . .]

The language of Article 7 [. . .] states that protecting IPRs should contribute to these goals rather than acknowledging that a failure to protect IPRs might also contribute to development objectives. [. . .] How broadly one should interpret the scope of this objective is subject to debate. [. . .] In this view, informal means of learning through imitation and copying would not constitute permissible transfers and the Agreement would not be structured to promote them. [. . .]

134. *See* Carlos M. Correa, Can the TRIPS Agreement Foster Technology Transfer to Developing Countries? in Keith E. Maskus & Jerome H. Reichman eds., *International Public Goods and the Transfer of Technology Under a Globalized Intellectual Property Regime*, Cambridge University Press (2005).

135. An additional important element is the extent to which foreign governments choose to place into the public domain the results of publicly funded research, but I do not consider that factor here.

It is also necessary to cast Article 7 as an objective for the global system. [. . .] The substantive obligations of TRIPS could be read against this objective. [. . .]

The most direct language on technology transfer arises in Article 66.2 [. . .] it requires only developed countries to provide such incentives, and only on behalf of the LDCs. No obligations or rights are created for the developing and transition countries. [. . .] Firms are likely to engage in ITT only where they can profit from it. In this regard, the LDCs greatly need to enhance their abilities to absorb information flows. [. . .]

Recognizing that developing countries and LDCs would face considerable difficulties in implementing TRIPS, Article 67 obligates the developed countries to technical assistance covering the entire agreement. [. . .]

B. TRIPS-Consistent Flexibilities in Intellectual Property Rights

[. . .] trademark protection can enhance the willingness of firms to license production and distribution rights and to extend their marketing efforts across space. [. . .] copyrights [. . .] can sort out complex contracting problems [. . .]. Patents and know-how are often the central components of technology transfer and legal certainty.

As always, however, IPRs are a two-sided sword for technology-importing nations and firms. [. . .]

Fundamentally, Article 27.2 and 27.3 permit countries to exclude certain important technologies from patentability, including plants and animals (except microorganisms).[136] [. . .]

Application and renewal fees for patents and trademarks could be set to promote innovation and dissemination of IPRs. It is possible to set lower patent application fees for small and medium-sized enterprises than for large firms. [. . .] countries could set high standards for the inventive step in order to prevent routine discoveries from being patented. [. . .]

Under limited circumstances set out in Article 31, governments may resort to compulsory licensing to promote public health, welfare, security, competition (a stipulation that would cover ITT), and other objectives.[137] [. . .] compulsory licensing procedures need to be transparent and well-defined in order not to discourage entry of foreign firms and development of new technologies by domestic firms. The restrictions imposed on compulsory licensing are seen by some observers as so rigorous as to eliminate nearly all prospects for effective technology transfer. [. . .] Indeed, there is little evidence that countries have successfully used this tool to gain access to international technologies. [. . .]

For purposes of encouraging learning and competition, it is important for developing countries to recognize reverse engineering as a fair competitive practice,

136. TRIPS Agreement, arts. 27.2 & 27.3.
137. TRIPS Agreement, art. 31.

consistent with TRIPS. This permits local rivals to use unpatented information but only at the cost of undertaking their own incremental R&D activity, which in itself can contribute to future technology transfer. [. . .]

TRIPS Article 40 sets out a general right for counties to define and enforce anti-monopoly policies in order to defeat abusive technology licensing practices.[138] [. . .]

In copyrights, TRIPS offers flexibility for defining fair use of unauthorized copies for purposes of achieving social and economic objectives. [. . .] Reverse engineering of computer programs for purposes of developing competing software is permissible under TRIPS. [. . .]

A. Market Channels

The first major channel through which technology is transferred across international boundaries is trade in goods and services. [. . .]

A second channel is foreign direct investment through multinational enterprises (MNEs). [. . .]

A third major channel is technology licensing, which may be done either within firms or between joint-venture partners or unrelated firms. [. . .] There are important differences between ITT within a multinational firm and market-mediated licensing. In the first case the MNE retains proprietary control of the intellectual property and know-how, while in the second case access to these assets must be provided to the licensee. [. . .] Where licensing contracts are reached through negotiation between buyer and seller, the transfer is voluntary. However, in cases in which the transfer is mandated through compulsory licensing, the relevant know-how that is embodied in the personal knowledge of engineers or trade secrets but not in patent rights may be difficult to acquire.

A final significant channel of ITT is cross-border movement of technical and managerial personnel. [. . .]

It is important to note that trade, FDI, licensing, joint ventures, and personnel movements are interdependent processes.

B. Non-Market Channels

Imitation may be achieved through product inspection, reverse engineering, and simple trial and error. [. . .] Imitation bears no compensation to the technology owner in formal markets. [. . .] However, imitation may be a costly process and tends to divert attention from local innovation, so a full accounting of its impacts is more complex.

A related form of learning is for technical and managerial personnel to leave employment within a MNE and join or start a rival firm based on knowledge gained there. [. . .]

138. TRIPS Agreement, art. 40.

A related source of information is confidential test data provided by patent applicants to governments. Government agencies may choose to share such data [. . .] much technology appears to be transferred through the temporary migration of students, scientists, and managerial and technical personnel to universities, laboratories, and conferences. Because education and training involve in-depth learning in science and engineering, this is a particularly long-lasting form of ITT. The challenge for developing countries in this context is to encourage their expatriate students and professionals to return home and undertake local scientific and business development.

C. Market Failures and the Need for Intervention

[. . .] In its purest form, a technology is both non-rival and non-excludable. Nonrivalry means that information may be shared among multiple users without diminishing its productivity for any one user. It is this feature of knowledge that lies at the heart of the modern theory of FDI and licensing. [. . .] Non-excludability means that an information developer may not be able to prevent others from using it without authorization. [. . .] firms have an interest in maintaining excludability in order to generate a market return on R&D investments. Excludability is the essence of intellectual property rights, which attempt to balance the returns to innovation against the needs for diffusion.

[. . .] transfers of technology are subject to asymmetric information problems that can significantly reduce incentives for trade. [. . .] Accordingly, many otherwise mutually beneficial technology transactions may fail. Here, policy should aim at two objectives. First, reduce this information asymmetry by increasing access of local buyers to the international stock of knowledge about available technologies. Second, increase the certainty with which technology owners can signal the true value and characteristics of their inventions to buyers without excessive concerns about losing that value without compensation.

A final problem inherent in technology-transfer markets is that owners of new technical information are likely to have market power because of lead times, brand loyalty, or the exercise of IPRs. [. . .] Unfortunately, it is difficult to implement the kinds of precise intervention that would expand technology transfers at lower cost, rather than simply induce technology developers to leave particular markets. [. . .] However, it is generally infeasible to intervene precisely in multiple markets, leaving governments the second-best policy task of reducing impediments to technology transfer for public goods.

III. Suggested Policies for Enhancing ITT

[. . .] Article 66.2 of TRIPS is well intentioned but it is not likely on its own merits to achieve significant increases in ITT.

[. . .]

A. Source-Country Policies

First, developed countries could provide indirect incentives for ITT. Perhaps the most powerful such incentive would be to provide significant market access in the developed economies for products in which poor countries have a comparative advantage [. . .]. An increase in such market access would encourage the transfer of IP-based agricultural inputs, including genetically engineered crop technologies and biotechnological plant varieties.

Second, [. . .] capacity building in IPRs should emphasize less the specification of protective laws and regulations and more the technical, judicial, and legal expertise underlying effective ITT. [. . .]

An alternative form of assistance could recognize that poor countries face major difficulties in developing and enforcing anti-monopoly laws. [. . .] one way for governments in developing countries to feel more confident about the system would be for authorities in the developed countries to undertake enforcement actions against firms headquartered or located in their jurisdictions. [. . .] this approach may require an agreement at the WTO over multilateral disciplines in competition policy, with enforcement to be shared between developed and developing countries. [. . .]

Governments could ensure also that tax deductions are available for contributions of technology to non-profit entities engaged in ITT. [. . .]

Fiscal incentives could be offered to encourage enterprises to employ, at least temporarily, recent scientific, engineering and management graduates from developing countries. [. . .]

Further, grant programs could be established for research into technologies that would be of greatest productivity in poor countries for social needs, such as water treatment, energy, and the environment. Technologies developed under such programs could be made publicly available if transferred through public resources.

B. Multilateral Policy Options

There are essentially two roles that international organizations can play in encouraging ITT. One is to serve as a coordinating mechanism for overcoming problems in private technology markets. The second is to serve as a forum for negotiating additional rights and obligations at the international level in order to reduce impediments to ITT. [. . .]

First, Article 66.2 of TRIPS could be expanded to include all developing countries, or at least those without a significant domestic science and technology base. [. . .]

Second, there may be scope for linking Article 66.2 and Article 67 to Article 7 in terms of obligations. Specifically, developing countries could argue that building a "sound and viable technological base" requires institutional reforms [. . .], infrastructure, and an effective science and technology policy, all of which are costly.

Third, because administrative costs are a central problem, it could be beneficial to establish a special fee on applications through the Patent Cooperation Treaty (PCT)

[. . . .] to resolve the collective-interest problem in TRIPS—that beneficiaries do not pay the costs—a special administrative fee at the PCT (and other international industrial-property registration organizations) is sensible.

Fourth, the WTO could increase its monitoring of developed-country efforts in ITT [. . .] the WTO could encourage collaboration and information sharing among member governments. [. . .]

Establishing trade policies to encourage cheaper prices in poor countries for medicines, software, education materials, agricultural inputs, and other technologies is attractive from the standpoint of ITT and Article 66.2. Thus, an extension of the basic approach in the August 2003 Waiver, combined with subsidies for provision of such technologies in the LDCs, could be beneficial.

Chapter 7

The Process and Value of the Unification of Commercial Law for International Trade and Investments

A. The Traditional Approach and Reliance on Conflict of Laws Rules
B. Movement to Adopt Common Rules for International Contracting
C. A Universal Approach: United Nations Convention on Contracts for the International Sale of Goods (UNCITRAL Sales Convention)
   1. Main Provisions of the Convention
      a. Conditions of Applicability
      b. Scope
      c. Offer and Acceptance
      d. Obligations of the Seller and of the Buyer
      e. Exemptions
   2. Distinguishing Features of the Convention
      a. Language
      b. Parties Agreement of Usage
      c. Writing
      d. Doctrine of Frustration
      e. Preservation of Goods
      f. Remedies for Breach of Contract by the Seller
      g. Passing of Risk
         Helen Kaminski Pty. Ltd. v. Marketing Australia Products, 1997 U.S. Dist. LEXIS 10630 (S.D.N.Y. July 23, 1997)
         Mitchell Aircraft Spares v. European Aircraft Service, 23 F. Supp. 2d 915 (N.D. Ill. 1998)
         MCC-Marble Ceramic Center, Inc. v. Ceramica Nuova D'Agostino, S.P.A. 144 F.3d 1384 (11th Cir. 1998), cert. denied, 526 U.S. 1087 (1999)
D. United Nations Convention on the Limitation Period in the International Sale of Goods (UNCITRAL Limitation Convention)
E. UNICTRAL Addressing Legal Barriers to Trade

A. The Traditional Approach and Reliance on Conflict of Laws Rules

Commercial activities in a country are governed by national legislation, but this does not have extra-territorial application to the non-national aspects of an international commercial transaction. The adoption of the United Nations Convention on the Limitation Period in the International Sale of Goods in 1974 ("UNCITRAL Limitation Convention") and the United Nations Convention on Contracts for the International Sale of Goods in 1980 (UNCITRAL Sales Convention or "CISG") effectively created a "global sale of goods law". Before this, international commercial practice in the U.S. relied on the Uniform Commercial Code and domestic contract law. For international contracting, the conflict of laws rules would be used where necessary to decide which set of laws would apply and the relevant court would observe. However, reliance on conflict of law rules meant unwelcome unpredictability and uncertainty for businesses, and provided governments with an incentive to seek a more harmonized approach to the conduct of international private law.

B. Movement to Adopt Common Rules for International Contracting

The UN Sales Convention or "CISG" sought to reconcile the substantively different approaches to commercial law under common law and civil law jurisdictions. It acts as an additional source of law to domestic contract law when dealing with sales contracts at an international level.

The UN Sales Convention, concluded in Vienna in 1980, followed an earlier attempt in The Hague to agree uniform laws on the international sale of goods. Although adopted in 1964, The Hague Uniform Laws were only ratified by a small number of countries.

© Muna Ndulo, *The Vienna Sales Convention 1980 and The Hague Uniform Laws on International Sale of Goods 1964: A Comparative Analysis*, International and Comparative Law Quarterly, vol. 38, pt. 1 (January 1989), reproduced with permission.

This article looks in depth at the origins and development of The Hague Uniform laws and the UN Sales Convention.

I. Introduction

[. . .] The Uniform Law on the International Sale of Goods (ULIS) and the Uniform Law on the Formation of Contracts of Sale (ULF) served as the underlying documents for the elaboration of the 1980 UN Sales Convention. Both the ULIS and the ULF did not fulfil the expectations which their signing in 1964 had ushered in. The number of States which have ratified the two Conventions has remained small. The UN Sales Convention has received the required number of ratifications or accessions and came into force on 1 January 1988.

II. Origins of the 1964 Hague Conventions and the 1980 UN Sales Convention

A. History

The UN Sales Convention is the outcome of a long process of unification whose origin goes back to the early days of the movement in respect of the unification of international trade law. [. . .]

In 1951 the government of the Netherlands organised a diplomatic conference on the international sale of goods in order to consider the draft prepared by UNIDROIT and to determine the means by which the work could be brought to a successful conclusion. [. . .]

In the meantime UNIDROIT had prepared a draft of the ULIS and the ULF. [. . .]

In 1966 the UN General Assembly created the United Nations Commission on International Trade Law (UNCITRAL).[139] [. . .]

At the first session of UNCITRAL, held in 1968, it was decided that in respect of the two 1964 Hague Conventions, which were then not yet in force, the Commission should determine the position of States in respect of those Conventions. Accordingly, the Commission requested the Secretary-General to send a questionnaire to member States of the UN and member States of any of its specialised agencies.[140] The replies and an analysis of the replies were submitted to the second session of the Commission in 1969.[141] After consideration of the replies, the Commission decided to create a working group on the international sale of goods, consisting of 14 member States, which was instructed to ascertain "which modifications of the existing texts might render them capable of wider acceptance by countries of different legal, social and economic systems, or whether it will be necessary to elaborate a new text for the same purpose".[142] The working group in both cases recommended the adoption of new texts. An analysis of the answers revealed that the existing texts of the ULIS and the ULF were unlikely to command such wider acceptance by many countries. Among the objections raised were the following.

1. The Hague Conference, at which the Conventions were adopted, had been attended by only 28 States and the socialist and the developing

139. G.A. Res. 2205 (XXI), Yearbook (1968–1970), Part 1, Chap. II, Section E.

140. G.A. Official Records, 23rd Session, Supp.16 (A/7216).

141. Replies and studies by States concerning the Hague Conventions of 1964: note by the Secretary-General (A/CN.9/11 and Corr. 1 and add. 4). *See also*, the analysis of these replies and studies prepared by the Secretariat: International Sale of Goods: The Hague Conventions of 1964: Analysis of the replies and studies received from governments: report of the Secretary-General (A/CN.9/17); Analysis of the studies and comments by Governments on the Hague Conventions of 1964: report of the Secretary-General (A/CN.9/13).

142. Official Records of the UN Conference on Contracts for the International Sale of Goods (A/CONF.97/19).

countries had not been adequately represented.[143] This seemed to encourage a belief that the Hague Conventions favoured the sellers of manufactured goods in the industrialised nations. In any case, without the adequate participation of the developing countries and socialist countries, the hope that the Hague Conventions would become internationally accepted could not be fulfilled.

2. The ULIS used abstract and complex concepts which could easily result in ambiguity and error and could not be easily understood by businessmen.
3. The ULIS pointed more to external trade between common boundary nations geographically near to each other, and insufficient attention had been given to international trade problems involving overseas shipments.
4. The scope of application was considered by many as too broad as it was to apply regardless of conflict rules.[144]

At its tenth session in 1977, UNCITRAL adopted the draft Convention on the International Sale of Goods.[145] [. . .] and in 1978 at its 11th session adopted the Rules on the Formation of Contracts for the International Sale of Goods [. . .]. UNCITRAL also decided to combine the draft Convention it had adopted at its tenth session and the Rules into a single instrument, the draft Convention on Contracts for the International Sale of Goods. This draft formed the basis of the UN Sales Convention.[146]

III. Sphere of Application

A. Scope

The Uniform Laws and the UN Sales Convention are both concerned primarily with the general principles of the law of sales. The special terms of the contract remain to be defined by the parties to the contract themselves. [. . .] Both the ULIS and the UN Sales Convention have similar provisions regarding scope.[147] The most important principle is that the texts cover only the relationship between the buyer and the seller. They do not regulate the rights of third parties. [. . .]

---

143. *Ibid.*, only Egypt and Yugoslavia participated from the Third World.

144. *See* H.J. Berman, *The Uniform Law on International Sale of Goods: A Constructive Critique*, 30 Law and Contemp. Probs (1966) 354.

145. G.A. Official Records, 32nd Session, Supp.17 (A/32117). The draft was published with a commentary prepared by the UNCITRAL Secretariat. It is the subject of several articles in a symposium on the work of UNCITRAL published in (1979) 27 A.J.C.L. 243.

146. The conference also adopted a protocol amending the Convention of the Limitation Period in the International Sale of Goods (New York, 1974) in order to harmonise the provisions of that Convention in respect of the sphere of application, with those of the UN Sales Convention. G.A. Official records, 33rd Session, Supp.17 (A/33/17). Final Act of the UN Conference on Contracts for the International Sale of Goods (A/CONF.97/18). The Convention is set forth in Annex I of the Final Act.

147. UN Sales Convention, Art. 4, and ULIS, Art. 8: *see also*, ULF, Art. 1.

It is expressly stated by the UN Sales Convention[148] and the ULIS[149] that, except as otherwise expressly provided in Convention, the validity of the contract is not covered. Examples of matters which are thus outside the scope of the Uniform Laws are: capacity of the parties; exchange control legislation; price control legislation; legislation requiring export licences for certain goods; rules concerning contracts *contra bonos mores*; rules regarding contracts against public policy; legislation intended to protect the weaker party; and questions of fraud, duress and mistake. The Convention in addition does not govern product liability.[150] [. . .]

B. Consumer Contracts, Auctions, Stocks and Securities Excepted

The UN Sales Convention and the ULIS exclude certain types of sales from the ambit of the Conventions.[151] They both exclude consumer sales. This is because in a number of countries consumer sales are subject to various types of national laws designed to protect consumers. [. . .] But there is a significant difference between the two Conventions. Article 2(a) of the UN Sales Convention states that the Convention does not apply to sales of goods bought for personal, family or household use, unless the seller, at any time before or at the conclusion of the contract, neither knew nor ought to have known that the goods were bought for any such use. The ULIS [. . .] differs in two important ways from the UN Sales Convention text. First, it does not exclude such contracts from the scope of the ULIS; it merely allows national mandatory provisions for the protection of the buyer to override the ULIS. Secondly, it identifies consumer transactions with instalment sales. This could cause some misunderstandings, in that many commercial sales provide for the payment to be made in instalments, especially in the case of expensive items of equipment, and much similar legislation applies even where the price is paid in a single instalment.

C. Uniform Character with Regard to the Civil or Commercial Character of the Legal Relationship

The Uniform Laws and the Convention apply irrespective of the civil or commercial character of the parties or the contract.[152] [. . .] Contracts for the supply of goods to be manufactured or produced are regarded as sales for the purpose of both Conventions. The relevant articles are Article 3(1) for the UN Sales Convention and Article 1(7) of the ULF. However, where the party ordering the goods undertakes to supply the materials, such a contract will not be covered by the UN Sales Convention (Article 3(1)) if he supplies a substantial part of the materials. [. . .] Sales of stocks, shares, investment securities, negotiable instruments or money, sales of

148. UN Sales Convention, Art. 4(a).

149. ULIS, Art. 8.

150. UN Sales Convention, Art. 5.

151. See UN Sales Convention, Art. 2(a), and ULIS, Art.5.

152. This rule is particularly necessary for those countries that apply commercial law rules to parties characterised as commercial parties and different rules to other parties. To some extent the non-application of the Convention and ULIS to consumer sales achieves the same purpose.

ships, aircraft or vessels and sales of electricity are also excluded.[153] The reason for the exclusions is that sales of this kind are usually subject to special national rules.

There are two differences between the UN Sales Convention text and the ULIS text. First, the former excludes auction sales and, second, the ULIS excludes ships, aircraft and vessels only if they are, or will be, subject to registration.[154] There is also a problem that what is meant by a vessel in the ULIS is not very clear, and domestic registration requirements differ greatly from country to country.

D. Application of the Convention on International Contracts of Sale of Goods

[. . .] the Uniform Laws and the Convention differ markedly in the sphere of their application. For the ULIS and the ULF to apply it is necessary that borders be crossed either in the formation or in the execution of the contract, or that formation and execution each take place in different countries. These requirements are not retained in the UN Sales Convention, whose application requires only that the parties' places of business be located in different States, even when formation and execution both took place in a single State.

[. . .] Another important difference which may be noted in this context is that Article 5 of the ULIS, which allowed a State to adopt the Uniform Laws on the basis that the relevant State will apply them only to contracts in which the parties have chosen the Convention as the law of the contract, is not retained in the Convention. This reservation was in fact made by the United Kingdom. The UN Sales Convention applies without any positive opting in. [. . .]

Under the Uniform Laws every signatory State promises to apply the Convention to all international sales which come before its courts whether or not the parties' States are parties to the Uniform Laws, to the extent that it does not affect the application of any mandatory provision of law which would have been applicable had the parties not chosen the Uniform Law. This is without regard to the rules of private international law, which Article 2 of the ULIS states shall be excluded for the purposes of the application of the ULIS, subject to any provision to the contrary in the ULIS. The application of the Convention in this situation could lead to the application of a law which was unpredictable at the time of the conclusion of the contract. By requiring that there be a substantial relationship between an international sales transaction and a State which ratifies or accedes to it, the UN Sales Convention seems to have resolved this problem, and its approach on the subject is much more appropriate and acceptable than that of the ULIS.

[. . .] The UN Sales Convention in Article 7(1) employs the concept of good faith as mentioned above. Although courts may consider it a vague concept capable of a wide variety of interpretations, the good faith principle can serve a number of useful purposes. It gives the courts the flexibility which is needed by any code to make

153. The relevant provisions are Art. 2(b)-(f) of the UN Sales Convention and Art. 5(a)-(d) of ULIS.

154. ULIS, Art. 5(b).

it work in practice. This allows tribunals to avoid over-literal interpretations which would provide inequitable results unintended by the drafters, and could prevent a too hasty resort to domestic law. Furthermore, the obligation of good faith itself may foster an atmosphere of mutual trust among businessmen.[155]

[. . .] The UN Sales Convention (Article 7(2)), like the ULIS, states that questions not expressly settled by the Convention are to be settled, in the first instance, in conformity with the general principles on which the Convention is based. But Article 7(2) adds that in the absence of such principles, such questions are to be settled "in conformity with the law applicable by virtue of the rules of private international law". Thus courts are to make reference to one or more systems of national law to fill gaps in the Convention. [. . .]

C. A Universal Approach: United Nations Convention on Contracts for the International Sale of Goods (UNCITRAL Sales Convention) (1989)

Where the UN Sales Convention applies, it replaces the use of conflict of law rules and becomes the source of applicable law for an international sales contract. The Convention addresses the full range of issues arising in contracts for the sale of goods, including the passing of risk, the transportation of goods, and acceptance and obligations of the buyer and the seller in an international contract. The United States has adopted and enacted the Sales Convention into United States law. Thus, the Convention automatically applies in the context of international sale contracts originating in the U.S. The emphasis is on place of business rather than nationality and place of incorporation. All major economies have ratified the Convention, except the United Kingdom,[156] Hong Kong, India and South Africa. However, where parties agree, freedom of contract prevails, and parties can choose and agree to specify another source of applicable law. Equally, the Convention can be chosen as a source of law, even if the parties' respective states have not ratified it.

1. Main Provisions of the Convention

a. Conditions of Applicability

Chapter I. Sphere of Application

Article 1

(1) This Convention applies to contracts of sale of goods between parties whose places of business are in different States:

155. *See*, Commentary on Article 7, UN Conference on Contracts for the International Sale of Goods, Vienna, 10 Mar. 11 Apr. 1980, UN Official Records (1981), 18.

156. Qi Zhou, The CISG and English Sales Law: An Unfair Competition in Larry A. Di Matteo (ed.) *International Sales Law: A Global Challenge* (2014).

(a) when the States are Contracting States; or

(b) when the rules of private international law lead to the application of the law of a Contracting State.

(2) The fact that the parties have their places of business in different States is to be disregarded whenever this fact does not appear either from the contract or from any dealings between, or from information disclosed by, the parties at any time before or at the conclusion of the contract.

(3) Neither the nationality of the parties nor the civil or commercial character of the parties or of the contract is to be taken into consideration in determining the application of this Convention.

b. Scope

Article 2

This Convention does not apply to sales:

(a) of goods bought for personal, family or household use, unless the seller, at any time before or at the conclusion of the contract, neither knew nor ought to have known that the goods were bought for any such use;

(b) by auction;

(c) on execution or otherwise by authority of law;

(d) of stocks, shares, investment securities, negotiable instruments or money;

(e) of ships, vessels, hovercraft or aircraft;

(f) of electricity.

Article 7

(1) In the interpretation of this Convention, regard is to be had to its international character and to the need to promote uniformity in its application and the observance of good faith in international trade.

(2) Questions concerning matters governed by this Convention which are not expressly settled in it are to be settled in conformity with the general principles on which it is based or, in the absence of such principles, in conformity with the law applicable by virtue of the rules of private international law.

c. Offer and Acceptance

Article 14

(1) A proposal for concluding a contract addressed to one or more specific persons constitutes an offer if it is sufficiently definite and indicates the intention of the offeror to be bound in case of acceptance. A proposal is sufficiently definite if it indicates the goods and expressly or implicitly fixes or makes provision for determining the quantity and the price.

(2) A proposal other than one addressed to one or more specific persons is to be considered merely as an invitation to make offers, unless the contrary is clearly indicated by the person making the proposal.

Article 16

(1) Until a contract is concluded an offer may be revoked if the revocation reaches the offeree before he has dispatched an acceptance.

(2) However, an offer cannot be revoked:

(a) if it indicates, whether by stating a fixed time for acceptance or otherwise, that it is irrevocable; or

(b) if it was reasonable for the offeree to rely on the offer as being irrevocable and the offeree has acted in reliance on the offer.

Article 17

An offer, even if it is irrevocable, is terminated when a rejection reaches the offeror.

Article 18

(1) A statement made by or other conduct of the offeree indicating assent to an offer is an acceptance. Silence or inactivity does not in itself amount to acceptance.

(2) An acceptance of an offer becomes effective at the moment the indication of assent reaches the offeror. An acceptance is not effective if the indication of assent does not reach the offeror within the time he has fixed or, if no time is fixed, within a reasonable time, due account being taken of the circumstances of the transaction, including the rapidity of the means of communication employed by the offeror. An oral offer must be accepted immediately unless the circumstances indicate otherwise.

(3) However, if, by virtue of the offer or as a result of practices which the parties have established between themselves or of usage, the offeree may indicate assent by performing an act, such as one relating to the dispatch of the goods or payment of the price, without notice to the offeror, the acceptance is effective at the moment the act is performed, provided that the act is performed within the period of time laid down in the preceding paragraph.

Article 19

(1) A reply to an offer which purports to be an acceptance but contains additions, limitations or other modifications is a rejection of the offer and constitutes a counter-offer.

(2) However, a reply to an offer which purports to be an acceptance but contains additional or different terms which do not materially alter the terms of the offer constitutes an acceptance, unless the offeror, without undue delay, objects orally to the discrepancy or dispatches a notice to that effect. If he does not so object, the terms of the contract are the terms of the offer with the modifications contained in the acceptance.

(3) Additional or different terms relating, among other things, to the price, payment, quality and quantity of the goods, place and time of delivery, extent of one party's liability to the other or the settlement of disputes are considered to alter the terms of the offer materially.

Article 20

(1) A period of time for acceptance fixed by the offeror in a telegram or a letter begins to run from the moment the telegram is handed in for dispatch or from the date shown on the letter or, if no such date is shown, from the date shown on the envelope. A period of time for acceptance fixed by the offeror by telephone, telex or other means of instantaneous communication, begins to run from the moment that the offer reaches the offeree.

(2) Official holidays or non-business days occurring during the period for acceptance are included in calculating the period. However, if a notice of acceptance cannot be delivered at the address of the offeror on the last day of the period because that day falls on an official holiday or a non-business day at the place of business of the offeror, the period is extended until the first business day which follows.

d. Obligations of the Seller and of the Buyer

Article 30

The seller must deliver the goods, hand over any documents relating to them and transfer the property in the goods, as required by the contract and this Convention.

Article 35

(1) The seller must deliver goods which are of the quantity, quality and description required by the contract and which are contained or packaged in the manner required by the contract. [. . .]

Article 39

(1) The buyer loses the right to rely on a lack of conformity of the goods if he does not give notice to the seller specifying the nature of the lack of conformity within a reasonable time after he has discovered it or ought to have discovered it.

(2) In any event, the buyer loses the right to rely on a lack of conformity of the goods if he does not give the seller notice thereof at the latest within a period of two years from the date on which the goods were actually handed over to the buyer, unless this time limit is inconsistent with a contractual period of guarantee.

Article 50

If the goods do not conform with the contract and whether or not the price has already been paid, the buyer may reduce the price in the same proportion as the value that the goods actually delivered had at the time of the delivery bears to the value that conforming goods would have had at that time. However, if the seller remedies any failure to perform his obligations in accordance with article 37 or article 48 or if the buyer refuses to accept performance by the seller in accordance with those articles, the buyer may not reduce the price.

Article 53

The buyer must pay the price for the goods and take delivery of them as required by the contract and this Convention.

Article 55

Where a contract has been validly concluded but does not expressly or implicitly fix or make provision for determining the price, the parties are considered, in the absence of any indication to the contrary, to have impliedly made reference to the price generally charged at the time of the conclusion of the contract for such goods sold under comparable circumstances in the trade concerned.

Article 64

(1) The seller may declare the contract avoided:

(a) if the failure by the buyer to perform any of his obligations under the contract or this Convention amounts to a fundamental breach of contract; or

(b) if the buyer does not, within the additional period of time fixed by the seller in accordance with paragraph (1) of article 63, perform his obligation to pay the price or take delivery of the goods, or if he declares that he will not do so within the period so fixed.

(2) However, in cases where the buyer has paid the price, the seller loses the right to declare the contract avoided unless he does so:

(a) in respect of late performance by the buyer, before the seller has become aware that performance has been rendered; or

(b) in respect of any breach other than late performance by the buyer, within a reasonable time:

(i) after the seller knew or ought to have known of the breach; or

(ii) after the expiration of any additional period of time fixed by the seller in accordance with paragraph (1) of article 63, or after the buyer has declared that he will not perform his obligations within such an additional period

e. Exemptions

Article 79

(1) A party is not liable for a failure to perform any of his obligations if he proves that the failure was due to an impediment beyond his control and that he could not reasonably be expected to have taken the impediment into account at the time of the conclusion of the contract or to have avoided or overcome it, or its consequences.

(2) If the party's failure is due to the failure by a third person whom he has engaged to perform the whole or a part of the contract, that party is exempt from liability only if:

(a) he is exempt under the preceding paragraph; and

(b) the person whom he has so engaged would be so exempt if the provisions of that paragraph were applied to him.

(3) The exemption provided by this article has effect for the period during which the impediment exists.

(4) The party who fails to perform must give notice to the other party of the impediment and its effect on his ability to perform. If the notice is not received by the other party within a reasonable time after the party who fails to perform knew or ought to have known of the impediment, he is liable for damages resulting from such non-receipt.

(5) Nothing in this article prevents either party from exercising any right other than to claim damages under this Convention.

2. Distinguishing Features of the Convention

Some of the unique features of the UN Convention, designed to promote a balanced approach to international sales contracts, are highlighted below.

a. Language

The language used in the Convention represents a compromise from multiple jurisdictions and especially between the common law and civil law traditions. For this reason, traditional common law approaches are not referred to by name, i.e., "consideration" or the doctrine of "frustration". Rather, the concepts are described as intended and not labeled by common law language or indeed the language of any other specific jurisdiction.

b. Parties' Agreement of Usage

Article 9 of the UN Sales Convention abandons the traditional common law approach to usage. This is an attempt to answer criticisms that usage in the common law systems was developed by western countries without the participation of developing states. The Convention emphasizes agreement in the international sphere.

Article 9

(1) The parties are bound by any usage to which they have agreed and by any practices which they have established between themselves.

(2) The parties are considered, unless otherwise agreed, to have impliedly made applicable to their contract or its formation a usage of which the parties knew or ought to have known and which in international trade is widely known to, and regularly observed by, parties to contracts of the type involved in the particular trade concerned.

c. Writing

Some jurisdictions worldwide do not recognize oral contracts. The Convention addresses this in Article 11 by implementing a common law approach but balancing this with the approach taken in non-common law jurisdictions. Article 96 (with reference to Article 12) allows for states to opt out from recognition of non-written agreements.

Article 11

A contract of sale need not be concluded in or evidenced by writing and is not subject to any other requirement as to form. It may be proved by any means, including witnesses.

Article 12

Any provision of article 11, article 29 or Part II of this Convention that allows a contract of sale or its modification or termination by agreement or any offer, acceptance or other indication of intention to be made in any form other than in writing does not apply where any party has his place of business in a Contracting State which has made a declaration under article 96 of this Convention. The parties may not derogate from or vary the effect of this article.

Article 96

A Contracting State whose legislation requires contracts of sale to be concluded in or evidenced by writing may at any time make a declaration in accordance with article 12 that any provision of article 11, article 29, or Part II of this Convention, that allows a contract of sale or its modification or termination by agreement or any offer, acceptance, or other indication of intention to be made in any form other than in writing, does not apply where any party has his place of business in that State.

d. Doctrine of Frustration

The doctrine of frustration is not referred to by name in the UN Sales Convention, but much of the substance under common law is found in Article 79, which deals with the question of the conditions under which a party is exempt from discharge of its contractual obligations. Again, the intention is to create a neutral approach, accommodating the different jurisdictional approaches to this issue.

Section IV. Exemptions
Article 79

(1) A party is not liable for a failure to perform any of his obligations if he proves that the failure was due to an impediment beyond his control and that he could not reasonably be expected to have taken the impediment into account at the time of the conclusion of the contract or to have avoided or overcome it, or its consequences.

(2) If the party's failure is due to the failure by a third person whom he has engaged to perform the whole or a part of the contract, that party is exempt from liability only if:

(a) he is exempt under the preceding paragraph; and

(b) the person whom he has so engaged would be so exempt if the provisions of that paragraph were applied to him.

(3) The exemption provided by this article has effect for the period during which the impediment exists.

(4) The party who fails to perform must give notice to the other party of the impediment and its effect on his ability to perform. If the notice is not received by the other party within a reasonable time after the party who fails to perform knew or ought to have known of the impediment, he is liable for damages resulting from such non-receipt.

(5) Nothing in this article prevents either party from exercising any right other than to claim damages under this Convention.

e. Preservation of Goods

There was much debate during the UNICTRAL process on whether a preservation of goods provision should be included in the Convention. In the end, the Convention introduced the concept that a seller has an obligation to preserve goods even when the buyer is rejecting because the goods do not conform to the order. The policy objective is to prevent unwarranted abandonment of goods, and especially, perishable goods in international trade.

Section VI. Preservation of the Goods

Article 85

If the buyer is in delay in taking delivery of the goods or, where payment of the price and delivery of the goods are to be made concurrently, if he fails to pay the price, and the seller is either in possession of the goods or otherwise able to control their disposition, the seller must take such steps as are reasonable in the circumstances to preserve them. He is entitled to retain them until he has been reimbursed his reasonable expenses by the buyer.

f. Remedies for Breach of Contract by the Seller

There are substantive differences between The Hague Uniform Laws and the UN Sales Convention, with the UN Sales Convention provisions generally less detailed and specific.

Article 46

(1) The buyer may require performance by the seller of his obligations unless the buyer has resorted to a remedy which is inconsistent with this requirement.

(2) If the goods do not conform with the contract, the buyer may require delivery of substitute goods only if the lack of conformity constitutes a fundamental breach of contract and a request for substitute goods is made either in conjunction with notice given under article 39 or within a reasonable time thereafter.

(3) If the goods do not conform with the contract, the buyer may require the seller to remedy the lack of conformity by repair, unless this is unreasonable having regard to all the circumstances. A request for repair must be made either in conjunction with notice given under article 39 or within a reasonable time thereafter.

Article 48

(1) Subject to article 49, the seller may, even after the date for delivery, remedy at his own expense any failure to perform his obligations, if he can do so without unreasonable delay and without causing the buyer unreasonable inconvenience or uncertainty of reimbursement by the seller of expenses advanced by the buyer. However, the buyer retains any right to claim damages as provided for in this Convention.

(2) If the seller requests the buyer to make known whether he will accept performance and the buyer does not comply with the request within a reasonable time, the seller may perform within the time indicated in his request. The buyer may not, during that period of time, resort to any remedy which is inconsistent with performance by the seller.

(3) A notice by the seller that he will perform within a specified period of time is assumed to include a request, under the preceding paragraph, that the buyer make known his decision.

(4) A request or notice by the seller under paragraph (2) or (3) of this article is not effective unless received by the buyer.

Article 49

(1) The buyer may declare the contract avoided:

(a) if the failure by the seller to perform any of his obligations under the contract or this Convention amounts to a fundamental breach of contract; or

(b) in case of non-delivery, if the seller does not deliver the goods within the additional period of time fixed by the buyer in accordance with paragraph (1) of article 47 or declares that he will not deliver within the period so fixed.

(2) However, in cases where the seller has delivered the goods, the buyer loses the right to declare the contract avoided unless he does so:

(a) in respect of late delivery, within a reasonable time after he has become aware that delivery has been made;

(b) in respect of any breach other than late delivery, within a reasonable time:

(i) after he knew or ought to have known of the breach;

(ii) after the expiration of any additional period of time fixed by the buyer in accordance with paragraph (1) of article 47, or after the seller has declared that he will not perform his obligations within such an additional period; or

(iii) after the expiration of any additional period of time indicated by the seller in accordance with paragraph (2) of article 48, or after the buyer has declared that he will not accept performance.

g. Passing of Risk

This is another important area where The Hague Uniform Laws and the UN Sales Convention differ significantly.

Article 66

Loss of or damage to the goods after the risk has passed to the buyer does not discharge him from his obligation to pay the price, unless the loss or damage is due to an act or omission of the seller.

Article 67

(1) If the contract of sale involves carriage of the goods and the seller is not bound to hand them over at a particular place, the risk passes to the buyer when the goods are handed over to the first carrier for transmission to the buyer in accordance with the contract of sale. If the seller is bound to hand the goods over to a carrier at a particular place, the risk does not pass to the buyer until the goods are handed over to the carrier at that place. The fact that the seller is authorized to retain documents controlling the disposition of the goods does not affect the passage of the risk.

(2) Nevertheless, the risk does not pass to the buyer until the goods are clearly identified to the contract, whether by markings on the goods, by shipping documents, by notice given to the buyer or otherwise.

Article 68

The risk in respect of goods sold in transit passes to the buyer from the time of the conclusion of the contract. However, if the circumstances so indicate, the risk is assumed by the buyer from the time the goods were handed over to the carrier who issued the documents embodying the contract of carriage. Nevertheless, if at the time of the conclusion of the contract of sale the seller knew or ought to have known that the goods had been lost or damaged and did not disclose this to the buyer, the loss or damage is at the risk of the seller.

Article 69

(1) In cases not within articles 67 and 68, the risk passes to the buyer when he takes over the goods or, if he does not do so in due time, from the time when the goods are placed at his disposal and he commits a breach of contract by failing to take delivery.

(2) However, if the buyer is bound to take over the goods at a place other than a place of business of the seller, the risk passes when delivery is due and the buyer is aware of the fact that the goods are placed at his disposal at that place.

(3) If the contract relates to goods not then identified, the goods are considered not to be placed at the disposal of the buyer until they are clearly identified to the contract.

The following extract describes why many contacting parties opt to exclude application of the UN Sales Convention (CISG) in favor of English sales law as the applicable law in international commercial transactions.

© Qi Zhou, The CISG and English Sales Law: An Unfair Competition in L.A. DiMatteo (ed), *International Sales Law: A Global Challenge* (Cambridge University Press, 2014). Published with permission of Cambridge University Press.

It has been more than thirty years since the adoption of the United Nations Convention on Contracts for the International Sale of Goods (CISG). It is also widely claimed in academic literature that the CISG is one of the most successful harmonization projects in the field of international commercial law. As of 2012, the CISG has been adopted by seventy-eight countries.[157] It is increasingly being applied both by national courts and by arbitration tribunals.[158] Despite its widespread adoption, there are a number of shortcomings to its claim of success. First, some major trading countries, such as the United Kingdom and India, have not ratified the CISG. Ironically, the United Kingdom played an influential role in drafting the CISG, but subsequently has refused to ratify it as UK law. British politicians and lawyers are worried that ratification of the CISG would undermine the dominant position of English commercial law in international trade.[159] The mainstream scholarly literature has argued that the proliferation of international trade and economic globalization makes a globally uniform contract law or sales law an imperative.

Second, although many states have adopted the CISG, a large number of businesses have opted to exclude the application of the CISG. Oftentimes, they choose English law, instead of the CISG, as applicable law. [. . .] As a result, English Sales Law is a competitor with the CISG as a suitable international sales law.

[. . .] the history of English Sales Law is inherently linked with the development of English commercial law. [. . .] Merchants had their own laws, such as commercial customs, usages, and *lex mercatoria* to govern their commercial transactions; they

157. Jon C. Kleefeld, Rethinking 'Like a lawyer': An Instrumentalist's Proposal for First-Year Curriculum Reform, 53 J. Leg. Ed. 254, 262 (2003).

158. *See*, Larry A. Di Matteo et al., *International Sale Law: A Critical Analysis of CISG Jurisprudence* (Cambridge: Cambridge University Press, 2001); Bruno Zeller, *CISG and the Unification of International Trade Law* (Sydney: Cavendish, 2009); Peter Huber and Alastair Mullis, *CISG: A New Textbook for Students and Practitioners* (Berlin: Sellier European Law Publishers, 2007); *Commentary on the UN Convention on the International Sale of Goods (CISG)*, 3rd ed. (ed. Peter Schlechtriem and Ingeborg Schwenzer) (Oxford: Oxford University Press, 2010).

159. Sally Moss, Why the United Kingdom Has Not Ratified the CISG, 2 J. of L. & Commerce 483, (2005–6); Angele Fort, The United Nations Convention on Contracts for the International Sale of Goods: Reason or Unreason in the United Kingdom, 26 Baltimore. L. Rev. 51 (1997); Nathalie Hofmann, Interpretation Rules and Good Faith as Obstacles to the UK's Ratification of the CISG and to the Harmonisation of Contract Law in Europe, 22 Pace Int'l L. Rev. 141 (2010); Barry Nicholas, The Vienna Convention on Contracts for the International Sale of Goods, 105 L. Quarterly Rev. 201 (1989); Robert G. Lee, The UN Convention on Contracts for the International Sale of Goods: OK for the UK?, J. Bus. L. 131 (1993).

established their own merchant courts to settle disputes arising from their commercial transactions.[160]

Gradually, judges adjusted traditional common law principles to meet the needs of merchants. [. . .] Lord Mansfield consolidated a vast body of case law on commercial disputes relating to sales, agency, bailment, and negotiable instruments. By the time of his retirement, English commercial law was much more advanced than the commercial laws in other countries. Lord Mansfield had laid a solid foundation for the Sale of Goods Act of 1893, enacted almost a century after his retirement. [. . .] critical textual changes were made by the Supply of Goods (Implied Terms) Act 1973, Consumer Credit Act 1974, and the Unfair Contract Terms Act 1977. Subsequently, the Sale of Goods Act 1979 consolidated all of these amendments and replaced the Sale of Goods Act of 1893. After 1979, further changes were made in 1994, 1995, and 2002.[161] [. . .]

The central role played by the city of London in international trade also aided the competitive advantage of English Sales Law. London had been an international trading center from Anglo-Saxon times, having a world reputation for its highly developed speciality markets in commodities, financial transactions, and transport and insurance services.[162] [. . .] The British political, business, and legal communities have recognized this competitive advantage. At a meeting convened by the British government in 2004 to discuss whether the UK should ratify the CISG, the major concern was the impact that the CISG would have on English commercial law's leading position in international trade, as well as London's standing in international arbitration and litigation.[163] Although certain leading academic lawyers argued in favor of the need to harmonize international private law, the majority of legal practitioners and judges did not share this view.[164] [. . .]

160. Frederic Sanborn, Origins of the Early English Maritime and Commercial Law (London: Century Co., 1930); Leon Trakman, The Law Merchant: The Evolution of Commercial Law (New York: Fred B Rothman & Co., 1983).

161. In 1994, the Sale of Goods (Amendment) Act 1994, ss. 1, 3(2) repealed the market over the exception to the *nemo dat* rule; the Sale and Supply of Goods Act 1994 revised the implied term of quality and the rules as to deemed acceptance. In 1995, the Sale of Goods (Amendment) Act 1995 made the prepaying buyer of an individual part of a bulk a co-owner of the bulk. In 2002 the Sale and Supply of Goods to Consumer regulation 2002 implemented the 1999 EC Consumer Sales Directive.

162. Pamela Nightingale, A Medieval Mercantile Community: The Grocers' Company and the Politics and Trade of London (New Haven: Yale University Press, 1995), 1000–483.

163. Sally Moss, Why the United Kingdom Has Not Ratified the CISG, 25 J. L. & Commerce 483, 485 (2005–6); John Hobhouse, International Conventions and Commercial Law: The Pursuit of Uniformity, 106 L. Quarterly Rev. 530 (1990); Roy Goode, Insularity or Leadership?: The Role of the United Kingdom in the Harmonisation of Commercial Law, 50 Int'l & Comp. L.Q. 751 (2001).

164. *See*, House of Lords, European Contract Law: The Draft Common Frame of Reference Report with Evidence (2009), available at http://www.publications.parliament.uk/pa/ld200809/ldselect/ldeucom/95/ 95.pdf.

V. Suggestions for Future Reform

[. . .] if the CISG intends to attract wide adoption by commercial parties, it is imperative that its primary users, international traders, play a leading role in the revision of the CISG. [. . .] The flaw in the drafting of the CISG was a lack of sufficient input from international traders. Consequently, although the CISG has been adopted by many states, international traders have deliberately excluded its application. This is simply because the CISG does not reflect their interests. To solve this problem, more involvement of commercial parties in the future reform of the CISG is necessary. [. . .]

Commercial law possesses a unique feature—by nature, it is private law, meaning the parties have the freedom to decide whether they would like to choose a national sales law or an international commercial law, such as the CISG, to govern their transactions. Generally, much of commercial law, especially sales law, is voluntary in nature (default rules), with few mandatory rules. Framing this problem from an economic perspective, it can be seen that the CISG's targeted audiences was nation states and not commercial traders. As a result, the CISG is widely adopted by states, but less often used in international trade. Therefore, to correct this mistake, the primary users of the CISG, commercial traders, should be invited to play a significant role in the future reform of the CISG.

[. . .] the hard law status of the CISG should be changed. As it stands now, the CISG is an international treaty, making it unable to meet new developments in the commercial world. The hard law status of the CISG undermines its ability to compete with English sales law. Sales law, in nature, is a part of a general law of contract. The non-mandatory nature of sales law, as noted earlier, is reflected in CISG Article 6, which provides that: "The parties may exclude the application of this Convention or subject to article 12, derogate from or vary the effect of any of its provisions."[165]

Helen Kaminski Pty. Ltd. v. Marketing Australia Products Inc., 1997 U.S. Dist. LEXIS 10630 (S.D.N.Y. July 23, 1997), M-47 (DLC) [21].[166]

Case Introduction

An Australian manufacturer of fashion accessories entered into a distribution agreement ("Agreement") with a U.S. distributor. The Agreement specified the terms on which the parties would do business, including methods of payment, delivery and warranties as to quality (article 14(1) CISG). The distributor agreed

165. Article 12 provides that any provision of Article 11, Article 29, or Part II of this Convention that allows a contract of sale or its modification or termination by agreement or any offer, acceptance, or other indication of intention to be made in any form other than in writing does not apply where any party has his place of business in a contracting state that has made a declaration under Article 96 of this CISG. These parties may not derogate from or vary this effect of this article.

166. District Court Case law on UNCITRAL texts (CLOUT) abstract no. 187.

to purchase accessories totaling a specified amount during the year following the conclusion of the Agreement. Soon after entering into the Agreement, the parties amended it to transfer the manufacturer's accessories that were already in the United States to the distributor.

The distributor subsequently ordered additional accessories, and the manufacturer sent notice that the accessories were ready for shipment. The distributor failed, however, to open a letter of credit before shipment as provided in the Agreement. The manufacturer thereupon sent notices to the distributor demanding that the distributor cure its default within a specified time (article 63 CISG). Before the time to cure expired, the distributor filed for bankruptcy in the United States. The bankruptcy court granted the distributor additional time to cure and ruled that the manufacturer was stayed from suing in an Australian court.

On appeal to the Federal District Court, the manufacturer argued that the CISG superseded the U.S. Bankruptcy Code and that, consequently, the bankruptcy court was not authorized to grant the distributor a "period of grace" (article 61(3) CISG). The Federal District Court affirmed the bankruptcy court's order, holding that the Agreement did not fall within the ambit of the CISG, because the Agreement did not cover the subsequently-ordered accessories. Although the Agreement had been amended to cover some specified goods, the amended Agreement did not refer specifically to the accessories in dispute.

Principal Points of the Judgment

Denis Cote, District Judge:

Appellant Helen Kaminski Pty. Ltd. ("Helen Kaminski") moves for leave to appeal an interlocutory order issued by the Bankruptcy Court for the Southern District of New York on March 3, 1997. Appellee Marketing Australian Products ("MAP") opposes this motion. For the reasons set forth below, the motion is denied.

Discussion

Although Helen Kaminski presents four issues it wishes to appeal, this Court will reformulate these questions into the questions it believes are presented in Helen Kaminiski's papers. Those questions are (1) whether the CISG applies to the Distributor Agreement, and if so, does the CISG supersede inconsistent provisions in the Bankruptcy Code, such that the bankruptcy court erred in giving MAP additional time to cure its default, and (2) if the CISG does not apply, whether the bankruptcy court erred in giving extra territorial effect to Section 362. I will discuss each issue in turn to ascertain whether either of these questions should be appealed on an interlocutory basis.

A. The CISG and the Distributor Agreement

The CISG is an international agreement that applies to sales of goods between parties in signatory nations, unless the parties expressly contract to be bound by another source of law. *Delchi Carrier SpA v. Rotorex Corp.*, 71 F.3d 1024, 1027-28 n.1 (2d Cir. 1995). There is no dispute that both the United States and Australia are signatories to the CISG.

If the CISG applies to the Distributor Agreement, as soon as MAP was in fundamental breach of the contract—and there does not appear to be a dispute that the failure to produce letters of credit was a fundamental breach—Helen Kaminski could declare the contract void and after it started an action for a breach of the contract, no court could extend MAP's time to cure the defect. CISG, Article 61(3), reprinted in 15 U.S.C. Appendix.

Thus, the dispositive issue is whether the CISG applies to the Distributor Agreement. Helen Kaminski maintains that it does, since the agreement, in addition to laying out the terms for the parties' commercial relationship, also governed the disposition of identified goods. Although it does not say so explicitly, it appears that Helen Kaminski is referring to the amendment in February 1996 which addressed specified goods already in the United States. MAP maintains that the Distributor Agreement is merely a "framework agreement" and that such agreements are not covered by the CISG. The Distributor Agreement requires MAP to purchase a minimum quantity of total goods, but does not identify the goods to be sold by type, date or price. In contrast, the CISG requires an enforceable contract to have definite terms regarding quantity and price.

While both sides cite various secondary sources, there appears to be no judicial authority determining the reach of the CISG and, in particular, whether it applies to distributor agreements. The parties do agree, however, that whether or not the CISG applies turns on whether the Distributor Agreement can be characterized as a contract for the sale of goods—that is, that it contained definite terms for specified goods. In this respect, the only contract for a specified set of goods to which Helen Kaminski points is the February 1996 amendment. As MAP correctly notes, however, these goods were not the subject of the breach. Rather, Helen Kaminski is claiming a breach for goods ordered but not shipped. Helen Kaminski makes no claim that these goods were identified in the Distributor Agreement.

For this reason, although I find that there is little to no case law on the CISG in general, and none determining whether a distributor agreement falls within the ambit of the CISG, Helen Kaminski's rationale for why the CISG applies to the debate about the breach for goods ordered but not shipped is not supported by the facts of the case. The identification in the Distributor Agreement of certain goods—about which there is no claim of breach—is insufficient to bring the Distributor Agreement within coverage of the CISG when the dispute concerns goods not specifically identified in the Distributor Agreement. Thus, while the question does present a controlling issue of law over which there may be substantial disagreement, it does not appear that a determination of the issue would materially advance the litigation as Helen Kaminski does not maintain that the general Distributor Agreement—absent the February amendment which does not concern the goods at issue—is definite enough to constitute a contract for the sale of goods.

B. Extra-territorial Effect of Section 362

Helen Kaminski cites no authority for its contention that Section 362 of the Bankruptcy Code should not have extra-territorial effect, other than an argument that such a stay is superseded by the CISG. Since I have held that, in the circumstances of this case at least, the CISG does not apply, I need not reach this second issue. I note, however, that it is a general principle that all claims against a debtor should be handled in a single proceeding to insure equitable and orderly distribution of debtor's property. *Allstate Life Insurance v. Linter Group Ltd.*, 994 F.2d 996 (2d Cir. 1993) (comity supported stay of U.S. litigation in favor of Australian bankruptcy proceeding); *Victrix Steamship Co., S.A. v. Salen Dry Cargo A.B.*, 825 F.2d 709 (2d Cir. 1987).

Conclusion

For the reasons given above, it is hereby

ORDERED that Helen Kaminski's motion for leave to appeal the March 3rd Order of the Bankruptcy Court is denied.

Mitchell Aircraft Spares, Inc. v. European Aircraft Service, 23 F. Supp. 2d 915 (N.D. Ill. 1998).

Case Introduction

A U.S. broker in the market for surplus commercial aircraft parts ("Plaintiff"), purchased three integrated drive generators from a Swedish dealer in aircraft parts ("Defendant"). There was a dispute between the parties as to whether the seller had in fact represented that the units were part number 729640. The two parties disputed the substance of the communications between them during negotiations. The buyer brought a legal action to recover damages for breach of the alleged representation. Each party moved for summary judgment.

The issue before the court was whether either the seller or the buyer was entitled to summary judgment in an action brought by the buyer to recover damages for breach of a sales contract.

Although the court confirmed its earlier order that the CISG applied generally to the contract between the parties, the court modified its order to apply Illinois state law to contract formation issues, because Sweden had declared that it was not a party to Part II of the CISG. Relying, nevertheless, on article 8(3) CISG, the court considered evidence of statements made during negotiations when determining whether there was a material dispute as to the terms of the contract.

The court concluded that there were unresolved issues of material fact that precluded it from granting either of the motions for summary judgment.

Memorandum Opinion and Order

James H. Alesia, District Judge

Before the court are the parties' cross-motions for summary judgment. For the following reasons, the court denies both motions.[167]

A. Choice-of-law issues and the court's subject matter jurisdiction

Before addressing the merits of the parties' motions, the court must address the issues raised with regard to choice-of-law and subject matter jurisdiction. After an initial review of this case, the court determined that it had diversity jurisdiction because the case is between a citizen of Illinois and a citizen of Sweden and the amount in controversy exceeds $75,000. 28 U S.C. § 1332(a)(2). Because it was a diversity case, [Seller] moved the court to determine whether the substantive law of Sweden, Illinois, or the CISG governed this contract dispute. [Seller] argued that the CISG governed. [Buyer] did not oppose the motion and did not argue that the CISG did not govern. Thus, the court determined that the CISG governed.

The parties then submitted their motions for summary judgment, in which each party raised an issue not raised in the parties' briefs regarding the choice-of-law determination. [Seller] argued for the first time that the court's subject matter jurisdiction is actually not based on diversity but is based on a federal question because the case arises under the CISG, a convention of the United States. See 28 U.S.C. § 1331. [Buyer] argued for the first time that issues of contract formation are governed by Illinois law because Sweden opted out of Part II of the CISG, which is the part that governs contract formation.

First, the court will address its basis for subject matter jurisdiction. As previously explained, it is clear that this court has subject matter jurisdiction over this case pursuant to 28 U.S.C. § 1332. Thus, this court has jurisdiction over the case regardless of whether the CISG provides an independent basis for subject matter jurisdiction. The court's opinion would not change in any way if it found that its jurisdiction were based on the CISG. Thus, the court need not reach the issue of whether the CISG provides an independent basis for subject matter jurisdiction.

Next, the court addresses the choice-of-law issues presented in this case. As previously discussed, the CISG governs most of the issues in this case because the United States, where [Buyer] has its place of business, and Sweden, where [Seller] has its place of business, are both States party to the CISG. CISG art. 1. As the parties agree, the CISG does not govern issues which are addressed in Part II (Formation of the Contract) of the CISG because Sweden declared in its instrument of ratification that it would not be bound by Part II. CISG Parties to the Convention n.16. Rather, as the parties also agreed, Illinois law governs the contract formation issues in this case.[168]

---

167. Unless otherwise indicated, the following facts are undisputed facts taken from the parties' Rule 12(M) and Rule 12(N) statements.

168. In the event that this court's subject matter jurisdiction is based on a federal question and not diversity, it is not clear that Illinois law would be the governing law. However, as the outcome of this opinion does not depend on whether Illinois law applies, the court need not address this issue.

B. Standard for deciding a motion for summary judgment

A motion for summary judgment is proper "if the pleadings, depositions, answers to interrogatories, and admissions on file, together with the affidavits, if any, show that there is no genuine issue as to any material fact and that the moving party is entitled to a judgment as a matter of law." Fed. R. Civ. P.56(c). A genuine issue of material fact exists for trial when, in viewing the record and all reasonable inferences drawn therefrom in a light most favorable to the non-moving party, a reasonable jury could return a verdict for the non-movant. *Anderson v. Liberty Lobby, Inc.*, 477 US. 242, 248, 91 L. Ed. 2d 202, 106 S. Ct. 2505 (1986); *Hedberg v. Indiana Bell Tel. Co.*, 47 F.3d 928, 931 (7th Cir. 1995).

The burden is on the moving party to show that no genuine issues of material fact exist. *Anderson*, 477 US. at 256; *Celotex Corp. v. Catrett*, 477 US. 317, 322, 91 L. Ed. 2d 265, 106 S. Ct. 2548 (1986). Once the moving party presents a prima facie showing that he is entitled to judgment as a matter of law, the non-moving party may not rest upon the mere allegations or denials in its pleadings but must set forth specific facts showing that a genuine issue for trial exists. *Anderson*, 477 US. at 256-57; *Celotex*, 477 US. at 324; *Schroeder v. Lufthansa German Airlines*, 875 F.2d 613, 620 (7th Cir. 1989).

C. [Buyer's] breach-of-contract claim

Both parties argue that they are entitled to summary judgment on [Buyer's] breach-of-contract claim. [Buyer] argues that the parties contracted for [Seller] to sell [Buyer] three IDGs part number 729640 and that [Seller] breached the contract when it sold [Buyer] IDGs which were not part number 729640. [Seller] argues that the parties contracted for [Seller] to sell [Buyer] the three IDGs that [Seller] had available for sale and not for [Seller] to sell IDGs part number 729640. [Seller] further argues that [Buyer] assumed the risk that the IDGs would not be part number 729640 and that [Buyer's] decision to purchase the IDGs was the direct result of [Buyer's] unilateral mistake in interpreting the information that [Seller] provided.

Under the CISG, "the seller must deliver goods which are of the quantity, quality and description required by the contract." CISG art. 35. The seller is liable in accordance with the contract and this Convention for any lack of conformity. CISG art. 36. Therefore, the issue is what specific goods the parties contracted for [Seller] to sell [Buyer].

1. Parol evidence and the CISG

Before analyzing the evidence submitted by the parties, the court must determine whether it can consider parol evidence in deciding the parties' dispute. [Buyer] argues that the court cannot because the contract, i.e., the purchase order, is clear and unambiguous. [Seller] argues that the court can because the contract is patently ambiguous. Neither [Buyer] nor [Seller] addressed whether parol evidence is admissible under the relevant provisions of the CISG.

This court was unable to find any case from the Seventh Circuit or a district court in the Seventh Circuit which has addressed the issue of whether a court can consider parol evidence in a contract dispute governed by the CISG. This is not surprising because "there is virtually no case law under the Convention." *Delchi Carrier SpA v. Rotorex Corp.*, 71 F.3d 1024, 1028 (2d Cir. 1995). Thus, the issue of whether the court can consider parol evidence in a contract dispute governed by the CISG is an issue of first impression for this court.

The Eleventh Circuit addressed this issue in its highly persuasive opinion in the case of *MCC-Marble Ceramic Center, Inc. v. Ceramica Nuova D'Agostino*, 144 F.3d 1384, 1389-90 (11th Cir. 1998). Because this court agrees with the holding and reasoning of *MCC-Marble* on this issue, the court will provide a detailed account of the MCC-Marble opinion.

In *MCC-Marble*, the plaintiff was suing the defendant for breach of contract. *Id.* at 1385. The CISG governed the breach-of-contract dispute. *Id.* at 1385. In addition to other defenses, the defendant relied on certain provisions contained in the pre-printed contract, which the defendant had prepared and the plaintiff had executed. *Id.* The plaintiff argued that the parties never intended for the provisions to apply to their agreements. *Id.* at 1386. In support of its argument, the plaintiff submitted an affidavit from the individual who signed the forms on the plaintiff's behalf. *Id.* The affiant stated that the plaintiff had no intent to be bound by the terms of the pre-printed forms and that the defendant was aware of that intent. *Id.* Applying the parol evidence rule and thus ignoring the evidence contained in the plaintiff's agent's affidavit, the district court granted summary judgment in favor of the defendant. *Id.* 1387.

The Eleventh Circuit reversed the district court. *Id.* at 1393. Addressing the parol evidence issue, the court first analyzed article 8 of the CISG. Article 8(1) provides: "For the purposes of this Convention statements made by and other conduct of a party are to be interpreted according to his intent where the other party knew or could not have been unaware what that intent was." The court read article 8(1) as requiring the court "to consider evidence of a party's subjective intent when signing a contract if the other party to the contract was aware of that intent at the time." *Id.* at 1388. The court also noted that article 8(3) "expressly directs courts to give 'due consideration . . . to all relevant circumstances of the case including the negotiations . . .' to determine the intent of the parties." *Id.* at 1389.

Having determined that much, the court then was forced to address the issue of "whether the parol evidence rule, which bars evidence of an earlier oral contract that contradicts or varies the terms of a subsequent or contemporaneous written contract, plays any role in cases involving the CISG." *Id.* Observing that the CISG contains no express statement on the role of parol evidence, the court stated: "It is clear, however, that the drafters of the CISG were comfortable with the concept of permitting parties to rely on oral contracts because they eschewed any statutes of fraud provision and expressly provided for the enforcement of oral contracts." *Id.* (citing article 11 of the CISG). The court then concluded: "Given article 8(1)'s directive to use the intent of the parties to interpret their statements and conduct, article 8(3) is a clear instruction to admit and consider parol evidence regarding the negotiations to the extent they reveal the parties' subjective intent." *Id.* The court thus held that CISG rejects the parol evidence rule and clearly instructs the court to admit and consider probative parol evidence regarding the parties' negotiations inasmuch as that evidence reveals the subjective intent of the parties. *Id.*

This court agrees with the Eleventh Circuit that article 8 of the CISG requires the court to consider parol evidence inasmuch as that evidence is probative of the subject intent of the parties. This conclusion is in accord with the great weight of persuasive authority on the issue. See *MCC-Marble*, 144 F.3d at 1390 and n.17 (citations omitted); *Claudi v. Olivieri Footwear Ltd.*, No. 96 Civ. 8052, 1998 WL 164824, at *5-6 (S.D.N.Y. Apr. 1, 1998) (stating that "contracts governed by the CISG are freed from the limits of the parol evidence rule and there is a wider spectrum of admissible evidence to consider in construing the terms of the parties' agreement"); see also *Filanto v. Chilewich Int'l Corp.*, 789 F. Supp. 1229, 1238, n.7 (S.D.N.Y. 1992).[169] Accordingly, the court finds that it must consider any evidence concerning any negotiations, agreements, or statements made prior to the issuance of the purchase order in this case in determining whether the parties contracted for [Seller] to sell [Buyer] three IDGs part number 729640 or, alternatively, to sell [Buyer] the three IDGs that [Seller] had available for purchase.

One might argue that Illinois law, not the CISG, governs the parol evidence issue in this case because the parol evidence rule is a rule of contract formation and, as discussed above, Illinois law governs contract formation issues in this case. *Mohr v. Metro East Mfg. Co.*, 711 F.2d 69, 71 (7th Cir. 1983). However, the issue of parol evidence is addressed in article 8 of the CISG, which is in Part I of the CISG. CISG art. 8. Neither Sweden nor the United States declared that it would not be bound by Part I of the CISG. See CISG Parties to the Convention nn.l6 and 19. Thus, the court finds that the CISG, not Illinois law, governs the parol evidence issue in this contract dispute.

Assuming that Illinois law would govern the parol evidence issue, however, parol evidence would still be admissible in this case. In Illinois, parol evidence is admissible when the contract is ambiguous. *Foxfield Realty Inc. v. Kubala*, 287 Ill. App. 3d 5l9, 678 N.E.2d 1060, 1063, 223 Ill. Dec. 52 (Ill. App. Ct. 1997). Whether an ambiguity exists is a question of law for the court to decide. *Id.* (citing *Hammel v. Ruby*, 139 Ill. App. 3d 241, 487 N.E.2d 409, 93 Ill. Dec.742 (1985)).

---

169. In *Beijing Metals & Minerals Import/Export Corp. v. American Bus. Ctr.*, 993 F.2d 1178 (5th Cir. 1993), the Fifth Circuit reached an opposite conclusion. However, the court did not conduct any analysis of the CISG to support its conclusion. Thus, the court finds that the *Beijing Metals* opinion is not persuasive on this issue. See *MCC-Marble*, 144 F.3d at 1389-90 (stating that the *Beijing Metals* opinion was "not particularly persuasive").

In this case, the purchase order is ambiguous. Although the purchase order describes the goods as IDGs part number 729640, it also states that the UNITS ARE TO BE AS DESCRIBED IN TELEFAX OF JUL 3." The July 3 fax never describes the IDGs as part number 729640; rather, the fax gives the part numbers for the generators and transmissions. [Seller] has submitted evidence that the part numbers given for the transmissions and the generators could never go together to form an IDG part number 729640. Therefore, the contract is ambiguous as to whether the parties contracted for [Seller] to sell [Buyer] IDG's part number 729640 or the three IDGs with the generator and transmission parts described in the July 3 fax, which were not IDG's part number 729640. Because the contract contains such an ambiguity, Illinois law allows the court to consider parol evidence in interpreting the contract.

2. The evidence in this case

Having determined that the CISG requires the court to consider the contract along with any evidence concerning any negotiations, agreements, or statements made prior to the issuance of the purchase order in this case, the court must now determine whether there is a genuine issue of fact as to whether the parties contracted for [Seller] to sell [Buyer] three IDGs part number 729640 or, alternatively, to sell [Buyer] the three IDGs that [Seller] had available for purchase. The court finds that there is.

On the one hand, there is evidence that the parties contracted for [Seller] to sell [Buyer] IDGs part number 729640. First the purchase order, invoice, and material certification all state that [Seller] is selling [Buyer] three IDGs part number 729640. Second, there is evidence that the information contained in the July 3 fax indicated that the part number of the IDGs was 729640. Finally, there is Fletcher's testimony that (1) the parts were listed on the ILD as three number 729640 IDGs; (2) at the time that the July 3 fax was sent, both [Seller] and [Buyer] knew that [Buyer] was only interested in purchasing IDGs with part number 729640; and (3) Fletcher asked Hedberg if [Seller] had any IDGs part number 729640 and Hedberg responded "Yes."

On the other hand, there is evidence that the parties contracted for [Seller] to sell the IDGs it had available for purchase, which were not part number 729640. First, the July 3 fax never identified the IDGs as part number 729640; rather, it simply listed the part numbers of the transmissions and the generators which went together to form the IDG. Second, the purchase order states that it is for the units described in the July 3 fax, which are the units [Seller] had available for purchase. Finally, there is Hedberg's testimony that (1) the parts were listed on the ILD with two or three alternative part numbers and not just part number 729640; (2) he and Fletcher did not discuss the part number of the IDGs in that first conversation; (3) he relied on Fletcher's expertise in IDGs in the negotiations; (4) he told Fletcher that [Seller] could not determine the exact part number of the IDGs available for sale and "made it clear" to Fletcher that he did not have the information necessary to determine whether the part number of the IDGs was 729640; (5) Fletcher requested information about the IDGs "to try to confirm" the part number of the units that [Seller] wished to sell and that [Buyer] wished to buy; (6) Hedberg sent Fletcher the July 3 fax "so that [Buyer] might make a determination" of the part number of the IDGs; and (7) Fletcher decided to buy the IDGs available after determining for himself that the IDGs were part number 729640.

Based on the above evidence, the court finds that there is a genuine issue of material fact which precludes summary judgment. There is evidence that the parties contracted for [Seller] to sell IDGs part number 729640. There is also evidence that the parties contracted for [Seller] to sell [Buyer] the IDGs that [Seller] had available for purchase. Accordingly, neither party is entitled to summary judgment on this issue.

[Seller] also argues that it is entitled to summary judgment because [Buyer] assumed the risk that the IDGs were not part number 729640 and made a unilateral mistake in determining that the IDGs were part number 729640. There is a genuine issue of fact, however, as to whether [Buyer] assumed the risk and whether the mistake was unilateral or bilateral.

As a preliminary matter, the court notes that these issues are moot if the parties contracted for [Seller] to sell [Buyer] the IDGs that [Seller] had available for purchase. If that is all that the parties agreed on, then the goods which [Seller] sent to [Buyer] would not be non-conforming and [Seller] would not be liable for breach of contract. Thus, these issues as to the assumption of risk and mistake are only issues if the parties contracted for [Seller] to sell [Buyer] IDGs part number 729640.

As to the assumption of risk issue, however, there is a genuine issue of fact as to whether [Buyer] assumed the risk. On the one hand, [Seller] submitted evidence that (1) the parts were listed on the ILD as three number 729640 IDGs; (2) Fletcher asked Hedberg if [Seller] had any IDGs part number 729640 and Hedberg responded "Yes"; and (3) one could tell from an external examination whether the IDGs were part number 729640 or 708524. This evidence would tend to show that [Buyer] did not assume the risk. On the other hand, there is evidence that (1) Hedberg relied on the information Fletcher's determination that the IDGs were part number 729640; and (2) Fletcher knew that Hedberg/[Seller] did not and could not determine the IDGs part number. This evidence tends to show that [Buyer] did assume the risk. Accordingly, neither party is entitled to summary judgment on this issue.

As to the mistake issue, there is also a genuine issue of fact as to whether the mistake was bilateral or unilateral. On the one hand, there is evidence that (1) Fletcher determined that the IDGs were part number 729640; (2) Fletcher knew that [Seller] could not determine what part number the IDGs were; and (3) the parties agreed that Fletcher would evaluate the information and then determine if he wanted the IDGs. This evidence would tend to show that the mistake was unilateral. On the other hand, there is evidence that (1) the parts were listed on the ILD as three number 729640 IDGs; and (2) Fletcher asked Hedberg if [Seller] had any IDGs part number 729640 and Hedberg responded "Yes." This evidence would tend to show that the mistake was bilateral. Therefore, neither party is entitled to summary judgment on this issue.

D. [Buyer's] breach of warranty claim

Both parties also argue that they are entitled to summary judgment on [Buyer's] breach of warranty claim. Their arguments mirror their arguments with respect to [Buyer's] breach of contract claim. [Buyer] argues that [Seller] breach[ed] its warranty to sell [Buyer] IDG's part number 729640. [Seller] argues that there was no warranty to sell [Buyer] IDGs part number 729640.

As with the breach of contract claim, the court finds that there is a genuine issue of fact as to whether [Seller] promised to sell [Buyer] IDGs part number 729640. See *supra* Part II.A.2. Accordingly, neither party is entitled to summary judgment on [Buyer's] breach of warranty claim.

E. [Buyer's] claim for damages

Both parties also move for summary judgment on the issue of damages. [Buyer] argues that it is entitled to a judgment of $120,000. [Seller] argues that [Buyer] is entitled to nothing.

The court need not reach the issue of damages at this stage of the litigation. As previously discussed, there is a genuine issue of fact as to liability. Accordingly, the issue of damages is premature.

Conclusion

In sum, there are several genuine issues of material fact which preclude summary judgment in this case. Accordingly, the court denies both parties' motions for summary judgment.

In the following case, the court considers oral evidence in a contract dispute governed by the United Nations Convention on Contracts for the International Sale of Goods ("CISG").

MCC-Marble Ceramic Center, Inc. v. Ceramica Nuova D'Agostino, S.P.A., 144 F.3d 1384 (11th Cir. 1998), cert. denied, 526 U.S. 1087 (1999).

Case Introduction

The plaintiff-appellant, MCC-Marble Ceramic, Inc. ("MCC"), is a Florida corporation engaged in the retail sale of tiles, and the defendant-appellee, CeramicaNuova d'Agostino S.p.A. ("D'Agostino"), is an Italian corporation engaged in the manufacture of ceramic tiles.

In October 1990, MCC's president, Juan Carlos Monzon, met representatives of D'Agostino at a trade fair in Bologna, Italy and negotiated an agreement to purchase ceramic tiles from D'Agostino based on samples he examined at the trade fair. Monzon, who spoke no Italian, communicated with Gianni Silingardi, then D'Agostino's commercial director, through a translator, Gianfranco Copelli, who was himself an agent of D'Agostino. The parties apparently arrived at an oral agreement on the crucial terms of price, quality, quantity, delivery and payment. The parties then recorded these terms on one of D'Agostino's standard, preprinted order forms, and Monzon signed the contract on MCC's behalf.

According to MCC, the parties also entered into a related but separate "requirements" contract in February 1991. D'Agostino thereby agreed to supply MCC with high-grade ceramic tile at specific discounts so long as MCC continued to purchase sufficient quantities of tile. MCC completed a number of additional order forms which thus requested tile deliveries pursuant to the discount agreement. Then this commercial dispute erupted. MCC brought suit against D'Agostino in a U.S. federal court, claiming that the defendant manufacturer breached the 1991 requirements discount contract by failing to fill orders that MCC placed in April, May, and August 1991.

Principal Points of the Judgment

[. . .] The parties to this case agree that the CISG governs their dispute because the United States, where MCC has its place of business, and Italy, where D'Agostino has its place of business, are both States Party to the Convention. Article 8 of the CISG governs the interpretation of international contracts for the sale of goods and forms the basis of MCC's appeal from the district court's grant of summary judgment in D'Agostino's favor.[170] MCC argues that the magistrate judge and the district court improperly ignored evidence that MCC submitted regarding the parties' subjective intent when they memorialized the terms of their agreement on D'Agostino's preprinted form contract, and that the magistrate judge erred by applying the parol evidence rule in derogation of the CISG.

I. Subjective Intent Under the CISG

Contrary to what is familiar practice in United States courts, the CISG appears to permit a substantial inquiry into the parties' subjective intent, even if the parties did not engage in any objectively ascertainable means of registering this intent.[171] Article 8(1) of the CISG instructs courts to interpret the "statements . . . and other

170. Article 8 provides: (1) For the purposes of this Convention statements made by and other conduct of a party are to be interpreted according to his intent where the other party knew or could not have been unaware what that intent was [thus allowing oral evidence which might be contrary to the terms in a written contract].

171. In the United States, the legislatures, courts, and the legal academy have voiced a preference for relying on objective manifestations of the parties' intentions. For example, Article Two of the Uniform Commercial Code, which most states have enacted in some form or another to govern contracts for the sale of goods, is replete with references to standards of commercial reasonableness. See e.g., U.C.C. § 2-206 (referring to reasonable means of accepting an offer); . . . Justice Holmes expressed the philosophy behind this focus on the objective in forceful terms: "The law has nothing to do with the actual state of the parties' minds. In contract, as elsewhere, it must go by externals, and [the law will] judge parties by their conduct." Oliver W. Holmes, "The Common Law" 242 (Howe ed.1963) quoted in John O. Honnold, Uniform Law for International Sales Under the 1980 United Nations Convention § 107 at 164 (2d ed.1991) (hereinafter Hannold, Uniform Law.)

conduct of a party . . . according to his intent" as long as the other party "knew or could not have been unaware" of that intent. The plain language of the Convention, therefore, requires an inquiry into a party's subjective intent as long as the other party to the contract was aware [or should have been aware] of that intent.

In this case, MCC has submitted three affidavits that discuss the purported subjective intent of the parties to the initial agreement concluded between MCC and D'Agostino in October 1990. All three affidavits discuss the preliminary negotiations and report that the parties arrived at an oral agreement for D'Agostino to supply quantities of a specific grade of ceramic tile to MCC at an agreed upon price. The affidavits state that the "oral agreement established the essential terms of quality, quantity, description of goods, delivery, price and payment." The affidavits also note that the parties memorialized the terms of their oral agreement on a standard D'Agostino order form, but all three affiants contend that the parties subjectively intended not to be bound by the terms on the reverse of that form despite a provision directly below the signature line that expressly and specifically incorporated those terms.

The terms on the reverse of the contract give D'Agostino the right to suspend or cancel all contracts in the event of a buyer's non-payment and require a buyer to make a written report of all defects within ten days. As the magistrate judge's report and recommendation makes clear, if these terms applied to the agreements between MCC and D'Agostino, summary judgment [on the law, which precludes the plaintiff's case from going to trial for the resolution of factual issues] would be appropriate because MCC failed to make any written complaints about the quality of tile it received and D'Agostino has established MCC's non-payment of a number of invoices amounting to $108,389.40 and 102,053,846.00 Italian lira.

Article 8(1) of the CISG requires a court to consider this evidence of the parties' subjective intent. Contrary to the magistrate judge's report, which the district court endorsed and adopted, article 8(1) does not focus on interpreting the parties' statements alone. Although we agree with the magistrate judge's conclusion that no "interpretation" of the contract's terms could support MCC's position, article 8(1) also requires a court to consider subjective intent while interpreting the conduct of the parties. The CISG's language, therefore, requires courts to consider evidence of a party's subjective intent when signing a contract if the other party to the contract was aware of that intent at the time. This is precisely the type of evidence that MCC has provided through the Silingardi, Copelli, and Monzon affidavits, which discuss not only Monzon's intent as MCC's representative but also discuss the intent of D'Agostino's representatives and their knowledge that Monzon did not intend to agree to the terms on the reverse of the form contract. [The defendant described them as disgruntled employees.] This acknowledgment that D'Agostino's representatives were aware of Monzon's subjective intent puts this case squarely within article 8(1) of the CISG, and therefore requires the court to consider MCC's evidence as it interprets the parties' conduct.

II. Parol Evidence and the CISG

Given our determination that the magistrate judge and the district court should have considered MCC's affidavits regarding the parties' subjective intentions, we must address a question of first impression in this circuit: [W]hether the parol evidence rule, which bars evidence of an earlier oral contract that contradicts or varies the terms of a subsequent or contemporaneous written contract,[172] plays any role in cases involving the CISG.

The CISG itself contains no express statement on the role of parol evidence. It is clear, however, that the drafters of the CISG were comfortable with the concept of permitting parties to rely on oral contracts because they eschewed any statutes of fraud provision and expressly provided for the enforcement of oral contracts. Compare CISG, art. 11 (a contract of sale need not be concluded or evidenced in writing) with U.C.C. § 2-201 (precluding the enforcement of oral contracts for the sale of goods involving more than $500). Moreover, article 8(3) of the CISG expressly directs courts to give "due consideration [. . .] to all relevant circumstances of the case including the negotiations [. . .]" to determine the intent of the parties. Given article 8(1)'s directive to use the intent of the parties to interpret their statements and conduct, article 8(3) is a clear instruction to admit and consider parol evidence regarding the negotiations to the extent they reveal the parties' subjective intent.

Despite the CISG's broad scope, surprisingly few cases have applied the Convention in the United States, see *Delchi Carrier SpA v. Rotorex Corp.*, 71 F.3d 1024, 1027-28 (2d Cir.1995) (observing that "there is virtually no case law under the Convention"), and only two reported decisions touch upon the parol evidence rule, both in dicta.

Our reading of article 8(3) as a rejection of the parol evidence rule [which prohibits proof of an oral agreement which varies a term in the parties' written contract] is in accordance with the great weight of academic commentary on the issue. As one scholar has explained:

> [T]he language of Article 8(3) that due consideration is to be given to all relevant circumstances of the case seems adequate to override any domestic rule that would bar a tribunal from considering the relevance of other agreements. [. . .] Article 8(3) relieves tribunals from domestic rules that might bar them from "considering" any evidence between the parties that is relevant. This added flexibility for interpretation is consistent with a growing body of opinion that the "parol evidence rule" has been an embarrassment for the administration of modern transactions. Honnold, Uniform Law § 110 at 170-71[. . .]

[A]lthough jurisdictions in the United States have found the parol evidence rule helpful to promote good faith and uniformity in contract, as well as an appropriate answer to the question of how much consideration to give parol evidence, a wide

---

172. The Uniform Commercial Code includes a version of the parol evidence rule applicable to contracts for the sale of goods in most states. U.C.C. § 2-202.

number of other [foreign] States Party to the CISG have rejected the rule in their domestic jurisdictions. One of the primary factors motivating the negotiation and adoption of the CISG was to provide parties to international contracts for the sale of goods with some degree of certainty as to the principles of law that would govern potential disputes and remove the previous doubt regarding which party's legal system might otherwise apply. [. . .] Courts applying the CISG cannot, therefore, [unwittingly] upset the parties' reliance on the Convention by substituting familiar principles of domestic law when the Convention requires a different result. We may only achieve the directives of good faith and uniformity in contracts under the CISG by interpreting and applying the plain language of article 8(3) as written and obeying its directive to consider this type of parol evidence.

This is not to say that parties to an international contract for the sale of goods cannot depend on written contracts or that parol evidence regarding subjective contractual intent need always prevent a party relying on a written agreement from securing summary judgment. To the contrary, most cases will not present a situation (as exists in this case) in which both parties to the contract acknowledge a subjective intent not to be bound by the terms of a pre-printed writing. In most cases, therefore, article 8(2) of the CISG will apply, and objective evidence will provide the basis for the court's decision. Consequently, a party to a contract governed by the CISG will not be able to avoid the terms of a contract simply by submitting an affidavit which states that he or she did not have the subjective intent to be bound by the contract's terms. Moreover, to the extent parties wish to avoid parol evidence problems they can do so by including a merger clause in their agreement that extinguishes any and all prior agreements and understandings not expressed in the writing.

Considering MCC's affidavits in this case, however, we conclude that the magistrate judge and the district court improperly granted summary judgment in favor of D'Agostino. Although the affidavits are, as D'Agostino observes, relatively conclusory and unsupported by facts that would objectively establish MCC's intent not to be bound by the conditions on the reverse of the form, article 8(1) requires a court to consider evidence of a party's subjective intent when the other party was aware of it, and the Silingardi and Copelli affidavits provide that evidence. This is not to say that the affidavits are conclusive proof of what the parties intended. A reasonable finder of fact, for example [at trial], could disregard testimony that purportedly sophisticated international merchants signed a contract without intending to be bound as simply too incredible to believe and hold MCC to the conditions printed on the reverse of the contract.[173] Nevertheless, the affidavits raise an issue of

173. D'Agostino attempts to explain and undermine the affidavit of its representatives during the transaction, by calling Silingardi a disgruntled former employee. Appellee's Br. at 11, 39. Silingardi's alleged feelings towards his former employer may indeed be relevant to undermine the credibility of his assertions, but that is a matter for the finder of fact, not for this court on summary judgment.

material fact regarding the parties' [arguable] intent to incorporate the provisions on the reverse of the form contract. If the finder of fact determines that the parties did not intend to rely on those provisions, then the more general provisions of the CISG will govern the outcome of the dispute. [. . .]

Conclusion

MCC asks us to reverse the district court's grant of summary judgment in favor of D'Agostino. The district court's decision rests on pre-printed contractual terms and conditions incorporated on the reverse of a standard order form that MCC's president signed on the company's behalf. Nevertheless, we conclude that the CISG, which governs international contracts for the sale of goods, precludes summary judgment in this case because MCC has raised an issue of material fact concerning the parties' subjective intent to be bound by the terms on the reverse of the pre-printed contract. The CISG also precludes the application of the parol evidence rule, which would otherwise bar the consideration of evidence concerning a prior or contemporaneously negotiated oral agreement.

Accordingly, we REVERSE the district court's grant of summary judgment and REMAND this case for further proceedings consistent with this opinion.

D. United Nations Convention on the Limitation Period in the International Sale of Goods (UNCITRAL Limitation Convention) (1990)

The concept of limitation periods relates to the time within which a party can bring an action arising from a certain contract. These periods differ from one area of law to another and from one country to another, and this may create significant difficulties at the international level. The UN Convention on the Limitation Period in the International Sale of Goods sought to eliminate the effect of these jurisdictional variations through a short and clearly-stated approach.

In addition to the diversity of limitation periods, there can also be different approaches from jurisdiction to jurisdiction over when an action can start. In some jurisdictions, the substantive effect is that a case cannot be brought after the limitation period has expired. In others, an action can be brought unless an objection is raised. In addition, it is quite common for contracting parties to agree on a shorter limitation period for the initiating of dispute settlement procedures under their contract.

SPHERE OF APPLICATION

Article 1

(1) This Convention shall determine when claims of a buyer and a seller against each other arising from a contract of international sale of goods or relating to its breach, termination or invalidity can no longer be exercised by reason of the expiration of

a period of time. Such a period of time is hereinafter referred to as "the limitation period".

THE DURATION AND COMMENCEMENT OF THE LIMITATION PERIOD

Article 8

The limitation period shall be four years.

Article 10

(1) A claim arising from a breach of contract shall accrue on the date on which such breach occurs.

(2) A claim arising from a defect or other lack of conformity shall accrue on the date on which the goods are actually handed over to, or their tender is refused by, the buyer.

(3) A claim based on fraud committed before or at the time of the conclusion of the contract or during its performance shall accrue on the date on which the fraud was or reasonably could have been discovered.

CONSEQUENCES OF THE EXPIRATION OF THE LIMITATION PERIOD

Article 24

Expiration of the limitation period shall be taken into consideration in any legal proceedings only if invoked by a party to such proceedings.

E. UNICTRAL Addressing Legal Barriers to Trade

This article addresses the trade policy objectives to be served by a unified approach to commercial law.

UNCITRAL calls for four key goals in this area: (i) clarity; (ii) flexibility; (iii) modernization; and (iv) fairness.

John O. Honnold (Secretary of UNCITRAL), *Goals of Unification in Uniform Commercial Law in the Twentieth-First Century: Proceedings of the Congress of the United Nations Commission on International Trade Law*, New York, 18–22 May 1992.

Clarity or, in other words, predictability

Perfect clarity and predictability in law, as most of you know all too well, is not for this world—[. . .]

International trade, crossing scores of different legal systems whose rules are expressed in a multitude of languages, has had to cope with formidable legal uncertainty. In response, those engaged in international commerce have developed useful tools for self-help, such as standard contracts for some well-organized areas of international trade, the International Chamber of Commerce (ICC) International Rules for the Interpretation of Trade Terms (Incoterms) and arbitration rules. [. . .] These self-help tools, however, cannot reach large areas of legal uncertainty that call for uniform international rules of law.

Can clear, predictable international law be made from the divergent rules of dozens of domestic legal systems, rules built with local legal idioms for which there are no equivalent terms in other languages? The answer, unhappily, is no, but that is not the end of the story.

As you might suppose, delegates nurtured in their domestic legal systems would come to UNCITRAL with a mission to get as much as possible of their cherished domestic legal culture into the uniform international text. [. . .]

Flexibility and adaptability to differing situations

[. . .] The most basic example of flexibility is in the choice among different unification techniques, as follows:

(a) Where maximum uniformity is important UNCITRAL employs the international treaty or convention. A notable example of this is the 1980 United Nations Convention on Contracts for the International Sale of Goods. This Convention has already been ratified by 33 countries, including States on each continent. The Convention provides for flexibility in many ways. One is by avoiding unnecessary detail. Another is the provision that the parties may exclude the Convention, and that the contract between the parties prevails over inconsistent provisions of the Convention. In addition, the Convention gives full effect to the practices established between the parties and to applicable trade usages. The Convention will be discussed in greater detail in the course of the proceedings, as well as other UNCITRAL conventions;

(b) Where there is need for greater adjustment to local conditions, instead of a convention UNCITRAL prepares a model law, for example the 1985 Model Law on International Commercial Arbitration, which the Congress will discuss during its proceedings;

(c) When even greater flexibility is needed, UNCITRAL prepares standard rules or provisions that the parties can make effective by contract—for example, the very successful UNCITRAL Arbitration Rules which become effective by a stroke of the pen of the parties concerned.

Modernization

[. . .] Such a "melting-pot" approach has fatal weaknesses. Some of the widely prevailing domestic codes are nearing the close of their second century and many are almost a century old. Worse, many were designed for domestic transactions that have no resemblance to today's international commerce.

Fairness

There is, I think, a consensus that commercial arrangements are developed most effectively in a competitive market by negotiation between experienced parties. However, in some situations the parties need help.

Parties often want to close contracts quickly, rather than hold up the transaction to negotiate solutions for every problem that might arise.

Uniform laws, like the United Nations Sales Convention, provide general rules that are designed fairly to fill these gaps in the contract. A widely representative body like UNCITRAL is well designed to develop rules that are fair to both parties; only rarely have delegates objected that draft rules favoured one side; when this has happened, the delegates' concern for widespread acceptance has led to satisfactory compromises.

For fair negotiations, both parties need to be well-informed. During the proceedings delegates will be able to consider the very successful UNCITRAL Legal Guide on Drawing up International Contracts for the Construction of Industrial Works, which, at the request of developing countries, was prepared to help in negotiating contracts for the construction of industrial works. [. . .]

Case Law on UNCITRAL Texts (CLOUT)

UNCITRAL provides a separate function from the World Trade Organization (WTO). The WTO is concerned with economic trade barriers, whereas UNCITRAL deals with legal barriers to trade. The policy objective of promoting international trade is the same, but the UNICTRAL focus is on identifying and addressing barriers to trade from a legal perspective.

In order to encourage the use of the UN Sales Convention, UNCITRAL has initiated the CLOUT case law system, which reports and assembles cases referred to the Convention on a worldwide basis.

Chapter 8

International Commercial Arbitration and International Settlement of Investment Disputes

World Duty Free Country Limited (Claimant) and The Republic of Kenya (Respondent), ICSID Case No. ARB/00/7

h. Permitting Attachments Pending Arbitration Proceedings
   Cooper v. Ateliers de la Motobecane S.A., 57 N.Y.2d 408 (1982)

E. Direct Investor to State Dispute Settlement: International Centre for Settlement of Investment Disputes (ICSID)
   1. Jurisdiction of the Centre
      a. Convention on the Settlement of Investment Disputes between States and Nationals of Other States
      b. Twofold Consent
         Liberian East Timber Corp (LETCO) v. Liberia, 650 F. Supp. 73 (S.D.N.Y. 1986)
      c. Establishing Jurisdiction: Foreign Control at the Time of Consent
         Vacuum Salt Products Limited v. Government of the Republic of Ghana, ICSID No. ARB/92/1 (1994)
      d. Establishing Jurisdiction: "Investment" Requirement
         Toto Construzioni Generali SpA v Republic of Lebanon, ICSID Case No. ARB/07/12
      e. Applicable Law Under ICSID
   2. The Energy Charter Treaty and Provision for Compulsory Arbitration
      Plama Consortium Limited v. Republic of Bulgaria, ICSID Case No. ARB/03/24, Decision on Jurisdiction (Feb. 8, 2005)
   3. ICSID Rules of Procedure for Arbitration Proceedings (Arbitration Rules)
      Hrvatska Elektroprivreda, d.d. v. The Republic of Slovenia, ICSID Case No. ARB/05/24, Order (May 6, 2008)
   4. Enforcement Mechanism under ICSID
   5. Annulment under ICSID
      Compania De Aguas Del Aconquija S.A. and Vivendi Universal (formerly Compagnie Générale Des Eaux) v. Argentine Republic, ICSID (2002) Case No. ARB/97/3

A. Out of Court Dispute Settlement

1. Negotiation, Mediation and Conciliation

In the event of an international investment dispute, a foreign investor will often seek first to resolve the dispute through voluntary negotiations, recognizing that formal court proceedings in the country of investment may be unpredictable and potentially costly. In many circumstances, a negotiated settlement is likely to represent the most effective outcome for the investor. Mediation or conciliation procedures may also be considered, if provided for in the agreement between the parties and/or if the parties so agree. However, if the dispute cannot be resolved through negotiation or other non-binding dispute resolution processes, the choice can be made either to take it through formal court proceedings or, if provided for in the agreement between the parties, to binding domestic or international arbitration.

2. International Arbitration

Provided that a contract includes an appropriately drafted dispute resolution clause, the foreign investor may elect to take the case to international arbitration in accordance with the contract provisions. Choices for the arbitration venue may include historically familiar locations such as Stockholm, London or New York, or emerging regional and international centers such as Hong Kong or Singapore. However, the option to refer to international arbitration will only be available if the counterparty has agreed to include such a provision in the relevant agreement. In reality, it can be difficult to convince a counterparty during contract negotiations that such a provision for international arbitration is both indispensable to the contract and in their wider commercial interest.

If a suitable dispute resolution provision is in place, arbitration can take place through ad hoc, institutional or treaty based mechanisms.

Ad hoc arbitration is arranged by the parties without the involvement of an organizing or rule setting institution. The United Nations Commission on International Trade Law (UNICTRAL) has elaborated arbitration rules to assist in ad hoc arbitration procedures.

Institutional arbitration is organized and administered by one of the many institutions specializing in international dispute resolution. In this area, the International Centre for Settlement of Investment Disputes (ICSID) plays an important reference role. ICSID was established by the Convention on the Settlement of Investment Disputes between States and Nationals of Other States (1966). It is a multilateral treaty, formulated by the Executive Directors of the World Bank, to further the Bank's objective of promoting international investment. ICSID seeks to act as an independent and depoliticized international dispute settlement institution. The public policy objective is to promote international investment, through strengthening the confidence of both investors and states in dispute resolution processes. ICSID is also available for resolution of state to state disputes under investment treaties and free trade agreements and as an administrative registry.

A crucial feature of ICSID is that its provisions for enforcement are self-contained within the treaty obligations and the ICSID process. In comparison, ad hoc or other institutional arbitrations need to look for enforcement to the New York Convention on the Recognition and Enforcement of Foreign Arbitral Awards (1958). This reminds that the successful enforcement of an award under ad hoc or institutional arbitration also relies on the existence and observance of international treaty provisions.

B. Arbitration in the Settlement of Investment Disputes

1. Advantages and Disadvantages

Enforceability under the New York Convention on the Recognition and Enforcement of Foreign Arbitral Awards (1958) is often cited as a core benefit of international arbitration. More than 145 states are party to this multilateral treaty for the enforcement of arbitral awards, under which an arbitral award is final and binding, with no appeal procedures and no precedent set. This is a particularly attractive feature for corporations, in ensuring a clear and final outcome to a dispute settlement process.

Foreign investors may also prefer not to submit to the jurisdiction of national courts for reasons of predictability and/or avoidance of possible political interference. International arbitration is designed to provide an acceptable neutral forum for dispute resolution. Arbitration rules are also streamlined, flexible and less complex than most national rules of civil procedure. This procedural flexibility may represent a particularly attractive feature for parties from different jurisdictional environments. Arbitration is also flexible in terms of the relevant practical arrangements, for example, when and where to convene the dispute settlement proceedings. Typically there is also less need for discovery (pre and post-trial paper work) than in formal litigation.

The ability to choose arbitrators for their technical expertise in the relevant business sector is often also cited as a valuable feature of arbitration procedures. Arbitrators can be selected for their familiarity with the relevant commercial practices, trade usages, legal structures and/or comparative law issues. Furthermore, subject to their agreement, the parties can design the dispute resolution process in accordance with the specific issues at stake, by selecting the governing law (substantive law), the place of arbitration, relevant aspects of arbitral procedure (rules), and the subject matter/expert arbitrators whom they believe will ensure a knowledgeable and fair hearing of their case.

Furthermore, the privacy of arbitral awards is an important consideration for commercial parties. Arbitral awards are not published unless agreed by the parties. The protection of confidential business transactions may be a significant attraction compared to the national courts.

Although the cost of arbitration is often perceived to be less than in litigation, this is not necessarily the case in practice. However, as there is no hierarchy of courts and no formal case law, the speed and clarity of determination may be seen by the parties as an advantage.

Equally, the perceived disadvantages of arbitration may include lack of binding precedent and the related uncertainty in predicting outcomes. Arbitration can also be expensive, as the required experts may be in demand and difficult to hire. Delays may occur with scheduling, as the leading experts are likely to have busy timetables. In terms of evidence, there is no coercive power equivalent to the power of the courts to subpoena witnesses, i.e., to order witnesses to appear. As there is no means of appeal, it may cause concern that there is no possibility for correction of errors in law or fact.

Finally, a remaining area of contention is whether attachments of assets should be allowed pending arbitral proceedings under the terms of the New York Convention. This will be further discussed later in this chapter.

2. Choice of Arbitration Rules

Many countries have arbitration laws which provide a legal framework for the conduct of commercial arbitrations. However, subject to the mandatory requirements of the applicable law, parties are free to agree on the arbitration procedures to be used between them. Rather than drafting a custom-made procedure for each contract, parties usually adopt a set of tried and tested standard arbitration rules. These rules are then interpreted in the context of the arbitration law of the seat (legal place) of arbitration.

The more widely used applicable rules include:

a) Ad hoc arbitration—this may be initiated where the parties do not have a prior agreement on applicable institutional/administrative rules. In this case, the respective lawyers will need to agree on the procedures to be used, which could include the UNCITRAL (UN Commission on International Trade Law) or ICSID (International Centre for Settlement of Investment Disputes) rules for ad hoc arbitration.

b) UN Commission on International Trade Law (UNCITRAL) rules.

c) International Centre for Settlement of Investment Disputes (ICSID) rules, noting that ICSID deals exclusively with disputes arising directly between a contracting state and an investor of another contracting state.

d) ICC (International Court of Arbitration of the International Chamber of Commerce) rules in Paris.

e) Rules of other international arbitration centers including the London Court of International Arbitration (LCIA), the Arbitration Institute of the Stockholm Chamber of Commerce (SCC), the Singapore International Arbitration Centre (SIAC) and the China International Economic and Trade Arbitration Commission (CIETAC).

International investors may also consider the use of national arbitration provisions that may be accessible for foreign parties, for example, in the People's Republic of China.

Before considering the use of international arbitration, foreign investors may wish to consider commercial arbitration in China itself.[174] The most popular forum for foreign investors is the China International Economic and Trade Arbitration

174. Abigail Chase, Commercial Dispute Resolution in China—A Practical Assessment, MA Law Thesis at the University of Sheffield (2012).

Commission (CIETAC). The possibility of commercial mediation under the People's Conciliation Law of 1st January 2011 is also attracting greater attention.

CIETAC was founded in 1956 and has its headquarters in Beijing and sub-commissions in Shanghai, Shenzhen, Chongqing and Tianjin. In 2010 it handled 1,352 cases, making it the busiest arbitration institution in the world, with around one third of the cases involving foreign parties.[175] Under revised rules adopted in February 2012, the CIETAC Secretariat has tried to incorporate global best practices, while operating within the framework of the Arbitration Law of the People's Republic of China. CIETAC is actively seeking to attract highly regarded national lawyers to deal with complex issues such as JV disputes and mergers and acquisitions. In May 2011, CIETAC appointed 218 foreign arbitrators under its three yearly review of arbitration panels.[176]

Important features of the 2012 rule changes are that the tribunal may, for the first time, order any interim measures deemed necessary in accordance with applicable Chinese law. It may also consolidate two or more separate arbitrations into a single procedure and designate a language for use in proceedings if the parties cannot agree.[177]

In 2012, internal conflict within CIETAC resulted in the split of the former branches in Shanghai[178] and Shenzhen[179] from the main body of CIETAC. Under Article 2(2) of the 2016 new arbitration rules of Shenzhen Court of International Arbitration (SCIA), the SCIA accepts arbitration cases related to investment disputes between states and nationals of other states.[180] The CIETAC split has created competition among the three arbitration institutions in the three most dynamic cities of China. In the longer run, this may have positive and productive effects for Chinese arbitration in general and for CIETAC in particular.

3. Arbitration Agreement

The arbitration clause or agreement incorporated into the contract between the parties is crucial, and the parties will often make use of model clauses selected from an institutional source such as the International Chamber of Commerce (ICC).[181] The arbitration clause or agreement will provide, for example, for the procedural

175. S Zhuang-Hui Wu, *International Arbitration for Chinese-Foreign Disputes: Emerging Choices*, 2012 International Law News, 41, 2, (Spring 2012) 1.

176. *Ibid.* p.2.

177. Freshfields Bruckhaus Deringer LLP, CIETAC Releases New Arbitration Rules (March 2012).

178. The Shanghai International Economic and Trade Arbitration Commission or Shanghai International Arbitration Center (SHIAC).

179. Shenzhen Court of International Arbitration (SCIA).

180. Shenzhen Court of International Arbitration Rules, Article 2(2).

181. "All disputes arising out of or in connection with the present contract shall be finally settled under the Rules of Arbitration of the International Chamber of Commerce by one or more arbitrators appointed in accordance with the said Rules."

and institutional rules to be used, the applicable law and the place (seat) of arbitration. The arbitration clause or agreement may also state the number of arbitrators to be appointed. This is normally either one arbiter or a panel of three, with each party choosing one arbiter and these two choosing the third. It is not uncommon for negotiations between the parties to lead to compromise in such areas as applicable law and the seat of arbitration in particular.

C. Substantive Law

The applicable law will normally be specified in the agreement between the parties. Arbitrators are bound to apply this law to the dispute. Where the arbitration clause is silent on the applicable law, the ICSID default position is that, where a state is involved, the arbitration will use the law of that state.

In the *Biloune* case, there was no Bilateral Investment Treaty (BIT) in place between the state of the investor (Syria) and the state in which the investment took place (Ghana). The investor consequently initiated an ad hoc tribunal, as provided for in the agreement between the parties, using UNCITRAL rules.

1. Appointing Authority

Centerra Gold Inc. and Kumtor Gold Company v. The Kyrgyz Republic, PCA Case No. 2007-01/AA278 UNCITRAL.

Case Introduction

The dispute concerned the exploration and development of certain gold mining sites and related assets in the Kyrgyz Republic. Centerra Gold Inc. and Kumtor Gold Company ("Claimants") argued that the Respondent's actions were in violation of protections and guarantees extended in a set of agreements and laws, including an Investment Agreement dated December 31, 2003 ("Investment Agreement") and Law No. 66 "On Investments in the Kyrgyz Republic" of March 27, 2003 ("Law No. 66").

Section 12.3(a) of the Investment Agreement and Article 18(2)(b) of Law No. 66 provide that disputes may be submitted to an Arbitrator appointed according to the Arbitration Rules of the United Nations Commission on International Trade Law ("UNCITRAL Rules"). Section 12.3(b) provides that the Arbitrator shall conduct the proceedings in accordance with the UNCITRAL Rules.

On April 10, 2007, the Secretary-General of the Permanent Court of Arbitration ("PCA") designated Mr. Jan Paulsson as appointing authority in accordance with Article 6(2) of the UNCITRAL Rules. On May 14, 2007, Mr. Paulsson appointed Professor Albert Jan van den Berg as Arbitrator in accordance with Article 6(3) of the UNCITRAL Rules.

At the request of the Parties, on November 1, 2007, the Arbitrator suspended the arbitration to enable the Parties to attempt an amicable settlement of their dispute.

On June 3, 2008, at the request of the Claimants, the Arbitrator lifted the suspension. The proceedings were eventually terminated in June 2009 after the parties amicably settled the dispute.

Biloune and Marine Drive Complex Ltd. v. Ghana Investment Centre and the Gov't of Ghana, UNCITRAL, Award on Jurisdiction and Liability (Oct. 27, 1989), 95 ILR 18429.

Case Introduction

In this case, the dispute arose out of an investment made by the claimant, Antoine Biloune, a Syrian national, involving the development of a hotel resort complex on Marine Drive in Accra, Ghana. Although Mr. Biloune had been a resident of Ghana for many years, his investments were made under a framework established by the Ghana Investments Centre, a government agency charged with the encouragement of foreign investment in Ghana. Construction of the hotel had proceeded substantially to completion when government officials issued a stop-work order, citing the lack of a building permit. The city government demolished part of the project. At the same time, Mr. Biloune and other investors were subjected to financial scrutiny by a "National Investigations Committee" charged with investigating alleged improprieties with the project. After Mr. Biloune submitted a required assets declaration form, he was arrested and detained for 13 days and then deported from the country. The government thereafter issued a notice stating that the site of the project was closed to access except for security forces. Mr. Biloune was not permitted to return to Ghana, and the project remained uncompleted. In the arbitration proceedings, Mr. Biloune submitted that the Ghana government through its various actions had nationalized his property. He also claimed damages for unlawful detention. Biloune argued that the norms of international law should be the applicable law, as it was likely that Ghana would seek to use local law in its favor.

Procedural Matters

The government of Ghana did not nominate an arbitrator and, after the tribunal verdict, sought to use this as a ground for the nullification of the award. No language of arbitration had been agreed between the parties.

Significance of Case

As no language of arbitration had been agreed on between the parties, the tribunal decided to use English. In order for an arbitration to work effectively, the refusal of one party to participate cannot be allowed to frustrate the process. The UNCITRAL rules avoid an impasse in the appointment of an arbitrator by empowering the General Secretary of the Permanent Court of Arbitration in The Hague to designate an arbitrator. The provision was invoked.

On applicable law, the tribunal held that the rights and obligations of the parties to the Ghana Investment Centre (GIC) Agreement were governed by the provisions of that Agreement, and Article 24 of the Agreement required the Tribunal to construe the Agreement "according to the laws of Ghana". The Tribunal also applied customary international law, as there was no "indication that Ghanaian law diverges on the central issue of expropriation from customary principles of international law" (95 ILR p.207).

On Biloune's human rights claims, the tribunal observed that an arbitration tribunal has no power to decide any dispute except that which the parties agreed to submit to arbitration. It held that it lacked the jurisdictional power under the arbitration clause to address the human rights claims, and limited its decision to the investment dispute which the parties had agreed to arbitrate.

The tribunal found that a series of actions by a number of governmental agencies prevented the claimant from pursuing the project. The tribunal held that this amounted to a constructive expropriation of the claimant's investment and awarded compensation for expropriation in favor of Biloune and against the government of Ghana.

D. United Nations Convention on the Recognition and Enforcement of Foreign Arbitral Awards (The New York Convention) (1958)

The New York Convention on the Recognition and Enforcement of Foreign Arbitral Awards is a treaty open to accession by any Member State of the United Nations, and any other state that is either a member of any specialized agency of the United Nations or a Party to the Statute of the International Court of Justice.[182] The New York Convention establishes uniform international standards for the enforcement of arbitration agreements.[183] The purpose is to make arbitral awards (institutional or ad hoc) rendered in a foreign state enforceable in any state that is party to the Convention.

The New York Convention binds its member states to observe two key principles:[184]

1. to respect parties' agreements to arbitrate: in practical terms, this means that their national courts must decline to hear disputes that parties have validly agreed to submit to arbitration; and

182. On 5 January 2016, the parliament of Myanmar adopted Union Law No.5/2016 ("the Arbitration Law") giving effect to its international law obligations under the New York Convention 1958. Based on UNCITRAL Model Law, the new legislation repealed the Myanmar Arbitration Act 1944 and positioned the country on the world stage as an arbitration-friendly jurisdiction.

183. The Convention's purpose is to "encourage the recognition and enforcement of commercial arbitration agreements in international contracts and to unify the standards by which agreements to arbitrate are observed and arbitral awards are enforced in the signatory countries." *TermoRio S.A. E.S.P. v. Electranta S.P.*, 487 F.3d 933-34 (D.C. Cir. 2007) (quoting *Scherk v. Alberto-Culver Co.*, 417 U.S. 506, 520 n.5)).

184. Robert Hunter, *Anticipating Trends in Dispute Resolution in International Commercial Arbitration—Developing Rules for the New Millennium*, ed. Odams de Zylva and Harrison, Jordans, 2000.

2. to recognize and enforce awards resulting from an arbitration in the same way they would enforce a judgment of their own national courts, subject only to being permitted a limited judicial review of the existence of an arbitration agreement and the observance of due process.

When acceding to the Convention, states may elect to restrict its application:[185]

1. to a reciprocity reservation, i.e. the recognition and enforcement of awards made only in the territory of another Contracting State; and

2. to a commercial reservation, i.e. differences arising out of "commercial" relationships (whether contractual or not).

The United States has ratified the New York Convention with both reservations. A list of all members, including details of whether or not they have chosen to make these reservations, is on the website of the United Nations Commission on International Trade Law (UNCTAD).[186] On 17 September, 2019, the Maldives became the 161st state to accede to the Convention.

1. Enforcement of Awards

a. The United States Arbitration Act (1925)

The United States Arbitration Act is more commonly referred to as the Federal Arbitration Act (FAA).[187] It is an act of Congress that provides for judicial facilitation of private dispute resolution through arbitration. Once an award is declared by an arbitrator or arbitration panel, it must be confirmed in a court of law.[188] The award may then be enforced by the winning party. Under the FAA, awards must be confirmed within one year.

The New York Convention on the Recognition and Enforcement of Foreign Arbitral Awards (1958) has been incorporated into Chapter 2 of the FAA.[189] This governs how U.S. courts should enforce arbitration agreements or arbitral awards in disputes between a U.S. citizen and a non-U.S. citizen of another country signatory to the Convention. Contracting states are to give effect to agreements to arbitrate, and also to recognize and enforce awards made in other states, subject to specific, limited exceptions.

---

185. Article 1(3).

186. http://www.uncitral.org/uncitral/en/uncitral_texts/arbitration/NYConvention_status.html. Currently there are 161 countries party to the Treaty.

187. 9 U.S.C. §§ 1–16.

188. NOTE: The UK Commercial Court is the principal supervisory court for London arbitration disputes. In *RJ v. HB* [2018] EWHC 2833 (Comm), the Commercial Court set aside an arbitral award on the basis that a serious irregularity caused the claimant substantial injustice. This is one of the few cases where a party has successfully challenged an arbitral award under section 68 of the Arbitration Act 1996.

189. 9 U.S.C.S. §§ 202–208.

Section 202. Agreement or award falling under the Convention

> An arbitration agreement or arbitral award arising out of a legal relationship, whether contractual or not, which is considered as commercial, including a transaction, contract, or agreement described in section 2 of this title, falls under the Convention. An agreement or award arising out of such a relationship which is entirely between citizens of the United States shall be deemed not to fall under the Convention unless that relationship involves property located abroad, envisages performance or enforcement abroad, or has some other reasonable relation with one or more foreign states. For the purpose of this section a corporation is a citizen of the United States if it is incorporated or has its principal place of business in the United States.

Section 207. Award of arbitrators; confirmation; jurisdiction; proceeding

> Chapter 1 applies to actions and proceedings brought under this chapter to the extent that chapter is not in conflict with this chapter or the Convention as ratified by the United States.

In 1975, the Inter-American Convention on International Commercial Arbitration, also known as the "Panama Convention", was adopted by a conference attended by countries belonging to the Organization of American States. Congress adopted the Panama Convention in 1990, and it became Chapter 3 of the FAA.[190] The New York Convention and the Panama Convention are the two main vehicles used to enforce foreign arbitration awards in the United States.

b. Scope of the Public Policy Exception

In the *Mitsubishi* case below, the U.S. Supreme Court confirmed that the Federal Arbitration Act is broad enough to require enforcement of arbitration awards arising from statutory as well as contractual claims.

Mitsubishi Motors Corp. v. Soler Chrysler-Plymouth, Inc., 473 U.S. 614 (1985).

Case Introduction

The parties were the Mitsubishi Motors Corporation ("Mitsubishi"), the product of a joint venture between Chrysler International S.A. ("CISA"), a wholly owned Swiss subsidiary of the Chrysler Corporation, Mitsubishi Heavy Industries, Inc. of Japan, and Soler Chrysler-Plymouth, Inc. ("Soler"), a Puerto Rican corporation. The parties entered into a Sales Procedure Agreement ("Sales Agreement") providing, in the event of a dispute, for arbitration in Tokyo in accordance with the rules and regulations of the Japan Commercial Arbitration Association.

190. 9 U.S.C.S. §§ 301–307.

Soler ran into sales difficulties and requested that Mitsubishi delay or cancel shipment of several orders. Soler also attempted to arrange for transshipment of some of its excess inventory of vehicles to other markets, but Mitsubishi refused to grant permission. Informal attempts to resolve the issues eventually failed, and Mitsubishi then brought an action against Soler in the United States District Court for the District of Puerto Rico under the Federal Arbitration Act ("FAA"). Mitsubishi sought to compel arbitration in accordance with the Sales Agreement and filed a request for arbitration before the Japan Commercial Arbitration Association. After conducting a hearing, the District Court ordered Mitsubishi and Soler to arbitrate the issues raised in the complaint. In doing so, the District Court held that the international character of the case required enforcement of the agreement to arbitrate, even with respect to the claim by Soler of alleged anti-trust violations under the Sherman Antitrust Act of 1890.

The United States Court of Appeals upheld the obligation on the parties to arbitrate but reversed the judgment concerning international arbitrability of the antitrust claims.

The United States Supreme Court subsequently upheld, by majority decision, the international arbitrability of the entire case including the antitrust claims. The case turned on whether international arbitration of a statutory claim should be allowable in view of the public policy importance of the relevant legislation.

Significance of Case

In reversing the decision of the Appeals Court regarding arbitration of a statutory claim, the Supreme Court explicitly accepted the need to recognize and strengthen international arbitration as an effective means of international commercial dispute resolution, in the context of the continuing growth of international trade. The Court considered that the national courts of the United States would still have the opportunity, at the enforcement stage, to ensure that the legitimate public policy interest represented by the U.S. antitrust laws would be adequately addressed.

However, in a dissenting opinion, Justice Stevens argued that antitrust claims were too complex and important to be left to arbitrators, and that in any event, these claims were not arbitrable even as a matter of ordinary contract interpretation.

Principal Points of the Judgment

Justice Blackmun delivered the opinion of the Court

II

Soler [. . .] argues that as a matter of law a court may not construe an arbitration agreement to encompass claims arising out of statutes designed to protect a class to which the party resisting arbitration belongs "unless [that party] has expressly agreed" to arbitrate those claims, by which Soler presumably means that the arbitration clause must specifically mention the statute giving rise to the claims that a party to the clause seeks to arbitrate. [. . .]

We do not agree, for we find no warrant in the Arbitration Act for implying in every contract within its ken a presumption against arbitration of statutory claims. [. . .] As this Court recently observed, "[t]he preeminent concern of Congress in passing the Act was to enforce private agreements into which parties had entered," a concern which "requires that we rigorously enforce agreements to arbitrate." *Dean Witter Reynolds Inc. v. Byrd*, 470 U.S. 213, 221 (1985).

Accordingly, the first task of a court asked to compel arbitration of a dispute is to determine whether the parties agreed to arbitrate that dispute. [. . .]

Thus, as with any other contract, the parties' intentions control, but those intentions are generously construed as to issues of arbitrability. There is no reason to depart from these guidelines where a party bound by an arbitration agreement raises claims founded on statutory rights. [. . .] Of course, courts should remain attuned to well-supported claims that the agreement to arbitrate resulted from the sort of fraud or overwhelming economic power that would provide grounds "for the revocation of any contract." 9 U.S.C. § 2; see *Southland Corp.* [*v. Keating*], 465 U.S., at 16, n. 11; [. . .] But, absent such compelling considerations, the Act itself provides no basis for disfavoring agreements to arbitrate statutory claims by skewing the otherwise hospitable inquiry into arbitrability. [. . .]

By agreeing to arbitrate a statutory claim, a party does not forgo the substantive rights afforded by the statute; it only submits to their resolution in an arbitral, rather than a judicial, forum. It trades the procedures and opportunity for review of the courtroom for the simplicity, informality, and expedition of arbitration. [. . .]

III

We now turn to consider whether Soler's antitrust claims are non-arbitrable even though it has agreed to arbitrate them. In holding that they are not, the Court of Appeals followed the decision of the Second Circuit in *American Safety Equipment Corp. v. J.P. Maguire & Co.*, 391 F.2d 821 (1968). Notwithstanding the absence of any explicit support for such an exception in either the Sherman Act or the Federal Arbitration Act, the Second Circuit there reasoned that "the pervasive public interest in enforcement of the antitrust laws, and the nature of the claims that arise in such cases, combine to make [. . .] antitrust claims [. . .] inappropriate for arbitration."

The Bremen [*v. Zapata Off-Shore Co.*, 407 U.S. 1(1972),] *supra* [. . .] recognizing that "agreeing in advance on a forum acceptable to both parties is an indispensable element in international trade, commerce, and contracting," the decision in *The Bremen* clearly eschewed a provincial solicitude for the jurisdiction of domestic forums.[. . .]

Thus, we must weigh the concerns of *American Safety* against a strong belief in the efficacy of arbitral procedures for the resolution of international commercial disputes and an equal commitment to the enforcement of freely negotiated choice-of-forum clauses.

At the outset, we confess to some skepticism of certain aspects of the *American Safety* doctrine. [. . .]

The mere appearance of an antitrust dispute does not alone warrant invalidation of the selected forum. [. . .] A party resisting arbitration of course may attack directly the validity of the agreement to arbitrate [. . .] that the agreement was "[a]ffected by fraud, undue influence, or overweening bargaining power." [. . .]

Next, potential complexity should not suffice to ward off arbitration. [. . .] In any event, adaptability and access to expertise are hallmarks of arbitration. The anticipated subject matter of the dispute may be taken into account when the arbitrators are appointed, and arbitral rules typically provide for the participation of experts either employed by the parties or appointed by the tribunal. [. . .] In sum, the factor of potential complexity alone does not persuade us that an arbitral tribunal could not properly handle an antitrust matter.

We decline to indulge the presumption that the parties and arbitral body conducting a proceeding will be unable or unwilling to retain competent, conscientious, and impartial arbitrators.

We are left, then, with the core of the *American Safety* doctrine—the fundamental importance to American democratic capitalism of the regime of the antitrust laws.

[. . .] "A claim under the antitrust laws is not merely a private matter. The Sherman Act is designed to promote the national interest in a competitive economy; thus, the plaintiff asserting his rights under the Act has been likened to a private attorney-general who protects the public's interest." [*Mitsubishi Motors Corp. v. Soler Chrysler-Plymouth*,] 723 F.2d, at 168 [1st Cir. 1983)], quoting *American Safety*, 391 F.2d, at 826.

[. . .] The importance of the private damages remedy, however, does not compel the conclusion that it may not be sought outside an American court. [. . .]

Having permitted the arbitration to go forward, the national courts of the United States will have the opportunity at the award-enforcement stage to ensure that the legitimate interest in the enforcement of the antitrust laws has been addressed. The Convention reserves to each signatory country the right to refuse enforcement of an award where the "recognition or enforcement of the award would be contrary to the public policy of that country" Art. V(2)(b). [. . .]

As international trade has expanded in recent decades, so too has the use of international arbitration to resolve disputes arising in the course of that trade. [. . .] If they are to take a central place in the international legal order, national courts will need to "shake off the old judicial hostility to arbitration," *Kulukundis Shipping Co. v. Amtorg Trading Corp.*, 126 F.2d 978, 985 (CA2 1942).

Justice Stevens, with whom *Justice Brennan* joins, and with whom *Justice Marshall* joins except as to Part II, dissenting.

This Court agrees with the Court of Appeals' interpretation of the scope of the arbitration clause, but disagrees with its conclusion that the clause is unenforceable insofar as it purports to cover an antitrust claim against a Japanese company. This Court's holding rests almost exclusively on the federal policy favoring arbitration of commercial disputes and vague notions of international comity arising from the fact that the automobiles involved here were manufactured in Japan. [. . .]

I

The federal policy favoring arbitration cannot sustain the weight that the Court assigns to it. A clause requiring arbitration of all claims "relating to" a contract surely could not encompass a claim that the arbitration clause was itself part of a contract in restraint of trade. *Cf. Paramount Famous Lasky Corp. v. United States,* 282 U.S. 30 (1930); *see also United States v. Paramount Pictures, Inc.,* 334 U.S. 131, 176 (1948). Nor in my judgment should it be read to encompass a claim that relies, not on a failure to perform the contract, but on an independent violation of federal law. The matters asserted by way of defense do not control the character, or the source, of the claim that Soler has asserted. Accordingly, simply as a matter of ordinary contract interpretation, I would hold that Soler's antitrust claim is not arbitrable.

II

The Court's opinions in *Alexander* [*v. Gardner-Denver Co.,* 415 U.S. 36 (1974)], *Barrentine* [*v. Arkansas-Best Freight System, Inc.,* 450 U.S. 728 (1981)], *McDonald* [*v. City of West Branch,* 466 U.S. 284 (1984)], and *Wilko* [*v. Swan,* 346 U.S. 427 (1953),] all explain why it makes good sense to draw a distinction between statutory claims and contract claims. In view of the Court's repeated recognition of the distinction between federal statutory rights and contractual rights, together with the undisputed historical fact that arbitration has functioned almost entirely in either the area of labor disputes or in "ordinary disputes between merchants as to questions of fact," *see* n. 11, *supra,* it is reasonable to assume that most lawyers and executives would not expect the language in the standard arbitration clause to cover federal statutory claims. Thus, in my opinion, both a fair respect for the importance of the interests that Congress has identified as worthy of federal statutory protection, and a fair appraisal of the most likely understanding of the parties who sign agreements containing standard arbitration clauses, support a presumption that such clauses do not apply to federal statutory claims.

c. Challenges to the Legality of a Contract as a Whole

Buckeye Check Cashing, Inc. v. Cardegna, 546 U.S. 440 (2006).

Case Introduction

John Cardegna and Donna Reuter entered into various deferred-payment transactions with petitioner Buckeye Check Cashing ("Buckeye"). The Respondents received cash in exchange for a personal check in the amount of the cash plus a finance charge. For each separate transaction, they signed a Deferred Deposit and Disclosure Agreement ("Agreement") which provided for arbitration in the event of disputes between the parties or third parties involved.

The Respondents sued in the Florida state court, alleging that Buckeye charged extortionate interest rates and that the Agreement violated various Florida laws rendering it illegal and criminal. The trial court denied Buckeye's motion to compel arbitration, holding that a court rather than an arbitrator should resolve a claim that a contract is illegal and void *ab initio.*

A state appellate court reversed the opinion but was in turn reversed by the Florida Supreme Court, which reasoned that enforcing an arbitration agreement in a contract challenged as unlawful would violate state public policy and contract law.

The United States Supreme Court was subsequently asked to decide whether a contract challenged as illegal can still be subject to the arbitration provisions contained in the contract.

Significance of Case

Justice Clarence Thomas dissented due to his long-held view that the FAA does not apply in state courts.

Principal Points of the Judgment

Justice Scalia delivered the opinion of the Court.

Held: Regardless of whether it is brought in federal or state court, a challenge to the validity of a contract as a whole, and not specifically to the arbitration clause within it, must go to the arbitrator, not the court. [. . .]

II

To overcome judicial resistance to arbitration, Congress enacted the Federal Arbitration Act (FAA), 9 U. S. C. §§ 1–16. Section 2 embodies the national policy favoring arbitration and places arbitration agreements on equal footing with all other contracts. [. . .]

Challenges to the validity of arbitration agreements [. . .] One type challenges specifically the validity of the agreement to arbitrate. See, e.g., *Southland Corp. v. Keating*, 465 U.S. 1, 4-5 (1984) [. . .] The other challenges the contract as a whole, either on a ground that directly affects the entire agreement (e.g., the agreement was fraudulently induced), or on the ground that the illegality of one of the contract's provisions renders the whole contract invalid. Respondents' claim is of this second type. The crux of the complaint is that the contract as a whole (including its arbitration provision) is rendered invalid by the usurious finance charge. [. . .]

Prima Paint [*Corp. v. Flood & Conklin Mfg. Co.*, 388 U.S. 395 (1967),] and *Southland* answer the question presented here by establishing three propositions. First, as a matter of substantive federal arbitration law, an arbitration provision is severable from the remainder of the contract. Second, unless the challenge is to the arbitration clause itself, the issue of the contract's validity is considered by the arbitrator in the first instance. Third, this arbitration law applies in state as well as federal courts. [. . .] Applying them to this case, we conclude that because respondents challenge the Agreement, but not specifically its arbitration provisions, those provisions are enforceable apart from the remainder of the contract. The challenge should therefore be considered by an arbitrator, not a court.

In declining to apply *Prima Paint's* rule of severability, the Florida Supreme Court relied on the distinction between void and voidable contracts. [. . .]

[. . .] *Southland* itself refused to "believe Congress intended to limit the Arbitration Act to disputes subject only to federal court jurisdiction." 465 U.S., at 15.

[. . .] This argument echoes Justice Black's dissent in *Prima Paint*: "Sections 2 and 3 of the Act assume the existence of a valid contract. They merely provide for enforcement where such a valid contract exists." 388 U.S., at 412-413. We do not read "contract" so narrowly. [. . .] There can be no doubt that "contract" as used this last time must include contracts that later prove to be void. [. . .]

Justice Thomas, dissenting.

I remain of the view that the Federal Arbitration Act (FAA), 9 U.S.C. § 1 et seq., does not apply to proceedings in state courts. See *Allied-Bruce Terminix Cos. v. Dobson*, 513 U.S. 265, 285-297 (1995) (Thomas, J., dissenting); *Doctor's Associates, Inc. v. Casarotto*, 517 U.S. 681, 689 (1996) (same); *Green Tree Financial Corp. v. Bazzle*, 539 U.S. 444, 460 (2003) (same). Thus, in state court proceedings, the FAA cannot be the basis for displacing a state law that prohibits enforcement of an arbitration clause contained in a contract that is unenforceable under state law. Accordingly, I would leave undisturbed the judgment of the Florida Supreme Court.

d. Judicial Review of Arbitral Awards at the Place of Arbitration

Article V(1)(e) of the New York Convention deals with an additional ground for refusing to enforce a foreign arbitral award, namely where an award has been challenged in the country where the award was made. Article V(1) and Article V(1)(e) together state that: "Recognition and enforcement of an award may be refused, at the request of the party against whom it is invoked, only if that party furnishes proof that [. . .] [t]he award has not yet become binding on the parties, or has been set aside or suspended by a competent authority of the country in which, or under the law of which, that award was made." In the following case, a court in the United States was asked to enforce an arbitral award, although it had been set aside by a court at the place of arbitration.

Chromalloy Aeroservices Corporation v. Arab Republic of Egypt, 939 F. Supp. 907 (D.D.C. 1996).

Case Introduction

This case concerns a military procurement contract between a U.S. Corporation, Chromalloy Aeroservices, Inc. ("CAS"), and the Air Force of the Arab Republic of Egypt. In June 1988, Egypt and CAS entered into a contract whereby CAS agreed to provide parts, maintenance and repair for Egyptian Air Force helicopters.

In December 1991, Egypt terminated the contact by notifying CAS representatives in Egypt and notifying CAS headquarters in Texas a couple of days later. CAS rejected the cancellation of the contract and commenced arbitration proceedings on the basis of the arbitration clause in their contract. In June 1992, the arbitration was initiated, and in August 1992, the arbitral panel ordered Egypt to pay to CAS over $17,000,000 plus interest.

In October 1994, CAS applied to the United States District Court, DC, for enforcement of the award, and in November of that year, Egypt filed an appeal with the Egyptian Court of Appeal, seeking nullification of the award. In March 1995, Egypt filed a motion with the United States District Court, DC, to adjourn CAS's petition. In December 1995, Egypt's Court of Appeal issued an order nullifying the award.

Principal Points of the Judgment

[. . .] This Court must grant CAS's Petition to recognize and enforce the arbitral award "unless it finds one of the grounds for refusal . . . of recognition or enforcement of the award specified in the Convention." 9 U.S.C. § 207. Under the Convention, "Recognition and enforcement of the award may be refused" if Egypt furnishes to this Court "proof that [t]he award has been set aside by a competent authority of the country in which, or under the law of which, that award was made." Convention, Article V(1) & V(1)(e).

In the present case, the award was made in Egypt, under the laws of Egypt, and has been nullified by the court designated by Egypt to review arbitral awards. Thus, the Court may, at its discretion, decline to enforce the award.

While Article V provides a discretionary standard, Article VII of the Convention requires that, "The provisions of the present Convention shall not deprive any interested party of any right he may have to avail himself of an arbitral award in the manner and to the extent allowed by the law of the country where such award is sought to be relied upon." In other words, under the Convention, CAS maintains all rights to the enforcement of this Arbitral Award that it would have in the absence of the Convention. Accordingly, the Court finds that if the Convention did not exist, the Federal Arbitration Act would provide CAS with a legitimate claim to enforcement of this arbitral award. [. . .]

An arbitral award will also be set aside if the award was made in "'manifest disregard' of the law." *First Options of Chicago v. Kaplan*, 514 U.S. 938, 942, 115 S.Ct. 1920, 1923, (1995). "Manifest disregard of the law may be found if (the] arbitrator[s] understood and correctly stated the law but proceeded to ignore it." [. . .]

In *A-Harbi v. Citibank*, 85 F.3d 680, 683 (D.C.Cir.1996), "the submission agreement under which the arbitrator decided the controversy mandated that the arbitrator apply 'the procedural and substantive laws of the Southern District of New York, U.S.A.'" *Id.* at 684. The arbitrator in *A-Harbi* ruled that a court applying the laws of New York would dismiss the case on *forum non conveniens* grounds. Appellant argued on appeal that the arbitrator had manifestly disregarded the substantive laws of New York by disposing of the case on procedural grounds. *Id.* The DC Circuit emphatically rejected this argument. [. . .]

Like the arbitrator in *A-Harbi*, the arbitrators in the present case made a procedural decision that allegedly led to a misapplication of substantive law. After considering Egypt's arguments that Egyptian administrative law should govern the contract, the majority of the arbitral panel held that it did not matter which substantive law they applied—civil or administrative. At worst, this decision constitutes a mistake of law, and thus is not subject to review by this Court. [. . .]

The Court's analysis thus far has addressed the arbitral award, and, as a of U.S. law, the award is proper [. . .] The Court now considers the question of whether the decision of the Egyptian court should be recognized as a valid foreign judgment. [. . .]

The Court has already found that the arbitral award is proper as a matter of U.S. law, and that the arbitration agreement between Egypt and CAS precluded an appeal in Egyptian courts. The Egyptian court has acted, however, and Egypt asks this Court to grant *res judicata* effect to that action.

The "requirements for enforcement of a foreign judgment . . . are that there be 'due citation' [i.e., proper service of process] and that the original claim not violate U.S. public policy." *Tahan v. Hodgson*, 662 F.2d 862, 864 (D.C. Cir. 1981). The U.S. public policy in favor of final and binding arbitration of commercial disputes is unmistakable, and supported by treaty, by statute, and by case law. The Federal Arbitration Act "and the implementation of the Convention in the same year by the amendment of the Federal Arbitration Act," demonstrate that there is an "emphatic federal policy in favor of arbitral dispute resolution," particularly "in the field of international commerce." *Mitsubishi v. Soler Chrysler-Plymouth*, [*supra*]. A decision by this Court to recognize the decision of the Egyptian court would violate this clear U.S. public policy.

"No nation is under an unremitting obligation to enforce foreign interests which are fundamentally prejudicial to those of the domestic forum." *Laker Airways Ltd. v. Sabena, Belgian World Airlines*, [731 F.2d 909 (D.C. Cir. 1984)].

[. . .]

Egypt argues that by choosing Egyptian law, and by choosing Cairo as the sight of the arbitration, CAS has for all time signed away its rights under the Convention and U.S. law. This argument is specious. When CAS agreed to the choice of law and choice of forum provisions, it waived its right to sue Egypt for breach of contract in the courts of the United States in favor of final and binding arbitration of such a dispute under the Convention. Having prevailed in the chosen forum, under the chosen law, CAS comes to this Court seeking recognition and enforcement of the award. The Convention was created for just this purpose. It is untenable to argue that by choosing arbitration under the Convention, CAS has waived rights specifically guaranteed by that same Convention. [. . .]

Article VII does not eliminate all consideration of Article V; it merely requires that this Court protect any rights that CAS has under the domestic laws of the United

States. There is no conflict between CAS use of Article VII to invoke the FAA and the language of the Convention. [. . .]

The Court concludes that the award of the arbitral panel is valid as a matter of U.S. law. The Court further concludes that it need not grant *res judicata* effect to the decision of the Egyptian Court of Appeal at Cairo. Accordingly, the Court GRANTS Chromalloy Aeroservices' Petition to Recognize and Enforce the Arbitral Award, and DENIES Egypt's Motion to Dismiss that Petition.

e. Limited Defenses to Recognition and Enforcement of an Arbitral Award

An action to enforce or confirm an award must commence within three years of an award's origin.[191] A party seeking to enforce an arbitration award can establish a prima facie case for enforcement by providing the original or a certified copy of the arbitration agreement and award.[192] Once a party has made a case for enforcement, a district court "shall confirm" the arbitration award unless one of the grounds for refusal specified in the New York Convention exists.[193] The seven grounds for refusal to recognize or enforce an arbitration award are listed in Article V of the New York Convention.

Parsons Whittemore Overseas Co. Inc. v. Societe Generale De L'Industrie Du Papier (RAKTA), 508 F.2d 969 (2d Cir. 1974).

Case Introduction

In November 1962, Parsons & Whittemore Overseas Co., Inc., ("Overseas"), an American corporation, contracted with Generale de L'Industrie du Papier ("RAKTA"), an Egyptian corporation, to construct and for one year to manage and supervise the operation of a paperboard mill in Alexandria, Egypt. The United States Agency for International Development (USAID) financed the project, by supplying RAKTA with funds to purchase letters of credit in Overseas' favour. An arbitration clause was agreed, providing for dispute settlement. There was also a "force majeure" clause which exempted delay in performance due to causes beyond Overseas' reasonable capacity to control.

Work proceeded until the Arab-Israeli Six Day War of 5th to 10th June 1967. On 6th June 1967, the Egyptian government broke diplomatic ties with the United States, and American citizens were expelled from Egypt, including the majority of Overseas' employees. Overseas subsequently abandoned the project and claimed this was excused through the force majeure clause. RAKTA disagreed and invoked arbitration under the rules of the International Chamber of Commerce (ICC), as

191. 9 U.S.C. §§ 207, 302.
192. 9 U.S.C. §§ 207, 302.
193. 9 U.S.C. § 207.

provided for in the contract with Overseas. The arbitral tribunal issued a preliminary award for damages, recognizing Overseas' force majeure defense as legitimate but only for the period from 28th May 1967 to 30th June 1967, after which Overseas had made "no more than a perfunctory effort to secure special visas". A final award was rendered in March 1973, and Overseas was held liable for breach of contract and payment to RATKA of $312,507.45 in damages and $30,000 for costs. Additionally, Overseas was held responsible for three-fourths of the arbitrator's compensation.

Subsequent to the final award, Overseas sought a declaratory judgment in the U.S. District Court to prevent RATKA from collecting the award, and RATKA counterclaimed. The Overseas defenses to the counterclaim were derived from the language of Article V of the New York Convention and included:

- enforcement of the award would violate the public policy of the United States (Article V(2)(b)).
- the award represented an arbitration of matters not appropriately decided by arbitration (Article V(2)(a)).
- the tribunal denied Overseas an adequate opportunity to present its case (Article V(1)(b)).
- the award was predicated upon a resolution of issues outside the scope of the contractual agreement to submit to arbitration (Article(1)(c)).
- the award was in manifest disregard of law (common law grounds).

Significance of Case

Overseas challenged the District Court's order granting summary judgment in favour of RAKTA in the Appeals Court. RATKA in turn sought double cost penalties against Overseas for pursuing a frivolous appeal. As the United States did not sign the New York Convention on the Recognition and Enforcement of Foreign Arbitral Awards (1958) until 1970, jurisdiction for this case was based on Paragraph 9 of the Federal Arbitration Act, which empowers federal district courts to hear cases for the recognition and enforcement of foreign arbitral awards.

The Appeals Court disallowed Overseas' public policy defense and affirmed the award to RAKTA. However, the court did not agree that the defenses presented by Overseas were frivolous and did not double the costs payable by Overseas.

Principal Points of the Judgment

J. Joseph Smith, Circuit Judge:

[. . .]

A. Public Policy

[. . . .] The general pro-enforcement bias informing the Convention and explaining its supersession of the Geneva Convention points toward a narrow reading of the public policy defense. [. . .] Additionally, considerations of reciprocity—considerations given express recognition in the Convention itself[194]—counsel courts to invoke the public policy defense with caution lest foreign courts frequently accept it as a defense to enforcement of arbitral awards rendered in the United States. [. . .]

We conclude, [. . .] that the Convention's public policy defense should be construed narrowly. Enforcement of foreign arbitral awards may be denied on this basis only where enforcement would violate the forum state's most basic notions of morality and justice. [. . .]

Under this view of the public policy provision in the Convention, Overseas' public policy defense may easily be dismissed. Overseas argues that various actions by United States officials [. . .] particularly, AID's withdrawal of financial support for the Overseas-RAKTA contract—required Overseas, as a loyal American citizen, to abandon the project. [. . .] Overseas' returning to work in defiance of these expressions of national policy would therefore allegedly contravene United States public policy. [. . .] To read the public policy defense as a parochial device protective of national political interests would seriously undermine the Convention's utility. This provision was not meant to enshrine the vagaries of international politics under the rubric of "public policy." Rather, a circumscribed public policy doctrine was contemplated by the Convention's framers and every indication is that the United States, in acceding to the Convention, meant to subscribe to this supranational emphasis. Cf. *Scherk v. Alberto-Culver Co.*, 417 U.S. 506, 94 S. Ct. 2449, 41 L. Ed. 2d 270 (1974).

To deny enforcement of this award largely because of the United States' falling out with Egypt in recent years would mean converting a defense intended to be of narrow scope into a major loophole in the Convention's mechanism for enforcement. We have little hesitation, therefore, in disallowing Overseas' proposed public policy defense.

B. Non-Arbitrability

Article V(2)(a) authorizes a court to deny enforcement, on a defendant's or its own motion, of a foreign arbitral award when "the subject matter of the difference is not capable of settlement by arbitration under the law of that (the forum) country." [. . .]

Resolution of Overseas' non-arbitrability argument, however, does not require us to reach such difficult distinctions between domestic and foreign awards. For

194. A Contracting State shall not be entitled to avail itself of the present Convention against other Contracting States except to the extent that it is itself bound to apply the Convention. Article XIV. Cf. Comment, [*International Commercial Arbitration under the United Nations Convention and the Amended Federal Arbitration Statute*,] *supra*, 47 Wash. L. Rev. 441 at 486-487: "In a system based upon reciprocity any tendency to take an overly narrow view of foreign arbitral awards will be balanced by a desire to obtain the widest acceptance of America's awards among the courts of other signatory states, which also have the public policy loophole available to them."

Overseas' argument, that "United States foreign policy issues can hardly be placed at the mercy of foreign arbitrators 'who are charged with the execution of no public trust' and whose loyalties are to foreign interests," Brief for Appellant at 23, plainly fails to raise so substantial an issue of arbitrability. The mere fact that an issue of national interest may incidentally figure into the resolution of a breach of contract claim does not make the dispute not arbitrable. [. . .] Finally, the Supreme Court's decision in favor of arbitrability in a case far more prominently displaying public features than the instant one, *Scherk v. Alberto-Culver Co.*, *supra*, compels by analogy the conclusion that the foreign award against Overseas dealt with a subject arbitrable under United States law. [. . .]

C. Inadequate Opportunity to Present Defense

Under Article V(1)(b) of the Convention, enforcement of a foreign arbitral award may be denied if the defendant can prove that he was "not given proper notice or was otherwise unable to present his case." This provision essentially sanctions the application of the forum state's standards of due process. [. . .]

Overseas seeks relief under this provision for the arbitration court's refusal to delay proceedings in order to accommodate the speaking schedule of one of Overseas' witnesses, David Nes, the United States Charge d'Affairs in Egypt at the time of the Six Day War. This attempt to state a due process claim fails for several reasons. First, inability to produce one's witnesses before an arbitral tribunal is a risk inherent in an agreement to submit to arbitration. By agreeing to submit disputes to arbitration, a party relinquishes his courtroom rights—including that to subpoena witnesses—in favor of arbitration "with all of its well known advantages and drawbacks." *Washington-Baltimore Newspaper Guild, Local 35 v. The Washington Post Co.*, 143 U.S. App. D.C. 210, 442 F.2d 1234, 1238 (1971). Secondly, the logistical problems of scheduling hearing dates convenient to parties, counsel and arbitrators scattered about the globe argues against deviating from an initially mutually agreeable time plan unless a scheduling change is truly unavoidable. [. . .] In fact, the tribunal did have before it an affidavit by Mr. Nes in which he furnished, by his own account, "a good deal of the information to which I would have testified." [. . .]

The arbitration tribunal acted within its discretion in declining to reschedule a hearing for the convenience of an Overseas witness. Overseas' due process rights under American law, rights entitled to full force under the Convention as a defense to enforcement, were in no way infringed by the tribunal's decision.

D. Arbitration in Excess of Jurisdiction

Under Article V(1)(c), one defending against enforcement of an arbitral award may prevail by proving that:

> The award deals with a difference not contemplated by or not falling within the terms of the submission to arbitration, or it contains decisions on matters beyond the scope of the submission to arbitration [. . .].

This defense to enforcement of a foreign award, like the others already discussed, should be construed narrowly. [. . .]

In making this defense as to three components of the award, Overseas must therefore overcome a powerful presumption that the arbitral body acted within its powers. Overseas principally directs its challenge at the $185,000 awarded for loss of production. Its jurisdictional claim focuses on the provision of the contract reciting that "neither party shall have any liability for loss of production." [. . .] the arbitration court interpreted the provision not to preclude jurisdiction on this matter. As in *United Steelworkers of America v. Enterprise Wheel & Car Corp., supra*, the court may be satisfied that the arbitrator premised the award on a construction of the contract and that it is "not apparent," 363 U.S. 593 at 598, 80 S. Ct. 1358 [(1960)], that the scope of the submission to arbitration has been exceeded.

The $30,000 in costs is equally unassailable, for the appellant's contention that this portion of the award is inconsistent with guidelines set by the International Chamber of Commerce [. . .] these guidelines [. . .] do not require, as a pre-condition to an award of expenses, express authority for such an award in the arbitration clause. The arbitration agreement's silence on this matter, therefore, is not determinative in the case under review. [. . .]

Although the Convention recognizes that an award may not be enforced where predicated on a subject matter outside the arbitrator's jurisdiction, it does not sanction second-guessing the arbitrator's construction of the parties' agreement. [. . .]

E. Award in "Manifest Disregard" of Law

Both the legislative history of Article V, and the statute enacted to implement the United States' accession to the Convention are strong authority for treating as exclusive the bases set forth in the Convention for vacating an award. On the other hand, the Federal Arbitration Act, specifically 9 U.S.C. § 10, has been read to include an implied defense to enforcement where the award is in 'manifest disregard' of the law. *Wilko v. Swan*, 346 U.S. 427, 436, 74 S. Ct. 182, 98 L. Ed. 168 (1953). [. . .]

This case does not require us to decide, however, whether this defense stemming from dictum in *Wilko*, supra, obtains in the international arbitration context. [. . .] Overseas in effect asks this court to read this defense as a license to review the record of arbitral proceedings for errors of fact or law—a role which we have emphatically declined to assume in the past and reject once again. "Extensive judicial review frustrates the basic purpose of arbitration, which is to dispose of disputes quickly and avoid the expense and delay of extended court proceedings." *Saxis Steamship Co.* [*v. Multifacs Int'l Traders, Inc.*], *supra*, 375 F.2d 577 at 582[(2d Cir. 1967)]. [. . .] We therefore affirm the district court's confirmation of award.

[. . .]

RAKTA also requests that this court award it damages and double costs as a penalty against Overseas for pursuing an allegedly frivolous appeal for purposes of delay. It is true that such an award has been made where an appellant presses a case of unquestionable frivolity, particularly where "the inference of an intent to delay is plausible." *South East Atlantic Shipping Ltd. v. Garnac Grain Co.*, 356 F.2d 189, 192-193 (2d Cir. 1966). [. . .] But although we are not persuaded by any of the appellant's numerous defenses to enforcement of the arbitral award, we would consider it harsh indeed to penalize by damages and double costs an effort of apparent honesty to explore the defense possibilities presented by a new and largely untested statute. We therefore reject RAKTA's invitation to supplement its judgment with the type of award reserved for fundamentally insincere appeals. [. . .]

f. Challenges to an Award Where the Tribunal Was Not Properly Constituted

The New York Convention allows courts to refuse to enforce an award where the tribunal was not properly constituted. The following case is interesting on that issue.

Noble Resources International Pte. Ltd v. Shanghai Good Credit International Trade Co. Ltd (2016) Hu 01 Xie Wai Ren No. 1.

In *Noble Resources International Pte. Ltd v. Shanghai Good Credit International Trade Co., Ltd.* (2016) Hu 01 Xie Wai Ren No. 1, the Shanghai No. 1 Intermediate People's Court in a judgment dated 11 August 2017 refused recognition and enforcement of a Singapore International Arbitration Centre ("SIAC") arbitral award under the New York Convention on the Recognition and Enforcement of Foreign Arbitral Awards 1958 ("New York Convention") on the basis that the composition of the arbitral tribunal and/or the arbitral procedure was not in accordance with the agreement of the parties.

The case arose out of the recently replaced SIAC 2013 arbitration rules ("SIAC Rules"). Article 5 of the SIAC Rules provided for the expedited procedure:

> 5.1 Prior to the full constitution of the Tribunal, a party may apply to the Registrar in writing for the arbitral proceedings to be conducted in accordance with the Expedited Procedure under this Rule where any of the following criteria is satisfied:
>
> - the amount in dispute does not exceed the equivalent amount of S$5,000,000, representing the aggregate of the claim, counterclaim and any set-off defense;
> - the parties so agree; or
> - in cases of exceptional urgency
>
> 5.2 When a party has applied to the Registrar under Rule 5.1, and when the President determines, after considering the views of the parties, that the arbitral proceedings shall be conducted in accordance with the Expedited Procedure, the following procedure shall apply:
>
> - The Registrar may shorten any time limits under these Rules;

- The case shall be referred to a sole arbitrator, unless the President determines otherwise;
- Unless the parties agree that the dispute shall be decided on the basis of documentary evidence only, the Tribunal shall hold a hearing for the examination of all witnesses and expert witnesses as well as for any argument;
- The award shall be made within six months from the date when the Tribunal is constituted unless, in exceptional circumstances, the Registrar extends the time; and
- The Tribunal shall state the reasons upon which the award is based in summary form, unless the parties have agreed that no reasons are to be given.

Under Article 5.1 of the SIAC Rules, a party may apply to the Registrar of SIAC for the arbitral proceedings to be conducted in accordance with the expedited procedure. If the expedited procedure applies, the arbitration is to be referred to a sole arbitrator, unless the President of SIAC determines otherwise. The Iron Ore Sale & Purchase Agreement dated 29 October 2014 ("Contract") between Noble Resources International Pte Ltd of Singapore ("Claimant") and Shanghai Good Credit International Trade Co., Ltd. of China ("Respondent") incorporated a Standard Iron Ore Trading Agreement ("Standard Agreement"). Article 16 of the Standard Agreement contained the arbitration agreement, and Article 16.1.1 provided for three arbitrators.

The dispute was in respect of the sale and purchase of iron ore. The Respondent failed to issue a letter of credit to the Claimant to pay for the goods as required under the Contract, and it was ultimately terminated. On 14 January 2015, the Claimant served a Notice of Arbitration and applied to SIAC for the proceedings to be conducted under the expedited procedure on the basis of the amount in dispute being under S$5 million. SIAC accepted the application for the arbitration to be conducted pursuant to the expedited procedure on 17 February 2015. On 20 April 2015, SIAC appointed a sole arbitrator for the case. On 16 July 2015, a hearing was conducted before the sole arbitrator. The Respondent objected to the expedited procedure and the appointment of a sole arbitrator but did not otherwise participate in the arbitration, and the Final Award was made in its absence. The Final Award was issued on 26 August 2015. The sole arbitrator awarded the sum of US$1,603,100 to the Claimant, representing damages for breach of contract.

When it came to recognition and enforcement of the arbitral award in Mainland China, the Respondent challenged enforcement under the New York Convention and Article 283 of the Civil Procedure Law of the PRC, based on a number of grounds.

One ground was the composition of the tribunal was not in accordance with the agreement of the parties as stipulated in the arbitration clause, as under the

Contract, it was expressly stated that the tribunal would comprise of three arbitrators, but in this case, only a sole arbitrator was appointed. The Respondent had not accepted the composition of the tribunal, and it had strongly opposed the appointment of a sole arbitrator, objecting on multiple occasions. Accordingly, the composition of the arbitral tribunal and/or the arbitral procedure was not in accordance with the agreement of the parties.

The court's reason for refusal of recognition and enforcement was Article V(1)(d) of the New York Convention—the composition of the arbitral tribunal or the arbitral procedure was not in accordance with the agreement of the parties.

First, the arbitration agreement in the Contract provided for three arbitrators. Accordingly, the arbitral proceedings and composition of the tribunal should have complied with the arbitration agreement.

Second, the adoption of the expedited procedure in this case was in line with Article 5.1 of the SIAC Rules as the disputed amount did not exceed S$5 million. Accordingly, the court was of the view that the adoption of the expedited procedure by SIAC was not contrary to the agreement of the parties.

Third, regarding the composition of the tribunal, the court commented that the 2013 SIAC Rules neither excluded the adoption of an alternative composition of the tribunal in proceedings conducted under the expedited procedure, nor do they specify that the President of SIAC can have the right to invoke Article 5.2(b) regarding the appointment of a sole arbitrator when the parties have agreed on the composition of the tribunal. Article 5.2(b) of the SIAC Rules stating "the case shall be referred to a sole arbitrator, unless the President determines otherwise" should not be interpreted that the President of SIAC has absolute discretion on the composition of the tribunal; on the contrary, when exercising its discretion, the President must give full consideration to the parties' agreement with respect to the composition of the tribunal in order to preserve party autonomy.

Since the parties had already expressly agreed in the arbitration agreement that the tribunal shall comprise of three arbitrators and did not exclude this composition of the tribunal in the expedited procedure, the adoption of the expedited procedure should have been referred to a three member tribunal. The court considered that use of the expedited procedure should not prevent the parties from exercising their fundamental rights to an arbitration comprised of three arbitrators as stipulated in the arbitration agreement. In this case, the court considered appointment of a sole arbitrator in accordance with Article 5.2 of the SIAC Rules was a breach of the arbitration agreement when the arbitration agreement had provided for three arbitrators and the Respondent had expressed its strong opposition against the appointment of a sole arbitrator. Accordingly, this fell within Article V(1)(d) of the New York Convention, and the award should not be recognized and enforced.

g. Enforcement and International Public Policy

In the following case, the arbitrators refused to enforce the contract on grounds that it was against international public policy to do so.

World Duty Free Country Limited (Claimant) and The Republic of Kenya (Respondent), ICSID Case No. ARB/00/7.

H.E. Judge Gilbert Guillaume President of the Tribunal Date: 31 August 2006

In 1989, Kenya concluded an agreement for the construction, maintenance, and operation of duty-free complexes at its Nairobi and Mombassa International Airports—with a company called the "House of Perfume" (incorporated under the laws of the Isle of Man, United Kingdom). The Claimant alleged that in order to do business with the Government of Kenya, a foreign owner was required to make a "personal donation" to Mr. Daniel arap Moi, then President of the Republic of Kenya. The "donation" was the equivalent of U.S. $2,000,000.

In 1992, President Moi allegedly required one of the Claimant's owners to assist with obtaining secret funds from abroad to finance Moi's re-election campaign. An assistant to Kenya's former president devised "a massive fraud through his [private] company to provide illicit funds for President Moi's campaign [. . .] accomplished through the fabrication of documentation purporting to evidence the export of gold and diamonds to a foreign consignee." On presentation of their documents to the Treasury and the Central Bank of Kenya, the related business entity was paid "export compensation." That payment, in Kenyan shillings, was the equivalent to the hard currency value shown for the exports.

Kenya submitted to the Tribunal an application alleging that the above 1989 agreement was unenforceable, because of its illegality. Kenya thus sought a dismissal of the Claimant's action. The following excerpts illustrate the evolution of bribery, and related corruption, as an international concern.

The British-based English spelling of certain words has been retained. Most citations to legal authorities have been omitted.

Arbitrators' Opinion:

106. The Respondent [. . .] contends that corrupting Governmental officials is in Kenya a crime punishable by up to 10 years' imprisonment and that, in Kenyan Law, "contracts tainted with illegality are unenforceable." [. . .]

107. The Respondent further submits that "Bribery of the type that the Claimant has now affirmed is contrary to international public policy". In support of this submission, the Respondent invokes the award given in ICC [International Chamber of Commerce] case no 1110 [. . .]; the interim Report of the ILA [International Law Association] Committee on International Commercial Arbitration of 2000; the OECD [Organization for Economic Cooperation and Development] Convention on combating bribery of foreign public officials in international business transactions

of 21 November 1997; and other conventions concluded or in preparation within the framework of the Council of Europe, the Organization of American States and the United Nations. [. . .]

110. [. . .] World Duty Free submits that the facts [. . .] do not amount to a confession of bribery; it stresses that "bribery is not a strict liability offence, *mens rea* [criminal intent] is relevant." Mr. Ali made a payment to President Moi that he believed lawful. At that time, it was routine practice to make such donations in advance of doing business in Kenya; said practice had cultural roots and was buttressed by the "Harambee" system, one which mobilized resources through private donations for public purposes. [. . .]

114. World Duty Free submits that the actions of President Moi and his colleagues were the action of the Government of Kenya. Thus Kenya negotiated the Contract with full knowledge of the payment it now seeks to impugn. In addition, Kenya later performed its side of the Contract and is estopped by conduct. In other words, rescission is not available to the Respondent; "it has already affirmed the House of Perfume Contract by its conduct between 1989 and 1998." [. . .]

116. In conclusion, World Duty Free requests the immediate dismissal of the Respondent's application of 19 March 2003.

V — Decision of the Tribunal

B — The Consequences of the Bribe

137. Kenya submits that as a matter of international public policy, as well as Kenyan and English law, the 1989 Agreement thus obtained "does not have force of law" and that World Duty Free's claims must therefore be dismissed.

1. International Public Policy

138. The concept of public policy ("ordre public") is rooted in most, if not all, legal systems. [. . .] This narrow concept is often referred to as "international public policy" ("ordre public international"). Although this name suggests that it is in some way a supranational principle, it is in fact no more than domestic public policy applied to foreign awards and its content and application remains subjective to each State.

139. The term "international public policy", however, is sometimes used with another meaning, signifying an international consensus as to universal standards and accepted norms of conduct that must be applied in all fora. It has been proposed to cover that concept in referring to "transnational public policy" or "truly international public policy."

140. Domestic courts generally refer to their own international public policy. One should nonetheless mention some judgments in which reference has been made, in one way or another, to a universal conception of public policy (*see*, for example, the Milan Court of Appeal decision dated 4 December 1992, reported in (1997) XXII Yearbook Com. Arb. 725; the judgment of the Paris Court of Appeal in *European Gas*

Turbines SA v. Westman International—30 September 1993—Revue de l'arbitrage 1994 p. 359; the decision of the Swiss Federal Tribunal in *W. -v- F. and V* dated 30 December 1994 (1995) Bull. ASA 217).

141. Arbitral tribunals have more often based their decisions on universal values in using various formulations such as "good morals," "bonas mores," "ethics of international trade" or "transnational public policy." [. . .]

142. In this respect, the Tribunal first notes that bribery or influence peddling, as well as both active and passive corruption, are sanctioned by criminal law in most, if not all, countries. This was the case in Kenya in particular in 1989, under the Kenyan Prevention of Corruption Act of 1956, and is still the case under the Anti-Corruption and Economic Crimes Act of 2003.

143. In order to render more effective this general condemnation, a number of international conventions were concluded during the last decade. The first was adopted within the framework of the Organization of American States on 29 March 1996. A convention on combating the bribery of foreign public officials in international business transactions was then concluded within the Organisation for Economic Cooperation and Development on 21 November 1997. It has thus far been ratified by 36 States. Afterwards, two conventions on corruption—one relating to criminal law and one dealing with civil law—were adopted by the Council of Europe on 27 January 1999 and 4 November 1999. The first has been supplemented by a Protocol of 15 May 2003. Those three instruments are in force. The first has been signed by 45 countries and ratified by 31 countries; the second has been signed by 39 countries and ratified by 25 countries.

144. The same trend can be observed in Africa: on 11 July 2003, in Maputo, Mozambique, the Heads of States and Governments of the African Union approved a Convention on Preventing and Combating Corruption, which has been signed by 39 African States (including Kenya) and has already been ratified by 11 of these 39 States. In this Convention, the Member States of the African Union declare themselves "concerned about the negative effects of corruption and impunity on the political, economic, social and cultural stability of African States and its devastating effects on the economic and social development of the African peoples." They "acknowledge that corruption undermines accountability and transparency in the management of public affairs as well as socio-economic development in the continent." Article 4 of the Convention lists the acts of corruption to which it applies and covers in particular "the solicitation or acceptance, directly or indirectly, by a public official or any other person, of any goods of monetary value or other benefit, such as a gift, favour, promise or advantage for himself or herself or for another person or entity, in exchange of any act or omission in the performance of his or her public functions." Under Article 5 of the Convention, legislative and other measures must be taken to establish such acts as offences.

145. For its part, the General Assembly of the United Nations adopted, on 16 December 1996, a Declaration against Corruption and Bribery in International

Commercial Transactions. It also established an ad hoc Committee for the preparation of a convention against corruption. This convention was later finalised and was approved by the General Assembly on 31 October 2003 (Resolution 58/4). It has been signed by 140 States and has already been ratified by 46 States (including Kenya). It entered into force on 14 December 2005. It should be noted that, in this Convention, the State Parties declared themselves "concerned about the seriousness of problems and threats posed by corruption to the stability and security of societies, undermining the institutions and values of democracy, ethical values and justice and jeopardizing sustainable development and the rule of law." In order "to prevent and combat corruption effectively," each State party to the Convention must adopt a number of legislative and other measures and it must in particular establish bribery of foreign public officials as a criminal offence (Article 16).

146. These various Conventions only bind State parties and do so only from the date States become parties. They deal mainly—and sometimes exclusively—with criminal law. In concluding these Conventions, States have shown their common will to fight corruption, not only through national legislation, as they did before, but also through international cooperation. In doing so, States not only reached a new stage in the fight against corruption, but also solidly confirmed their prior condemnation of it. [. . .]

156. The Tribunal notes that, in some of these [omitted domestic] cases, it was alleged that corruption is widespread either within the purchasing country or in the particular sector of activity. However, all arbitral tribunals concluded that such facts do no alter in any way the legal consequences dictated by the prohibition of corruption. [. . .] The present Tribunal agrees with such conclusion.

157. In light of domestic laws and international conventions relating to corruption, and in light of the decisions taken in this matter by courts and arbitral tribunals, this Tribunal is convinced that bribery is contrary to the international public policy of most, if not all, States or, to use another formula, to transnational public policy. Thus, claims based on contracts of corruption or on contracts obtained by corruption cannot be upheld by this Arbitral Tribunal.

188. In conclusion:

[. . .] 3) The Claimant is not legally entitled to maintain any of its pleaded claims in these proceedings as a matter of ordre public international and public policy under the contract's applicable laws.

h. Permitting Attachments Pending Arbitration Proceedings

The New York Convention seeks to provide for the reliable enforcement of arbitral awards on an international basis. However, one remaining area of contention is whether attachments should be permissible pending proceedings under the Convention. This issue is examined in the *Cooper* case below.

Cooper v. Ateliers de la Motobecane S.A., 57 N.Y.2d 408 (1982).

Case Introduction

Robert R. Cooper ("Cooper") and the French corporation Ateliers de la Motobecane, S.A. ("Motobecane") entered into a shareholder's agreement governing their joint ownership of Motobecane America, Ltd. ("Motobecane America"). The agreement provided that Cooper could tender their shares, according to a price-setting formula, to either Motobecane or the newly formed American subsidiary Motobecane America. The Agreement stated that if either seller or buyer believed the formula had "known adverse or favorable factors" substantially affecting the future profits of Motobecane America, the parties could resort to arbitration in Switzerland. Unsuccessful negotiations followed on this point, and Motobecane eventually requested the initiation of arbitration proceedings.

Cooper responded that Motobecane had not initiated arbitration within the time period recognized in their agreement and sought damages in court for the value of the shares. In addition, Cooper sought the attachment of a debt owed by the American subsidiary to Motobecane. This attachment was upheld by the New York Appellate Division but reversed by the New York Court of Appeals, which held that the New York Convention does not allow attachment pending arbitration proceedings.

Principal Points of the Judgment

Chief Judge Cooke

The United Nations Convention on the Recognition and Enforcement of Foreign Arbitral Awards was drafted to minimize the uncertainty of enforcing arbitration agreements and to avoid the vagaries of foreign law for international traders. This policy would be defeated by allowing a party, contrary to contract, to bring multiple suits and to obtain an order of attachment before arbitration. Therefore, the order of the Appellate Division should be reversed. [. . .]

The desirability of arbitration is enhanced in the context of international trade, where the complexity of litigation is often compounded by lack of familiarity with foreign procedures and law [. . .] Thus, resolving disputes through arbitration allows all parties to avoid unknown risks inherent in resorting to a foreign justice system. [. . .]

Generally, the UN Convention eased the difficulty in enforcing international arbitration agreements by minimizing uncertainties and shifting the burden of proof to the party opposing enforcement. [. . .] When an action is brought in court and a party asserts the arbitration agreement, the court "shall * * * refer the parties to arbitration, unless it finds that the said agreement is null and void, inoperative or incapable of being performed." (USCS Administrative Rules, Foreign Arbitral Awards Conv. Art. II, § 3; *see*, Contini, [*International Commercial Arbitration*, 8 Am J Comp L 283, 283-284,] op. cit. at p. 296). Moreover, foreign arbitration awards are to be enforced on the same terms as domestic awards (*see*, USCS Administrative Rules, Foreign Arbitral Awards Conv. Art. III; *see*, Contini, op. cit. at p. 297).

[. . .] Unlike the earlier Geneva Treaties, the UN Convention requires the party opposing enforcement to prove the award's invalidity, and it limits the grounds for objection. [. . .] Moreover, if enforcement is opposed, the proponent of the award may request that the other party be ordered to give suitable security. [. . .] This gives the courts a tool to discourage attempts to avoid arbitration awards which attempts are made merely as obstructionist tactics. [. . .]

The provisional remedy of attachment is, in part, a device to secure the payment of a money judgment. [. . .] It is available only in an action for damages [. . .] an order of attachment will remain valid if it was obtained with notice or has been confirmed in a contract action before a defendant obtains a stay of proceedings because the underlying controversy is subject to arbitration (See *American Reserve Ins. Co. v China Ins. Co.*, 297 N.Y. 322, 326-327). It should be noted, however, that attachment would not be available in a proceeding to compel arbitration (see CPLR 7503, subd [a]), as that is not an action seeking a money judgment.

It is open to dispute whether attachment is even necessary in the arbitration context. [. . .] Voluntary compliance with arbitral awards may be as high as 85% [. . .] Moreover, parties are free to include security clauses (e.g., performance bonds or creating escrow accounts) in their agreements to arbitrate. The UN Convention apparently considered the problem and saw no need to provide for prearbitration security. [. . .] Moreover, the list of signatory countries provides assurance to a contracting party that it will be able to enforce an arbitral award almost anywhere in the world. [. . .]

More important here, however, is the injection of uncertainty—the antithesis of the UN Convention's purpose—that would occur by permitting attachments and judicial proceedings. Once again, the foreign business entity would be subject to foreign laws with which it is unfamiliar.

[. . .] In *McCreary Tire & Rubber Co. v CEAT* (501 F.2d 1032) the Third Circuit ruled that the language "refer the parties to arbitration" (USCS Administrative Rules, Foreign Arbitral Awards Conv, art II, § 3) precludes the courts from acting in any capacity except to order arbitration, and therefore an order of attachment could not be issued. To hold otherwise would defeat the purpose of the UN Convention.

The issues raised by the *Cooper* decision are further examined in this article, in which it is argued that a preceding judgment in favor of attachment in *Carolina Power & Light Co. v. Uranex*, 451 F. Supp. 1044 (N.D. Cal. 1977), is more consistent with general international interpretation of the New York Convention.

© Peter. J. Fitzpatrick, *Attachment Prior to the Enforcement of International Arbitral Awards under the New York Convention*, 6 Fordham Int'l L.J. 556 (1982).

The narrow four-to-three margin in the *Cooper* decision suggests that the majority's interpretation of the New York Convention is not definitive. [. . .] The Convention's silence on attachment [. . .] should not be construed necessarily to mean that it would alter a traditional approach which permitted attachment pending domestic arbitral disputes.[195] [. . .] The implementing legislation for the Convention mandates that the Convention override the previously existing Federal Arbitration Law.[196] Thus, if the Convention is interpreted as prohibiting attachment pending arbitration, the Federal Arbitration Act can no longer allow for libel and seizure of vessels in maritime cases, because the Convention makes no distinction between maritime and non-maritime disputes.[197] It is contradictory to infer that the Convention would permit judicial action in one instance and proscribe it in another.[198]

[. . .] Attachment, according to the *Cooper* majority, may cause the defendant inconvenience and unnecessary expense, including legal fees, sheriff's fees, and bond premiums. It does not necessarily follow, however, that an attachment will cause delays. Attachment is a procedural device not related to the material dispute.[199] [. . .] The attachment is ancillary to the dispute and only provides that, in the event of an award, a party will have the ability to receive its just compensation.[200] Moreover, the security that attachment affords a concerned party outweighs the legal expenses and premiums that may be involved.[201]

[. . .] the complexity of contractual undertakings makes it unrealistic to assume that parties will seriously consider every detail of a future dispute including the need for provisional remedies if and when an arbitration occurs.[202]

---

195. Arbitration and attachment have long coexisted in the United States. *Atlas Chartering Servs.*[, *Inc. v. World Trade Group, Inc.*], 453 F. Supp. at 863 [(S.D.N.Y. 1978)]. New York permits attachment pending domestic arbitral disputes as long as certain criteria, are met.

196. 9 U.S.C. § 208 (1976).

197. See New York Convention, *supra*.

198. This point is argued in the *Cooper* dissent. 57 N.Y.2d at 416-17, 442 N.E.2d at 1243, 456 N.Y.S.2d at 732 (Meyer, J., dissenting).

199. Arbitral disputes concern the subject matter of the arbitration agreement, not the tangential issue of a party's effort to secure a possible award in its favor.

200. Attachment does not relate to the original purpose of arbitration agreements, which in most cases is to provide for non-judicial settlements of specified disputes in the future.

201. Without the possibility of attachment a party might attempt to avoid the arbitral process altogether.

202. When parties enter into a contract, most of their attention is directed to the business matter of the agreement. The minute details of providing for a provisional remedy in the event of an arbitration is too easily glossed over at this stage. Optimistic parties might presuppose that disputes will never arise and, therefore, not adequately prepare for them.

1. Policy Considerations

In most cases, the party seeking attachment fears that an arbitral award will be unenforceable and rendered meaningless should the other party transfer or hide its assets.[203] Attachment prevents a party from removing assets from a jurisdiction, thus ensuring that the assets will be available to satisfy the arbitration. [. . .]

2. Comparative Law Analysis

Available information concerning other signatories indicates that provisional remedies[204] are allowed in aid of arbitration. [. . .] at least twenty-three countries, all signatories to the Convention, already permit attachments when parties have agreed to arbitrate.[205] [. . .] One case, *Scherk Enterprises Aktiengesellschaft v. Société des Grandes Marques*,[206] was decided by the Italian Supreme Court. [. . .] The attachment favored a foreigner, the arbitral clause had not been written into the renewed agreement,[207] and the original arbitral clause had been written prior to Italy's becoming a signatory to the New York Convention.[208] Thus, the Court had motive to strictly interpret the New York Convention but still concluded that an attachment was not inconsistent with Convention-governed arbitrations. [. . .]

3. Treatment of the Issue by Rule Setting Bodies

The United Nations Commission of International Trade Law (UNCITRAL) arbitration rules[209] specifically provide for provisional remedies in aid of arbitration.[210] [. . .] The UNCITRAL rules were intended "to be compatible with all legal, social and economic systems throughout the world."[211]

---

203. Left unrestricted, a party which fears an award will be rendered against it has the option of removing its assets to a location where the award will not be enforced.

204. Provisional or interim measures other than attachment include court orders to provide testimony, produce documents, or grant injunctive relief.

205. As an example of the statutory support in other countries, the Israeli Knesset passed an arbitration law on July 30, 1968. It states that courts have the same powers in arbitration matters as in other court actions when it concerns "the attachment of property, the prevention of departure from Israel, security for the production of property, the appointment of a receiver, a mandatory injunction and a prohibitive injunction. Act of July 30, 1968, § 16(a), 22 Laws of the State of Israel 210, 213, reprinted in 2 INT'L COMM. ARB. (Oceana) pt. VII, at 14 (June 1979). Israel was one of the original signatories to the Convention. See Contracting States and Reservations, 2 INT'L COMM. ARB.: NEW YORK CONVENTION (Oceana) pt. VI.3 (Sept. 1980).

206. Judgment of May 12, 1977, Corte cass., Italy, 4 Y.B. COMM. ARB. 286 (1982).

207. *Id.* at 287.

208. *Id.* at 288.

209. Arbitration Rules of the United Nations Commission on International Trade Law, 31 U.N. GAOR Supp. (No. 17), U.N. Doc. A/31/17 (1976), reprinted in 2 Y.B. COM. ARB. 161 (1977) [hereinafter cited as UNCITRAL rules].

210. *Id.* art. 26(3).

211. Holtzmann, Introduction—Recent Contributions of Pieter Sanders to the Art of International Commercial Arbitration, in *The Art of Arbitration* at xi-xii (1982). The UNCITRAL rules play a significant role in international dispute settlement.

The International Chamber of Commerce arbitration rules, under which Cooper and Motobecane agreed to carry out their arbitrations,[212] also provide for interim or conservatory measures.[213] [. . .]

Reforming New York law on this issue is not enough absent a Supreme Court decision in favor of attachment. [. . .]

Conclusion

Attachment in aid of arbitration is acceptable to many countries that have signed the New York Convention. Thus, the *McCreary* [*Tire & Rubber Co. v CEAT*, 501 F.2d 1032,] court's broad interpretation of article 11(3) of the Convention and the Cooper court's reliance on *McCreary* are unwarranted. [. . .]

The decision in *Carolina Power*,[214] which allows for attachments pending arbitration, is more consistent with the views of judiciaries and legislatures of other signatory countries and serves to promote rather than disrupt the arbitral process. Parties to a contract will be more likely to enter into and adhere to arbitration agreements when they know that an award in their favor will be enforceable. Attachment can help provide this desired security.

E. Direct Investor to State Dispute Settlement: International Centre for Settlement of Investment Disputes (ICSID)

The ICSID Convention (1965) responded to a void in the legal framework for resolution of international disputes between states and foreign investors. A total of 162 states have to date joined the ICSID Convention, with the latest signatory being Mexico in July 2018. Mexico signed the ICSID Convention in the context of renegotiations of NAFTA with the U.S. and Canada, where investor-state dispute settlement is being discussed. Of these, a total of 154 have ratified the Convention and become contracting parties.

Chapter I of the Convention establishes the International Centre for Settlement of Investment Disputes (ICSID). Chapter II establishes the jurisdiction of the Centre, and Chapters III and IV set out the provisions for dispute settlement. The Convention purposefully includes only states and foreign investors as admissible parties to its dispute resolution procedures.

---

212. Record on Appeal, at 56, § 14.

213. Article 8(5) provides in pertinent part: Before the file is transmitted to the arbitrator, and in exceptional circumstances even thereafter, the parties shall be at liberty to apply to any competent judicial authority for interim or conservatory measures, and they shall not by so doing be held to infringe the agreement to arbitrate or to affect the relevant powers reserved to the arbitrator.

214. 451 F. Supp. 1044 (N.D. Cal. 1977).

1. Jurisdiction of the Centre

a. Convention on the Settlement of Investment Disputes between States and Nationals of Other States

Chapter II, Jurisdiction of the Centre

Article 25

(1) The jurisdiction of the Centre shall extend to any legal dispute arising directly out of an investment, between a Contracting State (or any constituent subdivision or agency of a Contracting State designated to the Centre by that State) and a national of another Contracting State, which the parties to the dispute consent in writing to submit to the Centre. When the parties have given their consent, no party may withdraw its consent unilaterally.

(2) "National of another Contracting State" means:

> (a) any natural person who had the nationality of a Contracting State other than the State party to the dispute on the date on which the parties consented to submit such dispute to conciliation or arbitration as well as on the date on which the request was registered pursuant to paragraph (3) of Article 28 or paragraph (3) of Article 36, but does not include any person who on either date also had the nationality of the Contracting State party to the dispute; and
>
> (b) any juridical person which had the nationality of a Contracting State other than the State party to the dispute on the date on which the parties consented to submit such dispute to conciliation or arbitration and any juridical person which had the nationality of the Contracting State party to the dispute on that date and which, because of foreign control, the parties have agreed should be treated as a national of another Contracting State for the purposes of this Convention.

(3) Consent by a constituent subdivision or agency of a Contracting State shall require the approval of that State unless that State notifies the Centre that no such approval is required.

(4) Any Contracting State may, at the time of ratification, acceptance or approval of this Convention or at any time thereafter, notify the Centre of the class or classes of disputes which it would or would not consider submitting to the jurisdiction of the Centre. The Secretary-General shall forthwith transmit such notification to all Contracting States. Such notification shall not constitute the consent required by paragraph (1).

Article 26

Consent of the parties to arbitration under this Convention shall, unless otherwise stated, be deemed consent to such arbitration to the exclusion of any other remedy. A Contracting State may require the exhaustion of local administrative or judicial remedies as a condition of its consent to arbitration under this Convention.

b. Twofold Consent

The concept of consent is fundamental to dispute settlement under ICSID and is granted in a twofold manner, first by states consenting to ICSID by signing the treaty, and then by the consent of both the state and private parties with respect to settlement of the given contract or dispute. The jurisdiction under which ICSID operates is examined more fully in the following article.

A. Consent as Establishing Agreement to Arbitrate

Consent has been referred to as the "cornerstone of the jurisdiction of the Centre". Article 25(1) limits ICSID jurisdiction to cases where both parties have specifically consented to submit their dispute to the Centre. Once both parties have consented to ICSID jurisdiction neither can revoke such consent unilaterally. As such, ICSID is fundamentally a voluntary arbitral regime. A State's ratification of the Convention alone does not obligate that State nor nationals of that State to use the Centre's facilities for the resolution of investment disputes. The State and the investor both must consent to ICSID arbitration with respect to a given contract or dispute. [. . .] For each jurisdictional issue raised [. . .] the answer is found, inevitably, by resort to the parties' arbitration agreement.

The only formal requirement for consent to ICSID arbitration is that the consent be in writing. [. . .] Several States have given consent to ICSID jurisdiction in provisions of legislation designed to encourage foreign investment. Many more countries have concluded bilateral investment treaties that give consent to ICSID jurisdiction. [. . .] Written consent, therefore, can be found in a number of types of instruments including foreign investment licenses or laws, bilateral agreements (e.g., bilateral investment treaties) and bilateral contracts.

Nothing requires that parties consent to ICSID jurisdiction prior to the development of a particular investment dispute. Consent in ICSID may represent either a *clause compromissoire* with respect to future disputes or a *compromis* regarding an existing dispute. Thus, while consent is required before a request for arbitration can be registered by the Centre, consent can be given before or after the dispute in question arises.

B. Consent as Establishing Scope of Arbitration

The terms of the parties' consent also defines the scope of the matters that may be arbitrated. [. . .] parties may do so in general terms, submitting to such arbitration any or all matters relating to the investment transaction or dispute in question. Or they may choose through their consent to make only certain such matters arbitrable. [. . .] Article 25(4) permits a Contracting State, on or after ratification of the Convention, to notify ICSID of the class or classes of disputes that it would or would not wish to consider submitting to the Centre. [. . .] As Article 25(4) of the

Convention itself makes clear, such notifications do not constitute consent to ICSID jurisdiction. Nor do they constitute reservations to the Convention.

C. Consent as Establishing Exclusive Remedy

According to Article 26 of the Convention, consent to ICSID arbitration is deemed to be consent to such arbitration to the exclusion of any other remedy unless the parties have provided otherwise. Article 26 makes it explicit that a State can, in particular, condition its consent to arbitration on the prior exhaustion of local administrative or judicial remedies. [. . .]

III. Jurisdiction Ratione Personae

A. Contracting States

[. . .] the home and host States of the investor must each be a Contracting State, i.e., a State that had, at least 30 days earlier, deposited an instrument of ratification, acceptance or approval with the World Bank.[215] Neither the governmental party nor the foreign national's State has to be a member of the Centre on the day of the agreement between the parties agreeing to ICSID arbitration, but they should be members of the Centre on the date of submission of the dispute to the Centre. The *Holiday Inns* case illustrates this point. [. . .]

B. Constituent Subdivisions and Agencies

Before a constituent subdivision or agency of a Contracting State can submit to ICSID jurisdiction, the subdivision or agency must, under Article 25(1) of the Convention, have been designated to the Centre by the State. In addition, any agreement by a designated subdivision or agency to submit disputes to ICSID must, under Article 25(3) of the Convention, be approved by the State or subdivision or agency unless that State notifies ICSID that no such approval is required. [. . .]

C. Investors that are Foreign Nationals

Article 25(2)(b) of the Convention, however, allows juridical persons who are nationals of the State party to the dispute to become parties to ICSID proceedings if the parties agreed to treat the juridical person as a national of another Contracting State where the juridical person is under foreign control.[216] [. . .]

Several ICSID tribunals have considered the Article 25(2)(b) exception. In the first case, *Holiday Inns v. Morocco* [ICSID Case No. ARB/72/1 (1972–1974)] the Moroccan Government submitted that the four local HISA subsidiaries were ineligible to be parties to the arbitration. Morocco argued that the Article 25(2)(b) exception departed from international law principles and represented a serious intrusion on the sovereign State's freedom from international suits by local nationals. Therefore, the necessary agreement should be found only where clearly stated and should not be presumed or admitted easily.

---

215. ICSID Convention, *supra*, at arts. 68 and 70.
216. ICSID Convention, *supra*, at art. 25(2)(b).

Holiday Inns argued that agreement did exist. They noted that the local subsidiaries were formed only at the request of the Moroccan Government and offered evidence that Morocco had always considered the HISA companies as foreign. Holiday Inns further noted that local law prohibited loans to be made to HISA alone, making local subsidiaries a necessary component of this foreign investment project. Given the Convention's purpose and the Government's actions, Morocco had agreed to treat the four subsidiaries as foreign.

Reading the Article 25(2)(b) exception somewhat narrowly, the *Holiday Inns* tribunal stated that, ordinarily, "one would expect that parties should express themselves clearly and explicitly with respect to such a derogation [. . .]. An implied agreement would only be acceptable in the event that the specific circumstances would exclude any other interpretation of the intention of the parties, which is not the case here". The Tribunal concluded that the parties, at the time the subsidiaries were created, did not foresee ICSID arbitration and, therefore, did not intend to include the subsidiaries in an arbitration agreement.

Eleven years later, in *Amco Asia et al. v. Indonesia*, [, ICSID Case No. ARB/81/1, Decision on Jurisdiction (Sept. 25, 1983),] the first Tribunal took a broader view of the Article 25(2)(b) exception, making it easier to find agreement to treat a local company as a foreign one. [. . .]

The first major question of the *Amco Asia* case was the jurisdictional one. Indonesia disagreed that the parties had agreed to treat P.T. Amco as being under foreign control and contended that Amco Asia and Pan American, although foreign corporations, were not parties to the agreement that included the ICSID arbitration clause.

Relying on *Holiday Inns*, Indonesia asserted that P.T. Amco had not been designated a national of another State under Article 25(2)(b) and, therefore, could not assert a right to ICSID arbitration.

The *Amco Asia* tribunal however held that the parties did agree to treat P.T. Amco as a foreign national and Amco Asia and Pan American as parties to the ICSID arbitration. The Tribunal observed that the concept of nationality in ICSID was "a classical one, based on the law under which the juridical person has been incorporated, the place of incorporation and the place of the social seat." The Tribunal then adopted a less stringent test for finding foreign corporation nationality. It held that "What is needed [. . .] is firstly that the juridical person, party to the dispute be legally a national of the Contracting State which is the other party and secondly that this juridical person being under foreign control, to the knowledge of the Contracting State, the parties agrees [sic] to treat it as a foreign juridical person."

The *Amco Asia* tribunal found that Indonesia agreed to treat P.T. Amco as a foreign national when Indonesia approved the investment license application (and the ICSID clause in it). The Tribunal explained that by approving the application referring to a "foreign business" it was "crystal clear that (Indonesia) agreed to treat P.T. Amco as a national of another Contracting State, for the purpose of the Convention." [. . .]

The *Amco Asia* tribunal's approach was reinforced by the next ICSID tribunal to rule on this issue, the first tribunal to be constituted in the *Klockner v. Cameroon*[217] case. [. . .]

A similar approach was taken by the Tribunal in a third ICSID case, *Liberian Eastern Timber Corp. (LETCO) et al. v. Liberia* [650 F. Supp. 73 (S.D.N.Y. 1986)]. [. . .]

V. Procedure For Examining Jurisdiction

[. . .] A party may make an objection to jurisdiction, but pursuant to Arbitration Rule 41, jurisdictional objections of a party must "be made as early as possible." Generally, objections must be filed with the Secretary-General "no later than the expiration of the time limit fixed for the filing of the counter-memorial or of the rejoinder [if the objection relates to an ancillary claim]."[218] [. . .]

On the raising of an objection relating to the dispute, the Arbitration Rules provide that the proceedings on the merits must be suspended and the parties must be given the opportunity to file observations on the jurisdictional issues. The tribunal then can "deal with the objection as a preliminary question or join it to the merits of the dispute."[219] If the objection is upheld and the dispute or claim is found not to be within the competence of the tribunal or within ICSID's jurisdiction, the tribunal must "render an award to that effect."[220]

Liberian Eastern Timber Corporation v. The Government of the Republic of Liberia, 650 F. Supp. 73 (S.D.N.Y. 1986).

Case Introduction

In 1970, the state of Liberia entered into a concession agreement granting the Liberian Eastern Timber Corporation ("LETCO"), a Liberian corporation owned and controlled by French nationals, use of over 400,000 acres of land for harvesting of timber. LETCO subsequently exploited its concession by processing and exporting timber. In 1980, Liberia reduced LETCO's concession area by 270,000 acres and later terminated the concession entirely. As provided for in the Concession Agreement, LETCO commenced arbitration under the ICSID Convention.

Liberia nominated an arbitrator and a law firm to represent it but refused to participate in the arbitration and commenced an action against LETCO in the Liberian courts. Nonetheless, the arbitration panel proceeded and awarded LETCO a total of $8,793,280 in damages, plus interest. The U.S. District Court was asked to decide whether the arbitration award could be enforced in the United States.

Principal Points of the Judgment

Edward Weinfeld, District Judge

---

217. ICSID ARB/81/2.
218. ICSID Arbitration Rule 41.
219. *Id.* at Rule 41(4).
220. *Id.* at Rule 41(5).

[. . .] The United States, as a signatory to the treaty, is such a state and the Foreign Sovereign Immunities Act is also applicable here. The broad questions presented are: whether the District Court had subject matter jurisdiction, under sections 1604 and 1605 of the FSIA, to enter judgment based upon the arbitration award,[221] and if so, whether it also had the power to issue executions, under sections 1609 and 1610 of the FSIA, upon property of Liberia to enforce the judgment. These issues require a determination of whether or not Liberia expressly or impliedly waived its sovereign immunity, and whether the property which LETCO seeks to execute the judgment upon is used for a commercial activity in the United States.

First, as to whether this Court has subject matter jurisdiction, reference has already been made to Article 54 of the Convention, which obligates the United States, as a signatory thereto, to recognize and enforce the pecuniary obligation of the award as if it were a final judgment of a court of the United States. [. . .]

Liberia, as a signatory to the Convention, waived its sovereign immunity in the United States with respect to the enforcement of any arbitration award entered pursuant to the Convention. When it entered into the concession contract with LETCO, with its specific provision that any dispute thereunder be settled by arbitration under the rules of ICSID and its enforcement provision thereunder, it invoked the provision contained in Article 54 of the Convention which requires enforcement of such an award by Contracting States. That action, and reading the treaty as a whole, leaves little doubt that the signatories to the Convention intended that awards made pursuant to its provisions be given full faith and credit in their respective jurisdictions subject to such rights as are reserved by signatories thereunder.[222] [. . .]

c. Establishing Jurisdiction: Foreign Control at the Time of Consent

Vacuum Salt Products Limited v. Government of the Republic of Ghana, ICSID No. ARB/92/1 (1994).

Case Introduction

Vacuum Salt is a corporation organized under the 1963 Companies Code of Ghana. Vacuum Salt was incorporated on 4 November 1966 by Mr. Gerassimos Alexis Panagiotopulos, a Greek national resident in Ghana since 1942, and his brothers. In November 1971, all shares were transferred to Samuel Christian Appenteng, a Ghanian national, who served as Managing Director of Vacuum Salt since that time. Upon its establishment in 1966, Mr. Panagiotopulos became a director of Vacuum Salt, and on 1 November 1976, Mr. Appenteng transferred 20 percent back to

221. *Verlinden B.V. v. Central Bank of Nigeria*, 461 U.S. 480, 493-94 n. 20, 103 S. Ct. 1962, 1971 n. 20, 76 L.Ed.2d 81 (1983).

222. *Cf. Frolova v. Union of Soviet Socialist Republics*, 761 F.2d 370 (7th Cir. 1985) [85 ILR 236]; *Tele-Oren v. Libyan Arab Republic*, 726 F.2d. 774 (D.C. Cir. 1984) (Bork, J., concurring), cert. denied, 470 U.S. 1003, 105 S. Ct. 1354, 84 L. Ed. 2d 377 (1985).

Mr. Panagiotopulos. Mrs. Panagiotopulos joined her husband as a director in 1978, and they both remained directors on 22 January 1988.

The parties agree that as of 22 January 1988, Mr. Panagiotopulos held 20 percent of the shares of Vacuum Salt. It is also agreed that on that date, three banks owned by Ghana, i.e., National Investment Bank, Development Finance and Holdings Limited and National Savings and Credit Bank, held ten percent each, and that the remaining 50 percent was held by private Ghanaian nationals. In the Lease Agreement, the parties agreed that, because Vacuum Salt is controlled by a Greek national,[223] it should be treated as a foreign corporation for the purposes of Article 25(2)(b) of the ICSID Convention. According to paragraph 36(a) of the Lease Agreement:

> Any dispute or difference between the parties arising out of or in connection with this Agreement or any agreed variation thereof or in respect of the interpretation or enforcement of the provisions of this document or any agreed variation or as to the rights, duties or liabilities of either party shall unless the parties agree to submit to any procedures available in Ghana for the settlement of such dispute be submitted at the instance of any party to the jurisdiction of the International Centre for the Settlement of Investment Disputes for settlement by reconciliation [sic] or arbitration pursuant to the Convention of [sic] the Settlement of Investment Disputes between States and Nationals of other States.

In the case at hand, Ghana objected to ICSID's jurisdiction on three grounds:

1. The Claimant was essentially a Ghanaian Company and therefore not foreign controlled and thus the conditions of Article 25(2)(b) of the ICSID Convention were not satisfied;
2. Submission of the Request had not been duly authorized by or on behalf of the Claimant;
3. The Claimant had agreed "to submit to [. . .] procedures available in Ghana for the settlement of such disputes" pursuant to Law No. 287 and under the terms of paragraph 36(a) of the 1988 lease agreement. thereby waived any right it might otherwise have had to ICSID arbitration.

Significance of Case

As noted by Professor Christoph Schreuer, the *Vacuum Salt* case underlines that foreign control at the time of consent is an objective requirement which must be examined by the tribunal to establish jurisdiction. Whereas an agreement on foreign nationality may be readily inferred from a consent agreement, no such inference is possible regarding foreign control. An agreement on foreign nationality will create a presumption that a factual condition of foreign control exists, but no more. This

223. The Request identified the Greek national as Gerassirnos Alexis Panagiotopulos, who, it is not disputed, held 20 percent of the shares of Vacuum Salt on 22 January 1988.

presumption is rebuttable. Foreign control must actually exist and cannot be construed by the parties or implied from an agreement between the parties.[224]

Principal Points of the Judgment

[. . .]

27. The parties diverge, however, on the threshold jurisdictional issue posed first by the Attorney-General of Ghana regarding whether "because of foreign control, the parties have agreed [that Vacuum Salt] should be treated as a national of another Contracting State [Greece] for the purposes of [the] Convention", specifically Article 25(2)(b). It is crucial to ICSID jurisdiction in this case and it is to this issue that the Tribunal first must turn.

28. Since it is agreed that Vacuum Salt is and has at all material times been a corporation organized under the 1963 Companies Code of Ghana and hence could not be regarded as "a national of another [ICSID] Contracting State" within the definition of the first clause of Article 25(2)(b) of the Convention, the Tribunal can have jurisdiction *ratione personae* in regard to Vacuum Salt only if in respect of it the requirements of the second clause of Article 25(2)(b) of the Convention are satisfied. [. . .]

> **Article 25**
>
> (2) "National of another Contracting State" means:
>
> (b) any juridical person which had the nationality of a Contracting State other than the State party to the dispute on the date on which the parties consented to submit such dispute to conciliation or arbitration and any juridical person which had the nationality of the Contracting State party to the dispute on that date and which, because of foreign control, the parties have agreed should be treated as a national of another Contracting State for the purposes of this Convention.

[. . .]

Unless the requirements of the second clause of Article 25(2)(b) have been fulfilled the Tribunal does not have jurisdiction. The Tribunal therefore must focus on this point.

29. The Tribunal discerns from the text of Article 25(2)(b) that the conditions of the second clause of Article 25(2)(b) must be fulfilled, at least initially, on the date of consent, in this case 22 January 1988. The antecedent to the phrase "on that date" in the second clause of Article 25(2)(b) necessarily is the reference in the first clause to "the date on which the parties consented to submit such dispute to [. . .] arbitration." The Tribunal therefore considers the situation as of 22 January 1988.

30. The issue, then, is whether at that date, "because of foreign control, the parties [. . .] agreed [that Vacuum Salt] should be treated as a national of another

224. Christoph H. Schreuer, *The ICSID Convention: A Commentary* (2009), p.316, para. 825.

Contracting State [Greece][225] for the purposes of this Convention." This divides into two parts: First, whether there was such agreement, and, second, whether such agreement was indeed "because of foreign control" within the meaning of the second clause of Article 25(2)(b).

31. Turning to the issue of agreement *vel non*, Ghana points out that the parties nowhere have referred to, let alone recited in *haec verba*, the second clause of Article 25(2)(b). Paragraph 36(a) of the 1988 lease agreement nowhere alludes to it. Certainly the better practice, as reflected in ICSID Model Clause 8,[226] would be for the parties at least to make some reference to foreign control.[227] The reported cases suggest, however, that such has not been the practice. *See, Amco Asia et al. v. Indonesia*, ICSID ARB/81/1 (decision on jurisdiction dated 25 Sept, 1983), para. 14(ii); *Kloeckner v. Cameroon*, ICSID ARB/81/2 (decision on jurisdiction dated 21 Oct, 1983); *Liberian Eastern Timber Corp. (LETCO) v. Liberia*, ICSID ARB/83/2 (award dated 31 March, 1986). [. . .] the very agreement by parties to an ICSID arbitration clause in circumstances such that ICSID jurisdiction can exist only on the basis of the second clause of Article 25(2)(b) necessarily implied their agreement to apply that clause. [. . .]

These cases are distinguishable from the instant case in that in none of them was the issue of consent separated from that of foreign control. In each of them the objective existence of foreign control was presumed, in particular because the foreign shareholding was 100 percent (or, in one case, 51 percent). *Amco Asia et al. v. Indonesia, supra* (100 percent foreign ownership); *Kloeckner v. Cameroon, supra* (51 percent foreign ownership); *LETCO v. Liberia, supra* (100 percent foreign ownership).

36. [. . .] The reference in Article 25(2)(b) to "foreign control" necessarily sets an objective Convention limit beyond which ICSID jurisdiction cannot exist and parties therefore lack power to invoke same no matter how devoutly they may have desired to do so. [. . .]

37. As the consent of the parties is in broad principle the "cornerstone of the jurisdiction of the Centre" (Report of the Executive Directors on the Convention on the Settlement of Investment Disputes between States and Nationals of Other States, ICSID Doc.2, 18 March 1965, para. 23, at 8), it is accorded considerable respect and is not lightly to be found to have been ineffective. [. . .]

---

225. Greece was a party to the Convention at that date, it having entered into force with respect to Greece on 21 May 1969.

226. "It is hereby agreed that, although the Investor is a national of the Host State, it is controlled by nationals of name(s) of other Contracting State(s) and shall be treated as a national of [that]/[those] State[s] for the purposes of the Convention." ICSID Model Clauses, ICSID Doc. 5/Rev. 2 (1 Feb. 1993).

227. This would facilitate, *inter alia*, identification of the State Party (or States Parties) to the Convention required by Article 27(1) to forego giving diplomatic protection in the circumstances.

38. Nevertheless the words "because of foreign control" have to be given some meaning and effect. These words are clearly intended to qualify an agreement to arbitrate and the parties are not at liberty to agree to treat any company of the host State as a foreign national: They may only do so "because of foreign control." The Tribunal concludes that the existence of consent to an arbitration clause such as paragraph 36(a) of the 1988 lease agreement in circumstances such that jurisdiction could be premised only on the second clause of Article 25(2)(b) raises a rebuttable presumption that the "foreign control" criterion of the second clause of Article 25(2)(b) has been satisfied on the date of consent. [. . .]

43. The Tribunal notes, and itself confirms, that "foreign control" within the meaning of the second clause of Article 25(2)(b) does not require, or imply, any particular percentage of share ownership. Each case arising under that clause must be viewed in its own particular context, on the basis of all of the facts and circumstances. [. . .] The question is whether the nationality chosen represents an exercise of a reasonable amount of control to warrant its choice on the basis of a reasonable criterion. [. . .]

44. Nonetheless, it must be true that the smaller the percentage of voting shares held by the asserted source of foreign control, the more one must look to other elements bearing on that issue. As one authority has said, "a tribunal [. . .] may regard any criterion based on management, voting rights, shareholding or any other reasonable theory as being reasonable for the purpose." [. . .] It is on this basis that Claimant has strongly advanced, and Respondent has sharply contested, arguments as to control based on the role Mr. Panagiotopulos personally played in Vacuum Salt on 22 January 1988.

45. [. . .] the Tribunal determined to hold oral proceedings [. . .] in regard to the issue under Article 25(2)(b) [. . .]

53. It is significant that nowhere does there appear to be any material evidence that Mr. Panagiotopulos either acted or was materially influential in a truly managerial rather than technical or supervisory vein. At all times he was subject to the direction of the Managing Director, Mr. Appenteng, who himself apparently controlled the largest single block of shares (31 percent held by Appenteng Mensah & Co.), and who in turn responded to the board of directors, of which Mr. and Mrs. Panagiotopulos were but two members. Nowhere in these proceedings is it suggested that Mr. Panagiotopulos, as holder of 20 percent of Vacuum Salt's shares, either through an alliance with other shareholders, through securing a significant power of decision or managerial influence or was in a position to steer, through either positive or negative action, the fortunes of Vacuum Salt. The fact that it was truly his "brainchild" and, if such be the case, that his technical advice generally was heeded, and even proved to be indispensable, does not fuse with his 20 percent shareholding to render him capable of strongly influencing critical decisions on important corporate matters. This is reflected in the board minutes under review, where he

invariably delivered the "technical report," and, while temporarily styled General Manager or Deputy Managing Director, also reported on the company's financial status. In the end, the entire proceedings, even viewed in the light most favorable to Claimant, are instinct with the sense that Mr. Panagiotopulos, for all his admitted talents, was not in any sense "in charge."

54. The Tribunal is constrained to conclude that the presumption from the fact of consent that the requirements of the second clause of Article 25(2)(b) were satisfied in this case on 22 January 1988 is rebutted. [. . .] The Tribunal finds the Request here, however, to be such a case. Simply stated, accepting jurisdiction in the particular circumstances of this case, in our view, "would permit parties to use the Convention for purposes for which it was clearly not intended." We do not find here indications of foreign control of Vacuum Salt such as to justify regarding it as a national of an ICSID Contracting State other than Ghana. [. . .]

55. For the reasons set forth above, the Tribunal finds that it lacks jurisdiction and, accordingly, the Request for Arbitration herein must be dismissed.

d. Establishing Jurisdiction: "Investment" Requirement

Toto Construzioni Generali SpA v. Republic of Lebanon, ICSID Case No. ARB/07/12), Decision on Jurisdiction.

Case Introduction

Toto Construzioni Generali S.p.A., ("Toto" or the "Claimant") is an Italian joint stock company registered at the commercial register of the Chamber of Commerce of Chieti and incorporated under the laws of Italy. The request for arbitration was submitted pursuant to the arbitration provisions contained in the Bilateral Treaty between the Italian Republic and the Lebanese Republic on the Promotion and Reciprocal Protection of Investments signed on November 7, 1997, and which entered into force on February 9, 2000 (the "Treaty").

The dispute arose in relation to a contract dated December 11, 1997 (the "Contract") between the Lebanese Republic-Conseil Exécutif des Grands Projets ("CEPG") and Toto to construct a portion of the Arab highway linking Beirut to Damascus (the "Project"). The Contract contained a forum selection clause in favour of Lebanese courts.

Toto alleged that the CEPG, and later its successor, the Council for Development and Reconstruction ("CDR"), both acting on behalf of the Lebanese Government, were responsible for several actions in relation to the Project, such as delaying the necessary expropriation of private property and changing the regulatory framework, which resulted in substantial delays to the construction of the highway. This jeopardized Toto's investment in Lebanon and the reputation of the Toto group.

Toto commenced proceedings in the Lebanese courts in accordance with the contractual jurisdiction clause and subsequently initiated arbitration against Lebanon at ICSID as provided for in the Bilateral Investment Treaty, alleging breach of the Treaty provisions for non-discrimination and fair and equitable treatment.

Lebanon raised a number of objections to the arbitral tribunal's jurisdiction including whether Toto had made an "investment" within the meaning of ICSID Convention Article 25(1).

Principal Points of the Judgment

[. . .]

81. The Tribunal finds that, regarding the issue of investment, the requirements for jurisdiction under the ICSID Convention are fulfilled in this case. However, the Tribunal wishes to make clear that it does not reach this conclusion strictly on the basis of the Salini test [*Salini Constuttori SPA and Italstrade SPA v. Kingdom of Morocco* (ICSID Case No. ARB/00/4), Decision on Jurisdiction, July 23, 2001], even if it agrees with Toto that in the present case that test is met, as demonstrated above. The Tribunal deviates from this commonly followed test in a desire to delineate the necessary features of an investment in a way that it considers more appropriate to the present case. [. . .]

83. As stated in *Biwater v. Tanzania* [*Biwater Gauff Ltd. v. United Republic of Tanzania*, ICSID No.ARB/05/22, Award (July 24, 2008)], in the ICSID Convention the term "investment" "was left intentionally undefined, with the expectation (inter alia) that a definition could be the subject of agreement as between Contracting States". And: "[g]iven that the Convention was not drafted with a strict, objective, definition of 'investment', it is doubtful that arbitral tribunals sitting in individual cases should impose one such definition which would be applicable in all cases and for all purposes."

84. In the absence of specific criteria or definitions in the ICSID Convention, the underlying concept of investment, which is economical in nature, becomes relevant: it implies an economical operation initiated and conducted by an entrepreneur using its own financial means and at its own financial risk, with the objective of making a profit within a given period of time. It has been argued that "investment" should include duration, e.g. a minimum duration of two years, although a shorter duration also may be conceivable, or that the investment should serve the public interest. [. . .] This is not a requirement of the ICSID Convention. [. . .]

86. In the present case, Toto's construction project meets the requirements deemed necessary by this Tribunal, i.e. a contribution by the investor, a profitability risk, a significant duration and a substantial contribution to the State's economic development, as follows:

> (a) Toto used its financial means before, during, and until completion of the works. At the start of the project, organizing personnel, machineries, and materials involved expenditures. The investment remains even though the contractor receives payments during the progress of the work. [. . .] Moreover, as the costs must be certified by the engineer in order to obtain payment, there is always a risk that the costs will not be approved. [. . .]

> (b) There is no guarantee that the price paid by Lebanon, the employer, will be sufficient to cover the actual costs of the contractor for the performance of its obligations, especially since many unknown factors might intervene.
>
> (c) Toto was involved in the investment for well over five years (and even well over six years if Toto's maintenance period is also included). Several activities were carried out during the period in order to perform its contractual obligations.

87. Thus, it is the considered conclusion of this Tribunal that the construction carried out by Toto in Lebanon was an "investment" according to Article 25 of the ICSID Convention, and as such, the disputes related to this construction qualify for the ICSID arbitration.

e. Applicable Law Under ICSID

The substantive rules of law for solving a dispute are not provided by the ICSID Convention. The Convention grants autonomy to the parties in choosing the law that ought to be applied to solve the dispute. The parties can also allow the tribunal to decide *ex aequo et bono.* In the absence of an agreement, the ICSID Convention designates the host state's law in conjunction with international law as the applicable law. The law of the host state is the typical choice for a contractual relationship concerning investment. The selection of the law of the investor's home country or of a third state is unusual. Such choices would create difficulties if the investment involves activities that are closely related to the host state's legal system such as tax law. An exception to this would be submission of loan contracts to the law of the lender's state or to the law of a third state that has an important financial center.

In order to protect the investor's interests in view of the uncertainties of the host state's law, the parties sometimes decide to internationalize their agreement. This is generally achieved by making a reference to international law or to general principles of law, jointly with the host state's law. In *AGIP v. Congo,*[228] the parties agreed on the principles of Congolese law supplemented by the principles of international law. After establishing that the Congolese ordinance, which had nationalized the claimant's property, was in breach of Congolese law, the Tribunal turned to international law. The tribunal stated:

> in the present case, it must be recalled, that according to Article 5 of the Agreement, Congolese law can be "supplemented" when the occasion arises by "principles of international law". It has been maintained by AGIP that the qualification of "supplemented" must be interpreted as implying the subordination of Congolese law to international law. Whenever the merits of this argument, it suffices for the Tribunal to note that the use of the word "supplemented" signifies at the very least that recourse to principles

228. Award (Nov. 30, 1979), 21 I.L.M. 726 (1982).

of international law can be made either to fill a lacuna in Congolese law, or to make any necessary additions to it.[229]

International law can be incorporated into domestic law through a variety of techniques. To the extent that it thereby becomes applicable internally, it may be seen as a part of a system of domestic law chosen by the parties and may be relied upon by an ICSID tribunal. On the question of whether international law will be taken into account by an ICSID Tribunal if it is not mentioned in an agreement on choice of law, in *Spp v. Egypt*,[230] there was disagreement as to whether a choice of Egyptian law had been made by the parties, and consequently, as to whether international law should be applied in conformity with the second sentence of Article 42(1). The Tribunal declared this disagreement immaterial, holding that international law was applicable either way. The Tribunal stated: "Finally, even accepting the respondent's view that the parties have implicitly agreed to apply Egyptian law, such an agreement cannot entirely exclude the direct applicability of international law in certain situations. The law of Egypt, like all municipal legal systems, is not complete or exhaustive, and where a lacuna occurs it cannot be said that there is agreement as to the application of a rule of law which ex hypothesis, does not exist. In such a case, it must be said that there is 'absence of agreement' and, consequently, the second sentence of article 42(1) would come into play".[231] The Tribunal proceeded to apply international law to defeat an Egyptian argument that certain acts of its officials were invalid under Egyptian law. It held that these acts created expectations protected by the application of the principle of international law regarding the international responsibility of states for unauthorized or ultra vires acts of officials having an official character. When municipal law contains a lacuna, or international law is violated by the exclusive application of municipal law, the Tribunal is bound in accordance with Article 42 of the ICSID Convention to apply directly the relevant principles and rules of international law.

The complete exclusion of international law as a consequence of an agreed choice of law containing only a domestic legal system would lead to undesirable consequences. It would mean that an ICSID tribunal would have to uphold discriminatory and arbitrary actions by the host state, or breaches of its undertakings which are evidently in bad faith or amount to a denial of justice as long as they conform to the applicable domestic law. It would mean that a foreign investor, by assenting to a choice of law clause, could sign away the minimum standards for the protection of aliens and their property developed in customary international law. The mandatory rules of international law which provide an international minimum standard of protection for aliens exist independently of any choice of law. The transaction

229. Award, 30 November 1979, ICSID, Reports 323.
230. Award, 20 May 1992, 3 ICSID Reports 189.
231. *Ibid.* p. 207.

remains governed by the domestic legal system chosen by the parties. However, this choice is subject to the application of mandatory international norms.

2. The Energy Charter Treaty (1994) and Provision for Compulsory Arbitration

The Energy Charter Treaty ("ECT") was the first multilateral treaty to provide as a general rule for the settlement of investor-state disputes by international arbitration. It has been signed by 54 states and by Euratom and the European Union, and has become widely used and referenced in international dispute settlement in the energy sector. It includes clear provisions for the settlement of investment disputes, with Article 26 ECT providing for investor-to-state disputes and Article 27 ECT for state to state disputes.

Investment arbitration proceedings under the ECT have increased considerably since 2013 and now total 124 cases.[232] Experienced arbitrators consider the ECT a robust and functioning mechanism, with appropriate checks and balances. The 2014 *Yukos* case, *Yukos Universal Ltd. v. Russian Fed'n* (*Isle of Man v. Russ.*), UNCITRAL, PCA No. AA 227 (Perm. Ct. Arb. 2014), shows that tribunals will apply the Treaty in good faith to prevent abusive and, in particular, expropriatory behavior, although enforcement is increasingly an issue. However, the judgments in favour of the state of Hungary in cases brought under the ECT by AES, Electrabel and EDF, also show that the ECT does not provide a "free ride" for investors, and tribunals will carefully weigh up legitimate regulatory considerations within the discretion allowed by the Treaty.

The *Plama Consortium* case below further examines the respective jurisdictions of the Energy Charter Treaty, the relevant Bilateral Investment Treaty and the ICSID Convention in an investor-to-state dispute.

Plama Consortium Limited v. Republic of Bulgaria, (2005) ICSID Case No. ARB/03/24). Decision on Jurisdiction.

Case Introduction

The Claimant, Plama Consortium Limited ("Plama"), a Cypriot company, was known at the time of the facts as Trammel Investment Limited ("Trammel"). Trammel purchased from EuroEnergy Holding OOD ("EEH") all (49,837,849) of its shares in Plama AD, which later changed its name to Nova Plama AD ("Nova Plama"). Nova Plama was a Bulgarian company owning an oil refinery in Bulgaria representing 97% of its capital. The share purchase agreement was concluded on 18th September 1998, and the transfer of shares took place on 18th December 1998.

232. As of 10/5/2019. The UNCTAD Investment Dispute Settlement Navigator.

The refinery's key industrial asset was a lubricants manufacturing unit, processing base oils produced by the refinery into a wide range of industrial and consumer lubricants. Plama Consortium claimed that the Bulgarian government, the national legislative and judicial authorities and other public authorities and agencies, deliberately created numerous grave problems for Nova Plama and/or refused or unreasonably delayed the adoption of adequate corrective measures. These actions caused material damage to the operations of the refinery and a direct negative impact on the reputations and market values of the Plama group companies.

Principal Points of the Judgment

21. [. . .] the Claimant alleges that [. . .] Bulgaria's actions and/or omissions violate the ECT, to which both Bulgaria and Cyprus are parties,[233] and the BIT. [. . .]

22. [. . .] Article 26, Part V, of the Treaty is devoted to dispute resolution and provides, *inter alia*, the right of Investors to resort to arbitration pursuant to the ICSID Convention.

23. The Respondent, in the first instance, argues that the claims made by the Claimant fall outside the jurisdiction of ICSID.

[. . .]

IV. Examination of the Parties' Submissions

116. [. . .] The Claimant contends that the Tribunal's jurisdiction is established under three instruments referred to at the outset of this Decision: (a) the Energy Charter Treaty (the "ECT"); (b) the Bilateral Investment Treaty between Bulgaria and Cyprus ("the BIT"); and (c) the ICSID Convention ("the ICSID Convention"). [. . .]

117. *Applicable Law*: All three instruments are treaties under international law; and their interpretation is governed by rules of international law, expressed in Articles 31 and 32 of the Vienna Convention on the Law of Treaties of 1969. [. . .]

121. The Claimant here rests its case on Article 26 ECT. Part V of the ECT regulates the settlements of disputes, with Article 26 providing for state-investor disputes and Article 27 for state-state disputes. [. . .] The ECT was the first multilateral treaty to provide as a general rule the settlement of investor-state disputes by international arbitration; and to date, it has been signed by at least 51 states and the European Communities. [. . .]

130. In any event, the Tribunal notes that the Respondent's charges of misrepresentation are not directed specifically at the parties' agreement to arbitrate found in Article 26 ECT. [. . .] It is not in these documents that the agreement to arbitrate is found. Bulgaria's agreement to arbitrate is found in the ECT, a multilateral treaty, a completely separate document. The Respondent has not alleged that the Claimant's purported misrepresentation nullified the ECT or its consent to arbitrate contained

233. Bulgaria ratified the ECT on 15 November 1996 and Cyprus, on 16 January 1998.

in the ECT. [. . .] so even if the parties' agreement regarding the purchase of Nova Plama is arguably invalid because of misrepresentation by the Claimant, the agreement to arbitrate remains effective. [. . .]

The Respondent's "Consent"

138. The Claimant contends that Bulgaria's signature and accession to the ECT constitutes the Respondent's "consent in writing" to ICSID arbitration, required by Article 25(1) of the ICSID Convention. [. . .]

140. [. . .] First, Article 26(3)(a) ECT provides that the Contracting Parties thereby give their "unconditional assent" to such state-investor arbitration (subject to specific exceptions which are here immaterial); and accordingly, as a Contracting Party, the Respondent thereby expressed unconditionally its written consent required under the ICSID Convention. [. . .] Third, under Article 25(1) of the ICSID Convention, when the parties have given their consent, no party "may withdraw its consent unilaterally"; and accordingly the Respondent's consent was also irrevocable from the date of the Claimant's Request for Arbitration. [. . .]

141. For all these reasons, Article 26 ECT provides to a covered investor an almost unprecedented remedy for its claim against a host state. The ECT has been described, together with NAFTA, as "the major multilateral treaty pioneering the extensive use of legal methods characteristic of the fledging regulation of the global economy", of which "perhaps the most important aspect of the ECT's investment regime is the provision for compulsory arbitration against governments at the option of foreign investors."[234] [. . .] By any standards, Article 26 is a very important feature of the ECT which is itself a very significant treaty for investors, marking another step in their transition from objects to subjects of international law.

The Tribunal's Conditional Conclusion on Article 26 ECT

142. In conclusion, subject to the major issue raised by the Respondent on Article 17(1) ECT (which is considered below), it follows from the decisions so far that this Tribunal decides that it would have jurisdiction to determine on its merits the present dispute between the Claimant and the Respondent under Article 26 ECT and the ICSID Convention, and that both parties to the dispute have given their written consent thereto within the meaning of Article 25(1) of the ICSID Convention. [. . .]

C. Jurisdiction of the Arbitral Tribunal under The Bulgaria-Cyprus BIT

185. The Tribunal notes at the outset that the Respondent does not seriously contest that the Claimant qualifies as an investor under the Bulgaria-Cyprus BIT. As a result, the question before the Tribunal is how the MFN provision in that BIT should be interpreted.

186. The Claimant's position appears to be prompted by the limited dispute settlement provisions in the Bulgaria-Cyprus BIT. [. . .]

---

234. Bamberger, Lineham and Wälde, *The Energy Charter Treaty in 2000*, Energy Law in Europe, ed. Roggenkamp (2000), 11, 31 and 32.

195. In the 1990s, after Bulgaria's communist regime changed, it began concluding BITs with much more liberal dispute resolution provisions, including resort to ICSID arbitration. [. . .] the Contracting Parties to the BIT themselves did not consider that the MFN provision extends to dispute settlement provisions in other BITs. [. . .]

198. [. . .] With the advent of bilateral and multilateral investment treaties since the 1980s (today estimated to be more than 1,500), the traditional diplomatic protection mechanism by home states for their nationals investing abroad has been largely replaced by direct access by investors to arbitration against host states. Nowadays, arbitration is the generally accepted avenue for resolving disputes between investors and states. Yet, that phenomenon does not take away the basic prerequisite for arbitration: an agreement of the parties to arbitrate. It is a well-established principle, both in domestic and international law, that such an agreement should be clear and unambiguous. In the framework of a BIT, the agreement to arbitrate is arrived at by the consent to arbitration that a state gives in advance in respect of investment disputes falling under the BIT, and the acceptance thereof by an investor if the latter so desires. [. . .]

227. For the foregoing reasons, the Tribunal concludes that the MFN provision of the Bulgaria-Cyprus BIT cannot be interpreted as providing consent to submit a dispute under the Bulgaria-Cyprus BIT to ICSID arbitration and that the Claimant cannot rely on dispute settlement provisions in other BITs to which Bulgaria is a Contracting Party in the present case. [. . .]

E. Registration by ICSID of the Request for Arbitration

231. The Respondent argues that ICSID, in registering the Claimant's Request for Arbitration, did so only with respect to the claims based on the ECT and not those based on the BIT. Consequently, says the Respondent, the Arbitral Tribunal has jurisdiction only over the claims under the ECT. [. . .]

V. The Decision

240. In light of the foregoing considerations, the Arbitral Tribunal makes the following decisions:

A. As to the jurisdictional issues with respect to the ECT:

(1) Under Article 26 ECT and the ICSID Convention, the Tribunal has jurisdiction to decide on the merits the Claimant's claims against the Respondent for alleged breaches of Part III of the ECT. [. . .]

C. The most favored nation provision of the Bulgaria-Cyprus BIT, read with other BITs to which Bulgaria is a Contracting Party (in particular the Bulgaria-Finland BIT), cannot be interpreted as providing the Respondent's consent to submit the dispute with the Claimant under the Bulgaria-Cyprus BIT to ICSID arbitration or entitling the Claimant to rely in the present case on dispute settlement provisions contained in these other BITs. [. . .]

3. ICSID Rules of Procedure for Arbitration Proceedings (Arbitration Rules)

The ICSID Rules of Procedure for Arbitration Proceedings (the "Arbitration Rules") were adopted by the Administrative Council of the Centre pursuant to Article 6(1)(c) of the Convention on the Settlement of Investment Disputes between States and Nationals of Other States (1966). The Arbitration Rules were adopted on 25th September 1967 and became effective as of 1st January 1968.

The Arbitration Rules have subsequently been amended three times, in 1984, 2002 (effective 1 January 2003), and 2006.

The rules provide for establishment of the Tribunal; the working of the Tribunal; general procedural provisions; written and oral procedures; particular procedures; the Award; and the post-Award remedies of Interpretation, Revision and Annulment of the Award.

The *Hrvatska Elektroprivreda* case below concerns the procedural integrity of the arbitral process under ICSID rules.

Hrvatska Elektroprivreda, d.d. v. The Republic of Slovenia, ICSID Case No. ARB/05/24, Order (May 6, 2008).

Case Introduction

The claimant, the national power company of the Republic of Croatia, formally requested arbitration against Slovenia on 4 November 2005. The Tribunal was constituted on 20 April 2006. A series of preliminary meetings took place during 2007 and 2008. In 2008, Allen & Overy representing the Respondent, sent to the Tribunal the Respondent's list of attendees for a two-week substantive hearing. Among those listed was Mr. David Milton QC of Essex Court Chambers. The Tribunal's President was a door tenant at the same Chambers. Subsequently, Hunter & Williams, acting for the Claimant, wrote to the Tribunal raising the "IBA Guidelines on Conflicts of Interest in International Arbitration" and requesting full disclosure of the details of the professional and personal relationship between the President of the Tribunal and Mr. Milton QC.

Referring to ICSID Arbitration Rule 18(1) and Rule 19, the Claimant sought an order from the Tribunal that the Respondent refrain from using the services of Mr. Milton QC.

Principal Points of the Judgment

12. [. . .] Does the Tribunal have the power to make such an order, and, if so, should it do so in the circumstances of this case? [. . .]

15. The Tribunal's obligation as guardian of the legitimacy of the arbitral process is to make every effort to ensure that the Award is soundly based and not affected by procedural imperfection. If the Tribunal grants the order sought it may later be

contended by the Respondent that there was a serious departure from a fundamental rule of procedure, i.e. the right to representation (ICSID Arbitration Rule 19) and the right to be given a full opportunity to present a case. On the other hand, if the order were refused the Claimant may later assert unfairness in that the President was not in a position to be relied upon to "judge fairly" as required by ICSID Arbitration Rule 6 or that there existed an impermissible appearance of partiality. [. . .]

17. Barristers are sole practitioners. Their Chambers are not law firms. Over the years it has often been accepted that members of the same Chambers, acting as counsel, appear before other fellow members acting as arbitrators. [. . .]

18. It is, however, equally true that this practice is not universally understood let alone universally agreed [. . .]

19. This evolution has been observed in the Background Information on the IBA Guidelines on Conflicts of Interest in International Arbitration. Paragraph 4.5 of that Background Information discusses the question of barristers who practise as arbitrators, and states:

> "While the peculiar nature of the constitution of barristers' chambers is well recognised and generally accepted in England by the legal profession and by the courts, it is acknowledged by the Working Group that, to many who are not familiar with the workings of the English Bar, particularly in light of the content of the promotional material which many chambers now disseminate, there is an understandable perception that barristers' chambers should be treated in the same way as law firms."

20. It is true that many parties would readily accept that a member of such a professional grouping would not be affected by any favouritism when considering submissions made by a fellow member, but by the same token other parties may take a different view. [. . .]

22. The ICSID Convention in Article 14 demands that arbitrators "be relied upon to exercise independent judgment." ICSID Arbitration Rule 6 requires them to "judge fairly". The objection in this case is not predicated on any actual lack of independence or impartiality, but on apprehensions of the appearance of impropriety. [. . .]

23. The consequences of this conclusion are not straightforward. For an international system like that of ICSID, it seems unacceptable for the solution to reside in the individual national bodies which regulate the work of professional service providers, because that might lead to inconsistent or indeed arbitrary outcomes depending on the attitudes of such bodies, or the content (or lack of relevant content) of their rules. It would moreover be disruptive to interrupt international cases to ascertain the position taken by such bodies.

24. The ICSID Convention and Rules do not, however, explicitly give the power to tribunals to exclude counsel. To the contrary, we readily accept that as a general rule

parties may seek such representation as they see fit—and that this is a fundamental principle.

25. Even fundamental principles must, however, give way to overriding exceptions. In this case, the overriding principle is that of the immutability of properly constituted tribunals (Article 56(1) of the ICSID Convention).

26. To be concrete: although the Respondent in this case was free to select its legal team as it saw fit prior to the constitution of the Tribunal, it was not entitled to subsequently amend the composition of its legal team in such a fashion as to imperil the Tribunal's status or legitimacy. [. . .]

28. The drafters of the ICSID Convention had no difficulty seeing that immutability was not absolute. It may be impossible to overcome the simple incapacity or even personal disinclination of an arbitrator to serve. The drafters nevertheless agreed that the immutability principle should be the norm, since it affects not only arbitrators. [. . .]

29. The present case involves precisely such an initiative undertaken by one of the litigants, which only at an extremely late stage has disclosed the involvement of counsel whose presence is for all practical purposes incompatible with the maintenance of the Tribunal in its present proper composition.

30. The Tribunal is concerned—indeed, compelled—to preserve the integrity of the proceedings and, ultimately, its Award. Undoubtedly, one of the "fundamental rules of procedure" referred to in Article 52(l)(d) of the ICSID Convention is that the proceedings should not be tainted by any justifiable doubt as to the impartiality or independence of any Tribunal member. [. . .]

31. The Tribunal does not believe there is a hard-and-fast rule to the effect that barristers from the same Chambers are always precluded from being involved as, respectively, counsel and arbitrator in the same case. Equally, however, there is no absolute rule to opposite effect. [. . .] Here, [. . .] the Respondent's conscious decision not to inform the Claimant or the Tribunal of Mr. Mildon's involvement in the case, following his engagement in February of this year, third, the tardiness of the Respondent's announcement of Mr. Mildon's involvement and, finally, the Respondent's subsequent insistent refusal to disclose the scope of Mr. Mildon's involvement, a matter of days before the commencement of the hearing on the merits. The last three matters were errors of judgment on the Respondent's part and have created an atmosphere of apprehension and mistrust which it is important to dispel.

33. The Tribunal disagrees with the contention of Respondent that it has no inherent powers in this regard. It considers that as a judicial formation governed by public international law, the Tribunal has an inherent power to take measures to preserve the integrity of its proceedings. In part, that inherent power finds a textual foothold in Article 44 of the Convention, which authorizes the Tribunal to decide

"any question of procedure" not expressly dealt with in the Convention, the ICSID Arbitration Rules or "any rule agreed by the parties". [. . .]

34. In light of the fundamental rule enshrined in Article 56(1) of the Convention and given its inherent procedural powers confirmed by Article 44, the Arbitral Tribunal hereby decides that the participation of Mr. Mildon QC in this case would be inappropriate and improper. [. . .]

RULING

In accordance with the foregoing, and after deliberations, the Tribunal hereby makes the following ruling:

1. Mr. David Mildon QC may not participate further as counsel in this case.

2. The hearing will proceed this afternoon with opening statements on all except quantum matters. It is clear from the written openings that there is an easy division, because each side has a section headed "Quantum" in their pre-hearing submissions. This will be followed by the hearing of evidence from witnesses who speak as to liability issues.[235]

4. Enforcement Mechanism under ICSID

The enforcement and annulment mechanisms under ICSID are found in Section 6 of the Convention.

Section 6 Recognition and Enforcement of the Award

Article 53

(1) The award shall be binding on the parties and shall not be subject to any appeal or to any other remedy except those provided for in this Convention. Each party shall abide by and comply with the terms of the award except to the extent that enforcement shall have been stayed pursuant to the relevant provisions of this Convention.

(2) For the purposes of this Section, "award" shall include any decision interpreting, revising or annulling such award pursuant to Articles 50, 51 or 52.

Article 54

(1) Each Contracting State shall recognize an award rendered pursuant to this Convention as binding and enforce the pecuniary obligations imposed by that award within its territories as if it were a final judgment of a court in that State. A Contracting State with a federal constitution may enforce such an award in or through

---

235. When directed by the Tribunal to disclose the nature and extent of Mr. Mildon QC's instructions it was indicated that he was "assisting . . . principally on matters of quantum. . . ." T.5: 10- 16.

its federal courts and may provide that such courts shall treat the award as if it were a final judgment of the courts of a constituent state.

(2) A party seeking recognition or enforcement in the territories of a Contracting State shall furnish to a competent court or other authority which such State shall have designated for this purpose a copy of the award certified by the Secretary-General. Each Contracting State shall notify the Secretary-General of the designation of the competent court or other authority for this purpose and of any subsequent change in such designation.

(3) Execution of the award shall be governed by the laws concerning the execution of judgments in force in the State in whose territories such execution is sought.

Article 55

Nothing in Article 54 shall be construed as derogating from the law in force in any Contracting State relating to immunity of that State or of any foreign State from execution.

5. Annulment under ICSID

Article 51

(1) Either party may request revision of the award by an application in writing addressed to the Secretary-General on the ground of discovery of some fact of such a nature as decisively to affect the award, provided that when the award was rendered that fact was unknown to the Tribunal and to the applicant and that the applicant's ignorance of that fact was not due to negligence.

(2) The application shall be made within 90 days after the discovery of such fact and in any event within three years after the date on which the award was rendered.

(3) The request shall, if possible, be submitted to the Tribunal which rendered the award. If this shall not be possible, a new Tribunal shall be constituted in accordance with Section 2 of this Chapter.

(4) The Tribunal may, if it considers that the circumstances so require, stay enforcement of the award pending its decision. If the applicant requests a stay of enforcement of the award in his application, enforcement shall be stayed provisionally until the Tribunal rules on such request.

Article 52

(1) Either party may request annulment of the award by an application in writing addressed to the Secretary-General on one or more of the following grounds:

(a) that the Tribunal was not properly constituted;

(b) that the Tribunal has manifestly exceeded its powers;

(c) that there was corruption on the part of a member of the Tribunal;

(d) that there has been a serious departure from a fundamental rule of procedure; or

(e) that the award has failed to state the reasons on which it is based.

(2) The application shall be made within 120 days after the date on which the award was rendered except that when annulment is requested on the ground of corruption such application shall be made within 120 days after discovery of the corruption and in any event within three years after the date on which the award was rendered.

(3) On receipt of the request the Chairman shall forthwith appoint from the Panel of Arbitrators an ad hoc Committee of three persons. None of the members of the Committee shall have been a member of the Tribunal which rendered the award, shall be of the same nationality as any such member, shall be a national of the State party to the dispute or of the State whose national is a party to the dispute, shall have been designated to the Panel of Arbitrators by either of those States, or shall have acted as a conciliator in the same dispute. The Committee shall have the authority to annul the award or any part thereof on any of the grounds set forth in paragraph (1).

(4) The provisions of Articles 41–45, 48, 49, 53 and 54, and of Chapters VI and VII shall apply mutatis mutandis to proceedings before the Committee.

(5) The Committee may, if it considers that the circumstances so require, stay enforcement of the award pending its decision. If the applicant requests a stay of enforcement of the award in his application, enforcement shall be stayed provisionally until the Committee rules on such request.

(6) If the award is annulled the dispute shall, at the request of either party, be submitted to a new Tribunal constituted in accordance with Section 2 of this Chapter.

Compania De Aguas Del Aconquija S.A. and Vivendi Universal (formerly Compagnie Générale Des Eaux) v. Argentine Republic, ICSID (2002) Case No. ARB/97/3.

Case Introduction

On 20th March 2001, Compagnie Générale des Eaux ("CGE") of France and its Argentinean affiliate Compania De Aguas Del Aconquija S.A. ("CAA"), collectively referred to as the "Claimants", filed an application in writing with the ICSID Secretary General for the partial annulment of a previous ICSID arbitral award relating to a water and sewage services Concession in the Province of Tucumán. The Application was made within the time period provided in Article 52(2) of the ICSID Convention. The Application sought partial annulment on three of the five grounds set out in Article 52(1) of the ICSID Convention, namely that the Tribunal making the Award had manifestly exceeded its powers; there had been a serious departure from a fundamental rule of procedure; and the Award failed to state the reasons on which it was based.

The Chairman of the Administrative Council proceeded to appoint an ad hoc Committee in accordance with Article 52(3) of the ICSID Convention. A two-day hearing in this annulment proceeding was held at ICSID on 31st January and 1st February 2002.

In the absence of any agreed request by the parties to vary the ICSID Convention rules of procedure, the annulment proceeding was conducted in accordance with the applicable provisions of Section 3 of Chapter IV of the ICSID Convention.

The Arbitration Award to which the Claimants sought partial annulment had been granted in November 2000. It concerned the alleged termination of a thirty-year concession contract by the Argentine Republic, in violation of the Bilateral Investment Treaty (BIT) between the Government of the Argentine Republic and Government of the Republic of France. The Claimants alleged that the Argentine Republic failed to prevent the Province of Tucumán from taking certain actions that consequently infringed the rights of the Claimants under the BIT.

After considering both the role of annulment under the ICSID Convention and the merits of the findings of the Tribunal with respect to the Award, the ad hoc Committee annulled that part of the Award that dealt with the Tucumán claims.

Principal Points of the Judgment

(2) The Role of Annulment Under the ICSID Convention

62. [. . .] Claimants and Respondent agree that an ad hoc Committee is not a court of appeal and that its competence extends only to annulment based on one or other of the grounds expressly set out in Article 52 of the ICSID Convention. It also appears to be established that there is no presumption either in favour of or against annulment,[236] a point acknowledged by Claimants as well as Respondent. [. . .]

64. A greater source of concern is perhaps the ground of "failure to state reasons," which is not qualified by any such phrase as "manifestly" or "serious." However, it is well accepted both in the cases and the literature that Article 52(1)(e) concerns a failure to state any reasons with respect to all or part of an award, not the failure to state correct or convincing reasons. [. . .]

65. In the Committee's view, annulment under Article 52(1)(e) should only occur in a clear case. This entails two conditions: first, the failure to state reasons must leave the decision on a particular point essentially lacking in any expressed rationale; and second, that point must itself be necessary to the tribunal's decision. [. . .]

66. Finally, it appears to be established that an ad hoc committee has a certain measure of discretion as to whether to annul an award, even if an annullable error is found. Article 52(3) provides that a committee "shall have the authority to annul the award or any part thereof," and this has been interpreted as giving committees

236. *Cf. MINE v. Guinea*, Decision on Annulment of 22 December 1989, (1989) 4 ICSID Rep. 79 at p. 86 (paras. 4.09-4.12); and *see also*, C. Schreuer, *The ICSID Convention: A Commentary* (Cambridge, Cambridge Unversity Press, 2001).

some flexibility in determining whether annulment is appropriate in the circumstances. Among other things, it is necessary for an ad hoc committee to consider the significance of the error relative to the legal rights of the parties. [. . .]

67. Another question, which was debated between the parties in this case, is whether an ad hoc committee is limited to the grounds for annulment relied on by a Claimant, or whether the Respondent may itself raise additional grounds for annulment. In their Application, Claimants sought only the partial annulment of the Award, on three grounds: (1) that the Tribunal manifestly exceeded its powers; (2) that there had been a serious departure from a fundamental rule of procedure; and (3) that the Award failed to state the reasons on which it is based. The Respondent not only resisted each of these contentions, it further argued that if any of them were to be upheld, the Award as a whole should be annulled, on the grounds either that the Tribunal had no jurisdiction at all, or that there was a fundamental contradiction in the Tribunal's reasoning as between that part which dealt with jurisdiction and that part which dealt with the merits. By way of reply, in their written pleadings, Claimants argued that what they called Respondent's "counterclaim" for annulment of the Award as a whole was inadmissible, on the ground that it was out of time and that Article 52 made no provision for counterclaims.

68. The Committee agrees with Claimants that a counterclaim for annulment, that is, a claim which is not raised by the party concerned as a separate request in accordance with Article 52(1) of the Convention, is inadmissible. [. . .]

(b) The Tribunal's Findings on the Merits

(i) Serious departure from a fundamental rule of procedure: Article 52(1)(d)

82. [. . .] Claimants argued that the Tribunal had departed from a fundamental rule of procedure in that its eventual decision, notably as to the dismissal of the Tucumán claims on grounds related to Article 16(4) of the Concession Contract, concerned a question not adequately canvassed in argument.

83. [. . .] Under Article 52(1)(d), the emphasis is clearly on the term "rule of procedure," that is, on the manner in which the Tribunal proceeded, not on the content of its decision. In the opinion of the Committee, the Tribunal proceeded with abundant care. It considered the issue of jurisdiction first, and it decided, in the exercise of its discretion, to join that issue to the merits of the dispute. It then considered the merits at length and rendered a densely reasoned award.

84. Claimants contend the Tribunal's decision came unannounced, and that they had no opportunity to present arguments on the decision to dismiss their claim on the merits on grounds related to Article 16(4) of the Concession Contract. [. . .] But even if true, this would by no means be unprecedented in judicial decision-making, either international or domestic, and it has nothing to do with the ground for annulment contemplated by Article 52(1)(d) of the ICSID Convention. [. . .]

85. From the record, it is evident that the parties had a full and fair opportunity to be heard at every stage of the proceedings. They had ample opportunity to consider and present written and oral submissions on the issues, and the oral hearing itself was meticulously conducted to enable each party to present its point of view. [. . .] For these reasons, the Committee finds no departure at all from any fundamental rule of procedure, let alone a serious departure.

(ii) Manifest excess of powers: Article 52(1)(b)

86. It is settled, and neither party disputes, that an ICSID tribunal commits an excess of powers not only if it exercises a jurisdiction which it does not have under the relevant agreement or treaty and the ICSID Convention, read together, but also if it fails to exercise a jurisdiction which it possesses under those instruments. One might qualify this by saying that it is only where the failure to exercise a jurisdiction is clearly capable of making a difference to the result that it can be considered a manifest excess of power. [. . .]

87. In the present case, Claimants contend that, far from considering their claims concerning breach of the BIT prior to purportedly dismissing them, the Tribunal actually declined to decide Claimants' allegations since it considered that, in order to do so, it would have had to address issues which, according to the Concession Contract, fell within the exclusive jurisdiction of the Tucumán courts. [. . .]

The federal claims

90. Claimants submit that, even if the Tribunal could be said to have considered the federal claims on their merits, its consideration was vitiated in that the Tribunal's handling of the federal and Tucumán claims was interdependent. Specifically, Claimants argue that if Tucumán's actions did in truth constitute a breach of the BIT, then Respondent was under a far more stringent obligation to respond and to correct the situation than the Tribunal found applied to it. Claimants contend that the Tribunal—always with its mind set on Article 16(4)—failed to consider this alternative. [. . .]

91. As to the Tribunal's findings of law, it may be that the Award lacks a detailed analysis of the relevant BIT provisions, as Claimants contend. Yet the gist of the Tribunal's reasoning is clear enough. On its face, Article 3 of the BIT imposes no more than an obligation on the Argentine Republic to take appropriate care. And the Tribunal's findings, taken together, are more than sufficient to provide a basis for the Tribunal's clear conclusion that the federal claims were not sustainable, and that there had been no breach of Article 3 as a result of any federal act or omission. [. . .]

The Tucumán claims

93. The second question in relation to Article 52(1)(b) is whether the Tribunal, having validly held that it had jurisdiction over the Tucumán claims, was entitled nonetheless to dismiss them as it did. Claimants, for their part, submit that the Tribunal

did not so much dismiss the Tucumán claims as decline to address them. They argue that the only reason those claims were dismissed was that they were held to be substantially identical with claims against Tucumán under the Concession Contract, which the Tribunal found it could not determine, and that the Tribunal's refusal to decide the Tucumán claims on this basis was a manifest excess of powers. [. . .]

95. As to the relation between breach of contract and breach of treaty in the present case, it must be stressed that Articles 3 and 5 of the BIT do not relate directly to breach of a municipal contract. Rather they set an independent standard. A state may breach a treaty without breaching a contract, and vice versa, and this is certainly true of these provisions of the BIT. [. . .]

96. Each of these claims will be determined by reference to its own proper or applicable law—in the case of the BIT, by international law; in the case of the Concession Contract, by the proper law of the contract, in other words, the law of Tucumán. For example, in the case of a claim based on a treaty, international law rules of attribution apply, with the result that the state of Argentina is internationally responsible for the acts of its provincial authorities. By contrast, the state of Argentina is not liable for the performance of contracts entered into by Tucumán, which possesses separate legal personality under its own law and is responsible for the performance of its own contracts. [. . .]

98. In a case where the essential basis of a claim brought before an international tribunal is a breach of contract, the tribunal will give effect to any valid choice of forum clause in the contract. [. . .]

102. In the Committee's view, it is not open to an ICSID tribunal having jurisdiction under a BIT in respect of a claim based upon a substantive provision of that BIT, to dismiss the claim on the ground that it could or should have been dealt with by a national court. In such a case, the inquiry which the ICSID tribunal is required to undertake is one governed by the ICSID Convention, by the BIT and by applicable international law. Such an inquiry is neither in principle determined, nor precluded, by any issue of municipal law, including any municipal law agreement of the parties.

103. Moreover the Committee does not understand how, if there had been a breach of the BIT in the present case (a question of international law), the existence of Article 16(4) of the Concession Contract could have prevented its characterisation as such. A state cannot rely on an exclusive jurisdiction clause in a contract to avoid the characterisation of its conduct as internationally unlawful under a treaty.

104. [. . .] According to the Respondent, it emerges clearly from the Award that the Claimants had no arguable case for a breach of Articles 3 or 5 of the BIT and that, at best, their claim was one for breach of contract: the issue of a treaty claim could only arise in the event that the contentious administrative tribunals of Tucumán denied Claimants justice, substantively or procedurally.

105. The question thus becomes how to characterize the Tribunal's decision. [. . .]

106. Claimants made a series of allegations as to the conduct of Tucumán, much of which, they claim, involved measures taken in bad faith. [. . .]

107. The Tribunal expressed views on some of these allegations, but by no means all. [. . .]

111. For these reasons, and despite certain passages of the Award in which the Tribunal seems to go further into the merits, the Committee can only conclude that the Tribunal, in dismissing the Tucumán claims as it did, actually failed to decide whether or not the conduct in question amounted to a breach of the BIT. [. . .] Moreover, it offered no interpretation whatsoever either of Article 3 or of Article 5 of the BIT, something which was called for if the claims were to be dismissed on their merits.

112. [. . .] In the Committee's view, the Tribunal, faced with such a claim and having validly held that it had jurisdiction, was obliged to consider and to decide it. Although the Tribunal expressed conclusions on certain aspects of the claim, it never expressed a conclusion as to the claim as a whole, still less did it assess Claimants' case against the requirements of Article 3 or 5 of the BIT.

114. [. . .] Claimants should not have been deprived of a decision, one way or the other, merely on the strength of the observation that the local courts could conceivably have provided them with a remedy, in whole or in part. Under the BIT they had a choice of remedies.

115. For all of these reasons, the Committee concludes that the Tribunal exceeded its powers in the sense of Article 52(1)(b), in that the Tribunal, having jurisdiction over the Tucumán claims, failed to decide those claims. Given the clear and serious implications of that decision for Claimants in terms of Article 8(2) of the BIT, and the surrounding circumstances, the Committee can only conclude that that excess of powers was manifest. It accordingly annuls the decision of the Tribunal so far as concerns the entirety of the Tucumán claims.

(iii) Failure to state reasons: Article 52(1)(e).

In view of the foregoing conclusion, it is unnecessary to consider the further ground of annulment relied on by Claimants, viz., that in dismissing the claim the Tribunal failed to state the reasons on which its decision was based. As to the federal claims, the Committee has already concluded that reasons for the dismissal of those claims were given. As to the Tucumán claims, in the Committee's view the Tribunal gave very full reasons for the step it took, viz., the dismissal of those claims without any overall consideration of their merits. The question of failure to state reasons would only arise if one took the view that the Tribunal actually did reach a conclusion adverse to Claimants under Articles 3 and 5 in respect of the Tucumán claims as a whole—a view the Committee has already rejected. Accordingly, nothing more needs to be said on this ground of annulment.

[. . .]

Chapter 9

Legal Issues in Joint Ventures

A. Joint Ventures as a Vehicle for Foreign Investment

The main legal vehicles for foreign direct investment are Joint Ventures ("JV") and Wholly Foreign Owned Enterprises ("WFOE"). JVs allow an investor to hold an equity interest with host country partners in the same limited liability company. Profits and losses are distributed in proportion to the ownership interests in the venture. Although a foreign investor's attention is often focused on obtaining a majority equity interest, in practice, this may not be sufficient to ensure effective management control.

Some countries have laws in place which allow foreigners to establish and operate wholly foreign-owned enterprises and make independent investments without the participation of a host country partner. Although a WFOE usually takes the form of a limited liability company, the Implementing Rules may permit other liability structures, subject to the approval of the relevant host country authorities.

In recent years, WFOEs rather than JVs have become the preferred vehicle for investment in countries such as China. The general reason is greater management autonomy, compared to the frequently ambiguous situation within JVs, and less exposure to actual or potential political interference. In China, for example, many large multinationals have been buying out or selling their JV interests over recent years and now have few JVs left in China.

Nevertheless, investors may still consider that cooperation with a local firm is indispensable. The benefits may include tangible contributions such as government land and intangible contributions including local relationships, expertise and industry knowledge. In addition, there may also be strategic or regulatory reasons why investment with a local JV partner continues to be necessary. This is most clearly the case in strategic sectors such as shipping or aviation, where foreign investors are often not permitted to hold full ownership or control and are limited to a specified percentage interest. These types of restrictions mean that foreign investors have no alternative except to link up with a local JV partner.

Disputes typically arise between JV partners over the management of a JV business and issues such as dividend entitlements, funding or capitalization, in particular if the JV partners want the business to develop in different ways. If the differences cannot be resolved, the JV may have to be wound up, with significant risks and exposures for the foreign investor.

Trading and contractual disputes may also arise over sale and purchase of goods, commodities or property, of which disputes over non-payment are the most common cause of contention. Practical problems may also arise from licensing or customs procedures, or the administrative complexities of capital transfer. Other sources of difficulty can include regulatory investigations by the securities or banking regulators, in particular where there is alleged misconduct by the JV company or its partners. Payment and quality disputes can also be caused by dishonesty, for example, a failure to disclose payments overdue, and cases have been reported of companies "disappearing" after provision of valuable technical information. Unfortunately, corruption is not uncommon and it is important for investors to be alert and seek professional advice. Where disputes involve allegations of fraudulent or corrupt behavior, related criminal proceedings may make it particularly difficult to wind up a Joint Venture undertaking.

The factory environment can also give rise to labor related problems in host countries. It is not uncommon in some countries for workers to live without family in dormitories on the premises of the factory. The focus is on maximizing earnings to send home, and this can be a setting for all kinds of labor related disputes. Common causes of difficulty include overtime, termination of contract, working conditions and problems arising from local labor regulations.

B. Historical Developments in the Law of Joint Ventures

1. Experience of CMEA Countries

The following article describes the joint venture relationship under The Council for Mutual Economic Assistance ("CMEA"), an economic organization led by the Soviet Union from 1949 to 1991, and comprising countries from the Warsaw Pact in Europe and a number of communist states elsewhere in the world.

Andrzej Burzynski, *The Concept of a Joint Venture and the Legal Context for Joint Ventures in CMEA Countries*, 5 FLA. INT'L L.J. [v] (1989–1990).

I. The Meaning of the Term "Joint Venture"

[. . .] In the broadest sense, the concept "joint venture" is understood to include all forms of agreements through which "the operation of two or more firms are partially, but not fully, functionally integrated in order to carry out activities in one or more areas".[237] This may consist of simple buying or selling of operations, development and production of natural resources, or research and development and construction projects. [. . .]

It is interesting to note in this context, however, that the use of this term in Council for Mutual Economic Assistance (CMEA) countries, as evidenced by national reports, is reserved for the particular relationship between a local and foreign party in which a new separate entity is created. [. . .]

The term "joint venture" usually is used in the broader sense in CMEA countries. Since at the earlier stage of foreign equity investment in these countries only joint ventures with local partners were permitted, the term "joint venture" became synonymous with "foreign investment".[238] [. . .]

II. Evolution of Legislation

European CMEA countries are latecomers to the international investment market. The first country allowing foreigners to operate inside its economy was Romania in 1971. [. . .] Among the laws of CMEA countries regulating foreign investment, Romanian law is the most stable one. It has not been changed for the last 18 years.

In contrast, Hungarian law on foreign joint ventures has been frequently changed. [. . .]

Poland decided to invite foreign investors in 1976. However, only small foreign businesses, limited both in scope and size, were invited. Ten years passed before the Polish legislature enacted a law allowing major foreign investment. [. . .]

In the Soviet Union, East-West joint ventures were authorized by two decrees of 1987. [. . .]

III. The Main Functions of Joint Venture Legislation

Multiple and complex reasons exist for the late start and guarded approach to foreign investment in CMEA countries. Political apprehensions were an important factor. [. . .] The economic system that developed in these countries during the post-war period was quite hostile toward any form of direct foreign participation

237. Organization for Economic Cooperation and Development, Competition Policy and Joint Venture 11 (1986).

238. Burzynski & Juergensmeyer, *East-West Industrial Cooperation: The Polish Example*, 1 LOY. L.A. INT'L & COMP. L. ANN. 37, 38–39 (1978).

in their economies. [. . .] Consequently, the legal and administrative framework for the economic life that was formulated during that period concentrated almost exclusively on regulating the organization and conduct of economic activities of the state-owned enterprises or cooperatives leaving little room for private initiative.

IV. Governmental Controls Over the Formation and Activities of Joint Ventures

Governmental control over the admission and activities of foreign investors is not an invention of CMEA countries. It is known and practiced also in many western European countries. In some of these countries, the governments reserve some measure of control under specific foreign investment acts.[239] In other countries, it is exercised under general procedures which have to be followed by anyone interested in obtaining the right to invest in the country.

Securing adequate governmental controls is also one of the main functions of CMEA countries' legislation allowing joint ventures. [. . .]

A common feature of the "first generation" of laws on foreign investment was the requirement of governmental approval for any joint venture project. [. . .] the requirement for the management of joint ventures to include nationals of the host country.[240]

The changes introduced to joint venture legislation in many CMEA countries at the end of 1988 indicate a tendency toward greater flexibility in providing for governmental control over joint ventures. [. . .]

Also, the proportion of shares allowed to be held by foreign companies has been liberalized. In Bulgaria, Poland, and Hungary, foreign investors may form wholly-owned subsidiaries. [. . .]

V. Protection of Rights and Property of Foreign Investors

[. . .] Increasing legislation containing guarantees against expropriation is evidence of the growing awareness among CMEA countries that inviting foreign investors without assuring them as to the security of their investment will not work.

[. . .] Apart from the fear of sudden expropriation, foreign investors are also very sensitive to foreign exchange restrictions which exist in all CMEA countries. The regulations on joint ventures in these countries contain guarantees as to the transfer of profits and capital abroad. With the exception of Hungary, however, in all CMEA countries foreign investors can only transfer abroad the amount in foreign currencies earned by their joint ventures. [. . .]

---

239. For instance in Greece, Italy, Portugal, Spain and Turkey.

240. For example the Polish Law of April 23, 1986 on Companies with Foreign Capital Participation, 1988 Dz. U., No. 17, provided in art. 17 that the company's manager, and in the case of a board of management, its president should be a Polish citizen who is a permanent resident in Poland.

VI. The Status of the Joint Venture in Legal and Economic System of the Host Country

Knowing foreign investors' tendencies toward economic planning, most of the foreign investment laws formally considered joint ventures as independent of the economic planning and administrative systems in the host country. This position was taken by the laws of the Soviet Union, Bulgaria, Czechoslovakia, Hungary and Poland. However, regarding domestic purchases, the same laws, with the exception of the Soviet Union, put joint ventures under the same conditions as state-owned enterprises.

Economic reform that is currently under way in some of the CMEA countries should render all of the problems connected with determining the status of the joint venture in the legal and economic system of Poland obsolete. Once the distinction between the rights and duties of state owned enterprises and other entities representing different forms of ownership is removed, the need for specific provisions determining the position of joint ventures will also disappear.

C. Establishing Joint International Business Ventures

International joint ventures can be initiated in three ways:

1. Foreign partner investment in an existing local company.
2. Local partner investment in an existing national operation of a foreign company.
3. Creation of an entirely new business venture.

Such joint ventures may take the form of an equity joint venture or a contractual joint venture. The equity JV is governed by corporate law and is the most commonly used form of joint venture. It may take several forms, often differentiated by the ownership provisions. A contractual JV is one in which no separate joint enterprise is formed, i.e. there is no actual partnership or joint corporate entity formed. Contractual arrangements are made for the supply of capital, equipment, industrial property and technical assistance by the foreign partner in return for royalties, which may depend on sales, etc. These types of arrangements are often used in countries with centrally planned economies, or in the exploration and development of natural resources, where the desire for national control is strong.

Often the host country partner provides land, machinery, industrial sites and facilities, and intangible contributions such as government contacts, environmental knowledge and customer contacts. The foreign investor usually provides technical skills and know-how, patents, marketing techniques, specialized personnel, production techniques and financial resources.

Joint venture contracts may take several forms, and there is no single standard prototype agreement. A basic joint venture agreement may incorporate only facts pertinent to formation and structure of the joint venture contract, with other matters covered in separate legal agreements. Matters such as the products the company is licensed to produce, the components each partner is to supply, and the territory in which the company may sell manufactured products, should be clearly defined in the contract. It is also advisable for the contract to clearly proscribe the procedures to be followed in the event of a dispute.

D. Structuring and Negotiating International Joint Ventures

When considering a possible joint venture, it is important to evaluate different options for ownership structure. A 50/50 partnership may help to create a strong feeling of partnership and equality, where profits and responsibilities are equally shared. Otherwise, the JV can be structured as a majority partnership or a minority partnership. A majority situation may be more attractive to a foreign partner, as many of the advantages of the wholly owned subsidiary can be gained and profits are proportionately higher. In addition, this structure implies a great degree of influence and decision making.

A majority ownership situation may also be attractive to the host country, as it reduces the use of national capital resources while giving protection against excessive foreign control. Foreign investors may also be willing to accept minority participation in a joint venture, if they feel the prospective partner is qualified and provides adequate safeguards. The extent of local participation in management may be linked to the proportion of national ownership.

Another consideration in the negotiation of an international joint venture is the marketing plan. It is best that this is clearly spelled out in advance, so that possible competitive conflicts and restrictive practices do not give rise to subsequent disappointment and conflict. Mutual consultation in areas such as export marketing strategy and supplier and customer relationships, as well as long term pricing policies, is important.

As many developing countries do not possess the necessary technologies and patents, it is customary for manufacturing joint ventures to be licensees of foreign patents. The scope of patent licensing agreements should also include future product developments.

© Michael E. Hooton, *Structuring and Negotiating International Joint Ventures*, Creighton University Law Review Vol. 27, Issue 4 (1993–1994), pp. 1013–1037, reprinted with permission. Copyright © 1994 by Creighton University.

i. Introduction

[. . .] Far from being a negative, though, the flexibility of the joint venture concept is one of its principle virtues. In turn, flexibility is essential in developing a joint venture relationship. Flexibility is also a critical component in the professional work—whether business development, finance or legal—required to organize and initiate a joint venture. A flexible approach will almost always result in the best possible outcome—for all concerned.

Just as flexibility is critical to structuring and negotiating joint ventures, fairness to both parties is crucial to the implementation and operation of the enterprise. [. . .]

The parties must be willing and able to push the negotiations forward creatively and steadily. They must also be willing to consider the other side's point of view and constraints. International joint ventures necessarily involve a meeting, and sometimes a clash, of two cultures. [. . .]

ii. Various Structures

At the outset of discussing alternative joint venture structures, it is important to note that the desired tax consequences will most likely be controlling. Because the tax results will vary greatly by jurisdiction and by the parent companies' tax situations, little can be provided in the way of general guidance.[241] If possible though it is important to make sure that the taxes paid by the joint venture company can be credited against the partners' home country tax liability arising when the joint venture company's earnings are repatriated.[242] [. . .]

The fundamental question then is who gets control and how much.[243] Usually, it is the party with the most money. When both partners have lots of money—which does not happen often—control may go to the partner contributing the scarcest resource. For example, if marketing or technical skills are critical, then control will follow the experienced marketer or high-technology contributor. If local marketing or distribution channels are more important, then control may vest in the local partner.

If a party is in the minority, then it will be critical for it to negotiate minority protection rights. For example, the minority partner would want to have a say in approving extraordinary transactions, such as a major capital expenditure, bank and other financing, the issuance of additional equity or call for additional capital, a major assets sale, development of a new line of business or territory, mergers, and amendment of the articles and bylaws. [. . .]

---

241. "[T]he choice of entity . . . will be based primarily on tax considerations." [Bernard L. Greer, Jr., et al., *Transnational Strategic Business Alliances: Some Observations*, in PRIVATE INVESTMENTS ABROAD— PROBLEMS AND SOLUTIONS IN INTERNATIONAL BUSINESS IN 1991 (Carol J. Holgren ed., 1991)], at 2-15.

242. Under United States federal income tax laws, dividends received by a United States parent company from a foreign subsidiary are fully taxed in the United States. The United States parent, however, is generally entitled to a tax credit against its United States tax liability on such dividends in an amount equal to the foreign income taxes paid with respect to such dividends, subject to certain limitations.

243. In general, one party or the other should have the lead in the ordinary course of business by, for example, being able to appoint the joint venture's chief executive officer. But even a substantial majority (80%) held by a multinational will not confer absolute control because the local partner's active participation and cooperation will usually be essential. A recalcitrant local partner, no matter how small its share, is still a force to be reckoned with.

iii. Preliminary Agreements

Finance transactions start with term sheets and acquisitions start with letters of intent. Likewise, international joint venture negotiations are often built on the foundation of a memorandum of understanding. [. . .] These types of agreements however are more important to joint venture practice because of the cross-cultural nature of joint ventures. Where the parties have less in common, it is more important to have a place to start.[244] [. . .]

These preliminary agreements can be signed or unsigned depending on the parties' desire to formalize the negotiations. In general, business people like to have these types of agreements signed in the hope that the other party will, or believe it will, be committed to the transaction.[245] In general, the lawyers for the parties, especially the multinational's lawyer, will prefer that these types of documents remain unsigned to avoid a commitment until all of the details can be negotiated into the definitive agreement.

Obviously, whether a signed or unsigned preliminary document is binding is a matter of local law.[246] A local lawyer must provide this advice. But if the negotiations are going well, the parties are dying to sign something, and local counsel advises that a preliminary document will not be treated as a binding contract (if indeed that is the intent), then it is acceptable to sign the memorandum. [. . .]

iv. Joint Venture Agreement

[. . .] There is no particularly right way to order the agreement. The order followed in this discussion is fairly standard. If, however, the joint venture agreement is being prepared pursuant to a specific joint venture law, then it is best to follow the order of the topics in the applicable law or regulations. [. . .]

Definitions. It is customary for American style transaction documents to lead off with the definitions. For people unaccustomed to working with such documents however

---

244. Before structuring and drafting [the joint venture agreement] begin, the parties should [. . .] outline the principal business terms of the venture in order to make the process as efficient as possible. A well-structured letter of intent will go a long way toward ensuring that the negotiating and drafting process is given a proper frame of reference and should minimize misunderstandings. The letter of intent stage should also expose any differences in basic viewpoint of the parties in terms of strategic objectives and relative contribution of the parties. All issues need not be resolved at the letter of intent stage, but in general it is a worthwhile exercise because the process will isolate the "deal breaker" points.

245. The parties should clearly identify preliminary letters as letters of intent and include a provision denying the enforceability of the obligations unless, of course, one is trying to "have his cake and eat it too." Such a party would undoubtedly adopt with enthusiasm the definition of a "gentleman's agreement" attributed by Professor Waddams to the English judge, Mr. Justice Vaisey: "A gentleman's agreement is an agreement which is not an agreement entered into between two persons, neither of whom is a gentleman, with each expecting the other to be strictly bound, while he himself has no intention of being bound at all." Richard B. Potter, *The Drafting and Enforcement of Canada/ United States Contracts: A Canadian Lawyer's Perspective*, 20 INT'L LAW. 3, 6 (1986).

246. *See*, *Texaco, Inc. v. Pennzoil Co.*, 729 S.W.2d 768 (Tex. Ct. App. 1987); *Keely v. Price*, 103 Cal. Rptr. 531 (1972); *Zimmerman v. Bank of Am. Nat'l Trust & Say.* Ass'n, 12 Cal. Rptr. 319 (1961).

this can be confusing and even irritating. It may therefore be advisable to include the definitions at the end of the agreement in a section covering miscellaneous items or even in an exhibit. The definitions will cover the parties, the joint venture itself, perhaps accounting terms, and the definitions that may be necessary for the termination provisions, such as "defaulting party" and "nondefaulting party." [. . .]

Purpose. [. . .] Not only is this sometimes a matter of local law, but it is often essential to make sure both parties are clear on the scope and scale of the joint venture's operations. It is not uncommon for the parties, especially the local partner, to have extremely ambitious plans for the business. It may therefore be appropriate for the multinational to attempt to get the specific purposes of the joint venture listed clearly and concisely. [. . .]

Joint Venture Company. This section would typically deal with the type of joint venture company to be formed. For example, a joint stock company or other limited liability company under local law. [. . .]

It may be appropriate in this section to include a reference to the government approvals necessary before the company can be formed. This section would also provide a reference to the joint venture company's articles of incorporation, which are usually included as an exhibit to the joint venture agreement.

It would also be appropriate to include a reference to the duration of the joint venture company. In general, multinationals prefer to incorporate the company for a perpetual term, although this can be a matter of local legal restrictions.[247] [. . .]

Funding and Capital. This section of the agreement should cover the parties' initial capital contributions, as well as the amount and responsibility for obtaining any debt financing for the joint venture. [. . .] to reference a funding agreement.

To the extent the parties contemplate contributions in-kind (land, equipment, site preparation, utilities), it is important to provide for a valuation method. [. . .]

Stock. [. . .] In most joint ventures the parties grant each other a right of first refusal with respect to the sale of their interests. [. . .] The agreement would typically provide that no pledge or other transfer of a party's shares or interests in the joint venture could be made without the consent of the other party. [. . .]

Other Responsibilities. [. . .]

Shareholders. [. . .]

Directors and Officers. The joint venture agreement would include provisions granting each party the right to appoint a certain number of the directors of the joint venture company. [. . .] This section of the agreement should also specify the senior officers of the joint venture company, and the party responsible for nominating them. [. . .]

247. Henry R. Zheng, *Business Organization and Securities Laws of the People's Republic of China*, 43 Bus. Law. 551, 599 (1988).

The critical control mechanism for the joint venture would also be included in this section if it is not already covered in the shareholder voting section. [. . .]

Corporate and Operating Procedures. This section of the agreement would provide for the accounting standards to be used for the joint venture and for audits by the company's regular auditors or a statutory auditor if required by local law. [. . .] This section of the agreement would also provide for the fiscal year of the joint venture company, with an indication as to whether the first year will be a short year (less than twelve months) or a long year (more than twelve months). The decision for a short or long year will depend on local law and tax policy.[248] In general, if losses are expected in the early years it is best to have a long first year to take full advantage of tax loss carry forwards.

Related Agreements. Usually a joint venture relationship will involve more than just the joint venture agreement. For example, it may be appropriate to have technology licenses, employment agreements, and various other agreements between one of the partners and the joint venture company itself. [. . .]

Confidentiality. The parties would also typically cover the confidential treatment of the information they disclose to each other and to the joint venture company. Moreover, it will normally be critical to provide that the joint venture company cannot use the confidential information of one of the contributing parties to the detriment of the disclosing party. [. . .]

Payments. A joint venture agreement may also include provisions for the priority of rights with respect to foreign currency. Typically, a multinational will require that the joint venture pay dividends and other distributions to the multinational in either its currency or another freely tradeable currency. [. . .]

Deadlock. Although parties to joint venture negotiations are not eager to confront the possibility of deadlock, it is always a good idea to include provisions governing what happens when the parties cannot agree. Typically, the agreement would include a provision calling for the parties to use their best efforts to resolve all disputes by mutual agreement. If this fails, then the parties may want to turn to mediation, arbitration, and ultimately termination of the joint venture. One technique is to provide a system whereby disagreements are referred to specific senior officers of the respective partners. For example, the agreement might provide for the dispute to be submitted to the chief executive officers of each of the partners for a certain period before the other dispute resolution mechanisms can be implemented.

Termination. The termination provisions for a joint venture are probably the most important terms of the entire document.[249] [. . .] The termination provisions

248. Once again, this will be a matter of local law. Indeed, local law and custom may require that the fiscal year be the calendar year, with the first year running from the start of the joint venture until the next December 31.

249. One of the most important provisions of a joint venture agreement is that which sets forth the procedure for terminating the venture and distributing the assets, leaving the venturers free to

might also cover the termination of the joint venture in the event of expropriation of the joint venture's assets. [. . .] On termination of the joint venture, it would be customary to provide a mechanism for one party to buy the other's interest, or for both parties to sell their interest to a third party, or for the joint venture to liquidate and distribute any proceeds to the partners in proportion to their interests. [. . .]

Additional Contributions. [. . .] the agreement should provide an adjustment mechanism. [. . .]

Noncompetition. [. . .] Noncompetition provisions are generally difficult to negotiate and, even assuming successful negotiation, may be unenforceable.[250] In addition, in certain jurisdictions, noncompetition provisions may be illegal. Similarly, due to local legal constraints, it may not be permissible to include provisions indicating that the joint venture will be the exclusive business operation of the partners in a certain country or area. [. . .]

Dispute Resolution, Governing Law.[251] Typically, a joint venture agreement for an international joint venture will include provisions requiring resolution of disputes through good faith negotiations for a period of time, such as thirty days. [. . .] Mediation is another possibility. It is customary to include arbitration provisions in joint venture agreements because it would most likely be difficult for a joint venture to survive litigation of a dispute between the partners.[252] If the local partner is a governmental agency or state company, then it may be appropriate to have it waive sovereign immunity in the agreement. [. . .] It may also be desirable to exclude from local jurisdiction disputes involving the intellectual property component of a joint venture (patents, trademarks or technology) where it is important to the contributing party (for example, the multinational) to make sure that disputes involving these assets are settled in its home jurisdiction.

Foreign Exchange. [. . .]

---

go their separate ways upon the occurrence of any number of events, including deadlock, lack of money, bankruptcy of one venturer, and any other matter that may disrupt the fundamentals of the venture relationship. This article also provides a discussion of various options on termination.

250. Just as in the United States, noncompetition (restraint of trade) contract provisions are disfavored in many other countries.

251. The importance of including dispute resolution procedures in the agreement can be summarized as follows: If the venture arrangements do not provide clearly for the resolution of [. . .] disputes, then what would probably end in an unhappy divorce in any event will become a messy and expensive divorce with much agonizing over property and custody. Thus it is imperative to prescribe clear dispute resolution mechanisms with clear, mandatory choice of law and choice of forum clauses and agreement on the language in which any dispute resolution proceeding will be conducted.

252. Arbitration of disputes between international companies has been a fertile area for discussion in law reviews and treatises. See Jay Lawrence Westbrook, *The Coming Encounter: International Arbitration and Bankruptcy*, 67 MINN. L. REV. 595 (1983); Roger R. Blanpain, The Kenneth M. Piper Lecture: *Transnational Regulation of the Labor Relations of Multinational Enterprises*, 58 CHI.-KENT. L. REV. 909 (1982). In general, it is best to provide for arbitration in a neutral country according to well-accepted rules. [. . .]

Change in Law. [. . .]

Compliance with Law. [. . .]

Miscellaneous. [. . .] The governing language of the agreement should also be specified.

v. Related Agreements

Typically, these agreements include technology licenses, trademark licenses or assignments, employment agreements, real estate purchase or lease agreements, construction contracts, finance documents, and operating agreements, such as supplier and distribution contracts. [. . .]

Although standard form agreements can provide a starting place for the negotiation of the related agreements, it is usually essential to consider local legal forms as well. [. . .] For example, it is critical in preparing employment agreements to take local law and custom into account.

In contrast, trademark and technology licenses are more often than not best based on the multinational's standard—at least at the outset. [. . .] In many international joint ventures, the greatest contribution the multinational can make to the long term success of the joint venture is in the area of advanced technology, business practices and trademarks.[253] Also, the multinational partner may have proprietary rights in intellectual property that is extremely valuable. [. . .]

vi. Additional Matters

There are a number of special issues that should also be noted in discussing the implementation of international joint ventures. Almost by definition, these joint ventures will involve the foreign investment laws of the host countries. The government approval process varies greatly from one country to another. Even where foreign investment laws are relatively easily satisfied, the country may restrict or prohibit foreign ownership of land or participation in certain businesses. At the outset, therefore, it is essential to determine the government's requirements and role in the process. Moreover, an evaluation of the time involved in obtaining the necessary approvals should be made at the outset so that a realistic transaction schedule can be prepared.

A related issue involves antitrust (merger control) notification procedures. [. . .]

In considering government review procedures, it is also appropriate to consider the possibility of obtaining government grants or tax holidays for the newly created joint venture. [. . .] In developing countries, there may be an array of incentives, including free enterprise zones, relief from custom duties for imported equipment,

253. There may be considerable debate regarding the value of a multinational's trademarks in developing countries because consumers in those countries may never have seen the trademark. Much depends on the trademark. For example, Coca-Cola, Marlboro and Heinz are recognized throughout the world. Also, part of the appeal, and consequent value, of such a trademark is in its overall look or presentation as a Western trademark in the English language and with a correspondingly stylized symbol, logo, and layout.

a tax holiday for the joint venture, or an exemption from withholding tax for technology royalties.[254] [. . .]

One area of international joint venture practice that should usually receive greater attention is the due diligence investigation process. No sophisticated company would undertake an acquisition without performing such an investigation. [. . .]

Prospective joint venture partners may be reluctant to investigate each other. After all, the partners are entering into a marriage of sorts and the thrill of the courtship may have overtaken the appropriate level of skepticism. Nevertheless, the parties should conduct a business, financial and legal investigation of each other — to the extent possible under the circumstances. In addition, if the joint venture will involve land, then the parties should undertake appropriate real estate title and environmental investigations. The same is true for other assets, whether tangible or intangible, that are to be contributed or licensed to the joint venture.

Political risk insurance is often available to Western investors in joint ventures in developing countries. This type of insurance would provide coverage in case of loss through war (and certain other calamities such as insurrection and civil disturbances), expropriation, or currency inconvertibility or non-transferability. [. . .]

E. Model Joint Venture Agreements

The Joint Venture Agreement below provides a good model covering key issues such as scope, formation, technology transfer and licensing, payment and dispute resolution.

1. Joint Venture Agreement between Innovative Technologies, Inc. of Charlottesville, Virginia, USA and the United Computer and Software Enterprises of Mexico

Article I — Definitions

[. . . .]

1.1.3. Products. The finished items to be assembled and manufactured by the Joint Venture consisting of:

(a) The HAL 69 Desk Top Computer

(b) The Video Scroller Terminal

(c) Multilayer Printed Circuit Boards

254. Tax exemptions, holidays and incentives are, of course, country specific. A good place to start in considering these matters for a specific project would be with the Price Waterhouse Guides. [. . .]

(d) Canterbury Disk Drives

(e) Floppy Diskettes

[. . .]

Article II — Object and Scope

2.1. The object of this Agreement is the establishing of an Equity Joint Venture in the form of a Limited Liability Joint Ownership Company to equip, construct, manage and operate the Plant to be established in Mexico for the assembly and manufacture of Products. The Joint Venture intends to market all of its Products solely through **IT** (**Europe**) which will have exclusive marketing rights all over the world including Mexico with all profits to be shared equally by the Joint Venture and **IT** (**Europe**) as set forth in the Marketing Agreement.

Article III — Formation of Joint Venture Company

3.1 Capitalization.

3.1.1. The initial equity capital of the Joint Venture Company is Forty Five Million Two Hundred Thousand United States Dollars (U.S. $45,200,000), to be committed and contributed in the proportion of seventy five percent (75%) for **UNITED** and twenty five percent (25%) for **IT**. IT's contribution to the equity of the Joint Venture consists of Eleven Million Three Hundred Thousand United States Dollars (U.S. $11,300,000). UNITED'S contribution to the equity of the Joint Venture consists of Thirty-Three Million Nine Hundred Thousand Dollars (U.S. $33,900,000).

3.1.2. The equity capital will be paid in by each party within thirty (30) days of any call or calls made by the Board of Directors. The Board may, at its discretion, require the equity capital to be paid all at once or in installments.

3.1.3. It is agreed that the Foreign Trade Bank of Mexico will guarantee each party's financing of its respective equity capital, and that this Agreement is subject to obtaining such guarantees. If the guarantee is exercised against Foreign Trade Bank of Mexico by either party's lending entity, then Foreign Trade Bank of Mexico shall have the right to that party's share of profits in the Joint Venture, until such time as the amounts owed to the Foreign Trade Bank of Mexico are paid off.

[. . .]

3.5.10. Officers, Managers and Section Chiefs. The following officers, managers and section chiefs will be appointed by the party indicated below, provided, however, that at a later date in the course of the Joint Venture, **UNITED** shall, with the consent of **IT**, appoint any or all of the personnel designated herein as **IT** appointees. The management personnel so appointed will be directly responsible to the Board, and will have primary operational responsibility in their designated areas:

A. To be appointed by **UNITED**, after consultation with **IT**:

1. Deputy Managing Director

2. Employee Relations Manager
3. Chief Production Engineer
4. Deputy Accounts Manager

B. To be appointed by **IT**, after consultation with **UNITED**:

1. Managing Director
2. Quality Control Supervisor
3. Accounts Manager
4. Training Manager
5. Maintenance Section Chief

All other management personnel, whether full-time or part-time, will be provided **by UNITED** unless otherwise determined by the Board. They will exercise such rights and authorities as the Board may from time to time direct. [. . .]

3.7. Quality Control.

3.7.1. It is recognized and agreed by the parties that the success of the Joint Venture is dependent upon the ability of the Joint Venture to maintain the quality control standards developed by **IT**. It is further recognized that the Joint Venture's Marketing Agreement with **IT (Europe)** makes **IT (Europe)** the exclusive distributor of all Joint Venture Products and requires **IT (Europe)** to accept only those Products which meet appropriate standards of quality. [. . .]

3.9. Bank Accounts and Convertibility.

3.9.1. The Joint Venture will maintain sufficient deposits in one or more bank accounts in United States Dollars or other foreign currencies with the Foreign Trade Bank of Mexico within Mexico. The Joint Venture shall, upon obtaining the necessary governmental approval, also open accounts with a bank or banks outside of Mexico acceptable to the parties, in order to provide for the Joint Venture's anticipated foreign currency requirements outside Mexico, as stated below, for such period as the Board may determine. All sales revenues generated **by IT (Europe)** purchase of Products which are not required to meet such foreign currency requirements shall be promptly remitted, in the same foreign currency as earned, to the Joint Venture's bank accounts in Mexico.

[. . .]

Article IV—Construction of Plant and Provision of Equipment and Components

4.1. Plant Location and Construction

4.1.1. The Plant will be constructed on land to be provided free of charge by **UNITED** at a site in Mexico to be selected by **IT** with the approval of **UNITED**.

[. . .]

4.2. Procurement and Installation of Capital Equipment.

4.2.1. The Joint Venture undertakes to purchase from **IT** all capital equipment relating to the multilayer board processes facility. This capital equipment is described in detail in Annex D to this Agreement. **IT** will be responsible for supervising the installation of the capital equipment for the multilayer board processes.

[. . .]

4.3. Procurement of Electronic Components

4.3.1. The Joint Venture undertakes to purchase from IT all necessary electronic components and sub-assemblies for the assembly and manufacture of Products, including the HAL 69 Desk Top Computer and the Video Scroller Terminal. The description of such components and sub-assemblies for each Product is set forth in Annex F to this Agreement.

[. . .]

Article V—License of Know-How, Transfer of Technology and Technical Assistance

5.1. License and Know-How. Subject to the terms and conditions herein, **IT** hereby grants to the Joint Venture the exclusive right and license to use the Know-how at the Plant in connection with the assembly and/or manufacture of Products.

5.2. Documentation.

5.2.1. IT shall deliver to the Joint Venture the documentary portion of Know-how licensed hereunder, including;

1. The blueprints for the construction of the Plant.

2. The production drawings for the assembly and manufacture of the Video Scroller Terminal.

3. The production drawings for the assembly and manufacture of the HAL 69 Desk Top Computer.

4. Specifications for fabrication of multilayer printed circuit boards, including assembly and testing procedures for the boards and injection molding and tooling.

5. Specifications for the manufacture of 5.25 inch floppy diskettes and 5.25 inch Canterbury disk drives including vertical recording media.

5.3. Limitations of Rights.

5.3.1. The Joint Venture shall utilize the Know-how granted hereunder solely in the manufacture of the Products at the Plant and in connection with the sale of Products to **IT (Europe)**, as specified in Paragraph 6.6. The Joint Venture shall not have the right to sublicense without IT's prior written approval, and **UNITED** shall not have or take any individual right or interest to or in the Know-how.

5.3.2. The Joint Venture and all Joint Venture personnel shall abide by the Trademark, quality control and marking procedures set forth in Article VI hereof, and shall likewise abide by the confidentiality rules set forth in Paragraph 11.1. hereof.

5.3.3. Should the Joint Venture or its personnel act contrary to or fail in any of the obligations specified in this Paragraph 5.3, and should **IT** notify the Joint Venture thereof, the Joint Venture shall cause any offending action to cease immediately or otherwise shall take steps satisfactory to **IT** within thirty (30) days of **IT**'s notice thereof. Should such offending action continue, **IT** shall have the right to terminate all or any part of this Agreement for cause and call for the liquidation of the Joint Venture, in addition to any other rights and remedies it may have.

5.4. Training of Mexican Personnel.

5.4.1. As part of the technical assistance and transfer of technology to the Joint Venture, IT shall develop a training program and in accordance therewith shall provide training for Mexican operations, management, maintenance and other personnel until the Plant is fully operational. **UNITED** shall bear the travel, transportation, living and other direct costs (but not salary or fringe benefits) of **IT** training personnel fulfilling their duties pursuant to this Paragraph 5.4., while in travel to or while in Mexico. Provided, however, should the training continue beyond eighteen (18) months, then **UNITED** shall also have to bear the salary and fringe benefits of **IT** training personnel.

5.4.2. The Joint Venture shall use its best efforts to provide trainees who speak and read English. However, to the extent trainees are not fluent in English, **UNITED**, on behalf of the Joint Venture, shall assure the availability of technically qualified interpreters and translators for both oral and written material.

5.4.3. It is understood that travel, transportation, living and other direct costs of Mexican trainees incurred in connection with their training, whether in or outside Mexico, as well as their salaries and any fringe benefits, shall be borne by **UNITED**.

Article VI — Trademarks, Markings, Quality Control and Sales

6.1. Grants. Subject to Paragraph 6.4. hereof, **IT** hereby grants to the Joint Venture (but not to any individual owner or holder of an interest therein) during its life, the night and license to use the Trademarks only in connection with the manufacture, promotion and sale of the Products. The above license, however, shall not prevent **IT**, its subsidiaries or licensees, from itself or themselves using the Trademarks to identify any products manufactured by it or by them outside Mexico for sale or resale anywhere in the world, including within Mexico. **IT** shall not grant a license for the use of Trademarks with respect to the Products to any other party in Mexico without the prior written consent of the Joint Venture.

6.2. Ownership and Registration.

6.2.1. All Trademarks now and hereafter used by the Joint Venture to identify the Products are and at all times shall remain the sole and exclusive property of **IT** and the use of the Trademarks by the Joint Venture shall inure solely to the benefit of **IT**. The Joint Venture shall not have the right to sublicense without **IT**'s prior written approval and **UNITED** shall not have or take any individual right or interest to or in the Trademarks.

[. . .]

6.4. Quality Control. The Joint Venture shall manufacture, assemble, and label the Products in strict accordance with the Know-how furnished hereunder and with this Article VI. [. . .]

Article VII — United's Responsibilities

7.1. UNITED shall give full cooperation and assistance to IT and to the Joint Venture so that all work can be accomplished in the most expeditious manner.

7.2. UNITED shall provide the site, free and clear of hindrances, and all physical structures relating to the Plant, adequately equipped with utilities and the like, all as specified in the designs to be furnished by IT pursuant to Paragraph 4.1.2. hereof. **UNITED** shall also make arrangements with the appropriate Mexican authorities for the initiation of service for all utilities necessary for the operation of the Plant, and shall seek to obtain such utilities at costs which do not exceed the costs which would be paid by Mexican enterprises.

[. . .]

Article VIII — Payment to it for Goods and Services

8.1. Method of Payment

8.1.1. The Joint Venture will establish, as of the Effective Date, an irrevocable, transferable, divisible and revolving letter of credit in favor of IT, payable at a bank within the United States acceptable to IT. The letter of credit will be issued or guaranteed by the Foreign Trade Bank of Mexico. [. . .]

8.2. Payment for Capital Equipment, Electronic Components and Transfer of Technical Know-How.

The Joint Venture shall pay the following amounts to **IT** by means of the letter of credit, upon **IT**'s presentation of the documents herein specified to the U.S. bank where the letter of credit is payable:

> (A) **Approval of License Application.** Five million U.S. dollars (U.S. $5,000,000) upon **IT**'s presentation of (i) a copy of the export license from the United States Department of Commerce approving the export of the commodities and technical data which are the subject of this Agreement (excluding the commodities and technical data pertaining to the Canterbury disk drives and floppy diskettes), certified as a true copy by **IT** and (ii) IT's certification to the Joint

Venture that it has delivered to the Joint Venture all production drawings for the Video Scroller Terminal.

B) Six (6) Months After Approval of Application for Export of License. [. . .]

(C) Twelve (12) Months After Approval of Application for Export License. [. . .]

(D) Delivery of Architectural Drawings. [. . .]

Article IX—Financial Affairs and Accounting

9.1. Fiscal Year. The Joint Venture shall have a fiscal year which coincides with the calendar year, that is, from January 1, to December 31.

9.2. Accrual Method of Accounting. The Joint Venture shall adopt the accrual basis of accounting.

9.3. Books in Both Mexican and English. The Joint Venture shall keep account books and related documentation both in Mexican and English.

9.4. Independent Certified Auditor. The Joint Venture shall employ an outside auditor from an internationally recognized accounting firm as provided in Paragraph 3.10.

Article X—Term and Liquidation

10.1. Coming into Force. This Agreement shall commence and come into force and all licenses granted hereunder shall take effect on the Effective Date, as defined in Paragraph 11.11, and shall remain in force until such time as the Joint Venture may be terminated or liquidated by the parties as hereinafter provided.

10.2. Duration of Joint Venture. The duration of the Joint Venture shall be thirty (30) years, but may be renewed if the parties decide to, in accordance with Mexican law.

10.3. Termination and Dissolution.

10.3.1. The Board of Directors, by a Major Decision, may decide at any time to terminate and liquidate the Joint Venture because:

(a) it is unable to continue profitable operations due to reasons of force majeure as provided by Paragraph 22.3;

(b) it is unable to carry out the purposes for which it was created; or

(c) it is unable to carry out operations due to heavy losses.

10.3.2. Termination by Election of Either Party. Either or both of the parties may at any time after the Joint Venture is in effect for thirty (30) years, elect to terminate and liquidate the Joint Venture. [. . .]

Article XI—General Provisions

11.1 Confidentiality. [. . .]

11.2 Industrial Property Rights. [. . .]

11.3. Force Majeure.

11.3.4. Requirement of Export License. It is expressly understood by the parties that this Agreement is subject to approval by the United States Government for export of the technology which is the subject of this Agreement. [. . .]

11.3.5. Requirement of Approval by the Ministry of Foreign Economic Relations and Trade. [. . .] UNITED, in consultation and with the assistance of IT, will make every effort to prepare and provide in an efficient and timely fashion all documentation [. . .]

11.4. Resolution of Disputes.

11.4.1. The parties express the intention that all disputes in connection with this Agreement and the execution hereunder shall be settled through friendly negotiations. In the event that, in the view of either party, no settlement can be reached through friendly negotiations, resort shall first be had to non-binding joint conciliation under the auspices of the American Arbitration Association and the Mexico Council for the Promotion of International Trade, to be held in Stockholm or such other place as the parties agree. One (1) conciliator shall be appointed by the American Arbitration Association and another conciliator shall be appointed by the Mexico Council for the Promotion of International Trade.

11.4.2. [. . .] termination or invalidity thereof shall be settled by arbitration. The records and files of the conciliators shall not be made available and may not used in the arbitration unless both parties agree otherwise.

1.4.3. The arbitration shall be held in Paris and shall be conducted in English in accordance with the UNCITRAL Arbitration Rules in effect on the date of this Agreement [. . .]

1.4.4. The number of arbitrators shall be three (3). Each party shall appoint one (1) arbitrator. [. . .]

11.5. Separability. Notwithstanding that any provision of this Agreement may prove to be illegal or unlawful, the remaining provisions of this Agreement shall continue in full force and effect, but in this event the parties shall attempt in good faith to replace such provision and thereby redefine their respective rights and obligations in the context of the new situation. Should the parties fail to agree on a redefinition of their rights and obligations, either party may invoke the termination and liquidation procedures set forth in Article X.

11.6. Waiver. The failure of either party hereto to insist upon a strict performance of any of the terms and provisions herein shall not be deemed a waiver of any subsequent breach or default in the terms or provisions herein.

11.7. Entire Agreement. This written Agreement, together with the Annexes attached hereto and any written amendments thereof, constitute the complete and exclusive agreement between the parties relating to the establishment and operation of the Joint Venture [. . .]

11.8. Language. The present Agreement is written in English and Spanish, both versions having equal weight. Each party will receive one (1) executed copy in each language.

[. . .]

Chapter 10

Emerging Issues in Foreign Direct Investment

A. Global Comprehensive Treaty on Foreign Investment

The Marrakesh Agreement establishing the World Trade Organization (WTO) in 1995 created a global multilateral and enforceable governance regime for international trade liberalization. However, there is no comparable global multilateral agreement or institutional structure for international investment. In early 2017, Roberto Azevêdo, Director-General of the World Trade Organization, emphasized how trade and investment are increasingly intertwined development issues. Discussions on the deepening relationship between trade and investment have taken place in almost every international economic fora—the G20,[255] UNCTAD, OECD, APEC—but not the WTO.[256]

The public policy objective is to encourage foreign direct investment (FDI) as an effective tool to foster economic growth and sustainable development and to equalize global economic development. FDI drives economic growth through job creation and competitiveness and can make an important contribution to growth in any economy. There is a need to address the role of FDI in sustainable economic development and to develop international policies to maximize the positive contribution investment can make to sustainable development.

However, investment by an investor of one country in the jurisdiction of another can create significant political risks for the investor. In principle, these risks should be reflected in the target rate of return sought for the investment. Consequently, there is a shared public policy interest in the management and reduction of risks through high-standard agreements for the promotion and protection of investment. Investment promotion and protection agreements provide essential assurance for investors putting their capital, intellectual property, management resources and reputation at risk outside the security of their home markets.

At present, international investment promotion and protection is achieved through a complex patchwork of bilateral and sometimes regional agreements of varying scope, quality and duration. A high-standard global multilateral framework on investment, comparable to the WTO Agreement in trade, has become a cherished goal of many international policy makers. There is a long-standing debate on the desired content of such an agreement, although negotiation of such a treaty is not currently on the agenda of any international organization.

Reform of investor-state dispute settlement (ISDS) systems has become a particular focus for various international initiatives in recent years. The United Nations Commission on International Trade Law (UNCITRAL) Working Group III was mandated in July 2017 to assess concerns regarding ISDS and seek possible solutions.

255. Note that in March 2017, the G20 dropped its pledge to "resist all kinds of protectionism" due to U.S. opposition.

256. 20 March 2017—WTO Speeches.

The 36th session in Vienna[257] concluded that reform is desirable in at least the three areas of consistency of arbitral rulings, diversity of arbitrators and decision-makers, and cost and duration of cases. However, the precise type of reform remains to be decided.

In keeping with previous sessions, and in view of the impact of foreign investment and ISDS on sustainable development, the Working Group stressed the need for ISDS reform to strike a balance between the rights of investors and the ability of states to regulate legitimate public welfare concerns, such as environmental and social protection. This also highlights the importance of inclusiveness with the participation of both developing and developed country states.

Although a multilateral rules-based agreement is not currently being negotiated, the European Commission has proposed the establishment of an EU Permanent Multilateral Investment Court System for resolving investment disputes. This is discussed later in this chapter.

© Surya P. Subedi, 2008, *International Investment Law: Reconciling Policy and Principle*, 2d Edition, Hart Publishing, Bloomsbury Publishing Plc.

The experience within the Doha Round and elsewhere demonstrates that states are reluctant to commit themselves to an international treaty unless they are fully satisfied with the provisions in such a treaty. Those very states that conclude a BIT or FTA with provisions favorable to foreign investors seem reluctant to do the same in the case of a multilateral international agreement with similar provisions. One reason for this could be that a BIT or an IIA has a limited or fixed lifespan—they are normally valid for 10 or 20 years—after which the unwilling state concerned would no longer be bound by the provisions of such a contractual treaty albeit the state would continue to be bound by the general principles enunciated in the treaty. States can also easily denounce a bilateral or other contractual treaty by giving advance notice. It is also easier to renegotiate such treaties since the number of states party to them are small. [. . .]

However, an ideal solution to address many of the problems in foreign investment law would, of course, be to have a comprehensive global investment treaty. It would be the preferred way of harmonizing the rules, trends and practices in foreign investment law, and it would bring about some consistency and uniformity in protecting foreign investors. Such a treaty, would, in principle, eliminate the need for individual BITs between two state parties, as do various WTO agreements on international trade law. At present there is a complex network of thousands of BITs, FTAs and other IIAs containing investment provisions, most of which contain a similar set of provisions. With the increased trend in forum-shopping, treaty-shopping and

---

257. United Nations Commission on International Trade Law, *Draft Report of Working Group III (Investor-State Dispute Settlement Reform) on the work of its thirty-sixth session*, A/CN.9/964. 6 November, 2018. https://uncitral.un.org/sites/uncitral.un.org/files/draft_report_of_wg_iii_for_the_website.pdf?utm_source=POLITICO.EU&utm_campaign=9d404ebd07-EMAIL_CAMPAIGN_2018_11_06_07_59&utm_medium=email&utm_term=0_10959edeb5-9d404ebd07-189512373.

nationality-shopping the picture is likely to get more complex. However, the negotiation of a global treaty on foreign investment law is not currently on the agenda of any international organization. Thus, it looks unlikely that a global comprehensive treaty on foreign investment law will be concluded in the near future. [. . .]

In the absence of both a global treaty and a hierarchy of international tribunals required to follow precedent, foreign investment law has remained controversial and the various tribunals seem to be free to interpret the law in a manner they deem appropriate. Some of the core principles relating to expropriation and the meaning and scope of terms such as 'just', 'adequate', 'full', 'prompt', 'effective', and 'fair', as well as the concepts of the 'due process of law', 'fair and equitable treatment' and 'full protection and security', have been applied to varying degrees by international courts and tribunals since there is still no internationally agreed definition of these terms. [. . .] What is needed is a balancing act that will preserve the regulatory authority of sovereign states under clearly and narrowly defined conditions when protecting foreign investors. [. . .] The irony is that even disputes between a state and an investor on a variety of investment matters are having massive impacts on public matters. [. . .] Therefore, a comprehensive international treaty on foreign investment prescribing uniform standards of treatment of foreign investors in host countries and the creation of an international court of foreign investment, modelled perhaps on the WTO's dispute settlement mechanism, are needed.

A global treaty could bring together generally accepted principles and norms on the regulation of foreign investment such as the notions of corporate social responsibly and corporate social governance to be found in 'soft law' instruments such as the UN Global Compact or OECD Guidelines. It could harmonize different trends in state practice, balancing environmental and human rights protection with investment protection. [. . .]

Perhaps what the world of foreign investment needs is at least a WTO DSB-styled quasi-judicial international investment court[258] that could balance competing interests as has, to certain extent, the WTO DSB, in spite of it being primarily a trade dispute settlement mechanism. A strict timetable-bound, efficient and speedy international investment court may be liked by investors too as they seem to get increasingly frustrated with the length of time taken by international investment tribunals to settle a dispute. For instance, the average time taken by an ICSID arbitration tribunal under NAFTA is three years. This is one year longer than the average time taken to resolve a trade dispute by a WTO DSB.

After all, the WTO DSB is a blend of diplomacy, negotiation, conciliation and arbitration designed to ensure an amicable and speedy resolution of trade disputes. The proposal made in this regard in the IISD's Model International Agreement on Investment for Sustainable Development offers a good model for the settlement of investment

258. Gus Van Harten also supports this idea: G Van Harten, *Investment Treaty Arbitration and Public Law* (Oxford, Oxford University Press, 2007) 180 et seq.

disputes. An international investment court would also have more legitimacy, accountability and transparency than would an ad hoc arbitration tribunal. [. . .]

There is a perception in public policy circles of a growing tendency towards investor "treaty or forum shopping" for favorable treaty treatment and/or nationality of establishment. While neither is new or illegal, this perception does not assist the public policy argument in favor of traditional arbitral dispute settlement proceedings and may support the case for a more harmonized and court-based global approach.

© Surya P. Subedi, 2008, *International Investment Law: Reconciling Policy and Principle*, 2d Edition, Hart Publishing, Bloomsbury Publishing Plc.

[. . .] Forum-selection is not new to the world of foreign investment as most BITs and investment contracts include provisions designed to offer the option of resorting to either national courts or international arbitration for the settlement of investment disputes, known as the 'fork-in-the-road' provision. [. . .] Relying on sufficiently broad-language provisions on dispute settlement in BITs, some treaty-based arbitral tribunals have established their jurisdiction even over contractual claims such as the performance of a contract. Thus, the trend towards expanding the scope of public international law arbitration to adjudicate even on certain matters of private law under contractual undertakings by invoking either the so called 'umbrella clause' in the BITs or the 'stabilization clause' in investment contracts, or by expanding the meaning of a substantive principle such as the MFN principle to cover even dispute settlement procedures, is gaining momentum. [. . .]

The expansion of the meaning of the MFN principle to cover even dispute settlement procedures has introduced yet another new trend towards treaty-shopping or forum-shopping among foreign investors. Although it is generally accepted that any arbitration requires explicit consent of the parties concerned, the trend in jurisprudence has been to resort to other means of deducing such consent of a host state party to the dispute by relying on not only the BIT in question but also on other treaties concluded by the state concerned by extending the nature, meaning and scope of the MFN principle. [. . .]

Since the nationality of the foreign investor is a crucial factor in making a valid claim under a BIT, and most BITs require companies to have their seat in the home country concerned to extend the BIT protection, there have been instances in which companies have relocated to another jurisdiction in order to avail themselves of such protection. For instance, Bechtel Corporation shifted its registration from the Cayman Islands to the Netherlands to sue the Government of Bolivia for the losses it incurred in Bolivia because the Cayman Islands did not have a BIT with Bolivia, whereas the Netherlands did.[259] This practice of shifting registration to acquire the

---

259. *Aguas del Tunari SA v. Republic of Bolivia*, ICSID Case No. ARB/02/3.

flag or nationality of convenience without having 'effective economic activities' in the home country concerned may encourage nationality-shopping or set up 'mail-box' operations to take advantage of the most investor-friendly BIT in existence if the laws of such home countries are lax in this regard. [. . .]

B. Dispute Resolution

1. UNCITRAL Rules on Transparency and Investor-State Dispute Settlement Reform

The UNCITRAL Rules on Transparency in Treaty-Based Investor-State Arbitration ("Rules on Transparency") came into effect on 1 April 2014 and provide for public transparency and accessibility of treaty-based investor-state arbitration where the arbitration is initiated under UNICITRAL Arbitration Rules. The Rules apply prior to 1 April 2014, where the parties agree to their application, and after 1 April 2014 as a matter of course, unless the parties agree otherwise. On 18 October 2017, the United Nations Convention on Transparency in Treaty-Based Investor-State Arbitration (the "Mauritius Convention on Transparency") entered into force. The Convention provides that the Rules of Transparency apply whether or not the arbitration was initiated under the UNCITRAL Rules. The Convention has been signed by 23 countries, including the United Kingdom and the United States, but ratified only by Cameroon, Canada, Gambia, Mauritius and Switzerland.

The Rules on Transparency were incorporated by new Article 1, paragraph 4 in the text of the UNCITRAL Arbitration Rules.

UNCITRAL Arbitration Rules (as revised in 2010)

Article 1

4. For investor-State arbitration initiated pursuant to a treaty providing for the protection of investments or investors, these Rules include the UNCITRAL Rules on Transparency in Treaty based Investor-State Arbitration ("Rules on Transparency"), subject to article 1 of the Rules on Transparency.

UNCITRAL Rules on Transparency in Treaty-Based Investor-State Arbitration

Article 1. Scope of application

Applicability of the Rules

1. The UNCITRAL Rules on Transparency in Treaty-based Investor-State Arbitration ("Rules on Transparency") shall apply to investor-State arbitration initiated under the UNCITRAL Arbitration Rules pursuant to a treaty providing for the

protection of investments or investors ("treaty")* concluded on or after 1 April 2014 unless the Parties to the treaty** have agreed otherwise.

2. In investor-State arbitrations initiated under the UNCITRAL Arbitration Rules pursuant to a treaty concluded before 1 April 2014, these Rules shall apply only when:

(a) The parties to an arbitration (the "disputing parties") agree to their application in respect of that arbitration; or

(b) The Parties to the treaty or, in the case of a multilateral treaty, the State of the claimant and the respondent State, have agreed after 1 April 2014 to their application.

Application of the Rules

3. In any arbitration in which the Rules on Transparency apply pursuant to a treaty or to an agreement by the Parties to that treaty:

(a) The disputing parties may not derogate from these Rules, by agreement or otherwise, unless permitted to do so by the treaty;

(b) The arbitral tribunal shall have the power, besides its discretionary authority under certain provisions of these Rules, to adapt the requirements of any specific provision of these Rules to the particular circumstances of the case, after consultation with the disputing parties, if such adaptation is necessary to conduct the arbitration in a practical manner and is consistent with the transparency objective of these Rules.

Discretion and authority of the arbitral tribunal

4. Where the Rules on Transparency provide for the arbitral tribunal to exercise discretion, the arbitral tribunal in exercising such discretion shall take into account:

(a) The public interest in transparency in treaty-based investor-State arbitration and in the particular arbitral proceedings; and

(b) The disputing parties' interest in a fair and efficient resolution of their dispute.

5. These Rules shall not affect any authority that the arbitral tribunal may otherwise have under the UNCITRAL Arbitration Rules to conduct the arbitration in such a manner as to promote transparency, for example by accepting submissions from third persons.

---

* For the purposes of the Rules on Transparency, a "treaty" shall be understood broadly as encompassing any bilateral or multilateral treaty that contains provisions on the protection of investments or investors and a right for investors to resort to arbitration against Parties to the treaty, including any treaty commonly referred to as a free trade agreement, economic integration agreement, trade and investment framework or cooperation agreement, or bilateral investment treaty.

** For the purposes of the Rules on Transparency, any reference to a "Party to the treaty" or a "State" includes, for example, a regional economic integration organization where it is a Party to the treaty.

6. In the presence of any conduct, measure or other action having the effect of wholly undermining the transparency objectives of these Rules, the arbitral tribunal shall ensure that those objectives prevail.

Applicable instrument in case of conflict

7. Where the Rules on Transparency apply, they shall supplement any applicable arbitration rules. Where there is a conflict between the Rules on Transparency and the applicable arbitration rules, the Rules on Transparency shall prevail. Notwithstanding any provision in these Rules, where there is a conflict between the Rules on Transparency and the treaty, the provisions of the treaty shall prevail.

8. Where any of these Rules is in conflict with a provision of the law applicable to the arbitration from which the disputing parties cannot derogate, that provision shall prevail.

9. These Rules are available for use in investor-State arbitrations initiated under rules other than the UNCITRAL Arbitration Rules or in ad hoc proceedings.

Article 2. Publication of information at the commencement of arbitral proceedings

Once the notice of arbitration has been received by the respondent, each of the disputing parties shall promptly communicate a copy of the notice of arbitration to the repository referred to under article 8. Upon receipt of the notice of arbitration from the respondent, or upon receipt of the notice of arbitration and a record of its transmission to the respondent, the repository shall promptly make available to the public information regarding the name of the disputing parties, the economic sector involved and the treaty under which the claim is being made.

Article 3. Publication of documents

1. Subject to article 7, the following documents shall be made available to the public: the notice of arbitration, the response to the notice of arbitration, the statement of claim, the statement of defence and any further written statements or written submissions by any disputing party; a table listing all exhibits to the aforesaid documents and to expert reports and witness statements, if such table has been prepared for the proceedings, but not the exhibits themselves; any written submissions by the non-disputing Party (or Parties) to the treaty and by third persons, transcripts of hearings, where available; and orders, decisions and awards of the arbitral tribunal.

2. Subject to article 7, expert reports and witness statements, exclusive of the exhibits thereto, shall be made available to the public, upon request by any person to the arbitral tribunal.

3. Subject to article 7, the arbitral tribunal may decide, on its own initiative or upon request from any person, and after consultation with the disputing parties, whether and how to make available exhibits and any other documents provided to, or issued by, the arbitral tribunal not falling within paragraphs 1 or 2 above. This may include, for example, making such documents available at a specified site.

4. The documents to be made available to the public pursuant to paragraphs 1 and 2 shall be communicated by the arbitral tribunal to the repository referred to under article 8 as soon as possible, subject to any relevant arrangements or time limits for the protection of confidential or protected information prescribed under article 7. The documents to be made available pursuant to paragraph 3 may be communicated by the arbitral tribunal to the repository referred to under article 8 as they become available and, if applicable, in a redacted form in accordance with article 7. The repository shall make all documents available in a timely manner, in the form and in the language in which it receives them.

5. A person granted access to documents under paragraph 3 shall bear any administrative costs of making those documents available to that person, such as the costs of photocopying or shipping documents to that person, but not the costs of making those documents available to the public through the repository.

Article 4. Submission by a third person

1. After consultation with the disputing parties, the arbitral tribunal may allow a person that is not a disputing party, and not a non-disputing Party to the treaty ("third person(s)"), to file a written submission with the arbitral tribunal regarding a matter within the scope of the dispute.

2. A third person wishing to make a submission shall apply to the arbitral tribunal, and shall, in a concise written statement, which is in a language of the arbitration and complies with any page limits set by the arbitral tribunal:

(a) Describe the third person, including, where relevant, its membership and legal status (e.g., trade association or other non-governmental organization), its general objectives, the nature of its activities and any parent organization (including any organization that directly or indirectly controls the third person);

(b) Disclose any connection, direct or indirect, which the third person has with any disputing party;

(c) Provide information on any government, person or organization that has provided to the third person (i) any financial or other assistance in preparing the submission; or (ii) substantial assistance in either of the two years preceding the application by the third person under this article (e.g. funding around 20 per cent of its overall operations annually);

(d) Describe the nature of the interest that the third person has in the arbitration; and

(e) Identify the specific issues of fact or law in the arbitration that the third person wishes to address in its written submission.

3. In determining whether to allow such a submission, the arbitral tribunal shall take into consideration, among other factors it determines to be relevant:

(a) Whether the third person has a significant interest in the arbitral proceedings; and

(b) The extent to which the submission would assist the arbitral tribunal in the determination of a factual or legal issue related to the arbitral proceedings by bringing a perspective, particular knowledge or insight that is different from that of the disputing parties.

4. The submission filed by the third person shall:

(a) Be dated and signed by the person filing the submission on behalf of the third person;

(b) Be concise, and in no case longer than as authorized by the arbitral tribunal;

(c) Set out a precise statement of the third person's position on issues; and

(d) Address only matters within the scope of the dispute.

5. The arbitral tribunal shall ensure that any submission does not disrupt or unduly burden the arbitral proceedings, or unfairly prejudice any disputing party.

6. The arbitral tribunal shall ensure that the disputing parties are given a reasonable opportunity to present their observations on any submission by the third person.

Article 5. Submission by a non-disputing Party to the treaty

1. The arbitral tribunal shall, subject to paragraph 4, allow, or, after consultation with the disputing parties, may invite, submissions on issues of treaty interpretation from a non-disputing Party to the treaty.

2. The arbitral tribunal, after consultation with the disputing parties, may allow submissions on further matters within the scope of the dispute from a non-disputing Party to the treaty. In determining whether to allow such submissions, the arbitral tribunal shall take into consideration, among other factors it determines to be relevant, the factors referred to in article 4, paragraph 3, and, for greater certainty, the need to avoid submissions which would support the claim of the investor in a manner tantamount to diplomatic protection.

3. The arbitral tribunal shall not draw any inference from the absence of any submission or response to any invitation pursuant to paragraphs 1 or 2.

4. The arbitral tribunal shall ensure that any submission does not disrupt or unduly burden the arbitral proceedings, or unfairly prejudice any disputing party.

5. The arbitral tribunal shall ensure that the disputing parties are given a reasonable opportunity to present their observations on any submission by a non-disputing Party to the treaty.

Article 6. Hearings

1. Subject to article 6, paragraphs 2 and 3, hearings for the presentation of evidence or for oral argument ("hearings") shall be public.

2. Where there is a need to protect confidential information or the integrity of the arbitral process pursuant to article 7, the arbitral tribunal shall make arrangements to hold in private that part of the hearing requiring such protection.

3. The arbitral tribunal shall make logistical arrangements to facilitate the public access to hearings (including where appropriate by organizing attendance through video links or such other means as it deems appropriate). However, the arbitral tribunal may, after consultation with the disputing parties, decide to hold all or part of the hearings in private where this becomes necessary for logistical reasons, such as when the circumstances render any original arrangement for public access to a hearing infeasible.

Article 7. Exceptions to transparency

Confidential or protected information

1. Confidential or protected information, as defined in paragraph 2 and as identified pursuant to the arrangements referred to in paragraphs 3 and 4, shall not be made available to the public pursuant to articles 2 to 6.

2. Confidential or protected information consists of:

(a) Confidential business information;

(b) Information that is protected against being made available to the public under the treaty;

(c) Information that is protected against being made available to the public, in the case of the information of the respondent State, under the law of the respondent State, and in the case of other information, under any law or rules determined by the arbitral tribunal to be applicable to the disclosure of such information; or

(d) Information the disclosure of which would impede law enforcement.

3. The arbitral tribunal, after consultation with the disputing parties, shall make arrangements to prevent any confidential or protected information from being made available to the public, including by putting in place, as appropriate:

(a) Time limits in which a disputing party, non-disputing Party to the treaty or third person shall give notice that it seeks protection for such information in documents;

(b) Procedures for the prompt designation and redaction of the particular confidential or protected information in such documents; and

(c) Procedures for holding hearings in private to the extent required by article 6, paragraph 2. Any determination as to whether information is confidential or protected shall be made by the arbitral tribunal after consultation with the disputing parties.

4. Where the arbitral tribunal determines that information should not be redacted from a document, or that a document should not be prevented from being made available to the public, any disputing party, non-disputing Party to the treaty or third person that voluntarily introduced the document into the record shall be permitted to withdraw all or part of the document from the record of the arbitral proceedings.

5. Nothing in these Rules requires a respondent State to make available to the public information the disclosure of which it considers to be contrary to its essential security interests.

6. Information shall not be made available to the public pursuant to articles 2 to 6 where the information, if made available to the public, would jeopardize the integrity of the arbitral process as determined pursuant to paragraph 7.

7. The arbitral tribunal may, on its own initiative or upon the application of a disputing party, after consultation with the disputing parties where practicable, take appropriate measures to restrain or delay the publication of information where such publication would jeopardize the integrity of the arbitral process because it could hamper the collection or production of evidence, lead to the intimidation of witnesses, lawyers acting for disputing parties or members of the arbitral tribunal, or in comparably exceptional circumstances.

Article 8. Repository of published information

The repository of published information under the Rules on Transparency shall be the Secretary-General of the United Nations or an institution named by UNCITRAL.

The UNCITRAL Rules on Transparency in Treaty-Based Investor-State Arbitration, adopted 2014 ("Rules on Transparency"), were applied for the first time in *Iberdrola, S.A. and Iberdrola Energia. S.A.U. v. Bolivia* (PCA Case No. 2015-05). According to the first procedural order issued by the arbitral tribunal, the parties to the disputes agreed to the application of the UNCITRAL Rules on Transparency to their proceeding, although the case was initiated under the 1976 UNCITRAL Arbitration Rules.

2. Lessons Learnt from Investor-State Dispute Settlement ("ISDS") under the Energy Charter Treaty

The Energy Charter Treaty (1994) established a comprehensive international agreement for the promotion and protection of investment in the energy sector, including strong investor-to-state dispute settlement procedures. Important investor claims initiated under the jurisdiction of the Treaty include the case brought by the Yukos Shareholders against the Russian Federation.

Yukos Universal Ltd. v. Russian Fed'n (Isle of Man v. Russ.), UNCITRAL, PCA No. AA 227 (Perm. Ct. Arb. 2014).

The Claimants in the *Yukos* case were the majority shareholders of the OAO Yukos Oil Company ("Yukos") namely, Yukos Universal Limited ("YUL"), Hulley Enterprises Limited ("Hulley") and Veteran Petroleum Limited ("VPL"). The Respondent was the Russian Federation. The seat of arbitration was the Permanent Court of Arbitration at The Hague, Netherlands, under the 1976 UNCITRAL Arbitration Rules. The value of the claim was US$114 billion, by far the largest brought under arbitral proceedings anywhere in the world.

The Tribunal found the Russian Federation liable to compensate the three companies for a series of acts that amounted to "indirect expropriation" of Yukos under Article 13(1) of the Energy Charter Treaty (Expropriation). In the view of the Tribunal, the actions of the Russian government were not supported by a clear public interest, were discriminatory against Yukos, were not carried out under due process of law and failed to provide due compensation. The Tribunal announced its decision on 18th July 2014 and awarded compensation for damages of US$50 billion against the Russian government.

On February 6, 2015, the Ministry of Finance for the Russian Federation announced that it would start judicial proceedings before the Hague District Court for setting aside the final awards, on the basis of jurisdiction, an inappropriate view of complex Russian rulings and the Tribunal's speculation. In accordance with Dutch law, the setting-aside proceedings did not suspend enforcement of the arbitral award.

Yukos' investors meanwhile continued to seek enforcement under the New York Convention on the Recognition and Enforcement of Foreign Arbitral Awards (1958) in other jurisdictions where assets owned by the Russian Federation are located, including in France, the U.S., the UK, Belgium and Germany. Under customary international law, domestic courts can seize assets owned by states and used for commercial purposes. However, assets owned by states which are used for the exercise of their sovereign powers are covered by sovereign immunity and cannot be seized.

On April 20, 2016, the Hague District Court unexpectedly set aside the arbitral award, on the basis that the arbitration panel did not have jurisdiction in this case,[260] as the Russian Federation had only signed and accepted provisional application but never formally ratified the Energy Charter Treaty.[261] Yukos shareholders immediately said they would appeal to the higher court in The Netherlands, and that the Dutch decision would need to be interpreted by national courts in other countries where Yukos' investors were seeking enforcement. In March 2018, through a series of judgments, the Brussels Court of Appeal has put an end to Yukos' attempts to enforce the Yukos Awards in Belgium and preclude it from seeking enforcement of the Yukos Awards in the future on the Belgian territory. Yukos have also abandoned their enforcement proceedings in France.

260. *Arbitration awards on multi-billion claims against Russia quashed*, https://www.yukoscase.com/wp-content/uploads/2017/03/6-20160420-Judgment-by-the-Hague-District-Court-setting-aside-the-award.pdf.

261. *Russia Wins Legal Victory over Yukos Damages*, http://www.ft.com/cms/s/0/2a23a352-06ce-11e6-a70d-4e39ac32c284.html#axzz46j5LUxdY.

3. Establishment of a European Union (EU) Permanent Multilateral Investment Court System

In June 2013, Presidents Obama (U.S.), Barroso (European Commission) and Van Rompuy (European Union) launched negotiations on a Transatlantic Trade and Investment Partnership (TTIP), an agreement meant to create growth and jobs in both the U.S. and Europe by stimulating trade and investment flows between them. The agreement was also widely heralded as having geostrategic implications, bringing the two largest supporters of democracy and the rule of law closer together.[262]

During 2015, the European Commission proposed a new investment court system under the Investor to State Dispute Settlement (ISDS) provisions of the Transatlantic Trade and Investment Partnership (TTIP) negotiations. The revised European Commission proposal replaced initial drafting based on the established form of arbitral tribunals and introduced a totally new approach to the negotiations in this area.

These apparently surprising developments should be seen largely in political terms. For the European Commission, the Lisbon Treaty (2009) confirmed EU competence over external trade but also extended this competence over international investment, superseding traditional member state jurisdiction. The Commission TTIP proposal could be seen as consolidating their right to negotiate investment agreements at the EU level on behalf of member states.

The Commission was also responding to strong public opinion and political concerns from NGO and trade union campaigning. These concerns were based on the perception that traditional ISDS provisions may prevent signatory states from regulating in the public interest and that companies may receive "special" treatment outside normal legal and democratic processes. In addition, concerns were expressed about such issues as perceived "forum shopping", lack of independence of arbitrators, and lack of transparency and precedent in arbitral proceedings.

> One of the major problems with the debate in Europe about ISDS is that it is described, even by such respected business-oriented publications as the *Financial Times*, as the right of a foreign investor to sue a government for lost profits. If that definition was accurate, everyone would be right to be concerned. Governments can and do take measures that affect corporate profitability as they work to protect consumers, workers and the environment. A system where such measures apply to everyone except foreign investors would be untenable and a fundamental violation of the rule of law. However, the presumption that investment protection and ISDS are about "lost profits" is simply wrong. Common sense alone demonstrates this. Investment treaties and ISDS were created by governments, for governments. And no government would ever create an instrument that so

262. Peter H. Chase, *TTIP, Investor-State Dispute Settlement and the Rule of Law*, EUROPEAN VIEW (2015), https://www.uschamber.com/issue-brief/ttip-investor-state-dispute-settlement-and-the-rule-law.

decidedly circumscribed its ability to adopt laws and regulations in the public interest.[263]

However, serious concerns have also been raised about the Commission "investment court" approach, on both a substantive and procedural basis. Chief among the concerns is whether ISDS does in any meaningful sense restrict the right of governments to regulate in the public interest. Other substantive concerns include the exclusion of the establishment phase of investment from ISDS, the proposed carve out related to state aids, and the definition of fair and equitable treatment ("FET").

The highlight of the proposed system is a procedural change that creates an "investment court system", under which the two governments involved appoint a standing body of 15 "judges" (5 from each nationality and 5 more of a third nationality); judges are selected on a "random" basis to hear complaints; provision is made for an appeals process formed of 6 panelists; and all are subject to strict ethical requirements.[264] Procedural concerns include the quasi-judicial reference to an "international court", the closed list of panelists, and the risk of nationality bias inherent in the proposed nomination process. The ICSID negotiators intentionally tried to avoid bias by stipulating that panelists may not be of the nationality of either the claimant or the respondent; in contrast, the Commission reinserted the nationality provision. Important questions raised by the European Commission proposal include the following:

i. Does the Commission proposal represent a fundamental change in legal approach?

Under the Commission proposals, private companies retain the right to sue governments for expropriation without due public policy reason and the payment of prompt and adequate compensation. In this respect, the Commission proposals do not change and arguably consolidate this right under international law.

Similarly, it can be argued that nothing in current bilateral and regional investment agreements prohibits governments from exercising the sovereign right to regulate. The issue is the extent of entitlement to compensation in the event of regulatory change. Some recent high profile cases have drawn attention to this concern, for example in tobacco advertising.[265] Many would argue that there is a legitimate balance to be found in investment protection law between the interest of the investor in a stable regulatory environment, and the democratic obligation for governments to respond to public policy concerns. In this respect, the question is then whether an explicit statement of a right to regulate is even necessary where governments in

---

263. Peter H. Chase, *TTIP, Investor-State Dispute Settlement and the Rule of Law*, EUROPEAN VIEW (2015), https://www.uschamber.com/issue-brief/ttip-investor-state-dispute-settlement-and-the-rule-law.

264. The proposal also enshrines other procedural "reforms", including on transparency, frivolous claims, binding interpretations of the parties, amicus briefs and so on, all of which are covered in the US model Bilateral Investment Treaty and the revised UNCITRAL rules.

265. *Phillip Morris Brands v. Republic of Uruguay*, ICSID Case No. ARB/10/7 (2010).

any case have this right, and whether an explicit statement either strengthens or weakens investor confidence.

ii. Does the Commission proposal affect enforcement?

A key question for investors is whether awards made by the proposed "investment court" would be enforceable under the New York Convention on the Recognition and Enforcement of Foreign Arbitral Awards (1958). Some have argued that the Commission is "walking away from international arbitration".[266] However, the TTIP proposal (and also the EU Agreements with Canada and Vietnam) made specific provision that the parties are obligated under the agreement to enforce awards, and that the awards rendered are meant to qualify as enforceable under the New York Convention. It is also noted that although only states can be signatories to ICSID, and the EU is consequently not a signatory, the TTIP proposal is "probably compatible" with the ICSID Convention.

It might consequently be questioned if the Commission TTIP proposal does in fact represent a substantive change in terms of policy, and whether it will be sufficient to satisfy those political constituencies that urged a change in the first place.

Finally, it may also be noted that the European Union is a signatory to the Energy Charter Treaty (ECT), and the implications for the "traditional" investor-to-state dispute settlement provisions under the ECT are far from clear.

iii. How is the U.S. going to respond?

This was at the time a central political question. A number of U.S. commentators questioned the need to change a well-functioning and familiar international dispute settlement system. There was also resistance to taking on board a solely European proposal designed mainly to handle a European political problem. At the present moment, this question has been put to one side because President Trump has removed the United States from TTIP negotiations as a whole. However, if at some point TTIP is resurrected, negotiators will undoubtedly come under considerable pressure to reach a compromise acceptable to both the EU and U.S. Whether this would then be sufficient to satisfy the European political constituencies that raised the ISDS concerns in the first place remains to be seen.

The Obama administration never formally responded to Europe's proposal before TTIP talks were indefinitely put on hold. Yet, as it happens, the EU was also finalizing a trade agreement with Canada (the Comprehensive Economic and Trade Agreement ("CETA")) at the same time, and a version of the investment court system made it into that deal.[267] Since then, Canada (along with the EU) have publicly advocated for this court and are actively seeking to recruit new members. The European Court

266. Céline Lévesque (University of Ottawa Faculty of law), *The European Union Commission Proposal for the Creation of an "Investment Court System": The Q and A that the Commission Won't Be Issuing*, Kluwer Arbitration Blog (April 6, 2016).

267. *CETA: EU and Canada agree on new approach on investment in trade agreement* (Brussels, 29 February 2016), http://europa.eu/rapid/press-release_IP-16-399_en.htm.

of Justice decided on 30 April 2019 that the mechanism for the resolution of disputes between investors and states provided for by the Free Trade Agreement between EU and Canada (CETA) is compatible with EU law.[268] The EU-Vietnam FTA agreed in July 2018 also included the EU's new investment court approach.[269]

Some of the Commission's proposals may indeed foreshadow possible future steps. For example, while ICSID has a procedure to annul rulings if necessary, some parties, such as the U.S., also consider that the introduction of an appeals process may make sense. There are considerable practical difficulties, however, as international investment law is an amalgam of three thousand different treaties, in which the parties have agreed on sometimes different wordings that may convey very different meanings and legal obligations.[270] Seen from this perspective, a single broad multilateral investment treaty could make sense, allowing disputes to be referenced everywhere to the same obligations on the parties.

4. Modifying the ICSID Convention under the Law of Treaties

Beyond the question of the proposed EU model, prospects for the institutional reform of ISDS include superimposing an appellate mechanism onto the existing arbitration framework. Article 41(1)(b) of the Vienna Convention on the Law of Treaties (VCLT)[271] allows Contracting States to agree to treaty modification *inter se* if the modification in question is not prohibited by the treaty and (i) does not affect the enjoyment by the other parties of their rights under the treaty or the performance of their obligation and (ii) does not relate to a provision, derogation from which it is incompatible with the effective execution of the object and purpose of the treaty as a whole.

Unlike "absolute" treaties such as human rights conventions, wherein effectiveness relies upon Members' adherence to every provision, *inter se* modification of reciprocal treaties is presumed to not affect the rights and obligations of other Members. Because the establishment of an appellate mechanism by some ICSID Members would not impede other Members and nationals thereof from utilizing the existing ICSID annulment regime, such modification *inter se* would not prejudice those third states under VCLT Article 41(1)(b)(i).[272]

---

268. http://curia.europa.eu/juris/document/document.jsf?text=&docid=213502&pageIndex=0&doclang=EN&mode=lst&dir=&occ=first&part=1&cid=707133&utm_source=POLITICO.EU&utm_campaign=32939f2e3e-EMAIL_CAMPAIGN_2019_04_30_09_08&utm_medium=email&utm_term=0_10959edeb5-32939f2e3e-189512373.

269. EU-Vietnam trade and investment agreements (authentic text as of August 2018), http://trade.ec.europa.eu/doclib/press/index.cfm?id=1437.

270. Hindelang, S. & C.P. Sassenrath, *The Investment Chapters of the EU's International Trade and Investment Agreements in a Comparative Perspective*, European Parliament, Directorate-General for External Policies (2015).

271. Vienna Convention on the Law of Treaties, May 23, 1969, 1155 U.N.T.S. 331.

272. Brian McGarry & Josef Ostřanský, *Is the Law of Treaties an Obstacle or a Conduit for the Reform of Investor-State Dispute Settlement?* Emory International Law Review, Vol. 32 (2017).

In any case, it can be considered whether the legal intricacies of modifying the ICSID Convention would be preferable to replacing the existing arbitration framework with a self-standing international court. The "new" ISDS court model in recent EU treaty texts (CETA, EU-Vietnam FTA, and draft TTIP) certainly raises the question of whether ICSID Members should establish an appellate mechanism. The importance of this question extends beyond the EU model, as discussed earlier in this chapter, to the broader desirability and feasibility of any appellate mechanism with multilateral aspirations.

C. Recent Developments in Investment Promotion and Protection

The Comprehensive Economic Trade Agreement ("CETA") between Canada and the European Union protects the state parties to the agreement from claims that may be brought as a result of investment losses arising from regulatory measures. The agreement expressly states that parties have the right to regulate within their territories to achieve legitimate policy objectives such as the protection of public health, safety, environment or public morals, social or consumer protection, or the promotion and protection of cultural diversity.

On 7 September 2017, Belgium requested the Court of Justice's opinion concerning the compatibility of the mechanism for the settlement of disputes (ISDS) with EU law. In essence, it expressed doubts as to the effects of that mechanism on the exclusive jurisdiction of the Court over the definitive interpretation of EU law, the general principle of equal treatment, the requirement that EU law is effective, and the right of access to an independent and impartial tribunal. On 29 January 2019, Advocate General Yves Bot delivered an opinion that ISDS does not adversely affect the autonomy of EU law and does not affect the principle that the Court of Justice has exclusive jurisdiction over the definitive interpretation of EU law.[273] As noted above, the European Court of Justice subsequently confirmed this opinion.

Further current developments include:

1. The Trans-Pacific Partnership ("TPP") Investment Provisions (U.S. abandoned 2018)

The text of the twelve-country Trans-Pacific Partnership (TPP) Agreement was publicly released in November 2015. The provisions for investment and investor-to-state dispute settlement (ISDS) became a "hot" political topic throughout the TPP negotiations. The proposals were contained in TPP's ninth chapter on Investment.

273. https://curia.europa.eu/jcms/upload/docs/application/pdf/2019-01/cp190006en.pdf?utm_source=POLITICO.EU&utm_campaign=e55585b65d-EMAIL_CAMPAIGN_2019_01_29_09_06&utm_medium=email&utm_term=0_10959edeb5-e55585b65d-189512373.

The chapter was divided into two sections: Section A focusing on applicable investment conditions and Section B on ISDS. The TPP parties agreed to provide national treatment and most-favored nation treatment, as well as a minimum-standard of treatment for investment, as defined under customary international law.

Regarding ISDS, a timetable and conditions for arbitration to occur was also outlined in the chapter. Provisions were also included for arbitration hearings and related documents to be made public, except where provided otherwise by the national security exception (Article 29.2) and the disclosure of information exception (Article 29.6).

Another additional element was the provision for *amicus curiae* "friend of the court" legal briefs (Article 9.23.3.) and expedited review of "frivolous claims" (Article 9.23.4). Regarding the possibility of appeal against an appellate decision, the parties could submit written comments on a proposed award within a defined time period (Article 9.23.10), but there was no proposal for a formal appellate mechanism. However, should such a mechanism for reviewing awards by ISDS tribunals be developed at a later stage "under other institutional arrangements", the TPP parties could then review whether awards should be subject to that appellate mechanism (Article 9.23.11).

Despite the withdrawal of the world's largest economy from the agreement, the remaining eleven countries reached agreement in January 2018 to conclude the now Comprehensive and Progressive Agreement for Trans-Pacific Partnership (CPTPP) or TPP11. Seven countries have now ratified the CPTPP (Mexico, Japan, Singapore, New Zealand, Canada, Australia and Vietnam), and the agreement entered into force on 30 December 2018.

CPTPP is now one of the largest free trade agreements in the world, representing nearly 13.5 percent of global gross domestic product (GDP).[274] Most of the original TPP text remains intact, and two-thirds of the CPTPP's 30 chapters are identical to TPP. The investor-state dispute settlement (ISDS) provisions in the investment chapter are still included, but the investment chapter removes agreements covering mining and raw materials from coverage. This means such investments will not necessarily be covered under investor-state dispute settlement and are therefore marginally riskier for foreign investors. Similarly, under the revised IP chapter, the length of patent protection for innovative medicines has been shortened.

A logical question is whether and when the United States will seek to join the agreement.

2. Resolving Investment Disputes after Brexit

The U.K. is at the present moment set to leave the European Union on 31 October 2019. This means an end to the jurisdiction of The Court of Justice of the

274. *CSIS: From TPP to CPTPP*, March 2018, https://www.csis.org/analysis/tpp-cptpp.

European Union (CJEU) in the United Kingdom. Prime Minister Theresa May acknowledged the need for a mechanism to resolve regulatory disputes arising within the future trade and investment relationships with the remaining EU-27. This is no simple matter, and dispute settlement may well cast a long shadow over the negotiations. The U.K. Trade Bill linked to Brexit is intended to enable the U.K. to replicate current trade agreements that the U.K. is party to as a member of the European Union after Brexit. It would also set up a Trade Remedies Authority to advise the government on trade remedies such as anti-dumping and safeguards currently handled at the EU level. The Bill also includes creation of a U.K. Dispute Resolution Authority, but it is not clear if this will cover investment as well as trade.

The U.K. and the EU could set up a new court or arbitration panel to settle disputes, potentially involving a combination of U.K. judges and European judges. Such proposals vividly illustrate the huge complexities introduced by the unprecedented Brexit decision, through which one entity is proposing to leave a well-established Customs Union of more than forty years standing.

3. NAFTA Renegotiations and Investment Protection

The North American Free Trade Agreement (NAFTA) was a multilateral agreement entered into by United States, Canada and Mexico to regulate trade and investment within the three countries. Shortly after it took office, the Trump Administration prompted Canada and Mexico to begin renegotiating NAFTA as required by the Trade Promotion Act. The successor United States-Mexico-Canada Agreement (USMCA) has been signed by the parties but not yet ratified.

While NAFTA was known primarily as a trade agreement, it also included important rules and regulations for governing cross-border investment between the three countries. NAFTA's Chapter 11 guaranteed investors the right to fair and equitable treatment, the ability to transfer profits abroad, and the right to compensation in the event of direct or indirect expropriation. Chapter 11 also provided for investor-state dispute settlement (ISDS). To date, there have been 66 such cases filed under NAFTA:* 17 against the U.S., 27 against Canada, and 22 against Mexico. While the U.S. has so far never lost an ISDS case, both Canada and Mexico have lost several, requiring payments to investors of over $100 million.[275]

The United States under President Trump would like to repatriate dispute resolution into the domestic legal system and out of the hands of international tribunals. The United States contends that NAFTA country investors in the U.S. should not be accorded greater substantive rights than domestic investors. This has the potential to undermine the idea of concrete standards judged by an independent, international tribunal. While this may please long-term critics of ISDS, it risks damaging

* https://investmentpolicy.unctad.org/investment-dispute-settlement.

275. Geoffrey Gertz, Brookings Institution, *Renegotiating NAFTA: Options for Investment Protection* (March 2017).

the appeal of the U.S. to foreign investors, with adverse consequences on growth and jobs.

As the CETA included a version of the investment court system in its agreement, it would be logical for Canada to seek to discuss the multilateral investment court in the context of NAFTA negotiations. However, in the light of Trump's distaste for multilateralism and for the shielding of American sovereignty, it is unlikely his administration would join a new international court. On 21 April 2018, the EU and Mexico reached a new agreement on trade and investment which includes the EU's new investment court approach.

Other options for the future of investment protection in NAFTA/USMCA could include upgrading the treaty's investment chapter, while leaving the main substantive and procedural aspects of investment protection in place, or shifting from an investor-state framework to a state-state framework, in which states would be responsible for legal enforcement of investment regulations.

D. Investment and Development

1. Encouraging Foreign Investment to Developing Countries

Investment, when accompanied by sound government policies, can be a productive instrument for raising the capital necessary for economic development. In recent times, emerging markets such as Brazil and India have become a more significant source of foreign investment, and there is an urgent policy need to increase developing countries' share of total foreign direct investment flows.[276] Furthermore, the limited share of FDI that goes to developing countries is spread unevenly, with two-thirds of total FDI flowing from OECD members to non-OECD countries going to Asia and Latin America. This illustrates the need to address the role of FDI in sustainable economic development and to develop international policies to maximize the positive contribution investment can make to sustainable development.

If developing countries wish to use an International Investment Agreement ("IIA") as part of their strategy for economic growth, for maximum sustainable benefit, this should be linked with improvement of the domestic regulatory framework for investment.[277]

---

276. FDI remains the largest external source of finance for developing economies. It makes up 39% of total incoming finance in developing economies as a group, but less than a quarter in the LDCs, with a declining trend since 2012. *2018 World Investment Report*, http://worldinvestmentreport.unctad.org/world-investment-report-2018/#key-messages.

277. Graham Mayeda, Sustainable International Investment Agreements: Challenges and Solutions for Developing Countries in Marie-Claire Cordonier Segger, Markus W. Gehring & Andrew Newcombe, eds., *Sustainable Development In World Investment Law*, Alphen aan den Rijn: Kluwer Law International (2011).

Controversy remains with regard to how FDI can be most effective in promoting sustainable development and whether IIAs are an effective strategy for attracting this class of investment. Experts suggest that it is tempting to see IIAs as generating an increase in economic growth that can then be redirected toward the promotion of other public goods. However, by creating an international legal framework within which to resolve conflicts between investors and the host state, IIAs are generally designed to limit the exposure of foreign investors to the dispute resolution mechanisms of the host state. This may lead to foreign investors seeing themselves as having a reduced stake in the domestic regulatory framework in the home state, and may also give rise to a conceptual separation between investment law, which is regulated by the IIA, and other areas of social policy, which are regulated by domestic law or other areas of international customary or treaty law.[278]

Accordingly, one of the best means for ensuring that IIAs are compatible with principles of sustainable development is for states to negotiate sustainable investment agreements. States can seek to negotiate IIAs with "development friendly" versions of the provisions currently found in most IIAs and/or to include new principles in future IIAs that promote the protection of the environment, human rights, labor rights, and the rights of indigenous peoples.

IIAs with "Development Friendly" Provisions

IIAs could seek to improve the ability of host states to promote sustainable development by incorporating provisions that provide host states with the flexibility to achieve their development goals. These may be supported by a formal statement of acknowledgment of the advancement of sustainable development as the primary goal of the IIA and recognizing the right to development in the IIA. A provision may also be made in the exceptions and reservations to the agreement that legitimate measures taken by the state to promote sustainable development do not violate the agreement.

Another approach could be the inclusion of obligations on the developed country home states of investors to promote investment in developing country host states and to require home states to provide related technical assistance. Investors may also be required to conduct rigorous environmental and social impact assessments and to enforce customary international norms with respect to human rights, the protection of indigenous peoples, and the prevention of bribery and other forms of corruption.

2. Role of the International Community in the Promotion of Investment

Market access and trade liberalization by developed states can contribute substantially to worldwide economic development, benefiting both developed and developing countries. An important share of FDI is contingent upon subsequent

278. *Ibid.*

trade between related enterprises. There is a need for developed states to assess the negative effects that their technology policies may have on the transfer of technologies to host countries and to minimize the obstacles to the flow of investment to developing countries.

Responsible corporate behavior is vital. While domestic law should remain the primary source for ensuring responsible business conduct and holding investors accountable, international rules on investor conduct can supplement and strengthen domestic legal frameworks. Voluntary international standards such as the OECD Guidelines are good examples.

Governments and investors should promote, protect and respect the human rights of citizens and communities in accordance with international human rights instruments. The international community should adopt measures to tackle tax avoidance strategies that exploit gaps and mismatches in tax rules to artificially shift profits to low-tax or no-tax locations (also referred to as base erosion and profit shifting (BEPS)).

In Ethiopia in 2015, the UN held its third international conference on financing for development. One hundred and ninety-three UN member state governments agreed to the ground-breaking Addis Ababa Action Agenda (Addis Agenda), resolving to adopt and implement investment promotion regimes for least developed countries and to offer financial and technical support.

This aspiration will be driven by seventeen sustainable development goals with six action areas to strengthen domestic public resources driven by economic growth; to foster domestic and international private business and finance; to reaffirm the importance of international development cooperation; to increase international trade as an engine for development; to ease debt and debt sustainability; and to address systemic issues to enhance global economic governance and foster a more inclusive international architecture for sustainable development. Other action agenda initiatives include introducing a technology facilitation mechanism to foster innovation and capacity-building.

The economic benefits of FDI are real, but they do not accrue automatically. To reap the maximum benefits from foreign corporate presence, a healthy enabling environment for business is paramount, which encourages domestic as well as foreign investment, provides incentives of skills and contributes to a competitive corporate climate.

As observed, a successful investment climate depends ultimately on the political and legal security of the country. Investors need to feel that there is little or no possibility of the creation of an unfavorable legal situation at a later date which will be harmful to their investments. Governments should seek to continually improve the independence and efficiency of their judicial processes, and ensure the availability of timely and meaningful domestic remedies in the event of a dispute.

International dispute settlement mechanisms relating to investments, when used, should be transparent, based on accountability and the rule of law, and free of conflict of interest. Regional cooperation should be encouraged and can do much for developing and implementing effective investment policies, including the mitigation of tax competition through tax incentive programs.

3. Chinese Investments in Africa: Impact on Economic Development

China's strategic focus on economic development in Africa has captured frequent headlines over the past years. It is undoubtedly the case that Chinese investment flows and technical expertise are becoming important change drivers in many parts of the world, and Africa is no exception. However, Kenyan Ambassador to the United Nations Macharia Kamau argues that concerns over China's increasing economic involvement in Africa are overstated.[279] In particular the frequent representation in the media of Chinese interest as little more than a "grab" for oil and other natural resources is inaccurate and oversimplified.

There is concern about China's economic intentions in Africa but Ambassador Kamau finds this misplaced, not least because Chinese economic links with Africa are not unprecedented. He highlights that China has been trading with Africa since the First Century AD, when Chinese merchants visited the continent seeking ivory, medicines and spices. The Chinese were followed by the Portuguese in the 14th century, the Arabs and Europeans in the 19th century and the Americans in the 20th century. In the 21st century China is prompting a huge and transformative impact on the African continent, including in important areas such as economic growth, fighting poverty and disease and bringing education.

In this sense, Ambassador Kamau argues that China has become a liberating force in Africa, although again this is not the image generally portrayed in the media. By 2009, after only about fifteen years of modern investment in Africa, China had overtaken the United States as the number one trading partner for Africa. According to the Ambassador, by 2012, Chinese investment in Africa was around $200 billion, double the amount from the United States. As Kamau points out, this is a huge transformation in a very short space of time. This investment is built around key areas for economic development such as infrastructure, manufacturing and construction. Where Chinese investors are engaged in mining of raw materials for China's industries, the terms of engagement are generous and part of a wider picture that also includes investment in education, health and social development.

Ambassador Kamau notes that European countries have also invested in Africa on an exploitative basis but without the commensurate benefits. Africa remains to this day the poorest, most exploited, most down-trodden continent on Earth, and that goes a long way to explaining why Africa has embraced the Chinese opportunity.

279. Kenyan Ambassador to the United Nations Macharia Kamau in an address to Cornell Law School on February 26, 2015 in Myron Taylor Hall.

Furthermore, contrary to the media portrayal, "Africa is not China's priority". Ambassador Kamau observes that only 3 percent of Chinese foreign direct investment goes to Africa, and only 4 percent of its trade. Around $25 billion, or 47 percent of China's investment on the continent, has been for "development assistance". In comparison, the total accumulated investment in development assistance in Africa from the rest of the world is about $90 billion. Once again this illustrates the huge transformative impact of Chinese investment on the continent. As Ambassador Kamau states repeatedly, "the terms of engagement [with China] have been amazingly generous".

Nevertheless, the Ambassador also concedes that "China is not doing this out of pure philanthropy", with 58 percent of its investment targeted at six countries with huge natural resource opportunities. However, while China's policy in Africa is clearly driven by its broader strategic agenda, this isn't necessarily a bad thing. China is setting out to make friends in the global community by supplying aid, fostering development and extending trade opportunities to achieve its national goals and further its interests. As Ambassador Kamau said, "There isn't a superpower in history that hasn't done that. Why wouldn't China?"

However, reliable figures on the levels of Chinese investment in Africa are hard to come by. Those published by the Chinese Ministry of Commerce suggest the net annual flow of Chinese direct investment into Africa increased eight-fold between 2005 and 2014, to $3.2 billion. The total stock of Chinese investments grew twenty-fold, to $32 billion. Direct comparisons to Western figures are harder still, but that makes China one of Africa's biggest investors.[280]

According to Deborah Brautigam, a professor at the School of Advanced International Studies in Washington DC, much of the hype about Chinese firms buying up vast amounts of industry in Africa is overblown. Chinese FDI to Africa constitutes less than 3% of all Chinese foreign investment: vastly more goes to other regions, especially Asia. Growth has slowed in recent years. And as Brautigam shows in her book investigating agricultural projects, *Will Africa Feed China?*, many heavily-reported Chinese projects do not amount to much.[281] A common problem is that Chinese firms "sort of assume that it works the way it does in China", says Brautigam. "In China, a company comes in, makes an arrangement with local government, and the government delivers." In Africa, they then discover that government promises to build infrastructure, provide power or supply land are not as credible as they thought. Public land turns out to be occupied by squatters, who may have farmed it for generations; private land may not be owned by the people selling it. Local politicians do not accept deals struck by national ones.

Increasingly, Chinese firms are adapting to these conditions. Chinese investors are now doing the sorts of things Western firms have long done. They are investing

280. *Chinese Investment in Africa, Not as Easy as it Looks*, The Economist (2015).

281. Deborah Brautigam, *Will Africa Feed China?* Oxford University Press (2015).

in corporate social responsibility programs, hiring African managers and doing reliable due diligence.[282]

The increasing importance of Africa for China is clearly evident in the intensified Chinese diplomatic activity in recent years. What is striking is the level of interest by China in African affairs, a level of interest that is concomitant with its rising importance in the world economy. In its relationship with African states, China has adopted a different approach from that which is associated with the West. In essence, as a Western analyst has noted, China has "increasingly regarded Africa as an opportunity, while Europe has long regarded Africa as a burden".[283]

a. Case Study: Chinese Investment in the Zambian Economy

Chinese investment in Zambia is a positive and welcome development. Zambia is one of the leading copper-producing countries in the world, and its economy is largely mineral-based. The real issue is whether Zambia's need for investment and China's need for raw materials can work for both countries to bring about economic development and alleviate poverty in both countries, a matter that is not wholly dependent on China alone.

One of the factors affecting development in Zambia, as elsewhere in Africa, is the availability of capital. Economic development is achieved through the productive employment of labor and the full utilization of natural resources. The productive employment of labor requires capital and presupposes an increase in the general level of education and the acquisition of technical skills, as well as the formation of a body of capable administrators and entrepreneurs. For the utilization of natural resources, a number of basic facilities are needed, such as roads, railways, harnessing of electric power and other forms of energy. For example, several countries in Africa, including Zambia, are facing serious power shortages, partly because they are beginning to experience modest economic growth, which increases the demand for electricity. In order to reverse this situation, a huge injection of external capital in the energy sector is required.

Since China and Zambia established diplomatic relations over 50 years ago, 200 Chinese companies have set up businesses in Zambia, ranging from mining, textile, construction, banking, agriculture, to medical clinics and restaurants. Some of the companies, such as China's Non-Ferrous Africa Mining Plc (NFC-Africa) and Zambia China Mulungushi Textile Company, are large sized and play an important role in the country's economy. Other Chinese investments in Zambia include the Chambishi Copper Mine, which China purchased during the privatization of the Zambian copper mines in the 1990s.

Zambia and China have also agreed to establish the Zambia-China Chambishi Trade and Economic Zone. In the zone, Zambia will exempt Chinese firms from

282. *Chinese Investment in Africa, Not as Easy as it Looks*, The Economist (2015).

283. B. Berger, *China Outwits the EU in Africa*, Asia Times, 13 December 2007.

import duties and value added taxes. China is also involved in the construction industry and has developed modern markets, using the build, operate and transfer approach. In addition to substantial capital investments, China has cancelled Zambian debt and is providing assistance in the form of agricultural training and education scholarships.

The major issue that arises in the context of Chinese investments in Zambia is whether the two countries can work constructively together to ensure that this is a win-win situation for both and what policies and mechanisms can be put in place to ensure this result.

It is alleged that the Chinese, in their dealings with Africa, bypass multilateral institutions like the World Bank and the International Monetary Fund, including their minimum standards of transparency, open bidding for contracts and environmental impact studies. Some ask whether China's willingness to spend whatever it needs in Africa without regard to fiscal prudence, democracy, honest business practices and human rights produces a replay of past booms, enriching local elites but leaving the continent poorer, its environment despoiled and its natural resources depleted. Major complaints have emerged in the field of labor relations. Chinese enterprises are often accused of exploiting workers through the payment of low wages and unsatisfactory working conditions, such as those relating to the health and safety of workers. One of the worst mining disasters in Zambian mining history occurred in 2006 at the Chinese-owned Chambishi mine, where 46 miners were killed. Chinese companies are further accused of importing Chinese labor for jobs that could be done by Zambians, especially in the construction industries.

Governance is central to all issues relating to the efficiency affecting government operations and economic development. Investors are not philanthropists driven by a moral code. They are typically large organizations, each with its own set of goals and objectives, motivated by profit and strategic interests, both national and corporate. It is the Zambian government that must put in place a framework to ensure the pursuit of profit is carried out in the context of respect for worker's rights and the protection of the environment. An example of this is the Zambian government's partnership with the International Labour Organization; together, they have completed the Zambia Decent Work Programme for improved working conditions and social protection for workers.

In general, the responsibility of the government is to create a conductive business and political climate and to perpetuate an atmosphere of trust between itself and investors. In short, investors have to be assured that they will receive, both today and in the future, legally defined and controlled treatment. However, as the Zambian government encourages investment, it should also implement measures that promote corporate governance. These measures should ensure the respect of workers' rights, the protection of the environment and the efficient management of investments as well as the continuous monitoring of operations and full documentation of all transactions. Zambia should strategically focus on the development of education, technology, science, energy and infrastructure as the method to drive economic growth, and it must direct Chinese investment in these areas. For Zambia to benefit effectively from its engagement with China, it needs to establish clear development objectives and identify priorities, identify mechanisms to meet the objectives and provide the institutional arrangements to implement the mechanisms, to include all relevant local stakeholders, especially the poor, in the policy formulation process.

These steps would allow Zambia to attract foreign investment, which is essential to reducing its capital deficit, invest heavily in infrastructure with particular emphasis on transportation and energy and improve competitiveness of Zambian goods and add value to raw materials produced in Zambia.

b. One Belt One Road Initiative

In 2017, China hosted its "One Belt One Road" Summit, showcasing its US$1 trillion spending plan for transport and other infrastructure connectivity projects throughout Asia, Africa and Europe. Some argue that domestic labor or social safeguards are not the responsibly of Chinese concession operators and funders. China's bilateral partners under the "One Belt One Road" initiative themselves will need to ensure that international environmental, labor and social safeguards form part of their domestic regulatory framework. In particular, under the International Covenant on Economic, Social and Cultural Rights, the obligation to protect requires states to adopt legislative, administrative and educational, as well as other appropriate means, to ensure effective protection against violation of Covenant rights linked to business activities. It would be an appropriate time for "One Belt One Road" initiative recipient countries to review and revisit the terms of their bilateral or regional investment treaties with China, to determine their institutional, practical and legal abilities. It is also for China's partner countries in its "One Belt One Road" initiative to be active investment partners conscious of their duties to ensure the protection of human rights and fundamental freedoms.

Section F looks in more detail at the protection of human rights in international investment law and the possibility of a new multilateral treaty on business and human rights.

E. Traditional Knowledge and the Protection of Intellectual Property

According to the World Intellectual Property Organization (WIPO), traditional knowledge is a living body of knowledge, know-how, skills and practices that are developed, sustained and passed on from generation to generation within a community often forming part of its cultural or spiritual identity. While there is not yet an accepted definition of traditional knowledge at the international level, it can be said that traditional knowledge in a general sense embraces the content of knowledge itself as well as traditional cultural expressions, including distinctive signs and symbols associated with traditional knowledge resulting from intellectual activity in a traditional context.

Traditional knowledge as well as biodiversity can be a valuable source of intellectual works. It has historical, cultural, scientific and economic value. Its community ownership characteristics can be considered individualistic, and this differentiates it from the typical intellectual property rights dealt with by the TRIPS Agreement. Such differences leave traditional knowledge unprotected by the core intellectual property laws and vulnerable to exploitation by companies that seek to own the knowledge as an intellectual property right by taking out patents and copyright registrations based on the traditional knowledge regardless of the interests of the community.

Several examples can be cited. For example, India (Council of Scientific and Industrial Research) won a petition against a US patent granted to two Indian born Americans who used the spice Kunyit, commonly known as "turmeric," for a wound-healing product. As a result, the U.S. Patent Office fully revoked the patent it had granted. India also stopped an attempt to register a patent of a mouthwash formula containing Nutmeg-Yayaphal herbal extract by Palmolive-Colgate. In Indonesia, some non-governmental organizations have questioned the validity of the Shiseido patents registered in Japan. There are allegations that the patents are not different from existing traditional knowledge in Indonesia. Another controversy surrounds the Hoodia plant indigenous to Southern Africa and used by Koi Koi as a medicinal plant. In this case, folk medicine practitioners believed the plant to be an appetite suppressant and to have other medicinal properties, such as treating indigestion and small infections. In 1977, the South African Council of Scientific and Industrial Research (CSIR) isolated the ingredient in Hoodia (now known as preparation P57), and it was patented in 1996. The CSIR then granted a United Kingdom pharmaceutical company a license, and they collaborated with Pfizer to isolate active ingredients from the extracts and look into synthesizing them for use as an appetite suppressant.

Efforts to protect traditional knowledge face many challenges, as such knowledge is in the public domain, it is easily accessible to anyone, the first creator is unknown, and the knowledge is collectively preserved by the community of origin. One of the legal issues that receives global attention is the lack of domestic legal instruments providing legal protection when the traditional knowledge is used by parties who are not responsible for its origination. At the international level, WIPO is currently working on a draft convention to protect traditional knowledge.[284]

284. The Protection of Traditional Knowledge; Draft Articles WIPO/GRTKF/IC/38/4.

1. The World Intellectual Property Organization Draft Convention to Protect Traditional Knowledge

WIPO, *The Protection of Traditional Knowledge*: Draft Articles—Background Brief.

The current international system for protecting intellectual property was fashioned during the age of industrialization in the West and developed subsequently in line with the perceived needs of technologically advanced societies. However, in recent years, indigenous peoples, local communities, and governments, mainly in developing countries, have demanded equivalent protection for traditional knowledge systems. In 2000, WIPO members established an Intergovernmental Committee on Intellectual Property and Genetic Resources, Traditional Knowledge and Folklore (IGC), and in 2009 they agreed to develop an international legal instrument (or instruments) that would give traditional knowledge, genetic resources and traditional cultural expressions (folklore) effective protection. Such an instrument could range from a recommendation to WIPO members to a formal treaty that would bind countries choosing to ratify it.

Traditional knowledge is not so-called because of its antiquity. It is a living body of knowledge that is developed, sustained and passed on from generation to generation within a community, often forming part of its cultural or spiritual identity. As such, it is not easily protected by the current intellectual property system, which typically grants protection for a limited period to inventions and original works by named individuals or companies. Its living nature also means that "traditional" knowledge is not easy to define.

Recognizing traditional forms of creativity and innovation as protectable intellectual property would be an historic shift in international law, enabling indigenous and local communities as well as governments to have a say over the use of their traditional knowledge by others. This would make it possible, for example, to protect traditional remedies, and indigenous art and music against misappropriation, and enable communities to control and benefit collectively from their commercial exploitation.

Although the negotiations underway in WIPO have been initiated and propelled mainly by developing countries, the discussions are not neatly divided along "North-South" lines. Communities and governments do not necessarily share the same views, and some developed country governments, especially those with indigenous populations, are also active.

Two types of intellectual property protection are being sought:

Defensive Protection

Defensive Protection aims to stop people outside the community from acquiring intellectual property rights over traditional knowledge. India, for example, has compiled a searchable database of traditional medicine that can be used as evidence of prior art by patent examiners when assessing patent applications. This followed a well-known case in which the U.S. Patent and Trademark Office granted a patent (later revoked) for the use of turmeric to treat wounds, a property well-known to traditional communities in India and documented in ancient Sanskrit texts. Defensive strategies might also be used to protect sacred cultural manifestations, such as sacred symbols or words, from being registered as trademarks.

Positive Protection

Positive protection is the granting of rights that empower communities to promote their traditional knowledge, control its uses and benefit from its commercial exploitation. Some uses of traditional knowledge can be protected through the existing intellectual property system, and a number of countries have also developed specific legislation. However, any specific protection afforded under national law may not hold for other countries, one reason why many indigenous and local communities as well as governments are pressing for an international legal instrument.

WIPO's work on traditional knowledge addresses three distinct yet related areas: traditional knowledge in the strict sense (technical know-how, practices, skills, and innovations related to, say, biodiversity, agriculture or health); traditional cultural expressions/expressions of folklore (cultural manifestations such as music, art, designs, symbols and performances); and genetic resources (genetic material of actual or potential value found in plants, animals and micro-organisms).

Although for many communities traditional knowledge, genetic resources and traditional cultural expressions form part of a single integrated heritage, from an intellectual property standpoint they raise different issues and may require different sets of solutions. In all three areas, in addition to work on an international legal instrument, WIPO is responding to requests from communities and governments for practical assistance and technical advice to enable communities to make more effective use of existing intellectual property systems and participate more effectively in the IGC's negotiations. WIPO's work includes assistance to develop and strengthen national and regional systems for the protection of traditional knowledge (policies, laws, information systems and practical tools) and the Creative Heritage Project which provides hands-on training for managing intellectual property rights and interests when documenting cultural heritage.

Traditional Knowledge

When community members innovate within the traditional knowledge framework, they may use the patent system to protect their innovations. However, traditional knowledge as such—knowledge that has ancient roots and is often informal and oral—is not protected by conventional intellectual property systems. This has prompted some countries to develop their own *sui generis* (specific, special) systems for protecting traditional knowledge.

There are also many initiatives underway to document traditional knowledge. In most cases the motive is to preserve or disseminate it, or to use it, for example, in environmental management, rather than for the purpose of legal protection. There are nevertheless concerns that if documentation makes traditional knowledge more widely available to the general public, especially if it can be accessed on the Internet, this could lead to misappropriation and use in ways that were not anticipated or intended by traditional knowledge holders.

At the same time, documentation can help protect traditional knowledge, for example, by providing a confidential or secret record of traditional knowledge reserved for the relevant community only. Some formal documentation and registries of traditional knowledge support *sui generis* protection systems, while traditional knowledge databases—such as India's database on traditional medicine—play a role in defensive protection within the existing IP system. These examples demonstrate the importance of ensuring that documentation of traditional knowledge is linked to an intellectual property strategy and does not take place in a policy or legal vacuum.

In the WIPO talks, many argue that use of traditional knowledge ought to be subject to free, prior and informed consent, especially for sacred and secret materials. However, others fear that granting exclusive control over traditional cultures could stifle innovation, diminish the public domain and be difficult to implement in practice.

Genetic Resources

Genetic resources themselves are not intellectual property (they are not creations of the human mind) and thus cannot be directly protected as intellectual property. However, inventions based on or developed using genetic resources (associated with traditional knowledge or not) may be patentable or protected by plant breeders' rights. In considering intellectual property aspects of use of genetic resources, WIPO's work complements the international legal and policy framework defined by the Convention on Biological Diversity (CBD), and its Nagoya Protocol, and the International Treaty on Genetic Resources for Food and Agriculture of the United Nations Food and Agriculture Organization. Issues under discussion at WIPO include:

Defensive Protection of Genetic Resources: This strand of the work aims at preventing patents being granted over genetic resources (and associated traditional knowledge) which do not fulfill the existing requirements of novelty and inventiveness. In this context, to help patent examiners find relevant prior art, proposals have been made that genetic resources and traditional knowledge databases could help patent examiners avoid erroneous patents and WIPO has improved its own search tools and patent classification systems. The other, more controversial, strand concerns the possible disqualification of patent applications that do not comply with CBD obligations on prior informed consent, mutually agreed terms, fair and equitable benefit-sharing, and disclosure of origin. "Biopiracy" is a term sometimes used loosely to describe biodiversity-related patents that do not meet patentability criteria or that do not comply with the CBD's obligations—but this term has no precise or agreed meaning.

Disclosure Requirements: A number of countries have enacted domestic legislation putting into effect the CBD obligations that access to a country's genetic resources should depend on securing that country's prior informed consent and agreeing to fair and equitable benefit-sharing. WIPO members are considering whether, and to what extent, the intellectual property system should be used to support and implement these obligations. Many, but not all, WIPO members want to make it mandatory for patent applications to show the source or origin of genetic resources, as well as evidence of prior informed consent and a benefit sharing agreement. Parallel discussions are also taking place in the World Trade Organization's Council on Trade Related Aspects of Intellectual Property (TRIPS).

WIPO also deals with the intellectual property aspects of mutually agreed terms for fair and equitable benefit-sharing. It has developed, and regularly updates, an online database of relevant contractual practices, and has prepared draft guidelines on intellectual property clauses in access and benefit-sharing agreements.

Traditional Cultural Expressions

Traditional cultural expressions (folklore) are seen as integral to the cultural and social identities of indigenous and local communities, embodying know-how and skills, and transmitting core values and beliefs. Protecting folklore contributes to economic development, encourages cultural diversity and helps preserve cultural heritage.

Traditional cultural expressions can sometimes be protected by existing systems, such as copyright and related rights, geographical indications, appellations of origin, trademarks and certification marks. For example, contemporary adaptations of folklore are copyrightable, while performances of traditional songs and music may come under the WIPO Performances and Phonograms Treaty. Trademarks can be used to identify authentic indigenous arts, as the Maori Arts Board in New Zealand, Te Waka Toi, has done. Some countries also have special legislation for the protection of folklore. Panama has established a registration system for traditional cultural expressions, while the Pacific Regional Framework for the Protection of Traditional Knowledge and Expressions of Culture gives "traditional owners" the right to authorize or prevent use of protected folklore and receive a share of the benefits from any commercial exploitation.

Developing an International Legal Instrument

Because the existing international intellectual property system does not fully protect traditional knowledge and traditional cultural expressions, many communities and governments have called for an international legal instrument providing *sui generis* protection.

An international legal instrument would define what is meant by traditional knowledge and traditional cultural expressions, who the rights holders would be, how competing claims by communities would be resolved, and what rights and exceptions ought to apply. Working out the details is complex and there are divergent views on the best ways forward, including whether intellectual property-type rights are appropriate for protecting traditional forms of innovation and creativity.

To take just one example, communities may wish to control all uses of their traditional cultural expressions, including works inspired by them, even if they are not direct copies. Copyright law, on the other hand, permits building on the works of others, provided there is sufficient originality. The text of the legal instrument will have to define where the line is to be drawn between legitimate borrowing and unauthorized appropriation.

On genetic resources, countries agree that intellectual property protection and the conservation of biodiversity should be mutually supportive, but differ on how this can be achieved and whether any changes to current intellectual property rules are necessary.

Representatives of indigenous and local communities are assisted by the WIPO Voluntary fund to attend the WIPO talks, and their active participation will continue to be crucial for a successful outcome. WIPO members have agreed to expedite their work so as to decide in late 2012 whether to convene a diplomatic conference for final adoption of one or more international instruments.

2. Additional Reading

Tustin, J. *Traditional Knowledge and Intellectual Property in Brazilian Biodiversity Law*, 2006 Texas Intellectual Property Law Journal, 14(2)13.

WIPO, *Intellectual Property Needs and Expectations of Traditional Knowledge Holders, WIPO Report on Fact Finding Missions on Intellectual Property and Traditional Knowledge* (1988–1999), Geneva, 2001.

F. Protection of Human Rights in International Investment Law

The relationship between international investment law and other public policy objectives, including the protection of human rights or the environment, raises many legal challenges as described in the following materials.

The right to self-determination is regarded as *jus cogens*, and states are under an obligation to take measures designed to protect such a right. Foreign companies also have an obligation to ensure that their activities do not undermine such human rights wherever they conduct their business. Equally, there is a vigorous debate on the extent of foreign companies' obligations to promote human rights in the countries where they do business.

New international treaties may introduce new rights requiring the states parties to enact laws and take other administrative measures to implement the provisions of such treaties. All natural and juridical persons, including foreign investors, may be required to abide by such measures, even if compliance with such measures may involve additional costs, and such costs may undermine the profitability of a foreign company doing business in the country concerned. For example, the Morocco-Nigeria BIT,[285] signed in late 2016, explicitly places human rights obligations on investors. In Article 18(2), the treaty stipulates that "Investors and investments shall uphold human rights in the host state". Article 18(3) requires investors to "act in accordance with core labor standards as required by the ILO Declaration on Fundamental Principles and Rights of Work, 1998".[286] Nevertheless, the question remains as to how affected individuals may obtain redress from investors. Both the Morocco-Nigeria BIT and the new Indian Model BIT[287] require state parties to allow investors to be subject to civil liability claims (e.g., tort) in their home state, for damage caused to third parties in the host state in the conduct of the investment. These provisions might improve the chances of victims having access to an effective remedy for human rights abuses caused by investor activity.

The core International Labour Organization Conventions ("ILO Conventions"), such as the Constitution of the ILO 1946, the 1948 Convention Concerning Forced or Compulsory Labour, the 1949 Convention Concerning the Application of the Principles of the Right to Organise and to Bargain Collectively, and the 1981 Convention Concerning Occupational Safety and Health and the Working Environment, provide for basic rights for workers. These rights include the freedom to bargain collectively, freedom of association, elimination of discrimination in the workplace, elimination of workplace abuse such as forced labor, adequate wages and proper working conditions. Since the provisions of these Conventions have to be implemented through national laws, a host state could adopt the necessary regulatory measures to this effect, and such measures may have financial implications for foreign companies in terms of higher wages or better working conditions, etc. Indeed, the revised OECD Guidelines of 2000 enshrine the provisions contained in the core ILO instruments mentioned above and, more significantly, have also created a mechanism for monitoring corporate behavior and investigating abuses.

Since 2014, discussions regarding a global treaty for regulating business impact on human rights have been taking place at the UN level.[288] Among the key disagreements is whether such a treaty should introduce direct human rights obligations for businesses under international law. Some argue that such obligations should

---

285. https://investmentpolicyhubold.unctad.org/Download/TreatyFile/5409.

286. https://www.ilo.org/wcmsp5/groups/public/---ed_norm/---declaration/documents/publication/wcms_467653.pdf.

287. https://www.mygov.in/sites/default/files/master_image/Model%20Text%20for%20the%20Indian%20Bilateral%20Investment%20Treaty.pdf.

288. Business and Human Rights Resource Centre, https://business-humanrights.org/en/binding-treaty.

not be a substitute for the state's duties to fulfill their human rights obligations. Others argue that effective legal protection requires the legal responsibility for businesses to respect human rights to be recognized in an internationally binding instrument.

1. Towards a New Treaty on Business and Human Rights

In June 2011, the United Nations Human Rights Council (UN HRC) unanimously endorsed the United Nations Guiding Principles on Business and Human Rights (UNGPs). Although these principles are not legally binding, they place certain responsibilities on businesses to respect human rights, and have become the first globally accepted standard covering the responsibilities of states and businesses in preventing and addressing business-related human rights abuse. They have established a common global platform for action, upon which cumulative progress has started to be recorded.

In 2014, at the 26th session of the UN HRC in Geneva, a resolution drafted by Ecuador and South Africa, and also signed by Bolivia, Cuba and Venezuela, was put forward to request a United Nations Global Treaty Regulating Business Impact on Human Rights. The resolution would have directed states "to establish an open-ended intergovernmental working group with the mandate to elaborate an international legally binding instrument on transnational corporations and other business enterprises with respect to human rights." Within the 47-members-large HRC, it was supported by 20 member states and opposed by 14 states (including the United States, the United Kingdom and the Member States of the European Union), with 13 member states of the HRC abstaining. Those skeptical of an international treaty maintained that the focus should be on implementing the UN Guiding Principles already in place, rather than creating new rules. In addition, the proposed treaty seemed to focus only on large transnational corporations, meaning that abuses committed by small and medium-sized enterprises may be overlooked.

In any case, adherence to the Principles has been slow and uneven from country to country, with only 14 of the 47 country members of the Human Rights Council having published their National Action Plans for domestic implementation. The Principles are not legally binding and seen by many as being "too weak", and the third pillar of the Principles, which says there must be access to a remedy for victims of business-related human rights abuses, has been largely unfulfilled.

The Morocco-Nigeria BIT and the new Indian Model BIT elevated human rights obligations to treaty level in their BITs. However, the bilateral nature of the commitments means the application of the standards is limited to investors from the BIT signatories. Unless taken up in BIT practice more broadly, for example by the EU, these provisions will not reach as many victims as they could. The possibility of a legally-binding international instrument in the area of business and human rights would extend the scope, responsibilities and obligations of state and non-state actors in this field and have meaningful benefits for victims across the world.

United Nations Guiding Principles on Business and Human Rights.

I. The State duty to protect human rights

A. Foundational principles

1. States must protect against human rights abuse within their territory and/or jurisdiction by third parties, including business enterprises. This requires taking appropriate steps to prevent, investigate, punish and redress such abuse through effective policies, legislation, regulations and adjudication.

2. States should set out clearly the expectation that all business enterprises domiciled in their territory and/or jurisdiction respect human rights throughout their operations.

B. Operational principles

General State regulatory and policy functions

3. In meeting their duty to protect, States should:

(a) Enforce laws that are aimed at, or have the effect of, requiring business enterprises to respect human rights, and periodically to assess the adequacy of such laws and address any gaps;

(b) Ensure that other laws and policies governing the creation and ongoing operation of business enterprises, such as corporate law, do not constrain but enable business respect for human rights;

(c) Provide effective guidance to business enterprises on how to respect human rights throughout their operations;

(d) Encourage, and where appropriate require, business enterprises to communicate how they address their human rights impacts.

The State-business nexus

4. States should take additional steps to protect against human rights abuses by business enterprises that are owned or controlled by the State, or that receive substantial support and services from State agencies such as export credit agencies and official investment insurance or guarantee agencies, including, where appropriate, by requiring human rights due diligence.

5. States should exercise adequate oversight in order to meet their international human rights obligations when they contract with, or legislate for, business enterprises to provide services that may impact upon the enjoyment of human rights.

6. States should promote respect for human rights by business enterprises with which they conduct commercial transactions.

Supporting business respect for human rights in conflict-affected areas

7. Because the risk of gross human rights abuses is heightened in conflict-affected areas, States should help ensure that business enterprises operating in those contexts are not involved with such abuses, including by:

(a) Engaging at the earliest stage possible with business enterprises to help them identify, prevent and mitigate the human rights-related risks of their activities and business relationships;

(b) Providing adequate assistance to business enterprises to assess and address the heightened risks of abuses, paying special attention to both gender-based and sexual violence;

(c) Denying access to public support and services for a business enterprise that is involved with gross human rights abuses and refuses to cooperate in addressing the situation;

(d) Ensuring that their current policies, legislation, regulations and enforcement measures are effective in addressing the risk of business involvement in gross human rights abuses.

Ensuring policy coherence

8. States should ensure that governmental departments, agencies and other State-based institutions that shape business practices are aware of and observe the State's human rights obligations when fulfilling their respective mandates, including by providing them with relevant information, training and support.

9. States should maintain adequate domestic policy space to meet their human rights obligations when pursuing business-related policy objectives with other States or business enterprises, for instance through investment treaties or contracts.

10. States, when acting as members of multilateral institutions that deal with business related issues, should:

(a) Seek to ensure that those institutions neither restrain the ability of their member States to meet their duty to protect nor hinder business enterprises from respecting human rights;

(b) Encourage those institutions, within their respective mandates and capacities, to promote business respect for human rights and, where requested, to help States meet their duty to protect against human rights abuse by business enterprises, including through technical assistance, capacity-building and awareness-raising;

(c) Draw on these Guiding Principles to promote shared understanding and advance international cooperation in the management of business and human rights challenges.

II. The corporate responsibility to respect human rights

A. Foundational principles

11. Business enterprises should respect human rights. This means that they should avoid infringing on the human rights of others and should address adverse human rights impacts with which they are involved.

12. The responsibility of business enterprises to respect human rights refers to internationally recognized human rights—understood, at a minimum, as those

expressed in the International Bill of Human Rights and the principles concerning fundamental rights set out in the International Labour Organization's Declaration on Fundamental Principles and Rights at Work.

13. The responsibility to respect human rights requires that business enterprises:

(a) Avoid causing or contributing to adverse human rights impacts through their own activities, and address such impacts when they occur;

(b) Seek to prevent or mitigate adverse human rights impacts that are directly linked to their operations, products or services by their business relationships, even if they have not contributed to those impacts.

14. The responsibility of business enterprises to respect human rights applies to all enterprises regardless of their size, sector, operational context, ownership and structure. Nevertheless, the scale and complexity of the means through which enterprises meet that responsibility may vary according to these factors and with the severity of the enterprise's adverse human rights impacts.

15. In order to meet their responsibility to respect human rights, business enterprises should have in place policies and processes appropriate to their size and circumstances, including:

(a) A policy commitment to meet their responsibility to respect human rights;

(b) A human rights due-diligence process to identify, prevent, mitigate and account for how they address their impacts on human rights;

(c) Processes to enable the remediation of any adverse human rights impacts they cause or to which they contribute.

B. Operational principles

Policy commitment

16. As the basis for embedding their responsibility to respect human rights, business enterprises should express their commitment to meet this responsibility through a statement of policy that:

(a) Is approved at the most senior level of the business enterprise;

(b) Is informed by relevant internal and/or external expertise;

(c) Stipulates the enterprise's human rights expectations of personnel, business partners and other parties directly linked to its operations, products or services;

(d) Is publicly available and communicated internally and externally to all personnel, business partners and other relevant parties;

(e) Is reflected in operational policies and procedures necessary to embed it throughout the business enterprise.

Human rights due diligence

17. In order to identify, prevent, mitigate and account for how they address their adverse human rights impacts, business enterprises should carry out human

rights due diligence. The process should include assessing actual and potential human rights impacts, integrating and acting upon the findings, tracking responses, and communicating how impacts are addressed. Human rights due diligence:

(a) Should cover adverse human rights impacts that the business enterprise may cause or contribute to through its own activities, or which may be directly linked to its operations, products or services by its business relationships;

(b) Will vary in complexity with the size of the business enterprise, the risk of severe human rights impacts, and the nature and context of its operations;

(c) Should be ongoing, recognizing that the human rights risks may change over time as the business enterprise's operations and operating context evolve.

18. In order to gauge human rights risks, business enterprises should identify and assess any actual or potential adverse human rights impacts with which they may be involved either through their own activities or as a result of their business relationships. This process should:

(a) Draw on internal and/or independent external human rights expertise;

(b) Involve meaningful consultation with potentially affected groups and other relevant stakeholders, as appropriate to the size of the business enterprise and the nature and context of the operation.

19. In order to prevent and mitigate adverse human rights impacts, business enterprises should integrate the findings from their impact assessments across relevant internal functions and processes, and take appropriate action.

(a) Effective integration requires that:

(i) Responsibility for addressing such impacts is assigned to the appropriate level and function within the business enterprise;

(ii) Internal decision-making, budget allocations and oversight processes enable effective responses to such impacts.

(b) Appropriate action will vary according to:

(i) Whether the business enterprise causes or contributes to an adverse impact, or whether it is involved solely because the impact is directly linked to its operations, products or services by a business relationship;

(ii) The extent of its leverage in addressing the adverse impact.

20. In order to verify whether adverse human rights impacts are being addressed, business enterprises should track the effectiveness of their response. Tracking should:

(a) Be based on appropriate qualitative and quantitative indicators;

(b) Draw on feedback from both internal and external sources, including affected stakeholders.

21. In order to account for how they address their human rights impacts, business enterprises should be prepared to communicate this externally, particularly when concerns are raised by or on behalf of affected stakeholders. Business enterprises

whose operations or operating contexts pose risks of severe human rights impacts should report formally on how they address them. In all instances, communications should:

(a) Be of a form and frequency that reflect an enterprise's human rights impacts and that are accessible to its intended audiences;

(b) Provide information that is sufficient to evaluate the adequacy of an enterprise's response to the particular human rights impact involved;

(c) In turn not pose risks to affected stakeholders, personnel or to legitimate requirements of commercial confidentiality.

Remediation

22. Where business enterprises identify that they have caused or contributed to adverse impacts, they should provide for or cooperate in their remediation through legitimate processes.

Issues of context

23. In all contexts, business enterprises should:

(a) Comply with all applicable laws and respect internationally recognized human rights, wherever they operate;

(b) Seek ways to honour the principles of internationally recognized human rights when faced with conflicting requirements;

(c) Treat the risk of causing or contributing to gross human rights abuses as a legal compliance issue wherever they operate.

24. Where it is necessary to prioritize actions to address actual and potential adverse human rights impacts, business enterprises should first seek to prevent and mitigate those that are most severe or where delayed response would make them irremediable.

III. Access to remedy

A. Foundational principle

25. As part of their duty to protect against business-related human rights abuse, States must take appropriate steps to ensure, through judicial, administrative, legislative or other appropriate means, that when such abuses occur within their territory and/or jurisdiction those affected have access to effective remedy.

B. Operational principles

State-based judicial mechanisms

26. States should take appropriate steps to ensure the effectiveness of domestic judicial mechanisms when addressing business-related human rights abuses, including considering ways to reduce legal, practical and other relevant barriers that could lead to a denial of access to remedy.

State-based non-judicial grievance mechanisms

27. States should provide effective and appropriate non-judicial grievance mechanisms, alongside judicial mechanisms, as part of a comprehensive State-based system for the remedy of business-related human rights abuse.

Non-State-based grievance mechanisms

28. States should consider ways to facilitate access to effective non-State-based grievance mechanisms dealing with business-related human rights harms.

29. To make it possible for grievances to be addressed early and remediated directly, business enterprises should establish or participate in effective operational-level grievance mechanisms for individuals and communities who may be adversely impacted.

30. Industry, multi-stakeholder and other collaborative initiatives that are based on respect for human rights-related standards should ensure that effective grievance mechanisms are available.

Effectiveness criteria for non-judicial grievance mechanisms

31. In order to ensure their effectiveness, non-judicial grievance mechanisms, both State based and non-State-based, should be:

(a) Legitimate: enabling trust from the stakeholder groups for whose use they are intended, and being accountable for the fair conduct of grievance processes;

(b) Accessible: being known to all stakeholder groups for whose use they are intended, and providing adequate assistance for those who may face particular barriers to access;

(c) Predictable: providing a clear and known procedure with an indicative timeframe for each stage, and clarity on the types of process and outcome available and means of monitoring implementation;

(d) Equitable: seeking to ensure that aggrieved parties have reasonable access to sources of information, advice and expertise necessary to engage in a grievance process on fair, informed and respectful terms;

(e) Transparent: keeping parties to a grievance informed about its progress, and providing sufficient information about the mechanism's performance to build confidence in its effectiveness and meet any public interest at stake;

(f) Rights-compatible: ensuring that outcomes and remedies accord with internationally recognized human rights;

(g) A source of continuous learning: drawing on relevant measures to identify lessons for improving the mechanism and preventing future grievances and harms; Operational-level mechanisms should also be:

(h) Based on engagement and dialogue: consulting the stakeholder groups for whose use they are intended on their design and performance, and focusing on dialogue as the means to address and resolve grievances.

2. The Role of Human Rights in Investment Arbitration

While the debate on the Business Human Rights Treaty is likely to continue, there are recent developments in international investment law addressing the international human rights obligations for businesses. The extent to which a state should be permitted to rely on its human rights obligations to defend claims that it breached its investment treaty obligation has received significant attention. There is a recent trend in foreign investment law to hold foreign companies accountable for human rights violations in the host countries concerned and to consider how investment treaties may be used to enforce compliance with human rights obligations.

In particular, the tribunal in *Urbaser S.A. v. Argentine Republic* countered the claimant's argument that the relevant BIT conferred no human rights obligations on the investor. In *Copper Mesa Mining Corp. v. Republic of Ecuador*, the Panel decided the case in favor of Copper Mesa but reduced the material compensation due to the company's activities, referring to human rights violations allegations.

Urbaser S.A. v. Argentine Republic, ICSID Case No. ARB/07/26, Award (Dec. 2016).

Case Introduction

The Claimants in this case were Urbaser S.A. and Consorcio de Aguas Bilbao Bizkaia, Bilbao Biskaia Ur Partzuergoa (the "Claimants", respectively "Urbaser" and "CABB"). The Claimants were shareholders in a concession for water and sewerage services which was granted in early 2000 in the Province of Buenos Aires (the "Concession").

The Concession ran into gridlock when Argentina suffered its economic crisis beginning in mid-2001. This crisis culminated in emergency measures taken in January 2002, including a conversion of 1:1 between USD and Argentine Peso, at a time when the Peso had depreciated by more than two thirds of its value.

The Claimants' repeated requests for a complete review of the Concession failed in large part because of the Province's lack of any serious commitment to bring the required renegotiation process to a successful end. Political reasons related to the fate of other concessions finally caused the Province to declare the Concession terminated in July 2006.

The Claimants filed a request with ICSID against the Argentine Republic. The Claimants submitted the Request pursuant to Article X of the Agreement on the Reciprocal Promotion and Protection of Investment between the Argentine Republic and the Kingdom of Spain, signed on October 3, 1991 ("Argentina-Spain BIT"). The Claimants alleged breach by Argentina of its fair and equitable treatment (BIT Article IV.1) and other obligations under the BIT.

Argentina counterclaimed for damages on the basis that the Claimants had failed to provide the necessary investment into the concession, thereby violating its commitments, and its obligations under international law based on the human right to water. Argentina filed its counterclaim based on Article 46 ICSID Convention and Rule 40(1) ICSID Arbitration Rules.

Article 46 ICSID states:

> Except as the parties otherwise agree, the Tribunal shall, if requested by a party, determine any incidental or additional claims or counterclaims arising directly out of the subject-matter of the dispute provided that they are within the scope of the consent of the parties and are otherwise within the jurisdiction of the Centre.

Significance of Case

In this case, the jurisdiction clause of the BIT was drafted broadly, allowing Argentina's counterclaim to be entertained. Nevertheless, the award in *Urbaser v. Argentina* undoubtedly creates a precedent for a host state human rights counterclaim in investment treaty arbitration. The Tribunal's finding of a human rights obligation applicable to corporations is novel and likely to be controversial.[289] The next stage will be to determine, with more precision, which rights are capable of forming the basis of host state human rights counterclaim.

Principal Points of the Judgment

Award

[. . .]

648. Within this context, the State had to continue to guarantee one of the most basic human rights: the human right to water, together with the right to access sanitation services.

[. . .]

693. In a different perspective, Claimants understand another argument of Respondent as supporting the contention that the Argentine Republic was under a duty to safeguard the interests of the population through the emergency measures affecting the Concession's tariff regime, and, therefore, had no other means available in order to preserve these fundamental interests. Claimants note that Respondent seems to argue that the fulfilment of its obligations intended to safeguard the human right to water was incompatible with the fulfilment of its obligations toward the Claimants. Claimants deny that this is true. Guaranteeing the human right to water is a duty of the State, not of private companies like the Claimants. They do not take issue with the fact that the Argentine Republic has obligations intended to provide drinking water and sewage services to its population.[290] What is inappropriate and is not provided for in any rule or legislation is that it is private companies, such as Claimants,

289. *Holding investors to account for human rights violations through counterclaims in investment treaty arbitration*, 30 January, 2017, http://www.allenovery.com/publications/en-gb/Pages/Holding-investors-to-account-for-human-rights-violations-through-counterclaims-in-investment-treaty-arbitration.aspx.

290. Cf. UN General Assembly Resolution of July 28, 2010, A/RES/64/292 (CUL 185).

who should have to undertake the costs of those State obligations. Invoking the human right to water will not aid Respondent in its attempt to exempt itself from any obligations towards the Concessionaire and the investors, as it is Respondent itself who must fulfil the burdens the right to water entails, as stated by the Committee on Economic, Social and Cultural Rights.[291]

694. Claimants further explain that Respondent has two kinds of obligations. These are its obligations regarding the population's right to water, and its obligations towards international investors. The Argentine Republic can and should fulfil both kinds of obligations simultaneously. Therefore, the Argentine Republic's obligations stemming from the human right to water does not operate as an obstacle to the fulfilment of its obligations towards the Claimants, nor does it mean that an alleged state of necessity will simply allow it to escape any commitment made to foreign investors.

[. . .]

XII. Respondent's Counterclaim

[. . .]

1110. Claimants observe at the outset that Respondent has chosen to assert an unexpected and surprising counterclaim. [. . .]

1111. Claimants submit that while it is correct that Arbitration Rule 40 allows Respondent to present a counterclaim not later than in the counter-memorial, Respondent's silence over more than seven years is an unmistakable symptom of the completely unfounded nature of an improvised counterclaim entirely devoid of foundation. The Counterclaim itself shows Respondent's lack of credibility. There can be no reason for waiting seven years since the termination of the Concession to raise a counterclaim for the first time. [. . .]

1117. Claimants accept that host States may be claimants in investment arbitration proceedings and, likewise, that they may file a counterclaim, as this is recognized in Article 46 of the ICSID Convention. However, said provision does not, by itself, vest the Arbitral Tribunal with competence over the Counterclaim. The jurisdiction and competence requirements to be satisfied are established in other provisions, including Article 25 of the ICSID Convention and the applicable BIT. The existence of jurisdiction over an ancillary claim is a precondition for the operation of Article 46 and of Arbitration Rule 40(1). [. . .]

1129. As regards the alleged violation of international law, Article X of the BIT does not authorize a decision by the Arbitral Tribunal either. As the *Biloune* Tribunal put it, a ruling on human rights violations is outside the scope of its jurisdiction.[292]

291. Cf. General Comment No. 15 (2002), E/C.12/2002/11, January 20, 2003 (CUL-186).

292. *Antoine Biloune and Marine Drive Complex Ltd. v. Ghana Investment Centre and the Government of Ghana*, Awards of October 27, 1989 and June 30, 1990, Yearbook Commercial Arbitration XIX (1994) p. 11 (CUL-207).

Besides this point, the rules of international law are directly binding on States but not on private parties. [. . .]

1150. The Tribunal therefore finds that the BIT accepts a possibility for Respondent to raise a counterclaim in the instant case. It understands Claimants' surprise that such claim 307 was raised many years after they had given notice of a dispute and that Respondent did not reveal even a hypothesis of such initiative when the Parties agreed upon a set of procedural rules governing this proceeding in preparation of the Tribunal's first session. Nonetheless, such surprise and disappointment has no legal effect given the provision of Arbitration Rule 40(2) permitting submission of a counterclaim no later than in the counter-memorial. The Parties had not agreed on any waiver of this procedural right nor did they agree on another time factor. The Tribunal accepts therefore that Respondent's Counterclaim was filed on time in compliance with Arbitration Rule 40(2). It does not share either Claimants' view that the late submission of this claim, or the fact that no similar claim was raised by the Argentine Republic in the *Impregilo* case [*Impregilo S.p.A. v. The Argentine Republic*, ICSID/ARB/07/17, Award of July 21, 2011 (LARA-77, CUL 126)], had to be understood somehow as a clear sign of its "completely unfounded nature."

1151. One of Claimants' main objections is that Respondent's Counterclaim has no connection with Claimants' claims under the BIT. The Tribunal observes that the factual link between the two claims is manifest. Both the principal claim and the claim opposed to it are based on the same investment, or the alleged lack of sufficient investment, in relation to the same Concession. This would be sufficient to adopt jurisdiction over the Counterclaim as well. The legal connection is also established to the extent the Counterclaim is not alleged as a matter based on domestic law only. Respondent argues indeed that Claimants' failure to provide the necessary investments caused a violation of the fundamental right for access to water, which was the very purpose of the investment agreed upon in the Regulatory Framework and the Concession Contract and embodied in the protection scheme of the BIT. It would be wholly inconsistent to rule on Claimants' claim in relation to their investment in one sense and to have a separate proceeding where compliance with the commitment for funding may be ruled upon in a different way. Reasonable administration of justice cannot tolerate such a potential inconsistent outcome. [. . .]

1157. When relying for the purposes of its Counterclaim upon international law and the human right to water contained therein, Respondent objects above all to Claimants' view that the Argentine Republic would be the "true guarantor" of human rights and that such rules, as they are part of international law, are directly binding on States but not on private parties. Claimants argue that guaranteeing the human right to water is a duty of the State, not of private companies like the Claimants. Respondent denies: Claimants' most important obligation during the Concession term was to guarantee the access to water and thus to comply with a fundamental human right.

1158. The Universal Declaration of Human Rights of 1948 is part of customary international law. The commitment of the Argentine Republic with this Declaration is evident. The regulatory nature of this Declaration is acknowledged by Claimants when they state that "there are international rules that include specific obligations having to do with drinking water." Respondent submits—further referring to the *Goetz* Award[293]—that the BIT is to be considered by the Tribunal not on its own basis but by including all relevant rights and obligations of the Argentine Republic under international law.

1159. The Declaration avoids making reference to who would be responsible for the rights and obligations arising therefrom. However, upon reading the Declaration, it is evident that obligations arising therefrom do not lie exclusively on States. The Preamble expressly sets forth that the duties would lie both on institutions and on individuals. Article 1 states that its provisions apply to individuals even in private relationships. Article 30 declares that nothing in the Declaration may be interpreted as implying for any State, group or person any right to engage in any activity or to perform any act aimed at the destruction of the rights and freedoms set forth herein. Article 29 sets forth that everyone has duties to the community. Therefore, business companies and international corporations are affected by the obligations included in international human rights law. [. . .]

b. The BIT's relation to international law and human rights

1191. As has been stated above, the definition of disputes capable of being submitted to arbitration and, hence, the possible scope of claims to be submitted to arbitration under Article X is not limited to rights directly based on the application (or interpretation) of the BIT. If Claimants' view of the BIT as a closed system strictly preserving investors' rights under the BIT would be correct, it would not fully reflect the terms of Article X(1), which have a broader scope, as explained above; therefore, Claimants' understanding of the BIT would deprive this provision of part of its meaning. [. . .]

1199. At this juncture, it is therefore to be admitted that the human right for everyone's dignity and its right for adequate housing and living conditions are complemented by an obligation on all parts, public and private parties, not to engage in activity aimed at destroying such rights.

1200. The Tribunal further retains that the Convention has to be interpreted in the light of the rules set out in the Vienna Convention on the Law of Treaties of May 23, 1969, and that Article 31 § 3 (c) of that Treaty indicates that account is to be taken of "any relevant rules of international law applicable in the relations between the parties." The BIT cannot be interpreted and applied in a vacuum. The Tribunal must certainly be mindful of the BIT's special purpose as a Treaty promoting foreign

293. *Antoine Goetz v. République du Burundi ("Goetz v. Burundi")*, ICSID Case No. ARB/95/03, Award of 10 February, 1999 (LARA-126, CUL-106).

investments, but it cannot do so without taking the relevant rules of international law into account. The BIT has to be construed in harmony with other rules of international law of which it forms part, including those relating to human rights.[294]

1203. Another illustration is given by peremptory norms of general international law (jus cogens) to the extent they may be of interest in an investment matter. If so, such norms must certainly prevail over any contrary provision of the BIT, as per the express statement in Article 53 of the Vienna Convention.[295]

1204. Beyond these sources of law, it remains to be examined, in light of the openly framed provision of Article 31 § 3 (c) of the Vienna Convention, whether other parts of international law may be relevant in the instant case. This leads to the question whether the human right to water and sanitation as part of the general notion of human rights is pertinent in the instant case and, in particular, whether such right is completed by a corresponding obligation on part of Claimants as investors. [. . .]

1206. However, this does not answer the question whether Claimants' as investors were bound by an obligation based on international law to provide the population living on the territory of the Concession with drinking water and sanitation services. Respondent does not, in fact, go so far. Indeed, it argues that such human right was incumbent on Claimants because providing for water and sewage was AGBA's and therefore its shareholders' obligation under the Concession. Even if this obligation could be imposed upon Claimants, Respondent does not state that such obligation is based on international law. It merely asserts that the performance obligation under the Concession had the effect of supplying the services that are part of the population's human right to access water. Respondent also states that Claimants had violated human rights obligations clearly applicable to international companies. This argument does not reference any particular international law obligation, but relies only on AGBA's obligations based on the Concession Contract. And while Respondent correctly introduces the principle of *pacta sunt servanda* as a principle of international law, it identifies the relevant *pactum* as Claimants' obligation to invest in expansion work, thus relying again on the Concession Contract and admitting that international law does not provide a cause of action for the Counterclaim.

1208. Respondent does not explain the basis of such obligations under international law other than by emphasizing Claimants' duty to ensure AGBA's performance in

---

294. Cf. *Tulip Real Estate and Development Netherlands B.V. v. Republic of Turkey*, ICSID Case No. ARB/11/28, Decision on Annulment of December 30, 2015, paras. 86–92, where the ad hoc Committee refers to the "principle of systemic integration," stating that resort to authorities stemming from the field of human rights is a "legitimate method of treaty interpretation".

295. As this has been stated in *Phoenix*, taking an extreme example, "nobody would suggest that ICSID protection should be granted to investments made in violation of the most fundamental rules of protection of human rights, like investments made in pursuance of torture or genocide or in support of slavery or trafficking of human organs." *Phoenix Action, Ltd. v. The Czech Republic*, ICSID Case No. ARB/06/5, para. 78 (LARA-68).

providing water and sewage services as if such duty were based on the human right to water and thus on international law. This is incorrect. The human right to water entails an obligation of compliance on the part of the State, but it does not contain an obligation for performance on part of any company providing the contractually required service. Such obligation would have to be distinct from the State's responsibility to serve its population with drinking water and sewage services.

1209. This obligation, as all others retained in the Covenant referred to above, "imposes a duty on each State party to take whatever steps are necessary to ensure that everyone enjoys the right to water, as soon as possible." This includes establishing "accountability mechanisms to ensure the implementation of the strategy." The necessary step is therefore that a host State accepting investments in the domain of the provision of water relies on the BIT to have the investor participating to its obligation under international law. It thus complies with the conclusion of the UN Committee on Economic, Social and Cultural Rights that "States parties should ensure that the right to water is given due attention in international agreements." This includes the possibility to consider matters related to the human right to water in the dispute resolution mechanisms provided for in such agreements. However, the investor's obligation to ensure the population's access to water is not based on international law. This obligation is framed by the legal and regulatory environment under which the investor is admitted to operate on the basis of the BIT and the host State's laws.

1210. While it is thus correct to state that the State's obligation is based on its obligation to enforce the human right to water of all individuals under its jurisdiction, this is not the case for the investors who pursue, it is true, the same goal, but on the basis of the Concession and not under an obligation derived from the human right to water. Indeed, the enforcement of the human right to water represents an obligation to perform. Such obligation is imposed upon States. It cannot be imposed on any company knowledgeable in the field of provision of water and sanitation services. In order to have such an obligation to perform applicable to a particular investor, a contract or similar legal relationship of civil and commercial law is required. In such a case, the investor's obligation to perform has as its source domestic law; it does not find its legal ground in general international law. The situation would be different in case an obligation to abstain, like a prohibition to commit acts violating human rights would be at stake. Such an obligation can be of immediate application, not only upon States, but equally to individuals and other private parties. This is not a matter for concern in the instant case.[296]

1220. [. . .] The Tribunal adds that such failure can also be explained by the lack of any legal ground based on international law that would entitle a group of individuals to raise a claim for performance for delivery of water and sewage services

296. Therefore, Respondent's reliance on the case *Filártiga v. Peña-Irala*, U.S. Court of Appeals, Second Circuit, 630 F.2d 876 (2d Cir., June 30 1980) (ALRA 307) is not convincing.

directed against a company or any other private party. Accordingly, there does not exist a claim for compensation in case of lack of such performance not based on an obligation under international law.

1221. For the reasons given above, Respondent's Counterclaim must fail.

Copper Mesa Mining Corp. v. Republic of Ecuador (*Can. v. Ecuador*), UNCITRAL, PCA No. 2012-2 (Perm. Ct. Arb. 2016).

Case Introduction

Copper Mesa Mining Corporation (the "Claimant") was a Canadian corporation established under the laws of the province of British Columbia, Canada. The Claimant commenced arbitral proceedings against the Republic of Ecuador (the "Respondent") under the UNCITRAL Arbitration Rules 1976 (the "UNCITRAL Rules") pursuant to Article XIII(4)(c) of the Agreement between the Government of Canada and the Government of the Republic of Ecuador for the Promotion and Reciprocal Promotion of Investments, signed in 1996 (the "Treaty").

The factual chronology set out in the arbitration covers a period of thirty years, beginning in 1981 and ending in 2011. Between 1991 and 1997, the first sophisticated geological tests were conducted in the Junín area of Northwestern Ecuador. The final technical report confirmed large deposits of copper and noted potential environmental impacts of a proposed mine. Since then, an increasing number of local residents became concerned about the deleterious impacts of mining and organized to resist the activity.

In 2002 Ecuador granted the Junín concession to an Ecuadorian national. In 2005, Canadian company Copper Mesa Mining Corporation Exploration (Copper Mesa), through Barbadian and Ecuadorian subsidiaries, acquired the Junín concession, the neighbouring Chaucha concession and an option for the Telimbela concession. The dispute at hand in the arbitration arises from these three mining concessions granted by the Respondent in Junín, Chaucha and Telimbela.

The Claimant's principal concessions were situated in the Junín area and extended over 12,900 hectares. The Junín area lies within the larger Intag area. Opposition to the mining was concentrated in the Junín area, while strong support was expressed by local politicians in the Cotacachi area of Intag. From 2005 onwards, Copper Mesa made a series of expenditures in relation to the concessions. In particular, it commissioned a geological report, acquired a neighboring concession and surface land in and around the concession areas, prepared and submitted an environmental impact study (EIS) for the exploration phase, employed a team of Ecuadorian staff and committed resources to providing social services and community development.

In April 2008, Ecuador's Constituent Assembly passed legislation known as the Mining Mandate, which declared that mineral substances were "to be exploited to suit national interests". Ecuador's Under-Secretary of Mines subsequently ordered the termination of the Junín and Chaucha concessions due to a lack of prior consultation with the local residents.

The Claimant alleged that the Respondent unlawfully revoked or terminated the concessions, thereby depriving the Claimant of the entire value of its investments in its project companies and causing it to suffer substantial damages. The Claimant contended that the Respondent's actions and omissions violated its obligations to the Claimant and the Claimant's investments under the Treaty and international law, as the applicable law.

In the arbitration proceedings, Ecuador argued that the suspension of the mining contracts with Copper Mesa occurred because the company violated the human rights of the community affected by the mining project.

The Tribunal decided the case in favor of Copper Mesa and ordered Ecuador to compensate the Canadian company for expropriation of two of the three mineral concessions. The alleged expropriation of the company's option interest in a third concession was dismissed. However, in the light of contributory negligence by the company's executives and referring to human rights violations allegations, the tribunal discounted damages by 30 per cent. On this point, the Tribunal references the *Yukos* Tribunal discussed earlier in this chapter. The parties were ordered to bear their own legal costs and to share arbitration costs equally.

In May 2018, the Republic of Ecuador urged a Washington DC federal court to deny Copper Mesa's petition to confirm the $24.4 million arbitral award, claiming the company violated Ecuadorean law, and therefore, an investment treaty with Canada did not govern the dispute. Ecuador contended that the bilateral investment treaty between it and Canada does not apply to the dispute, as the Canadian company did not qualify as an investor.

Principal Points of the Judgment

1.71. The Claimant advances its claims under the Treaty, alleging violations by the Respondent of its international obligations under Article II (as to fair and equitable treatment ["FET"] and full protection and security ["FPS"] standards); Article IV (as to national treatment) and Article VIII (as to expropriation). In respect of all three concessions at Junín, Chaucha and Telimbela, the Claimant claims compensation for its losses in a total principal sum of U.S. $70 million, together with compound interest and costs.

1.72. The Respondent objects to the Tribunal's jurisdiction and, in regard to the Junín concessions, also to the admissibility of the Claimant's claims. As to the merits in regard to three concessions, the Respondent denies any liability to the Claimant, including causation, compensation, interest and costs. [. . .]

1.110. *The 2008 Mining Mandate*: On 18 April 2008, the Respondent's Constituent Assembly (Asamblea Constituyente) passed Constituent Mandate No. 6 (Mandato Constituyente No. 6, the "Mining Mandate") declaring that mineral substances were "to be exploited to suit national interests" and provided for the termination (extinción) "without economic compensation" of mining concessions falling into a number of categories, including those "without any investment in project development having been made in their exploration stage by December 31, 2007 or without their environmental impact study having been submitted or without a prior referendum process having been conducted, including those pending an administrative resolution" (Article 1).

Part 2—The Principal Issues

A: Introduction

2.1. This list of issues is largely derived from the consolidated list originally prepared by the Parties, as modified substantially by the Tribunal for present purposes. It should be read as an incomplete checklist of the principal issues arising in the arbitration, rather than a comprehensive description of all the issues arising from the Parties' many written and oral submissions.

2.2. Moreover, as will be evident from later parts of this Award, the Tribunal did not think it necessary to address and decide specifically all issues listed in this checklist, still less all issues arising from the Parties' respective submissions. Moreover, the Tribunal considers that many of the decisive issues turn on the specific facts of this case. Having determined those facts, other issues become irrelevant or otiose. [. . .]

2.7. Is the Respondent estopped or otherwise precluded from alleging any breach of Ecuadorian law or any breaches of the doctrines of international public policy and unclean hands? [. . .]

2.9. Regarding Article 1(g) of Treaty again, whether the Claimant "owned and controlled" its investments in accordance with Ecuadorian law, including international human rights law as incorporated in Ecuadorian law, so that the Tribunal has jurisdiction pursuant to Article 1(g) of the Treaty, and whether this obligation of legality extends beyond the acquisition or making of an investment?

2.10. After the making of an investment, what is the scope of the application of the doctrine of unclean hands? [. . .]

2.15. Whether Ascendant Ecuador (as the Claimant's agent) and the Claimant, committed human rights violations in 2006 and 2007; and what is the legal standard applicable to such determination (prima facie or otherwise)?

2.16. Whether Ascendant Ecuador and the Claimant failed to obtain the required social licence to operate the Junín concessions; and whether such failure was wholly attributable to the Claimant? [. . .]

4.115. *1 April 2005*—A Resolution is made by the Cantonal Unity Assembly of Cotacachi and the Development and Action Council. It is entitled "With a single voice: NO TO MINING"; and it is signed by Mayor Tituaña and representatives of the Council. It merits here citing at length, as one of several turning points during this period:

> [. . .] To avoid more problems of this kind, we request the Central Government, through the Ministry of Energy and Mines to:

> 1) Respect the independence and autonomy of Cotacachi Canton's local governments.
>
> 2) Abstain from violating human rights recognized in the Political Constitution of Ecuador and especially those that guarantee the right to prior consultations in connection with the exploitation of non-renewable natural resources and that may affect our environmental and social rights. [. . .]

The Tribunal's Chronology 1981 to 2011

4.39. *5 June 1998*—A new constitution is promulgated by the Respondent. In brief, it grants more extensive powers to local government. In particular, Article 86 provides (*inter alia*) that the State shall protect the right of its people to live in a healthy and ecologically balanced environment to ensure sustainable development, ensure that this right is not affected and guarantee the preservation of nature. Article 88 obliges the State to consult in relation to decisions that may affect the environment.

4.40. *1999*—The Association of Coffee Growers of Rio Intag is created. Several hundred local families are part of the association. It is or soon becomes anti-mining. [. . .]

4.47. *18 August 2000*—An Amendment is made to the 1991 Mining Law, part of the 'Law on Investment Promotion and Citizen Participation'. [. . .]

4.54. *March 2003*—Unified Environmental Rules of the Respondent's Ministry of Environment are enacted (the "TULAS"). [. . .]

4.57. *May 2003—On 12 May 2003*, local communities in the Junín area (represented by Mayor Tituaña) seek urgent constitutional protection in the Court of Imbabura against the granting of the Junín concessions, in legal proceedings against MEM and Dr Bustamante. The Imbabura Court, by its judgment of 27 May 2003, grants the following relief:

> [Article 5]: "From the above, and having analysed the evidence adduced by the parties, it becomes apparent that the mining concession granted by the Pichincha Regional Mining Directorate to Mr Roque Bernardo Bustamante Espinoza, would have brought serious consequences and impacts such as on an environmental and ecological level in rivers and streams and to the flora and fauna, and social impacts, and others. Moreover, it is not apparent from proceedings that [by: sic] the Pichincha Regional Mining Directorate has taken into account the provisions of Article 88 of the National Constitution, i.e.: that the criteria of the community were not previously considered; because, as has previously been said, the inhabitants of the six parishes of Intag in this canton have resolutely objected to said mining concession occurring. Wherefore, above without requiring further analysis, and since this Judge estimates that constitutional provisions have been violated, such as Article 86 and 88 of the National Constitution; the Fundamental rights protection measure is accepted, submitted by the Attorney Generals and representatives of the Municipality of Cotacachi and it is resolved to rescind

> the mining Concession previously granted to the Pichincha Regional Mining Directorate in favour of Mr Roque Bernardo Bustamante Espinoza, namely in the areas known as Golden 1, of an area of about four thousand hectares of mining and Golden 2, of an area of three thousand hectares of mining, located in the García Moreno parish, Cotacachi Canton, Imbabura province, for which purpose the representative of the Pichincha Regional Mining Directorate will be served, by means of a letter rogatory addressed to one of the Judges of the Civil Court of Pichincha with its seat in Quito Canton; the Commercial and Property Registrar of the canton will likewise be notified, to cancel the registration of the mining concession in the name of Mr Roque Bernardo Bustamante Espinoza, and, where that mining concession has not been registered, no such registration will be made for the aforementioned mining concession . . .".

4.61. *7 November 2003*—Ascendex is granted the Chaucha (Janeth 1) concession by MEM.

4.62. *28 November 2003*—Ascendex is granted the Telimbela concession (San Pablo 1) by MEM.

4.63. *9 December 2003*—Ecuador's Constitutional Court overturns by a majority (5–4) the judgment dated 27 May 2003 of the Imbabura Court. The Court also (in resolution 3) "urges the Ecuadorian State to respect the rights of nature and protect the families that inhabit the sites where the concession will have an effect." [. . .]

4.67. *5 May 2004*—The Claimant (then named Ascendant Copper Corporation) is incorporated in British Columbia, Canada (the company's name was later changed to Copper Mesa Mining Corporation, i.e. the named Claimant, on 3 July 2008). Its original sole shareholder is Ascendant Holdings Ltd, a company controlled by Mr Grist and Mr Jurika.

4.68. *14 May 2004*—At a meeting in Chalguayacu Alto, Ascendex officially announces to the local communities that it is now the owner of the Junín concessions. For Ascendex, its representatives include Mr Andrade, a former member of Parliament and General Villacís, a retired military officer. It was a controversial meeting and, insofar as it aimed at establishing good relations between Ascendex and the local anti-miners, it was not successful. At the end of the meeting, according to representatives attending from the local communities, General Villacís "implied that it would be a simple task to send troops to protect the interests of the company." [. . .]

4.73. *17 July 2004*—At La Armenia, one of Mr Andrade's bodyguards (Carlos Alonso Cedeño) and others allegedly threaten to kill Francisco Quilca, an anti-miner. Mr Quilca said: "he told me he would kill me with a bullet or a machete." (This allegation subsequently becomes part of local criminal proceedings, which are inconclusive). [. . .]

4.83. *17 October 2004*—Mayor Tituaña is re-elected in Cotacachi (for a third term). He stands on an anti-mining policy; and he defeats (*inter alios*) Mr Andrade's party called "Todos por Intag" (All for Intag), which promotes a pro-mining policy. [. . .]

4.95. 2004—Summary: By the end of 2004, it is clear that the communities in the Junín remained sorely divided between pro-mining and anti-mining activists, with allegations of violent and other unlawful conduct freely made by each side, often with cause. It is equally clear that conduct by individual pro-miners cannot, without more, be attributed to AE (or Ascendant Copper). The hostilities between pro-miners and anti-miners pre-existed the granting of the Junín concessions; and certain anti-miners were not angels, as evidenced by the arson attack on Bishimetal. Nor can the conduct of the anti-miners be attributed to the Respondent. To the contrary, the Government in Quito supported AE and its Junín concessions; and it remained unequivocally promining. However, as already indicated, governmental agencies, including the forces of law and order, were only thinly present in the Junín area. [. . .]

4.97. At this point, AE was aware (with Ascendant Copper) that it faced severe troubles in the Junín area, sufficient to imperil the further development of its concessions. Whilst MEM and the Government in Quito as a whole were pro-mining, AE knew that the Government's powers in the Junín area were weak, if not (for most practical purposes) non-existent, and therefore easily exploited by both pro-miners and anti-miners with an increasing risk of social conflict. For AE and Ascendant Copper, all this required a new strategy: increased efforts, particularly with social funding, to gain genuine support for the Junín project amongst the local communities (with CODEGAM's involvement); and a program of land acquisition both to secure such support and also to gain ready access to the Junín concessions. [. . .]

4.100. In 2005, AE begins its program of land acquisition. AE purchases surface rights. These purchases were made at fair market values from local residents; and AE denies that it participated in or had any knowledge of unlawful land trafficking. The program started with the acquisition of La Florida farm. AE bought over 50 plots of land. Several of those who sold their land became employees of AE. The program was initiated by Mr Rosanía (a senior officer of AE based in Quito). [. . .]

4.104. *20 January 2005*—A mining concession is granted by MEM to Ascendex in respect of the Magdalena 1 concession in the parish of García Moreno, in the canton of Cotacachi in the province of Imbabura. It will later form part of AE's Junín concessions.

4.105. *1 February 2005*—A written contract is made in Quito between AE (for Ascendant Copper) and CODEGAM, entitled "Agreement of Work between [CODEGAM] and Ascendant Copper Corp." signed by Mr Andrade and Mr Bolaños (then the latter's general manager). Ascendant Copper agrees to make monthly payments to CODEGAM in return for CODEGAM planning and executing community development initiatives, at the rate of U.S. $9,000 per month. Mr Davis acknowledged that, in Ecuador, this was a "sizable amount" and that CODEGAM "had a fairly free rein as to what they actually invested in."

4.106. *2 February 2005*—The MEM's Regional Director of Mining approves the transfer of the Junín concession Golden 2 from Ascendex to AE. (It is assumed, from other undisputed evidence, that like approval was granted in respect of Golden 1).

4.107. *5 February 2005*—An anti-mining demonstration of over 300 people takes place in Junín.

4.108. *22 February 2005*—By letter, responding to an inquiry of 27 December 2004, the Under-Secretary of Mines confirms to the office of the President of Ecuador that the Junín concessions have been legally granted by the Respondent; and that the concessionaire's presence in the parish of García Moreno was "in line with the rights granted by the Ecuadorian state, with whose backing it will carry out tasks that are specifically allowed by the mining/environmental laws . . .". The letter also refers to the concessionaire's obligation to carry out an EIS. It is clear that MEM was here expressing, unequivocally, support for AE and Ascendant Copper, including its own confirmation of the legal validity of the Junín concessions. [. . .]

4.116. Around *1 April 2005*—Mr Giovanni Rosanía is appointed as the general manager of AE. He had previous experience as the head of another copper project. In the Tribunal's view, as later events would demonstrate, his appointment was another turning point. [. . .]

4.132. *9 May 2005*—MEM sends a letter to Ascendant Copper recording that MEM supports the preparation of the EIS for the Golden 1 and 2 concessions. The letter also refers to the local communities approving the performance of these studies at the meeting on 5 March 2005 in García Moreno, attended by MEM (see above). Its terms are unambiguously supportive of the Junín project; and the letter was doubtless drafted for local publication in Junín. Thus, the Government in Quito remains pro-mining.

4.133. *12 May 2005*—Mayor Tituaña of Cotacachi files an extraordinary administrative claim with MEM requesting the nullification of the Junín concessions. [. . .]

4.143. *25 June 2005*—Mr Davis travels to Junín and meets Mr Pérez and others. The meeting was filmed, apparently by DECOIN. It shows Mr Davis taking a conciliatory approach. Mr Davis states there is no doubt in his mind that the company had made mistakes to this point; and he expresses his apologies if there had been threats and abuses. He accepts that Ascendant Copper had funded CODEGAM and that the latter had done things with its money which Ascendant Copper would not tolerate. He refuses to identify the amount of funding provided by Ascendant Copper, as being an internal company matter. He says CODEGAM was originally set up as a clearing house for community input. The meeting lasts for about one hour; but none of Mr Davis' explanations of the proposed development are shown in the video made by DECOIN. During his oral evidence, Mr Davis testified: "The [video] footage, if it says that what is stated, that I apologized for wrong doing that is incorrect. I said if there had been any wrongdoing or any abuses, for that I was sorry. I had no knowledge whatsoever that there had been [any wrongdoing]". Mr Davis went on to say that CODEGAM had been trying to divide the community—that was something which his company did not stand for and was not in the interest of the company.

4.144. In the Tribunal's view, having seen and heard Mr Davis as an oral witness in this arbitration, it is highly unlikely that Mr Davis was seeking at this meeting to deceive Mr Pérez and his colleagues. It is also highly likely that Mr Davis was not fully informed as to what had actually taken place in the Junín area, attributed (rightly or wrongly) to his company and its predecessors-in-title. Mr Davis, so the Tribunal decides on the evidence available, was genuinely trying at this meeting to calm down what had become a difficult situation for his company, with the sincere intention of starting anew its relations with the affected communities of the Junín area. He also genuinely believed that the Junín project could benefit these communities as a whole. Unfortunately, given the events that had already transpired, members of those communities did not believe or trust him or the company and remained resolutely anti-mining. [. . .]

4.149. *10 August 2005*—A legal opinion of the State Attorney General in Quito is addressed to Mayor Tituaña of Cotacachi. It states that a breach of the consultation obligations established by the State would not serve as grounds for nullification of a mining title or concession rights, but only for a suspension in the exercise of such activities. [. . .]

4.154. *December 2005*—There is increasing conflict between anti-miners and pro-miners in the Junín area. At a community meeting, over 300 local residents vote "to burn down a mining camp building after ensuring that it was empty of people as a reaction to the aggressive tactics employed by [Ascendant Copper/AE]". [. . .]

4.264. ***2006—Summary***: It is appropriate here to take stock of Ascendant Copper's position as at the end of 2006. In brief, the situation for Ascendant Copper in the Junín area, difficult from the outset, had become significantly worse: Ascendant Copper's successive attempts (with AE) at conciliation and confrontation with the anti-miners had all failed to meet Ascendant Copper's objectives. The hostility to mining from anti-miners was now greater in the Junín area than at any time since the forced departure of Bishimetal almost ten years earlier. The divisions within the local communities and the social conflicts between anti-miners and pro-miners (with the latter actively supported by AE and Ascendant Copper) were becoming increasingly strident, for which Ascendant Copper was being held responsible. MEM, for the first time, was no longer supporting Ascendant Copper unequivocally: MEM's rejection of AE's EIS for the Junín concessions was problematic: it was not entirely clear how AE and Ascendant Copper were now to meet successfully MEM's criticisms regarding further attempts at consultation with the local communities; and such consultations were of paramount importance for the EIS. As a result, MEM's acceptance of AE's EIS remained in abeyance; and without such acceptance, the Junín concessions could not move forward.

4.265. Worse than any of this, however, was the reckless escalation of violence which AE (by itself and by its contractors and sub-contractors) had introduced into the Junín area in its own name and also that of Ascendant Copper, particularly with the employment of organised armed men in uniform using tear gas canisters and firing weapons at local villagers and officials. It was miraculous that no-one had been killed during one or more of these violent incidents. Certain of the anti-miners were certainly not angels, as already noted; but Mr Pérez (with CDC) appears to have done his best to restrain his supporters during these incidents. That could not be said of AE. As a result, AE and Ascendant Copper had now acquired, irrevocably, a malign reputation for intimidation, threats, deception, mendacity and violence amongst members of the local communities in the Junín area. It was a place from which there could be no easy return; and there was soon to be an important change in the country's political administration in Quito, unfavourable to mining concessions. [. . .]

4.297. *8 August 2007*—At a meeting between the Minister for Mines (Mr Chiriboga) and his officers (including Ms Ruiz), anti-mining and pro-mining representatives (the latter including Mr Veintimilla), Ascendant Copper is asked to suspend all forms of activity in the Junín area. As Ms Ruiz testified: "what the minister asked the company was to act in an environment of peace for the EIS to be prepared; it must be stated that 10 months almost had elapsed where the activities and the relationship had permanently deteriorated. This, because of the fact that there was no peace." [. . .]

4.307. *25 January 2008*—*Nullification Resolutions*: The newly appointed Regional Director of Mining of Pichincha (Santiago Pazmiño) nullifies by resolutions Ascendant Copper's concessions at Junín. These "Nullification Resolutions" are issued without any prior notice to Ascendant Copper.

4.308. *1 February 2008*—Ascendant Copper appeals the Regional Director's Nullification Resolutions to the National Mining Director.

4.309. *11 February 2008*—The Regional Mining Director applies to the Constitutional Court requesting a declaration that the Mining Law is unconstitutional. (The application is declared inadmissible on 12 June 2008).

4.310. *18 April 2008*—The "Mining Mandate" (Constituent Mandate No 6) is promulgated by the Respondent's Constituent Assembly. By Article 1, "Termination, without economic compensation, is declared for all mining concessions without any investment in project development having been made in their exploration stage by December 31, 2007 or without their [EIS] having been submitted or without a prior referendum process having been conducted, including those pending an administrative resolution."

4.311. *18 April 2008*—Ascendant Copper suspends work on the Chaucha (Janeth 1) concession.

4.312. *July 2008*—Ascendant Copper receives an unsolicited offer from a hedge fund based in New York, Platinum Partners. It decides to pursue the negotiations; but no agreement is reached.

4.313. *30 July 2008*—Ascendant Copper changes its name to Copper Mesa Mining Corporation. [. . .]

4.316. *7 October 2008*—The Under-Secretary of Mines (Mr Serrano) orders the Regional Director of Pichincha to declare the termination of the Junín concessions (Golden 1 and 2) "without any compensation whatsoever" on the basis of Article 1 of the Mining Mandate. The reasons stated are that consultations have not been carried out by the concessionaire.

4.317. *12 November 2008*—Termination Resolutions: By resolutions of the new Regional Mining Director of Pichincha (Eduardo Sandoya Sánchez), Copper Mesa's Junín concessions are terminated without any economic compensation (the "Termination Resolutions"). No prior notice is given to Copper Mesa. These resolutions address Golden 1 and 2; but their effect extends to Magdalena, as Mr Davis testified. [. . .]

4.319. *18 November 2008*—Copper Mesa appeals against the Termination Resolutions to the National Mining Director. [. . .]

4.321. ***2008 Summary***: For all practical purposes, following the Termination Resolutions, AE and Copper Mesa have lost the Junín concessions, unless the Termination Resolutions can be annulled in Ecuadorian legal or administrative proceedings. [. . .]

4.324. *15 January 2009*—Copper Mesa applies to the Constitutional Court for an 'extraordinary measure of protection'.

4.325. *29 January 2009*—The 2009 Mining Law is enacted. Article 24 provides: "The mining areas and mining projects where the State of Ecuador conducted geological research, exploration or prefeasibility study or feasibility studies shall be returned to the State."

4.326. *20 March 2009*—Copper Mesa receives an offer from Entrée Gold—it is withdrawn three days later. [. . .]

4.328. *4 June 2009*—Copper Mesa's application to the Constitutional Court for an extraordinary measure of protection is rejected as being inadmissible. [. . .]

4.331. *24 June 2009*—Copper Mesa issues a press release (repeated in its later financial statements), as required by Canadian securities laws, reporting the cloud on its title to the Chaucha (Janeth 1) concession. Mr Davis testified that Copper Mesa was now insolvent: ". . . with the Junín Concessions expropriated and the Chaucha and Telimbela projects publicly designated for reversion to the State, there was no longer any prospect of raising any additional financing from a public offering of securities or a sale of its Ecuadorian assets. Nortec's withdrawal from its proposed acquisition of Ascendant Barbados had confirmed that no mining company would be interested in Copper Mesa's Ecuadorian projects and no investors would provide any significant amounts of financing in these circumstances." [. . .]

4.335. *10 September 2009*—A newspaper article indicates that the Chaucha concession is to be run by MEM and Codelco, the Chilean state mining company. [. . .]

4.337. ***2009—Summary***: For all practical purposes, subject to further legal proceedings in Ecuador, the Claimant has lost (for one reason or another) its beneficial interests in the Junín and Chaucha concessions, save for the possibility of a fire-sale of its legal interests in the project companies to one or more third parties. [. . .]

4.343. *July 2010*—Copper Mesa's shares cease to trade in Canada.

4.344. *24 August 2010*—The Constitutional Court rejects Copper Mesa's appeal from the dismissal of its application for extraordinary protection.

4.350. The interests shown by ENAMI and the Chilean state mining company in Junín take place in 2011 long after Copper Mesa's loss of its Junín and Chaucha concessions, i.e. with the Termination Resolutions of 12 November 2008 and the events of June 2009 respectively.

4.351. By this time, Copper Mesa had begun these arbitration proceedings, by its Notice of Arbitration dated 21 January 2011. [. . .]

5.4. In brief, the Respondent does not dispute these factors. However, the Respondent has challenged the jurisdiction of this Tribunal, contending that: (i) the Claimant failed to comply with Article XIII(12) of the Treaty by not obtaining the consents and waiver of other remedies from the Ecuadorian project companies that the Claimant contends sustained damage, and (ii) the Claimant failed to establish that it had made any investments in Ecuador that would qualify for protection under the Treaty. The Respondent contends that the claims of the Claimant relating to the Junín concessions fall outside the Tribunal's jurisdiction because: (i) these were not investments made and operated in accordance with the applicable law (Ecuadorian law); and (ii) the Claimant is approaching this Tribunal with "unclean hands" (under international law). The Respondent further contends that the Claimant has not proven ownership of the Ecuadorian project companies at critical dates.

5.5. The Claimant, on the contrary, submits that this Tribunal has jurisdiction and that it has met all the requirements for the Tribunal's jurisdiction under the Treaty: *ratione temporis, ratione personae* and *ratione materiae*. [. . .]

5.9. The Respondent's principal jurisdictional objection is based on Article XIII(12) of the Treaty. According to the Respondent, the Claimant is bringing a claim under Article XIII(12)(a) concerning damage to the (alleged) local subsidiaries of the Claimant in Ecuador (i.e. the three project companies), and not a claim under Article XIII(3). Therefore, according to the Respondent, the Claimant must comply with the requirements of Article XIII(12) and the local subsidiaries must separately consent to arbitration and waive any rights each may have under the local law (here Ecuadorian law) against the measures taken by the host State (here the Respondent) of which the investor (here the Claimant) complains.

5.10. In brief, the Respondent submits that Article XIII(12) is an "improved version of a fork-in-the-road clause", establishing a unity of interest between the foreign investor and its local subsidiary. If the latter chooses to initiate or continue local or other proceedings, no claim under the Treaty may be brought by the foreign investor; but if the foreign investor chooses to initiate an arbitration under the Treaty for damages caused to the subsidiary, these proceedings are considered to have been brought on behalf of the local subsidiary. Pursuant to Article XIII(12)(b) of the Treaty, the only exception to these conditions would be when the host State has unlawfully deprived the foreign investor of the control of its local subsidiary. Such is not this case.

5.11. The Respondent contends that Article XIII(12) seeks to eliminate the risk of parallel litigation as the foreign investor and the local subsidiary have separate legal personalities; and, therefore, each has the capacity to sue in its own right. The Respondent further contends that: "[h]aving elected to organize its investment in Ecuador in the form of local subsidiaries which had their own legal personality and could act in their own name, the Claimant is not entitled to pierce the corporate veil and claim for losses allegedly sustained by those subsidiaries" [. . .]

5.17. The Claimant refers to the NAFTA Chapter 11 arbitration in *UPS v. Canada* [*United Parcel Service of America Inc. v. Canada*, UNCITRAL, Award on the Merits, 24 May 2007,] where the tribunal dismissed the objection that the claimant could not assert damage on its own behalf under Article 1116 where the impugned measures related solely to the treatment of its local subsidiary, UPS Canada. The Claimant further cites another NAFTA Chapter 11 arbitration award in *Pope & Talbot Inc. v. Canada* [UNCITRAL (NAFTA), Arb. Trib. (2000–2002),] where the Tribunal accepted a claim brought by the investor on its own behalf for damages to the local subsidiary that it owned and controlled. It cites the decision of the ICSID annulment committee in *Azurix v. Argentina* [ICSID Case No. ARB/01/12, Decision on the Application for Annulment, 1 September 2009,] to similar effect. [. . .]

E: Unclean Hands

5.36. According to the Respondent, the Claimant's claims are inadmissible *ratione materiae* as the Claimant approaches the Tribunal with "unclean hands" having failed to comply with applicable Ecuadorian and international laws. This fourth jurisdictional objection relates only to the Junín concessions. In its post-hearing brief, the Respondent re-confirmed that its case on "unclean hands" only applies to the Claimant's claims concerning the Junín concessions and not to the Chaucha and Telimbela concessions.

5.37. In brief, according to the Claimant, the Respondent is estopped from raising any case based on "unclean hands", because it failed at the material time to investigate any "unclean hands" committed by the Claimant. The Claimant submits that no contemporary statement was ever made by the Respondent or its officials regarding any alleged violations of human rights by the Claimant prior to this arbitration. [. . .]

5.42. The Respondent replies that it does not contend that "any breach" of the law is relevant and that "a trivial violation of the law that is unrelated to the merits would not be relevant". However, the Respondent contends that such is not the case here. The Respondent submits that the Claimant and its subsidiary, Ascendant Ecuador, "have committed flagrant breaches of Ecuadorian and international human rights law and international public policy" in circumstances that are not "unrelated to the merits of the claim", rather "the Claimant's claim arise directly out of the circumstances in which the breaches were committed and thus form the very subject matter of the dispute before this Tribunal". Further, the Respondent contends that it is not estopped from challenging the Claimant's claims on the basis of illegality. [. . .]

5.60. *Unclean Hands*: The Tribunal does not consider that the Claimant was guilty of any wrongdoing, whether it amounted to "unclean hands" or any other like impropriety, at the time when it acquired the Junín concessions in 2004. The Tribunal does not understand the Respondent's case on "unclean hands" to extend to the Chaucha and Telimbela concessions. Accordingly, the Respondent's case on unclean hands is limited to the alleged misconduct of the Claimant (by itself, its agents and employees) after its indirect acquisition of the Junín concessions in 2004.

5.61. The Respondent has adduced an impressive amount of expert testimony and materials relating to the legal doctrine of unclean hands under international law, including the obligations of foreign investors on human rights in the broadest sense.[297] The Tribunal has studied this testimony and materials, including (in particular) the expert testimony of Professor Murphy. Nevertheless, this is not the place to address these materials in detail, for two cumulative reasons.

5.62. First, the Tribunal considers that the Respondent's case on unclean hands is not a jurisdictional objection, but rather an objection to the admissibility of the Claimant's claims based upon its alleged post-acquisition misconduct. In regard to the latter, if correct, the Tribunal would have jurisdiction, but it could not exercise that jurisdiction in favour of the Claimant's claim. An objection as to admissibility necessarily assumes that a tribunal has jurisdiction.

5.63. Second, the Respondent's case involves grave allegations against the Claimant of violations of international law, particularly during the post-acquisition period from 2005 to 2007. All, or almost all, of such alleged conduct took place in Ecuador, openly and in view of the Respondent's governmental authorities both in the Junín area and in Quito. Yet, as regards international law, international public policy and human rights, not a single complaint was made by the Respondent against the Claimant at the time. Such a complaint surfaced for the first time after the commencement of this arbitration. [. . .]

5.65. The Tribunal has decided to join what remains of the Respondent's case on admissibility to the merits of the Claimant's claims in regard the Junín concessions. As will appear below, the Tribunal there prefers to take into account the Claimant's case not in the form of the doctrine of unclean hands as such, but rather under analogous doctrines of causation and contributory fault applying to

297. The Tribunal's reference to "human rights" includes civil and political rights and economic, social and cultural rights.

the merits of the Claimant's claims arising from events subsequent to the acquisition of its investment. That result, based on the Respondent's case on the merits, strikes the Tribunal as more legally appropriate to this case than an outright dismissal of the Claimant's claims (in regard to the Junín concessions) on the ground of inadmissibility. [. . .]

6.91. *Contributory Fault*: As to "contributory fault", the Tribunal refers to Article 39 of the ILC Articles on State Responsibility, entitled "Contribution to the Injury" as being declaratory of international law. It provides: "In the determination of reparation, account shall be taken of the contribution to the injury by wilful or negligent action or omission of the injured State or any person or entity in relation to whom reparation is sought." In the ILC Commentary (paragraph 1), Article 39 is described as dealing "with the situation where damage has been caused by an intentionally wrongful act of a State, which is accordingly responsible for the damage in accordance with Articles 1 and 28, but where [. . .] the individual victim of the breach has materially contributed to the damage by some willful or negligent act or omission. Its focus is on situations which in national law systems are referred to as 'contributory negligence', 'comparative fault', 'faute de la victime' etc." [. . .]

6.93. *Unclean Hands*: As to the Respondent's remaining case on "unclean hands", the Tribunal refers to the ECT tribunal's three awards in the *Yukos* cases of 18 July 2014. These awards add nothing new to the state of international law; and the Tribunal cites them only as a useful illustration of existing legal principles. The *Yukos* tribunal there concluded (in similar terms for each award): "In the view of the Tribunal, Claimants should pay a price for their abuse . . . which contributed in a material way to the prejudice which they subsequently suffered at the hands of the Russian Federation."[298] The *Yukos* tribunal cited Article 39 of the ILC Articles on State Responsibility, *MTD v Chile* and *Occidental v Ecuador* (as did the Respondent in this case).[299]

6.94. The *Yukos* tribunal also stated: "[1636]. The Tribunal agrees with the ICSID Annulment Committee in the *MTD v. Chile* case that 'the role of the two parties contributing to the loss [is] [. . .] only with difficulty commensurable and the Tribunal [has] a corresponding margin of estimation' [footnote omitted]. However, the Tribunal, as other tribunals have done, must reach a decision and it has done so on the basis of all the evidence which it has reviewed." The *Yukos* tribunal then decided that the claimants had contributed to the extent of 25 percent to the

298. *Hulley Enterprises Limited (Cyprus) v. The Russian Federation*, PCA Case No. AA 226, UNCITRAL, Final Award of 18 July 2014 (Fortier, Poncet, Schwebel) para. 1634; *Yukos Universal Limited (Isle of Man) v. The Russian Federation*, PCA Case No. AA 227, UNCITRAL, Final Award of 18 July 2014 (Fortier, Poncet, Schwebel) para. 1634; *Veteran Petroleum Limited (Cyprus) v. The Russian Federation*, PCA Case No. AA 228, UNCITRAL, Final Award of 18 July 2014 (Fortier, Poncet, Schwebel) para. 1634 ["*Yukos v. Russia*"].

299. *MTD v. Chile* [ICSID Case No. ARB/01/7, Decision on Annulment, 21 March 2007,] paras. 242 ff; *Occidental v. Ecuador*, paras. 659 ff.

prejudice which they had suffered as a result of the respondent State's destruction of their investments. [. . .]

6.96. As was cited by the *Yukos* tribunal, the *MTD* committee held that the role of the two parties contributing to the loss was only with difficulty commensurable; and that the tribunal had "a corresponding margin of estimation" (paragraph 101). The *Occidental* tribunal decided likewise that it had "a wide margin of discretion in apportioning fault." (paragraph 670). The Tribunal does not discount the difficulty in estimating a contribution by way of percentage contribution; but it prefers to interpret these references to "margin" and "discretion" as requiring the same exercise for any issue of causation. In the present case, that issue is essentially factual.

6.97. For present purposes, the Tribunal considers that the general approach taken in all these decisions, whether treated as causation, contributory fault (based on wilful or negligent act or omission) or unclean hands, is materially the same, deriving from a consistent line of international legal materials. The Tribunal decides to apply that general approach in this case. As further explained below, it decides that the Claimant's injury was caused both by the Respondent's unlawful expropriation and also by the Claimant's own contributory negligent acts and omissions and unclean hands. Given that the Tribunal draws no distinction between these different concepts for this case, it prefers to refer only to Article 39 of the ILC Articles.

6.98. In the Tribunal's view, Article 39 requires a factual assessment as regards the Claimant's conduct from mid-2006 to late-2006. Given all the events leading up to November 2008, the issue is whether and, if so, to what extent, the Claimant's worsening situation as the concessionaire in the Junín area was caused (in whole or in part) by its own acts or omissions. Much of the detailed factual evidence has already been described in Part 4 above; and what follows should be read with those findings of fact.

6.99. By December 2006, by the acts of its agents in Ecuador, the Claimant had substantially reduced its chances of turning its Junín concessions into a commercial success. In short, a foreign investor, by its local agents, whatever the illegal provocations by local residents in the form of road-blocks, violence, arson and other impediments, should not resort to recruiting and using armed men, firing guns and spraying mace at civilians, not as an accidental or isolated incident but as part of premeditated, disguised and well-funded plans to take the law into its own hands. Yet, this is what happened. The Claimant's decisions to do so from mid-July to December 2006 remain both unexplained and inexplicable to the Tribunal, save as a sustained act of folly. It was bound to fail and to make the situation far worse for the Claimant; and it did.

6.100. In the Tribunal's view, the evidence establishes that several of the Claimant's senior personnel in Quito were guilty of directing violent acts committed on its behalf, in violation of Ecuadorian criminal law. Their resort to subterfuge and mendacity aggravated those acts. The consequences could have led to serious injury and loss of life. The adverse response from members of the local communities, already hostile, was inevitable. That is not to say that the Claimant's senior management in Canada was fully privy to the planning and execution of these acts. On the evidence, the Tribunal prefers to base its decision on the Claimant's negligence, rather than the wilful conduct of its Canadian senior management. If it were based on the latter's own wilful conduct as the Claimant's alter ego, the result, as regards Article 39, would be much graver for the Claimant's case.

6.101. By 13 November 2008, almost a year later than these critical events, the Claimant's situation had not improved in the Junín area. Indeed, the Claimant had by then acquired a pariah-like status in the local community and in Quito — hence, doubtless, its change of corporate name in July 2008, to no avail.

6.102. Taking all these factors into account, including the provocations by certain anti-miners, the Tribunal assesses the Claimant's contribution to its own injury as at November 2008, for the purpose of applying Article 39 of the ILC Articles, at 30 per cent. On the facts of this case, it could not be less. [. . .]

Chapter 11

Project Financing

A. Introduction

Project financing as a vehicle for foreign direct investment is an important growth area. As foreign direct investment (FDI) does not add to the debt of a country, many developing countries, as well as more developed nations, are turning to FDI to provide essential infrastructure without increasing the burden on national finances. Project financing involves multiple contracts which bring together many of the topics covered in this book.

1. Allocation of Risk

In project financing, the financial risk is in principle carried only by the project itself, i.e. the financers can only recover money from the project and its revenues and not from other assets or businesses of the owners.

Important considerations in the assessment and allocation of such risks are country and political risk, consents, change of law and currency risks. Country and political risks may impact the investor through the legal and regulatory frameworks in such areas as taxation, import controls, currency conversion, repatriation of profits and tariff policy. Given these risks, it is important to consider whether political risk insurance is available (*see* Chapter 3).

2. Types of Financing

If the investors form a project company, the project will be based on twin negotiations with government for concession agreements and with lenders on credit and security arrangements.

A common option in project financing is Build Operate Transfer (BOT), where the investor receives the revenues of the project for a defined period before handing over ownership to the relevant national authority. BOT projects are generally financed by the private sector.

B. Project Financing in Emerging Markets

1. Build Operate Transfer (BOT)

The BOT vehicle for project financing is widely used, especially when investing in emerging markets. The major commercial contracts involved in a BOT structure are between the project company and the sponsors, lenders, government, suppliers, contractors, operator and product off-takers.

The following article illustrates the type of agreements entered into in a BOT project and considers the risks that each party may hold.

© Christopher Rushton, Damien McNair, Allen & Overy, *Public Projects: Private Finance, Project Financing in Emerging Markets* (1994). Printed with permission of Thomson Reuters.

The rapid development of economies in the emerging markets of Eastern Europe, Asia and South America in the last two to three years has placed unprecedented demands on the existing infrastructure most noticeably in the energy fields. It is clear that the demand for development of the infrastructure in many countries will far outstrip the availability of traditional sources of financing from the public sector.

As a result, a significant amount of new capacity is likely to come from privately financed projects using project financing techniques [. . .]

A technique which is particularly suited to large scale infrastructure projects is the Build Operate Transfer (BOT) structure.

What is BOT?

Under a BOT structure, a government typically grants a concession to a project company under which the project company has the right to build and operate a facility, for instance, an oil refinery, power station or water treatment plant; or to construct new roads and bridges—an area that would previously have seen direct funding. The project company (the employer under the construction contract) borrows from lending institutions in order to finance the construction of the facility. The loans are repaid from "tariffs" paid by the government during the life of the concession. At the end of the concession period, the facility is usually transferred back to the government, hopefully after the project company has obtained a return for its equity investors. This type of structure is popular with governments in emerging markets as it enables them to develop infrastructure projects without committing their limited resources to particular projects.

Strictly speaking, a BOT structure is a form of non-recourse financing (lenders are repaid solely from the cash flow generated by the project and their only security is in that revenue and the assets of the project). However, pure non-recourse financing is rare as lenders are seldom willing to commit the large amounts needed for today's international projects solely on the basis of a project's expected cash flow or assets. [. . .]

Accordingly, most international project financing [. . .] tends to be financed on a basis which, while relying primarily on the project company's cash flow to service the debt and security provided over the assets of the project company, also minimizes the lender's risks by incorporating a number of back-up or secondary means of credit support provided by the host government, sponsors, purchasers or other interested third parties. [. . .]

The Parties

Government/ Government Authority

Infrastructure projects in emerging markets will normally involve the local government either acting through its ministries or an appropriate government authority. It is normally the pivotal player. It will initiate the project, conduct the tendering process and evaluation of tenders and will grant the project company the concession. It will also either grant a long term lease of, or sell the site for, the project to the project company and will often acquire most or all of the services provided by the facility. [. . .]

Project Company

The project company will usually be a company, partnership or limited partnership, a joint venture or a combination of them. This will be influenced by the legal and regulatory framework of the host government. [. . .]

Many BOT projects are structured separately to insulate the project company from as many risks as possible. In such cases, the project company is intended to be a mere financing vehicle and risks will be passed through it and allocated to parties which have the capacity or expertise to bear those risks.

Sponsors/Shareholders

The project sponsors are those companies, agencies or individuals who promote the project and bring together the various parties and consents necessary to get it under way. [. . .]

The support provided by project sponsors varies from project to project and includes the giving of comfort letters, cash injection undertakings, both pre- and post-competition, as well as the provision of competition support through letters of credit. [. . .]

Lenders/Banks

The financing for a BOT will usually involve, due to the sheer scale of the project, a syndicate of banks and, from within that syndicate, an arranging bank or banks which will take the lead role in negotiating the project and finance documents. The syndicate will most likely include banks from the host country, particularly if there are restrictions on foreign banks taking security over project assets.

The syndicate will necessarily undertake a review of all core project documents to assess the allocation of risks and how that allocation impacts upon its credit approval. These will often be evaluated in conjunction with an experienced engineering firm which will assess the design of the project and the technical aspects of the contracts. [. . .] principal concerns the lenders will have [. . .] will be to ensure that they can take effective security over all of the principal assets of the project.

Multilateral and Export Credit Agencies

Numerous projects in emerging markets are co-financed by the World Bank or its private sector lending arm, the International Finance Corporation (IFC), or by regional development agencies, for instance, the Asian Development Bank (ADB) or the European Bank for Reconstruction and Development (EBRD). These multilateral agencies are able to enhance the bankability of a project by providing international commercial banks with protection against a variety of political risks including the failure of host governments to make agreed payments or to provide foreign exchange, as well as the failure of the host government to grant necessary regulatory approvals or to ensure the performance of certain participants in a project. [. . .]

The participation of these agencies may alleviate some of the concerns about the inherent political risks in the host country. Their presence in a project often assists in financing, as the project is seen by private financiers as having international political clout thereby reducing the level of political risk associated with a project.

Construction Company

[. . .] depending upon the nature of the infrastructure, the commissioning risk (that is, the risk that the technology will work and that the infrastructure will operate to predetermined performance standards), is often allocated to the construction company. [. . .]

The Contractual Framework

A BOT is a very complex structure with a large number of elements which need to be combined and integrated. It requires an extensive network of interrelated and often inter-conditional contracts.

A BOT will usually include all or at least a majority of the following agreements:

- A concession agreement, license or mineral lease between the government authority and the project company. This is the cornerstone of the structure as it effectively gives the project company the right to carry out the project. Concession agreements in emerging markets vary enormously. In some cases, the right to carry out the project is sourced in special legislation enacted by the relevant government. But in other cases the concession agreement will be a very loosely drafted document where parties will rely more on the goodwill of the host government (and its need to develop projects in the future) than on the contractual terms of the concession agreement. [. . .]

- An offtake agreement/take or pay sales agreement between the government authority and the project company in which the government authority agrees to purchase, over a specific period, a minimum quantity of the project company's product at an agreed price. [. . . .] Although the structure of these agreements does not generally cause a problem under English law, this is not always the case in countries which do not have an English law background. In a number of jurisdictions, the adequacy of consideration in a contract is of great importance. [. . .] Advice on local law should be taken regarding proposed off-take agreements, not only in relation to their enforceability but also in relation to their structure. Another consideration which may arise in some of the more regulated economies in the region is whether an adequate offtake agreement can be negotiated. For example, if as in China or some Eastern European countries, electricity prices are subject to central controls, it may not be possible to simply "pass through" costs to the offtaker.
- A construction contract between the project company and the construction company. This will usually be in the form of a comprehensive turnkey contract which provides for the project to be handed over and to be ready for immediate operation. [. . .]
- A fuel supply agreement between the project company and the fuel supplier. Of course, this would not be necessary where the project company provides its own raw materials or the project concerns the extradition of natural resources. In many projects the terms of supply agreements are notoriously difficult to negotiate because the fuel is being provided by monopolistic suppliers. [. . .]
- A credit agreement between the banks and the project company in which the banks will advance funds to the project company together with any associated security documents. Parties will need to consider the currency of the loans. [. . .]
- A shareholders' agreement between the sponsors which sets out the respective rights and obligations of the sponsors with respect to each other and the project company. [. . .]

Risk Sharing

BOTs are generally structured on a basis that requires all parties to share the risks of the project. [. . .] Each project has its own unique set of risks. In identifying the risks, parties generally look at the project in three stages:

- Development/financing
- Construction
- Operation

Within each of these stages multiple sources of risk exist. [. . .] Once the project's risks are identified, the likelihood of their occurrence assessed and their impact on the project determined, the risks are allocated to the appropriate parties. Therefore, the primary consideration at the outset in analyzing risk sharing is that the risk must be placed with a party to the BOT structure which is willing to accept that risk. At its most basic allocation, risk in a BOT will be apportioned as follows: market risk (that the product generated is able to produce revenue) will be borne by the sponsors: detailed design, construction and commissioning risk will, to a large extent, be taken by the construction company; operating risk will be taken by the operator, and all residual risks, including those risks arising as a result of the mismatching of risks among participants, will be taken by the project company.

Risk Analysis

Country and Political Risk

Most developing countries have, in the past, lacked clearly defined policies for the role of private infrastructure projects, particularly in politically sensitive fields like energy generation. However, as a matter of necessity, there is evidence of a general move in these countries towards establishing appropriate structures for investment in privately financed infrastructure projects. A recent example is the partial privatization of Tenaga Nasional and the subsequent award of four licences for independent power projects in Malaysia.

Nevertheless, it is usually not enough to establish the mechanism for private investment without also establishing a regime which provides indirect support. The necessary requirements to convince the parties, and the banks, of the long term viability of these projects include a legal and regulatory framework which addresses issues such as tax, import controls, conversion and reparation of profits, and commercially based tariffs which permit a reasonable return on investment. [. . .]

Currency

It is not unusual for a project to incur expenditure in a number of currencies, generate revenues in another—pay taxes and royalties in a third and fund debt service in yet another currency. Most BOTs in emerging markets will have to address the problem of a mismatch between the currency generated by a project and foreign currency required to meet the project company's commitments. [. . .]

Change of Law

Dramatic changes of law through nationalization or expropriation are a part of the sovereign risk of doing business in emerging markets. [. . .] subtle changes of law or regulations may have a significant impact upon project economics. For example, the host government may impose additional tariffs on imports of plant and machinery or materials, or the health and safety requirements may change during the course of construction leading to design change, both of which may increase the cost of construction of the facility. This can only be dealt with by negotiations on political risk.

Security

In some countries, for example, China and Vietnam, the legal framework for taking the level of security commonly required in Western project financing is still evolving. In other countries legal structures are more developed, particularly where there is an inheritance from the colonial past, as in the former British and Spanish empires, or, in parts of central Europe, from the country's own pre-socialist tradition. However, even in these countries there may be difficulties associated with taking security, for example, in Malaysia there are restrictions on holding foreign currency earnings in offshore accounts, thereby limiting the ability to take security over those accounts without accepting country/political risk on those moneys. Furthermore, in Thailand the nature of the security which is available is very limited. For example, there is no concept of a general floating charge, a concept frequently used in UK-based project financing. It is therefore necessary to adapt the security structure to the particular market.

Environmental Issues

This is an extremely important area. Lenders and sponsors will be keen to ensure that the project in which they are involved is unlikely to contravene existing or future environmental legislation, and, even more importantly, that it will not impose any liability on them. This is of particular concern to lenders when they exercise their security rights. [. . .] Planning for environmental approvals should start from the beginning of the project, particularly if the project is looking for support from multilateral agencies such as the World Bank and Asian Development Bank, which require environmental standards as a condition to their involvement.

The Right Approach

[. . .] the practical aspects rather than the conceptual aspects, are the backbone of a successful project. Success not only depends on the ability of the project participants to identify, allocate and manage the risks they have accepted but also on the ability of the participants to adapt structures they have used in the past to meet the challenges thrown up in emerging markets. Participants must cast a critical eye over the structures they use and resist the impulse to insist on the inclusion of relevant structures simply on the basis that it worked well in the past. This is particularly important in emerging markets where the regional, contractual and financing aspects of projects, including projects structured around the BOT model, are considerably more complicated than in Europe, UK or the US.

2. Benefits and Disadvantages for Host Country

The core advantage of BOT projects is that the asset ultimately reverts to the ownership of the host country, but acquisition does not add to the national debt. National economic efficiency can be improved through the provision of adequate incentives to private investors for the construction and operation of much-needed infrastructure. Competitive bidding at the concession stage can reduce the total project cost, and the resulting private sector involvement may stimulate reduced bureaucracy and more efficient performance by state-owned utilities.

Further advantages for the host country are that a large-scale infrastructure project which is too costly for the public sector can be made possible by attracting private investment. Countries can also expect some transfer of advanced technology to maintain and operate the facility, and are entitled to own the facility after the specified operation period.

A disadvantage for the host country is that the net positive cash flow to the national finances from the development will be decreased because of repayment of foreign loans and repatriation of dividends. Furthermore, most of the revenue from the project will be converted into hard currency during the project period, which may put pressure on the balance of payments of the host country. Inflation, devaluation and other cost increases will be reflected in an increase in the fees, tolls or tariffs charged and, as a result, local consumers may have to pay higher charges.

BOTs are a complex arrangement, and some observers argue that the overall project cost may be higher than for an equivalent publicly funded project.

3. Criteria for a Successful BOT Project

The readings in this chapter highlight a number of areas as critical for a successful BOT project. Firstly, the project must be financially sound, feasible and affordable, and the country risks must be manageable. There should be strong government support, and the project(s) must rank high on the host government's list of priority infrastructure projects. It is beneficial if the legal framework is stable and the administrative framework is relatively efficient and predictable. Crucially, the public bidding procedure must be fair and transparent.

BOT transactions need to be structured for completion of cost recoveries within a reasonable time and with a reasonable profit provision. The sponsors must be experienced and reliable and have sufficient financial strength. The construction contractors should have sufficient experience and resources to undertake what are often complex engineering projects. The project risk needs to be allocated rationally amongst the parties. The financial structure should provide the lenders with adequate security and currency, while foreign exchange and inflation issues need to be adequately assessed and resolved.

At the core of these criteria is that the BOT contractual framework should be well coordinated and reflect the basic economics of the project.

© Don Wallace, *Private Participation in Infrastructure and the Provision of Public Services—Inevitable and Difficult*, 18 Transnat'l Law. 117 (2004–2005).

[. . .] The reason there is a need for a legal framework is because private sector participation in infrastructure—roads, public schools, jails, public housing, power plants, telecom, and all other things that the (International Finance Corporation) "IFC" and "OPIC" (Overseas Private Investment Corporation) work on—is inevitable and difficult. Why is it inevitable? Because of money. Public lenders, such as the World Bank, only have a limited amount of money. [. . .]

Privately financed infrastructure is objectively difficult; it is not just ignorance in the West about host countries that makes it difficult. [. . .] Eight factors illustrate this. The first is lack of sufficient policy and negotiating experience, as well as capacity, in many host countries. It is a vicious circle because when governments are unable to coordinate their efforts, the risks for investors and lenders increase, causing the investors to become nervous and demanding. When investors become more nervous and demanding, governments have a harder time coordinating their efforts, thus creating a vicious circle. Many countries lack experience because provision of infrastructure is the government's primary role. For example, during an oil crisis in Argentina, President Frondizi stated, "oil is Argentina's sovereign mission". So the government's mission is to provide roads, and public services. Governments in many developing countries cannot turn these services over to foreign businesses. It is the sacred public duty of the government itself to perform the services. If a country would discharge its sacred duty, the country would not need foreign and private investors. Populations are growing and the country would not need foreign and private investors. Populations are growing and the pressures are mounting—there is demand for higher standards. Consumers across the globe desire cellular phones and other products and services. It is difficult for the "PTTs" (Ministries of Post, Telephone and Telegraph) to provide these types of services when they cannot even provide the landline telephones. [. . .]

[. . .] my second point, [. . .]. Many countries, such as France, China and previously Turkey, have a statist tradition which is not communism. It means that the people will collectively provide for itself whether in a monarchy, a democracy, or the Governing Council of Iraq.

Ideological resistance is a kind of post-socialist, Marxist idea. In the 1980s, Lady Margaret Thatcher and Ronald Reagan changed the world. The past orthodoxy of elites, professors, and in the case of the French, the top civil servants who are called the Ecoliens, guided the fate of countries (in a very interventionist, from the top down, way). The Stalinist experience in Russia has completely discredited that practice. However, the intelligentsia, in developing countries and elsewhere, has not yet grasped that concept. So a resistance persists in terms of going to the market. "Marketism" like Marxism will create problems, if it seen as an absolute answer that can solve everything. Some of the resistance is visceral or innate in the person resisting the change. It is simply irrational.

The government and the people need to come to a realization. Abraham Lincoln stated, "we have to disenthrall ourselves of the dogmas of the past". One way to begin this re-infrastructure is to have the people decide via the legislatures to enact a general concession law, and possibly sector specific laws. Enacting an enabling law (a framework) is a means to overcome public resistance and signal a movement into a new era. Of course, there will be resistance from trade unions because they fear loss of public sector jobs. In addition, there are ideological flavors, such as the romantic successor to Marxism, which is the position that the people must be involved in the decisions. Examples of various ideas exist in Argentina with Peronism, and also in Venezuela with Populism. While people should be involved in the decision-making, problems continue to obstruct the movement forward.

A subsequent problem comes from the French, [. . .] which has given us administrative law [. . .]. Unfortunately, that interventionist law survives with BOT in Argentina, Latin America, Turkey, and parts of Africa. This law gives the government unilateral powers, including the right to order changes to projects. The French removes some of its features and rigidities, but some Latins have not. These unilateral powers include giving governments the right to change a contract for a two-lane road into an agreement for a four-lane road, and make a project unbankable. [. . .] Governments in these countries really have extraordinary powers. The expression that is used is "extraordinary clauses". [. . .]

A third point is structured competitive selection of concessionaires. [. . .] Countries must have a structured variety of competitive selection. However, the French have occasionally said no, the state can do this project. So, why can we not delegate it to whom we want? This is the French position—delegation. Why is that not corrupt? Indeed, it could be very corrupt. Admittedly, in a country such as France that is very rich and able—corruption is one thing—but corruption in Mauritania and Mali might be disastrously worse. Thus, competitive selection must be open and transparent. [. . .]

A sixth point is that in theory, project finance is non-recourse. [. . .]

Seventh, dispute settlement is a major issue. [. . .]

An eighth point relates to capacity. [. . .] gaining experience is difficult and takes time. This is an area where training can make a contribution, but it is training of a rather elaborate variety. One must be sensitive that accepting private and foreign participation in infrastructure may impinge on national history and self-image.

Conclusion

Private participation in public infrastructure will continue to be difficult, despite its necessity. [. . .]

C. Dispute Resolution in International Project Finance Transactions

Dispute settlement is generally provided for in the multiple contracts for a project-financed development. Project participants will normally choose to draft in appropriate arbitration clauses, and usually, the parties agree to arbitration in the case of a dispute. International arbitration is very attractive in international projects due to its flexibility regarding the resolution of multi-party disputes.

© Christopher Dugué, *Dispute Resolution in International Project Finance Transactions*, 24 Fordham Int'l L.J. 1064 (2000).

Most of the legal issues raised in international project financing have been discussed in various studies published on the subject. One angle, however, has been kept in the dark: dispute resolution. The anticipation of disputes and the method of resolving them seem to be perceived by international financiers as a rather automatic and not complex routine consisting of the incorporation of a model dispute resolution clause into the transactions. The reality is quite different. International projects imply many participants. Each participant brings into the project what other participants are lacking: financing ability, political authority, technical know-how, procurement of supplies, human resources, etc. Therefore, setting up a project implies dealing with numerous contracts entered into by various participants from different countries, either bilaterally or multilaterally. Because those contracts are signed in an international context of increased political and credit and exchange-rate risks, the risk of disputes arising between the participants is, in turn, increased. [. . .]

When providing for dispute resolution mechanisms, international financiers have a first option between non-binding (mainly, conciliation and mediation) and binding (judicial forums and arbitration) means. Non-binding mechanisms traditionally offer the flexibility that international market participants require while binding mechanisms offer the judicial implementation of the rules set forth in applicable statutory law and in the relevant contracts. Presuming that the parties will choose to resolve their disputes through a binding dispute resolution method, a second option for international financiers is between, on the one hand, the domestic courts of individual states where the parties are located or where the transactions are to be applied and, on the other hand, international fora.

Although international financiers have had a clear preference for domestic courts, practice has slowly evolved towards a better recognition of international arbitration in the field of project financing. [. . .] the assessment of the most effective forum cannot dismiss what this author considers as an essential feature of international project financing, i.e., its transactional unity. As a result, international arbitration is the most appropriate mechanism to deal with corollary specificities of international project financing, such as multi-party disputes. [. . .]

I. Dispute Resolution in Light of the Transactional Unity of International Project Financing

International project financing is a method of private financing classically structured in capital-absorbing industries, especially in the fields of energy (e.g., gas, electricity), mining, resort, transportation, or telecommunications.' It has been a particularly attractive method of financing industrial projects for developing countries, but is not limited to those countries. [. . .]

The common denominator between all international projects, in spite of their inevitable individuality, is that the participants negotiate multiple and separate contracts that will form a global structure with links, both from a business and a legal perspective. [. . .]

A. The Practical View: Negotiating Multiple and Separate Contracts

The basic structure of project financing consists of the establishment of a project company by a group of "sponsors," who are the shareholders of that company and who therefore participate in equity. [. . .] The project company's debt is said to be non-recourse i.e., its repayment depends on the cash flow sourcing from the revenue-producing contracts of the project and the assets of the project company are used as collateral for the debt. [. . .]

Therefore, a multitude of other mechanisms have to be set up to ensure the viability of the project company and its capacity to repay the project debt. Because project finance participants use a contractual framework to achieve such goals, including the transfer of unavoidable risks to third parties and the undertaking of guarantees, the negotiation of an international project finance structure leads to the setting up of an aggregate of multiple, sometimes intertwining, contracts and documents. [. . .]

1. The Underlying Documents

The corporate structure of the project company, which will be the borrower in the international loan agreements, may be determined by a preliminary series of agreements between the sponsors, instituting either a single corporate subsidiary of the shareholders or a joint venture in the form of a partnership between multiple sponsors. Depending on the type of project, the participants then negotiate a series of contracts in relation to the construction and the operation of the project company, such as site lease, sales contracts, supply contracts, construction contracts and subcontracts, technology or license agreements, and administrative agreements and documents (environmental consents, concession agreements, or documents regarding title to land, etc.). There are yet other agreements to be concluded regarding the management of the project.

2. The Financing and Supporting Documents

The heart of international project financing is the loan structure. The negotiation of loan agreements needs to take into consideration many important issues, in particular the limitations on recourse to the sponsors, the future application of cash flows, protective clauses (market disruption, political risks, expropriation guarantees, and stabilization clauses), events of default, or assignment and transfer provisions. The main financing agreements may be completed by security and support documents, such as intercreditor agreements, completion guarantee and other guarantees and comfort letters, insurance coverage, or security documents. They also may be completed by financial instruments, such as swaps or credit derivatives, aimed at controlling external economic risks beyond the control of the participants that are allocated to third parties. [. . .]

B. The Legal View: The Unity of Transactional Documents

It is international financiers' common knowledge that setting up a project financing structure involves negotiating the above-mentioned contracts and documents. It also is common knowledge that there are two levels to each type of project financing contract or document: a loan agreement and a sales agreement or a construction sub-contract. Each agreement is concluded between different parties and has a different purpose. Therefore, they each have a separate economic and legal philosophy. At a more global level, that of the project financing structure as a whole, however, each transaction contributes to the general purpose of the project: the economic viability of the project company and its capacity to make profits and to repay its loans.

The global nature of international project financing is essential in understanding the originality of the mechanism. There are no general negotiations to enter into a single contract, but a series of contracts, which, once entered into, will define the global structure of the project. Therefore, it appears imperative to this author that the participants recognize the concept of unity with respect to the resolution of their disputes and reflect this unity in their future transactions. Any failure to do so would dissolve the transactional unity of the structure and jeopardize the project's viability. [. . .]

In addition, international project finance participants need to assess, among all types of risks, the legal risk associated with an erroneous determination of the competent court that will resolve future disputes. Given the transactional unity of project financing, the non-application or the defective application of a given contract may have an economic, as well as a legal, impact on other contracts or mechanisms and, eventually, on the project as a whole. For example, in a project regarding the construction, maintenance, and operation of a petroleum facilities in country A, the scheduling clauses in the construction contract are fundamental to the implementation of a petroleum sales agreement entered into between the project company (in country A) and the purchasing corporation (in country B). Obviously, project financing allows for contractual mechanisms aimed at ensuring the timely completion of the construction phase, such as completion guarantee provisions or documents, liquidated damages provisions in the construction contract, or a fixed-price turnkey contract. The mere existence of these mechanisms, however, does not preclude the occurrence of disputes regarding their enforcement. A dispute regarding the failure to comply with the completion date on the part of the construction contractor may have a consequence on the implementation of the sales agreement and the applicability of the dispute resolution clause in that agreement. In this example, the effective resolution of the overall dispute depends on two elements to be considered by the parties: (1) choosing the appropriate court to resolve the dispute between the project company and the construction contractor and (2) anticipating the likely connections and the possible differences in approach by the competent courts regarding the dispute between the construction agreement (the competent courts being, for instance, the courts of Country A where the project company has its seat) and the dispute regarding the sales agreement (the competent courts being, for instance, the courts of Country B, where the purchasing corporation has its seat).

This simple example shows that dispute resolution in international project financing requires that the participants have an accurate understanding of the project as a whole in order to draft an appropriate dispute resolution clause in their contracts. Such an approach is consistent with the philosophy of project financing and constitutes an effective guarantee against the uncertainty of the outcome.

II. The Different Types of Dispute Resolution Mechanisms in International Project Financing Transactions

There are mainly two types of forums open to the parties to an international contract: domestic courts and international arbitral tribunals. In this regard, international project finance transactions are no exception to the rule.

When negotiating their contracts, the first danger that international financiers should avoid is the failure to draft a dispute resolution clause and, therefore, the failure to select a forum. In such a case, once the dispute has arisen, it can be resolved through a binding method, either by the application of conflict rules of private international law referring the dispute to the competent domestic court or by the signature of an arbitration agreement. The parties could, however, find their dispute brought in an undesirable forum and be confronted with an uncertain outcome. In reality, international project financing participants and their counsels are sophisticated enough to understand the necessity of drafting the most favorable dispute resolution clause. The practical difficulty to which they are confronted relates, rather, to the choice between domestic courts and international arbitration.

A. Recourse to Domestic Courts

[. . .] The jurisdiction of domestic courts is reinforced in project financing by the fact that some of the underlying agreements are governed by local laws. As a result, the jurisdictional risk in the implementation of project finance transactions is twofold: the selection of an unfavorable forum and the fragmentation of the resolution of multi-party disputes into as many fora as the number of agreements involved, along with parallel proceedings.

As far as the risk of selecting an unfavorable forum is concerned, the parties to project finance transactions are often sophisticated and know the risk of having their future disputes resolved by a local court, the court of the seat of the project company for instance, which may not be familiar with the complex issues involved in the transactions. Such risk is enhanced by possible difficulties regarding the enforcement of the judgment eventually rendered in a different country. Practice, however, has developed the trend towards the selection of U.S. or English courts (in particular the courts of New York), mainly because of the parties' relation with financial centers in New York or London and the applicability of New York or English law to the agreement under consideration (especially to loan agreements, where there is a stronger protection of the rights of the creditors). [. . .]

As far as the risk of the fragmentation of the dispute resolution process is concerned, [. . .] it is thus essential for international financiers at the drafting stage to have a good understanding of the general structure of the project and to be attentive to the dispute resolution clauses of the most important transactions-those that have an impact on the implementation of the agreement under consideration. They could combine either compatible forum selection clauses or forum selection clauses with international arbitration clauses. They could also aim to better control the whole dispute resolution mechanism by selecting international arbitration. [. . .]

B. Recourse to International Arbitration

In avoiding the proliferation and dissipation of their potential future disputes, project financing participants have slowly evolved towards international arbitration as a truly neutral alternative to domestic courts. [. . .] The past reluctance of many international operators due to the arbitral tribunals' lack of authority to order provisional measures has been swept away by the adoption by the major arbitration institutions of rules allowing for such measures.[300] [. . .]

This general trend towards arbitration has indisputably been reinforced by the fact that even when an arbitral tribunal is set up, domestic courts may remain competent[301] they may assist the arbitration process, either upstream by compelling a reluctant party to arbitrate or by ordering interim measures, or downstream by enforcing interim measures or a final arbitral award ordered by an arbitral tribunal.[302]

1. Transactional Unity of International Project Financing and Multi-party Disputes

[. . .] The global, multi-contractual, multi-party aspect of the transactions may, in cases of difficulty, call for multi-party disputes. [. . .] In a first situation, a dispute

300. *See* International Chamber of Commerce ("ICC"), Rules of Arbitration, art. 23, at http:// www.iccwbo.org/court/english/arbitration/rules.asp [hereinafter ICC Rules]; London Court of International Arbitration Rules ("LCIA"), art. 25, at http:// www.lcia-arbitration.com/lcia /usergyde/usergyde.htm#21 [hereinafter LCIA Rules]; International Centre for Settlement of Investment Disputes, Rules of Procedure for Arbitration Proceedings ("ICSID"), art. 39, at http:// www.worldbank.org/icsid/basicdoc/ 63.htm [hereinafter ICSID Rules]; see also United Nations Commission on International Trade Law Model Law on International Commercial Arbitration, art. 39, at http:// www.uncitral.org/en-index.htm [hereinafter UNCITRAL Rules] (regarding ad hoc arbitration).

301. *See, e.g.*, William W. Park, International Forum Selection 105 et seq. (1995) (discussing possible combination of litigation and arbitration).

302. *See, e.g.*, Richard H. Kreindler, *Supervision and Support of Arbitration by Courts: A Comparative Approach*, 7 Int'l Arb. Rep. 14 (1992). However, some jurisdictions are hostile to arbitration and the courts in those jurisdiction, if called upon to intervene, may obstruct the arbitral process; international financiers should therefore avoid locating the seat of the arbitration in such jurisdictions and turn to other pro-arbitration jurisdictions. *See* Emmanuel Gaillard, *Interference of National Courts in the International Arbitral Process*, N.Y.L.J., Jan. 29, 2001, at 3 (providing recent examples) [hereinafter Emmanuel Gaillard, *Interference of National Courts*].

may arise between multiple parties to a single multilateral agreement (a consortium agreement for instance) containing a single arbitration clause; in a second situation, a dispute may arise between different parties to multiple bilateral agreements containing different arbitration clauses. [. . .]

Where, for instance, a contractual structure including a master agreement and subsidiary agreements exists, an arbitral tribunal that has jurisdiction over the master agreement may also have jurisdiction, on the basis of the theory of unified transaction, over the subsidiary agreements, whereas a competent domestic court may not have jurisdiction over those agreements. [. . .] As a general rule, however, since international arbitration is based on the parties' consent, multi-party arbitrations are initiated with the consent of the parties and to the extent allowed for by the arbitration clauses or the arbitration rules of major international arbitration institutions such as the International Chamber of Commerce ("ICC") in Paris. [. . .]

Therefore, to fully benefit from the advantages offered by international arbitration, the project participants may wish to consider incorporating multi-party arbitration into the dispute resolution clause of their contracts. [. . .]

In addition, the finality of arbitral awards and their better enforcement, as compared to the difficulties encountered in the enforcement of domestic judgments, makes international arbitration a trustworthy alternative to domestic courts.

2. Drafting an Effective Arbitration Clause

[. . .] The negotiation and drafting of an arbitration clause should take into consideration many features including, classically, the seat of arbitration, the modalities of the nomination of the arbitrators, and the choice between ad hoc or institutional arbitration. Firstly, in project financing as in any other field, it is essential for the parties to choose a seat where both national legislation and judicial tradition favor arbitration. Secondly, international financiers should take the opportunity offered by international arbitration to select specialized arbitrators, especially with regard to the technicality and complexity of project financing. [. . .]

As far as the enforcement of the award is concerned, it is important for international financiers to predict the country where they will seek the enforcement of a future award. [. . .] the applicability of the New York Convention and make sure that the State where they would like the award to be enforced is a party to the New York Convention [. . .] international financiers may be interested in ICSID [. . .] the enforcement of ICSID awards is not dependent on the applicability of any other convention than the Washington Convention itself. [. . .]

Conclusion

Because dispute resolution clauses are fundamental to the effective implementation of international project finance transactions, they should be one of international financiers' first concerns when they enter into negotiations. Drafting a dispute resolution clause, whether referring the parties to domestic courts or to international arbitration, requires that project participants possess comprehensive knowledge of the project, an accurate anticipation of the risks incurred-including the judicial risk and a thorough understanding of dispute resolution mechanisms. Given the complexity and the uniquely global nature of international project financing, international arbitration clearly appears as the most fitting avenue for project participants. Because it allows for flexibility in the dispute resolution process and for effectiveness in the enforcement of the outcome, international arbitration optimizes, both legally and economically, the implementation of project finance transactions and the protection of the parties' rights.

Chapter 12

International Efforts Against Corruption in International Business Transactions

A. Introduction

The possibility of corruption in association with foreign direct investment is unfortunately a persistent and important topic. This chapter identifies some of the problems related to corruption that may arise in foreign direct investment projects. Corruption is a criminal offence in most countries, but the challenge invariably lies in successful prosecution. In this chapter, some of the leading legislation in place at the domestic and international level is analyzed, and the international institutions engaged in the battle against corruption are introduced.

Corruption undermines democracy, good governance and social cohesion, distorts the allocation of resources, and discourages responsible investment. Foreign investors are cautious about locations with a reputation for massive corruption. The promotion of corrupt interests may lead to misallocation of funds and resources and to distortion of trade, as well as erosion of public confidence in democratic government and institutions.

It has been argued by some economists that corruption can contribute to efficiency in underdeveloped countries through accelerating growth. However, this argument no longer appears credible. For example, the accumulation by President Suharto and his family in Indonesia of a $30 billion fortune through ignoring lower cost tenders in competitive bidding processes resulted in major economic distortions that helped to cripple domestic competition and significantly reduced foreign investment, contributing to Indonesia's 1998 economic crisis.

The most common form of corruption is acceptance of bribes. Other forms of corruption may include collusion in tendering processes, conflicts of interest, embezzlement, fraud, extortion and money laundering.

The well-known organization Transparency International (TI), founded by two former World Bank individuals and headquartered in Belgium, plays an important role in monitoring and drawing attention to corruption. It issues annual country corruption scores and rankings that attract wide attention and can affect the granting of loans and interest rates.

1. Foreign Corrupt Practices Act

The United States was the first country to criminalize corruption by its corporations acting abroad, through the Foreign Corrupt Practices Act (FCPA), passed in 1977 during the Jimmy Carter Presidency. Some companies complained that this disadvantaged U.S. corporations, and there was resistance to the legislation. The United States subsequently started to work towards internationalization of this approach.

The United States Department of Justice, Foreign Corrupt Practices Act.

An Overview

The Foreign Corrupt Practices Act of 1977, as amended, 15 U.S.C. § 78dd-1, et seq. ("FCPA"), was enacted for the purpose of making it unlawful for certain classes of persons and entities to make payments to foreign government officials to assist in obtaining or retaining business. Specifically, the anti-bribery provisions of the FCPA prohibit the willful use of the mails or any means of instrumentality of interstate commerce corruptly in furtherance of any offer, payment, promise to pay, or authorization of the payment of money or anything of value to any person, while knowing that all or a portion of such money or thing of value will be offered, given or promised, directly or indirectly, to a foreign official to influence the foreign official in his or her official capacity, induce the foreign official to do or omit to do an act in violation of his or her lawful duty, or to secure any improper advantage in order to assist in obtaining or retaining business for or with, or directing business to, any person.

Since 1977, the anti-bribery provisions of the FCPA have applied to all U.S. persons and certain foreign issuers of securities. With the enactment of certain amendments in 1998, the anti-bribery provisions of the FCPA now also apply to foreign firms and persons who cause, directly or through agents, an act in furtherance of such a corrupt payment to take place within the territory of the United States.

The FCPA also requires companies whose securities are listed in the United States to meet its accounting provisions. See 15 U.S.C. § 78m. These accounting provisions, which were designed to operate in tandem with the anti-bribery provisions of the FCPA, require corporations covered by the provisions to (a) make and keep books and records that accurately and fairly reflect the transactions of the corporation and (b) devise and maintain an adequate system of internal accounting controls.

United States v. Kozeny, 582 F. Supp. 2d 535 (S.D.N.Y. 2008).

Case Introduction

SOCAR is the state oil company of the Republic of Azerbaijan. In the mid-1990s, Azerbaijan began a program of privatization which gave the President of Azerbaijan discretionary authority as to whether and when to privatize SOCAR.

Defendant Frederic Bourke, Jr. and others allegedly violated the FCPA by making payments to Azeri officials to encourage the privatization of SOCAR and to permit them to participate in that privatization.

Bourke argued that the alleged payments were legal under Azeri law and thus under the FCPA (which provides an affirmative defense for payments that are legal under relevant foreign law) because they were the product of extortion. He also argues that pursuant to Azeri law, any criminality associated with the payments was excused when he reported them to the President of Azerbaijan.

Bourke requested that the court make determinations as to the content of applicable law in Azerbaijan and instruct the jury on certain defenses that might be available under the law of Azerbaijan. The Government and Bourke were unable to agree on the contents or applicability of that law. To resolve this disagreement, the court held a hearing on September 11, 2008. This Opinion and Order contains the court's determinations.

Principal Points of the Judgment

B. The Legal System of Azerbaijan

Azerbaijan, a sovereign nation in the Caspian Sea region that borders Russia, was formerly integrated as a Republic of the Soviet Union. Azerbaijan declared independence in 1991.[303] The current criminal code of Azerbaijan took effect in 2000. In Azerbaijan, decisions of most courts are not considered binding authority; however, the highest court in Azerbaijan has the authority to give official interpretations of the Azeri Constitution and laws.

---

303. *See* The Constitutional Act on Restoration of the State Independence of the Republic of Azerbaijan (Oct. 18, 1991).

III. Legal Standard

A. The FCPA

The FCPA prohibits giving something of value for the purpose of "(i) influencing any act or decision of [a] foreign official in his official capacity, (ii) inducing such foreign official to do or omit any act in violation of the lawful duty of such official, or (iii) securing any improper advantage . . . to obtain or retain business for or with . . . any person."[304] The law provides an affirmative defense for payments that are "lawful under the written laws and regulations" of the country.[305]

B. Foreign Law

"Though foreign law once was treated as an issue of fact, it now is viewed as a question of law and may be determined through the use of any relevant source, including expert testimony."[306] Rule 26.1 of the Federal Rules of Criminal Procedure provides that "[a] party intending to raise an issue of foreign law must provide the court and all parties with reasonable written notice. Issues of foreign law are questions of law, but in deciding such issues a court may consider any relevant material or source—including testimony—without regard to the Federal Rules of Evidence."

IV. Discussion

During the relevant period, Article 170 of the Azerbaijan Criminal Code ("ACC") provided that "[t]he receiving by an official [. . .] of a bribe in any form whatsoever for the fulfillment or the failure to fulfill any action in the interest of the person giving the bribe which the official should have or might perform with the use of his employment position [. . .] shall be punished by deprivation of freedom [. . .]." Professor Stephan [Bourke's expert] asserts that during the same period, Article 171 of the ACC provided that "[g]iving a bribe shall be punished by deprivation of freedom for a term of from three to eight years [. . .] A person who has given a bribe shall be free from criminal responsibility if with respect to him there was extortion of the bribe or if that person after giving the bribe voluntarily made a report of the occurrence." Professor Butler [Government's expert] believes that a more accurate translation of the last clause is "[a] person who has given a bribe shall be relieved from criminal responsibility if extortion of the bribe occurred with respect to him or if this person after giving the bribe voluntarily stated what happened."

The Supreme Court of the U.S.S.R. interpreted Article 171 in a Resolution published in 1990.[307] The parties agree that the Resolution is relevant to the Azeri courts' interpretation of the Article. It defines extortion as "a demand by an official for a bribe under the threat of carrying out actions that could do damage to the legal interests of the briber [. . . .]" The Resolution further explains that "a voluntary

304. 15 U.S.C. § 78dd-2(a)(1)(A).

305. *Id.* § 78dd-2(c).

306. *United States v. Vilar*, No. 05 Cr. 621, 2007 WL 1075041, at *55 n. 35 (S.D.N.Y. Apr. 4, 2007).

307. See *Resolution of the Plenum of the Supreme Court of the U.S.S.R. of March 30, 1990, No. 3, "On Court Practice in Bribery Cases,"* ("Res.") Ex. C to Stephan Decl.

declaration of having committed the crime absolves from criminal responsibility not only the bribe giver but his accomplices." Finally, the Resolution provides that "[t]he absolution of a bribe-giver from criminal responsibility because of extortion of the bribe or the voluntary declaration of the giving of the bribe [. . .] does not signify an absence in the actions of such persons of the elements of an offense. For that reason, they cannot be considered victims and are not entitled to claim restitution of the items of value given as bribes."

As a threshold matter, I must determine the meaning of "relieved (or free) from criminal responsibility." Bourke contends that if an individual is relieved of criminal responsibility, his action was "lawful" and he may thus avail himself of the FCPA's affirmative defense. I disagree.

For purposes of the FCPA's affirmative defense, the focus is on the payment, not the payer.[308] A person cannot be guilty of violating the FCPA if the payment was lawful under foreign law. But there is no immunity from prosecution under the FCPA if a person could not have been prosecuted in the foreign country due to a technicality (e.g., time-barred) or because a provision in the foreign law "relieves" a person of criminal responsibility. An individual may be prosecuted under the FCPA for a payment that violates foreign law even if the individual is relieved of criminal responsibility for his actions by a provision of the foreign law.

A. The Reporting Exception

As Professor Butler observes, the structure of the reporting exception to liability in Article 171 illustrates that the initial payment of a bribe was certainly not lawful. The ACC relieves the payer of a bribe from criminal liability if the bribe is properly reported not because such an action retroactively erases the stain of criminality, but because the state has a strong interest in prosecuting the government official who received the bribe. By waiving liability for reporting payers, the state increases the likelihood that it will learn of the bribery.

But at the moment that an individual pays a bribe, the individual has violated Article 171. At that time, the payment was clearly not "lawful under the written laws" of Azerbaijan.[309] If the individual later reports the bribe, she can no longer be prosecuted for that payment. But it is inaccurate to suggest that the payment itself suddenly became "lawful"—on the contrary, the payment was unlawful, though

---

308. The FCPA focuses on payments, not payers, throughout its structure. For example, it provides that there is no liability for "any facilitating or expediting payment to a foreign official [. . .] the purpose of which is to expedite or to secure the performance of a routine governmental action by a foreign official [. . .]." 15 U.S.C. § 78dd-2(b). The purpose of this subsection was to "acknowledge [. . .] that some payments that would be unethical or even illegal within the United States might not be perceived similarly in foreign countries, and those payments should not be criminalized." *United States v. Castle*, 925 F.2d 831, 834 (5th Cir. 1991).

309. In this sense, the relief from liability operates in a fashion similar to that of a statute of limitations in the United States. If an individual commits a crime but that individual is not prosecuted within the statute of limitations, the individual's actions do not become "lawful", rather, the criminal cannot be prosecuted.

the payer is relieved of responsibility for it. This is why the Resolution provides that the payer cannot receive restitution. Further, if the payment were retroactively lawful, the official who received the payment could not be prosecuted for receiving it. This cannot be correct because the purpose of the reporting exception is to enable the government to pursue the official. Thus, the relief from liability in Article 171 operates to excuse the payer, not the payment.

B. The Extortion Exception

The exception for extortion contained in the same sentence must operate in the same manner.[310] A payment to an Azeri official that is made under threat to the payer's legal interests is still an illegal payment, though the payer cannot be prosecuted for the payment.

This conclusion does not preclude Bourke from arguing that he cannot be guilty of violating the FCPA by making a payment to an official who extorted the payment because he lacked the requisite corrupt intent to make a bribe.[311] The legislative history of the FCPA makes clear that "true extortion situations would not be covered by this provision."[312] Thus, while the FCPA would apply to a situation in which a "payment [is] demanded on the part of a government official as a price for gaining entry into a market or to obtain a contract," it would not apply to one in which payment is made to an official "to keep an oil rig from being dynamited," an example of "true extortion." The reason is that in the former situation, the bribe payer cannot argue that he lacked the intent to bribe the official because he made the "conscious decision" to pay the official. In other words, in the first example, the payer could have turned his back and walked away—in the latter example, he could not.

If Bourke provides an evidentiary foundation for the claim that he was the victim of "true extortion," I will instruct the jury on what constitutes a situation of "true extortion" such that Bourke would not be found to have possessed the "corrupt" intent required for a violation under the FCPA. In any event, the jury will be instructed regarding the "corrupt" intent that the Government must prove he possessed beyond

310. While in the American system, it is generally accepted that a payment that was extorted was not a "bribe," the language of Article 171 clearly indicates that Azeri law considers extorted payments to be bribes. Otherwise, the phrase "[a] person who has given a bribe shall be free from criminal responsibility if with respect to him there was extortion of the bribe" would make no sense.

311. By the same token, an individual who is forced to make payment on threat of injury or death would not be liable under the FCPA. Federal criminal law provides that actions taken under duress do not ordinarily constitute crimes. See generally *United States v. Gonzalez*, 407 F.3d 118, 122 (2d Cir. 2005) ("Three discrete elements must be met to establish coercion or duress. These are: (1) a threat of force directed at the time of the defendant's conduct; (2) a threat sufficient to induce a well-founded fear of impending death or serious bodily injury; and (3) a lack of a reasonable opportunity to escape harm other than by engaging in the illegal activity.") (citing *United States v. Podlog*, 35 F.3d 699, 704 (2d Cir. 1994)). If a payment was obtained under duress, no liability attaches under the FCPA.

312. *See* S.Rep. No. 95-114, at 10–11 (1977), reprinted in 1977 U.S.C.C.A.N. 4098, 4108.

a reasonable doubt he possessed.[313] Such instruction will define "corrupt" intent as "having an improper motive or purpose" and will explain that the payment must have been intended to "induce the recipient to misuse his official position" in discharging an official act. The charge will also emphasize that the proper focus is on Bourke's intent and that the Government is not required to show that "the official accepted the bribe," that the "official had the power or authority to perform the act sought" or that the "defendant intended to influence an official act which was lawful."

V. Conclusion

For the reasons stated above, the Court will not instruct the jury on the exceptions to criminal liability in Article 171. However, if Bourke provides an evidentiary foundation for "true extortion," the Court will instruct the jury on what constitutes a "true extortion" situation such that Bourke would not be found to possess the "corrupt" intent required for a violation under the FCPA.[314] The Court will, in any case, instruct the jury on the requisite elements of the crime of bribery under the FCPA, including the element of "corrupt" intent.

SO ORDERED.

United States v. Hoskins, 902 F.3d 69 (2d Cir. 2018).

Case Introduction

The United States government alleged that several defendants, including Lawrence Hoskins, a non-U.S. citizen, were part of a scheme to bribe officials in Indonesia so that their company could secure a $118 million contract from the Indonesian government. Hoskins worked for Alstom S.A. ("Alstom"), a global company headquartered in France that provides power and transportation services. During the relevant time, which was from 2002 to 2009, Hoskins was employed by Alstom's UK subsidiary, but was assigned to work with another subsidiary called Alstom Resources Management, which is in France.

The government alleged that although Hoskins never traveled to the U.S. during the scheme, he was one of the persons responsible for approving the selection of the consultants and authorizing payments to them with knowledge that portions of the payments were intended as bribes.

The district court dismissed portions of the indictment, in relevant part, finding that Hoskins could not be liable for conspiracy if he could not be liable for a direct violation of the statute.[315]

313. *See United States v. Alfisi*, 308 F.3d 144, 150 n. 1 (2d Cir. 2002) (citing *United States v. Kahn*, 472 F.2d 272, 279 (2d Cir. 1973)) (finding that the issue of extortion or "economic coercion" is addressed by instructing the jury on the requisite intent of bribery).

314. If Bourke demonstrates an evidentiary foundation for an affirmative defense of duress, the Court will also instruct the jury on its elements. See *Gonzalez*,407 F.3d at 122 ("A defendant is entitled to an instruction on an affirmative defense only if the defense has 'a foundation in the evidence'") (quoting *Podlog*, 35 F.3d at 704).

315. *United States v. Hoskins*, 123 F. Supp. 3d 316, 327 (D. Conn. 2015).

Significance of Case

Given the scarcity of judicial opinions construing the FCPA, decisions such as *Hoskins* provide valuable guidance as to the elements and scope of liability under the statute. The *Hoskins* decision demonstrates an unwillingness on the part of certain courts to expand FCPA-related liability beyond the categories of persons explicitly subject to the statute. It potentially places a significant limitation on the application and extraterritorial reach of the FCPA and jeopardizes the government's ability to charge foreign companies and individuals who have conspired to violate the FCPA, but who are not agents, employees, directors, or officers of any company that issues stock on a U.S. exchange or any other U.S. company and have not taken any action in furtherance of the FCPA violation while in the United States.[316]

As the *Hoskins* decision makes clear, the government frequently takes an expansive view of the doctrine of agency. It is therefore possible that the government will be able to avoid the practical effect of the decision's holding in many cases by using agency theories to charge foreign individuals and companies that otherwise would have been charged as conspirators or accomplices before *Hoskins*. The DOJ's continued pursuit of such a theory against *Hoskins* will provide some indication of the future viability of that path as an alternative to conspiracy liability in cases in which a defendant's agency relationship is unclear.[317]

Principal Points of the Judgment

[. . .]

In this case, we are asked to decide whether the government may employ theories of conspiracy or complicity to charge a defendant with violating the Foreign Corrupt Practices Act ("FCPA"), even if he is not in the category of persons directly covered by the statute.[318] We determine that the FCPA defined precisely the categories of persons who may be charged for violating its provisions. The statute also stated clearly the extent of its extraterritorial application.

The FCPA establishes three clear categories of persons who are covered by its provisions: (1) Issuers of securities registered pursuant to 15 U.S.C. § 78l or required to file reports under Section 78o(d), or any officer, director, employee, or agent of such issuer, or any stockholder acting on behalf of the issuer, using interstate commerce in connection with the payment of bribes, 15 U.S.C. § 78dd-1; (2) American companies and American persons using interstate commerce in connection with the payment of bribes, U.S.C. § 78dd-2; and (3) foreign persons or businesses taking acts

316. Sullivan & Cromwell LLP 2018, *United States v. Hoskins—Second Circuit Rejects DOJ's Attempt to Expand the Extraterritorial Reach of the FCPA through Conspiracy and Complicity Doctrines* (August 27, 2018).

317. *Ibid.*

318. Because the question before us is whether conspiracy and complicity charges can be used to extend liability beyond the categories delineated in the statute, we assume that Hoskins is not an agent of Alstom U.S. only for the sake of arguments advanced on appeal and express no views on the scope of agency under the FCPA.

to further certain corrupt schemes, including ones causing the payment of bribes, while present in the United States, 15 U.S.C. 3 § 78dd–3.

Because we agree with the district court that the FCPA's carefully-drawn limitations do not comport with the government's use of the complicity or conspiracy statutes in this case, we AFFIRM the district court's ruling barring the government from bringing the charge in question. We REVERSE the district court's holding on the Second Object of the Conspiracy, because the government's intention to prove that Hoskins was an agent of a domestic concern places him squarely within the terms of the statute and takes that provision outside our analysis on the other counts.

[. . .]

The alleged bribery scheme centers on Alstom's American subsidiary, Alstom Power, Inc. ("Alstom U.S."), headquartered in Connecticut. The 13 allegations are that Alstom U.S. and various individuals associated with Alstom S.A. retained two consultants to bribe Indonesian officials who could help secure the $118 million power contract for the company and its associates. Hoskins never worked for Alstom U.S. in a direct capacity. But the government alleges that Hoskins, while working from France for Alstom Resources Management, was "one of the people responsible for approving the selection of, and authorizing payments to, [the consultants], knowing that a portion of the payments to [the consultants] was intended for Indonesian officials in exchange for their influence and assistance in awarding the [contract.]"

The government alleges that several parts of the scheme occurred within the United States. The indictment alleges that one of the consultants kept a bank account in Maryland. In some cases, funds for bribes allegedly were paid from bank accounts held by Alstom and its business partners in the United States, and deposited in the consultant's account in Maryland, for the purpose of bribing Indonesian officials. The indictment also states that several executives of Alstom U.S. held meetings within the United States regarding the bribery scheme and discussed the project by phone and email while present on American soil. [. . .]

The Third Superseding Indictment, the operative one in the case, brings twelve counts against Hoskins. This appeal concerns the first seven counts of the indictment.

Count one charges Hoskins with conspiring to violate the FCPA. It alleges that Hoskins is liable because he was an agent of Alstom U.S., an American company, and, in that capacity, committed acts that violated the statute. It also alleges that, independently of his agency relationship with an American company, Hoskins conspired with the company and its employees, as well as foreign persons, to violate the FCPA, and also aided and abetted their violations. The Count focuses on two objects of the conspiracy, which correspond to two provisions of the FCPA that Hoskins supposedly violated as an accomplice and also conspired to violate. The first of the two FCPA provisions prohibits American companies and American persons, as well as their agents, from using interstate commerce in connection with the payment of bribes. 15 U.S.C. § 78dd-2. The second prohibits foreign persons or businesses from taking acts to further certain corrupt schemes, including ones causing the payment of bribes, while present in the United States. 15 U.S.C. § 78dd-3.

Counts two through seven charge substantive violations of the FCPA, focusing on particular wire transfers from Alstom U.S.'s bank account to the consultants' accounts. These counts all charge Hoskins with violations of 15 U.S.C. § 78dd-2. The counts allege that Hoskins violated this provision as "an agent" of an American company or person, and also "by aiding and abetting" such a company or person.

[. . .]

II. The FCPA and the First Object of the Conspiracy

The central question of the appeal is whether Hoskins, a foreign national who never set foot in the United States or worked for an American company during the alleged scheme, may be held liable, under a conspiracy or complicity theory, for violating FCPA provisions targeting American persons and companies and their agents, officers, directors, employees, and shareholders, and persons physically present within the United States. In other words, can a person be guilty as an accomplice or a co-conspirator for an FCPA crime that he or she is incapable of committing as a principal?

A. Conspiracy Liability

For purposes of this appeal, we assume that Hoskins was neither an employee nor an agent of a domestic concern and therefore does not fall within the terms of the statute. But accomplice and conspiracy liability are generally not so limited. A getaway driver for a bank robbery team can still be prosecuted even though he has not "by force and violence . . . take[n] . . . from the person or presence of another . . . any property . . . belonging to . . . any bank." 18 U.S.C. 16 § 2113(a). As the common law has long recognized, persons who intentionally direct or facilitate the crimes physically executed by others must be held accountable for their actions. This recognition was effectuated by developing the doctrines of conspiracy and complicity, principles that are now codified in statutes. Under 18 U.S.C. § 2(a), a person who does not personally commit the acts constituting an offense is liable as a principal if he or she "aids, abets, counsels, commands, induces or produces" the commission of those acts by another. In addition, 18 U.S.C. § 371 punishes anyone who "conspire[s]" with another to commit the offense. Thus, by the plain language of the general statutes regarding conspiracy and accessorial liability—which nothing in the language of the FCPA purports to overrule or limit—if Hoskins did what the indictment charges, he would appear to be guilty of conspiracy to violate the FCPA and (as an accomplice) of substantive violations of that statute.

Conspiracy and complicity statutes do not cease to apply simply because a statute specifies particular classes of people who can violate the law. It is well established in federal criminal law that "[a] person . . . may be liable for conspiracy even though he was incapable of committing the substantive offense." *Salinas v. United States*, 522 U.S. 52, 64 (1998). That principle was already deeply ingrained when the

Supreme Court unanimously ruled in 1915 that persons not themselves bankrupt could be guilty of conspiring with someone who had declared bankruptcy to hide assets of the bankrupt's estate from the bankruptcy trustee, even if a non-bankrupt party could not be convicted of the principal offense. *United States v. Rabinowich*, 238 U.S. 78, 86 (1915). [. . .]

Thus the firm baseline rule with respect to both conspiracy and complicity is that where the crime is so defined that only certain categories of persons, such as employees of a particular sort of entity, may commit the crime through their own acts, persons not within those categories can be guilty of conspiring to commit the crime or of the substantive crime itself as an accomplice. [. . .]

B. The Affirmative-Legislative-Policy Exception

[. . .]

Here the government concedes that the common law principle of conspiracy liability admits of exceptions but argues that the FCPA falls outside those exceptions. Hoskins, by contrast, contends that the FCPA demonstrates "an affirmative Congressional intent to exclude certain persons from liability" under the statute. Appellee's Br. at 20 (emphasis omitted). The parties' dispute focuses on two cases, *Gebardi v. United States*, 287 U.S. 112 (1932), and *United States v. Amen*, 831 F.2d 373 (2d Cir. 1987), and it is thus profitable to consider both in some detail.

1. Gebardi

In *Gebardi*, the Supreme Court considered a conviction under the Mann Act, a statute that imposes a penalty upon:

> any person who shall knowingly transport or cause to be transported, or aid or assist in obtaining transportation for, or in transporting, in interstate or foreign commerce any woman or girl for the purpose of prostitution or debauchery, or for any other immoral purpose.

287 U.S. at 118 (quoting 18 U.S.C. § 398 (1932)). The Mann Act criminalizes such transportation "with or without [the woman's] consent." *Id.* The government convicted both a man and woman for conspiracy to violate the Mann Act, on the theory that the woman conspired to transport a person—herself—merely by consenting to the man's transportation of her.

The Supreme Court reversed the convictions. The Court first noted that the Mann Act plainly covered cases where "the woman consents to her own transportation," rather than just cases where her transportation was forced, "[y]et it does not specifically impose any penalty upon her, although it deals in detail with the person by whom she is transported." *Id.* at 119. Because it would be obvious that women would participate in many violations of the statute, but the statute discussed no punishment for the women, the Court concluded that Congress intended for the women not to be liable for at least some class of violations of the Act. In particular, the Court determined it could not "infer that the mere acquiescence of the woman transported was intended to be condemned by the general language punishing those who aid and assist the transporter." *Id.* "The penalties of the statute are too clearly directed against the acts of the transporter" to support the view that Congress intended the woman always to be liable. *Id.*

Having decided that Congress intended to leave the woman unpunished when she merely acquiesced in her own illegal transportation, the Court next considered whether she could be convicted of conspiring to violate the statute in such circumstances. *Id.* at 119–23. The Court concluded that she could not. The Court emphasized, again, that "Congress set out in the Mann Act to deal with cases which frequently, if not normally, involve consent and agreement on the part of the woman to the forbidden transportation," but that "this acquiescence . . . was not made a crime under the Mann Act itself." *Id.* at 121. Consequently, the Court "perceive[d] in the failure of the Mann Act to condemn the woman's participation in those transportations which are effected with her mere consent, evidence of an affirmative legislative policy to leave her acquiescence unpunished." *Id.* at 123. [. . .]

2. Amen

We applied the reasoning of *Gebardi* in *United States v. Amen*, 831 F.2d 373 14 (2d Cir. 1987). In Amen, the Court considered the "continuing criminal enterprise" statute, 21 U.S.C. § 848, a provision "designed to reach the 'top brass' in the drug rings," *Garrett v. United States*, 471 U.S. 773, 781 (1985), or, to put it differently, the "kingpin" in an enterprise. *Amen*, 831 F.2d at 382. A defendant was convicted on the theory that he conspired with, and aided and abetted, an enterprise's "kingpin," even though the defendant himself was not the "kingpin." *Id.*

The government conceded that the statute did not apply to an enterprise's employees. *Id.* at 381. It nevertheless attempted to distinguish between "mere employees and those who otherwise 'help' the kingpin," and to argue that "non-employees who knowingly provide direct assistance to the head of the organization in supervising and operating the criminal enterprise can be . . . punished" for violating the "kingpin" statute under conspiracy and aiding-and abetting theories. *Id.* at 381–82.

We explained, however, that the government's theory "lack[ed] support in legislative history" and "seem[ed] totally unworkable" because many employees would provide greater assistance to the "kingpin" than non-employee third parties, and that it made little sense to extend the government's theory to one group if it concededly could not reach the other. *Id.* at 382. This application of complicity and conspiracy would disrupt the carefully defined statutory gradation of offenses; the low-level henchman would find himself subject to the more severe penalties applicable to the "kingpin." Because the Court determined that Congress did not intend for the "kingpin" statute to apply to the class of individuals involved in the case, the defendant's conviction was overturned. *Id.*

C. The Affirmative Legislative Policy Regarding the FCPA's Coverage

Applying the teachings of *Gebardi* and *Amen* to the FCPA, we find the "something more" that evinces an affirmative legislative policy to leave the category of defendants omitted from the statutory framework unpunished. In particular, the carefully tailored text of the statute, read against the backdrop of a well-established principle that U.S. law does not apply extraterritorially without express congressional authorization and a legislative history reflecting that Congress drew lines in the FCPA out of specific concern about the scope of extraterritorial application of the statute, persuades us that Congress did not intend for persons outside of the statute's carefully delimited categories to be subject to conspiracy or complicity liability. Our conclusion is consistent with the reasoning of other courts that have addressed this question. See *United States v. Castle*, 925 F.2d 831 (5th Cir. 1991); *United States v. Bodmer*, 342 F. Supp. 2d 176 7 (S.D.N.Y. 2004).

1. Text of the FCPA

[. . .] the FCPA contains no provision assigning liability to persons in the defendant's position—nonresident foreign nationals, acting outside American territory, who lack an agency relationship with a U.S. person, and who are not officers, directors, employees, or stockholders of American companies. See 15 U.S.C. §§ 78dd-1; 78dd-2; 78dd-3. [. . .] But the Court stated in *Gebardi*, much as it did in [*United States v.*] *Holte*, [236 U.S. 140 (1915)], that the Mann Act would cover the woman to the extent she were to "'aid or assist' someone else in transporting or in procuring transportation" for her. *Id.* Thus, the statute created at least some potential for liability where a woman did more than exhibiting "mere agreement . . . to the transportation." *Id.* In the present case, by contrast, there is no text that creates any liability whatsoever for the class of persons in question.

2. Structure of the FCPA

A second piece of evidence—the structure of the FCPA—confirms that Congress's omission of the class of persons under discussion was not accidental, but instead was a limitation created with surgical precision to limit its jurisdictional reach. The statute includes specific provisions covering every other possible combination of nationality, location, and agency relation, leaving excluded only nonresident foreign nationals outside American territory without an agency relationship with a U.S. person, and who are not officers, directors, employees, or stockholders of American companies. [. . .]

3. Legislative History

The question thus becomes whether there is "something more," a policy basis for Congress to exclude Hoskins's category of defendants from criminal liability—something akin to the Mann Act's decision not to punish the woman who is frequently, if not normally involved in the offense or 21 U.S.C. § 848's gradation of punishment based on leadership in a criminal enterprise. We think there is. "It is a basic premise of our legal system that, in general, United States law governs domestically but does not rule the world." *RJR Nabisco, Inc. v. European Cmty.*, 136 S. Ct. 2090, 2100 (2016) (internal quotation marks omitted). Courts will therefore not apply a U.S. law extraterritorially unless "the affirmative intention of the Congress [is] clearly expressed." *E.E.O.C. v. Arabian Am. Oil Co.*, 499 U.S. 244, 248 (1991). This principle stems from the risk of "unintended clashes between our laws and those of other nations which could result in international discord." *Id.* The legislative history of the FCPA makes it clear that Congress was attuned to these risks and carefully delimited the statute accordingly.

[. . .] Although it hoped to pass aggressive anti-bribery legislation, the [Carter] Administration recognized that a statute focusing on criminalization, rather than disclosure, required a delicate touch where extraterritorial conduct and foreign nationals were concerned. [. . .]

ii. Language of the OECD Convention

The government's argument—that Congress must have intended to cover foreign nationals acting abroad who are not employees or agents of an American company—focuses heavily on the OECD Convention with which Congress intended to make American law comply. The government first contends that the OECD Convention shows that the United States agreed to "take such measures as may be necessary to establish that it is a criminal offence under its law for *any person* intentionally to" engage in bribery of foreign officials. Convention on Combating Bribery and Foreign Public Officials in International Business Transactions art. 1.1, Dec. 17, 1997, S. Treaty Doc. No. 105-43, 37 I.L.M. 1 (1998) 7 (hereinafter "OECD Convention") (emphasis added). The government reads the words "any person" to apply expansively, including to nonresident foreign nationals who do not have direct connections to American businesses.

The government's argument falters for two reasons. First, the requirement that intentional bribery by "any person" is illegal is a highly general one; it does not require approval of the precise type of complicity or conspiracy theory involved in this case. Second, Congress carefully considered the "any person" language, and interpreted it in a way that does not involve the government's theory of liability here. The Senate's Committee Report first noted that the "any person" text was effectuated by expanding the FCPA to include conduct by foreign nationals within the United States:

> [T]he OECD Convention calls on parties to cover "any person"; the current FCPA covers only issuers with securities registered under the 1934 Securities Exchange Act and "domestic concerns." The Act, therefore, expands the FCPA's coverage to include all foreign persons who commit an act in furtherance of a foreign bribe while in the United States. [. . .]

The difficulty with the government's position, however, is that this provision covers the content of substantive law—the particular acts prohibited by it—not the law's jurisdictional aspects. A separate part of the Convention addresses jurisdictional questions. See OECD Convention art. 4. Moreover, adopting the government's view that the jurisdictional reach of the FCPA must be coterminous with that of bribery of American officials would transform the FCPA into a law that purports to rule the world. The defendant notes, for example, that bribery statutes covering American officials prohibit not only crimes with foreign national conspirators acting overseas, therefore, under the government's theory, these statutes likely cover situations in which the entire offense occurred overseas—that is, where there is no U.S. nexus at all except that the official to be bribed is stateside. The government does not dispute this point. Consequently, if read as the government proposes, the above-quoted provision of the Convention would cover conspiracies to bribe foreign officials consisting entirely of actions taken abroad. That is obviously not consistent with the legislation Congress wrote, and it cannot be what the OECD Convention requires.

III. The Second Object of the Conspiracy

Notwithstanding this Court's conclusion that Hoskins cannot be held liable under the FCPA if he is not in the categories of persons directly covered by the statute, the government argues that it was error for the district court to dismiss the second object of the conspiracy. We agree.

The second object alleges that Hoskins willfully conspired with various codefendants to, "while in the territory of the United States," commit acts in furtherance of bribing foreign officials in violation of Section 78dd-3. Indictment ¶ 26(b). The district court held that, because "it is undisputed that Mr. Hoskins never entered the territory of the United States and thus could not be prosecuted under this section," *Gebardi* barred the government from charging Hoskins with the second object of the conspiracy. *Hoskins*, 123 F. Supp. 3d at 327 n.14. This Court agrees that Hoskins cannot be directly liable under Section 78dd-3. However, the government "maintains that it still intends to prove that [Hoskins] acted as an agent of a domestic concern liable as a principal for the substantive FCPA counts charged in the indictment" in violation of Section 78dd-2. *Id.* Provided that the government makes this showing, there is no affirmative legislative policy to leave his conduct unpunished, nor is there an extraterritorial application of the FCPA. Accordingly, the government should be allowed to argue that, as an agent, Hoskins committed the first object by conspiring with employees and other agents of Alstom U.S. and committed the second object by conspiring with foreign nationals who conducted relevant acts while in the United States.

Accordingly, the district court erred in concluding that Hoskins was incapable of conspiring to violate Section 78dd-3 because he was never in the United States and we reverse this portion of the holding with instructions for the district court to reinstate the second object of the conspiracy.

Conclusion

We have considered the government's remaining arguments and find them to be without merit. Accordingly, the district court's orders are AFFIRMED in part and REVERSED in part.

B. International Framework

1. OECD Convention on Combating Bribery of Foreign Public Officials in International Business Transactions (1997)

The OECD took up and embraced the American approach of criminalizing corruption by corporations. Countries who joined the OECD Convention undertook to pass similar legislation in their own jurisdictions.

2. Inter-American Convention Against Corruption (1996)

Around the same time as the OECD Convention was enacted, the Inter-American Convention Against Corruption was adopted under the auspices of the Organization of American States.

3. United Nations Convention Against Corruption (2004)

Both the new Conventions required member states to punish overseas corporations found guilty of corruption, thereby illustrating the power of the U.S. Foreign Corrupt Practices Act. Arguably, however, the most effective achievement in the movement against corruption was the United Nations Convention Against Corruption. The UN Convention generally reflects the principles found in the United States FCPA but has broader scope and intent. In particular, it requires the signatory states to criminalize corruption and seek implementation on a global basis. The Convention has been signed by 175 countries, but the acknowledged challenge remains in implementation.

The UN Convention is comprehensive in scope, both in defining corruption and specifying the types of offenses to be criminalized in domestic legislation. The scope covers favours and preferential treatment as well as outright financial inducement. The Convention requires states to adopt an anti-corruption strategy and to set up anti-corruption bodies in their own jurisdictions, e.g., commissions or agencies independent from other government bodies.

In addition the Convention advocates for and invites states to criminalize unexplained wealth (Article 20: Illicit Enrichment). It also sets up an asset recovery system (Chapter V: Asset Recovery), enabling countries to recover money stolen under its jurisdiction. Successful examples of recovery include from the family of former President Ferdinand Marcos of the Philippines and from the Swiss deposits of former Nigerian President General Sani Abacha.

Chapter II
Preventive measures

Article 5. Preventive anti-corruption policies and practices

1. Each State Party shall, in accordance with the fundamental principles of its legal system, develop and implement or maintain effective, coordinated anti-corruption policies that promote the participation of society and reflect the principles of the

rule of law, proper management of public affairs and public property, integrity, transparency and accountability.

2. Each State Party shall endeavour to establish and promote effective practices aimed at the prevention of corruption.

3. Each State Party shall endeavour to periodically evaluate relevant legal instruments and administrative measures with a view to determining their adequacy to prevent and fight corruption.

4. States Parties shall, as appropriate and in accordance with the fundamental principles of their legal system, collaborate with each other and with relevant international and regional organizations in promoting and developing the measures referred to in this article. That collaboration may include participation in international programmes and projects aimed at the prevention of corruption.

Article 6. Preventive anti-corruption body or bodies

1. Each State Party shall, in accordance with the fundamental principles of its legal system, ensure the existence of a body or bodies, as appropriate, that prevent corruption by such means as:

(a) Implementing the policies referred to in article 5 of this Convention and, where appropriate, overseeing and coordinating the implementation of those policies;

(b) Increasing and disseminating knowledge about the prevention of corruption.

2. Each State Party shall grant the body or bodies referred to in paragraph 1 of this article the necessary independence, in accordance with the fundamental principles of its legal system, to enable the body or bodies to carry out its or their functions effectively and free from any undue influence. The necessary material resources and specialized staff, as well as the training that such staff may require to carry out their functions, should be provided.

3. Each State Party shall inform the Secretary-General of the United Nations of the name and address of the authority or authorities that may assist other States Parties in developing and implementing specific measures for the prevention of corruption.

Article 20. Illicit enrichment

Subject to its constitution and the fundamental principles of its legal system, each State Party shall consider adopting such legislative and other measures as may be necessary to establish as a criminal offence, when committed intentionally, illicit enrichment, that is, a significant increase in the assets of a public official that he or she cannot reasonably explain in relation to his or her lawful income.

Chapter V Asset recovery

Article 51. General provision

The return of assets pursuant to this chapter is a fundamental principle of this Convention, and States Parties shall afford one another the widest measure of cooperation and assistance in this regard.

Article 52.

Prevention and detection of transfers of proceeds of crime

1. Without prejudice to article 14 of this Convention, each State Party shall take such measures as may be necessary, in accordance with its domestic law, to require financial institutions within its jurisdiction to verify the identity of customers, to take reasonable steps to determine the identity of beneficial owners of funds deposited into high-value accounts and to conduct enhanced scrutiny of accounts sought or maintained by or on behalf of individuals who are, or have been, entrusted with prominent public functions and their family members and close associates. Such enhanced scrutiny shall be reasonably designed to detect suspicious transactions for the purpose of reporting to competent authorities and should not be so construed as to discourage or prohibit financial institutions from doing business with any legitimate customer.

2. In order to facilitate implementation of the measures provided for in paragraph 1 of this article, each State Party, in accordance with its domestic law and inspired by relevant initiatives of regional, interregional and multilateral organizations against money-laundering, shall:

> (a) Issue advisories regarding the types of natural or legal person to whose accounts financial institutions within its jurisdiction will be expected to apply enhanced scrutiny, the types of accounts and transactions to which to pay particular attention and appropriate account-opening, maintenance and record-keeping measures to take concerning such accounts; and
>
> (b) Where appropriate, notify financial institutions within its jurisdiction, at the request of another State Party or on its own initiative, of the identity of particular natural or legal persons to whose accounts such institutions will be expected to apply enhanced scrutiny, in addition to those whom the financial institutions may otherwise identify.

Article 53. Measures for direct recovery of property

Each State Party shall, in accordance with its domestic law:

(a) Take such measures as may be necessary to permit another State Party to initiate civil action in its courts to establish title to or ownership of property acquired through the commission of an offence established in accordance with this Convention;

(b) Take such measures as may be necessary to permit its courts to order those who have committed offences established in accordance with this Convention to pay compensation or damages to another State Party that has been harmed by such offences; and

(c) Take such measures as may be necessary to permit its courts or competent authorities, when having to decide on confiscation, to recognize another State

Party's claim as a legitimate owner of property acquired through the commission of an offence established in accordance with this Convention.

[. . .]

4. Implementing the United Nations Convention on Corruption: Recommended Legal Framework[319]

It is widely acknowledged that corruption is a major challenge to the development and wellbeing of many countries. As the UNDP Report, *Tackling Corruption, Transforming Lives*[320] (2008) underscores, corruption undermines democratic institutions, retards economic development and contributes to government instability. It attacks the foundation of democratic institutions by distorting electoral processes, perverting the rule of law and creating bureaucratic quagmires whose only reason for existence is the soliciting of bribes. Economic development is stunted because outside direct investment is discouraged and small businesses within the country often find it impossible to overcome the "startup costs" required because of corruption. In procurement and construction the ordinary people end up getting inferior quality goods as corruption advantages bribe givers at the expense of quality. Tragically, as former United Nations Secretary General Kofi Annan observed: "corruption hurts the poor disproportionately by diverting resources intended for development, undermining a government's ability to provide basic services, feeding inequality and injustice, and discouraging foreign investment and aid.[321]

Corruption has many other damaging effects; *inter alia*, weakened national institutions, inequitable social services, and blatant injustice in the courts, along with widespread economic inefficiency and unchecked environmental exploitation which again hits hardest at the poor, who often depend heavily on public services and the natural environment and are least able to pay bribes for essential services that should be theirs by right. Corruption distorts the marketplace by substituting corruption for competition in the allocation of businesses and business contracts. Instead of quality, price and service the willingness to pay bribes determines who wins and who loses contracts. Governments whose officials accept bribes are deprived of access to those who can supply the best and lowest cost of goods and services.

An essential element in any discussion on efforts to combat corruption is the legal and juridical framework within which the scourge of corruption is being fought. It is unquestionable that a sound legal framework though not the answer to all

319. Muna B. Ndulo, Occasional Paper, Southern African Institute for Policy and Research (Saipar) 2018.

320. United Nations Development Program (UNDP, Tackling Corruption, Transforming Lives: Accelerating Human Development in Asia and the Pacific, (2008).

321. *Ibid.*

corruption problems is crucial in the fight against corruption. In several countries, a number of instruments are typically put in place to fight corruption. These include the Anti-Corruption Commission Act, the Money Laundering Act, the Whistle Blower Act, The Plea Negotiations and Agreements Act, the Financial Intelligence Center Act, and the Forfeiture of the Proceeds of Crime Act. It is important to point out that in any event these pieces of legislation would be required as a result of a country's international and regional commitments as per the standards set by international and regional anti-corruption instruments that a country is expected to ratify. These include: the United Nations Convention against Corruption[322] and for an African Country the African Union (AU Convention on the Prevention and Combating of Corruption.[323] And for a Latin American Country, the Latin American Convention on Corruption.

The need to effectively curb corruption through legislation and effective institutions goes without saying because of the threat corruption poses to good governance, democracy and the rule of law and ultimately, it's potential to hinder economic, social and political development. As the South African Constitutional Court observed with respect to the impact of corruption on economic development in South Africa: *"There can be no gainsaying that corruption threatens to fell at the knees virtually everything we hold dear and precious in our hard won constitutional order. It blatantly undermines the democratic ethos, the institutions of democracy, the rule of law and the foundational values of our nascent constitutional project. It fuels maladministration and public fraudulence and imperils the capacity of the state to fulfill its obligations to respect, protect, promote and fulfill all the rights enshrined in the bill of rights. When corruption and organized crime flourish, sustainable development and economic growth are stunted. And in turn, the stability and security of society is put at risk."*[324] Indeed, the demonstrated inability of many resource-rich states to attain a decent level of development commensurate with their resources is attributable to the corruption plague that infects many of them. Although its prevalence may differ from one state to the other, no state can claim to be completely immune from corruption.[325]

---

322. The United Nations Convention against Corruption was recognized by the General Assembly in its resolution 55/61 of 4 December 2000 as an effective international legal instrument against corruption, independent of the United Nations Convention against Transnational Organized Crime.

323. The *African Union Convention* on *Preventing and Combating Corruption* (*AU Convention*) was adopted in Maputo on 11 July 2003.

324. *In the Matter between: Hugh Glenister and President of South Africa, Minister for Safety and Security, Minister for Justice and Constitutional Development, Director of Public Prosecutions, South African Government and Helen Suzman Foundation*, Constitutional Court of South Africa, Case CCT 48/10, Para. 166.

325. W. Paati Ofosu-Amaah et al., Combating Corruption; a Comparative Review of Selected Legal Aspects of State Practice and Major International Initiatives (The World Bank 1999) vi.

The deleterious impact of corruption on societies and the need to combat it effectively is widely recognized in public discourse. It is also recognized in regional[326] and international conventions.[327] In a statement preceding the text of the United Nations Convention against Corruption former United Nations Secretary-General, Kofi Annan observed: "*The evil phenomenon is found in all countries big and small, rich and poor but it is in the developing world that its effects are most destructive. Corruption hurts the poor disproportionately by diverting funds intended for development, undermining a government's ability to provide basic services, feeding inequality and injustice, and discouraging foreign investments and aid. Corruption is a key element in economic under performance, and a major obstacle to poverty alleviation and development.*"[328]

The preamble to the African Union Convention acknowledges that corruption undermines accountability and transparency in the management of public affairs as well as social-economic development on the continent.[329] Africa has suffered particularly badly from corruption because the proceeds of corruption tend to be banked or spent outside of the continent. Capital flight is possibly Africa's biggest financial problem. The African Union estimates that $48 billion a year leaves the continent because of corruption.[330] This represents a quarter of the Continent's GDP. Furthermore, in Africa's case the outflow of illicit money tends to be permanent.[331] The money that leaves the continent through corruption typically does not return and is instead invested in real estate and businesses abroad.

From a functional perspective, the different techniques and institutions adopted in order to combat corruption can be broadly categorized as either preventive or curative measures.[332] Preventive instruments are upstream legal rules and norms of good behavior conducive to the establishment of a corruption free environment, while curative measures seek to provide appropriate remedies to sanction acts of corruption.[333] States adopt preventive instruments to deter corruption through direct and indirect techniques which are most appropriate to their economic, cultural and sociopolitical situation.[334] Indirect techniques include allusion to national commitment, leadership codes, declaration of assets, codes of conduct and the

326. Southern African Development Community Protocol against Corruption adopted on 14 August 2001.

327. United Nations Convention against Corruption, 2004 and African Union Convention on Preventing and Combating Corruption, 2004.

328. http://www.undodc.org/documents/treaties/UNCA/Publications/Convention/08-50026E.pdf.

329. The AU Convention was adopted on 11 July 2003.

330. All African Parliamentary Group (AAPG), *The Other Side of the Coin: The UK and Corruption in Africa*, 2006, London, p12-14.

331. *Ibid.*

332. W. Paati Ofosu-Amaah et al., Combating Corruption; a Comparative Review of Selected Legal Aspects of State Practice and Major International Initiatives (The World Bank 1999) vi.

333. *Id.*

334. *Id.* P. 5.

media.[335] Direct preventive techniques on the other hand pertain to financial management, procurement regulations and laws, and campaign finance laws and aim at transparency and accountability of public figures.[336]

The curative approach refers to the legal framework adopted to combat corruption. One of the most basic anti-corruption measures expected of a country which has an anti-corruption policy is to ensure that various corrupt acts are outlawed-either as part of general legislation, or as laws against specific forms of corruption. Legislation can also cover issues such as money laundering, public procurement and ethical codes. This has to be supplemented by the protection of whistle blowers-individuals who disclose information leading to the exposure of corruption. In the interest of avoiding complications and inconsistency, anti-corruption legislation needs to be easy to understand and simple to apply.

However, in as much as the instruments themselves are important, arguably the adequacy of anti-corruption legislation depends heavily on the availability of effective, transparent and capable enforcement institutions and complementary legal and institutional reforms aimed at prevention. In this regard, complementary laws such as freedom of information and reformed libel laws should be resorted to. Codes of conduct and ethical standards are aimed at ensuring the honesty and technical competence of the enforcers. It should not be forgotten that a government determined to eradicate corruption must not only enact legislation, promote civic values and establish institutions and agencies, but must also denote formal political commitment to implement legislation comprehensively, impartially and sustainably. For the fight against corruption to succeed government efforts have to go beyond legislation. The fight against corruption requires strong institutions, the provision of adequate resources to those institutions and above all the existence of a determined political will to end corruption in all its forms regardless of the perpetrator. In this article we look at the main issues in anti-corruption legislation. We will cite examples of legislation from a number of countries to illustrate the main features of corruption legislation.

International Conventions and Anti-Corruption Legal Framework

The international community has long recognized the need for a global, legally-binding instrument dealing with corruption.[337] That goal was realized—in 2003 when the members of the United Nations adopted the UN Convention against Corruption (UNCAC). The Convention entered into force in December 2005. As of August 2018, 186 parties have ratified or acceded to the Convention. The UN Office on Drugs and Crime (UNODC) has developed a Legislative Guide for the Implementation of the United Nations Conventions against Corruption. The UNODC, with

335. *Id.*

336. *Id.* P. 21.

337. W. Paatii Ofusu-Amaah, Raj Soopramanien & Kishor Uprety, Combating Corruption: A Comparative Review of Selected Aspects of State Practice and Major International Initiatives, 1999, p.3.

the UN Interregional Crime and Justice Research Institute (UNICRI), prepared a Technical Guide to provide practical support to State Parties in implementing the main provisions under the UN Convention. The United Nations Convention against corruption requires state parties to develop and implement or maintain effective, coordinated anti-corruption policies that promote the participation of society and reflect the principles of the rule of law, proper management of public affairs and public property, integrity, transparency and accountability.[338] Similarly, the African Union Convention on Preventing and Combating Corruption states its objectives as among others to promote and strengthen the development in Africa by each state party, of mechanisms required to prevent, detect, punish and eradicate corruption and related offences in the public and private sectors.[339]

The UNCAC is the most comprehensive international anti-corruption convention to date as it covers the broadest range of corruption offences, including the active and passive bribery of domestic and foreign public officials, obstruction of justice, illicit enrichment, and embezzlement.[340] In addition, the UNCAC addresses preventive measures, international co-operation, and technical assistance.[341] One of the most important features of the Convention is its provisions on asset recovery, which is expressly recognized as "a fundamental principle of the Convention."[342] Several provisions specify the forms of co-operation and assistance, e.g. embezzled public funds that have been confiscated must be returned to the requesting state.[343] The adoption of some of the provisions of the Convention are mandatory (e.g., adoption of the offences of active and passive bribery of a national public official, and the active bribery of foreign public officials and officials of public international organizations); some however, are optional and only require signatories to consider their implementation. The UNCAC contemplates a process for the periodic review of the implementation of the Convention by States Parties. The States Parties discussed the issue in the first Conference of States Parties in December 2006 and will take further decisions in this regard.[344]

The United Nations Convention imposes an obligation on each member state party to establish and provide effective practices aimed at the prevention of corruption.[345] It further requires the existence of a body or bodies tasked with the prevention of corruption in all the territories of state parties to the Countries.[346] Moreover, Article 6(2) provides that: "each state party shall grant the body or bodies referred to in paragraph 1 of this article the necessary independence, in accordance with the

338. United Nations Convention against Corruption, article 5 (1).
339. African Union Convention on Preventing and Combating Corruption, article 2.
340. United Nations Convention against Corruption, articles 15, 16, & 17.
341. *Ibid.*, articles 43, 44, 46, & 48.
342. United Nations Convention against Corruption, article 51.
343. *Ibid.*, articles 51, 54, 55 & 57.
344. State Parties, Conference, Dead Sea, Jordan, 2006.
345. United Nations Convention against Corruption, article 2.
346. *Ibid*, article 6 (1).

fundamental principles of its legal system, to enable the body or bodies to carry out its or their functions effectively and free from any undue influence. The necessary material resources and specialized staff, as well as the training that such staff may require to carry out their functions, should be provided." The AU Convention provides in Article 5(3) that states parties undertake to "establish, maintain and strengthen independent national anti-corruption authorities or agencies" Article 20 (4) reinforces the importance of independence in a more direct terms, it states that "The national authorities or agencies shall be allowed the necessary independence and autonomy, to be able to carry out their duties effectively."

The OECD[347] has identified the main criteria for effective anti-corruption agencies to be independent, specialized and to receive adequate training and resources. The OECD report defined independence as follows: "independence primarily means that the anti-corruption bodies should be shielded from undue political interference. To this end, genuine political will to fight corruption is the key to the prerequisite to the establishment of independent institutions. Such political will must be embedded in a comprehensive anti-corruption strategy. The level of independence can vary according to specific needs and conditions. Experience suggests that it is the structural and operational autonomy that is important, along with a clear basis and mandate for a special body, department or unit. This is particularly important for law enforcement bodies. Transparent procedures for appointment and removal of the director and other officers running anti-corruption regimes together with proper resources management and internal controls are important elements to prevent undue interference."[348] The report further adds that: "one of the prominent and mandatory features of specialized institutions is not full independence but rather an adequate level of structural and operational autonomy secured through institutional and legal mechanisms aimed at preventing undue political interference as well as promoting "pre-emptive obedience". In short, "independence" first of all entails de-politicization of anti-corruption institutions. Adequate level of independence or autonomy depends on the type and mandate of an anti-corruption institution. Institutions in charge of investigation and prosecution of corruption normally require a higher level of independence than those charged with preventive functions."[349]

The obligations that would result from a country acceding to these conventions are clear and unequivocal. Firstly they impose an obligation to: adopt such legislative and other measures as may be necessary to establish as a criminal offence, when committed intentionally, the promise, offering, or giving to a foreign official or an official of a public international organization, directly or indirectly, of an undue advantage, for the official himself or herself or another person or entity, in order that the official act or refrain from acting in the exercise of his or her official

347. OECD: Specialized Anti-corruption Institutions: Review of Models (OECD Report).
348. http://www.oecd.org/dataoecd/7/4/39971975.pdf
349. *Id.*, p. 17.

duties, in order to obtain or retain business or other undue advantage in relation to the conduct of international business; and adopting such legislative and other measures as may be necessary to establish as criminal offences, when committed intentionally:[350] (a) The promise, offering or giving to a public official or any other person, directly or indirectly, of an undue advantage in order that the public official or the person abuse his or her real or supposed influence with a view to obtaining from an administration or public authority of the State Party an undue advantage for the original instigator of the act or for any other person; (b) The solicitation or acceptance by a public official or any other person, directly or indirectly, of an undue advantage for himself or herself or for another person in order that the public official or the person abuse his or her real or supposed influence with a view to obtaining from an administration or public authority of the state party an undue advantage.[351] Further they impose on a member state a duty in international law to create an anti-corruption agency that has the necessary independence to be an effective instrument in the fight against corruption. A member state would therefore under international law be under an obligation to pass legislation implementing the conventions in its domestic law. In the following sections the paper will examine the features of a number of pieces of legislation that are typically adopted to fight corruption.

The Anti-Corruption Commission Act

a. Suggested Scope of the Act

According to the (UNCAC), the Anti-Corruption Commission Act should create an agency to fight corruption in a country. This should be an autonomous agency. The Commission should be a body corporate with perpetual succession and a common seal, capable of suing and of being sued in its corporate name and with power to do all such acts and things as a body corporate may do or perform by law. It's functions should be to: Prevent and take necessary and effective measures for the prevention of corruption in public and private bodies, including, in particular, measures for: (a) Examining the practices and procedures of public and private bodies in order to facilitate the discovery of opportunities of corrupt practices and secure the revision of methods of work or procedures which, in the opinion of the Commission, may be prone or conducive to corrupt practices;[352] (b) advise both public and private bodies on ways and means of preventing corrupt practices, and on changes in methods of work or procedures of such public bodies and private bodies compatible with the effective performance of their duties, which the Commission considers necessary to reduce the likelihood of the occurrence of corrupt practices;[353] (c) disseminate information of the evil and dangerous effects of corrupt practices on society; (d) creation of committees in various national institutions for monitoring corruption

350. Article 16.1 United Nations Convention against Corruption.

351. Article 18, *Ibid.*

352. The Anti-Corruption Commission Act of Zambia, section, 6.

353. *Ibid*, section 6(1)(a)(ii).

in the institutions;[354] and (e) enlist and foster public confidence and support against corrupt practices.[355]

The agency should also be authorized to: (a) initiate, receive, and investigate complaints of alleged or suspected corrupt practices, and, (b) subject to the directions of the Director of Public Prosecutions, prosecute offences under the Anti-Corruption Commission Act; and such other offences under any other written law as may have come to the notice of the commission during the investigation of an offence under the Act. It is a good approach that the Commission is empowered to investigate other offences, besides corruption and this should be emphasized in its operations. This is extremely important because a corruption crime may not exist in isolation. It may occur and be intermingled with other crimes such as cheating, commercial crimes, etc. Therefore any anti-corruption agency must have the power to question suspects on the full range of offences, otherwise there will be severe limits placed on investigations and the accused person will probably be able to get away from the punishment that he or she deserves. This is not to suggest that the Commissions should have the same powers as the police. The work of the Commission should complement the work of the police. It is to investigate any conduct of any public officer which, in the opinion of the Commission, may be connected with or conducive to corrupt practices; be the lead agency in matters of corruption; cooperate with other institutions authorized to investigate, prosecute, prevent, and combat corrupt practices so as to implement an integrated approach to the eradication of corruption; consult, cooperate, and exchange information with appropriate bodies of other countries that are authorized to conduct inquiries or investigations in relation to corrupt practices; and do all such things as are incidental or conducive to the attainment of its functions.

b. Recovery of Assets

It is important that the Anti-Corruption Act contains provisions on recovery of assets this is required by the United Nations Convention provisions (Article 31). Investigating officers should be allowed in the course of an investigation into an offence, upon obtaining a warrant, to seize property where he or she reasonably suspects that it was derived from corrupt practices or is the subject matter of an offence or is evidence relating to an offence. The provisions of the UN Convention on asset recovery have been praised as being the "highlights" or fundamental principles of the convention.[356] This can be inferred from the fact that as per the preamble of the convention, state parties undertake to prevent, detect and deter in a more effective manner international transfers of illicitly acquired assets and to strengthen international cooperation

354. *Ibid.*, section 6(1)(a)(iii).

355. *Ibid.*, section 6(1)(a)(v).

356. Institute for Security Studies, Handbook: A Comparative Analysis: SADC Protocol Against Corruption (2001), AU Convention on Preventing and Combating Corruption (2003) &UN Convention Against Corruption (2003) (November 2004) 84.

in asset recovery.[357] As asserted by the UN Office on Drugs and Crime, provisions on asset recovery are particularly important for developing countries because plundering of the nation's wealth and resources are attributable to the high level corruption and they are indispensable for reconstruction and rehabilitation.[358] Article 31 of the UN Convention states that each state party has the responsibility to take measures necessary to enable confiscation of proceeds of crime derived from offences established in accordance with the convention and property used in or destined for use of offences in the convention. In accordance with this requirement, measures need to be taken to enable the identification, tracing, freezing or seizure of these items. Moreover where such proceeds of crime have been transformed or converted, in part or in full, into other property, such property shall be liable to the measures referred to in this article instead of the proceeds or where the proceeds have been intermingled with property acquired from legitimate sources, such property shall, without prejudice to any powers relating to freezing or seizure, be liable to confiscation up to the assessed value of the intermingled proceeds.

The Unexplained Wealth/Illicit Enrichment Provisions

a. Overview of Concept

Corruption laws adopted by several countries involve the introduction of special rules of evidence, the effect of which is to ease the burden of proof resting on the prosecution and in so doing increase the odds of securing convictions. These provisions are generally referred to as "unexplained wealth" provisions. They generally require public servants to explain sudden unexplained wealth. This section critically evaluates the role of unexplained wealth provisions, the consistence of such provisions with the constitutional rights against self-incrimination and presumption of innocence. In the main it is argued that these provisions mandated by international conventions are useful in the fight to combat corruption and are consistent with and do not violate the right against self-incrimination and presumption of innocence. They are a legally appropriate technique and deal with corruption's increasingly complexity.

b. International Conventions and Unexplained Wealth Provisions

Article 20 of the United Nations Convention against Corruption provides that: "subject to its constitution and the fundamental principles of its legal system, each state Party shall consider adopting such legislative measures as may be necessary to establish as a criminal offence, when committed intentionally, illicit enrichment, that is, a significant increase in the assets of a public official that he or she cannot reasonably explain in relation to his or her lawful income". In similar vein the African Union Convention on Preventing and Combating Corruption,[359] in article 8 provides that:

---

357. Institute for Security Studies, Handbook: A Comparative Analysis: SADC Protocol Against Corruption (2001), AU Convention on Preventing and Combating Corruption (2003) &UN Convention Against Corruption (2003) (November 2004) 84.

358. See http://www.unodc.org/unodc/en/crime_convention_corruption.html.

359. African Union Convention on Prevention and Combating Corruption, adopted by the 2nd Ordinary Session of the Assembly of the Union, Maputo, 11 July 2003.

"(1) subject to the provisions of their domestic law, state parties undertake to adopt necessary measures to establish under their laws an offence of illicit enrichment; (2) for state parties that have established illicit enrichment as an offence under their domestic law, such offence shall be considered an act of corruption or a related offence for the purposes of this Convention." Several other international Conventions and national legislation take a similar position. The Inter-American Convention Against Corruption, in article 9 states that: "Subject to its constitution and the fundamental principles of its legal system, each state party that has not yet done so shall take the necessary measures to establish under its laws as an offence a significant increase in the assets of a government official that he cannot reasonably explain in relation to his lawful earnings during the performance of his functions."[360]

Hong Kong is said to be the home of the most effective and best known of all anti-corruption agencies. With the complete inclusion of the United Nations Convention article 20 concept of "illicit enrichment" in its anti-corruption legal framework, the Independent Commission Against Corruption (ICACs) power to prosecute "illicit enrichment without having to prove specific acts of corruption constitutes the core of its effectiveness in achieving the UNCAs aims. Unexplained wealth laws are relatively recent development in the world in the fight against corruption.[361] Those who object to the illicit enrichment provisions do so on the grounds that they are inconsistent with the constitution and violate the presumption of innocence, relaxed the normal burden on the prosecution to establish a case beyond reasonable doubt and violated the right of an accused person to remain silent. Article 20 of the United Nations Convention against Corruption, also acted as detection mechanism since it requires the accused to account for his or her incommensurate standard of living and to explain the disproportion between the amount of pecuniary resources and other assets in his or her control at the charge date and his total official emoluments up to the same date.

Unexplained wealth/illicit enrichment is defined as a significant increase in the assets of a public official that he or she cannot reasonably explain in relation to his or her lawful income. By placing the onus of proof on the individual whose wealth is in dispute the concept raises a presumption that the wealth was obtained corruptly. In other words, in jurisdictions with unexplained wealth laws, it is not necessary to demonstrate beyond reasonable doubt that the wealth has been obtained by criminal activity, but instead, the state places the onus on an individual to prove that their wealth was acquired by legal means. It is "a legal device that aims at overcoming the difficulties of meeting the burden of proof in corruption-related offenses.[362] It must, however, be emphasized that even though the accused party bears the bur-

---

360. Inter-American Convention against Corruption, adopted, March 29, 1996.

361. They are widely in use in Australia, where they are in place in Northern Territory, Western Australia, New South Wales and South Austria. See Treads & Issues in Crime and Criminal Justice, Australian Government, No. 395, July 2010.

362. Guillermo Jorge, The Romanian Legal Framework in Illegal Enrichment, ABA, 2007 at Para 167.

den of proof on this one issue, the standard of proof that applies in the case of the accused is merely an evidential burden of adducing sufficient evidence to rebut the legal presumption created by such a provision which operates in favor of the prosecution. The following sections evaluate the arguments that are advanced against the "unexplained/illicit enrichment" provisions especially those relating to shifting the burden of proof, the right to silence and look at the practice in other jurisdictions. The discussion below will demonstrate that the presumption of innocence and the right to silence are not absolute rights. On the contrary, inroads into these rights have been permitted subject to specific limitations.

c. The Reversal of the Burden of Proof Argument

In the last two decades, there has been a revolution in criminal law and in law enforcement theory. Since the 18th century and until a few decades ago law has been governed by a relatively steady paradigm centered at determining under what conditions the state would be able to deprive a human being of his fundamental right to freedom. In the era of what others have termed "acquisitive crimes" (crimes that generate profits) however, there has been a shift from traditional theory towards a new "profit oriented paradigm of criminal law." This approach is concerned about confiscation of ill-gotten gains.

Fundamental rights provisions in most constitutions around the world guarantee the presumption of innocence in criminal trials. The fundamental rights provisions on due process and fair hearing have been sought to be deployed by persons accused of corruption by claiming that their refusal to explain the sources of their wealth was justified by the constitutional right to remain silent and not incriminate themselves. The effect of this is to impose an almost impossible task for the prosecution to discharge its burden of proving its case beyond reasonable doubt. The idea of reversing the burden of proof was first internationalized in the 1988 United Nations Convention against the Illicit Traffic of Narcotic Drugs and Psychotropic Substances. Article 5 of the Convention required states to confiscate proceeds of drug trafficking as well as to internationally cooperate to that end. Article 7 provided that: "state parties consider ensuring that the onus of proof be reversed regarding the lawful origin of alleged proceeds or other property liable to confiscation, to the extent that action is consistent with principles of its domestic law and with the nature of judicial proceedings and other proceedings." Guillermo argues that the underlying theory is quite straightforward: increasing the effectiveness of legal instruments to detect, seize and confiscate ill-gotten gains will reduce the motivation for engaging in these criminal activities. When connected to criminal organizations, it will also reduce the operative capital for continuing the illegal activities."[363]

There are several countries of different legal traditions that have adopted and implemented this approach in their anti-corruption legislation. France has recently

363. Guillermo Jorge, *The Romanian Legal Framework in Illegal Enrichment*, ABA, 2007, at Para 21.

introduced in its Penal Code several offences allowing the reversal of the burden of proof as a central element of the crime. Article 225-6, paragraph 3 of the Criminal Code against profiting from prostitution businesses criminalizes any person "being unable to account for an income compatible with one's lifestyle while living with a person engaged in prostitution or while entertaining habitual relationship with one or more persons engaged in prostitution. Romania had illicit enrichment legislation: the Romanian law 18/1968 (former) which was an illicit enrichment law that applied to *all citizens* (not just public officials). The burden of proof was reversed if data showed a "clear disproportion" between a person's wealth and income. The person had 10 days to justify the disproportion.[364] The current Romanian law 115/1996 aims to control illicit wealth of only certain classes of public officials. Creates a disclosure system—disclosure of official's assets (and spouse's and dependent children) required upon taking office and upon leaving office (or every four years). The burden of proof is still on the prosecution, but this makes it easier for prosecution to prove (w/o having to resort to more intrusive means of investigation—i.e., wiretapping, etc.) In Italy section 12 of Legislative Decree 306 of 8 June 1992 adopts a similar approach for drug trafficking and organized criminal offences. The onus of proving that the assets are legitimate is placed on the defendant if the prosecution established that the assets are not commensurate with the defendant's income or economic resources. The Dutch Criminal Code article 36 allows a partial reversal of the burden of proof with regard to the illicit origin of the proceeds of several crimes. On a constitutional challenge based on the right to innocence, the Dutch Supreme Court held that the provision is compatible with the presumption of innocence of Article 6 (2) of the European Convention on Human Rights. The most important factor considered by the Dutch Supreme Court in reaching this conclusion was the fact that "once a presumption of criminal origin of proceeds has been established by the prosecution, the defense can always reverse the presumption. A mere denial will not be sufficient, however. Once the criminal origin of the proceeds has been made probable, the burden to rebut, not simply deny this presumption lies with the defense.

The important point to remember is that the presumption does not operate automatically but has to be established by the prosecution by demonstrating that the criminal origin of the proceeds though not proven is probable. Several Australian states have enacted what in Australia are termed the "unexplained wealth laws (illicit enrichment)". Western Australia was the first Australian jurisdiction to introduce unexplained wealth laws with the Criminal Property Confiscation Act, 2000. The Australian legislation requires courts to make an order seizing property if satisfied that a person's total wealth is greater that the lawfully acquired wealth. Courts have minimal discretion in making such orders, reversal of the onus of proof in favor of the prosecution providing that "any property, service, advantage or benefit that is a constituent of the respondent's wealth is presumed not to have been lawfully

364. *Ibid*, Para, 39.

acquired unless the respondent establishes the contrary. The Australian legislation is broad and covers more than just public officials. The European Court of Human Rights has made an important ruling in this matter. The Court has observed that generally the prosecution must prove the accused person's guilt beyond reasonable doubt. Such abstract formulation is more or less far from being absolute the court observed. In *Salabiaku v. France*[365] The European Court of Human rights stated: "in principle the contracting states may under certain conditions, penalize a simple or objective fact as such irrespective of whether it results from criminal intent or from negligence. These are not cases of reversal burden of proof, but rather cases where the prosecution is not obliged to prove the subjective part showing the will and knowledge elements of the crime."

A slightly different case is that of regulatory offences, in these cases usually once the prosecution has proven the existence of a duty, the accused has a reverse burden to prove that he had complied with the duty. An example of this is driving license cases. Further, when issuing confiscation orders, being against an accused or a third party, there may be a reversal of the burden of proof with regard to the assets that are the proceeds of crime. With regard to offences that partially reverse the burden of proof, which is the case of illicit enrichment, the European Court observed: "presumptions of fact or of law operate in every legal system clearly the convention does not prohibit such presumptions in principle." It does, however, require a state to remain within certain limits. It requires the state to confine this approach within reasonable limits which take into account the importance of what is at stake to maintain the rights of the defense.[366]

The House of Lords has interpreted this approach as authorizing a "proportionality" test. Common law jurisdictions use a "proportionality test" when carving out statutory exceptions to the presumption of innocence. In *R. v. Lambert*,[367] the court took the view that: "legislative interference with the presumption of innocence requires justification and must not be greater than is necessary. The principle of proportionality must be observed." Lord Steyn stated: "in a constitutional democracy limited iron roads into a presumption of innocence may be justified. The approach to be adopted as stated by the European Court of Human Rights in *Silabiaku v. France* (1988) is the proportionality test. It follows that a legislative interference with the presumption of innocence requires justification. The principle of proportionality must be observed." Canadian courts have adopted a similar approach. The Canadian Supreme Court: *In R. v. Chaulk*, [[1990] 3 SCR 1303,] drew a two prong test: "1. The objective of the impugned provision must be of sufficient importance to warrant overriding a constitutionally protected right of freedom; it must [be] related to concerns which are pressing and substantial in a free and democratic society before it can be characterized as sufficiently important and 2. Assuming that a sufficiently

365. A 141-A Para. 27 (1988).

366. *Salabiaku v. France*, A Para 28 (1988).

367. All ER 577-672, Para. 34.

important objective has been established, the means chosen to achieve the objective must pass a proportionality test; that is to say they must: (a) be "rationally connected" to the objective and not be arbitrary, unfair or based on irrational considerations; (b) impair the right in question "as little as possible", and (c) be such that their effects on the limitations of rights and freedoms are proportional to the objective." A similar approach has been adopted in South Africa. The South African Supreme Court, in, In re. *S v. Coetzee*[368] observed that such presumption should be open to challenge and held that the presumption of innocence must be balanced with the advantage for the prosecution.

Further support can be found in national constitutions among several African constitutions. In African Constitutions, there is often an "out" for the presumption of innocence. In Nigeria it is provided that: "Every person who is charged with a criminal offence . . ." Shall be presumed to be innocent until he is proved guilty; Provided that nothing in this section shall invalidate any law by reason only that the law imposes upon any such person the burden of proving particular facts." Nig. Const. § 36(5). The Unites States of America has reverse burden of proof for criminal asset forfeiture—confiscation of property that is alleged to be criminal proceeds or an instrument of criminality. "[T]he burden shifts to the defendant once the government shows that the defendant acquired the property around the time of the crime, and no other likely source existed."[369] In sum, directly holding officials criminally liable for unexplained increases in their wealth has considerable support in the jurisprudence of several countries.

d. Right to Silence

Another argument often used to resist the illicit enrichment provisions is that they are a violation of the right to silence. In most constitutions an accused person is guaranteed a right not to incriminate him or herself when charged with a crime. The privilege against self-incrimination is made up of the right to silence or the right to remain silent and the right not to be compelled to produce exculpatory evidence. The right protects the accused against improper compulsion by the authorities, reducing the risk of miscarriage of justice. In principle, the prosecution must prove its case without resort to evidence obtained through coercion or oppression. Any compulsion to produce incriminating evidence becomes an infringement of the right to silence. This right is not absolute. All states and the European Human Rights Court have recognized the fact that the right is not absolute. One of the most important decisions made on this issue is the European Court of Human Rights decision of *Murray v. UK.*[370] In this case the court observed: "on the one hand it is self-evident that it is incompatible with the immunities under consideration to base a conviction solely or mainly on the accused's silence or on a refusal to answer questions or to give evidence himself. On the other hand it seems equally obvious that

368. *S v. Coetzee & Others* (CCT 50795), 1997 (4) BCLR437.

369. http://www.law.cornell.edu/background/forfeiture.

370. No. 18731/9/ (8 February 1996).

these immunities cannot and should not prevent the fact that the accused's silence in situations which clearly call for an explanation from him be taken into account in assessing the persuasiveness of evidence adduced by the prosecution. Whenever the line between these two extremes is to be drawn, it follows from this understanding of the right to silence that the question whether the right is absolute must be answered in the negative."

The unexplained wealth laws have three objectives, namely: (a) to deter those who contemplate criminal activity by reducing the possibility of gaining or keeping a profit from that activity; (b) to prevent crime by diminishing the capacity of offenders to finance any future criminal activity that they might engage in and (c) to remedy the unjust enrichment of criminals who profit at society's expense. In Australia the Australian Federal Police noted that investigations can often be frustrated through lack of evidence against people with significant wealth and no apparent source of legitimate income. Laws of this nature, if applied successfully, remove the financial incentive to commit corruption. In a submission to the Australian Senate Legal and Constitutional Affairs Committee (SLCAC), Professor Rod Broadhurst observed: "tainted or unexplained wealth may be the only means to reliably identify criminal entrepreneurs whose involvement in crime is usually indirect in terms of actual commission. Indeed, unexplained wealth laws are one of the most effective means to investigate/prosecute the otherwise very difficult offences of corruption and bribery."[371]

e. Due Process Arguments

There are a number of other arguments against unexplained wealth provisions. Clarke for example argues that in a democratic state depriving citizens of privately-owned assets is a highly intrusive act of state.[372] Such conduct is *prima facie* in conflict with norms such as the sanctity of property ownership, freedom of citizens from unnecessary interference by the state and the right to privacy. The other argument is that the reversal of the onus of proof raises the risk of confiscating assets from innocent people. Many of the foregoing concerns can be ameliorated through appropriate legislative drafting and administrative processes. The argument that the unexplained wealth provisions undermine the due process of law in that it relaxes the normal burden on the prosecution to establish the offense: beyond reasonable doubt is not entirely correct. The question is not so much one of the burden of proof; but the appropriate evidence to establish the offense. If you define the offense of taking bribes based on receipt of a payment coupled with other elements and not on proving the corrupt intention of what is in the head of the bribe-taker, there is no infringement on the accusers right to a fair trial.

371. Senate Legal and Constitutional Affairs Committee (SAGAC), 2009. Report on the Crimes Legislation Amendment (Serious and Organized Crime,) Bill 2009, Canberra: SACAC.

372. Clarke B. *A man's home is his castle or is it? How to take people's homes without convicting them of anything: The Criminal Property Confiscation Act 2000* (WA) Criminal Law Journal 28: 263–286.

The aim of pursuing the corrupt through effective detection and investigation is enabled by legislation that embodies United Nations Convention against Corruption Article 20 because it provides the power to prosecute "illicit enrichment" without having to prove specific acts of corruption. In the Tanzanian Prevention of Corruption Act the appropriate authorities are empowered by notice in writing to require any public officer to provide a full and true account of properties that such public officer may have or have had in his possession, including a true account of how such property has been acquired. Failure to provide such a full and true account as required in the notice is in itself an offence punishable with imprisonment of up to two years.[373] Moreover where a public officer is found to be or to have been in possession of property, or to have received the benefit of services that he is reasonably suspected of having corruptly acquired or received while holding public office, he may be charged with an offence under the Act. He is also required to satisfy a court of law that he did not corruptly acquire the property or receive the benefit of services as the case maybe, failing which he may be deemed to have corruptly acquired the property or received the benefit of services, as the case may be. Similarly in the Malawi Corrupt Practices Act there are provisions pertaining to a public officer who maintains a standard of living, or has pecuniary resources or property, that is not commensurate with his official emoluments, past or present, or other known sources of income, or is in receipt of the benefits of services which he is reasonably suspected of having received corruptly or under circumstances that may amount to an offense under the Act.[374] Although the Act does not appear to make it an offense as such for a public officer to maintain such a standard of living or to have such pecuniary resources or property, or to be in receipt of such benefit of services, it does require the officer, upon receipt of a notice in writing to that effect, to provide a satisfactory explanation of such standard of living, pecuniary resources or property, or receipt of the benefit of services, as the case may be.

The Public Interest Disclosure (Protection of Whistleblowers) Act

a. Suggested Features of the Act

Typically, a Public Interest Disclosure (Protection of Whistleblowers) Act provides a framework within which persons who make a public interest disclosure shall be protected. The objective of such legislation is to provide for the disclosure of conduct adverse to the public interest in the public and private sectors. It aims at setting up a framework within which public interest disclosures shall be independently and rigorously dealt with. The procedures aim to provide the terms under which employees in both the private and the public sectors are protected should they wish to disclose information regarding unlawful or irregular conduct of employers or employees at their places of work. It should include within its scope conduct that is adverse to the public interest in both private and public sectors. Moreover, it should provide for disclosure of "unlawful or irregular" conduct whether it be done by high

373. Tanzania Prevention of Corruption Act, section 9(1).

374. Malawi Corrupt Practices Act of 1995 (No. 18 of 1995), section 32(1).

level officials or employers or by fellow employees. It should ensure that whistleblowers are protected and corruption is dealt with broadly. In section 10, the Zambian Whistleblower Protection Act provides that an employer shall not subject an employee to any occupational detriment on account, or partly on account of the employee having made a protected disclosure or public interest disclosure. In addition, the act explicitly provides that it applies to government agencies, private or public companies, institutions, any organization, body or organ registered, established or incorporated by any law.[375]

In addition, the Whistle Blower Act should seek to cover both disclosures that are formally made as well as disclosures that leak laterally as part of another case. In the Zambian legislation, section 5 provides that where information that could amount to a public interest disclosure is disclosed in the course of any proceedings of a court or tribunal, the court or tribunal shall refer the information to an interested authority. It ensures effective protection in this regard. The protected disclosures should include disclosures to investigating authorities and anonymous disclosures. In Zambian legislation, in the case of anonymous disclosures, the person making the disclosure, shall identify him or herself to the head of an investigating authority and request that that person's identity be kept confidential by the investigating authority. By keeping their identity confidential through its permission of anonymous disclosures, the law encourages whistleblowers to come forward and report corrupt or suspicious conduct without fear of repercussions for their disclosure.

The Whistleblower Protection Law should prohibit agreements in a contract of employment which go against the provisions of the Act.[376] The Act should state that such agreements would be null and void.[377] In that way the unequal bargaining power of the employer weighed against that of the potential employee is curbed which in turn would encourage the employee to come forward without fear of potential lawsuit for breach of contract.

b. Malicious, Frivolous or Vexatious Disclosures

The Act although designed to protect whistleblowers, should discourage the making of frivolous and vexatious disclosures. For example, the Zambian legislation in section 13(1) criminalizes public interest disclosure that is malicious, frivolous, vexatious, or made in bad faith. Disclosure for pecuniary gain or other illegal purpose is also excluded. The law provides a remedy for victims of malicious disclosure by asserting that the victims of such disclosures shall be compensated and reinstated in their employment (section 13(4)). For a disclosure to be protected by the Act it

---

375. The Public Interest Disclosure (Protection of Whistleblowers) Act, 2010, section 10.

376. *Ibid.*, section 4.

377. *Ibid.* section 4 provider: Any provision in a contract of employment or other agreement between an employer and an employee is void in so far as it—(a) purports to exclude any provision of this Act, including an agreement to refrain from instituting or continuing any proceeedings under this Act or any proceedings for breach of contract ; or (b) purports to preclude the employee or has the effect of discouraging the employee, from making a protected disclosure.

has to satisfy the following conditions: (1) it is made in good faith; (2) made by a person who reasonably believes that the information disclosed, and any allegations contained in it, are substantially true; (3) who does not make the disclosure for purposes of personal gain, excluding any reward payable in terms of reward and (4) in all the circumstances of the case it is reasonable to make the disclosure. Sections 22(1)(a, b, c) and 13(1) provides that an investigating authority may decline to act on a public interest disclosure where it considers that the disclosure is malicious, frivolous, vexatious or made in bad faith, where the disclosure is misconceived or lacking in substance, trivial, there is a more appropriate method of dealing with the disclosure reasonably available, the disclosure has already been dealt with adequately or the disclosure is made for pecuniary gain or other illegal purpose. The focus on good faith or bad faith could divert the attention from the information to the intention of the whistleblower.

c. Concluding Observations

Whistleblower protection laws are meant to encourage public interest disclosures so that disclosures will be made without any fear that the person who makes the disclosure will be subjected to ill treatment. In such a way, whistleblowing is an important means of reducing corruption and dangerous situations in addition to improving the management, efficiency and the overall internal organizational culture of organizations.[378] Not only is it a means of bringing to light corrupt acts but also preventing harmful mistakes and disasters.[379] Whistleblowing has proven to be an effective tool in the fight against corruption, in countries such as in Kenya, where the theft of millions of dollars of public money was revealed through whistleblowing.[380] Notwithstanding the purposes that whistleblowing serves, it may result in serious repercussions for some whistleblowers.[381] Whistleblowing not only promotes accountability but also protects against sanctions. In this regard, some distinguish between internal and external disclosures. Whereas internal whistleblowing is made to higher ranking officials in the organization, external whistleblowing is made to external bodies, such as regulatory bodies, ombudsmen, anti-corruption commissioners, elected officials and the media.[382] Moreover, whistleblowing promotes the right to free speech as well as serving as an administrative control mechanism, by ensuring that organizations are more open and accountable to their employees, shareholders and the greater public in their activities.[383]

Because of the danger that whistleblowers could be subjected to criminal charges for violation of employment laws, they could be ostracized or in some extreme

378. David Banisar, *Whistleblowing International Standards and Developments, Estudio Especializado para la Primera Conferencia Internacional: Debatiendo las Fronteras entre Estado, Mercado y Sociedad*, Ciudad de Mexico, 23-25 de marzo de 2006, p. 2

379. *Id.*

380. *Id.* P. 2.

381. *Id.* P. 3.

382. *Id.* P. 7, 8.

383. *Id.* P. 8.

cases they may be in physical danger, the need to protect whistleblowers has been recognized in many anti-corruption treaties. The way in which they are protected however varies from one state to the next. An examination of various jurisdictions reveals that some choose to adopt laws that are specifically geared towards whistleblower protection while others resort to the use of other legislation including labor laws or public sector employment rules.[384]

Notwithstanding the diversity of the form of protection granted, there is a general agreement that all whistleblower protection laws have two major themes; a proactive and a protective or prohibitive aspect.[385] The proactive aspect of the law is aimed at changing the behavior of individuals. By making disclosure of information culturally acceptable, it seeks to alter the culture of organizations and to facilitate the disclosure of information on negative activities in the organization. The protective/ prohibitive aspect on the other hand, consists of a series of protections and incentives that would encourage people to disclose information without fear of suffering for their disclosures.[386] The effectiveness of whistleblower protection laws is a function of several elements, including *inter alia*, the scope of the laws and the clarity of the definitions provided.

The Financial Intelligence Center Act

a. Overview of the Act

Countries are encouraged to enact legislation to establish the Financial Intelligence Center. Zambian legislation is instructive in this regard. The Zambian Financial Intelligence Center Act of 2010 establishes a center to detect suspicious financial transactions. The center is established as a body corporate with perpetual succession and common seal, capable of suing and being sued in its corporate name and with power to do all such things as a body corporate may do or perform by law. It is the sole designated agency responsible for the receipt, requesting, analyzing, and disseminating of the disclosure of suspicious transaction reports. Its functions include: to receive, request, and analyze suspicious transaction reports required to be made under the Act or any other written law, including information from any foreign designated authority; analyze and evaluate suspicious transaction reports and information so as to determine whether there is sufficient basis to transmit reports for investigation by the law enforcement agencies or a foreign designated authority; disseminate information to law enforcement agencies, where there are reasonable grounds to suspect money laundering or financing of terrorism; provide information relating to suspicious transactions in accordance with the Act to any foreign designated authority, subject to such conditions as the Director may determine; provide information, advice, and assistance to law enforcement agencies in furtherance of an investigation; enter into any agreement or arrangement,

384. *Id.* P. 3.
385. *Id.*
386. *Id.* P. 4.

in writing, with a foreign designated authority which the center considers necessary or desirable for the discharge or performance of its functions; conduct inquiries on behalf of foreign designated authorities and notify them of the outcome; inform the public and reporting entities of their obligation and measures that have been or might have taken to detect, prevent, and deter money laundering and financing of terrorism; access directly or indirectly, on a timely basis financial, administrative, or law enforcement information, required for the better carrying out of its functions under this Act.[387]

The center has wide powers. Where it reasonably suspects that a transaction relates to money laundering, terrorist financing or any other serious offence or the commission of a serious offence, it may order a reporting entity to freeze an account or suspend a transaction.[388] The center in section 15 prohibits reporting entities from establishing or maintaining anonymous accounts or any account in a fictitious name. A reporting entity is required to identify its customers and verify its customers identities by means of reliable and independent source of document (section 16(1)). The center may issue policy directives to reporting entities regarding their obligations under measures that have been or might be taken to detect, prevent, and deter the commission of any offences connected to proceeds of crime; enter into and facilitate cooperation agreements with foreign designated authorities; and perform such other functions as are necessary to give effect to this Act. The reporting companies shall not establish or maintain an anonymous account or any account in a fictitious name; shall identify its customers and verify its customers' identities by means of reliable and independent source documents or information; may rely on an intermediary or other third party to perform the customer identification required' shall, where conducting any business relationship or executing transaction with a customer that is not physically present for purposes of identification, take adequate measures to address the specific risk of money laundering financing of terrorism and any other serious offence; ensure that the due diligence conducted is no less effective than where the customer appears in person; and require additional documentary evidence or supplementary measures to verify or certify the documents supplied by the customer, or confirmatory certification from financial institutions or other documentary evidence or measures as may be prescribed.[389] The reporting companies are required to have; appropriate risk management systems for high risk customers; have systems for identification and account opening for cross-border correspondent banking relationship; maintain all the books and records with respect to their customers and transactions and shall ensure that such records and the underlying information are available, on a timely basis, to the center; develop and implement programs for the prevention of money laundering, financing of terrorism, and any other serious offences; shall exercise ongoing

---

387. The Financial Intelligence Centre Act, 2010, section 5(1), (2)a, b, c, d, e, f, g, h.

388. *Ibid.*, section 6.

389. *Ibid.*

due diligence with respect to any business relationship with a customer; shall have systems for special monitoring of certain transactions; shall have certain obligations regarding wire transfers; require its foreign branches and majority owned subsidiaries to implement the requirements to the extent that domestic applicable laws of the host country so permit; shell banks shall not be established or permitted to operate in or through the territory of Zambia.

The reporting entity or a director, principal, officer, partner, professional, or employee has an obligation to report suspicious transactions to the center. They are further required to promptly submit a report to the center on any currency transactions in an amount equal to or above the prescribed amount, whether conducted as a single transaction or several transactions that appear to be linked. Where it appears to a supervisory authority that a reporting entity, or any of its directors, officers, or employees, is not complying or has not complied, with the obligations set out in this Act, it shall immediately inform the center accordingly. No secrecy or confidentiality provision in any other law shall prevent a reporting entity from fulfilling its obligations under the Act.[390] A reporting entity shall not disclose to its customer or a third party that a report or any other information concerning suspected money laundering, financing of terrorism, or any other serious offense shall be, or it being, or has been, submitted to the center, or that a money laundering, financing of terrorism, or any other serious offence investigation is being, or has been, carried out. Reporting entities are required to protect the identity of persons and information relating to suspicious transaction reports. Where a supervisory authority has reasonable grounds to believe that a business transaction indicates that a person has or may have been engaged in money laundering, the financing of terrorism, or any other serious offence, it shall disclose, or cause to be disclosed, that information to the center.[391] The supervisory authority shall take all reasonable steps to ensure the reporting entity's compliance with its obligations under the Act. The center may communicate anything disclosed to it under the Act to a foreign designated authority if there is in existence an arrangement between Zambia and the foreign state and the center is satisfied that the foreign designated authority has given appropriate undertakings.[392] No order for the production of information, document, or evidence shall be issued in respect of the center or against the Minister, Director, officers, or other staff of the center or any person engaged pursuant to this Act. The Act creates a number offences and penalties as follows: (a) failure to comply with identification requirements; (b) failure to maintain or provide access to records; (c) failure to fulfill due diligence obligations or maintain internal controls; (d) failure to submit a report to the center with regard to a suspicious transaction or other reporting; (e) false or misleading

390. *Ibid.*, section 32, provides: No secrecy or confidential provisions in any law shall prevent a reporting agency from fulfilling its obligations under this Act.

391. *Ibid.*, section 29(1).

392. *Ibid.*, section 40.

statements; (f) confidentiality violation and setting up shell banks. The standard of guilty is: intentionally or negligently doing any of the specified acts.[393]

b. Evaluation of the Concept of Financial Intelligence Center

Money transfers are the handmaiden of international corruption and efforts to curb suspicious transactions are indispensable to the fight against corruption. The linkage is clear: those who take bribes must find safe domestic and international channels through which they can move and bank their ill-gotten gains. The effective use of intelligence is key to a successful anti money laundering regime. Such a system should be run by well-resourced and well-trained personnel. The reporting entity plays an important part in the implementation of the act. Among other things, the act provides that the reporting entity aims at prevention of money laundering, terrorist financing and other serious offences through some of its robust provisions including those prohibiting the establishment of anonymous accounts (section 15), requiring identification of customers (section 16(3)), reliance on third party for identification (section 17), identification of high risk customers (section 19), cross-border correspondent banking relationships (section 20), record keeping, internal programs within the reporting entities to combat money laundering (section 23), financing of terrorism and other serious offences (section 23), ongoing due diligence (section 24), special monitoring of certain transactions (section 25), obligations regarding wire transfers, compliance by foreign subsidiaries and branches (section 27), prohibition against the establishment of shell banks (section 28), obligation to report suspicious transactions (section 29), obligations to report currency transactions (section 30), disclosure of information regarding compliance (section 31), inapplicability of confidentiality provisions (section 32), prohibition against tipping off (section 33). In addition, with regard to the protection of disclosers, the act provides for protection of identity of persons and information relating to suspicious transaction reports (section 34) and exemption from liability for good faith reporting of suspicious transactions (section 35). The entity is made subject to supervision by the supervisory authorities who have the power to enforce compliance (Section 38).

Although one of the major functions of the Financial Intelligence Center is the investigation of suspicious transactions, there is no explicit definition provided for suspicious transactions. Although there is a definition of suspicious transaction reports, in the interest of clarity and for effective implementation of the law, it would be advisable to provide a specific definition of the terminology. Section 5 of the Act states that the center shall be the sole designated agency responsible for the receipt, requesting, analyzing and disseminating of the disclosure of suspicious transaction reports. Suspicious transaction reports have earlier been defined as reports submitted on suspected money laundering, financing of terrorism or other serious offence or attempted money laundering, financing of terrorism or other

393. *Ibid.*, section 42(a), 43, 44, & 54.

serious offence, whether in form of a data message or otherwise.[394] The provision fails to include the proceeds of corruption within the list of crimes. Although it is possible to read corruption within the meaning of other serious offence, in so far as one of the major purposes of the Financial Intelligence Center is to curb corruption, it would be more effective to be specific about it.

Forfeiture of Proceeds of Crime Act

a. Suggested Features of the Act

The Zambian Forfeiture of Proceeds of Crime Act of 2010 provides for the confiscation of the proceeds of crime; deprivation of any person of any proceed, benefit, or property derived from the commission of any serious offence; facilitate the tracing of any proceeds, benefit, and property derived from the commission of any serious offence.[395] The Zambian legislation in this field is intended to domesticate provisions of the United Nations Convention against Corruption relating to the forfeiture of proceeds of crime.[396] In section 4(1) the Act provides that where a person is convicted of a serious offence, a public prosecutor may apply to the court for a forfeiture order against property that is tainted property in respect of the offence and/or a confiscation order against the person in respect of benefits derived by the person from the commission of the offence. Where an application under section 4(1) is finally determined, no further application for a forfeiture order or a confiscation order may be made in respect of the offence for which the person was convicted unless the court grants leave for making of a new application on being satisfied: (a) that the property or benefit to which the new application relates was identified after the previous application was determined; (b) that necessary evidence became available only after the previous application was determined; or (c) that it is in the interests of justice that the new application be made. Under section 5 of the Act, the court has jurisdiction to make a forfeiture order irrespective of the value of the property. The amount to be recovered under any confiscation order is the amount which the court assesses to be the value of the person's benefit from the offence or, if more than one, all the offences in respect of which the order may be made. The forfeiture order is made pursuant to an application by the public prosecutor (section 6). The Public prosecutor shall give written notice of the application to the person and any other person who the public prosecutor has reason to believe may have an interest in the property.

Any other person, who claims an interest in the property, may appear and adduce evidence at the hearing of the application and the court may at any time before the final determination of the application, direct the public prosecutor to give notice of the application to ant person who, in the opinion of the court, appears to have an interest in the property; or to publish in the Gazette and in a daily newspaper

394. *Ibid.*, section 2(2).

395. The Fofeiture of Proceeds of Crime Act, 2010, preamble.

396. *Ibid.*

of general circulation in Zambia, notice of the application, in the manner and containing such particulars and within the time that the court considers appropriate. Where a public prosecutor applies for a confiscation order against a person the public prosecutor shall give the person written notice of the application; and the person may appear and adduce evidence at the hearing of the application. Section 9(1) provides that where a person absconds in connection with a serious offence committed after the coming into force of the Act, a public prosecutor may, within a period of six months after the person so absconds, apply to the court for a forfeiture order in respect of any tainted property. Where a public prosecutor applies to the court for an order against any property and the court is satisfied that the property is tainted property, the court may order that the property or such of the property as is specified by the court in the order, be forfeited to the State. Where the court makes a forfeiture order against any property, the property vests absolutely in the state by virtue of the order.[397]

The Act provides protection for third parties. It provides in section 12(1) that where an application is made for a forfeiture order against any property, a person who claims an interest in the property may apply to the court, before the forfeiture order is made, for a recognition of his or her interest. The court may make an order declaring the nature, extent and value, of the applicant's interest. Where a court makes a forfeiture order in reliance on a person's conviction of an offence and the conviction is subsequently quashed, the quashing of the conviction discharges the order.[398] Where the court is satisfied that a forfeiture order cannot be executed because (a) the property cannot be located; (b) the property has been transferred to a third party in circumstances that do not give rise to a reasonable inference that the title or interest was transferred for the purpose of avoiding the forfeiture of the property, (c) is located outside Zambia; (d) has been mixed with other property that cannot be divided without difficulty; or (e) has been transferred to a bona fide third party purchaser for fair value without notice, the court may instead order the person to pay to the state an amount equal to the value of the property or interest[399].

The Forfeiture Act in section 19(1) empowers courts to issue confiscation order. Such an order can be issued where a public prosecutor applies to the court for a confiscation order against a person in respect of that person's conviction of a serious offense and the court is satisfied that the person has benefited from the offence. Where a confiscation order is issued the convicted person is required to pay into court an amount equal to the value of the person's benefits from the offence or such lesser as the court certifies.[400] In assessing the value of benefits derived by a person from the commission of an offence or offences, the court may treat as prop-

397. Section 11(1) Forfeiture of Proceeds of Crime Act, 2010.

398. Section 13 (1), Forfeiture of Proceeds of Crime Act, 2010.

399. Section 15(a), (b), (c), (d), (e).

400. Section 22(1) Forfeiture of Proceeds Act, 2010.

erty of the person any property that, in the opinion of the court, is subject to the effective control of the person and may lift the corporate veil to determine questions of ownership of property.[401] The Act has several other routine provisions such as those dealing with the registration of foreign forfeiture orders and restraining the disposal of tainted property.[402]

b. Evaluation of the Proceeds of Crime Act

Corruption is a far reaching, continuing and extremely profitable criminal enterprise which as we observed earlier diverts significant amounts of public money for illicit purposes. Public corruption-related schemes persist. This is despite legislation which facilitates the actual prosecution and imprisonment of individual participants. In order to further discourage corruption it is important to effectively reach the money and other assets generated by such schemes. It is therefore necessary to supplement existing sanctions by mandating forfeiture of money and other assets generated by public corruption-related activities. As pointed out earlier Forfeiture of Proceeds of Crime Acts are aimed at the domestication of the provisions relating to forfeiture of proceeds of corruption in the United Nations Convention Against Corruption. One of its stated objectives is to deprive any person of any proceeds, benefit or property derived from the commission of any serious crime, facilitate the tracing of any proceeds, benefit and property derived from the commission of a crime. The threat of confiscation of proceeds of crime provides an important tool in the fight against corruption. It is designed to deter those who contemplate committing corruption crimes by reducing the possibility of gaining or keeping the profit from crime and to remedy the unjust enrichment of criminals who profit at the society's expense. Forfeiture diminishes the financial incentives which encourage and sustain corruption.

Prohibition and Prevention of Money Laundering (Amendment) Act

a. Overview of the Act

The last piece of legislation the article discusses is legislation to prohibit and prevent money laundering. In Zambia the Prohibition and Prevention of Money Laundering (Amendment) Act, 2010 defines money laundering as: where a reasonable inference may be drawn, having regard to the objective factual circumstances, any activity by a person (a) who knows or has reason to believe that the property is the proceeds of a crime; or (b) without reasonable excuse, fails to take reasonable steps to ascertain whether or realized directly or indirectly, by any person from the commission of a crime; where the person (i) engages, directly or indirectly, in a transaction that involves proceeds of a crime; (ii) acquires, receives, possesses, disguises, transfers, converts, exchanges, carries, disposes, uses, removes from or brings into Zambia proceeds of a crime; or (iii) conceals, disguises, or impedes the establishment of the true nature, origin, location, movement, disposition, title of,

401. Section 24, Forfeiture of Proceeds Act, 2010.
402. Section 18, Forfeiture Act, 2010.

rights with respect to, or ownership of, proceeds of any illegal activity.[403] It further defines proceeds of crime as: property or benefit that is wholly or partly derived or realized from a disposal or other dealing with proceeds of a crime; wholly or partly acquired proceeds of a crime; and includes, on a proportional basis, property into which any property derived or realized directly from the illegal activity is later converted, transformed, or intermingled, and any income, capital or other economic gains derived or realized from the property at any time after the crime; or any property that is derived or realized, directly or indirectly, by any person from any act or omission that occurred outside Zambia and would if the act or omission had occurred in Zambia, have constituted a crime.[404] Under the Act it a criminal offence to engage in any activities relating to money laundering.

Best Practices with Regards to Anti-Corruption Agencies

As we saw in the discussion in the preceding pages the various new pieces of legislation create special commissions and agencies as structures in the fight against corruption. This approach as explained earlier is recommended by international and regional conventions. Commissions have become an important mechanism for fighting corruption. Yet commissions by themselves cannot be an answer to corruption. To be effective they have to be properly constituted, and functionally and operationally independent. This section examines the factors that guarantee an independent and effective anti-corruption commission. There are general points that can be made to strengthen the commissions and other anti-corruption agencies. On the major points is the need to ensure the independency of those that are charged to fight corruption. For example to ensure that members of commissions do not seek to act in such a way as to secure reappointment to the commissions, they could be appointed for single terms and should not be eligible for reappointment. The grounds for the removal of commissioners should be specified. For example it could be provided that commissioners may be removed from office only for: (a) serious violation of the constitution or any other law; (b) gross misconduct, whether in the performance of the members or office holders functions or otherwise; (c) physical or mental incapacity to perform the functions of office or (incompetence or bankruptcy). The removal procedure should be clearly spelt out. Another weakness of the system as currently structured is that the various Commissions are not accountable to Parliament. It is important that the Commissions are accountable to a body outside the executive. It could be provided that after the end of each financial year, each commission and each holder of an independent office shall submit a report to the President and to the National Assembly.

Another matter that needs to be elaborated is a code of conduct for state officials. It is important to develop a code that will govern the conduct of state officials whether in public and official life, in private life or in association with other persons in a

403. Prohibition and Prevention of Money Laundering (Amendment) Act, 2010, section, 3(a)(b).

404. *Ibid*, section 3(c).

manner that avoids: (a) any conflict between personal interest and public or official duties; (b) compromising and public or official interest in favor of a personal interest. To further ensure financial probity of government officials it is necessary to have a law which requires state officials to declare gifts received by them and also to declare that gifts above a certain value are deemed to be gifts to the State and shall be delivered to the state unless exempted under an Act of Parliament.

One of the key factors that determines the autonomy and effectiveness of an oversight institution is its membership, including the process and criteria for appointment. This calls for the adoption of appointment procedures which ensure that commissioners are independent and are subject to public scrutiny before appointment. The essence of the appointment procedure should be that it is a confidence building exercise for government, citizens and civil society alike in the integrity, independence and ability of the commissioners. It follows that undue executive influence over the process can undermine the effectiveness of a national institution. The process of appointment should not begin and end with the President. The procedures adopted for appointment should be geared towards maximizing checks and balances among government organs and securing the independence of the institutions from each other so that they can act as effective checks on each other. A good appointment process for watchdog institutions is one that is transparent and involves effective consultation with civil society groups in order to identify good candidates to serve on Boards of such institutions. It follows that undue executive influence over the appointment process can undermine the effectiveness of the institution. One factor that must be considered in the selection of members of Boards is diversity. In countries with ethnic or religious tensions, it is important that the composition of the Boards reflects that diversity. Likewise gender balance serves to underline the importance of women's rights and the importance of Boards representing the whole community. In Boards that exercise quasi-judicial powers there might be need to provide for qualifications for appointment to such Boards. The major concern must remain the need to appoint demonstrably independent and able persons. In addition, adequate protection against arbitrary removal from office is vital for the work of the institution.

A country determined to fight corruption must have the political will to change laws, to change the structure of government institutions, to not tolerate corrupt conduct and to allocate resources to investigate and prosecute corruption. The question then arises as to how to persuade a government to develop the political will. First, it is through increasing media consciousness about what is corrupt conduct and how the criminal justice system should be strengthened. Second, it is through the involvement of civil society, which uses democratic means to pressure governments to prosecute corruption. Civil society also creates public awareness about the need to resist corruption. It is stated that in a democracy there can be no greater voice than that of the people. For civil society and the public to play an effective role, there are two important oversights instruments that need to be in place. Procurement regulations must keep contracting and government purchasing open and fair. A Freedom of Information Act is the other instrument that must be in place. These laws permit citizens to request information as members of the public and use it to ensure the accountability of government agencies. In addition there is need to strengthen the role of parliament as monitor of the executive and scrutinizer of government budgets, particularly public accounts. The ability of the Anti-Corruption Commission to work in an unbiased way will depend on appropriate checks and balances as well as constant scrutiny through various oversight mechanisms. Hong Kong's Independent Commission Against Corruption (ICAC) for example has its activities examined by four independent committees which include representatives from civil society, in addition to an independent ICAC complaints Committee which receives, monitors and reviews all complaints against the Commission. Another way to enhance oversight over an Anti-Corruption Commission is to make it accountable to more than one authority. Many countries have decided to shift reporting lines from a single-person institution such as the president to the parliament, allowing various political parties to scrutinize the activities of the Anti-Corruption Commission. In a constitutional democracy, Parliament is supposed to operate as a counter-weight to the executive, and its committee system, in which diverse voices are represented across the spectrum of political views. Parliament should also assist in ensuring that questions are asked, that conduct is scrutinized and that motives are questioned.

C. Dodd-Frank Wall Street Reform and Consumer Protection Act (2010)

Particular corruption concerns have often revolved around exploitation of raw materials, including oil and gas, but also minerals and gem stones from areas of armed conflict. The Dodd-Frank Act[405] passed in the wake of the U.S. financial crisis of 2008 included a specific section on these so-called conflict minerals (Section 1502). This imposes a disclosure requirement that calls on companies to determine whether their products contain conflict minerals and to report this to the Securities and Exchange Commission (SEC), with the intention of discouraging corrupt practices in mineral exploitation in locations such as eastern Congo.

Sec. 1502. Conflict Minerals.

(a) SENSE OF CONGRESS ON EXPLOITATION AND TRADE OF CONFLICT MINERALS ORIGINATING IN THE DEMOCRATIC REPUBLIC OF THE CONGO.—It is the sense of Congress that the exploitation and trade of conflict minerals originating in the Democratic Republic of the Congo is helping to finance conflict characterized by extreme levels

405. Please note that The House Financial Services Committee under the Trump Administration 2017 approved a bill to repeal and roll back significant pieces of the Dodd-Frank Wall Street Reform and Consumer Protection Act.

of violence in the eastern Democratic Republic of the Congo, particularly sexual-and gender-based violence, and contributing to an emergency humanitarian situation therein, warranting the provisions of section 13(p) of the Securities Exchange Act of 1934, as added by subsection (b).

(b) DISCLOSURE RELATING TO CONFLICT MINERALS ORIGINATING IN THE DEMOCRATIC REPUBLIC OF THE CONGO.—Section 13 of the Securities Exchange Act of 1934 (15 U.S.C. §78m), as amended by this Act, is amended by adding at the end the following new subsection:

(p) DISCLOSURES RELATING TO CONFLICT MINERALS ORIGINATING IN THE DEMOCRATIC REPUBLIC OF THE CONGO. [. . .]

D. Other Actors in the Fight against Corruption

This article further discusses the origins of corruption and the types of alliance that can help to support anti-corruption initiatives.

© George, Barbara Crutchfield & Lacey, Kathleen A., *A Coalition of Industrialized Nations, Developing Nations, Multilateral Development Banks, and Non-Governmental Organizations: A Pivotal Complement to Current Anti-Corruption Initiatives*, Cornell International Law Journal: Vol. 33: Iss. 3, Article 5 (2000). Printed with permission of Cornell International Law Journal.

A. World Bank

The Bank with its divisions, the International Bank for Reconstruction and Development ("IBRD") and the International Development Agency ("IDA") was created to "assist in reconstruction after World War II. Reconstruction has remained an important focus of the Bank's work, given the increasing number of natural disasters, complex humanitarian emergencies, and post-conflict rehabilitation needs that have characterized the developing and transition economies." The Bank stimulates productive investment in developing countries by lending capital to the countries for infrastructure projects, financing banking and corporate reform, and engaging in other projects intended to provide a social cushion to the poor and unemployed in transition economy nations. In addition, the Bank is a key player in the battle against corruption in the public procurement process within developing nations.

The Bank, through a number of mechanisms, has recently intensified its focus on preventing corruption. In 1997, the Bank published a report evaluating its role in combating corruption, stating that while it cannot formally take "a coercive stance," it can lawfully withhold aid or other funding to countries that have not adequately addressed corruption.

The World Bank Institute (WBI), as part of the World Bank Group, "facilitates action-oriented and participatory programs to promote good governance and curb corruption in client countries." To combat corruption in client countries, the WBI cooperates with other World Bank Group entities, outside organizations, and stakeholders within client countries to conduct diagnostic surveys and organize coalitions.

In May 1998, the World Bank created the Oversight Committee on Fraud and Corruption to review allegations of corruption by any member. Through the Economic Development Institute, the World Bank conducts Integrity Workshops and procurement seminars. In October 1998, the World Bank established a telephone hotline to facilitate the reporting of fraud and corruption. The Bank also conducts ongoing research to diagnose the extent and character of corruption in a given country.

The Bank has been mindful of corruption within its own organization too. Accordingly, it authorized independent audits of fifty-four of its own projects in the last two years. The audit revealed that the Bank had been involved in "misprocurement on about 40 contracts with a total contract value of $40 million."

In part due to the findings of the audit, the Bank has strengthened its anti-corruption stance by banning firms that offer bribes from participating in future Bank-financed procurement projects. In addition, it maintains the right to cancel loans to governments whose officials solicited bribes and require borrowing countries and their contractors to comply with anticorruption guidelines as a prerequisite to aid.

The guidelines provide that, upon discovery of fraudulent or corrupt conduct by a bidder or, once financing has been granted, by a borrower, the bank will reject the bidder's proposals for awards, cancel the remaining portions of loans, and debar the borrower from future World Bank financing for a stated period of time or indefinitely.

Thus, if a bidder is found to have engaged in corrupt behavior, the Bank can bar it from future bids; and if a borrower has engaged in corruption, the remaining portions of the loan may be cancelled. The development of guidelines calling for specific economic and financial consequences when corruption is detected reflects the growing reluctance of international agencies to provide capital to nations riddled with corruption. The guidelines also evidence the agencies' efforts to reduce corruption in the procurement process of emerging countries.

B. International Monetary Fund

[. . .]

As a creditor, the IMF has the power to attach certain conditions to the money that it provides; for instance, it may insist that an applicant adopt institutional reform measures intended to eliminate corrupt practices which undermine economic stability. Thus, the IMF possesses significant leverage to require that developing nations reduce internal corruption.[406]

---

406. The IMF funding pool is the sum of subscriptions by the IMF's 182 member nations, which essentially keep a share of their national currencies on deposit with the IMF. The IMF deals only with a recipient country's central bank, feeding money directly into that institution and thus bolstering the financial reserves ultimately backing the government. *See*, Petruno, [*The Financial "White Knight": IMF Demystified*, L.A. Times, Nov.22, 1997,] *supra*, at Al.

In August 1997 the IMF adopted stringent guidelines to promote public sector transparency and accountability. These guidelines were adopted to improve efficiency and support sustained economic growth. According to the guidelines, the IMF has adopted a "more proactive approach in advocating policies" and actively pursues "the development of institutions and administrative systems that aim to eliminate the opportunity for corruption [and] fraudulent activity in the management of public resources." The IMF's aims to achieve "an evenhanded treatment of governance issues in all member countries," "enhanced collaboration with other multilateral institutions, in particular the World Bank" and an improved "use of complementary areas of expertise [among anti-corruption initiatives]." [. . .]

IV. Transparency International, the Leading Non-governmental Institution in the Fight Against Corruption

TI gathers data regarding the perceived extent of corruption, develops systems to combat corruption, engages various multinational organizations to encourage the passage of conventions aimed at eliminating corruption, and organizes conferences for the exchange of information about current levels of corruption world-wide.[407] In sum, "TI builds national, regional and global coalitions, embracing the state, civil society and the private sector, in order to fight domestic and international corruption." TI's formation of coalitions is a critical step towards eradicating corruption.

[. . .] TI is convinced that anti-corruption efforts are sustainable only "with the involvement of all the stakeholders [including] the state, civil society and the private sector." TI's aim thus is to achieve cooperation among diverse non-governmental entities. It focuses its energies upon the formation of coalitions, including the construction of information-sharing systems. Finally, TI strives to operate in a non-confrontational way, and, accordingly, it does not "name names" or publicize individual cases of corruption. [. . .]

TI's Integrity Pacts (IPs) are an important part of its grassroots-level initiative. An IP results when a national government and bidding companies mutually promise not to engage in corrupt public procurement practices; bidding companies publicly pledge not to use bribes, while government agencies pledge total transparency on the part of its officials in awarding the contract. The IP is designed to ensure the absence of corruption in the handling of selected contracts with International Financing Institutions and selected external donor-financed projects. [. . .]

TI must educate nations regarding its IP program and assist national efforts to implement the IPs. One example of a failed attempt to implement an IP-like

407. *See*, [Transparency Int'l, Mission Statement (last modified Feb. 9, 2000), http://www.transparency.de/mission.html]. TI's Mission Statement includes a statement of purpose: "TI assists in the design and the implementation of effective integrity systems [and] . . . collects, analyses and disseminates information and raises public awareness on the damaging impact of corruption (especially in low-income countries) on human and economic development." *Id.*

program involved a coalition of African nations obtaining construction funds from the World Bank. In 1998, the Chairman for Global Coalition for Africa, Robert McNamara, and the Executive Secretary of the Global Coalition of Africa, Ould Abdallah, received a commitment from the governments of seven African states Benin, Malawi, Ethiopia, Tanzania, Mali, Mozambique and Uganda to participate in an IP. The states submitted a written request to the World Bank that future construction projects be subject to the IP. [. . .]

V. Coalitions Necessary to Successfully Eradicate Bribery and Corruption: Involvement of Civil Society, Government and Private Sector in Campaign Against Corruption.

The three social institutions most responsible for and affected by globalization are government, business, and civil society. However, government and business institutions are often the perpetrators of corruption—with business as the bribe-giver and government the bribe-taker. These groups may therefore be less able or inclined to establish and maintain anti-corruption agendas. As noted by Peter Eigen, of the three institutions, only civil society organizations have the public mandates and the global potential to both declare the improvement of people's lives as the paramount priority, and to do something meaningful about it. Only civil society organizations can provide the impetus, the force, and the leadership to wage the global war against corruption.

It is impossible, however, for civil society to remedy corruption alone. A coalition of the three pillars of the social structure—business, government, and civil society—is of paramount importance in the fight against corruption. Each of these sectors has the capacity, based on its unique characteristics, to make critical contributions. Government, when, accountable to democratic control, and whose legitimacy thus is derived from the people, can establish the legislative framework to criminalize corrupt conduct. Government is also uniquely situated to provide the access, leadership and resources necessary to reform governmental systems and institute measures to ensure transparency and accountability.

For any campaign against corruption to succeed, it is also necessary to enlist the cooperation and support of the business community. The private sector can assist in identifying problematic issues and is the ultimate "testing ground for anti-corruption models—no rules and regulations will check corruption if the gap between ethical standards and competitive forces is too wide to be bridged."

The legitimacy of civil society, like that of democratic government, also emanates from the people; people who, without the profit motivation of the private sector or the political self-interest of government, are concerned with the broadest issues of social welfare in the local, regional, national, and global communities. Civil society can provide the initiative and leadership to build pivotal alliances among these three principal entities. These alliances are absolutely essential to the eradication of bribery and corruption.

The alliance between government, business, and civil society is developing through the mechanisms already established by TI, OECD, OAS, and other organizations with various representative groups of civil society. As noted by Peter Eigen, "I wish to leave no doubt that Transparency International's highest priority is strengthening its national chapters and contributing to the humanitarian and anti-corruption endeavors of civil society worldwide." Transparency International seeks to empower civil society to function successfully. TI has developed a number of mechanisms to involve local communities in its anti-corruption agenda, through utilizing mechanisms such as the Integrity Pact, the National Chapters and other efforts previously discussed. [. . .]

Finally, a coalition of the industrialized nations, developing and transitional nations, multilateral development banks, and NGOs representing civil society, plus other pertinent entities at the multilateral, national, and grassroots levels are pivotal complements to current anticorruption initiatives. Such a coalition would ideally utilize the following means: multilateral conventions and international treaties (with their associated harmonization of domestic legislation that carry penalties with a high level of severe enforcement); anticorruption guidelines tied to funding in the public procurement process; activities of NGOs (like TI with its Integrity Pacts in the public procurement process and Corruption/Bribery Perception Indices); and grassroots initiatives by civil society that work to alter cultural attitudes toward business corruption. The dynamic energy and focus of such coalitions, utilizing these various strategies, will contribute greatly to the fight against corrupt business activities.

E. Anti-Corruption Law and Investment Disputes

The World Duty Free case is discussed in detail in Chapter 8. In this case, a contract secured by bribe was voidable on the basis of being contrary to international public policy.

© Surya P. Subedi, 2008, *International Investment Law: Reconciling Policy and Principle*, 2d Edition, Hart Publishing, Bloomsbury Publishing Plc.

Since international investment tribunals are willing to venture into private law areas by elevating contractual disputes to BIT disputes, they should also be prepared, at the same time, to look into credible claims of corruption by foreign investors, especially MNEs, regarding either securing lop-sided investment contracts from corrupt politicians and senior civil servants or other corrupt business practices. This is because international treaties such as the UN anti-corruption Convention, the OECD's anti-bribery Convention and other soft law instruments such as the UN Global Compact and other guidelines outlaw corrupt business practices by TNCs.

It can be argued that such anti-corruption laws are now becoming part of the corpus of international foreign investment law. In the *Enron* case, the ICSID tribunal held that it has broad powers to adjudicate on the matters before it.[408] If such tribunals can claim such broad powers, there is no reason why they should not take into account the background leading to the conclusion of investment contracts including corruption on the part of state and company officials in concluding such contracts.

Article 34 of the 1985 Model Law of UNCITRAL on International Commercial Arbitration states that a national court of the seat of arbitration can set aside an arbitral award made by an arbitral tribunal sitting under the UNCITRAL rules if the award is in conflict with the public policy of the state concerned. Although there is no internationally agreed definition of the phrase 'public policy', it would cover, as stated by Redfern and others, 'the possibility of setting aside an award if the arbitral tribunal has been corrupted in some way, or if it has been misled by corrupt evidence'.[409]

In one of the recent cases decided by an ICSID tribunal it was held that investment contracts concluded through corrupt practices stand to be rejected by such tribunals. In the case between *World Duty Free Company v. Kenya*, the ICSID tribunal held that a payment made by the company to the former President of Kenya, Arap Moi, to obtain a contract was a bribe. Since such a contract secured by using bribe was voidable in law, the ICSID tribunal would not enforce it, stating that bribery was contrary to international public policy.[410] Although the Vienna Convention on the Law of Treaties would not apply to investment contracts between a state and a foreign company, it applies to BITs. Under the Convention, fraud and corruption are valid reasons to declare a treaty null and void.[411] By applying this analogy, it would be logical to deny protection under such treaties for companies engaged in fraudulent and corrupt practices. [. . .]

Some other ICSID tribunals [. . .] have been reluctant to get involved in allegations of corruption by the companies concerned when adjudicating on investment matters, examples include *Empress Lucchetti*,[412] *SGS v Pakistan*[413] and *Methanex*.[414]

---

408. *Enron Corporation and Ponderosa Assets, L.P. v. Argentine Republic*, ICSID Case No. ARB/01/3, Decision on Jurisdiction of January 2004, 32-34.

409. A. Redfern et al., *Law and Practice of International Commercial Arbitration,* 4th ed., London: Sweet & Maxwell (2004).

410. *World Duty Free Co. Ltd. v. Republic of Kenya* (ICSID Case No. ARB/00/7) Award, 4 October 2006.

411. Arts. 49 and 50 of the Vienna Convention on the Law of Treaties of 1969.

412. *Empresas Lucchetti*, Award of 7 Febuary 2005, 17 and 19.

413. *SGS Société Générale de Surveillance SA v. Islamic Republic of Pakistan*, ICSID Case No ARB/01/13, Award of 8 September 2003, 330, 350.

414. *Methanex Corporation v. United States of America* (Final Award of the Tribunal on Jurisdiction and Merits of 3 August 2005).

Chapter 13

Documents

A. United Nations Convention on the Recognition and Enforcement of Foreign Arbitral Awards ("New York Convention"), New York, 10 June 1958
B. Convention on the Settlement of Investment Disputes Between States and Nationals of Other States, International Centre for Settlement of Investment Disputes Convention, Regulations and Rules ("ICSID Convention"), Washington DC, October 14, 1966 (amended effective April 10, 2006)
C. Convention Establishing the Multilateral Investment Guarantee Agency ("MIGA Convention"), Seoul, April 12, 1988
D. The Agreement on Trade-Related Aspects of Intellectual Property Rights ("TRIPS"), World Trade Organization, Uruguay 1994

A. New York Convention (1958)

Article I

1. This Convention shall apply to the recognition and enforcement of arbitral awards made in the territory of a State other than the State where the recognition and enforcement of such awards are sought, and arising out of differences between persons, whether physical or legal. It shall also apply to arbitral awards not considered as domestic awards in the State where their recognition and enforcement are sought.

2. The term "arbitral awards" shall include not only awards made by arbitrators appointed for each case but also those made by permanent arbitral bodies to which the parties have submitted.

3. When signing, ratifying or acceding to this Convention, or notifying extension under article X hereof, any State may on the basis of reciprocity declare that it will apply the Convention to the recognition and enforcement of awards made only in the territory of another Contracting State. It may also declare that it will apply the Convention only to differences arising out of legal relationships, whether contractual or not, which are considered as commercial under the national law of the State making such declaration.

Article II

1. Each Contracting State shall recognize an agreement in writing under which the parties undertake to submit to arbitration all or any differences which have arisen

or which may arise between them in respect of a defined legal relationship, whether contractual or not, concerning a subject matter capable of settlement by arbitration.

2. The term "agreement in writing" shall include an arbitral clause in a contract or an arbitration agreement, signed by the parties or contained in an exchange of letters or telegrams.

3. The court of a Contracting State, when seized of an action in a matter in respect of which the parties have made an agreement within the meaning of this article, shall, at the request of one of the parties, refer the parties to arbitration, unless it finds that the said agreement is null and void, inoperative or incapable of being performed.

Article III

Each Contracting State shall recognize arbitral awards as binding and enforce them in accordance with the rules of procedure of the territory where the award is relied upon, under the conditions laid down in the following articles. There shall not be imposed substantially more onerous conditions or higher fees or charges on the recognition or enforcement of arbitral awards to which this Convention applies than are imposed on the recognition or enforcement of domestic arbitral awards.

Article IV

1. To obtain the recognition and enforcement mentioned in the preceding article, the party applying for recognition and enforcement shall, at the time of the application, supply:

(a) The duly authenticated original award or a duly certified copy thereof;

(b) The original agreement referred to in article II or a duly certified copy thereof.

2. If the said award or agreement is not made in an official language of the country in which the award is relied upon, the party applying for recognition and enforcement of the award shall produce a translation of these documents into such language. The translation shall be certified by an official or sworn translator or by a diplomatic or consular agent.

Article V

1. Recognition and enforcement of the award may be refused, at the request of the party against whom it is invoked, only if that party furnishes to the competent authority where the recognition and enforcement is sought, proof that:

(a) The parties to the agreement referred to in article II were, under the law applicable to them, under some incapacity, or the said agreement is not valid under the law to which the parties have subjected it or, failing any indication thereon, under the law of the country where the award was made; or

(b) The party against whom the award is invoked was not given proper notice of the appointment of the arbitrator or of the arbitration proceedings or was otherwise unable to present his case; or

(c) The award deals with a difference not contemplated by or not falling within the terms of the submission to arbitration, or it contains decisions on matters beyond the scope of the submission to arbitration, provided that, if the decisions on matters submitted to arbitration can be separated from those not so submitted, that part of the award which contains decisions on matters submitted to arbitration may be recognized and enforced; or

(d) The composition of the arbitral authority or the arbitral procedure was not in accordance with the agreement of the parties, or, failing such agreement, was not in accordance with the law of the country where the arbitration took place; or

(e) The award has not yet become binding on the parties, or has been set aside or suspended by a competent authority of the country in which, or under the law of which, that award was made.

2. Recognition and enforcement of an arbitral award may also be refused if the competent authority in the country where recognition and enforcement is sought finds that:

(a) The subject matter of the difference is not capable of settlement by arbitration under the law of that country; or

(b) The recognition or enforcement of the award would be contrary to the public policy of that country.

Article VI

If an application for the setting aside or suspension of the award has been made to a competent authority referred to in article V (1) (e), the authority before which the award is sought to be relied upon may, if it considers it proper, adjourn the decision on the enforcement of the award and may also, on the application of the party claiming enforcement of the award, order the other party to give suitable security.

Article VII

1. The provisions of the present Convention shall not affect the validity of multilateral or bilateral agreements concerning the recognition and enforcement of arbitral awards entered into by the Contracting States nor deprive any interested party of any right he may have to avail himself of an arbitral award in the manner and to the extent allowed by the law or the treaties of the country where such award is sought to be relied upon.

2. The Geneva Protocol on Arbitration Clauses of 1923 and the Geneva Convention on the Execution of Foreign Arbitral Awards of 1927 shall cease to have effect between Contracting States on their becoming bound and to the extent that they become bound, by this Convention.

Article VIII

1. This Convention shall be open until 31 December 1958 for signature on behalf of any Member of the United Nations and also on behalf of any other State which is

or hereafter becomes a member of any specialized agency of the United Nations, or which is or hereafter becomes a party to the Statute of the International Court of Justice, or any other State to which an invitation has been addressed by the General Assembly of the United Nations.

2. This Convention shall be ratified and the instrument of ratification shall be deposited with the Secretary-General of the United Nations.

Article IX

1. This Convention shall be open for accession to all States referred to in article VIII.

2. Accession shall be effected by the deposit of an instrument of accession with the Secretary-General of the United Nations.

Article X

1. Any State may, at the time of signature, ratification or accession, declare that this Convention shall extend to all or any of the territories for the international relations of which it is responsible. Such a declaration shall take effect when the Convention enters into force for the State concerned.

2. At any time thereafter any such extension shall be made by notification addressed to the Secretary-General of the United Nations and shall take effect as from the ninetieth day after the day of receipt by the Secretary-General of the United Nations of this notification, or as from the date of entry into force of the Convention for the State concerned, whichever is the later.

3. With respect to those territories to which this Convention is not extended at the time of signature, ratification or accession, each State concerned shall consider the possibility of taking the necessary steps in order to extend the application of this Convention to such territories, subject, where necessary for constitutional reasons, to the consent of the Governments of such territories.

Article XI

In the case of a federal or non-unitary State, the following provisions shall apply:

(a) With respect to those articles of this Convention that come within the legislative jurisdiction of the federal authority, the obligations of the federal Government shall to this extent be the same as those of Contracting States which are not federal States;

(b) With respect to those articles of this Convention that come within the legislative jurisdiction of constituent states or provinces which are not, under the constitutional system of the federation, bound to take legislative action, the federal Government shall bring such articles with a favourable recommendation to the notice of the appropriate authorities of constituent states or provinces at the earliest possible moment;

(c) A federal State Party to this Convention shall, at the request of any other Contracting State transmitted through the Secretary-General of the United Nations, supply a statement of the law and practice of the federation and its constituent units in regard to any particular provision of this Convention, showing the extent to which effect has been given to that provision by legislative or other action.

Article XII

1. This Convention shall come into force on the ninetieth day following the date of deposit of the third instrument of ratification or accession.

2. For each State ratifying or acceding to this Convention after the deposit of the third instrument of ratification or accession, this Convention shall enter into force on the ninetieth day after deposit by such State of its instrument of ratification or accession.

Article XIII

1. Any Contracting State may denounce this Convention by a written notification to the Secretary-General of the United Nations. Denunciation shall take effect one year after the date of receipt of the notification by the Secretary-General.

2. Any State which has made a declaration or notification under article X may, at any time thereafter, by notification to the Secretary-General of the United Nations, declare that this Convention shall cease to extend to the territory concerned one year after the date of the receipt of the notification by the Secretary-General.

3. This Convention shall continue to be applicable to arbitral awards in respect of which recognition and enforcement proceedings have been instituted before the denunciation takes effect.

Article XIV

A Contracting State shall not be entitled to avail itself of the present Convention against other Contracting States except to the extent that it is itself bound to apply the Convention.

Article XV

The Secretary-General of the United Nations shall notify the States contemplated in article VIII of the following:

(a) Signatures and ratifications in accordance with article VIII;

(b) Accessions in accordance with article IX;

(c) Declarations and notifications under articles I, X and XI;

(d) The date upon which this Convention enters into force in accordance with article XII;

(e) Denunciations and notifications in accordance with article XIII.

Article XVI

1. This Convention, of which the Chinese, English, French, Russian and Spanish texts shall be equally authentic, shall be deposited in the archives of the United Nations.

2. The Secretary-General of the United Nations shall transmit a certified copy of this Convention to the States contemplated in article VIII.

B. Convention on the Settlement of Investment Disputes Between States and Nationals of Other States (1966, Amended 2006)

Preamble

The Contracting States

Considering the need for international cooperation for economic development, and the role of private international investment therein;

Bearing in mind the possibility that from time to time disputes may arise in connection with such investment between Contracting States and nationals of other Contracting States;

Recognizing that while such disputes would usually be subject to national legal processes, international methods of settlement may be appropriate in certain cases;

Attaching particular importance to the availability of facilities for international conciliation or arbitration to which Contracting States and nationals of other Contracting States may submit such disputes if they so desire;

Desiring to establish such facilities under the auspices of the International Bank for Reconstruction and Development;

Recognizing that mutual consent by the parties to submit such disputes to conciliation or to arbitration through such facilities constitutes a binding agreement which requires in particular that due consideration be given to any recommendation of conciliators, and that any arbitral award be complied with; and

Declaring that no Contracting State shall by the mere fact of its ratification, acceptance or approval of this Convention and without its consent be deemed to be under any obligation to submit any particular dispute to conciliation or arbitration,

Have agreed as follows:

Chapter I
International Centre for Settlement of Investment Disputes

Section 1
Establishment and Organization

Article 1

(1) There is hereby established the International Centre for Settlement of Investment Disputes (hereinafter called the Centre).

(2) The purpose of the Centre shall be to provide facilities for conciliation and arbitration of investment disputes between Contracting States and nationals of other Contracting States in accordance with the provisions of this Convention.

Article 2

The seat of the Centre shall be at the principal office of the International Bank for Reconstruction and Development (hereinafter called the Bank). The seat may be moved to another place by decision of the Administrative Council adopted by a majority of two-thirds of its members.

Article 3

The Centre shall have an Administrative Council and a Secretariat and shall maintain a Panel of Conciliators and a Panel of Arbitrators.

Section 2
The Administrative Council

Article 4

(1) The Administrative Council shall be composed of one representative of each Contracting State. An alternate may act as representative in case of his principal's absence from a meeting or inability to act.

(2) In the absence of a contrary designation, each governor and alternate governor of the Bank appointed by a Contracting State shall be ex officio its representative and its alternate respectively.

Article 5

The President of the Bank shall be ex officio Chairman of the Administrative Council (hereinafter called the Chairman) but shall have no vote. During his absence or inability to act and during any vacancy in the office of President of the Bank, the person for the time being acting as President shall act as Chairman of the Administrative Council.

Article 6

(1) Without prejudice to the powers and functions vested in it by other provisions of this Convention, the Administrative Council shall:

(a) adopt the administrative and financial regulations of the Centre;

(b) adopt the rules of procedure for the institution of conciliation and arbitration proceedings;

(c) adopt the rules of procedure for conciliation and arbitration proceedings (hereinafter called the Conciliation Rules and the Arbitration Rules);

(d) approve arrangements with the Bank for the use of the Bank's administrative facilities and services;

(e) determine the conditions of service of the Secretary-General and of any Deputy Secretary-General;

(f) adopt the annual budget of revenues and expenditures of the Centre;

(g) approve the annual report on the operation of the Centre.

The decisions referred to in sub-paragraphs (a), (b), (c) and (f) above shall be adopted by a majority of two-thirds of the members of the Administrative Council.

(2) The Administrative Council may appoint such committees as it considers necessary.

(3) The Administrative Council shall also exercise such other powers and perform such other functions as it shall determine to be necessary for the implementation of the provisions of this Convention.

Article 7

(1) The Administrative Council shall hold an annual meeting and such other meetings as may be determined by the Council, or convened by the Chairman, or convened by the Secretary-General at the request of not less than five members of the Council.

(2) Each member of the Administrative Council shall have one vote and, except as otherwise herein provided, all matters before the Council shall be decided by a majority of the votes cast.

(3) A quorum for any meeting of the Administrative Council shall be a majority of its members.

(4) The Administrative Council may establish, by a majority of two-thirds of its members, a procedure whereby the Chairman may seek a vote of the Council without convening a meeting of the Council. The vote shall be considered valid only if the majority of the members of the Council cast their votes within the time limit fixed by the said procedure.

Article 8

Members of the Administrative Council and the Chairman shall serve without remuneration from the Centre.

Section 3
The Secretariat

Article 9

The Secretariat shall consist of a Secretary-General, one or more Deputy Secretaries-General and staff.

Article 10

(1) The Secretary-General and any Deputy Secretary-General shall be elected by the Administrative Council by a majority of two-thirds of its members upon the nomination of the Chairman for a term of service not exceeding six years and shall be eligible for re-election. After consulting the members of the Administrative Council, the Chairman shall propose one or more candidates for each such office.

(2) The offices of Secretary-General and Deputy Secretary-General shall be incompatible with the exercise of any political function. Neither the Secretary-General nor any Deputy Secretary-General may hold any other employment or engage in any other occupation except with the approval of the Administrative Council.

(3) During the Secretary-General's absence or inability to act, and during any vacancy of the office of Secretary-General, the Deputy Secretary-General shall act

as Secretary-General. If there shall be more than one Deputy Secretary-General, the Administrative Council shall determine in advance the order in which they shall act as Secretary-General.

Article 11

The Secretary-General shall be the legal representative and the principal officer of the Centre and shall be responsible for its administration, including the appointment of staff, in accordance with the provisions of this Convention and the rules adopted by the Administrative Convention Council. He shall perform the function of registrar and shall have the power to authenticate arbitral awards rendered pursuant to this Convention, and to certify copies thereof.

Section 4
The Panels

Article 12

The Panel of Conciliators and the Panel of Arbitrators shall each consist of qualified persons, designated as hereinafter provided, who are willing to serve thereon.

Article 13

(1) Each Contracting State may designate to each Panel four persons who may but need not be its nationals.

(2) The Chairman may designate ten persons to each Panel. The persons so designated to a Panel shall each have a different nationality.

Article 14

(1) Persons designated to serve on the Panels shall be persons of high moral character and recognized competence in the fields of law, commerce, industry or finance, who may be relied upon to exercise independent judgment. Competence in the field of law shall be of particular importance in the case of persons on the Panel of Arbitrators.

(2) The Chairman, in designating persons to serve on the Panels, shall in addition pay due regard to the importance of assuring representation on the Panels of the principal legal systems of the world and of the main forms of economic activity.

Article 15

(1) Panel members shall serve for renewable periods of six years.

(2) In case of death or resignation of a member of a Panel, the authority which designated the member shall have the right to designate another person to serve for the remainder of that member's term.

(3) Panel members shall continue in office until their successors have been designated.

Article 16

(1) A person may serve on both Panels.

(2) If a person shall have been designated to serve on the same Panel by more than one Contracting State, or by one or more Contracting States and the Chairman, he

shall be deemed to have been designated by the authority which first designated him or, if one such authority is the State of which he is a national, by that State.

(3) All designations shall be notified to the Secretary-General and shall take effect from the date on which the notification is received.

Section 5
Financing the Centre

Article 17

If the expenditure of the Centre cannot be met out of charges for the use of its facilities, or out of other receipts, the excess shall be borne by Contracting States which are members of the Bank in proportion to their respective subscriptions to the capital stock of the Bank, and by Contracting States which are not members of the Bank in accordance with rules adopted by the Administrative Council.

Section 6
Status, Immunities and Privileges

Article 18

The Centre shall have full international legal personality. The legal capacity of the Centre shall include the capacity:

(a) to contract;

(b) to acquire and dispose of movable and immovable property;

(c) to institute legal proceedings.

Article 19

To enable the Centre to fulfil its functions, it shall enjoy in the territories of each Contracting State the immunities and privileges set forth in this Section.

Article 20

The Centre, its property and assets shall enjoy immunity from all legal process, except when the Centre waives this immunity.

Article 21

The Chairman, the members of the Administrative Council, persons acting as conciliators or arbitrators or members of a Committee appointed pursuant to paragraph (3) of Article 52, and the officers and employees of the Secretariat

(a) shall enjoy immunity from legal process with respect to acts performed by them in the exercise of their functions, except when the Centre waives this immunity;

(b) not being local nationals, shall enjoy the same immunities from immigration restrictions, alien registration requirements and national service obligations, the same facilities as regards exchange restrictions and the same treatment in respect of travelling facilities as are accorded by Contracting States to the representatives, officials and employees of comparable rank of other Contracting States.

Article 22

The provisions of Article 21 shall apply to persons appearing in proceedings under this Convention as parties, agents, counsel, advocates, witnesses or experts; provided, however, that sub-paragraph (b) thereof shall apply only in connection with their travel to and from, and their stay at, the place where the proceedings are held.

Article 23

(1) The archives of the Centre shall be inviolable, wherever they may be.

(2) With regard to its official communications, the Centre shall be accorded by each Contracting State treatment not less favourable than that accorded to other international organizations.

Article 24

(1) The Centre, its assets, property and income, and its operations and transactions authorized by this Convention shall be exempt from all taxation and customs duties. The Centre shall also be exempt from liability for the collection or payment of any taxes or customs duties.

(2) Except in the case of local nationals, no tax shall be levied on or in respect of expense allowances paid by the Centre to the Chairman or members of the Administrative Council, or on or in respect of salaries, expense allowances or other emoluments paid by the Centre to officials or employees of the Secretariat.

(3) No tax shall be levied on or in respect of fees or expense allowances received by persons acting as conciliators, or arbitrators, or members of a Committee appointed pursuant to paragraph (3) of Article 52, in proceedings under this Convention, if the sole jurisdictional basis for such tax is the location of the Centre or the place where such proceedings are conducted or the place where such fees or allowances are paid.

Chapter II
Jurisdiction of the Centre

Article 25

(1) The jurisdiction of the Centre shall extend to any legal dispute arising directly out of an investment, between a Contracting State (or any constituent subdivision or agency of a Contracting State designated to the Centre by that State) and a national of another Contracting State, which the parties to the dispute consent in writing to submit to the Centre. When the parties have given their consent, no party may withdraw its consent unilaterally.

(2) "National of another Contracting State" means:

(a) any natural person who had the nationality of a Contracting State other than the State party to the dispute on the date on which the parties consented to submit such dispute to conciliation or arbitration as well as on the date on which the request was registered pursuant to paragraph (3) of Article 28 or paragraph (3) of Article 36, but does not include any person who on either date also had the nationality of the Contracting State party to the dispute; and

(b) any juridical person which had the nationality of a Contracting State other than the State party to the dispute on the date on which the parties consented to submit such dispute to conciliation or arbitration and any juridical person which had the nationality of the Contracting State party to the dispute on that date and which, because of foreign control, the parties have agreed should be treated as a national of another Contracting State for the purposes of this Convention.

(3) Consent by a constituent subdivision or agency of a Contracting State shall require the approval of that State unless that State notifies the Centre that no such approval is required.

(4) Any Contracting State may, at the time of ratification, acceptance or approval of this Convention or at any time thereafter, notify the Centre of the class or classes of disputes which it would or would not consider submitting to the jurisdiction of the Centre. The Secretary General shall forthwith transmit such notification to all Contracting States. Such notification shall not constitute the consent required by paragraph (1).

Article 26

Consent of the parties to arbitration under this Convention shall, unless otherwise stated, be deemed consent to such arbitration to the exclusion of any other remedy. A Contracting State may require the exhaustion of local administrative or judicial remedies as a condition of its consent to arbitration under this Convention.

Article 27

(1) No Contracting State shall give diplomatic protection, or bring an international claim, in respect of a dispute which one of its nationals and another Contracting State shall have consented to submit or shall have submitted to arbitration under this Convention, unless such other Contracting State shall have failed to abide by and comply with the award rendered in such dispute.

(2) Diplomatic protection, for the purposes of paragraph (1), shall not include informal diplomatic exchanges for the sole purpose of facilitating a settlement of the dispute.

Chapter III
Conciliation

Section 1
Request for Conciliation

Article 28

(1) Any Contracting State or any national of a Contracting State wishing to institute conciliation proceedings shall address a request to that effect in writing to the Secretary-General who shall send a copy of the request to the other party.

(2) The request shall contain information concerning the issues in dispute, the identity of the parties and their consent to conciliation in accordance with the rules of procedure for the institution of conciliation and arbitration proceedings.

(3) The Secretary-General shall register the request unless he finds, on the basis of the information contained in the request, that the dispute is manifestly outside the jurisdiction of the Centre. He shall forthwith notify the parties of registration or refusal to register.

Section 2
Constitution of the Conciliation Commission

Article 29

(1) The Conciliation Commission (hereinafter called the Commission) shall be constituted as soon as possible after registration of a request pursuant to Article 28.

(2) (a) The Commission shall consist of a sole conciliator or any uneven number of conciliators appointed as the parties shall agree.

(b) Where the parties do not agree upon the number of conciliators and the method of their appointment, the Commission shall consist of three conciliators, one conciliator appointed by each party and the third, who shall be the president of the Commission, appointed by agreement of the parties.

Article 30

If the Commission shall not have been constituted within 90 days after notice of registration of the request has been dispatched by the Secretary-General in accordance with paragraph (3) of Article 28, or such other period as the parties may agree, the Chairman shall, at the request of either party and after consulting both parties as far as possible, appoint the conciliator or conciliators not yet appointed.

Article 31

(1) Conciliators may be appointed from outside the Panel of Conciliators, except in the case of appointments by the Chairman pursuant to Article 30.

(2) Conciliators appointed from outside the Panel of Conciliators shall possess the qualities stated in paragraph (1) of Article 14.

Section 3
Conciliation Proceedings

Article 32

(1) The Commission shall be the judge of its own competence.

(2) Any objection by a party to the dispute that that dispute is not within the jurisdiction of the Centre, or for other reasons is not within the competence of the Commission, shall be considered by the Commission which shall determine whether to deal with it as a preliminary question or to join it to the merits of the dispute.

Article 33

Any conciliation proceeding shall be conducted in accordance with the provisions of this Section and, except as the parties otherwise agree, in accordance with the Conciliation Rules in effect on the date on which the parties consented to conciliation.

If any question of procedure arises which is not covered by this Section or the Conciliation Rules or any rules agreed by the parties, the Commission shall decide the question.

Article 34

(1) It shall be the duty of the Commission to clarify the issues in dispute between the parties and to endeavour to bring about agreement between them upon mutually acceptable terms. To that end, the Commission may at any stage of the proceedings and from time to time recommend terms of settlement to the parties. The parties shall cooperate in good faith with the Commission in order to enable the Commission to carry out its functions, and shall give their most serious consideration to its recommendations.

(2) If the parties reach agreement, the Commission shall draw up a report noting the issues in dispute and recording that the parties have reached agreement. If, at any stage of the proceedings, it appears to the Commission that there is no likelihood of agreement between the parties, it shall close the proceedings and shall draw up a report noting the submission of the dispute and recording the failure of the parties to reach agreement. If one party fails to appear or participate in the proceedings, the Commission shall close the proceedings and shall draw up a report noting that party's failure to appear or participate.

Article 35

Except as the parties to the dispute shall otherwise agree, neither party to a conciliation proceeding shall be entitled in any other proceeding, whether before arbitrators or in a court of law or otherwise, to invoke or rely on any views expressed or statements or admissions or offers of settlement made by the other party in the conciliation proceedings, or the report or any recommendations made by the Commission.

Chapter IV
Arbitration

Section 1
Request for Arbitration

Article 36

(1) Any Contracting State or any national of a Contracting State wishing to institute arbitration proceedings shall address a request to that effect in writing to the Secretary-General who shall send a copy of the request to the other party.

(2) The request shall contain information concerning the issues in dispute, the identity of the parties and their consent to arbitration in accordance with the rules of procedure for the institution of conciliation and arbitration proceedings.

(3) The Secretary-General shall register the request unless he finds, on the basis of the information contained in the request, that the dispute is manifestly outside the jurisdiction of the Centre. He shall forthwith notify the parties of registration or refusal to register.

Section 2
Constitution of the Tribunal

Article 37

(1) The Arbitral Tribunal (hereinafter called the Tribunal) shall be constituted as soon as possible after registration of a request pursuant to Article 36.

(2) (a) The Tribunal shall consist of a sole arbitrator or any uneven number of arbitrators appointed as the parties shall agree.

(b) Where the parties do not agree upon the number of arbitrators and the method of their appointment, the Tribunal shall consist of three arbitrators, one arbitrator appointed by each party and the third, who shall be the president of the Tribunal, appointed by agreement of the parties.

Article 38

If the Tribunal shall not have been constituted within 90 days after notice of registration of the request has been dispatched by the Secretary-General in accordance with paragraph (3) of Article 36, or such other period as the parties may agree, the Chairman shall, at the request of either party and after consulting both parties as far as possible, appoint the arbitrator or arbitrators not yet appointed. Arbitrators appointed by the Chairman pursuant to this Article shall not be nationals of the Contracting State party to the dispute or of the Contracting State whose national is a party to the dispute.

Article 39

The majority of the arbitrators shall be nationals of States other than the Contracting State party to the dispute and the Contracting State whose national is a party to the dispute; provided, however, that the foregoing provisions of this Article shall not apply if the sole arbitrator or each individual member of the Tribunal has been appointed by agreement of the parties.

Article 40

(1) Arbitrators may be appointed from outside the Panel of Arbitrators, except in the case of appointments by the Chairman pursuant to Article 38.

(2) Arbitrators appointed from outside the Panel of Arbitrators shall possess the qualities stated in paragraph (1) of Article 14.

Section 3
Powers and Functions of the Tribunal

Article 41

(1) The Tribunal shall be the judge of its own competence.

(2) Any objection by a party to the dispute that that dispute is not within the jurisdiction of the Centre, or for other reasons is not within the competence of the Tribunal, shall be considered by the Tribunal which shall determine whether to deal with it as a preliminary question or to join it to the merits of the dispute.

Article 42

(1) The Tribunal shall decide a dispute in accordance with such rules of law as may be agreed by the parties. In the absence of such agreement, the Tribunal shall apply the law of the Contracting State party to the dispute (including its rules on the conflict of laws) and such rules of international law as may be applicable.

(2) The Tribunal may not bring in a finding of non liquet on the ground of silence or obscurity of the law.

(3) The provisions of paragraphs (1) and (2) shall not prejudice the power of the Tribunal to decide a dispute ex aequo et bono if the parties so agree.

Article 43

Except as the parties otherwise agree, the Tribunal may, if it deems it necessary at any stage of the proceedings,

(a) call upon the parties to produce documents or other evidence, and

(b) visit the scene connected with the dispute, and conduct such inquiries there as it may deem appropriate.

Article 44

Any arbitration proceeding shall be conducted in accordance with the provisions of this Section and, except as the parties otherwise agree, in accordance with the Arbitration Rules in effect on the date on which the parties consented to arbitration. If any question of procedure arises which is not covered by this Section or the Arbitration Rules or any rules agreed by the parties, the Tribunal shall decide the question.

Article 45

(1) Failure of a party to appear or to present his case shall not be deemed an admission of the other party's assertions.

(2) If a party fails to appear or to present his case at any stage of the proceedings the other party may request the Tribunal to deal with the questions submitted to it and to render an award. Before rendering an award, the Tribunal shall notify, and grant a period of grace to, the party failing to appear or to present its case, unless it is satisfied that that party does not intend to do so.

Article 46

Except as the parties otherwise agree, the Tribunal shall, if requested by a party, determine any incidental or additional claims or counterclaims arising directly out of the subject-matter of the dispute provided that they are within the scope of the consent of the parties and are otherwise within the jurisdiction of the Centre.

Article 47

Except as the parties otherwise agree, the Tribunal may, if it considers that the circumstances so require, recommend any provisional measures which should be taken to preserve the respective rights of either party.

Section 4
The Award

Article 48

(1) The Tribunal shall decide questions by a majority of the votes of all its members.

(2) The award of the Tribunal shall be in writing and shall be signed by the members of the Tribunal who voted for it.

(3) The award shall deal with every question submitted to the Tribunal, and shall state the reasons upon which it is based.

(4) Any member of the Tribunal may attach his individual opinion to the award, whether he dissents from the majority or not, or a statement of his dissent. (5) The Centre shall not publish the award without the consent of the parties.

Article 49

(1) The Secretary-General shall promptly dispatch certified copies of the award to the parties. The award shall be deemed to have been rendered on the date on which the certified copies were dispatched.

(2) The Tribunal upon the request of a party made within 45 days after the date on which the award was rendered may after notice to the other party decide any question which it had omitted to decide in the award, and shall rectify any clerical, arithmetical or similar error in the award. Its decision shall become part of the award and shall be notified to the parties in the same manner as the award. The periods of time provided for under paragraph (2) of Article 51 and paragraph (2) of Article 52 shall run from the date on which the decision was rendered.

Section 5
Interpretation, Revision and Annulment of the Award

Article 50

(1) If any dispute shall arise between the parties as to the meaning or scope of an award, either party may request interpretation of the award by an application in writing addressed to the Secretary-General.

(2) The request shall, if possible, be submitted to the Tribunal which rendered the award. If this shall not be possible, a new Tribunal shall be constituted in accordance with Section 2 of this Chapter. The Tribunal may, if it considers that the circumstances so require, stay enforcement of the award pending its decision.

Article 51

(1) Either party may request revision of the award by an application in writing addressed to the Secretary-General on the ground of discovery of some fact of such a nature as decisively to affect the award, provided that when the award was rendered that fact was unknown to the Tribunal and to the applicant and that the applicant's ignorance of that fact was not due to negligence.

(2) The application shall be made within 90 days after the discovery of such fact and in any event within three years after the date on which the award was rendered.

(3) The request shall, if possible, be submitted to the Tribunal which rendered the award. If this shall not be possible, a new Tribunal shall be constituted in accordance with Section 2 of this Chapter.

(4) The Tribunal may, if it considers that the circumstances so require, stay enforcement of the award pending its decision. If the applicant requests a stay of enforcement of the award in his application, enforcement shall be stayed provisionally until the Tribunal rules on such request.

Article 52

(1) Either party may request annulment of the award by an application in writing addressed to the Secretary-General on one or more of the following grounds:

(a) that the Tribunal was not properly constituted;

(b) that the Tribunal has manifestly exceeded its powers;

(c) that there was corruption on the part of a member of the Tribunal;

(d) that there has been a serious departure from a fundamental rule of procedure; or

(e) that the award has failed to state the reasons on which it is based.

(2) The application shall be made within 120 days after the date on which the award was rendered except that when annulment is requested on the ground of corruption such application shall be made within 120 days after discovery of the corruption and in any event within three years after the date on which the award was rendered.

(3) On receipt of the request the Chairman shall forthwith appoint from the Panel of Arbitrators an ad hoc Committee of three persons. None of the members of the Committee shall have been a member of the Tribunal which rendered the award, shall be of the same nationality as any such member, shall be a national of the State party to the dispute or of the State whose national is a party to the dispute, shall have been designated to the Panel of Arbitrators by either of those States, or shall have acted as a conciliator in the same dispute. The Committee shall have the authority to annul the award or any part thereof on any of the grounds set forth in paragraph (1).

(4) The provisions of Articles 41–45, 48, 49, 53 and 54, and of Chapters VI and VII shall apply mutatis mutandis to proceedings before the Committee.

(5) The Committee may, if it considers that the circumstances so require, stay enforcement of the award pending its decision. If the applicant requests a stay of enforcement of the award in his application, enforcement shall be stayed provisionally until the Committee rules on such request.

(6) If the award is annulled the dispute shall, at the request of either party, be submitted to a new Tribunal constituted in accordance with Section 2 of this Chapter.

Section 6
Recognition and Enforcement of the Award

Article 53

(1) The award shall be binding on the parties and shall not be subject to any appeal or to any other remedy except those provided for in this Convention. Each party shall abide by and comply with the terms of the award except to the extent that enforcement shall have been stayed pursuant to the relevant provisions of this Convention.

(2) For the purposes of this Section, "award" shall include any decision interpreting, revising or annulling such award pursuant to Articles 50, 51 or 52.

Article 54

(1) Each Contracting State shall recognize an award rendered pursuant to this Convention as binding and enforce the pecuniary obligations imposed by that award within its territories as if it were a final judgment of a court in that State. A Contracting State with a federal constitution may enforce such an award in or through its federal courts and may provide that such courts shall treat the award as if it were a final judgment of the courts of a constituent state.

(2) A party seeking recognition or enforcement in the territories of a Contracting State shall furnish to a competent court or other authority which such State shall have designated for this purpose a copy of the award certified by the Secretary-General. Each Contracting State shall notify the Secretary-General of the designation of the competent court or other authority for this purpose and of any subsequent change in such designation.

(3) Execution of the award shall be governed by the laws concerning the execution of judgments in force in the State in whose territories such execution is sought.

Article 55

Nothing in Article 54 shall be construed as derogating from the law in force in any Contracting State relating to immunity of that State or of any foreign State from execution.

Chapter V
Replacement and Disqualification of Conciliators and Arbitrators

Article 56

(1) After a Commission or a Tribunal has been constituted and proceedings have begun, its composition shall remain unchanged; provided, however, that if a conciliator or an arbitrator should die, become incapacitated, or resign, the resulting vacancy shall be filled in accordance with the provisions of Section 2 of Chapter III or Section 2 of Chapter IV.

(2) A member of a Commission or Tribunal shall continue to serve in that capacity notwithstanding that he shall have ceased to be a member of the Panel.

(3) If a conciliator or arbitrator appointed by a party shall have resigned without the consent of the Commission or Tribunal of which he was a member, the Chairman shall appoint a person from the appropriate Panel to fill the resulting vacancy.

Article 57

A party may propose to a Commission or Tribunal the disqualification of any of its members on account of any fact indicating a manifest lack of the qualities required by paragraph (1) of Article 14. A party to arbitration proceedings may, in addition, propose the disqualification of an arbitrator on the ground that he was ineligible for appointment to the Tribunal under Section 2 of Chapter IV.

Article 58

The decision on any proposal to disqualify a conciliator or arbitrator shall be taken by the other members of the Commission or Tribunal as the case may be, provided that where those members are equally divided, or in the case of a proposal to disqualify a sole conciliator or arbitrator, or a majority of the conciliators or arbitrators, the Chairman shall take that decision. If it is decided that the proposal is well-founded the conciliator or arbitrator to whom the decision relates shall be replaced in accordance with the provisions of Section 2 of Chapter III or Section 2 of Chapter IV.

Chapter VI
Cost of Proceedings

Article 59

The charges payable by the parties for the use of the facilities of the Centre shall be determined by the Secretary-General in accordance with the regulations adopted by the Administrative Council.

Article 60

(1) Each Commission and each Tribunal shall determine the fees and expenses of its members within limits established from time to time by the Administrative Council and after consultation with the Secretary-General.

(2) Nothing in paragraph (1) of this Article shall preclude the parties from agreeing in advance with the Commission or Tribunal concerned upon the fees and expenses of its members.

Article 61

(1) In the case of conciliation proceedings the fees and expenses of members of the Commission as well as the charges for the use of the facilities of the Centre, shall be borne equally by the parties. Each party shall bear any other expenses it incurs in connection with the proceedings.

(2) In the case of arbitration proceedings the Tribunal shall, except as the parties otherwise agree, assess the expenses incurred by the parties in connection with the proceedings, and shall decide how and by whom those expenses, the fees and

expenses of the members of the Tribunal and the charges for the use of the facilities of the Centre shall be paid. Such decision shall form part of the award.

Chapter VII
Place of Proceedings

Article 62

Conciliation and arbitration proceedings shall be held at the seat of the Centre except as hereinafter provided.

Article 63

Conciliation and arbitration proceedings may be held, if the parties so agree,

(a) at the seat of the Permanent Court of Arbitration or of any other appropriate institution, whether private or public, with which the Centre may make arrangements for that purpose; or

(b) at any other place approved by the Commission or Tribunal after consultation with the Secretary-General.

Chapter VIII
Disputes Between Contracting States

Article 64

Any dispute arising between Contracting States concerning the interpretation or application of this Convention which is not settled by negotiation shall be referred to the International Court of Justice by the application of any party to such dispute, unless the States concerned agree to another method of settlement.

Chapter IX
Amendment

Article 65

Any Contracting State may propose amendment of this Convention. The text of a proposed amendment shall be communicated to the Secretary-General not less than 90 days prior to the meeting of the Administrative Council at which such amendment is to be considered and shall forthwith be transmitted by him to all the members of the Administrative Council.

Article 66

(1) If the Administrative Council shall so decide by a majority of two-thirds of its members, the proposed amendment shall be circulated to all Contracting States for ratification, acceptance or approval. Each amendment shall enter into force 30 days after dispatch by the depositary of this Convention of a notification to Contracting States that all Contracting States have ratified, accepted or approved the amendment.

(2) No amendment shall affect the rights and obligations under this Convention of any Contracting State or of any of its constituent subdivisions or agencies, or of any national of such State arising out of consent to the jurisdiction of the Centre given before the date of entry into force of the amendment.

Chapter X
Final Provisions

Article 67

This Convention shall be open for signature on behalf of States members of the Bank. It shall also be open for signature on behalf of any other State which is a party to the Statute of the International Court of Justice and which the Administrative Council, by a vote of two-thirds of its members, shall have invited to sign the Convention.

Article 68

(1) This Convention shall be subject to ratification, acceptance or approval by the signatory States in accordance with their respective constitutional procedures.

(2) This Convention shall enter into force 30 days after the date of deposit of the twentieth instrument of ratification, acceptance or approval. It shall enter into force for each State which subsequently deposits its instrument of ratification, acceptance or approval 30 days after the date of such deposit.

Article 69

Each Contracting State shall take such legislative or other measures as may be necessary for making the provisions of this Convention effective in its territories.

Article 70

This Convention shall apply to all territories for whose international relations a Contracting State is responsible, except those which are excluded by such State by written notice to the depositary of this Convention either at the time of ratification, acceptance or approval or subsequently.

Article 71

Any Contracting State may denounce this Convention by written notice to the depositary of this Convention. The denunciation shall take effect six months after receipt of such notice.

Article 72

Notice by a Contracting State pursuant to Articles 70 or 71 shall not affect the rights or obligations under this Convention of that State or of any of its constituent subdivisions or agencies or of any national of that State arising out of consent to the jurisdiction of the Centre given by one of them before such notice was received by the depositary.

Article 73

Instruments of ratification, acceptance or approval of this Convention and of amendments thereto shall be deposited with the Bank which shall act as the depositary of this Convention. The depositary shall transmit certified copies of this Convention to States members of the Bank and to any other State invited to sign the Convention.

Article 74

The depositary shall register this Convention with the Secretariat of the United Nations in accordance with Article 102 of the Charter of the United Nations and the Regulations thereunder adopted by the General Assembly.

Article 75

The depositary shall notify all signatory States of the following:

(a) signatures in accordance with Article 67;

(b) deposits of instruments of ratification, acceptance and approval in accordance with Article 73;

(c) the date on which this Convention enters into force in accordance with Article 68;

(d) exclusions from territorial application pursuant to Article 70;

(e) the date on which any amendment of this Convention enters into force in accordance with Article 66; and

(f) denunciations in accordance with Article 71.

DONE at Washington, in the English, French and Spanish languages, all three texts being equally authentic, in a single copy which shall remain deposited in the archives of the International Bank for Reconstruction and Development, which has indicated by its signature below its agreement to fulfil the functions with which it is charged under this Convention.

C. MIGA Convention (1988)

Preamble

The Contracting States

Considering the need to strengthen international cooperation for economic development and to foster the contribution to such development of foreign investment in general and private foreign investment in particular;

Recognizing that the flow of foreign investment to developing countries would be facilitated and further encouraged by alleviating concerns related to noncommercial risks;

Desiring to enhance the flow to developing countries of capital and technology for productive purposes under conditions consistent with their development needs, policies and objectives, on the basis of fair and stable standards for the treatment of foreign investment;

Convinced that the Multilateral Investment Guarantee Agency can play an important role in the encouragement of foreign investment complementing national and regional investment guarantee programs and private insurers of non-commercial risk; and

Realizing that such Agency should, to the extent possible, meet its obligations without resort to its callable capital and that such an objective would be served by continued improvement in investment conditions.

Have agreed as follows:

Chapter I
Establishment, Status, Purposes and Definitions

Article 1. Establishment and Status of the Agency

(a) There is hereby established the Multilateral Investment Guarantee Agency (hereinafter called the Agency).

(b) The Agency shall possess full juridical personality and, in particular, the capacity to:

(i) contract;

(ii) acquire and dispose of movable and immovable property; and

(iii) institute legal proceedings.

Article 2. Objective and Purposes

The objective of the Agency shall be to encourage the flow of investments for productive purposes among member countries, and in particular to developing member countries, thus supplementing the activities of the International Bank for Reconstruction and Development (hereinafter referred to as the Bank), the International Finance Corporation and other international development finance institutions.

To serve its objective, the Agency shall:

(a) issue guarantees, including coinsurance and reinsurance, against non-commercial risks in respect of investments in a member country which flow from other member countries;

(b) carry out appropriate complementary activities to promote the flow of investments to and among developing member countries; and

(c) exercise such other incidental powers as shall be necessary or desirable in the furtherance of its objective.

The Agency shall be guided in all its decisions by the provisions of this Article.

Article 3. Definitions

For the purposes of this Convention:

(a) **"Member"** means a State with respect to which this Convention has entered into force in accordance with Article 61.

(b) **"Host country"** or **"host government"** means a member, its government, or any public authority of a member in whose territories, as defined in Article 66, an investment which has been guaranteed or reinsured, or is considered for guarantee or reinsurance, by the Agency is to be located.

(c) A "**developing member country**" means a member which is listed as such in Schedule A hereto as this Schedule may be amended from time to time by the Council of Governors referred to in Article 30 (hereinafter called the Council).

(d) A "**special majority**" means an affirmative vote of not less than two-thirds of the total voting power representing not less than fifty-five percent of the subscribed shares of the capital stock of the Agency.

(e) A "**freely usable currency**" means (i) any currency designated as such by the International Monetary Fund from time to time and (ii) any other freely available and effectively usable currency which the Board of Directors referred to in Article 30 (hereinafter called the Board) may designate for the purposes of this Convention after consultation with the International Monetary Fund and with the approval of the country of such currency.

Chapter II
Membership and Capital

Article 4. Membership

(a) Membership in the Agency shall be open to all members of the Bank and to Switzerland.

(b) Original member shall be the States which are listed in Schedule A hereto and become parties to this Convention on or before October 30, 1987.

Article 5. Capital

(a) The authorized capital stock of the Agency shall be one billion Special Drawing Rights (SDR 1,000,000,000). The capital stock shall be divided into 100,000 shares having a par value of SDR 10,000 each, which shall be available for subscription by members. All payment obligations of members with respect to capital stock shall be settled on the basis of the average value of the SDR in terms of United States dollars for the period January 1, 1981 to June 30, 1985, such value being 1.082 United States dollars per SDR.

(b) The capital stock shall increase on the admission of a new member to the extent that the then authorized shares are insufficient to provide the shares to be subscribed by such member pursuant to Article 6.

(c) The Council, by special majority, may at any time increase the capital stock of the Agency.

Article 6. Subscription of Shares

Each original member of the Agency shall subscribe at par to the number of shares of capital stock set forth opposite its name in Schedule A hereto. Each other member shall subscribe to such number of shares of capital stock on such terms and conditions as may be determined by the Council, but in no event at an issue price of less than par. No member shall subscribe to less than fifty shares. The Council may prescribe rules by which members may subscribe to additional shares of the authorized capital stock.

Article 7. Division and Calls of Subscribed Capital

The initial subscription of each member shall be paid as follows:

(i) Within ninety days from the date on which this Convention enters into force with respect to such member, ten percent of the price of each share shall be paid in cash as stipulated in Section (a) of Article 8 and an additional ten percent in the form of non-negotiable, non-interest-bearing promissory notes or similar obligations to be encashed pursuant to a decision of the Board in order to meet the Agency's obligations.

(ii) The remainder shall be subject to call by the Agency when required to meet its obligations.

Article 8. Payment of Subscription of Shares

(a) Payments of subscriptions shall be made in freely usable currencies except that payments by developing member countries may be made in their own currencies up to twenty-five percent of the paid-in cash portion of their subscriptions payable under Article 7(i).

(b) Calls on any portion of unpaid subscriptions shall be uniform on all shares.

(c) If the amount received by the Agency on a call shall be insufficient to meet the obligations which have necessitated the call, the Agency may make further successive calls on unpaid subscriptions until the aggregate amount received by it shall be sufficient to meet such obligations.

(d) Liability on shares shall be limited to the unpaid portion of the issue price.

Article 9. Valuation of Currencies

Whenever it shall be necessary for the purposes of this Convention to determine the value of one currency in terms of another, such value shall be as reasonably determined by the Agency, after consultation with the International Monetary Fund.

Article 10. Refunds

(a) The Agency shall, as soon as practicable, return to members amounts paid on calls on subscribed capital if and to the extent that:

(i) the call shall have been made to pay a claim resulting from a guarantee or reinsurance contract and thereafter the Agency shall have recovered its payment, in whole or in part, in a freely usable currency; or

(ii) the call shall have been made because of a default in payment by a member and thereafter such member shall have made good such default in whole or in part; or

(iii) the Council, by special majority, determines that the financial position of the Agency permits all or part of such amounts to be returned out of the Agency's revenues.

(b) Any refund effected under this Article to a member shall be made in freely usable currency in the proportion of the payments made by that member to the total amount paid pursuant to calls made prior to such refund.

(c) The equivalent of amounts refunded under this Article to a member shall become part of the callable capital obligations of the member under Article 7(ii).

Chapter III
Operations

Article 11. Covered Risks

(a) Subject to the provisions of Sections (b) and (c) below, the Agency may guarantee eligible investments against a loss resulting from one or more of the following types of risk:

(i) *Currency Transfer*

any introduction attributable to the host government of restrictions on the transfer outside the host country of its currency into a freely usable currency or another currency acceptable to the holder of the guarantee, including a failure of the host government to act within a reasonable period of time on an application by such holder for such transfer;

(ii) *Expropriation and Similar Measures*

any legislative action or administrative action or omission attributable to the host government which has the effect of depriving the holder of a guarantee of his ownership or control of, or a substantial benefit from, his investment, with the exception of non-discriminatory measures of general application which governments normally take for the purpose of regulating economic activity in their territories;

(iii) *Breach of Contract*

any repudiation or breach by the host government of a contract with the holder of a guarantee, when (a) the holder of a guarantee does not have recourse to a judicial or arbitral forum to determine the claim of repudiation or breach, or (b) a decision by such forum is not rendered within such reasonable period of time as shall be prescribed in the contracts of guarantee pursuant to the Agency's regulations, or (c) such a decision cannot be enforced; and

(iv) *War and Civil Disturbance*

any military action or civil disturbance in any territory of the host country to which this Convention shall be applicable as provided in Article 66.

(b) In addition, the Board, by special majority, may approve the extension of coverage under this Article to specific non-commercial risks other than those referred to in Section (a) above, but in no case to the risk of devaluation or depreciation of currency.

(c) Losses resulting from the following shall not be covered:

(i) any host government action or omission to which the holder of the guarantee has agreed or for which he has been responsible; and

(ii) any host government action or omission or any other event occurring before the conclusion of the contract of guarantee.

Article 12. Eligible Investments

(a) Eligible investments shall include equity interests, including medium- or long-term loans made or guaranteed by holders of equity in the enterprise concerned, and such forms of direct investment as may be determined by the Board.

(b) Loans other than those mentioned in Section (a) above are eligible for coverage

(i) if they are made to finance or are otherwise related to a specific investment or project in which some other form of direct investment is present, whether or not guaranteed by the Agency and regardless of when such other investment was made, or

(ii) as may be otherwise approved by the Board by special majority.

(c) The Board, by special majority, may extend eligibility to any other medium- or long-term form of investment.

(d) Guarantees shall generally be restricted to investments the implementation of which begins subsequent to the registration of the application for the guarantee by the Agency or receipt by the Agency of other satisfactory evidence of investor intent to obtain guarantees from the Agency. Such investments may include:

(i) a transfer of foreign exchange made to modernize, expand, or develop an existing investment, in which case both the original investment and the additional investment may be considered eligible for coverage;

(ii) the use of earnings from existing investments which could otherwise be transferred outside the host country;

(iii) the acquisition of an existing investment by a new eligible investor;

(iv) existing investments where an eligible investor is seeking to insure a pool of existing and new investments;

(v) existing investments owned by an eligible investor where there is an improvement or enhancement of the underlying project or the investor otherwise demonstrates medium- or long-term commitment to the project, and the Agency is satisfied that the project continues to have a high developmental impact in the host country; and

(vi) such other investments as may be approved by the Board by special majority.

(e) In guaranteeing an investment, the Agency shall satisfy itself as to:

(i) the economic soundness of the investment and its contribution to the development of the host country;

(ii) compliance of the investment with the host country's laws and regulations;

(iii) consistency of the investment with the declared development objectives and priorities of the host country; and

(iv) the investment conditions in the host country, including the availability of fair and equitable treatment and legal protection for the investment.

Article 13. Eligible Investors

(a) Any natural person and any juridical person may be eligible to receive the Agency's guarantee provided that:

(i) such natural person is a national of a member other than the host country;

(ii) such juridical person is incorporated and has its principal place of business in a member or the majority of its capital is owned by a member or members or nationals thereof, provided that such member is not the host country in any of the above cases; and

(iii) such juridical person, whether or not it is privately owned, operates on a commercial basis.

(b) In case the investor has more than one nationality, for the purposes of Section (a) above the nationality of a member shall prevail over the nationality of a non-member, and the nationality of the host country shall prevail over the nationality of any other member.

(c) Upon the joint application of the investor and the host country, the Board, by special majority, may extend eligibility to a natural person who is a national of the host country or a juridical person which is incorporated in the host country or the majority of whose capital is owned by its nationals, provided that the assets invested are transferred from outside the host country.

Article 14. Eligible Host Countries

Investments shall be guaranteed under this Chapter only if they are to be made in the territory of a developing member country.

Article 15. Host Country Approval

The Agency shall not conclude any contract of guarantee before the host government has approved the issuance of the guarantee by the Agency against the risks designated for cover.

Article 16. Terms and Conditions

The terms and conditions of each contract of guarantee shall be determined by the Agency subject to such rules and regulations as the Board shall issue, provided that the Agency shall not cover the total loss of the guaranteed investment. Contracts of guarantee shall be approved by the President under the direction of the Board.

Article 17. Payment of Claims

The President under the direction of the Board shall decide on the payment of claims to a holder of a guarantee in accordance with the contract of guarantee and such policies as the Board may adopt. Contracts of guarantee shall require holders of guarantees to seek, before a payment is made by the Agency, such administrative remedies as may be appropriate under the circumstances, provided that they are readily available to them under the laws of the host country. Such contracts may require the lapse of certain reasonable periods between the occurrence of events giving rise to claims and payments of claims.

Article 18. Subrogation

(a) Upon paying or agreeing to pay compensation to a holder of a guarantee, the Agency shall be subrogated to such rights or claims related to the guaranteed investment as the holder of a guarantee may have had against the host country and other obligors. The contract of guarantee shall provide the terms and conditions of such subrogation.

(b) The rights of the Agency pursuant to Section (a) above shall be recognized by all members.

(c) Amounts in the currency of the host country acquired by the Agency as subrogee pursuant to Section (a) above shall be accorded, with respect to use and conversion, treatment by the host country as favorable as the treatment to which such funds would be entitled in the hands of the holder of the guarantee. In any case, such amounts may be used by the Agency for the payment of its administrative expenditures and other costs. The Agency shall also seek to enter into arrangements with host countries on other uses of such currencies to the extent that they are not freely usable.

Article 19. Relationship to National and Regional Entities

The Agency shall cooperate with, and seek to complement the operations of, national entities of members and regional entities the majority of whose capital is owned by members, which carry out activities similar to those of the Agency, with a view to maximizing both the efficiency of their respective services and their contribution to increased flows of foreign investment. To this end, the Agency may enter into arrangements with such entities on the details of such cooperation, including in particular the modalities of reinsurance and coinsurance.

Article 20. Reinsurance of National and Regional Entities

(a) The Agency may issue reinsurance in respect of a specific investment against a loss resulting from one or more of the noncommercial risks underwritten by a member or agency thereof or by a regional investment guarantee agency the majority of whose capital is owned by members. The Board, by special majority, shall from time to time prescribe maximum amounts of contingent liability which may be assumed by the Agency with respect to reinsurance contracts. In respect of specific investments which have been completed more than twelve months prior to receipt of the application for reinsurance by the Agency, the maximum amount shall initially be set at ten percent of the aggregate contingent liability of the Agency under this Chapter. The conditions of eligibility specified in Articles 11 to 14 shall apply to reinsurance operations, except that the reinsured investments need not be implemented subsequent to the application for reinsurance.

(b) The mutual rights and obligations of the Agency and a reinsured member or agency shall be stated in contracts of reinsurance subject to such rules and regulations as the Board shall issue. The Board shall approve each contract for reinsurance covering an investment which has been made prior to receipt of the application for reinsurance by the Agency, with a view to minimizing risks, assuring that the Agency receives premiums commensurate with its risk, and assuring that the reinsured entity is appropriately committed toward promoting new investment in developing member countries.

(c) The Agency shall, to the extent possible, assure that it or the reinsured entity shall have the rights of subrogation and arbitration equivalent to those the Agency would have if it were the primary guarantor. The terms and conditions of reinsurance shall require that administrative remedies are sought in accordance with Article 17 before a payment is made by the Agency. Subrogation shall be effective with respect to the host country concerned only after its approval of the reinsurance by the Agency. The Agency shall include in the contracts of reinsurance provisions requiring the reinsured to pursue with due diligence the rights or claims related to the reinsured investment.

Article 21. Cooperation with Private Insurers and with Reinsurers

(a) The Agency may enter into arrangements with private insurers in member countries to enhance its own operations and encourage such insurers to provide coverage of noncommercial risks in developing member countries on conditions similar to those applied by the Agency. Such arrangements may include the provision of reinsurance by the Agency under the conditions and procedures specified in Article 20.

(b) The Agency may reinsure with any appropriate reinsurance entity, in whole or in part, any guarantee or guarantees issued by it.

(c) The Agency will in particular seek to guarantee investments for which comparable coverage on reasonable terms is not available from private insurers and reinsurers.

Article 22. Limits of Guarantee

(a) Unless determined otherwise by the Council by special majority, the aggregate amount of contingent liabilities which may be assumed by the Agency under this Chapter shall not exceed one hundred and 50 percent of the amount of the Agency's unimpaired subscribed capital and its reserves plus such portion of its reinsurance cover as the Board may determine. The Board shall from time to time review the risk profile of the Agency's portfolio in the light of its experience with claims, degree of risk diversification, reinsurance cover and other relevant factors with a view to ascertaining whether changes in the maximum aggregate amount of contingent liabilities should be recommended to the Council. The maximum amount determined by the Council shall not under any circumstances exceed five times the amount of the Agency's unimpaired subscribed capital, its reserves and such portion of its reinsurance cover as may be deemed appropriate.

(b) Without prejudice to the general limit of guarantee referred to in Section (a) above, the Board may prescribe:

(i) maximum aggregate amounts of contingent liability which may be assumed by the Agency under this Chapter for all guarantees issued to investors of each individual member. In determining such maximum amounts, the Board shall give due consideration to the share of the respective member in the capital of the Agency and the need to apply more liberal limitations in respect of investments originating in developing member countries; and

(ii) maximum aggregate amounts of contingent liability which may be assumed by the Agency with respect to such risk diversification factors as individual projects, individual host countries and types of investment or risk.

Article 23. Investment Promotion

(a) The Agency shall carry out research, undertake activities to promote investment flows and disseminate information on investment opportunities in developing member countries, with a view to improving the environment for foreign investment flows to such countries. The Agency may, upon the request of a member, provide technical advice and assistance to improve the investment conditions in the territories of that member. In performing these activities, the Agency shall:

(i) be guided by relevant investment agreements among member countries;

(ii) seek to remove impediments, in both developed and developing member countries, to the flow of investment to developing member countries; and

(iii) coordinate with other agencies concerned with the promotion of foreign investment, and in particular the International Finance Corporation.

(b) The Agency also shall:

(i) encourage the amicable settlement of disputes between investors and host countries;

(ii) endeavor to conclude agreements with developing member countries, and in particular with prospective host countries, which will assure that the Agency, with respect to investment guaranteed by it, has treatment at least as favorable as that agreed by the member concerned for the most favored investment guarantee agency or State in an agreement relating to investment, such agreements to be approved by special majority of the Board; and

(iii) promote and facilitate the conclusion of agreements, among its members, on the promotion and protection of investments.

(c) The Agency shall give particular attention in its promotional efforts to the importance of increasing the flow of investments among developing member countries.

Article 24. Guarantees of Sponsored Investments

In addition to the guarantee operations undertaken by the Agency under this Chapter, the Agency may guarantee investments under the sponsorship arrangements provided for in Annex I to this Convention.

Chapter IV
Financial Provisions

Article 25. Financial Management

The Agency shall carry out its activities in accordance with sound business and prudent financial management practices with a view to maintaining under all circumstances its ability to meet its financial obligations.

Article 26. Premiums and Fees

The Agency shall establish and periodically review the rates of premiums, fees and other charges, if any applicable to each type of risk.

Article 27. Allocation of Net Income

(a) Without prejudice to the provisions of Section (a)(iii) of Article 10, the Agency shall allocate net income to reserves until such reserves reach five times the subscribed capital of the Agency.

(b) After the reserves of the Agency have reached the level prescribed in Section (a) above, the Council shall decide whether, and to what extent, the Agency's net income shall be allocated to reserves, be distributed to the Agency's members or be used otherwise. Any distribution of net income to the Agency's members shall be made in proportion to the share of each member in the capital of the Agency in accordance with a decision of the Council acting by special majority.

Article 28. Budget

The President shall prepare an annual budget of revenues and expenditures of the Agency for approval by the Board.

Article 29. Accounts

The Agency shall publish an Annual Report which shall include statements of its accounts and of the accounts of the Sponsorship Trust Fund referred to in Annex I to this Convention, as audited by independent auditors. The Agency shall circulate to members at appropriate intervals a summary statement of its financial position and a profit and loss statement showing the results of its operations.

Chapter V
Organization and Management

Article 30. Structure of the Agency

The Agency shall have a Council of Governors, a Board of Directors, a President and staff to perform such duties as the Agency may determine.

Article 31. The Council

(a) All the powers of the Agency shall be vested in the Council, except such powers as are, by the terms of this Convention, specifically conferred upon another organ of the Agency. The Council may delegate to the Board the exercise of any of its powers, except the power to:

(i) admit new members and determine the conditions of their admission;

(ii) suspend a member;

(iii) decide on any increase or decrease in the capital;

(iv) increase the limit of the aggregate amount of contingent liabilities pursuant to Section (a) of Article 22;

(v) designate a member as a developing member country pursuant to Section (c) of Article 3;

(vi) classify a new member as belonging to Category One or Category Two for voting purposes pursuant to Section (a) of Article 39 or reclassify an existing member for the same purposes;

(vii) determine the compensation of Directors and their Alternates;

(viii) cease operations and liquidate the Agency;

(ix) distribute assets to members upon liquidation; and

(x) amend this Convention, its Annexes and Schedules.

(b) The council shall be composed of one Governor and one Alternate appointed by each member in such manner as it may determine. No Alternate may vote except in the absence of his principal. The Council shall select one of the Governors as Chairman.

(c) The Council shall hold an annual meeting and such other meetings as may be determined by the Council or called by the Board. The Board shall call a meeting of the Council whenever requested by five members or by members having 25 percent of the total voting power.

Article 32. The Board

(a) The Board shall be responsible for the general operations of the Agency and shall take, in the fulfillment of this responsibility, any action required or permitted under this Convention.

(b) The Board shall consist of not less than twelve Directors. The number of Directors may be adjusted by the Council to take into account changes in membership. Each Director may appoint an Alternate with full power to act for him in case of the Director's absence or inability to act. The President of the Bank shall be ex officio Chairman of the Board, but shall have no vote except a deciding vote in case of an equal division.

(c) The Council shall determine the term of office of the Directors. The first Board shall be constituted by the Council at its inaugural meeting.

(d) The Board shall meet at the call of its Chairman acting on his own initiative or upon request of three Directors.

(e) Until such time as the Council may decide that the Agency shall have a resident Board which functions in continuous session, the Directors and Alternates shall receive compensation only for the cost of attendance at the meetings of the Board and the discharge of other official functions on behalf of the Agency. Upon the establishment of a Board in continuous session, the Directors and Alternates shall receive such remuneration as may be determined by the Council.

Article 33. President and Staff

(a) The President shall, under the general control of the Board, conduct the ordinary business of the Agency. He shall be responsible for the organization, appointment and dismissal of the staff.

(b) The President shall be appointed by the Board on the nomination of its Chairman. The Council shall determine the salary and terms of the contract of service of the President.

(c) In the discharge of their offices, the President and the staff owe their duty entirely to the Agency and to no other authority. Each member of the Agency shall respect the international character of this duty and shall refrain from all attempts to influence the President or the staff in the discharge of their duties.

(d) In appointing the staff, the President shall, subject to the paramount importance of securing the highest standards of efficiency and of technical competence, pay due regard to the importance of recruiting personnel on as wide a geographical basis as possible.

(e) The President and staff shall maintain at all times the confidentiality of information obtained in carrying out the Agency's operations.

Article 34. Political Activity Prohibited

The Agency, its President and staff shall not interfere in the political affairs of any member. Without prejudice to the right of the Agency to take into account all the circumstances surrounding an investment, they shall not be influenced in their decisions by the political character of the member or members concerned. Considerations relevant to their decisions shall be weighed impartially in order to achieve the purposes states in Article 2.

Article 35. Relations with International Organizations

The Agency shall, within the terms of this Convention, cooperate with the United Nations and with other inter-governmental organizations having specialized responsibilities in related fields, including in particular the Bank and the International Finance Corporation.

Article 36. Location of Principal Office

(a) The principal office of the Agency shall be located in Washington, D.C., unless the Council, by special majority, decides to establish it in another location.

(b) The Agency may establish other offices as may be necessary for its work.

Article 37. Depositories for Assets

Each member shall designate its central bank as a depository in which the Agency may keep holdings of such member's currency or other assets of the Agency or, if it has no central bank, it shall designate for such purpose such other institution as may be acceptable to the Agency.

Article 38. Channel of Communication

(a) Each member shall designate an appropriate authority with which the Agency may communicate in connections with any matter arising under this Convention. The Agency may rely on statements of such authority as being statements of the member. The Agency, upon the request of a member, shall consult with that member with respect to matters dealt with in Articles 19 to 21 and related to entities or insurers of that member.

(b) Whenever the approval of any member is required before any act may be done by the Agency, approval shall be deemed to have been given unless the member presents an objection within such reasonable period as the Agency may fix in notifying the member of the proposed act.

Chapter VI
Voting, Adjustments of Subscriptions and Representation

Article 39. Voting and Adjustments of Subscriptions

(a) In order to provide for voting arrangements that reflect the equal interest in the Agency of the two Categories of States listed in Schedule A of this Convention, as well as the importance of each member's financial participation, each member shall have 177 membership votes plus one subscription vote for each share of stock held by that member.

(b) If at any time within three years after the entry into force of this Convention the aggregate sum of membership and subscription votes of members which belong to either of the two Categories of States listed in Schedule A of this Convention is less than 40 percent of the total voting power, members from such a Category shall have such number of supplementary votes as shall be necessary for the aggregate voting power of the Category to equal such a percentage of the total voting power. Such supplementary votes shall be distributed among the members of such Category in the proportion that the subscription votes of each bears to the aggregate of subscription votes of the Category. Such supplementary votes shall be subject to automatic adjustment to ensure that such percentage is maintained and shall be canceled at the end of the abovementioned three-year period.

(c) During the third year following the entry into force of this Convention, the Council shall review the allocation of shares and shall be guided in its decision by the following principles:

(i) the votes of members shall reflect actual subscriptions to the Agency's capital and the membership votes as set out in Section (a) of this Article;

(ii) shares allocated to countries which shall not have signed the Convention shall be made available for reallocation to such members and in such manner as to make possible voting parity between the above-mentioned Categories; and

(iii) the Council will take measures that will facilitate members' ability to subscribe to share allocated to them.

(d) Within the three-year period provided for in Section (b) of this Article, all decisions of the Council and Board shall be taken by special majority, except that decisions requiring a higher majority under this Convention shall be taken by such higher majority.

(e) In case the capital stock of the Agency is increased pursuant to Section (c) of Article 5, each member which so requests shall be authorized to subscribe a proportion of the increase equivalent to the proportion which its stock theretofore subscribed bears to the total capital stock of the Agency, but no member shall be obligated to subscribe any part of the increased capital.

(f) The Council shall issue regulations regarding the making of additional subscriptions under Section (e) of this Article. Such regulations shall prescribe reasonable time limits for the submission by members of requests to make such subscriptions.

Article 40. Voting in the Council

(a) Each Governor shall be entitled to cast the votes of the member he represents. Except as otherwise specified in this Convention, decisions of the Council shall be taken by a majority of the votes cast.

(b) A quorum for any meeting of the Council shall be constituted by a majority of the Governors exercising not less than two-thirds of the total voting power.

(c) The Council may by regulation establish a procedure whereby the Board, when it deems such action to be in the best interests of the Agency, may request a decision of the Council on a specific question without calling a meeting of the Council.

Article 41. Election of Directors

(a) Directors shall be elected in accordance with Schedule B.

(b) Directors shall continue in office until their successors are elected. If the office of a Director becomes vacant more than ninety days before the end of his term, another Director shall be elected for the remainder of the term by the Governors who elected the former Director. A majority of the votes cast shall be required for election. While the office remains vacant, the Alternate of the Former Director shall exercise his powers, except that of appointing an Alternate.

Article 42. Voting in the Board

(a) Each Director shall be entitled to cast the number of votes of the members whose votes counted towards his election. All the votes which a Director is entitled to cast shall be cast as a unit. Except as otherwise specified in this Convention, decisions of the Board shall be taken by a majority of the votes cast.

(b) A quorum for a meeting of the Board shall be constituted by a majority of the Directors exercising not less than one-half of the total voting power.

(c) The Board may by regulation establish a procedure whereby its Chairman, when he deems such action to be in the best interests of the Agency, may request a decision of the Board on a specific question without calling a meeting of the Board.

Chapter VII
Privileges and Immunities

Article 43. Purposes of Chapter

To enable the Agency to fulfill its functions, the immunities and privileges set forth in this Chapter shall be accorded to the Agency in the territories of each member.

Article 44. Legal Process

Actions other than those within the scope of Articles 57 and 58 may be brought against the Agency only in a court of competent jurisdiction in the territories of a member in which the Agency has an office or has appointed an agent for the purpose of accepting service or notice of process. No such action against the Agency shall be brought:

(i) by members or persons acting for or deriving claims from members or

(ii) in respect of personnel matters.

The property and assets of the Agency shall, wherever located and by whomsoever held, be immune from all forms of seizure, attachment or execution before the delivery of the final judgment or award against the Agency.

Article 45. Assets

(a) The property and assets of the Agency, wherever located and by whomsoever held, shall be immune from search, requisition, confiscation, expropriation or any other form of seizure by executive or legislative action.

(b) To the extent necessary to carry out its operations under this Convention, all property and assets of the Agency shall be free from restrictions, regulations, controls and moratoria of any nature; provided that property and assets acquired by the Agency as successor to or subrogee of a holder of a guarantee, a reinsured entity or an investor insured by a reinsured entity shall be free from applicable foreign exchange restrictions, regulations and controls in force in the territories of the member concerned to the extent that the holder, entity or investor to whom the Agency was subrogated was entitled to such treatment.

(c) For purposes of this Chapter, the term "assets" shall include the assets of the Sponsorship Trust Fund referred to in Annex I to this Convention and other assets administered by the Agency in furtherance of its objective.

Article 46. Archives and Communications

(a) The archives of the Agency shall be inviolable, wherever they may be.

(b) The official communications of the Agency shall be accorded by each member the same treatment that is accorded to the official communications of the Bank.

Article 47. Taxes

(a) The Agency, its assets, property and income, and its operations and transactions authorized by this Convention, shall be immune from all taxes and customs duties.

The Agency shall also be immune from liability for the collection or payment of any tax or duty.

(b) Except in the case of local nationals, no tax shall be levied on or in respect of expense allowances paid by the Agency to Governors and their Alternates or on or in respect of salaries, expense allowances or other emoluments paid by the Agency to the Chairman of the Board, Directors, their Alternates, the President or staff of the Agency.

(c) No taxation of any kind shall be levied on any investment guaranteed or reinsured by the Agency (including any earnings therefrom) or any insurance policies reinsured by the Agency (including any premiums and other revenues therefrom) by whomsoever held:

(i) which discriminates against such investment or insurance policy solely because it is guaranteed or reinsured by the Agency; or

(ii) if the sole jurisdictional basis for such taxation is the location of any office or place of business maintained by the Agency.

Article 48. Officials of the Agency

All Governors, Directors, Alternates, the President and staff of the Agency:

(i) shall be immune from legal process with respect to acts performed by them in their official capacity;

(ii) not being local nationals, shall be accorded the same immunities from immigration restrictions, alien registration requirements and national service obligations, and the same facilities as regards exchange restrictions as are accorded by the members concerned to the representatives, officials and employees of comparable rank of other members; and

(iii) shall be granted the same treatment in respect of travelling facilities as is accorded by the members concerned to representatives, officials and employees of comparable rank of other members.

Article 49. Application of the Chapter

Each member shall take such action as is necessary in its own territories for the purpose of making effective in terms of its own law the principles set forth in this Chapter and shall inform the Agency of the detailed action which it has taken.

Article 50. Waiver

The immunities, exemptions and privileges provided in this Chapter are granted in the interest of the Agency and may be waived, to such extent and upon such conditions as the Agency may determine, in cases where such a waiver would not prejudice its interests. The Agency shall waive the immunity of any of its staff in cases where, in its opinion, the immunity would impede the course of justice and can be waived without prejudice to the interests of the Agency.

Chapter VIII
Withdrawal, Suspension of Membership and Cessation of Operations

Article 51. Withdrawal

Any member may, after the expiration of three years following the date upon which this Convention has entered into force with respect to such member, withdraw from the Agency at any time by giving notice in writing to the Agency at its principal office. The Agency shall notify the Bank, as depository of this Convention, of the receipt of such notice. Any withdrawal shall become effective ninety days following the date of the receipt of such notice by the Agency. A member may revoke such notice as long as it has not become effective.

Article 52. Suspension of Membership

(a) If a member fails to fulfill any of its obligations under this Convention, the Council may, by a majority of its members exercising a majority of the total voting power, suspend its membership.

(b) While under suspension a member shall have no rights under this Convention, except for the right of withdrawal and other rights provided in this Chapter and Chapter IX, but shall remain subject to all its obligations.

(c) For purposes of determining eligibility for a guarantee or reinsurance to be issued under Chapter III or Annex I to this Convention, a suspended member shall not be treated as a member of the Agency.

(d) The suspended member shall automatically cease to be a member one year from the date of its suspension unless the Council decides to extend the period of suspension or to restore the member to good standing.

Article 53. Rights and Duties of States Ceasing to be Members

(a) When a State ceases to be a member, it shall remain liable for all its obligations, including its contingent obligations, under this Convention which shall have been in effect before the cessation of its membership.

(b) Without prejudice to Section (a) above, the Agency shall enter into an arrangement with such State for the settlement of their respective claims and obligations. Any such arrangement shall be approved by the Board.

Article 54. Suspension of Operations

(a) The Board may, whenever it deems it justified, suspend the issuance of new guarantees for a specified period.

(b) In an emergency, the Board may suspend all activities of the Agency for a period not exceeding the duration of such emergency, provided that necessary arrangements shall be made for the protection of the interests of the Agency and of third parties.

(c) The decision to suspend operations shall have no effect on the obligations of the members under this Convention or on the obligations of the Agency towards holders of a guarantee or reinsurance policy or towards third parties.

Article 55. Liquidation

(a) The Council, by special majority, may decide to cease operations and to liquidate the Agency. Thereupon the Agency shall forthwith cease all activities, except those incident to the orderly realization, conservation and preservation of assets and settlement of obligations. Until final settlement and distribution of assets, the Agency shall remain in existence and all rights and obligations of members under this Convention shall continue unimpaired.

(b) No distribution of assets shall be made to members until all liabilities to holders of guarantees and other creditors shall have been discharged or provided for and until the Council shall have decided to make such distribution.

(c) Subject to the foregoing, the Agency shall distribute its remaining assets to members in proportion to each member's share in the subscribed capital. The Agency shall also distribute any remaining assets of the Sponsorship Trust Fund referred to in Annex I to this Convention to sponsoring members in the proportion which the investments sponsored by each bears to the total of sponsored investments. No member shall be entitled to its share in the assets of the Agency or the Sponsorship Trust Fund unless that member has settled all outstanding claims by the Agency against it. Every distribution of assets shall be made at such times as the Council shall determine and in such manner as it shall deem fair and equitable.

Chapter IX
Settlement of Disputes

Article 56. Interpretation and Application of the Convention

(a) Any question of interpretation or application of the provisions of this Convention arising between any member of the Agency and the Agency or among members of the Agency shall be submitted to the Board for its decision. Any member which is particularly affected by the question and which is not otherwise represented by a national in the Board may send a representative to attend any meeting of the Board at which such question is considered.

(b) In any case where the Board has given a decision under Section (a) above, any member may require that the question be referred to the Council, whose decision shall be final. Pending the result of the referral to the Council, the Agency may, so far as it deems necessary, act on the basis of the decision of the Board.

Article 57. Disputes between the Agency and Members

(a) Without prejudice to the provisions of Article 56 and of Section (b) of this Article, any dispute between the Agency and a member or an agency thereof and any dispute between the Agency and a country (or agency thereof) which has ceased to be a member, shall be settled in accordance with the procedure set out in Annex II to this Convention.

(b) Disputes concerning claims of the Agency acting as subrogee of an investor shall be settled in accordance with either:

(i) the procedure set out in Annex II to this Convention, or

(ii) an agreement to be entered into between the Agency and the member concerned on an alternative method or methods for the settlement of such disputes. In the latter case, Annex II to this Convention shall serve as a basis for such an agreement which shall, in each case, be approved by the Board by special majority prior to the undertaking by the Agency of operations in the territories of the member concerned.

Article 58. Disputes Involving Holders of a Guarantee or Reinsurance

Any dispute arising under a contract of guarantee or reinsurance between the parties thereto shall be submitted to arbitration for final determination in accordance with such rules as shall be provided for or referred to in the contract of guarantee or reinsurance.

Chapter X
Amendments

Article 59. Amendment by Council

(a) This Convention and its Annexes may be amended by vote of three-fifths of the Governors exercising four-fifths of the total voting power, provided that:

(i) any amendment modifying the right to withdraw from the Agency provided in Article 51 or the limitation on liability provided in Section (d) of Article 8 shall require the affirmative vote of all Governors; and

(ii) any amendment modifying the losssharing arrangement provided in Articles 1 and 3 of Annex I to this Convention which will result in an increase in any member's liability thereunder shall require the affirmative vote of the Governor of each such member.

(b) Schedules A and B to this Convention may be amended by the Council by special majority.

(c) If an amendment affects any provision of Annex I to this Convention, total votes shall include the additional votes allotted under Article 7 of such Annex to sponsoring members and countries hosting sponsored investments.

Article 60. Procedure

Any proposal to amend this Convention, whether emanating from a member or a Governor or a Director, shall be communicated to the Chairman of the Board who shall bring the proposal before the Board. If the proposed amendment is recommended by the Board, it shall be submitted to the Council for approval in accordance with Article 59. When an amendment has been duly approved by the Council, the Agency shall so certify by formal communication addressed to all members. Amendments shall enter into force for all members ninety days after the date of the formal communication unless the Council shall specify a different date.

Chapter XI
Final Provisions

Article 61. Entry into Force

(a) This Convention shall be open for signature on behalf of all members of the Bank and Switzerland and shall be subject to ratification, acceptance or approval by the signatory States in accordance with their constitutional procedures.

(b) This Convention shall enter into force on the day when not less than five instruments of ratification, acceptance or approval shall have been deposited on behalf of signatory States in Category One, and not less than fifteen such instruments shall have been deposited on behalf of signatory States in Category Two; provided that total subscriptions of these States amount to not less than one-third of the authorized capital of the Agency as prescribed in Article 5.

(c) For each State which deposits its instrument of ratification, acceptance or approval after this Convention shall have entered into force, this Convention shall enter into force on the date of such deposit.

(d) If this Convention shall not have entered into force within two years after its opening for signature, the President of the Bank shall convene a conference of interested countries to determine the future course of action.

Article 62. Inaugural Meeting

Upon entry into force of this Convention, the President of the Bank shall call the inaugural meeting of the Council. This meeting shall be held at the principal office of the Agency within sixty days from the date on which this Convention has entered into force or as soon as practicable thereafter.

Article 63. Depository

Instruments of ratification, acceptance or approval of this Convention and amendments thereto shall be deposited with the Bank which shall act as the depository of this Convention. The depository shall transmit certified copies of this Convention to States members of the Bank and to Switzerland.

Article 64. Registration

The depository shall register this Convention with the Secretariat of the United Nations in accordance with Article 102 of the Charter of the United Nations and the Regulations thereunder adopted by the General Assembly.

Article 65. Notification

The depository shall notify all signatory States and, upon the entry into force of this Convention, the Agency of the following:

(a) signatures of this Convention;

(b) deposits of instruments of ratification, acceptance and approval in accordance with Article 63;

(c) the date on which this Convention enters into force in accordance with Article 61;

(d) exclusions from territorial application pursuant to Article 66; and

(e) withdrawal of a member from the Agency pursuant to Article 51.

Article 66. Territorial Application

This Convention shall apply to all territories under the jurisdiction of a member including the territories for whose international relations a member is responsible, except those which are excluded by such member by written notice to the depository of this Convention either at the time of ratification, acceptance or approval or subsequently.

Article 67. Periodic Reviews

(a) The Council shall periodically undertake comprehensive reviews of the activities of the Agency as well as the results achieved with a view to introducing any changes required to enhance the Agency's ability to serve its objectives.

(b) The first such review shall take place five years after the entry into force of this Convention. The dates of subsequent reviews shall be determined by the Council.

DONE at Seoul, in a single copy which shall remain deposited in the archives of the International Bank for Reconstruction and Development, which has indicated by its signature below its agreement to fulfill the functions with which it is charged under this Convention.

Annex I
Guarantees of Sponsored Investments Under Article 24

Article 1. Sponsorship

(a) Any member may sponsor for guarantee an investment to be made by an investor of any nationality or by investors of any or several nationalities.

(b) Subject to the provisions of Sections (b) and (c) of Article 3 of this Annex, each sponsoring member shall share with the other sponsoring members in losses under guarantees of sponsored investments, when and to the extent that such losses cannot be covered out of the Sponsorship Trust Fund referred to in Article 2 of this Annex, in the proportion which the amount of maximum contingent liability under the guarantees of investments sponsored by it bears to the total amount of maximum contingent liability under the guarantees of investments sponsored by all members.

(c) In its decisions on the issuance of guarantees under this Annex, the Agency shall pay due regard to the prospects that the sponsoring member will be in a position to meet its obligations under this Annex and shall give priority to investments which are co-sponsored by the host countries concerned.

(d) The Agency shall periodically consult with sponsoring members with respect to its operations under this Annex.

Article 2. Sponsorship Trust Fund

(a) Premiums and other revenues attributable to guarantees of sponsored investments, including returns on the investment of such premiums and revenues, shall be held in a separate account which shall be called the Sponsorship Trust Fund.

(b) All administrative expenses and payments on claims attributable to guarantees issued under this Annex shall be paid out of the Sponsorship Trust Fund.

(c) The assets of the Sponsorship Trust Fund shall be held and administered for the joint account of sponsoring members and shall be kept separate and apart from the assets of the Agency.

Article 3. Calls on Sponsoring Members

(a) To the extent that any amount is payable by the Agency on account of a loss under a sponsored guarantee and such amount cannot be paid out of assets of the Sponsorship Trust Fund, the Agency shall call on each sponsoring member to pay into such Fund its share of such amount as shall be determined in accordance with Section (b) of Article 1 of this Annex.

(b) No member shall be liable to pay any amount on a call pursuant to the provisions of this Article if as a result total payments made by that member will exceed the total amount of guarantees covering investments sponsored by it.

(c) Upon the expiry of any guarantee covering an investment sponsored by a member, the liability of that member shall be decreased by an amount equivalent to the amount of such guarantee; such liability shall also be decreased on a pro rata basis upon payment by the Agency of any claim related to a sponsored investment and shall otherwise continue in effect until the expiry of all guarantees of sponsored investments outstanding at the time of such payment.

(d) If any sponsoring member shall not be liable for an amount of a call pursuant to the provisions of this Article because of the limitation contained in Sections (b) and (c) above, or if any sponsoring member shall default in payment of an amount due in response to any such call, the liability for payment of such amount shall be shared pro rata by the other sponsoring members. Liability of members pursuant to this Section shall be subject to the limitation set forth in Sections (b) and (c) above.

(e) Any payment by a sponsoring member pursuant to a call in accordance with this Article shall be made promptly and in freely usable currency.

Article 4. Valuation of Currencies and Refunds

The provisions on valuation of currencies and refunds contained in this Convention with respect to capital subscriptions shall be applied mutatis mutandis to funds paid by members on account of sponsored investments.

Article 5. Reinsurance

(a) The Agency may, under the conditions set forth in Article 1 of this Annex, provide reinsurance to a member, an agency thereof, a regional agency as defined in

Section (a) of Article 20 of this Convention or a private insurer in a member country. The provisions of this Annex concerning guarantees and of Article 20 and 21 of this Convention shall be applied mutatis mutandis to reinsurance provided under this Section.

(b) The Agency may obtain reinsurance for investments guaranteed by it under this Annex and shall meet the cost of such reinsurance out of the Sponsorship Trust Fund. The Board may decide whether and to what extent the loss-sharing obligation of sponsoring members referred to in Section (b) of Article 1 of this Annex may be reduced on account of the reinsurance cover obtained.

Article 6. Operational Principles

Without prejudice to the provisions of this Annex, the provisions with respect to guarantee operations under Chapter III of this Convention and to financial management under Chapter IV of this Convention shall be applied mutatis mutandis to guarantees of sponsored investments except that:

(i) such investments shall qualify for sponsorship if made in the territories of any member, and in particular of any developing member, by an investor or investors eligible under Section (a) of Article 1 of this Annex, and

(ii) the Agency shall not be liable with respect to its own assets for any guarantee or reinsurance issued under this Annex and each contract of guarantee or reinsurance concluded pursuant to this Annex shall expressly so provide.

Article 7. Voting

For decisions relating to sponsored investments, each sponsoring member shall have one additional vote for each 10,000 Special Drawing Rights equivalent of the amount guaranteed or reinsured on the basis of its sponsorship, and each member hosting a sponsored investment shall have one additional vote for each 10,000 Special Drawing Rights equivalent of the amount guaranteed or reinsured with respect to any sponsored investment hosted by it. Such additional votes shall be cast only for decisions related to sponsored investments and shall otherwise be disregarded in determining the voting power of members.

Annex II
Settlement of Disputes Between a Member and the Agency Under Article 57

Article 1. Application of the Annex

All disputes within the scope of Article 57 of this Convention shall be settled in accordance with the procedure set out in this Annex, except in the cases where the Agency has entered into an agreement with a member pursuant to Section (b)(ii) of Article 57.

Article 2. Negotiation

The parties to a dispute within the scope of this Annex shall attempt to settle such dispute by negotiation before seeking conciliation or arbitration. Negotiations shall be deemed to have been exhausted if the parties fail to reach a settlement within a period of one hundred and twenty days from the date of the request to enter into negotiation.

Article 3. Conciliation

(a) If the dispute is not resolved through negotiation, either party may submit the dispute to arbitration in accordance with the provisions of Article 4 of this Annex, unless the parties, by mutual consent, have decided to resort first to the conciliation procedure provided for in this Article.

(b) The agreement for recourse to conciliation shall specify the matter in dispute, the claims of the parties in respect thereof and, if available, the name of the conciliator agreed upon by the parties. In the absence of agreement on the conciliator, the parties may jointly request either the Secretary-General of the International Centre of Settlement of Investment Disputes (hereinafter called ICSID) or the President of the International Court of Justice to appoint a conciliator. The conciliation procedure shall terminate if the conciliator has not been appointed within ninety days after the agreement for recourse to conciliation.

(c) Unless otherwise provided in this Annex or agreed upon by the parties, the conciliator shall determine the rules governing the conciliation procedure and shall be guided in this regard by the conciliation rules adopted pursuant to the Convention on the Settlement of Investment Disputes between States and Nationals of Other States.

(d) The parties shall cooperate in good faith with the conciliator and shall, in particular, provide him with all information and documentation which would assist him in the discharge of his functions; they shall give their most serious consideration to his recommendations.

(e) Unless otherwise agreed upon by the parties, the conciliator shall, within a period not exceeding one hundred and eighty days from the date of his appointment, submit to the parties a report recording the results of his efforts and setting out the issues controversial between the parties and his proposals for their settlement.

(f) Each party shall, within sixty days from the date of the receipt of the report, express in writing its views on the report to the other party.

(g) Neither party to a conciliation proceeding shall be entitled to have recourse to arbitration unless:

- (i) the conciliator shall have failed to submit his report within the period established in Section (e) above; or
- (ii) the parties shall have failed to accept all of the proposals contained in the report within sixty days after its receipt; or
- (iii) the parties, after an exchange of views on the report, shall have failed to agree on a settlement of all controversial issues within sixty days after receipt of the conciliator's report; or
- (iv) a party shall have failed to express its views on the report as prescribed in Section (f) above.

(h) Unless the parties agree otherwise, the fees of the conciliator shall be determined on the basis of the rates applicable to ICSID conciliation. These fees and the other costs of the conciliation proceedings shall be borne equally by the parties. Each party shall defray its own expenses.

Article 4. Arbitration

(a) Arbitration proceedings shall be instituted by means of a notice by the party seeking arbitration (the claimant) addressed to the other party or parties to the dispute (the respondent). The notice shall specify the nature of the dispute, the relief sought and the name of the arbitrator appointed by the claimant. The respondent shall, within thirty days after the date of receipt of the notice, notify the claimant of the name of the arbitrator appointed by it. The two parties shall, within a period of thirty days from the date of appointment of the second arbitrator, select a third arbitrator, who shall act as President of the Arbitral Tribunal (the Tribunal).

(b) If the Tribunal shall not have been constituted within sixty days from the date of the notice, the arbitrator not yet appointed or the President not yet selected shall be appointed, at the joint request of the parties, by the Secretary-General of ICSID. If there is not such joint request, of if the Secretary-General shall fail to make the appointment within thirty days of the request, either party may request the President of the International Court of Justice to make the appointment.

(c) No party shall have the rights to change the arbitrator appointed by it once the hearing of the dispute has commenced. In case any arbitrator (including the President of the Tribunal) shall resign, die, or become incapacitated, a successor shall be appointed in the manner followed in the appointment of his predecessor and such successor shall have the same powers and duties of the arbitrator he succeeds.

(d) The Tribunal shall convene first at such time and place as shall be determined by the President. Thereafter, the Tribunal shall determine the place and dates of its meetings.

(e) Unless otherwise provided in this Annex or agreed upon by the parties, the Tribunal shall determine its procedure and shall be guided in this regard by the arbitration rules adopted pursuant to the Convention on the Settlement of Investment Disputes between States and Nationals of Other States.

(f) The Tribunal shall be the judge of its own competence except that, if an objection is raised before the Tribunal to the effect that the dispute falls within the jurisdiction of the Board or the Council under Article 56 or within the jurisdiction of a judicial or arbitral body designated in an agreement under Article 1 of this Annex and the Tribunal is satisfied that the objection is genuine, the objection shall be referred by the Tribunal to the Board or the Council or the designated body, as the case may be, and the arbitration proceedings shall be stayed until a decision has been reached on the matter, which shall be binding upon the Tribunal.

(g) The Tribunal shall, in any dispute within the scope of this Annex, apply the provisions of this Convention, any relevant agreement between the parties to the dispute, the Agency's by-laws and regulations, the applicable rules of international law, the domestic law of the member concerned as well as the applicable provisions of the investment contract, if any. Without prejudice to the provisions of this Convention, the Tribunal may decide a dispute ex aequo et bono if the Agency and the member concerned so agree. The Tribunal may not bring a finding of non liquet on the ground of silence or obscurity of the law.

(h) The Tribunal shall afford a fair hearing to all the parties. All decisions of the Tribunal shall be taken by a majority vote and shall state the reasons on which they are based. The award of the Tribunal shall be in writing, and shall be signed by at least two arbitrators and a copy thereof shall be transmitted to each party. The award shall be final and binding upon the parties and shall not be subject to appeal, annulment or revision.

(i) If any dispute shall arise between the Parties as to the meaning or scope of an award, either party may, within sixty days after the award was rendered, request interpretation of the award by an application in writing to the President of the Tribunal which rendered the award. The President shall, if possible, submit the request to the Tribunal which rendered the award and shall convene such Tribunal within sixty days after receipt of the application. If this shall not be possible, a new Tribunal shall be constituted in accordance with the provisions of Sections (a) to (d) above. The Tribunal may stay enforcement of the award pending its decision on the requested interpretation.

(j) Each member shall recognize an award rendered pursuant to this Article as binding and enforceable within its territories as if it were a final judgment of a court in that member. Execution of the award shall be governed by the laws concerning the execution of judgments in force in the State in whose territories such execution is sought and shall not derogate from the law in force relating to immunity from execution.

(k) Unless the parties shall agree otherwise, the fees and remuneration payable to the arbitrators shall be determined on the basis of the rates applicable to ICSID arbitration. Each party shall defray its own costs associated with the arbitration proceedings. The costs of the Tribunal shall be borne by the parties in equal proportion unless the Tribunal decides otherwise. Any question concerning the division of the costs of the Tribunal or the procedure for payment of such costs shall be decided by the Tribunal.

Article 5. Service of Process

Service of any notice or process in connection with any proceeding under this Annex shall be made in writing. It shall be made by the Agency upon the authority designated by the member concerned pursuant to Article 38 of this Convention and by that member at the principal office of the Agency.

Schedule A
Membership and Subscriptions

[. . .]

D. TRIPS (1994)

Preamble

Members,

Desiring to reduce distortions and impediments to international trade, and taking into account the need to promote effective and adequate protection of intellectual property rights, and to ensure that measures and procedures to enforce intellectual property rights do not themselves become barriers to legitimate trade;

Recognizing, to this end, the need for new rules and disciplines concerning:

(a) the applicability of the basic principles of GATT 1994 and of relevant international intellectual property agreements or conventions;

(b) the provision of adequate standards and principles concerning the availability, scope and use of trade-related intellectual property rights;

(c) the provision of effective and appropriate means for the enforcement of trade-related intellectual property rights, taking into account differences in national legal systems;

(d) the provision of effective and expeditious procedures for the multilateral prevention and settlement of disputes between governments; and

(e) transitional arrangements aiming at the fullest participation in the results of the negotiations;

Recognizing the need for a multilateral framework of principles, rules and disciplines dealing with international trade in counterfeit goods;

Recognizing that intellectual property rights are private rights;

Recognizing the underlying public policy objectives of national systems for the protection of intellectual property, including developmental and technological objectives;

Recognizing also the special needs of the least-developed country Members in respect of maximum flexibility in the domestic implementation of laws and regulations in order to enable them to create a sound and viable technological base;

Emphasizing the importance of reducing tensions by reaching strengthened commitments to resolve disputes on trade-related intellectual property issues through multilateral procedures;

Desiring to establish a mutually supportive relationship between the WTO and the World Intellectual Property Organization (referred to in this Agreement as "WIPO") as well as other relevant international organizations;

Hereby agree as follows:

Part I—General Provisions and Basic Principles

Article 1—Nature and Scope of Obligations

1. Members shall give effect to the provisions of this Agreement. Members may, but shall not be obliged to, implement in their law more extensive protection than is required by this Agreement, provided that such protection does not contravene the provisions of this Agreement. Members shall be free to determine the appropriate method of implementing the provisions of this Agreement within their own legal system and practice.

2. For the purposes of this Agreement, the term "intellectual property" refers to all categories of intellectual property that are the subject of Sections 1 through 7 of Part II.

3. Members shall accord the treatment provided for in this Agreement to the nationals of other Members. (1) In respect of the relevant intellectual property right, the nationals of other Members shall be understood as those natural or legal persons that would meet the criteria for eligibility for protection provided for in the Paris Convention (1967), the Berne Convention (1971), the Rome Convention and the Treaty on Intellectual Property in Respect of Integrated Circuits, were all Members of the WTO members of those conventions. (2) Any Member availing itself of the possibilities provided in paragraph 3 of Article 5 or paragraph 2 of Article 6 of the Rome Convention shall make a notification as foreseen in those provisions to the Council for Trade-Related Aspects of Intellectual Property Rights (the "Council for TRIPS").

Article 2—Intellectual Property Conventions

1. In respect of Parts II, III and IV of this Agreement, Members shall comply with Articles 1 through 12, and Article 19, of the Paris Convention (1967).

2. Nothing in Parts I to IV of this Agreement shall derogate from existing obligations that Members may have to each other under the Paris Convention, the Berne Convention, the Rome Convention and the Treaty on Intellectual Property in Respect of Integrated Circuits.

Article 3—National Treatment

1. Each Member shall accord to the nationals of other Members treatment no less favourable than that it accords to its own nationals with regard to the protection (3) of intellectual property, subject to the exceptions already provided in, respectively, the Paris Convention (1967), the Berne Convention (1971), the Rome Convention or the Treaty on Intellectual Property in Respect of Integrated Circuits. In respect of performers, producers of phonograms and broadcasting organizations, this obligation only applies in respect of the rights provided under this Agreement. Any Member availing itself of the possibilities provided in Article 6 of the Berne Convention (1971) or paragraph 1(b) of Article 16 of the Rome Convention shall make a notification as foreseen in those provisions to the Council for TRIPS.

2. Members may avail themselves of the exceptions permitted under paragraph 1 in relation to judicial and administrative procedures, including the designation of an address for service or the appointment of an agent within the jurisdiction of a Member, only where such exceptions are necessary to secure compliance with laws and regulations which are not inconsistent with the provisions of this Agreement and where such practices are not applied in a manner which would constitute a disguised restriction on trade.

Article 4—Most Favoured Nation Treatment

With regard to the protection of intellectual property, any advantage, favour, privilege or immunity granted by a Member to the nationals of any other country shall be accorded immediately and unconditionally to the nationals of all other Members. Exempted from this obligation are any advantage, favour, privilege or immunity accorded by a Member:

(a) deriving from international agreements on judicial assistance or law enforcement of a general nature and not particularly confined to the protection of intellectual property;

(b) granted in accordance with the provisions of the Berne Convention (1971) or the Rome Convention authorizing that the treatment accorded be a function not of national treatment but of the treatment accorded in another country;

(c) in respect of the rights of performers, producers of phonograms and broadcasting organizations not provided under this Agreement;

(d) deriving from international agreements related to the protection of intellectual property which entered into force prior to the entry into force of the WTO Agreement, provided that such agreements are notified to the Council for TRIPS and do not constitute an arbitrary or unjustifiable discrimination against nationals of other Members.

Article 5—Multilateral Agreements on Acquisition or Maintenance of Protection

The obligations under Articles 3 and 4 do not apply to procedures provided in multilateral agreements concluded under the auspices of WIPO relating to the acquisition or maintenance of intellectual property rights.

Article 6—Exhaustion

For the purposes of dispute settlement under this Agreement, subject to the provisions of Articles 3 and 4 nothing in this Agreement shall be used to address the issue of the exhaustion of intellectual property rights.

Article 7—Objectives

The protection and enforcement of intellectual property rights should contribute to the promotion of technological innovation and to the transfer and dissemination of technology, to the mutual advantage of producers and users of technological knowledge and in a manner conducive to social and economic welfare, and to a balance of rights and obligations.

Article 8 — Principles

1. Members may, in formulating or amending their laws and regulations, adopt measures necessary to protect public health and nutrition, and to promote the public interest in sectors of vital importance to their socio-economic and technological development, provided that such measures are consistent with the provisions of this Agreement.

2. Appropriate measures, provided that they are consistent with the provisions of this Agreement, may be needed to prevent the abuse of intellectual property rights by right holders or the resort to practices which unreasonably restrain trade or adversely affect the international transfer of technology.

Part II — Standards concerning the availability, scope and use of Intellectual Property Rights

Section 1: Copyright and Related Rights

Article 9 — Relation to the Berne Convention

1. Members shall comply with Articles 1 through 21 of the Berne Convention (1971) and the Appendix thereto. However, Members shall not have rights or obligations under this Agreement in respect of the rights conferred under Article 6bis of that Convention or of the rights derived therefrom.

2. Copyright protection shall extend to expressions and not to ideas, procedures, methods of operation or mathematical concepts as such.

Article 10 — Computer Programs and Compilations of Data

1. Computer programs, whether in source or object code, shall be protected as literary works under the Berne Convention (1971).

2. Compilations of data or other material, whether in machine readable or other form, which by reason of the selection or arrangement of their contents constitute intellectual creations shall be protected as such. Such protection, which shall not extend to the data or material itself, shall be without prejudice to any copyright subsisting in the data or material itself.

Article 11 — Rental Rights

In respect of at least computer programs and cinematographic works, a Member shall provide authors and their successors in title the right to authorize or to prohibit the commercial rental to the public of originals or copies of their copyright works. A Member shall be excepted from this obligation in respect of cinematographic works unless such rental has led to widespread copying of such works which is materially impairing the exclusive right of reproduction conferred in that Member on authors and their successors in title. In respect of computer programs, this obligation does not apply to rentals where the program itself is not the essential object of the rental.

Article 12 — Term of Protection

Whenever the term of protection of a work, other than a photographic work or a work of applied art, is calculated on a basis other than the life of a natural person, such term shall be no less than 50 years from the end of the calendar year of authorized publication, or, failing such authorized publication within 50 years from the making of the work, 50 years from the end of the calendar year of making.

Article 13—Limitations and Exceptions

Members shall confine limitations or exceptions to exclusive rights to certain special cases which do not conflict with a normal exploitation of the work and do not unreasonably prejudice the legitimate interests of the right holder.

Article 14—Protection of Performers, Producers of Phonograms (Sounds Recordings) and Broadcasting Organizations

1. In respect of a fixation of their performance on a phonogram, performers shall have the possibility of preventing the following acts when undertaken without their authorization: the fixation of their unfixed performance and the reproduction of such fixation. Performers shall also have the possibility of preventing the following acts when undertaken without their authorization: the broadcasting by wireless means and the communication to the public of their live performance.

2. Producers of phonograms shall enjoy the right to authorize or prohibit the direct or indirect reproduction of their phonograms.

3. Broadcasting organizations shall have the right to prohibit the following acts when undertaken without their authorization: the fixation, the reproduction of fixations, and the rebroadcasting by wireless means of broadcasts, as well as the communication to the public of television broadcasts of the same. Where Members do not grant such rights to broadcasting organizations, they shall provide owners of copyright in the subject matter of broadcasts with the possibility of preventing the above acts, subject to the provisions of the Berne Convention (1971).

4. The provisions of Article 11 in respect of computer programs shall apply mutatis mutandis to producers of phonograms and any other right holders in phonograms as determined in a Member's law. If on 15 April 1994 a Member has in force a system of equitable remuneration of right holders in respect of the rental of phonograms, it may maintain such system provided that the commercial rental of phonograms is not giving rise to the material impairment of the exclusive rights of reproduction of right holders.

5. The term of the protection available under this Agreement to performers and producers of phonograms shall last at least until the end of a period of 50 years computed from the end of the calendar year in which the fixation was made or the performance took place. The term of protection granted pursuant to paragraph 3 shall last for at least 20 years from the end of the calendar year in which the broadcast took place.

6. Any Member may, in relation to the rights conferred under paragraphs 1, 2 and 3, provide for conditions, limitations, exceptions and reservations to the extent permitted by the Rome Convention. However, the provisions of Article 18 of the Berne Convention (1971) shall also apply, mutatis mutandis, to the rights of performers and producers of phonograms in phonograms.

Section 2: Trademarks

Article 15—Protectable Subject Matter

1. Any sign, or any combination of signs, capable of distinguishing the goods or services of one undertaking from those of other undertakings, shall be capable of constituting a trademark. Such signs, in particular words including personal names, letters, numerals, figurative elements and combinations of colours as well as any combination of such signs, shall be eligible for registration as trademarks. Where signs are not inherently capable of distinguishing the relevant goods or services, Members may make registrability depend on distinctiveness acquired through use. Members may require, as a condition of registration, that signs be visually perceptible.

2. Paragraph 1 shall not be understood to prevent a Member from denying registration of a trademark on other grounds, provided that they do not derogate from the provisions of the Paris Convention (1967).

3. Members may make registrability depend on use. However, actual use of a trademark shall not be a condition for filing an application for registration. An application shall not be refused solely on the ground that intended use has not taken place before the expiry of a period of three years from the date of application.

4. The nature of the goods or services to which a trademark is to be applied shall in no case form an obstacle to registration of the trademark.

5. Members shall publish each trademark either before it is registered or promptly after it is registered and shall afford a reasonable opportunity for petitions to cancel the registration. In addition, Members may afford an opportunity for the registration of a trademark to be opposed.

Article 16—Rights Conferred

1. The owner of a registered trademark shall have the exclusive right to prevent all third parties not having the owner's consent from using in the course of trade identical or similar signs for goods or services which are identical or similar to those in respect of which the trademark is registered where such use would result in a likelihood of confusion. In case of the use of an identical sign for identical goods or services, a likelihood of confusion shall be presumed. The rights described above shall not prejudice any existing prior rights, nor shall they affect the possibility of Members making rights available on the basis of use.

2. Article 6bis of the Paris Convention (1967) shall apply, mutatis mutandis, to services. In determining whether a trademark is well-known, Members shall take account of the knowledge of the trademark in the relevant sector of the public, including knowledge in the Member concerned which has been obtained as a result of the promotion of the trademark.

3. Article 6bis of the Paris Convention (1967) shall apply, mutatis mutandis, to goods or services which are not similar to those in respect of which a trademark is registered, provided that use of that trademark in relation to those goods or services would indicate a connection between those goods or services and the owner of the

registered trademark and provided that the interests of the owner of the registered trademark are likely to be damaged by such use.

Article 17—Exceptions

Members may provide limited exceptions to the rights conferred by a trademark, such as fair use of descriptive terms, provided that such exceptions take account of the legitimate interests of the owner of the trademark and of third parties.

Article 18—Term of Protection

Initial registration, and each renewal of registration, of a trademark shall be for a term of no less than seven years. The registration of a trademark shall be renewable indefinitely.

Article 19—Requirement of Use

1. If use is required to maintain a registration, the registration may be cancelled only after an uninterrupted period of at least three years of non-use, unless valid reasons based on the existence of obstacles to such use are shown by the trademark owner. Circumstances arising independently of the will of the owner of the trademark which constitute an obstacle to the use of the trademark, such as import restrictions on or other government requirements for goods or services protected by the trademark, shall be recognized as valid reasons for non-use.

2. When subject to the control of its owner, use of a trademark by another person shall be recognized as use of the trademark for the purpose of maintaining the registration.

Article 20—Other Requirements

The use of a trademark in the course of trade shall not be unjustifiably encumbered by special requirements, such as use with another trademark, use in a special form or use in a manner detrimental to its capability to distinguish the goods or services of one undertaking from those of other undertakings. This will not preclude a requirement prescribing the use of the trademark identifying the undertaking producing the goods or services along with, but without linking it to, the trademark distinguishing the specific goods or services in question of that undertaking.

Article 21—Licensing and Assignment

Members may determine conditions on the licensing and assignment of trademarks, it being understood that the compulsory licensing of trademarks shall not be permitted and that the owner of a registered trademark shall have the right to assign the trademark with or without the transfer of the business to which the trademark belongs.

Section 3: Geographical Indications

Article 22—Protection of Geographical Indications

1. Geographical indications are, for the purposes of this Agreement, indications which identify a good as originating in the territory of a Member, or a region or

locality in that territory, where a given quality, reputation or other characteristic of the good is essentially attributable to its geographical origin.

2. In respect of geographical indications, Members shall provide the legal means for interested parties to prevent:

(a) the use of any means in the designation or presentation of a good that indicates or suggests that the good in question originates in a geographical area other than the true place of origin in a manner which misleads the public as to the geographical origin of the good;

(b) any use which constitutes an act of unfair competition within the meaning of Article 10bis of the Paris Convention (1967).

3. A Member shall, ex officio if its legislation so permits or at the request of an interested party, refuse or invalidate the registration of a trademark which contains or consists of a geographical indication with respect to goods not originating in the territory indicated, if use of the indication in the trademark for such goods in that Member is of such a nature as to mislead the public as to the true place of origin.

4. The protection under paragraphs 1, 2 and 3 shall be applicable against a geographical indication which, although literally true as to the territory, region or locality in which the goods originate, falsely represents to the public that the goods originate in another territory.

Article 23—Additional Protection of Geographical Indications for Wines and Spirits

1. Each Member shall provide the legal means for interested parties to prevent use of a geographical indication identifying wines for wines not originating in the place indicated by the geographical indication in question or identifying spirits for spirits not originating in the place indicated by the geographical indication in question, even where the true origin of the goods is indicated or the geographical indication is used in translation or accompanied by expressions such as "kind", "type", "style", "imitation" or the like.

2. The registration of a trademark for wines which contains or consists of a geographical indication identifying wines or for spirits which contains or consists of a geographical indication identifying spirits shall be refused or invalidated, ex officio if a Member's legislation so permits or at the request of an interested party, with respect to such wines or spirits not having this origin.

3. In the case of homonymous geographical indications for wines, protection shall be accorded to each indication, subject to the provisions of paragraph 4 of Article 22. Each Member shall determine the practical conditions under which the homonymous indications in question will be differentiated from each other, taking into account the need to ensure equitable treatment of the producers concerned and that consumers are not misled.

4. In order to facilitate the protection of geographical indications for wines, negotiations shall be undertaken in the Council for TRIPS concerning the establishment of

a multilateral system of notification and registration of geographical indications for wines eligible for protection in those Members participating in the system.

Article 24—International Negotiations, Exceptions

1. Members agree to enter into negotiations aimed at increasing the protection of individual geographical indications under Article 23. The provisions of paragraphs 4 through 8 below shall not be used by a Member to refuse to conduct negotiations or to conclude bilateral or multilateral agreements. In the context of such negotiations, Members shall be willing to consider the continued applicability of these provisions to individual geographical indications whose use was the subject of such negotiations.

2. The Council for TRIPS shall keep under review the application of the provisions of this Section; the first such review shall take place within two years of the entry into force of the WTO Agreement. Any matter affecting the compliance with the obligations under these provisions may be drawn to the attention of the Council, which, at the request of a Member, shall consult with any Member or Members in respect of such matter in respect of which it has not been possible to find a satisfactory solution through bilateral or plurilateral consultations between the Members concerned. The Council shall take such action as may be agreed to facilitate the operation and further the objectives of this Section.

3. In implementing this Section, a Member shall not diminish the protection of geographical indications that existed in that Member immediately prior to the date of entry into force of the WTO Agreement.

4. Nothing in this Section shall require a Member to prevent continued and similar use of a particular geographical indication of another Member identifying wines or spirits in connection with goods or services by any of its nationals or domiciliaries who have used that geographical indication in a continuous manner with regard to the same or related goods or services in the territory of that Member either (a) for at least 10 years preceding 15 April 1994 or (b) in good faith preceding that date.

5. Where a trademark has been applied for or registered in good faith, or where rights to a trademark have been acquired through use in good faith either:

(a) before the date of application of these provisions in that Member as defined in Part VI; or

(b) before the geographical indication is protected in its country of origin;

measures adopted to implement this Section shall not prejudice eligibility for or the validity of the registration of a trademark, or the right to use a trademark, on the basis that such a trademark is identical with, or similar to, a geographical indication.

6. Nothing in this Section shall require a Member to apply its provisions in respect of a geographical indication of any other Member with respect to goods or services for which the relevant indication is identical with the term customary in common language as the common name for such goods or services in the territory of that Member. Nothing in this Section shall require a Member to apply its provisions in

respect of a geographical indication of any other Member with respect to products of the vine for which the relevant indication is identical with the customary name of a grape variety existing in the territory of that Member as of the date of entry into force of the WTO Agreement.

7. A Member may provide that any request made under this Section in connection with the use or registration of a trademark must be presented within five years after the adverse use of the protected indication has become generally known in that Member or after the date of registration of the trademark in that Member provided that the trademark has been published by that date, if such date is earlier than the date on which the adverse use became generally known in that Member, provided that the geographical indication is not used or registered in bad faith.

8. The provisions of this Section shall in no way prejudice the right of any person to use, in the course of trade, that person's name or the name of that person's predecessor in business, except where such name is used in such a manner as to mislead the public.

9. There shall be no obligation under this Agreement to protect geographical indications which are not or cease to be protected in their country of origin, or which have fallen into disuse in that country.

Section 4: Industrial Designs

Article 25 — Requirements for Protection

1. Members shall provide for the protection of independently created industrial designs that are new or original. Members may provide that designs are not new or original if they do not significantly differ from known designs or combinations of known design features. Members may provide that such protection shall not extend to designs dictated essentially by technical or functional considerations.

2. Each Member shall ensure that requirements for securing protection for textile designs, in particular in regard to any cost, examination or publication, do not unreasonably impair the opportunity to seek and obtain such protection. Members shall be free to meet this obligation through industrial design law or through copyright law.

Article 26 — Protection

1. The owner of a protected industrial design shall have the right to prevent third parties not having the owner's consent from making, selling or importing articles bearing or embodying a design which is a copy, or substantially a copy, of the protected design, when such acts are undertaken for commercial purposes.

2. Members may provide limited exceptions to the protection of industrial designs, provided that such exceptions do not unreasonably conflict with the normal exploitation of protected industrial designs and do not unreasonably prejudice the legitimate interests of the owner of the protected design, taking account of the legitimate interests of third parties.

3. The duration of protection available shall amount to at least 10 years.

Section 5: Patents

Article 27 — Patentable Subject Matter

1. Subject to the provisions of paragraphs 2 and 3, patents shall be available for any inventions, whether products or processes, in all fields of technology, provided that they are new, involve an inventive step and are capable of industrial application. Subject to paragraph 4 of Article 65, paragraph 8 of Article 70 and paragraph 3 of this Article, patents shall be available and patent rights enjoyable without discrimination as to the place of invention, the field of technology and whether products are imported or locally produced.

2. Members may exclude from patentability inventions, the prevention within their territory of the commercial exploitation of which is necessary to protect ordre public or morality, including to protect human, animal or plant life or health or to avoid serious prejudice to the environment, provided that such exclusion is not made merely because the exploitation is prohibited by their law.

3. Members may also exclude from patentability:

(a) diagnostic, therapeutic and surgical methods for the treatment of humans or animals;

(b) plants and animals other than micro-organisms, and essentially biological processes for the production of plants or animals other than non-biological and microbiological processes. However, Members shall provide for the protection of plant varieties either by patents or by an effective *sui generis* system or by any combination thereof. The provisions of this subparagraph shall be reviewed four years after the date of entry into force of the WTO Agreement.

Article 28 — Rights Conferred

1. A patent shall confer on its owner the following exclusive rights:

(a) where the subject matter of a patent is a product, to prevent third parties not having the owner's consent from the acts of: making, using, offering for sale, selling, or importing (6) for these purposes that product;

(b) where the subject matter of a patent is a process, to prevent third parties not having the owner's consent from the act of using the process, and from the acts of: using, offering for sale, selling, or importing for these purposes at least the product obtained directly by that process.

2. Patent owners shall also have the right to assign, or transfer by succession, the patent and to conclude licensing contracts.

Article 29 — Conditions on Patent Applicants

1. Members shall require that an applicant for a patent shall disclose the invention in a manner sufficiently clear and complete for the invention to be carried out by a person skilled in the art and may require the applicant to indicate the best mode for carrying out the invention known to the inventor at the filing date or, where priority is claimed, at the priority date of the application.

2. Members may require an applicant for a patent to provide information concerning the applicant's corresponding foreign applications and grants.

Article 30—Exceptions to Rights Conferred

Members may provide limited exceptions to the exclusive rights conferred by a patent, provided that such exceptions do not unreasonably conflict with a normal exploitation of the patent and do not unreasonably prejudice the legitimate interests of the patent owner, taking account of the legitimate interests of third parties.

Article 31—Other Use without Authorization of the Right Holder

Where the law of a Member allows for other use (7) of the subject matter of a patent without the authorization of the right holder, including use by the government or third parties authorized by the government, the following provisions shall be respected:

(a) authorization of such use shall be considered on its individual merits;

(b) such use may only be permitted if, prior to such use, the proposed user has made efforts to obtain authorization from the right holder on reasonable commercial terms and conditions and that such efforts have not been successful within a reasonable period of time. This requirement may be waived by a Member in the case of a national emergency or other circumstances of extreme urgency or in cases of public non-commercial use. In situations of national emergency or other circumstances of extreme urgency, the right holder shall, nevertheless, be notified as soon as reasonably practicable. In the case of public non-commercial use, where the government or contractor, without making a patent search, knows or has demonstrable grounds to know that a valid patent is or will be used by or for the government, the right holder shall be informed promptly;

(c) the scope and duration of such use shall be limited to the purpose for which it was authorized, and in the case of semi-conductor technology shall only be for public non-commercial use or to remedy a practice determined after judicial or administrative process to be anti-competitive;

(d) such use shall be non-exclusive;

(e) such use shall be non-assignable, except with that part of the enterprise or goodwill which enjoys such use;

(f) any such use shall be authorized predominantly for the supply of the domestic market of the Member authorizing such use;

(g) authorization for such use shall be liable, subject to adequate protection of the legitimate interests of the persons so authorized, to be terminated if and when the circumstances which led to it cease to exist and are unlikely to recur. The competent authority shall have the authority to review, upon motivated request, the continued existence of these circumstances;

(h) the right holder shall be paid adequate remuneration in the circumstances of each case, taking into account the economic value of the authorization;

(i) the legal validity of any decision relating to the authorization of such use shall be subject to judicial review or other independent review by a distinct higher authority in that Member;

(j) any decision relating to the remuneration provided in respect of such use shall be subject to judicial review or other independent review by a distinct higher authority in that Member;

(k) Members are not obliged to apply the conditions set forth in subparagraphs (b) and (f) where such use is permitted to remedy a practice determined after judicial or administrative process to be anti-competitive. The need to correct anti-competitive practices may be taken into account in determining the amount of remuneration in such cases. Competent authorities shall have the authority to refuse termination of authorization if and when the conditions which led to such authorization are likely to recur;

(l) where such use is authorized to permit the exploitation of a patent ("the second patent") which cannot be exploited without infringing another patent ("the first patent"), the following additional conditions shall apply:

(i) the invention claimed in the second patent shall involve an important technical advance of considerable economic significance in relation to the invention claimed in the first patent;

(ii) the owner of the first patent shall be entitled to a cross-licence on reasonable terms to use the invention claimed in the second patent; and

(iii) the use authorized in respect of the first patent shall be non-assignable except with the assignment of the second patent.

Article 32—Revocation/Forfeiture

An opportunity for judicial review of any decision to revoke or forfeit a patent shall be available.

Article 33—Term of Protection

The term of protection available shall not end before the expiration of a period of twenty years counted from the filing date.

Article 34—Process Patents: Burden of Proof

1. For the purposes of civil proceedings in respect of the infringement of the rights of the owner referred to in paragraph 1(b) of Article 28, if the subject matter of a patent is a process for obtaining a product, the judicial authorities shall have the authority to order the defendant to prove that the process to obtain an identical product is different from the patented process. Therefore, Members shall provide, in at least one of the following circumstances, that any identical product when produced without the consent of the patent owner shall, in the absence of proof to the contrary, be deemed to have been obtained by the patented process:

(a) if the product obtained by the patented process is new;

(b) if there is a substantial likelihood that the identical product was made by the process and the owner of the patent has been unable through reasonable efforts to determine the process actually used.

2. Any Member shall be free to provide that the burden of proof indicated in paragraph 1 shall be on the alleged infringer only if the condition referred to in subparagraph (a) is fulfilled or only if the condition referred to in subparagraph (b) is fulfilled.

3. In the adduction of proof to the contrary, the legitimate interests of defendants in protecting their manufacturing and business secrets shall be taken into account.

Section 6: Layout-designs (topographies) of integrated circuits

Article 35 — Relation to the IPIC Treaty

Members agree to provide protection to the layout-designs (topographies) of integrated circuits (referred to in this Agreement as "layout-designs") in accordance with Articles 2 through 7 (other than paragraph 3 of Article 6), Article 12 and paragraph 3 of Article 16 of the Treaty on Intellectual Property in Respect of Integrated Circuits and, in addition, to comply with the following provisions.

Article 36 — Scope of the Protection

Subject to the provisions of paragraph 1 of Article 37, Members shall consider unlawful the following acts if performed without the authorization of the right holder: importing, selling, or otherwise distributing for commercial purposes a protected layout-design, an integrated circuit in which a protected layout-design is incorporated, or an article incorporating such an integrated circuit only in so far as it continues to contain an unlawfully reproduced layout-design.

Article 37 — Acts Not Requiring the Authorization of the Right Holder

1. Notwithstanding Article 36, no Member shall consider unlawful the performance of any of the acts referred to in that Article in respect of an integrated circuit incorporating an unlawfully reproduced layout-design or any article incorporating such an integrated circuit where the person performing or ordering such acts did not know and had no reasonable ground to know, when acquiring the integrated circuit or article incorporating such an integrated circuit, that it incorporated an unlawfully reproduced layout-design. Members shall provide that, after the time that such person has received sufficient notice that the layout-design was unlawfully reproduced, that person may perform any of the acts with respect to the stock on hand or ordered before such time, but shall be liable to pay to the right holder a sum equivalent to a reasonable royalty such as would be payable under a freely negotiated licence in respect of such a layout-design.

2. The conditions set out in subparagraphs (a) through (k) of Article 31 shall apply mutatis mutandis in the event of any non-voluntary licensing of a layout-design or of its use by or for the government without the authorization of the right holder.

Article 38—Term of Protection

1. In Members requiring registration as a condition of protection, the term of protection of layout-designs shall not end before the expiration of a period of 10 years counted from the date of filing an application for registration or from the first commercial exploitation wherever in the world it occurs.

2. In Members not requiring registration as a condition for protection, layout-designs shall be protected for a term of no less than 10 years from the date of the first commercial exploitation wherever in the world it occurs.

3. Notwithstanding paragraphs 1 and 2, a Member may provide that protection shall lapse 15 years after the creation of the layout-design.

Section 7: Protection of undisclosed information

Article 39

1. In the course of ensuring effective protection against unfair competition as provided in Article 10bis of the Paris Convention (1967), Members shall protect undisclosed information in accordance with paragraph 2 and data submitted to governments or governmental agencies in accordance with paragraph 3.

2. Natural and legal persons shall have the possibility of preventing information lawfully within their control from being disclosed to, acquired by, or used by others without their consent in a manner contrary to honest commercial practices so long as such information:

> (a) is secret in the sense that it is not, as a body or in the precise configuration and assembly of its components, generally known among or readily accessible to persons within the circles that normally deal with the kind of information in question;
>
> (b) has commercial value because it is secret; and
>
> (c) has been subject to reasonable steps under the circumstances, by the person lawfully in control of the information, to keep it secret.

3. Members, when requiring, as a condition of approving the marketing of pharmaceutical or of agricultural chemical products which utilize new chemical entities, the submission of undisclosed test or other data, the origination of which involves a considerable effort, shall protect such data against unfair commercial use. In addition, Members shall protect such data against disclosure, except where necessary to protect the public, or unless steps are taken to ensure that the data are protected against unfair commercial use.

Section 8: Control of anti-competitive practices in contractual licences

Article 40

1. Members agree that some licensing practices or conditions pertaining to intellectual property rights which restrain competition may have adverse effects on trade and may impede the transfer and dissemination of technology.

2. Nothing in this Agreement shall prevent Members from specifying in their legislation licensing practices or conditions that may in particular cases constitute an abuse of intellectual property rights having an adverse effect on competition in the relevant market. As provided above, a Member may adopt, consistently with the other provisions of this Agreement, appropriate measures to prevent or control such practices, which may include for example exclusive grantback conditions, conditions preventing challenges to validity and coercive package licensing, in the light of the relevant laws and regulations of that Member.

3. Each Member shall enter, upon request, into consultations with any other Member which has cause to believe that an intellectual property right owner that is a national or domiciliary of the Member to which the request for consultations has been addressed is undertaking practices in violation of the requesting Member's laws and regulations on the subject matter of this Section, and which wishes to secure compliance with such legislation, without prejudice to any action under the law and to the full freedom of an ultimate decision of either Member. The Member addressed shall accord full and sympathetic consideration to, and shall afford adequate opportunity for, consultations with the requesting Member, and shall cooperate through supply of publicly available non-confidential information of relevance to the matter in question and of other information available to the Member, subject to domestic law and to the conclusion of mutually satisfactory agreements concerning the safeguarding of its confidentiality by the requesting Member.

4. A Member whose nationals or domiciliaries are subject to proceedings in another Member concerning alleged violation of that other Member's laws and regulations on the subject matter of this Section shall, upon request, be granted an opportunity for consultations by the other Member under the same conditions as those foreseen in paragraph 3.

Part III — Enforcement of Intellectual Property Rights

Section 1: General Obligations

Article 41

1. Members shall ensure that enforcement procedures as specified in this Part are available under their law so as to permit effective action against any act of infringement of intellectual property rights covered by this Agreement, including expeditious remedies to prevent infringements and remedies which constitute a deterrent to further infringements. These procedures shall be applied in such a manner as to avoid the creation of barriers to legitimate trade and to provide for safeguards against their abuse.

2. Procedures concerning the enforcement of intellectual property rights shall be fair and equitable. They shall not be unnecessarily complicated or costly, or entail unreasonable time-limits or unwarranted delays.

3. Decisions on the merits of a case shall preferably be in writing and reasoned. They shall be made available at least to the parties to the proceeding without undue delay.

Decisions on the merits of a case shall be based only on evidence in respect of which parties were offered the opportunity to be heard.

4. Parties to a proceeding shall have an opportunity for review by a judicial authority of final administrative decisions and, subject to jurisdictional provisions in a Member's law concerning the importance of a case, of at least the legal aspects of initial judicial decisions on the merits of a case. However, there shall be no obligation to provide an opportunity for review of acquittals in criminal cases.

5. It is understood that this Part does not create any obligation to put in place a judicial system for the enforcement of intellectual property rights distinct from that for the enforcement of law in general, nor does it affect the capacity of Members to enforce their law in general. Nothing in this Part creates any obligation with respect to the distribution of resources as between enforcement of intellectual property rights and the enforcement of law in general.

Section 2: Civil and administrative procedures and remedies

Article 42 — Fair and Equitable Procedures

Members shall make available to right holders civil judicial procedures concerning the enforcement of any intellectual property right covered by this Agreement. Defendants shall have the right to written notice which is timely and contains sufficient detail, including the basis of the claims. Parties shall be allowed to be represented by independent legal counsel, and procedures shall not impose overly burdensome requirements concerning mandatory personal appearances. All parties to such procedures shall be duly entitled to substantiate their claims and to present all relevant evidence. The procedure shall provide a means to identify and protect confidential information, unless this would be contrary to existing constitutional requirements.

Article 43 — Evidence

1. The judicial authorities shall have the authority, where a party has presented reasonably available evidence sufficient to support its claims and has specified evidence relevant to substantiation of its claims which lies in the control of the opposing party, to order that this evidence be produced by the opposing party, subject in appropriate cases to conditions which ensure the protection of confidential information.

2. In cases in which a party to a proceeding voluntarily and without good reason refuses access to, or otherwise does not provide necessary information within a reasonable period, or significantly impedes a procedure relating to an enforcement action, a Member may accord judicial authorities the authority to make preliminary and final determinations, affirmative or negative, on the basis of the information presented to them, including the complaint or the allegation presented by the party adversely affected by the denial of access to information, subject to providing the parties an opportunity to be heard on the allegations or evidence.

Article 44—Injunctions

1. The judicial authorities shall have the authority to order a party to desist from an infringement, inter alia to prevent the entry into the channels of commerce in their jurisdiction of imported goods that involve the infringement of an intellectual property right, immediately after customs clearance of such goods. Members are not obliged to accord such authority in respect of protected subject matter acquired or ordered by a person prior to knowing or having reasonable grounds to know that dealing in such subject matter would entail the infringement of an intellectual property right.

2. Notwithstanding the other provisions of this Part and provided that the provisions of Part II specifically addressing use by governments, or by third parties authorized by a government, without the authorization of the right holder are complied with, Members may limit the remedies available against such use to payment of remuneration in accordance with subparagraph (h) of Article 31. In other cases, the remedies under this Part shall apply or, where these remedies are inconsistent with a Member's law, declaratory judgments and adequate compensation shall be available.

Article 45—Damages

1. The judicial authorities shall have the authority to order the infringer to pay the right holder damages adequate to compensate for the injury the right holder has suffered because of an infringement of that person's intellectual property right by an infringer who knowingly, or with reasonable grounds to know, engaged in infringing activity.

2. The judicial authorities shall also have the authority to order the infringer to pay the right holder expenses, which may include appropriate attorney's fees. In appropriate cases, Members may authorize the judicial authorities to order recovery of profits and/or payment of pre-established damages even where the infringer did not knowingly, or with reasonable grounds to know, engage in infringing activity.

Article 46—Other Remedies

In order to create an effective deterrent to infringement, the judicial authorities shall have the authority to order that goods that they have found to be infringing be, without compensation of any sort, disposed of outside the channels of commerce in such a manner as to avoid any harm caused to the right holder, or, unless this would be contrary to existing constitutional requirements, destroyed. The judicial authorities shall also have the authority to order that materials and implements the predominant use of which has been in the creation of the infringing goods be, without compensation of any sort, disposed of outside the channels of commerce in such a manner as to minimize the risks of further infringements. In considering such requests, the need for proportionality between the seriousness of the infringement and the remedies ordered as well as the interests of third parties shall be taken into account. In regard to counterfeit trademark goods, the simple removal of the trademark unlawfully affixed shall not be sufficient, other than in exceptional cases, to permit release of the goods into the channels of commerce.

Article 47—Right of Information

Members may provide that the judicial authorities shall have the authority, unless this would be out of proportion to the seriousness of the infringement, to order the infringer to inform the right holder of the identity of third persons involved in the production and distribution of the infringing goods or services and of their channels of distribution.

Article 48—Indemnification of the Defendant

1. The judicial authorities shall have the authority to order a party at whose request measures were taken and who has abused enforcement procedures to provide to a party wrongfully enjoined or restrained adequate compensation for the injury suffered because of such abuse. The judicial authorities shall also have the authority to order the applicant to pay the defendant expenses, which may include appropriate attorney's fees.

2. In respect of the administration of any law pertaining to the protection or enforcement of intellectual property rights, Members shall only exempt both public authorities and officials from liability to appropriate remedial measures where actions are taken or intended in good faith in the course of the administration of that law.

Article 49—Administrative Procedures

To the extent that any civil remedy can be ordered as a result of administrative procedures on the merits of a case, such procedures shall conform to principles equivalent in substance to those set forth in this Section.

Section 3: Provisional Measures

Article 50

1. The judicial authorities shall have the authority to order prompt and effective provisional measures:

(a) to prevent an infringement of any intellectual property right from occurring, and in particular to prevent the entry into the channels of commerce in their jurisdiction of goods, including imported goods immediately after customs clearance;

(b) to preserve relevant evidence in regard to the alleged infringement.

2. The judicial authorities shall have the authority to adopt provisional measures inaudita altera parte where appropriate, in particular where any delay is likely to cause irreparable harm to the right holder, or where there is a demonstrable risk of evidence being destroyed.

3. The judicial authorities shall have the authority to require the applicant to provide any reasonably available evidence in order to satisfy themselves with a sufficient

degree of certainty that the applicant is the right holder and that the applicant's right is being infringed or that such infringement is imminent, and to order the applicant to provide a security or equivalent assurance sufficient to protect the defendant and to prevent abuse.

4. Where provisional measures have been adopted inaudita altera parte, the parties affected shall be given notice, without delay after the execution of the measures at the latest. A review, including a right to be heard, shall take place upon request of the defendant with a view to deciding, within a reasonable period after the notification of the measures, whether these measures shall be modified, revoked or confirmed.

5. The applicant may be required to supply other information necessary for the identification of the goods concerned by the authority that will execute the provisional measures.

6. Without prejudice to paragraph 4, provisional measures taken on the basis of paragraphs 1 and 2 shall, upon request by the defendant, be revoked or otherwise cease to have effect, if proceedings leading to a decision on the merits of the case are not initiated within a reasonable period, to be determined by the judicial authority ordering the measures where a Member's law so permits or, in the absence of such a determination, not to exceed 20 working days or 31 calendar days, whichever is the longer.

7. Where the provisional measures are revoked or where they lapse due to any act or omission by the applicant, or where it is subsequently found that there has been no infringement or threat of infringement of an intellectual property right, the judicial authorities shall have the authority to order the applicant, upon request of the defendant, to provide the defendant appropriate compensation for any injury caused by these measures.

8. To the extent that any provisional measure can be ordered as a result of administrative procedures, such procedures shall conform to principles equivalent in substance to those set forth in this Section.

Section 4: Special Requirements Related to Border Measures

Article 51

Suspension of Release by Customs Authorities

Members shall, in conformity with the provisions set out below, adopt procedures to enable a right holder, who has valid grounds for suspecting that the importation of counterfeit trademark or pirated copyright goods may take place, to lodge an application in writing with competent authorities, administrative or judicial, for the suspension by the customs authorities of the release into free circulation of such goods. Members may enable such an application to be made in respect of goods which involve other infringements of intellectual property rights, provided that the requirements of this Section are met. Members may also provide for corresponding procedures concerning the suspension by the customs authorities of the release of infringing goods destined for exportation from their territories.

Article 52—Application

Any right holder initiating the procedures under Article 51 shall be required to provide adequate evidence to satisfy the competent authorities that, under the laws of the country of importation, there is prima facie an infringement of the right holder's intellectual property right and to supply a sufficiently detailed description of the goods to make them readily recognizable by the customs authorities. The competent authorities shall inform the applicant within a reasonable period whether they have accepted the application and, where determined by the competent authorities, the period for which the customs authorities will take action.

Article 53—Security or Equivalent Assurance

1. The competent authorities shall have the authority to require an applicant to provide a security or equivalent assurance sufficient to protect the defendant and the competent authorities and to prevent abuse. Such security or equivalent assurance shall not unreasonably deter recourse to these procedures.

2. Where pursuant to an application under this Section the release of goods involving industrial designs, patents, layout-designs or undisclosed information into free circulation has been suspended by customs authorities on the basis of a decision other than by a judicial or other independent authority, and the period provided for in Article 55 has expired without the granting of provisional relief by the duly empowered authority, and provided that all other conditions for importation have been complied with, the owner, importer, or consignee of such goods shall be entitled to their release on the posting of a security in an amount sufficient to protect the right holder for any infringement. Payment of such security shall not prejudice any other remedy available to the right holder, it being understood that the security shall be released if the right holder fails to pursue the right of action within a reasonable period of time.

Article 54—Notice

The importer and the applicant shall be promptly notified of the suspension of the release of goods according to Article 51.

Article 55—Duration of Suspension

If, within a period not exceeding 10 working days after the applicant has been served notice of the suspension, the customs authorities have not been informed that proceedings leading to a decision on the merits of the case have been initiated by a party other than the defendant, or that the duly empowered authority has taken provisional measures prolonging the suspension of the release of the goods, the goods shall be released, provided that all other conditions for importation or exportation have been complied with; in appropriate cases, this time-limit may be extended by another 10 working days. If proceedings leading to a decision on the merits of the case have been initiated, a review, including a right to be heard, shall take place upon request of the defendant with a view to deciding, within a reasonable period, whether these measures shall be modified, revoked or confirmed.

Notwithstanding the above, where the suspension of the release of goods is carried out or continued in accordance with a provisional judicial measure, the provisions of paragraph 6 of Article 50 shall apply.

Article 56 — Indemnification of the Importer and of the Owner of the Goods

Relevant authorities shall have the authority to order the applicant to pay the importer, the consignee and the owner of the goods appropriate compensation for any injury caused to them through the wrongful detention of goods or through the detention of goods released pursuant to Article 55.

Article 57 — Right of Inspection and Information

Without prejudice to the protection of confidential information, Members shall provide the competent authorities the authority to give the right holder sufficient opportunity to have any goods detained by the customs authorities inspected in order to substantiate the right holder's claims. The competent authorities shall also have authority to give the importer an equivalent opportunity to have any such goods inspected. Where a positive determination has been made on the merits of a case, Members may provide the competent authorities the authority to inform the right holder of the names and addresses of the consignor, the importer and the consignee and of the quantity of the goods in question.

Article 58 — Ex Officio Action

Where Members require competent authorities to act upon their own initiative and to suspend the release of goods in respect of which they have acquired prima facie evidence that an intellectual property right is being infringed:

(a) the competent authorities may at any time seek from the right holder any information that may assist them to exercise these powers;

(b) the importer and the right holder shall be promptly notified of the suspension. Where the importer has lodged an appeal against the suspension with the competent authorities, the suspension shall be subject to the conditions, mutatis mutandis, set out at Article 55;

(c) Members shall only exempt both public authorities and officials from liability to appropriate remedial measures where actions are taken or intended in good faith.

Article 59 — Remedies

Without prejudice to other rights of action open to the right holder and subject to the right of the defendant to seek review by a judicial authority, competent authorities shall have the authority to order the destruction or disposal of infringing goods in accordance with the principles set out in Article 46. In regard to counterfeit trademark goods, the authorities shall not allow the re-exportation of the infringing goods in an unaltered state or subject them to a different customs procedure, other than in exceptional circumstances.

Article 60 — De Minimis Reports

Members may exclude from the application of the above provisions small quantities of goods of a non-commercial nature contained in travellers' personal luggage or sent in small consignments.

Section 5: Criminal Procedures

Article 61

Members shall provide for criminal procedures and penalties to be applied at least in cases of willful trademark counterfeiting or copyright piracy on a commercial scale. Remedies available shall include imprisonment and/or monetary fines sufficient to provide a deterrent, consistently with the level of penalties applied for crimes of a corresponding gravity. In appropriate cases, remedies available shall also include the seizure, forfeiture and destruction of the infringing goods and of any materials and implements the predominant use of which has been in the commission of the offence. Members may provide for criminal procedures and penalties to be applied in other cases of infringement of intellectual property rights, in particular where they are committed willfully and on a commercial scale.

Part IV
Acquisition and Maintenance of Intellectual Property Rights and Related Inter-partes Procedures

Article 62

1. Members may require, as a condition of the acquisition or maintenance of the intellectual property rights provided for under Sections 2 through 6 of Part II, compliance with reasonable procedures and formalities. Such procedures and formalities shall be consistent with the provisions of this Agreement.

2. Where the acquisition of an intellectual property right is subject to the right being granted or registered, Members shall ensure that the procedures for grant or registration, subject to compliance with the substantive conditions for acquisition of the right, permit the granting or registration of the right within a reasonable period of time so as to avoid unwarranted curtailment of the period of protection.

3. Article 4 of the Paris Convention (1967) shall apply mutatis mutandis to service marks.

4. Procedures concerning the acquisition or maintenance of intellectual property rights and, where a Member's law provides for such procedures, administrative revocation and inter partes procedures such as opposition, revocation and cancellation, shall be governed by the general principles set out in paragraphs 2 and 3 of Article 41.

5. Final administrative decisions in any of the procedures referred to under paragraph 4 shall be subject to review by a judicial or quasi-judicial authority. However, there shall be no obligation to provide an opportunity for such review of decisions in cases of unsuccessful opposition or administrative revocation, provided that the grounds for such procedures can be the subject of invalidation procedures.

Article 63—Transparency

1. Laws and regulations, and final judicial decisions and administrative rulings of general application, made effective by a Member pertaining to the subject matter of this Agreement (the availability, scope, acquisition, enforcement and prevention of the abuse of intellectual property rights) shall be published, or where such publication is not practicable made publicly available, in a national language, in such a manner as to enable governments and right holders to become acquainted with them. Agreements concerning the subject matter of this Agreement which are in force between the government or a governmental agency of a Member and the government or a governmental agency of another Member shall also be published.

2. Members shall notify the laws and regulations referred to in paragraph 1 to the Council for TRIPS in order to assist that Council in its review of the operation of this Agreement. The Council shall attempt to minimize the burden on Members in carrying out this obligation and may decide to waive the obligation to notify such laws and regulations directly to the Council if consultations with WIPO on the establishment of a common register containing these laws and regulations are successful. The Council shall also consider in this connection any action required regarding notifications pursuant to the obligations under this Agreement stemming from the provisions of Article 6ter of the Paris Convention (1967).

3. Each Member shall be prepared to supply, in response to a written request from another Member, information of the sort referred to in paragraph 1. A Member, having reason to believe that a specific judicial decision or administrative ruling or bilateral agreement in the area of intellectual property rights affects its rights under this Agreement, may also request in writing to be given access to or be informed in sufficient detail of such specific judicial decisions or administrative rulings or bilateral agreements.

4. Nothing in paragraphs 1, 2 and 3 shall require Members to disclose confidential information which would impede law enforcement or otherwise be contrary to the public interest or would prejudice the legitimate commercial interests of particular enterprises, public or private.

Article 64—Dispute Settlement

1. The provisions of Articles XXII and XXIII of GATT 1994 as elaborated and applied by the Dispute Settlement Understanding shall apply to consultations and the settlement of disputes under this Agreement except as otherwise specifically provided herein.

2. Subparagraphs 1(b) and 1(c) of Article XXIII of GATT 1994 shall not apply to the settlement of disputes under this Agreement for a period of five years from the date of entry into force of the WTO Agreement.

3. During the time period referred to in paragraph 2, the Council for TRIPS shall examine the scope and modalities for complaints of the type provided for under subparagraphs 1(b) and 1(c) of Article XXIII of GATT 1994 made pursuant to this

Agreement, and submit its recommendations to the Ministerial Conference for approval. Any decision of the Ministerial Conference to approve such recommendations or to extend the period in paragraph 2 shall be made only by consensus, and approved recommendations shall be effective for all Members without further formal acceptance process.

Part VI — Transitional Arrangements

Article 65 — Transitional Arrangements

1. Subject to the provisions of paragraphs 2, 3 and 4, no Member shall be obliged to apply the provisions of this Agreement before the expiry of a general period of one year following the date of entry into force of the WTO Agreement.

2. A developing country Member is entitled to delay for a further period of four years the date of application, as defined in paragraph 1, of the provisions of this Agreement other than Articles 3, 4 and 5.

3. Any other Member which is in the process of transformation from a centrally-planned into a market, free-enterprise economy and which is undertaking structural reform of its intellectual property system and facing special problems in the preparation and implementation of intellectual property laws and regulations, may also benefit from a period of delay as foreseen in paragraph 2.

4. To the extent that a developing country Member is obliged by this Agreement to extend product patent protection to areas of technology not so protectable in its territory on the general date of application of this Agreement for that Member, as defined in paragraph 2, it may delay the application of the provisions on product patents of Section 5 of Part II to such areas of technology for an additional period of five years.

5. A Member availing itself of a transitional period under paragraphs 1, 2, 3 or 4 shall ensure that any changes in its laws, regulations and practice made during that period do not result in a lesser degree of consistency with the provisions of this Agreement.

Article 66 — Least-Developed Country Members

1. In view of the special needs and requirements of least-developed country Members, their economic, financial and administrative constraints, and their need for flexibility to create a viable technological base, such Members shall not be required to apply the provisions of this Agreement, other than Articles 3, 4 and 5, for a period of 10 years from the date of application as defined under paragraph 1 of Article 65. The Council for TRIPS shall, upon duly motivated request by a least-developed country Member, accord extensions of this period.

2. Developed country Members shall provide incentives to enterprises and institutions in their territories for the purpose of promoting and encouraging technology transfer to least-developed country Members in order to enable them to create a sound and viable technological base.

Article 67 — Technical Cooperation

In order to facilitate the implementation of this Agreement, developed country Members shall provide, on request and on mutually agreed terms and conditions, technical and financial cooperation in favour of developing and least-developed country Members. Such cooperation shall include assistance in the preparation of laws and regulations on the protection and enforcement of intellectual property rights as well as on the prevention of their abuse, and shall include support regarding the establishment or reinforcement of domestic offices and agencies relevant to these matters, including the training of personnel.

Part VII — Institutional Arrangements; Final Provisions

Article 68 — Council for Trade-Related Aspects of Intellectual Property Rights

The Council for TRIPS shall monitor the operation of this Agreement and, in particular, Members' compliance with their obligations hereunder, and shall afford Members the opportunity of consulting on matters relating to the trade-related aspects of intellectual property rights. It shall carry out such other responsibilities as assigned to it by the Members, and it shall, in particular, provide any assistance requested by them in the context of dispute settlement procedures. In carrying out its functions, the Council for TRIPS may consult with and seek information from any source it deems appropriate. In consultation with WIPO, the Council shall seek to establish, within one year of its first meeting, appropriate arrangements for cooperation with bodies of that Organization.

Article 69 — International Cooperation

Members agree to cooperate with each other with a view to eliminating international trade in goods infringing intellectual property rights. For this purpose, they shall establish and notify contact points in their administrations and be ready to exchange information on trade in infringing goods. They shall, in particular, promote the exchange of information and cooperation between customs authorities with regard to trade in counterfeit trademark goods and pirated copyright goods.

Article 70 — Protection of Existing Subject Matter

1. This Agreement does not give rise to obligations in respect of acts which occurred before the date of application of the Agreement for the Member in question.

2. Except as otherwise provided for in this Agreement, this Agreement gives rise to obligations in respect of all subject matter existing at the date of application of this Agreement for the Member in question, and which is protected in that Member on the said date, or which meets or comes subsequently to meet the criteria for protection under the terms of this Agreement. In respect of this paragraph and paragraphs 3 and 4, copyright obligations with respect to existing works shall be solely determined under Article 18 of the Berne Convention (1971), and obligations with respect to the rights of producers of phonograms and performers in existing phonograms shall be determined solely under Article 18 of the Berne Convention (1971) as made applicable under paragraph 6 of Article 14 of this Agreement.

3. There shall be no obligation to restore protection to subject matter which on the date of application of this Agreement for the Member in question has fallen into the public domain.

4. In respect of any acts in respect of specific objects embodying protected subject matter which become infringing under the terms of legislation in conformity with this Agreement, and which were commenced, or in respect of which a significant investment was made, before the date of acceptance of the WTO Agreement by that Member, any Member may provide for a limitation of the remedies available to the right holder as to the continued performance of such acts after the date of application of this Agreement for that Member. In such cases the Member shall, however, at least provide for the payment of equitable remuneration.

5. A Member is not obliged to apply the provisions of Article 11 and of paragraph 4 of Article 14 with respect to originals or copies purchased prior to the date of application of this Agreement for that Member.

6. Members shall not be required to apply Article 31, or the requirement in paragraph 1 of Article 27 that patent rights shall be enjoyable without discrimination as to the field of technology, to use without the authorization of the right holder where authorization for such use was granted by the government before the date this Agreement became known.

7. In the case of intellectual property rights for which protection is conditional upon registration, applications for protection which are pending on the date of application of this Agreement for the Member in question shall be permitted to be amended to claim any enhanced protection provided under the provisions of this Agreement. Such amendments shall not include new matter.

8. Where a Member does not make available as of the date of entry into force of the WTO Agreement patent protection for pharmaceutical and agricultural chemical products commensurate with its obligations under Article 27, that Member shall:

(a) notwithstanding the provisions of Part VI, provide as from the date of entry into force of the WTO Agreement a means by which applications for patents for such inventions can be filed;

(b) apply to these applications, as of the date of application of this Agreement, the criteria for patentability as laid down in this Agreement as if those criteria were being applied on the date of filing in that Member or, where priority is available and claimed, the priority date of the application; and

(c) provide patent protection in accordance with this Agreement as from the grant of the patent and for the remainder of the patent term, counted from the filing date in accordance with Article 33 of this Agreement, for those of these applications that meet the criteria for protection referred to in subparagraph (b).

9. Where a product is the subject of a patent application in a Member in accordance with paragraph 8(a), exclusive marketing rights shall be granted, notwithstanding the provisions of Part VI, for a period of five years after obtaining marketing

approval in that Member or until a product patent is granted or rejected in that Member, whichever period is shorter, provided that, subsequent to the entry into force of the WTO Agreement, a patent application has been filed and a patent granted for that product in another Member and marketing approval obtained in such other Member.

Article 71 — Review and Attachment

1. The Council for TRIPS shall review the implementation of this Agreement after the expiration of the transitional period referred to in paragraph 2 of Article 65. The Council shall, having regard to the experience gained in its implementation, review it two years after that date, and at identical intervals thereafter. The Council may also undertake reviews in the light of any relevant new developments which might warrant modification or amendment of this Agreement.

2. Amendments merely serving the purpose of adjusting to higher levels of protection of intellectual property rights achieved, and in force, in other multilateral agreements and accepted under those agreements by all Members of the WTO may be referred to the Ministerial Conference for action in accordance with paragraph 6 of Article X of the WTO Agreement on the basis of a consensus proposal from the Council for TRIPS.

Article 72 — Reservations

Reservations may not be entered in respect of any of the provisions of this Agreement without the consent of the other Members.

Article 73 — Security Exceptions

Nothing in this Agreement shall be construed:

(a) to require a Member to furnish any information the disclosure of which it considers contrary to its essential security interests; or

(b) to prevent a Member from taking any action which it considers necessary for the protection of its essential security interests;

(i) relating to fissionable materials or the materials from which they are derived;

(ii) relating to the traffic in arms, ammunition and implements of war and to such traffic in other goods and materials as is carried on directly or indirectly for the purpose of supplying a military establishment;

(iii) taken in time of war or other emergency in international relations; or

(c) to prevent a Member from taking any action in pursuance of its obligations under the United Nations Charter for the maintenance of international peace and security.

Index